# MATTERS
# OF
# LIFE AND DEATH

# MATTERS OF LIFE AND DEATH

## New Introductory Essays in Moral Philosophy

### SECOND EDITION

TOM L. BEAUCHAMP
HUGO ADAM BEDAU
J. BAIRD CALLICOTT
JOEL FEINBERG
JAN NARVESON
ONORA O'NEILL
JAMES RACHELS
PETER SINGER
DONALD VANDEVEER

## Edited by Tom Regan

NORTH CAROLINA STATE UNIVERSITY AT RALEIGH

 RANDOM HOUSE     NEW YORK

Second Edition
98765432
Copyright © 1980, 1986 by Random House, Inc.

**Library of Congress Cataloging-in-Publication Data**
Main entry under title:

Matters of life and death

Bibliography: p.
Includes index.
1. Ethics—Addresses, essays, lectures.   2. Social ethics—Addresses, essays, lectures.   I. Beauchamp, Tom L.   II. Regan, Tom.
BJ1012.M37  1985        179'.1        85–18411
ISBN 0–394–34297–6

Manufactured in the United States of America

The following page constitutes an extension of the copyright page.

# ACKNOWLEDGMENTS

*Grateful acknowledgment is made to the following authors and publishers for permission to reprint selections from copyrighted material:*

From Stewart Alsop, "The Right to Die with Dignity." Copyright © 1974 by Stewart Alsop. Reprinted from *Good Housekeeping Magazine.*

From Joseph V. Sullivan, "The Immorality of Euthanasia" in Marvin Kohl, ed., *Beneficent Euthanasia* (Buffalo, N.Y.: Prometheus Books, 1975), pp. 14, 19. Reprinted by permission of the publisher.

From Philippa Foot, "Euthanasia," *Philosophy and Public Affairs* 6, no. 2 (Winter 1977). Copyright © 1977 by Philippa Foot. Excerpts reprinted by permission of the author and Princeton University Press.

From "The Definition of Suicide." © 1968 by The New York Times Company. Reprinted by permission.

From Tom L. Beauchamp, William T. Blackstone, and Joel Feinberg, ed., *Philosophy and the Human Condition,* © 1980, pp. 250–265. Adapted by permission of Prentice-Hall, Inc., Englewood Cliffs, N.J.

From Judith Jarvis Thomson, "A Defense of Abortion," *Philosophy and Public Affairs* 1, no. 1 (Fall 1971). Copyright © 1971 by Princeton University Press. Excerpts reprinted by permission.

News item cited in Tom L. Beauchamp, "Suicide," date lined Phoenix, Arizona, Feb. 6. Copyright © 1968 by The New York Times Company. Reprinted by permission.

To the Memory of
WILLIAM T. (BILL) BLACKSTONE

# PREFACE

As was true of the first, this second edition of *Matters of Life and Death* consists of original essays that illustrate the application of moral theory to topics of vital practical concern—to matters of life and death. It is intended primarily for persons taking their first course in moral philosophy or philosophy in general.

Eight of the essays in the present edition are revised versions of essays that were originally commissioned for the first edition. The extent of revision varies, from a few pages in some places to almost totally new essays in others. So even if this second edition were otherwise the same as the first, it would be a much different book. In fact, however, there are two newly commissioned essays in the present volume. The first—Donald VanDeVeer's "Whither Baby Doe?"—explores a number of the troubling ethical questions occasioned by the treatment or nontreatment of defective newborns, babies who may lack anything from a toe to a brain. In the first edition, these questions were not addressed at the length or with the care they deserve; with VanDeVeer's essay in this second edition, they are. Ethical questions about the environment were examined at length in the first edition, but the essay devoted to them was not a finished, finely tuned piece of scholarship, the author, William T. Blackstone, having tragically died before the essay was completed. J. Baird Callicott has retained Blackstone's title, "The Search for an Environmental Ethic," but the essay he has written for the present volume bears his own distinctive mark throughout.

There is no single order in which the essays must be read. The present arrangement has been selected for the following reasons. The force of a moral question is perhaps clearest when, as individuals, we are told that it is wrong to do something that does not cause anyone else any obvious harm. Why should our individual liberty be morally limited if its exercise does not wrong others? The essays on euthanasia and suicide raise this question in especially clear terms and so have been placed first.

The point of a moral question also is clear when an individual person or persons have been mistreated or harmed. It is natural to ask what morality will allow us to do to the persons causing the harm, including what forms of punishment or harmful responses are morally justifiable. What morality allows us to do when people are violently assaulted, whether in peacetime or during war, and whether the war is conventional or nuclear, are the central questions considered in "At Arms' Length: Violence and War." The morality of one form of punishment—capital punishment—is the central focus of the essay that follows.

Morality, however, arguably requires that we widen our horizons and think about the harm done to those who have not done any wrong themselves and who have no means of protecting themselves. Within the human moral community, this class of question requires that we think through the perplexities of the kind of treatment or nontreatment we should extend to defective newborns, of the policies we should or should not support regarding abortion, and of the nature and stringency of our obligations to the innocent human victims of widespread famine. The essays devoted to examining these perplexities are thus placed next.

The difficulties we might encounter in trying to discern the moral ties that bind us to those distant strangers currently starving to death halfway around the world are likely to be compounded when we are challenged to think about the ethics of how animals are treated in our own society—for example, in commercial animal agriculture. But think about these matters we must if we are to discharge our obligation to eat with our minds, not just our bodies. The ninth essay, "Animals and the Value of Life," examines this and related questions about the ethics of our treatment of animals.

The last essay, "The Search for an Environmental Ethic," occupies its position not because it is of least importance but because it canvasses a set of issues we are better advised to work toward than to begin with. If, as some have speculated, it is difficult for human beings to be unselfish and to act on behalf of the interests of other human beings, how much more difficult is it likely to be for us to consider and act on behalf of the interests of the natural environment.

The introduction has two principal aims. First, it attempts to explain some assumptions that are common to the several essays—for example, some assumptions that concern how not to answer moral questions. Second, by tracing some of the major ideas current in moral philosophy, it formulates sets of questions that might help readers work their way more confidently through the essays themselves. The hope is that people will better understand the discussion of a particular ethical question when it is viewed against the backdrop of moral philosophy generally, and vice versa.

It is a pleasure to thank all the contributors for their help and cooperation; Steve Pensinger of Random House for his advice and guidance; Heidi Thaens, for her skill in copyediting the manuscript; Ann Rives for her help in preparing the manuscript for publication; my wife, Nancy, for her expert typing and research assistance; and my children, Bryan and Karen, for their benign indulgence.

Raleigh, North Carolina                                         TOM REGAN
6 January 1985

# CONTENTS

## 3. SUICIDE  *Tom L. Beauchamp*  77

# 4. AT ARMS' LENGTH: VIOLENCE AND WAR
## *Jan Narveson 125*

# 5. CAPITAL PUNISHMENT  *Hugo Adam Bedau*  175
§1 Introduction

---

## 6. WHITHER BABY DOE? *Donald VanDeVeer* 213

## 7. ABORTION *Joel Feinberg 256*

## 8. THE MORAL PERPLEXITIES OF FAMINE AND WORLD HUNGER   *Onora O'Neill* 294

§1 Are Famine and World Hunger New Moral Problems?

---

# 9. ANIMALS AND THE VALUE OF LIFE
## *Peter Singer 338*

# 10. THE SEARCH FOR AN ENVIRONMENTAL ENVIRONMENTAL ETHIC  *J. Baird Callicott 381*

# MATTERS
## OF
# LIFE AND DEATH

# I

# Introduction

## TOM REGAN

§1 KILLING AND LETTING DIE

The essays in this volume deal with questions about the value of life
and the morality of killing and letting die. It is difficult to imagine
more important questions. We live amid a sea of death-by-killing,
something we are reminded of every day by stories in the news. A
husband decapitates his wife and children, then leaps to his own death.
A convicted murderer is executed by a firing squad or by lethal injection. Wars between nations break out and the death toll of combatants
and civilians mounts daily. In hospitals and clinics, millions of human
fetuses are aborted every year. Elsewhere, a fatally ill woman,
wracked by unrelenting, untreatable pain, is given an overdose of
sleeping pills by her son and dies quietly in her sleep. Familiar stories
all. We know them well, at least at a distance. They are what people
talk about. A lot.

How ought we to think about these cases of killing? In the case of
suicide, for example, ought we to think that all suicides are wrong and
should be prevented? Or is it more reasonable to think that no one has
a right to stop people from doing what they want, including taking
their own lives? Does a person's age make any difference? And what
of the suicide's mental condition? Or imagine: A close friend has been
in an automobile accident. His face is permanently disfigured. He has
lost both arms. He will never walk again, never even leave his bed. He
is in almost constant pain. He pleads with us to kill him. Ought we to
do so? Since he is not going to die soon as a result of his injuries,
wouldn't we be guilty of murder if we killed him? And isn't murder
always wrong? The questions come easily. Answers, and the means of
defending them, may not.

3

The issues we must face go beyond just those that involve killing, however. Imagine that a baby is lying face down in a shallow pond. We can save the child if we but lift her from the water. Suppose we don't and the child drowns. Here there is no question of our *killing* the baby. But we *have* let the baby die. And sometimes letting someone die seems to be a terribly immoral thing to do. Yet an estimated ten thousand human beings die every day from lack of food. If we are doing nothing to prevent this, are we then just as guilty as someone who would let a small baby drown when this could be prevented? Or, again, unknown numbers of "defective" newborns are denied the necessary care that would prolong their lives: they are "allowed to die," sometimes over a period of days, often in apparently acute pain. Can this be justified? And if it can, why not simply kill these infants outright by painless means rather than allow their lingering, pointless suffering? Like the questions about the morality of suicide, these questions cannot be omitted from an examination of the morality of killing and letting die.

But not just human beings are killed; not just human beings are allowed to die. In all large cities, vast numbers of animals are killed every day to supply people with the meat they are accustomed to eating. More than five billion animals are killed every year, just in the United States, to be eaten as steaks and chops, drumsticks and roasts. In these same cities, moreover, scientists are daily at work testing the safety of new products, such as deodorants and eye shadow, by using laboratory animals. Can this use of animals be justified? Or is their routine use as "models" morally objectionable? Ought it to be stopped? If we are seriously to think about the morality of killing and letting die, the killing and letting die of animals cannot escape our notice.

But there is more. Virgin forests and wilderness areas are destroyed to make room for roads, pipelines, resort complexes. Rivers become clogged avenues of waste and pollution, and myriad forms of complex vegetative and animal life are destroyed. Entire species are rendered extinct. There is even talk of the oceans "dying." Are we doing anything wrong when we treat nature in this way, and if so, why? Is it possible to develop an environmental ethic in which trees and fields, the creatures of the sea and sagebrush have a *right* to life? Or is the idea of a right necessarily restricted to human beings?

The essays in this volume explore these and related questions. The authors are moral philosophers. Moral philosophers are persons who take a special interest in thinking carefully about questions that concern moral right and wrong, good and bad, duty and obligation. Their objectives include understanding questions like those posed in the preceding paragraphs and in giving what they think are the most reasonable answers to them.

Like others who seek to replace opinion with understanding, these philosophers do not always agree on what is true. Some affirm that individuals have value; others deny this. Some argue that people have rights; others fail to see them. So we must not expect to find unanimity on all important questions in the pages that lie ahead. But despite the presence of some vital disagreements, the contributors to this volume agree about many essential matters; for example, they think that some tempting ways to answer moral questions are mistaken and confused. Agreement at this level is important. Without it the present collection of essays would have as much organization as Joe, Curley, and Moe have when they try to enter a door at the same time. The remainder of this introduction attempts to highlight some of the shared assumptions the contributors bring to their work, assumptions that more often than not go unstated. The hope is that by understanding what they do not say we might better understand what they do.

# I. META-ETHICS

## §2 CONCEPTUAL ANALYSIS

The first idea that requires attention is that of conceptual analysis. Philosophers frequently use the words "conceptual analysis" to refer to the activity of clarifying our concepts or ideas. Since we use words to express our concepts, the goal of conceptual analysis is to reach a clearer understanding of the meaning of words. Achieving such clarity is absolutely vital. If we do not have a clear understanding of the meanings of words, we will not have a clear understanding of our questions. And if we do not understand our questions, we will not understand what count as answers to them. This is especially true in the case of questions that ask whether something is morally right or wrong—for example, whether the use of violence is wrong. If we do not understand what violence is, how can we even begin to consider the question of its morality?

One way to think about conceptual analysis is in terms of necessary and sufficient conditions. If $x$ is a necessary condition of $y$, then $y$ cannot be the case if $x$ is not the case; in other words, if not $x$, then not $y$. Being a plane closed figure or having interior angles, for example, is a necessary condition of something's being a triangle. A sufficient condition is different. If $a$ is a sufficient condition of $b$, then $b$ will be the case if $a$ is the case; that is, if $a$, then $b$. Being a plane closed figure with only three sides or only three interior angles, for example, is a sufficient condition of something's being a triangle.

A necessary condition may not also be sufficient, and vice versa. For example, while being a plane closed figure is a necessary condition of something's being a triangle, it is not sufficient: There are many plane closed figures that are not triangles—e.g., rectangles. Again, that something is a Cadillac Seville is a sufficient condition of its being a car, but being a Cadillac Seville is not a necessary condition of being a car: There are many cars that are not Cadillac Sevilles.

The ideas of necessary and sufficient conditions relate to the activity of conceptual analysis in the following way. Conceptual analysis can be understood as the attempt to state the necessary and sufficient conditions of the correct use of a given concept. The aims of conceptual analysis, on this view, are thus (1) to state, so far as it is possible, those conditions which, if they are *not* satisfied, prevent the concept in question from being correctly applied—the necessary conditions of correct use—and (2) to state those conditions which, if they *are* satisfied, permit the concept to be correctly applied—the sufficient conditions of correct use. In this view of conceptual analysis, an analysis is itself correct to the extent that it states the necessary and sufficient conditions of correct use.

Now, sometimes it is not possible to give a complete set of necessary and sufficient conditions, and sometimes the conditions given cannot be very precise. For example, though a triangle must have no more nor less than three interior angles, how many hairs a person must be missing to be bald is far less precise. We should not expect all concepts to be analyzable in the way concepts in mathematics are. Some "defy analysis" in the sense that it is not possible to give a complete set of quite precise necessary and sufficient conditions. However, even in the case of these concepts, one ought to strive to reach the highest degree of completeness and precision possible. The more complete and exact we can make our understanding of a given concept, the more likely we will be to understand those questions in which the concept figures.

If we think of the concepts that play central roles in the essays in this volume—suicide, euthanasia, and punishment, for example—we can anticipate some difficulties for conceptual analysis. Unlike 'triangle', these concepts are not very precise. Take suicide. Many people think that a necessary and sufficient condition of a man's act being a suicide is that he killed himself intentionally. But both these ideas—'intentional' and 'self-killing'—are not as precise as 'three interior angles', which makes it necessary to think hard about them to see just what they do and do not mean. In his essay on this topic, Tom L. Beauchamp discusses this analysis of suicide and considers cases that call its correctness into question—for example, a case where a terminally ill man refuses medical treatment that would prolong his life and dies as a result. Here there seems to be no reason to say that the man killed himself—the disease killed him. And yet, might it not be true to say that he committed suicide?

The reasons that can be given for or against competing analyses of the concept of suicide must await a reading of Beauchamp's essay. And similar remarks apply to alternative analyses of the other important concepts that dot the landscape in each of the essays. In the essays by Donald VanDeVeer and Joel Feinberg, for example, the concept 'person' is examined at length, and the view that being a human being is a necessary and sufficient condition of being a person is subjected to a critical review. As these examples suggest, philosophers do not always agree on what the correct analysis of a given concept is, even when they agree that conceptual analysis is important. The merits of alternative analyses will have to be considered in the essays that lie ahead.

## §3 IS THERE A CORRECT METHOD FOR ANSWERING MORAL QUESTIONS?

The conceptual analysis of key moral concepts is one part of what is called "meta-ethics." The other major component of meta-ethics is the inquiry into the *correct method* for answering moral questions. Such a method would function in the case of moral questions in ways that are analogous to how the scientific method functions in the case of scientific questions. This latter method does not itself contain answers to particular questions (for example, about what happens to the pressure of a gas when the temperature is raised). Rather, the scientific method can be understood as specifying how we must approach particular questions *if we are to give scientific answers* to them; it defines, one might say, what it is to think about questions "from the scientific point of view." Well, if there is a correct method for answering moral questions, similar things would be true of it: It would not itself contain answers to particular moral questions (for example, whether wilderness should be preserved only if it is economically profitable to do so); rather, it would specify how we must approach questions *if we are to give moral answers* to them—if, that is, we are to give answers "from the moral point of view."

Whether there even exists such a method, not surprisingly, is a very controversial question. Some philosophers think there is; others think not. And among those who think there is, some think it is one thing while others think it is something different.

It will not be possible to examine these controversies in all the detail they deserve. Instead a rough sketch will be given of some of the central issues. Two ideas in particular are important. First, there is the matter of how *not* to answer moral questions; this idea is explored in §4. Second, there is the idea of an ideal moral judgment; this is discussed in §5. The relevance of these ideas to the essays will be explained as we proceed.

## §4 SOME WAYS NOT TO ANSWER MORAL QUESTIONS

*Moral Judgments and Personal Preferences*  Some people like classical music; others do not. Some people think bourbon is just great; others detest its taste. Some people will go to a lot of trouble to spend an afternoon in the hot sun at the beach; others can think of nothing worse. In all these cases disagreement in preference exists. Someone likes something; someone else does not. Are moral disagreements, disagreements over whether something is morally right or wrong, good or bad, just or unjust, the same as disagreements in preference?

It does not appear so. For one thing, when a person (say, Jack) says he likes something, he is not denying what another person (Jill) says if she says she does not like it. Suppose Jack says "I (Jack) like bourbon," and Jill says "I (Jill) do not like bourbon." Then clearly Jill does not deny what Jack says. To deny what Jack says, Jill would have to say "You (Jack) do not like bourbon," which is not what she says. So, in general, when two persons express different personal preferences, the one does not deny what the other affirms. It is perfectly possible for two opposing expressions of personal preference to be true at the same time.

When two people express conflicting judgments about the morality of something, however, the disagreement is importantly different. Suppose Jack says, "War is always wrong," while Jill says, "War is sometimes permissible." Then Jill *is* denying what Jack affirms; she is *denying* that war is always wrong, so that if what she said were true, what Jack said would have to be false. Some philosophers have denied this. They have maintained that moral judgments should be understood as expressions of personal preferences. Though this view deserves to be mentioned with respect, it is doubtful that it is correct. When people say that something is morally right or wrong, it is always appropriate to ask them to give reasons to justify their judgment, reasons for accepting their judgment as *correct*. In the case of personal preferences, however, such requests are inappropriate. If Jack says he likes to go to the beach, it hardly seems apt to press him to give reasons to justify what he says. If he says abortion is always wrong, however, it is highly relevant to test Jack's judgment by examining the reasons he gives for thinking what he does.

This difference between expressions of differing personal preference and conflicting moral judgments points to one way not to answer moral questions. Given that moral judgments are not just expressions of personal preference, it follows that moral right and wrong cannot be determined just by finding out about the personal preferences of some particular person—say, Jack. This is true even in the case of our own preferences. Our personal preferences are certainly important, but we do not answer moral questions just by saying what we like or dislike.

*Moral Judgments and Feelings*   Closely connected with personal preferences are a person's feelings, and some philosophers have maintained that words like 'right' and 'wrong' are devices we use merely to express how we feel about something. In this view, when Barbie says that we ought to permit capital punishment, what she conveys is that she has certain positive feelings toward having the death penalty; whereas when Ken says that we ought not to have it, what he expresses is that he has feelings of disapproval. It is as if what Barbie says is, "Death penalty, hurray!"—while what Ken says is, "Death penalty, boo!"

This position encounters problems of the same kind as those raised in the previous section. It is not appropriate to ask for justification in the case of mere expressions of feeling. True, if Ken is sincere, one can infer that he has strong negative feelings toward the death penalty. But his saying that we ought not to have it does not appear to be simply a way of venting his feelings (or of eliciting ours). As in the case of a person's preferences, so also in the case of a person's feelings: neither by itself provides answers to moral questions.

*Why Thinking It So Does Not Make It So*   The same is true about what someone thinks. Quite aside from her feelings, Bonnie, if she is sincere, does think that we who are well off ought to make sacrifices to help feed the many starving people in the world if she says that we ought to do so. Nevertheless, if her judgment is a *moral* judgment, what she means cannot be "I (Bonnie) think we who are well off ought to make sacrifices to help feed the many starving people in the world." If it were, then she would not be affirming something that Clyde denies, when he says "We who are well off ought not to make such sacrifices." Each would merely be stating that each thinks something, and it is certainly possible for it *both* to be true that Bonnie thinks that we ought to make sacrifices for those who are starving *and,* at the same time, that Clyde thinks we ought not. So if Clyde is denying what Bonnie affirms, he cannot merely be stating that *he* thinks that we ought not to make sacrifices for these people. Thus, the fact that Clyde happens to think what he does is just as irrelevant to establishing whether we ought or ought not to make sacrifices to help those who are starving as are Ken's feelings about the death penalty. And the same is true concerning what *we* happen to think. Our thinking something right or wrong is not what makes it so.

*The Irrelevance of Statistics*   Someone might think that though what one person happens to think or feel about moral issues does not settle matters, what all or most people happen to think or feel does. A single individual is only one voice; what most or all people think or feel is a great deal more. There is strength in numbers. Thus, the correct method for answering questions about right and wrong is to find out what most or all people think or feel. Opinion polls should be conducted, statistics compiled. That will reveal the truth.

This approach to moral questions is deficient. All that opinion polls can reveal is what all or most people happen to think or feel about some moral question—for example, "Should the government penalize hospitals that withhold life-prolonging treatment for defective newborns?" What such polls cannot determine is whether what all or most people happen to think about such an issue is reasonable or true, *or* that what all or most people happen to feel is appropriate. There may be strength in numbers, but not truth, at least not necessarily. This does not mean that "what we think (or feel)" is irrelevant to answering moral questions. Later on, in fact (in §7, below), we will see how, given that certain conditions have been met, "what we think" provides us with a possible place from which to begin the search for what makes acts right or wrong as well as a possible test of the adequacy of competing theories of right and wrong. Nevertheless, *merely* to establish that all (or most) people happen to think that the government should penalize hospitals that withhold life-prolonging treatment from defective newborns is not to establish that the government *should* do this. In times past, most (possibly even all) people thought the world was flat. But the question of its shape wasn't answered merely by finding out what most people happened to think or feel. There is no reason to believe moral questions differ in this respect. Questions of right and wrong cannot be answered just by counting heads.

*The Appeal to a Moral Authority*   Suppose it is conceded that we cannot answer moral questions just by finding out what Jack or Jill or Ken or Barbie happen to think or feel, or by finding out what all or most people happen to think or feel. After all, single individuals like Jack or Jill, or most or all people like them, might think or feel one way when they should think or feel differently. But suppose there is a person who never is mistaken when it comes to moral questions: if this person judges that something is morally right, it *is* morally right; if it is judged wrong, it *is* wrong. No mistakes are made. Let us call such a person a "moral authority." Might appealing to the judgments of a moral authority be the correct method for answering moral questions?

Most people who think there is a moral authority think this authority is not an ordinary person but a god. This causes problems immediately. Whether there is a god (or gods) is a very controversial question, and to rest questions of right and wrong on what an alleged god says (or the gods say) is already to base morality on an intellectually unsettled foundation. The difficulties go deeper than this, however, since even if there is a god who is a moral authority, very serious questions must arise concerning whether people always understand what this authority says about right and wrong. The difficulties that exist when Jews and Christians consult the Bible can be taken as illustrative. Problems of interpretation abound. Some who think that we were created to be vegetarians think they find evidence in the Bible that God thinks so too; others think they find evidence that He does not. Some who think that God allows us to exploit nature without regard to its values cite what they think are supporting chapters and verses; others cite other chapters and verses they think show that God does not allow this, or they cite the same passages and argue that they should be interpreted differently. The gravity of these and kindred problems of interpretation should not be underestimated. Even if there is a moral authority, and even if the God Jews and Christians worship should happen to be this authority, that would not make it a simple matter to find out what is right and wrong. The problem of finding out what God thinks on these matters would still remain and would be especially acute in areas where the Bible offers very little, if any, direct guidance—on the ethics of the use of life-sustaining technology for the irreversibly comatose, for example.

Problems of interpretation aside, it is clear that the correct method for answering moral questions cannot consist merely in discovering what some alleged moral authority says. Even if there is a moral authority, those who are not moral authorities can have no good reason for thinking that there is one unless the judgments of this supposed authority can be checked for their truth or reasonableness without relying on these judgments themselves *as grounds* for their truth or reasonableness, and it is not possible to do this unless what is true or reasonable regarding right and wrong can be known independently of what this supposed authority says. An example from another quarter might make this point clearer. A plumber proves his "authority as a plumber" not merely by what he says but by the quality of his work, which can be verified independently of what he says in any particular case. *After* we have come to know, on independent grounds, that a particular plumber's judgment is reliable, *then* we have reason to rely on his judgment in the future. The same is true of the authority of one's judgment in, say, science, economics, the law, and morality. One's "credentials" can be established in the case of moral judgment only if there are independent ways of testing moral judgment against what is known to be true or reasonable. Thus, since in the nature of the case there must be some independent way of knowing what judgments are true or reasonable in order to test for the authority of another's moral judgments, to appeal to this or that "moral authority" cannot itself be the method that we seek for answering moral questions.

## §5 THE IDEAL MORAL JUDGMENT

The ideas discussed in §4 are relevant to the essays in this volume because the authors never argue that something is right or wrong merely on the grounds of their personal preferences, or merely because they personally feel one way or another, or just because they think it right or wrong, or only because all or most people happen to feel or think a certain way, or because some alleged moral authority has said or revealed that something is right or wrong. It is important to realize the ways that these philosophers do not argue; it is also important to understand some of the arguments that can be given against arguing in these ways. This is what has been briefly explained in §4. What now needs to be described is an approach to moral questions that is not open to the objections raised against the methods considered so far.

The approach described in what follows turns on how the following question is answered: "What requirements would someone have to meet to make an ideal moral judgment?" Considered ideally, that is, what are the conditions that anyone would have to satisfy to reach a moral judgment as free from fault and error as possible? Now, by its very nature, an *ideal* moral judgment is just that—an ideal. Perhaps no one ever has or ever will completely meet all the requirements set forth in the ideal. But that does not make it irrational to strive to come as close as possible to fulfilling it. If we can never quite get to the finish, we can still move some distance from the starting line.

There are at least six different ideas that must find a place in our description of the ideal moral judgment. A brief discussion of each follows.

*Conceptual Clarity*   This idea was mentioned earlier (§2). Its importance is obvious. If someone asserts that the human fetus has a right to life, for example, we cannot determine whether that statement is true or reasonable before we understand what is meant by a *right*, a question explored by a number of the contributors. Similar remarks apply to other issues. In James Rachels's essay, for example, we find a careful examination of the concept of euthanasia as a preliminary to the moral question "Is euthanasia always morally wrong?" Who can reasonably say without first taking the time to ask what "euthanasia" means? Clarity by itself may not be enough, but rational thought cannot get far without it.

*Information*   We cannot answer moral questions in our closets. Moral questions come up in the real world, and a knowledge of the real-world setting in which they arise is essential if we are seriously to seek rational answers to them. For example, in the debate over the morality of capital punishment, some people argue that convicted murderers ought to be executed because, if they are not, they may be (and often are) paroled; and if they are paroled, they are more likely to kill again than are other released prisoners. Is this true? Is this a fact? We have to come out of our closets to answer this (or to find the answer others have reached on the basis of their research); and answer it we must if we are to reach an informed judgment about the morality of capital punishment. It and related questions are surveyed in Hugo Bedau's essay on that topic. The importance of getting the facts, of being informed, is not restricted just to the case of capital punishment by any means. It applies all across the broad sweep of moral inquiry.

*Rationality*   Rationality is a multifaceted concept. The one aspect that concerns us here is when rationality is understood as the ability to recognize the connection between different ideas—the ability to recognize, that is, that if some statements are true, then some other statements must be true while others must be false. Now, it is in logic that rules are set forth that specify when statements follow from others, and it is because of this that a person who is rational often is said to be logical. When we speak of the need to be rational, then, we are saying that we need to observe the rules of logic. To reach an ideal moral judgment, therefore, we must not only strive to make our judgment against a background of information and conceptual clarity; we must also take care to explore how our beliefs are logically related to other things that we do or do not believe. For example, assume that a person accepts the statements *(a)* "Suicide is not wrong if it brings a merciful end to the suicide's life" and *(b)* "Harriet's suicide would bring her life to a merciful end"; that person *logically* is committed to the statement *(c)* "Harriet's suicide would not be wrong." Were Ozzie to accept *a* and *b*, in other words, he would have no rational choice but to accept *c*. To affirm *a* and *b* and to deny *c* would be tantamount to asserting a contradiction, and a contradiction by definition *cannot possibly* be true. To fall short of the ideal moral judgment by committing oneself to a contradiction is to fall as short as one possibly can.

*Impartiality* Partiality involves favoring someone or something above others. For example, if a father is partial to one of his children, then he will be inclined to give the favored child more than he gives his other children. In some cases, partiality is a fine thing; but a partiality that excludes even thinking about or taking notice of others is far from what is needed in an ideal moral judgment. The fact that someone has been harmed, for example, always seems to be a relevant consideration, whether this someone is favored by us or not. In striving to reach the correct answers to moral questions, therefore, we must strive to guard against extreme, unquestioned partiality; otherwise we shall run the risk of having our judgment clouded by bigotry and prejudice.

The idea of impartiality is at the heart of what is sometimes referred to as the formal principle of justice: justice is the similar, and injustice the dissimilar, treatment of similar cases. This principle is said to express the *formal* principle of justice because by itself it does not specify what factors are relevant for determining what makes cases similar or dissimilar. To decide this, one must supplement the formal principle of justice with a substantive or normative interpretation of justice. More will be said on this matter (§8). Even at this juncture, however, we can recognize the rich potential the formal principle of justice can have in arguments about moral right and wrong. Were we to approve of practices that cause unnecessary suffering to farm animals while denouncing such practices when those who suffer are human beings, it would be apposite to ask why the two cases are judged dissimilar. For they must be dissimilar if, as we are assuming, dissimilar treatment is allowed. If, in reply to our question, we were told that the difference is that human beings belong to one species while farm animals belong to others, it would again be apposite to ask how this difference in species membership *can* make any moral difference to the morality of the treatment in the two cases. To sanction practices that cause unnecessary suffering to farm animals while disapproving of similar practices in the case of humans because of species membership seems to be a symptom of unjustified partiality (what some call speciesism), a point made by Peter Singer in his essay, "Animals and the Value of Life." While the formal principle of justice does not by itself tell us what are the relevant factors for determining when treatment is similar or dissimilar, that principle must be observed if we are to make the ideal moral judgment. Not to observe it is a symptom of prejudice or bias, rational defects that must be identified and overcome if we are to make the best moral judgment we can.

*Coolness*   All of us know what it is like to do something in the heat of anger that we later regret. No doubt we have also had the experience of getting so excited that we do something that later on we wish we had not done. Emotions are powerful forces, and though life would be a dull wasteland without them, we need to appreciate that the more volatile among them can mislead us; strong emotion is not a reliable guide to doing (or judging) what is best. This brings us to the need to be "cool." "Being cool" here means "not being in an emotionally excited state, being in an emotionally calm state of mind." The idea is that the hotter (the more emotionally charged) we are, the more likely we are to reach a mistaken moral conclusion, while the cooler (the calmer) we are, the greater the chances that we will avoid making mistakes.

This position is borne out by common experience. People who are in a terribly excited state may not be able to retain their rationality; because of their deep emotional involvement, they may not be able to attain impartiality; and when they are in an excited, emotional state, they may not even care about what happened or why. Like the proverb about shooting first and asking questions later, a lack of coolness can easily lead people to judge first and ask about the facts afterward. The need to be cool, then, seems to merit a place on our list.

*Valid Moral Principles*   The concept of a moral principle has been analyzed in different ways. At least this much seems clear, however: for a principle to qualify as a *moral* principle (as distinct from, say, a scientific or a legal principle), it must prescribe conduct for all moral agents. Moral agents are those who can bring impartial reasons (i.e., reasons that respect the requirement of impartiality) to bear on deciding how they ought to act. They are thus conceived to be both rational and autonomous. Individuals who lack the ability to understand or act on the basis of impartial reasons (e.g., young children) fail to qualify as moral agents. They cannot meaningfully be said to have obligations to do, or to refrain from doing, what is morally right or wrong. Only moral agents can have this status, and moral principles can apply only to the determination of how moral agents should behave. Normal adult human beings are the paradigmatic instance of moral agents.

How does the idea of a valid moral principle relate to the concept of an ideal moral judgment? In an ideal moral judgment, it is not enough that the judgment be based on complete information, complete impartiality, complete conceptual clarity, and so on. It is also essential that the judgment be based on a *valid* or *correct* moral principle. Ideally, one wants not only to make the correct judgment but to make it for the correct reasons. The idea of valid moral principles will be discussed more fully below in part II, Normative Ethics.

## §6 NO DOUBLE STANDARDS ALLOWED

The portrait of the ideal moral judgment drawn in §5, or something very like it, forms the background of the several essays in this anthology. The authors do not always explicitly say that, for example, impartiality or rationality are ideals worth striving for; but the manner in which they argue makes it clear that these ideals play an important role in their examinations of the views of others. Accordingly, these philosophers imply that it would be fair to apply these same ideals to their own thinking. In the case of each essay, therefore, we can ask:

1.  Have important concepts been analyzed, and, if so, have they been analyzed correctly?
2.  Does the author argue from a basis of knowledge of the real-life setting(s) in which a moral question arises?
3.  Is the author rational? (Do the arguments presented observe the rules of logic?)
4.  Is there a lack of impartiality? (Is someone, or some group, arbitrarily favored over others?)
5.  Are things argued for in a state of strong emotion? (Are deep feelings rhetorically vented in the place of hard thinking?)
6.  Are the moral principles used valid ones? (Is any effort expended to show that they meet the appropriate criteria?)

These six questions, then, though they do not exhaust all possibilities, at least provide a place to begin. It is pertinent to ask how our authors pose these questions of the persons whose views they examine. But fairness requires that these same questions be asked of each author's views too. No double standards are allowed.

## II. NORMATIVE ETHICS

Earlier, meta-ethics was characterized as the inquiry into the meaning of key concepts (for example, 'autonomy' and 'rights') as well as the inquiry into whether there is a correct method for answering moral questions. Meta-ethical questions, however, by no means exhaust a moral philosopher's interest in ethics. A second main area of inquiry is commonly referred to as *normative ethics.* Philosophers engaged in normative ethics attempt to go beyond the questions concerning meaning and method that arise in meta-ethics; the goal they set themselves is nothing short of determining *what moral principles are valid* —those principles, that is, by which all moral agents ought morally to be guided. There is, then, an important connection between the goal of normative ethics and the concept of an ideal moral judgment. An ideal moral judgment, we have said, must be based on valid moral principles, and it is just the question, "What principles *are* the valid ones?" that is at the heart of normative ethics. Unless the normative ethical philosopher succeeds in disclosing what moral principles are valid, therefore, a vital part of the ideal moral judgment will be unfulfillable because unknown.

Which moral principles *are* valid? Not surprisingly, a variety of answers have been offered. Not all of them can be considered here, and no one can be considered in much detail. But enough can be said to make important ideas intelligible.

## §7 CONSEQUENTIALIST THEORIES

One way to begin the search for the valid moral principle(s) is to begin with our considered beliefs (also referred to by some as our "reflective intuitions"). These beliefs or intuitions are not to be identified with what we just happen to believe independent of our critical reflection; rather, our considered beliefs are those beliefs we have about right and wrong, good and bad, justice and injustice *after* we have made a conscientious effort to think about these beliefs with an eye to four of the five requirements of the ideal moral judgment explained in §5. Such beliefs are considered beliefs or reflective intuitions, in other words, only if we have made our best effort to think about them with maximal conceptual clarity, coolly and impartially, and against the backdrop of the ideal of complete information. Those moral beliefs we continue to hold or come to hold *after* we have thought about them in these terms are our considered beliefs, and it is at least in part by appeal to such beliefs, or so many moral philosophers think, that normative moral philosophy can get under way and against which its possible success can be fairly tested. Not all moral philosophers, it is true, not even all those who have contributed to this volume, are in agreement on this fundamental methodological point. But let us see how this point of agreement in theory, where it obtains, might work in practice.

Suppose we could reach agreement about a body of considered beliefs; then we would believe, on reflection, that certain acts are right or wrong, just or unjust, and the like. Assuming this much we could then ask how this body of beliefs could be unified; we could ask, in other words, what general moral principle(s) unify these intuitions by identifying their plausible common ground. By way of example, suppose George and Gracie each operate farms and sell their produce at roadside stands. George's business has suffered of late because of the recent competition offered by Gracie's new stand, and he decides to eliminate the competition by hiring a professional arsonist with whom he has had dealings in the past. Fire inspectors rule that the fire that gutted Gracie's house was due to faulty wiring, George's business regains its former vitality, and Gracie, who barely had enough money to start her enterprise and had no insurance, is left in a state of abject poverty. Suppose we judge that what George did was wrong, and suppose we make this judgment not only initially but after we have made a conscientious effort to think about the case coolly, impartially, and so on. What could plausibly illuminate the wrongness of George's act? Well, Gracie experiences some unhappiness certainly. When she thinks about her former business she is distraught and frustrated, and the enjoyment she would have had, if the business had continued to grow, is canceled. Gracie, then, is worse off than she would have been, both in terms of the unhappiness of her present condition and in terms of lost enjoyment. Thinking along these lines has led some philosophers to theorize that what makes George's (and the arsonist's) act wrong is that it is the cause of bad results, in this case the frustration, anger, disappointment, and general unhappiness caused Gracie.

Next imagine this case. Suppose people accepted a general rule whose observance gave unequal care to terminally ill patients. This rule requires that the terminally ill receive medical care when they are male but not when they are female; in the latter case they receive no care at all. Such a rule must strike us as radically unjust. But why? Well, imagine how women who are not terminally ill are likely to feel. It is not implausible to suppose that they will feel angry, fearful, and envious. These feelings (anger, fear, envy) are not desirable. Moreover, those females who are terminally ill, because they receive no care at all, are very likely to suffer grievously in many cases. As in the earlier example of George and Gracie, then, we again have a situation where (1) we would judge, on reflection, that something is wrong and (2) what we judge to be wrong causes bad results.

Many philosophers have not stopped with just these sorts of cases. Roughly speaking, the one common and peculiar characteristic of every wrong action, they have theorized, is that it leads to bad results, whereas the one common and peculiar characteristic of every right action, again roughly speaking, is that it leads to good results. Philosophers who accept this type of view commonly are referred to as *consequentialists,* an appropriate name given their strong emphasis on results or consequences. Theories of this type also are called *teleological theories,* from the Greek *telos,* meaning "end" or "purpose," another fitting name since, according to these thinkers, actions are not right or wrong in themselves; they are right or wrong, according to these theories, if they promote or frustrate the purpose of morality—namely, to bring about the greatest possible balance of good over evil consequences. Acts are, as it were, arrows we shoot: right acts hit the target (that is, cause the best results); wrong acts do not.

Now, in normative ethics, when someone advances a principle that states what makes all right acts right and all wrong acts wrong, they do so in the course of advancing a *normative ethical theory.* Considered abstractly, there are at least three different types of teleological normative ethical theories.

1. *Ethical egoism:* According to this theory, roughly speaking, whether any person (A) has done what is morally right or wrong depends solely on how good or bad the consequences of A's action are *for* A. How *others* are affected is irrelevant, unless how they are affected in turn alters the consequences for A.

2. *Ethical altruism:* According to this theory, roughly speaking, whether any person (B) has done what is morally right or wrong depends solely on how good or bad the consequences of B's action are *for everyone except* B. How B is affected is irrelevant, unless how B is affected in turn alters the consequences for anyone else.

3. *Utilitarianism:* According to this theory, roughly speaking, whether any person (C) has done what is morally right or wrong depends solely on how good or bad the consequences of C's action are *for everyone affected.* Thus, how C is affected is relevant; but so is how *others* are affected. How *everyone* concerned is affected by the good or bad consequences is relevant.

These are not very exact statements of these three types of teleological normative ethical theories, but enough has been said about two of them—namely, ethical egoism and ethical altruism—to enable us to understand why most philosophers find them unsatisfactory. Both seem to fall far short of the ideal of impartiality, ethical egoism because it seems to place arbitrary and exclusive importance on the good or welfare of the individual agent, and ethical altruism because it seems to place arbitrary and exclusive importance on the good or welfare of everyone else. Moreover, both theories arguably lead to consequences that clash with a broad range of reflective intuitions. This is perhaps clearest in the case of ethical egoism. Provided only that, all considered, torching Gracie's house led to consequences that were as good *for George* as any that would have resulted had he acted otherwise, what he did was not morally wrong according to ethical egoism. But that is something we would most likely deny, not only in a case involving arson but in many other sorts of cases (e.g., murder or rape, which also would not be wrong if the consequences *for the agent* were at least as good as those that would have resulted if the agent had acted otherwise). Faced with the choice between accepting ethical egoism or giving up a large class of considered beliefs, most philosophers choose to reject the theory and retain the convictions.

An important variation on the main theme of ethical egoism deserves brief mention. *Contractarianism* is the name usually given to a cluster of normative theories, each of which is traceable to the plausible assumption that any individual (A) has a *good reason* to favor what is in that individual's own self-interest. Imagine, then, that A is being asked to decide what policies or rules to accept and support. For example, suppose A is asked about the rule (M) "Do not murder." Then A will have a good reason to accept and support M if it is in A's self-interest to do so. And who can doubt that it *would* be in A's self-interest to accept and support this rule, or other, familiar rules— for example, "Do not steal" and "Do not lie"?

Unlike ethical egoism proper, however, all forms of contractarianism necessarily involve considerations on the part of *at least two* different individuals—the so-called contractors. Not only must A agree to accept and support M, because to do so is in A's self-interest, but at least one other individual (B) must do the same because it is in *B's* self-interest to do the same. For obvious reasons there is no upper limit on the number of people who can be parties to the contract—who can, that is, agree to accept and support one or more rules because it is in the self-interest of each contractor to do so. In fact, in some versions of contractarianism rules are viewed as morally binding if and only if each rational individual, seeking to maximize his or her own self-interest, would have just as good a reason to accept and support each rule as every other rational, self-interested individual would have. This is the version of contractarianism (sometimes called "rational egoism") that Jan Narveson seems to favor in his essay, "At Arms' Length: Violence and War." It is a normative theory not to be summarily dismissed, requiring, as it does, very careful evaluation before we may reasonably give or withhold our informed assent. Certainly it is not open to the criticisms, mentioned earlier, to which standard versions of ethical egoism are vulnerable. But whatever our final judgment of the merits of contractarian theories happens to be, it is utilitarianism, within the class of consequentialist normative ethical theories, that historically has and, in the present climate of thought, continues to have the largest number of philosophical adherents. It is to the task of offering a somewhat lengthier characterization of its possible strengths and weaknesses that we must now turn.

## §8 UTILITARIANISM

"The Principle of Utility" is the name given to the fundamental principle advocated by those who are called utilitarians. This principle has been formulated in different ways. Here is a common formulation.

> Acts are right if they bring about the greatest possible balance of
> intrinsic good over intrinsic evil for everyone concerned; otherwise
> they are wrong.

Already it must be emphasized that utilitarians do not agree on everything. In particular, they do not all agree on what is intrinsically good
and evil. Some philosophers (called *value hedonists*) think that pleasure and pleasure alone is intrinsically good (or good in itself), whereas
pain, or the absence of pleasure, and this alone, is intrinsically evil (or
evil in itself). Others (so-called preference utilitarians) believe that the
satisfaction of one's desires or preferences is what is good and their
frustration bad. The classical utilitarians—Jeremy Bentham (1748–
1832) and John Stuart Mill (1806–1873)—favor hedonistic utilitarianism. Most recent utilitarians, especially those who seek to apply
economic theory to ethical issues, favor preference utilitarianism.
Whether either of these views regarding intrinsic value is adequate is
a question we can bypass at this juncture, since the ideas of special
importance for our present purposes can be discussed independently
of whether value hedonism, for example, is a reasonable position.

*Act- and Rule-Utilitarianism*    One idea of special importance is the
difference between act-utilitarianism and rule-utilitarianism. *Act-
utilitarianism* is the view that the Principle of Utility should be applied to individual actions; *rule-utilitarianism* states that the Principle
of Utility should be applied mainly to rules of action. The act-
utilitarian says that whenever people have to decide what to do, they
ought to perform that act which will bring about the greatest possible
balance of intrinsic good over intrinsic evil. The rule-utilitarian says
something different: People are to do what is required by justified
moral rules. These are rules, some rule-utilitarians maintain, that
would lead to the best possible consequences, all considered, *if* everyone were to abide by them. The rules recognized as valid by these
rule-utilitarians, in other words, need not be rules that most people
*do* accept and act on—what we might call conventional morality.
Rules recognized as valid are those everyone *should* act on because
everyone's doing so would lead to the best results. If a justified rule
unambiguously applies to a situation, and if no other justified moral
rule applies, then the person in that situation ought to choose to do
what the rule requires, even if in that particular situation performing
this act will not lead to the best consequences. Thus, act-utilitarians
and rule-utilitarians can reach opposing moral judgments. An act that
is wrong according to the rule-utilitarian, because it is contrary to a
justified moral rule, might not be wrong according to the act-
utilitarian's position.

*Some Problems for Act-Utilitarianism*    Is act-utilitarianism correct?
Many philosophers answer no. One reason given against this theory is
that act-utilitarianism clashes with a broad range of our considered

beliefs. Recall the arson example. According to act-utilitarianism, whether George's hiring of the arsonist was wrong or not depends on this and this alone: Were the net consequences for everyone affected by the outcome at least as good as the net consequences that would have resulted if he had done anything else? It is not *just* the bad results Gracie has to live with (her frustration, anger, and the like) that are relevant. How *others* are affected also is relevant, given act-utilitarianism, and there is no reason why, just because Gracie is made worse off than she would have been as a result of George's decision, *the sum or total* of the good and bad consequences for everyone involved might not "hit" the utilitarian target. The benefits George derives from eliminating Gracie's competition, the income the arsonist earns, and the possible pleasures and satisfactions others derive (for example, perhaps George's son can now go to college and the arsonist's wife can have her teeth capped)—these pleasures and satisfactions, too, not just Gracie's misery, have to be taken into account. In principle, then, there is no reason why the consequences, all considered, might not add up to the best balance of good over evil, or at least equal a balance that is as good as any other that would have resulted if George had acted otherwise.

Suppose the consequences are at least as good as any that would have obtained had George acted otherwise. Then act-utilitarianism implies that what he did was right. And yet his involvement in the destruction of Gracie's business is likely to strike us as wrong. Thus, we again seem to be faced with a choice between (1) retaining a considered belief or (2) accepting a particular normative ethical theory. And the same choice would recur in a host of other cases involving our reflective intuitions (e.g., intuitions about the wrongness of murder and rape, individual cases of which arguably could lead to the best balance of good results over bad, when the good and bad for the involved individuals are totaled). There are, that is, *many* sorts of cases where the implications of act-utilitarianism are or seem to be in conflict with our considered beliefs. In the face of such conflicts, many come down on the side of retaining our convictions and rejecting the theory.

Act-utilitarians actively defend their position against this line of criticism. The debate is among the liveliest and most important in normative ethics. The point that bears emphasis here is that *rule-*utilitarians do not believe that *their* version of utilitarianism can be refuted by the preceding argument. On their view what George did was wrong because it violated a valid moral rule—the rule against destroying another's property. Thus, rule-utilitarians hold that their position not only does not lead to a conclusion that clashes with the conviction that what George did was wrong; this position actually illuminates *why* it was—namely, because it violates a rule whose adoption by everyone can be defended by an appeal to the Principle of Utility.

*Some Problems for Rule-Utilitarians*   One success does not guarantee that all goes well, however, and many philosophers think that rule-utilitarianism, too, is inadequate. One of the most important objections turns on considerations about justice. The point of the objection is that rule-utilitarianism arguably could justify the adoption of rules that would be grossly unjust. To make this clearer, recall the rule that figured in our earlier example about health care: terminally ill men are to receive medical care but women are not. The injustice of this rule (R) jumps out at us. It is unjust to discriminate against people in the way R requires. And yet might not this rule be justified by appeal to rule-utilitarianism? Certainly it seems possible that, when the good and bad consequences for each affected individual are taken into account and totaled, we might find that adopting R would bring about the best balance of good over bad results. Granted, the envy, resentment, fear, and anger of women must be taken into account. But so, too, must the benefits that males secure. So, *on balance,* the "minuses" for women *might* be more than offset by the "pluses" for men. If, then, rule-utilitarianism could sanction unjust rules, not only in health care but across the broad sweep of social policies (for example, in education, voting, and employment, where women might be denied benefits offered to men in the name of the "general welfare")—if this is true, then rule-utilitarianism is not the adequate ethical theory its proponents suppose.

Can the rule-utilitarian meet this challenge? Philosophers are not unanimous in their answer. As was the case with the debate over the correctness of act-utilitarianism, this debate is too extensive to be examined further here. Nevertheless, enough has been said to suggest the importance of utilitarianism and to anticipate some of the ways it surfaces in the essays.

To begin with, some of the philosophers in this anthology are utilitarians—for example, Singer holds this theory. Moreover, even those who are not utilitarians (or are not clearly so) often use utilitarian arguments to support their position. Beauchamp, for example, argues that a rule permitting suicide under certain conditions can be defended on a rule-utilitarian basis. Moreover, even those philosophers who are most clearly not utilitarians—for example, O'Neill—discuss this theory. In a word, there is not a single essay in which utilitarianism does not put in an appearance, so that the following questions can be asked of each.

1.   Is the philosopher being read a utilitarian?
2.   If so, of what kind—act or rule?
3.   If the philosopher is a utilitarian, are persuasive arguments adduced in support of the utilitarian answers given?
4.   Is the possible clash between justice and utility examined?
5.   If the philosopher being read is not a utilitarian, then what arguments, if any, are given against the correctness of the

principle of utility and how rationally compelling are these arguments?

6. Moreover, if the philosopher is not a utilitarian, what other principle (or principles), if any, is (are) subscribed to?

7. How rationally compelling are the arguments, if any, that are given in support of the principle(s)?

## §9 NONCONSEQUENTIALIST THEORIES

'Nonconsequentialism' is a name frequently given to normative ethical theories that are not forms of consequentialism. In other words, any theory that states that moral right and wrong are *not* determined solely by the relative balance of intrinsic good over intrinsic evil commonly is called a nonconsequentialist theory. Theories of this type are also called *deontological* theories, from the Greek *deon,* meaning "duty." Such theories might be either (a) extreme or (b) moderate. An extreme deontological theory holds that the intrinsic good and evil of consequences are totally irrelevant to determining what is morally right or wrong. A moderate nonconsequentialist theory holds that the intrinsic good and evil of consequences *are relevant* to determining what is morally right and wrong but that they are not the *only* things that are relevant and may not be of the greatest importance in some cases. A great variety of nonconsequentialist theories, both extreme and moderate, have been advanced. Why have some philosophers been attracted to such theories?

*The Problem of Justice* A central argument advanced against all forms of consequentialism by many nonconsequentialists is that no consequentialist theory (no form of ethical egoism, ethical altruism, or utilitarianism) can account for basic convictions about justice and injustice—for example, that it is unjust to allow policies that discriminate against people on the basis of race or sex. The point these deontologists make is that such discrimination is not only wrong; harming the people who are discriminated against wrongs them. Fundamentally, according to these thinkers, it is because people are wronged when treated unjustly, quite apart from the value of the consequences for the victim or others, that all consequentialist theories ultimately prove to be deficient.

Suppose these deontologists are correct—a large assumption! Some deontological theory would then be called for. A number of such theories have been advanced. The one associated with the German philosopher Immanuel Kant (1724–1804) is unquestionably the most influential. In Kant's view, all persons (that is, all rational, autonomous individuals) have a distinctive kind of value, a unique worth or dignity. The value these people have, Kant may be interpreted to believe, is not reducible to the value of their mental states (e.g., their pleasure) and is, in fact, incommensurate with this latter kind of value; one cannot meaningfully ask how much pleasure the value of an individual is equal to. That would be like trying to compare apples and oranges. Moreover, the worth of a person is not reducible to that individual's talents (for example, at sports or music) or to that individual's utility or service to others (a surgeon has neither more nor less worth than a dishwasher, a saint neither more nor less than an unscrupulous used car salesman), nor to how others relate to that individual (the loved and admired are neither more nor less valuable than the despised and forsaken). All who have worth or value as individuals, in short, have this value equally. Now, in order to treat such individuals as morality requires, we must never treat them in ways that fail to show proper respect for their unique value. Yet this is precisely what we would be guilty of if, in an effort to justify treating some people in a given way, we claimed that doing so gave rise to the best aggregate balance of pleasure over pain, or preference satisfactions over frustrations, for all affected by the outcome. For Kant, this is tantamount to ignoring the distinctive kind of value people have as individuals; it is to treat them as *mere means* to promote the ends others have, not as ends in themselves. Any and all such disrespectful treatment is wrong, for Kant, whatever the consequences.

This Kantian approach to moral questions offers a strikingly different interpretation of equality than the one offered by utilitarians. For Kant, it is *individuals* who are equal in value, whereas, for utilitarians, what is equal in value are similar pleasures or preference satisfactions. Moreover, Kant's position provides a very different way to approach questions of just treatment, something we can illustrate by recalling the rule (R) that terminally ill men are to receive medical care but women are not. As was suggested earlier (§7), a utilitarian justification of adopting R is at hand *if* observing R would produce the best aggregate balance of good over bad for all those affected by the outcome, assuming that the preferences or pleasures of all have been considered and weighted equitably. The fact that, if this rule were adopted, women would experience more pain, fear, and so on than would men *by itself* is no objection to adopting it, given utilitarian theory. What each person is due is equal consideration and weighting of their pleasures or preferences, and as that is what each gets in this case, there should be no cry of injustice.

Kant would be of a different mind. The very approach to R's justification prescribed by utilitarians is morally flawed from the outset. What all people are due is respect for their value *as individuals*, something we would fail to show if we attempted to decide the morality of acts or rules by asking which among them causes the best aggregate balance of good over bad (e.g., pleasure over pain) for all affected by the outcome. If, then, the justification of R is that its adoption "would promote the general welfare," those who follow Kant would decry its adoption. Conduct prescribed by the rule in question is wrong because it treats women with something less than the respect they are due, treating them *as if their value* as individuals could be ignored if doing so would bring about the best consequences.

## §10 LEGAL AND MORAL RIGHTS

Philosophers sympathetic with Kant can use his views concerning the unique value of the individual as a foundation on which to rest their positions about the rights of the individual. To make this clearer, it will be useful first to explain some of the differences between the concept of legal and moral rights.

First, moral rights, if there are any, are *universal,* while legal rights need not be. Legal rights depend upon the law of this or that country, and what is a matter of legal right in one country may not be so in another. For example, in the United States any citizen eighteen years old or older has the legal right to vote in federal elections; but not everyone in every nation has this same legal right. If, however, persons living in the United States have a moral right to, say, life, then *every* person in every nation has this same moral right, whether or not it is also recognized as a legal right.

Second, unlike legal rights, moral rights are *equal* rights. If all persons have a moral right to life, then all have this right equally; it is not a right that some (for example, males) can possess to a greater extent than others (for example, females). Neither, then, could this moral right be possessed to a greater extent by the inhabitants of one country (for example, one's own) than by the inhabitants of some other country (for example, a country poor in agricultural resources with a burgeoning human population and widespread famine).

Third, moral rights often are said to be *inalienable,* meaning they cannot be transferred to another—for example, they cannot be lent or sold. If Frankie has a moral right to life, then it is hers and it cannot become anyone else's. Frankie may give her life for her country, sacrifice it in the name of science, or destroy it herself in a fit of rage or despair. But she cannot give, sacrifice, or destroy her right to life. Legal rights, on the other hand, are paradigmatically transferable, as when Frankie transfers her legal right to an inheritance to Johnnie or gives him her car.

Fourth, moral rights are sometimes said to be "natural" rights, not in the sense that they are discoverable by closely studying nature from the scientific point of view but in that they are not conventional—are not, that is, as are legal rights, created by the acts of ordinary human beings.

Kant's view of the unique worth of persons dovetails with these four characteristics of the concept of a moral right: (1) *all* persons have unique worth (that is, this value is *universal* among persons); (2) no one person has this value *to any greater degree* than any other (that is, all who have this value have it *equally*); (3) those who have this unique value *cannot transfer* it to anyone else, or buy or sell it (that is, this unique value is *inalienable*); and, finally, (4) the value or dignity persons possess is theirs *independently of the acts or decisions of anyone else* (is, that is, "natural," in the sense explained). Small wonder, then, that those philosophers enamored of the view that individuals have moral rights should find a strong ally in Kant's views about the value of the individual.

## §11 LEGAL AND MORAL JUSTICE

Moral and legal rights are connected in important ways with moral and legal justice. Legal justice requires that one respect the legal rights of everyone, while moral justice demands that everyone's moral rights be honored. The two—legal justice and moral justice—do not necessarily coincide. Critics of "the law" frequently claim that certain laws are morally unjust. For example, a country might have a law that allows companies owned by whites to pollute but not those owned by blacks. Then *legal* justice might be done in this country if this law is enforced. If people have moral rights, however, it would not follow that moral justice is done. That would depend not on whether there is a particular law in this country but on whether the law recognizes and protects the moral rights of the country's inhabitants. If it does, then the law is both legally and morally just; if it does not, then, though the law may be legally just, it lacks moral justice. Thus, this law in particular and "the law" in general are appropriate objects of moral assessment, a theme that emerges in a number of the essays.

## §12 WHAT ARE RIGHTS?

Whether rights are moral or legal, the question remains: What are rights? How is the concept of a right to be analyzed? Various answers have been given, ranging from the view that rights are an individual's entitlements to be treated in certain ways to the view that they are valid claims that individuals can make, or have made on their behalf, to have their interests or welfare taken into account. What is common to these answers is that a right involves the idea of a *justified constraint upon how others may act*. If Margaret has a right to X, then Pierre and others are constrained not to interfere with her pursuit or possession of X, at least so long as her pursuit or possession of X does not come into conflict with their rights. If it does, Margaret may be exceeding her rights, and a serious moral question would arise. But aside from cases of exceeding one's rights and, as may sometimes be the case, of forfeiting them, the possession of a right by one individual places a justified limit on how other individuals may treat the person possessing the right. Whether rights are entitlements or valid claims, they involve a justified constraint or limitation on how others may act.

## §13 NEGATIVE AND POSITIVE RIGHTS

Even were we to agree that people themselves have a unique sort of value and moral rights grounded in this value, we might still disagree on what rights they have. Though the terminology frequently differs, philosophers who defend the validity of moral rights all seem to agree that some of these rights are *liberty rights;* in many cases, that is, to have a right is simply *to be at liberty* to act as one chooses (for example, to go to a concert, or to stay at home). Other rights are *claim rights;* those who have such rights *have a valid claim to be treated in certain ways* (for example, not to be injured, or have lies spread about them, or be killed). Both sorts of rights have correlative duties. If Eleanor is at liberty to have the chocolate cake rather than the strawberry yogurt, then Franklin has a duty not to deny her the exercise of her liberty when she makes her choice, something he would be doing if he coerced or forced her to choose as *he* wished. If, in addition, Eleanor has a right to life, then Franklin has a duty not to kill her except, perhaps, in quite exceptional circumstances (as in self-defense).

Now, both those duties correlated with liberty rights and those correlated with claim rights are *negative duties.* They prescribe what people *are not to do,* how they *are not to act,* given that others have such rights. As such, it seems that we can fulfill these duties by doing nothing. If, that is, Franklin does not personally kill Eleanor, then he seems to do all that is required to respect her right to life, while if he does not personally interfere with the exercise of her liberty, then he seems to do all he is obliged to do to respect her right to liberty. So-called *welfare rights,* however, if there are such rights, differ fundamentally. If people have welfare rights, we have a *duty to help them,* not merely a duty not to harm them or not to interfere with their liberty. And the performance of this duty to help, if this duty is correlated with welfare *rights,* is something that we *owe* to those who need it, is something *they deserve,* and so is their due as a matter of moral justice.

Debates about our duties to the victims of famine frequently turn on the position different people take concerning welfare or, as these are sometimes called, positive rights. If those who are starving to death have only negative rights, then people who do not choose to help them are not guilty of violating the victims' rights. People may, of course, choose to help even if those who are starving have no right to be helped, and the charitable acts of those who do decide to do this no doubt should be praised. But people need not help if they choose not to, preferring to do something else instead—say, spend a month at the beach or a week gambling in Las Vegas. If the victims of famine have no right to our help, then morality simply does not require that the more affluent lend a hand. If, however, the victims of famine have a welfare or positive right to our assistance, then people do wrong if they fail to help; indeed, if the victims have a right to be helped, then others (for example, national governments or, perhaps, international agencies) could be morally authorized to coerce the more affluent to help, using the threat of force, punishment, or some other sanction to encourage compliance on the part of the better off. It is no idle question to ask, therefore, whether the victims of famine have a right to be helped, a question Onora O'Neill considers at length in her contribution to the present volume. But the importance of the notion of welfare or positive rights by no means is confined to the particular issue of famine. It makes its presence felt in virtually every important debate about social policy, from education and employment to voting rights and health care, and is, indeed, a sort of litmus test for the type of political philosophy one accepts. *Libertarianism,* for example, is the view, roughly speaking, that each rational individual has a basic negative moral right to liberty, a right that morally can be limited only by the liberty rights of others. In other words, I am at liberty to do anything I wish so long as I do not violate your rights in the process; and the same is true of you. You may not like what I do; you may even think it wrong. But that does not give you a license to interfere with my legitimate exercise of my liberty. The proper role of the state, then, according to libertarianism, is to protect this fundamental negative right of its citizens, and this it does, at least in part, by itself avoiding reliance on coercive programs that assume that people have positive rights—for example, rights to food, clothing, or shelter. The citizens of a state may freely choose to help the needy; to do so is one way in which they may choose to exercise their liberty; and those who do so may even be praised for the beneficence. But no one, not even the state, is morally authorized to force or compel another to help those who need it. The shadow libertarianism casts across the moral-political landscape, at the levels of both theory and practice, certainly will be visible in several of the essays.

## §14 THE CRITERIA OF RIGHT-POSSESSION

Suppose the concept of a moral right is clear and that some beings have moral rights. Many questions would still remain to be explored. One in particular stands out: What are the criteria of right-possession? Or, in terms explained earlier (§2), What are the necessary and sufficient conditions of right-possession? Again, many different answers have been proposed. Here are some examples: (a) All and only free, rational beings have moral rights; (b) All and only sentient beings (that is, individuals capable of experiencing pleasure and pain) have moral rights; (c) All and only beings who are able to use a language have moral rights; (d) All and only beings who have a concept of themselves as an enduring identity (that is, who have a concept of their identity as the same self over time) have moral rights.

How might one rationally choose among these alternatives? This methodological question is hotly disputed, but one way to proceed here is as follows. Suppose that not only "normal" adult human beings but also infants, the senile, and the mentally enfeebled of all ages have moral rights. If this much were granted, there would be powerful grounds for denying the correctness of some of the proposed criteria of right-possession listed above. Infants, for example, presumably do not have a concept of themselves as an enduring entity, so that, if they have moral rights, this proposed criterion cannot be correct; having a concept of oneself as an enduring entity cannot be a *necessary* condition of having rights, granting the assumption about infants, etc., having rights. Neither could being free and rational be correct, since many mentally enfeebled humans lack these capacities. And the same is true of the ability to use a language, since it sets as a necessary condition of right-possession a capacity that many human beings (some of the mentally enfeebled, again) fail to satisfy. In this way, then, an argument could be developed against the correctness of various proposed criteria of right-possession. To argue in favor of the correctness of a proposed criterion would consist, at least in part, in asking whether any given criterion sets forth conditions that those humans assumed to have rights (infants, the enfeebled, etc.) can satisfy. If there is such a criterion, then its claim to correctness is to that degree a strong one, given our assumptions. The criterion of sentience, for example, arguably passes this test, and thus, given our assumptions, must be considered to be a strong candidate for the correct criterion of right-possession.

## §15 WHAT BEINGS POSSESS WHAT MORAL RIGHTS?

Suppose that the criterion of being sentient is the correct criterion of right-possession; then *only* those beings who are sentient and *all* those beings who are sentient have moral rights. Now, if this is true, a position would have been reached that is fraught with enormous practical implications. To begin with, there are many nonhumans who are sentient—namely, many nonhuman animals. If all sentient beings have moral rights, then these animals have moral rights; and if these animals have moral rights, we must seriously stop to inquire whether we are doing anything that violates their rights when we eat or experiment upon them. This is a question that is pursued in considerable depth by Singer in his essay. Moreover, there are some *human* beings who lack sentiency—namely, those who are comatose. If a being must be sentient to have moral rights, then has the comatose individual lost all rights? This is an issue discussed in James Rachels's essay on euthanasia.

Still, *is* sentience a necessary condition of right-possession? Recall that the reason underlying the introduction of the idea of moral rights was that it seems possible to act in ways that harm or wrong people. But why must the ideas of harming or wronging be limited to people or to sentient beings? Might it not be possible to harm or wrong any living thing? If a tree is killed or the sagebrush is destroyed, have they not been harmed? And if they have, might not the idea that living but nonsentient entities have moral rights demand serious consideration? Perhaps life itself is inherently valuable? Perhaps all living things have a right to life?

Short of extending moral rights to trees or sagebrush, there may be grounds for rejecting the view that sentience is a necessary condition of right-possession. Possibly the *potential* for sentience must be added, an addition that at once *excludes* trees and sagebrush and *includes* many more beings than are included if just sentience is accepted. In particular, adding the *potential* for sentience would necessitate including many human *fetuses* in the class of beings having moral rights. And if these beings are included, how can one avoid the conclusion that abortion violates the fetus's right to life? The debate revolving around this idea is a central theme in the essay on abortion. Clearly, to ask about the criteria of right-possession is not an idle, merely theoretical question like asking how many angels can dance on the head of a pin.

To establish what beings can and do have moral rights, however, may not necessarily establish all the moral rights they have. Consider the three rights enshrined in the American Declaration of Independence: the rights to life, liberty, and the pursuit of happiness. Someone who argues that a given being, A, has a right to life, does not necessarily have to believe that A also has the right to liberty. If, for example, sense can be made of the idea of extending a right to life to trees and plants, it would not follow that a right to liberty must also be attributed. This would be meaningless, since plants lack the power to exercise choice. Or consider the status of animals. Perhaps it is possible to argue in support of the view that they have a moral right not to be made to suffer unnecessary pain. Still, it does not follow necessarily that they have *other* moral rights—for example, a right to life. The question of *what* moral rights a being has must be examined separately from the question of what beings satisfy the criteria for the possession of moral rights.

## §16 WHEN RIGHTS CONFLICT

One final question relating to the topic of rights deserves our attention. It sometimes happens that one person's rights conflict with another's. The case of abortion illustrates this well. Suppose that both the fetus and the pregnant woman have a right to life. And suppose that, as sometimes happens, the medical situation is such that if the fetus is permitted to be born, the woman will die, whereas if steps are taken to enable the woman to live, the fetus will die. Since both rights cannot prevail, whose, the fetus's or the woman's, ought to? One way of thinking about conflicting rights will be described here.

*The Idea of Innocence*   Innocence is an important moral idea. In the case of punishment, for example, it is morally wrong to punish someone who is known to be innocent. Innocence might be extremely important in some cases where rights conflict. Suppose the right to life of two beings, A and B, conflict; and suppose, further, that A is innocent of any wrongdoing whereas B is in this situation because B has not acted responsibly—for example, perhaps B has been negligent. Then ought not A's right to life prevail over B's? Ought not such cases of conflict be settled by appealing to the following rule: "Whenever the right to life of two beings conflict, the right to life of the innocent party must always take precedence over the right to life of the party who is not innocent"?

Unfortunately, the situation is not so simple. For though innocence always is a relevant moral consideration, it is not clear that it should always be given a place of preeminence. To make this clearer, let us apply the previous argument to the case of abortion. The fetus, it is agreed, is innocent. Let us assume, however, that the woman and the prospective father have acted irresponsibly: they have not taken due precautions to avoid pregnancy. Thus, it hardly seems fair to abort the fetus. But suppose we know that the fetus, if it is permitted to develop, will become a grossly deformed child—no arms or legs, blind, and acutely mentally defective. Is the fact that the fetus is innocent, while the potential parents are not, a sufficiently weighty reason to insist that, morally speaking, the fetus ought not to be aborted? Are there not other, possibly weightier, reasons in addition to the comparative innocence of the parties in question? Many philosophers think so. Feinberg explores some of their arguments in his essay on abortion. But the kind of problem just described, where rights conflict, is to be met with in many of the essays.

## §17 MORAL ATOMISM AND HOLISM

Despite their many differences, all of the normative ethical theories discussed so far are "atomistic"; that is, each holds it is of crucial moral importance that *individuals* be considered equitably. Some of the theories, it is true, emphasize the importance of considering the rights or worth of individuals, while others emphasize consideration of individual interests or preferences. Still, all take the notion of the importance of the individual as a sort of moral datum in terms of which we must do our thinking about moral right and wrong. As so often happens in philosophy, a widely shared assumption has given rise to a cadre of critics, persons who for a variety of reasons argue that the traditional importance attached to the individual in moral theory is misplaced at best and morally perverse at worst. In place of the pervasive "atomistic" emphasis in moral theory, these critics would have us develop a "holistic" vision, a vision that locates ultimate value in systems rather than in the individuals who comprise them. It is, on this view, the balance, sustainability, diversity, integrity—the beauty, even—of more or less large ecosystems or communities of living things that should be the focus of our moral thinking. The importance of the individual, like the emperor of lore, has no clothes.

This assault by holistic thinkers on the importance traditionally attached to the individual, and the growing debate over animal rights, are perhaps the most significant recent developments in the general area of environmental ethics. Nonanthropocentric well beyond those who argue for the rights of animals, these holistic thinkers are attempting to articulate a radical transformation of how we do ethics, or at least environmental ethics, and their possible success in this endeavor would, if it came to pass, have enormously important implications for virtually all of the issues discussed in this anthology. For example, a great deal of recent thought has been devoted to questions about the existence and stringency of our obligations to future generations. To the extent that we suppose that issues about environmental policy depend on obligations to future generations, however, to that extent at least it is arguable that we continue to perpetuate the "atomistic" vision of morality holistic critics are determined to replace. In their view, or so it seems, concern about the welfare and rights of the individual, even including those of our descendants, is too narrow, focusing as it does on the rights, interests, or value of the individual rather than on the beauty, stability, balance, and sustainability of ecosystems. Should we accept this "paradigm shift" away from the individual to the ecosystem? It is not easy to say. But it should come as no surprise that the grounds and implications of this holistic approach to environmental ethics should be the object of critical scrutiny in this volume (see, in particular, the essay by J. Baird Callicott).

## §18 THE VALUE OF LIFE

One idea mentioned earlier (§15) is that of the value of life. Many questions must be asked about this idea. Is life itself valuable, or is it rather that life is a necessary condition of other kinds of value? If life itself is valuable, why is it, and what kind of value does it have? If it is life itself that is valuable, are the lives of all living beings equally valuable? If it is said that only the lives of certain beings (say, human beings) are valuable, then what are the grounds for restricting the value of life in this way? These questions demand close scrutiny and are examined in many of the essays.

The idea of life's value is connected with most of the ideas discussed in this introduction. Its relevance to the question of moral rights will have to serve as illustrative. Suppose that the life of any human being (Bill) has a kind of value that does not depend on anyone else happening to find Bill useful or fun to be with; in other words, suppose Bill's life, and the life of any other person, is *inherently* valuable. Then it might be possible to argue that Bill and other persons have a moral right to life *because* their lives are inherently valuable. And this, if it were true, could have direct implications for debates over the morality of capital punishment, euthanasia, suicide, etc. If it is morally wrong to destroy an inherently valuable life, why are not all cases of capital punishment, euthanasia, and suicide morally wrong? As we might expect, just this question is considered in the essays on these respective topics. But the idea of life's value finds a place in each essay. To ask about the role that this idea plays in the several essays, therefore, is to formulate a final question that can be asked of each.

## §19 A FINAL SET OF QUESTIONS

The discussions of ideas in the preceding sections provide few, if any, answers, but like earlier discussions, they enable us to formulate a set of questions which we can take to the readings that follow. Here are some examples.

1. Does the author being read make use of the idea of individual rights and, if so, are the rights invoked legal or moral rights?
2. Is any effort expended to say what rights are (that is, how the notion of a right, whether moral or legal, is to be analyzed?) If so, how adequate is the analysis that is offered?
3. If moral rights are invoked, are they negative rights, or positive (welfare) rights, or both? And is any argument offered in support of recognizing the validity of the rights appealed to?
4. Does the author address the question of the scope of rights (that is, the question of who or what has rights)? For example, is the question concerning animal rights examined and, if so, how is it answered?
5. Does the author implicitly or explicitly subscribe to an anthropocentric vision of morality? Are human interests and rights, and *only* human interests and rights, assumed to be the measure of right and wrong?
6. Does the author implicitly or explicitly endorse an atomistic vision of morality, one that places the rights and interests of the *individual* at the center of our moral thinking, or is a holistic vision advocated, one that places value in the integrity and stability of whole systems or, perhaps, the entire biosphere? In either case, what arguments, if any, are offered to support the author's vision of the moral scheme of things, and how rationally compelling are these arguments?

As before, when we put our questions in terms of, say, the rights of the individual or the value of ecosystems or their nonhuman inhabitants, this final set of questions hardly exhausts those we can ask of the philosophers whose work we will be reading. Like the previous questions, however, those just given provide us with a map of sorts, helping to guide us through the thicket of ideas that lies ahead by reminding us of some of the questions we will need to ask if we are to understand where we are and where we are going. Philosophy, Aristotle remarks, begins in wonder, and to wonder is seriously to ask "What?" "Why?" "How?"—is, that is, seriously to question. To have a store of questions at our disposal, therefore, questions we will seriously pose of the essays that follow, is already to have begun the journey that is philosophy.

# 2

# Euthanasia

## JAMES RACHELS

In this essay we shall discuss the major moral and legal questions concerning euthanasia. Is euthanasia morally permissible, or is it morally wrong? Should it be against the law, or should it be legal?

## I. INTRODUCTION

It would be useful if we could define at the outset exactly what we mean by the word 'euthanasia'. But that is not an easy task. The word derives from two Greek words that mean, literally, "a good death," but we mean much more by it than that. The nearest English synonym for 'euthanasia' is 'mercy killing', which is close. Beyond that, it is hard to give a precise definition because the word is used in connection with a wide variety of cases.

### §1 THE CENTRAL CASE

Let's begin by looking at a case that illustrates perfectly what euthanasia is. (Incidentally, all the examples of euthanasia that I use throughout this essay are taken from real life.)

> Albert A., a hospital patient, was dying of cancer, which had spread throughout his body. The intense pain could no longer be controlled. Every four hours he would be given a painkiller, but over many months of treatment he had built up a tolerance for the drug, until now it would relieve the pain for only a few minutes each time. Albert knew that he was going to die anyway, for the cancer could not be cured. He did not want to linger in agony, so he asked his

doctor to give him a lethal injection to end his life without further suffering. His family supported this request.

It would have been illegal for the doctor to grant this request—in fact, it would have been first degree murder—so Albert was not given the injection.

If the doctor had killed Albert, it would have been a perfect example of euthanasia. The case would have had these five important features:

1.  The patient would have been deliberately killed.
2.  The patient was going to die soon anyway.
3.  The patient was suffering terrible pain.
4.  The patient asked to be killed.
5.  The killing would have been an act of mercy; that is, the *reason* for the killing would have been to prevent further needless suffering and to provide the patient with a "good death," or at least as good as it could be under the circumstances.

When all these features are present, we have the clearest possible case of euthanasia.

It is easy to find other examples of the same kind. Here is one in which the patient's request *was* granted:

> Barbara B. was a multiple amputee and diabetic in constant pain, who was told that she could live for only a few more months. She begged her husband to kill her, and he did, by electrocution. The husband was charged with murder and was convicted. On sentencing day the judge wept. Mr. B., who could have spent decades in prison, was sentenced to a year and a day. He never wavered in his opinion that he had done the right thing, and he said that his act was an act of love.

## §2 RELATED CASES

There are many other cases in which the above five features are *not* all present to which the word 'euthanasia' is also commonly applied. For example:

> Charles C. begged to be killed after being paralyzed from the neck down in an automobile accident. The doctors ignored the request, but his brother did not. The brother brought a sawed-off shotgun into the hospital and fatally wounded him.

This case is different from the previous ones because Charles C. was not going to die soon anyway, and he wanted to be killed, not because he was in pain, but because he did not want to live as a hopeless invalid. Other people, of course, might have had a different preference. Others might prefer to live paralyzed, rather than not to live at all. But not Charles C.; he preferred to die.

Donald D. had been a jet pilot and a rodeo performer and was in the prime of life when he was severely burned over 67 percent of his body by an exploding gas line. He was grotesquely disfigured, blinded, lost the use of both his arms and legs, and was in constant horrible pain for many months as all the most sophisticated techniques of modern medicine were used to keep him alive. When rational, he would ask to be killed—specifically, he wanted an overdose of heroin. He refused to give permission for treatment, and so a psychiatrist was called in to declare him "incompetent" to withhold consent. After interviewing Donald, the psychiatrist decided that he was in fact competent. But, having won his point, Donald suddenly changed his mind and consented to further treatment. He eventually regained partial use of his limbs and went to law school.

In all the cases I have mentioned so far, the patient is conscious, at least arguably rational, and requests death. In the following case, however, the patient is not rational and makes no such request:

Edward E., eighty-nine years old, had suffered three heart attacks, had bad kidneys, suffered various other ailments, and was hopelessly senile. He was hospitalized for his heart condition, and most of the time was only semiconscious. He was unable even to recognize members of his own family. There was no expectation of significant improvement in his condition. The attending physician instructed the hospital staff that if he should suffer another attack, nothing should be done to save him. Shortly afterwards, Edward's heart failed, no action was taken, and he died.

This is a very common sort of case, in which doctors have to decide how much is to be done to prolong lives that have become meaningless even to the patients themselves. In addition to the fact that the patient is not rational and that death is not requested, there are two other important features of this case that should be noted. First, the patient is not killed but is merely allowed to die. And second, the reason for allowing the patient to die is not as a kindness to him. The patient is not allowed to die for his own good, since he is not suffering. Rather, he is allowed to die because it is felt that there is simply no longer any point in keeping him alive. The case of Edward E. is similar in these ways to the following case:

Frances F. was in a permanent coma, being kept alive by machines and fed intravenously. She had suffered such severe brain damage that she could never wake up. She could be kept alive indefinitely by the use of artificial life-support systems, but if these machines were turned off she would die. The machines were turned off, and she died.

Like Edward, Frances did not ask to die, and like him, she was really unable to express an opinion in the matter. The attending physician judged that there was no point in keeping her alive—death would be neither kind nor cruel for her, since it would make no difference at all as far as *she* was concerned—so she was allowed to die.

Finally, we may note in passing a widely publicized recent case that raises some of the same issues as the above cases. In September 1983 Elizabeth Bouvia, a twenty-six-year-old cerebral palsy victim, checked into the Riverside (California) General Hospital and informed the staff that she wished to die of starvation while they made her comfortable by administering painkillers. (Lacking use of her limbs, she maintained this was the only means of suicide available to her.) The hospital refused this request, and a court battle ensued. While the case was being heard in court, she was force-fed through a nasogastric tube. In April 1984 she checked out of that hospital and went to a Mexican hospital that specializes in Laetrile and other treatments for cancer patients and made the same request. Again, she was refused. Then, in a dramatic reversal, she apparently changed her mind and began to eat voluntarily, saying to one newspaper reporter that she would "try" to "get better."

Elizabeth Bouvia was not a terminally ill patient; with adequate care, she could live indefinitely. But she did not want to go on living because she could not have a family, because she could not work, and because she had become so dependent on other people: at the court hearing, she said, "I hate to have someone care for every personal need . . . it's humiliating. It's disgusting, and I choose to no longer do that." The case raises several issues. Did she have a right to commit suicide? Would it have been permissible for the hospital to aid her as she requested? Did the hospital have a *duty* to provide that aid—that is, was it wrong for the hospital *not* to comply? (Even if you think it would have been permissible for the hospital to help her, it still does not follow that they were wrong not to help her.)

## §3 SOME DISTINCTIONS

At this point I want to introduce a bit of terminology. The phrase '*active* euthanasia' is used to refer to cases in which the patient is killed —for example, by being given a lethal injection. The phrase '*passive* euthanasia' refers to cases in which the patient is not killed but merely allowed to die. In passive euthanasia we simply refrain from doing anything to keep the patient alive—for example, we may refuse to perform surgery, administer medication, give a heart massage, or use a respirator—and let the person die of whatever ills are already present. It is important to note this distinction, because many people believe that, although active euthanasia is immoral, passive euthanasia is morally all right. They believe that, while we should never actually kill patients, it is sometimes all right to let them die.

In addition to the distinction between active and passive euthanasia, it is important to bear in mind the difference between voluntary, nonvoluntary, and involuntary euthanasia. *Voluntary* euthanasia occurs whenever the patient requests death. The cases of Barbara B. and Charles C. are both examples of voluntary euthanasia, since both patients asked to be killed. *Nonvoluntary* euthanasia occurs when the patient is unable to form a judgment or voice a wish in the matter and, therefore, expresses no desire whatever. The cases of Edward E. and Frances F. are both instances of nonvoluntary euthanasia; Edward was senile and only semiconscious, while Frances was permanently comatose, so neither could form a preference.

Finally, *involuntary* euthanasia occurs when the patient says that he or she does not want to die but is nevertheless killed or allowed to die. In this essay I will not be concerned with involuntary euthanasia. My view is that it is simply murder and that it is not justified. If a person *wants* to live on, even in great pain and even with the certainty of a horrible end, that is the individual's right. I believe that most people would agree with this judgment, but at any rate, I will not discuss this sort of case any further. Rather, attention will be focused primarily on voluntary euthanasia, and, to a somewhat lesser extent, on nonvoluntary euthanasia.

## §4 THE MAIN ISSUES

We have now looked at a number of cases and noted some of the important similarities and differences among them. Now let us return to our original question: What are we to understand by the word 'euthanasia'? Primarily it means killing someone—or letting someone die—who is going to die soon anyway, at the person's own request, as an act of kindness. This is the central case. The other cases I have described are called "euthanasia" because of their similarities to it.

In what follows we will be concerned mainly with the morality of euthanasia in the central case. The two main issues are: first, is it morally permissible to kill or let die someone who is going to die soon anyway, at the person's own request, as an act of kindness? And second, should such killing or letting die be against the law?

Along the way I will also discuss the morality of killing, or letting die, in the other cases I have described, since many of the same problems are involved. However, it is primarily the central case that will concern us.

Let me add one word of caution: We must be careful not to confuse the question of whether euthanasia *is* against the law with the very different question of whether it *ought to be* against the law. As a matter of fact, in the United States, active euthanasia is against the law. But it does not follow from this fact that active euthanasia ought to be against the law, for it *could be* that this is an unwise law that ought to be stricken from the books. The law itself can be the object of moral criticism. Once, for example, it was against the law in the southern United States for black people and white people to eat together in restaurants. But this legal rule was clearly a bad one, and it was changed after moral objections were raised forcefully against it. In the same spirit, we will ask whether the law prohibiting active euthanasia is a good one or a bad one, and whether it ought to be changed.

## II. AN HISTORICAL PERSPECTIVE

We cannot conclude that any practice is morally right simply because people believe that it is right, or because historically the practice has been accepted. What we believe, or what our culture accepts, may be wrong. Nevertheless, in order to place our convictions in context, it is useful to reflect on the history of those beliefs and to compare them with the beliefs of people who live, or who have lived, in societies different from our own.

### §5 ATTITUDES FROM THE ANCIENT WORLD

The people of ancient Greece took an attitude toward human life that is very different from our own. They did not believe that all human life is precious or that it must be preserved at all costs. In Sparta, for example, it was required by law that deformed infants be put to death —this was considered better than an unhappy life for them and their parents. The approval of infanticide was not limited to Sparta; in Athens, which we consider to have been a more enlightened community, the destruction of deformed or unhealthy babies was also approved. The Athenians did not *require* that they be killed, but there was no condemnation of the practice either. It is worth remembering that we are not talking about a crude, backward society but about one of the world's great civilizations, which produced some of our finest literature, art, and philosophy as well as virtually inventing science and mathematics.

  The fact that the Greeks approved infanticide is not a sign that they placed little value on human life. They were not a murderous people, and they took a stern view of some other types of killing. In general, they did not approve of suicide: Pythagoras, Plato, and Aristotle all rejected it as a cowardly way of avoiding life's hardships and one's duties to self and state. However, all three of these philosophers thought it foolish to prohibit suicide in *every* situation, and they allowed that in cases of incurable disease accompanied by great pain, a person has the right to choose an earlier death. Unfortunately, the Greek whose views are most often remembered on this subject was not really representative. Hippocrates, sometimes counted as the "father of medicine," was the author of an oath that is still taken by new doctors; in it, the doctors pledge that "If any shall ask of me a drug to produce death I will not give it, nor will I suggest such counsel." This part of the Hippocratic Oath would not have been endorsed without qualification by the majority of Greek thinkers.

The Romans adopted many of the Greeks' attitudes. The Stoic philosopher Seneca, for example, wrote without apology that "We destroy monstrous births, and drown our children if they are born weakly and unnaturally formed."[1] If anything, the Romans regarded killing—in special circumstances—even more indifferently than the Greeks. The Stoic and Epicurean philosophers thought suicide an acceptable option *whenever* one no longer cared for life. The most famous statement of this attitude is by Epictetus: "If the room is smoky, if only moderately, I will stay; if there is too much smoke I will go. Remember this, keep a firm hold on it, the door is always open."[2] To those with such a frame of mind, it seemed obvious that euthanasia was preferable to a miserable, lingering death. Seneca, again, wrote:

> I will not relinquish old age if it leaves my better part intact. But if it begins to shake my mind, if it destroys my faculties one by one, if it leaves me not life but breath, I will depart from the putrid or the tottering edifice. If I know that I must suffer without hope of relief I will depart not through fear of the pain itself but because it prevents all for which I would live.[3]

## §6 THE EARLY CHRISTIAN VIEW

The coming of Christianity caused vast changes in these attitudes. The early Church was resolutely pacifist and opposed the killing of humans in *every* context. Infanticide was prohibited, for it was thought that all who are born of woman, no matter how monstrous or miserable, have immortal souls. Suicide was forbidden because one's life was viewed as a trust from God, and only God has the right to take it. Considering the nonpacifist views of most modern Christians, the reader may be surprised to learn that participation in warfare was also condemned by the early Church. The Church fathers—Lactantius, Tertullian, Origen—were in agreement on all of this. Of war, Tertullian wrote: "Can it be lawful to handle the sword, when the Lord himself has declared that he who uses the sword shall perish by it?"[4]

The Church continued to denounce infanticide and suicide, but it soon modified its position on war. A sympathetic interpretation of this change might be that Christians came to recognize a valid moral difference between killing in a just war and other forms of killing. A less sympathetic view is taken by the sociologist-philosopher Edward Westermarck, who remarked in his classic work *Christianity and Morals:*

> A divine law which prohibited all resistance to enemies could certainly not be accepted by the State, especially at a time when the Empire was seriously threatened by foreign invaders. Christianity could therefore never become a State religion unless it gave up its attitude towards war. And it gave it up.[5]

The early Church had also condemned capital punishment, which was not surprising considering the number of Church figures, including Jesus himself and St. Peter, who had been executed. But this position, too, was soon modified, bringing the Church's stance more into line with political requirements. The imposition of death by the State was said to be all right so long as priests took no part in the proceedings.

But the Church's opposition to euthanasia continued, and—under its influence—what for the Greek and Roman philosophers had been a compassionate solution to the problem of lingering, degrading death became a mortal sin. Suffering, no matter how horrible or seemingly pointless, came to be viewed as a burden imposed by God himself, for purposes known to Him, which men and women must bear until the "natural" end. This attitude prevailed throughout the Middle Ages and was not seriously challenged until the sixteenth century.

## §7 OTHER RELIGIONS AND CULTURES

But I do not want to give the impression that the prohibition of euthanasia is exclusively a Christian doctrine. Jewish law also forbids it. In fact, we find a rare consensus among rabbinic authorities on this subject. The medieval Jewish theologians were no less emphatic than their Christian counterparts: The great Maimonides, for example, wrote in the twelfth century that "One who is in a dying condition is regarded as a living person in all respects. . . . He who touches him (thereby causing him to expire) is guilty of shedding blood."[6] The Islamic tradition is also uncompromising, for the Koran explicitly states that the suicide "shall be excluded from heaven forever," and voluntary euthanasia is regarded as simply a form of assisted suicide.[7] So not only Christianity but all these religious traditions conspire to withhold a merciful death from those who suffer—or, to look at things from an opposite point of view, conspire to affirm the preciousness of life even when life is most wretched.

If we turn for a moment to the experience of other cultures, we find a striking contrast. While these developing Western traditions were opposing euthanasia, most Eastern peoples were comfortably accepting it. In China, Confucian ethics had always allowed voluntary death in the case of hopeless disease, and the great Eastern religions, including Shintoism and Buddhism, took a similar attitude. In *The Dialogues of Buddha* there are described two holy men who commit suicide to escape incurable illness, and this is said to be no obstacle to their attaining "nirvana," the spiritual goal of all Buddhist endeavor. Among so-called primitive societies, there is a wide range of attitudes toward euthanasia, but it is easy to compile long lists of cultures in which the suicide or killing of those with intolerable illness is approved; one historian mentions eighteen such societies in the space of two pages.[8]

## §8 DISSENTERS

But now let us return to our historical sketch of Western attitudes. As I said, after Christianity became a state religion, opposition to euthanasia—as well as to suicide, infanticide, and abortion—took a firm hold on the minds of almost everyone who bothered to think seriously about it. Throughout the Middle Ages, the prohibition on these practices was virtually unchallengeable. Not until 1516 do we find an important defense of mercy killing. In that year Sir Thomas More, later to be made a saint of the Church, wrote in his *Utopia* that in the imaginary perfect community:

> When any is taken with a torturing and lingering pain, so that there is no hope either of cure or ease, the priests and magistrates come and exhort them, that, since they are now unable to go on with the business of life, are become a burden to themselves and all about them, and they have really outlived themselves, they should no longer nourish such a rooted distemper, but choose rather to die since they cannot live but in such misery.[9]

Remarkably, More advocates in this passage not only that euthanasia be permitted but that it be *urged* on the desperately ill, even when they are reluctant to accept it. This certainly seems to be going too far; I do not know of any other advocate of euthanasia who would agree with More about *that*. Nevertheless, More adds that a person who refuses euthanasia is to be cared for as well as possible.

Gradually, more and more thinkers came to believe that the prohibition on euthanasia ought to be relaxed. It was, however, a very slow movement, and those who favored the relaxation remained in a distinct minority. After Thomas More, the next notable proponent of euthanasia was Francis Bacon, credited as one of the founders of modern philosophy. A hundred years after More's *Utopia,* Bacon defined the role of the physician as "not only to restore the health, but to mitigate pain and dolours; and not only when such mitigation may conduce to recovery, but when it may serve to make a fair and easy passage."[10]

## §9 MODERN SECULAR THOUGHT

*Seventeenth- and Eighteenth-Century Thought* During the seventeenth and eighteenth centuries, philosophers began to move away from the idea that morality requires a religious foundation. Although most were still theists and God still held a prominent place in their understanding of the universe, they did not think that right and wrong consisted in following God's commandments and did not look to the Church as a primary source of moral guidance. Instead, human reason and the individual conscience were regarded as the sources of moral insight. This did not mean, however, that these thinkers abandoned

all traditional moral views. Although they were revolutionary in their
ideas concerning the *sources* of morality, often they were not so radical in their particular moral opinions. The most famous German
philosophers, Kant (1724–1804) and Hegel (1770–1831), held that
moral truths are known through the use of reason alone; but when
they exercised their reason on such matters as suicide and euthanasia,
they discovered that the Church had been right all along. A notable
exception to this way of thinking was the greatest British philosopher,
David Hume (1711–1776), who argued vigorously that one has the
right to end one's life when he or she pleases. Hume, who was a sceptic
about religion, particularly tried to refute theological arguments to
the contrary.

It is one thing for a philosopher to argue that morality is separate
from religion or that the basis of morality is not necessarily religious,
but it is quite a different matter for those ideas to affect popular
thinking. In spite of the growing secularization of philosophical
thought in the seventeenth and eighteenth centuries, in the popular
mind, ethics was still very much tied to religion. The Protestant Refor-
mation had created many churches where before there had been the
one Church; and for Protestants the authority of the Church had been
replaced by the individual believer's direct relationship with God. But
still, people's moral duties were conceived as the outgrowth of their
religious beliefs, and the purpose of the moral life was still thought to
be the service of God. Then in the nineteenth century a remarkable
thing happened: a philosophical movement, utilitarianism, not only
captured the imaginations of philosophers but revolutionized popular
thinking as well.

*Utilitarianism*  Jeremy Bentham (1748–1832) argued that the purpose of morality is not the service of God or obedience to abstract
moral rules but the promotion of the greatest possible happiness for
creatures on earth. What we ought to do is calculate how our actions,
laws, and social policies will actually affect people (and other animals,
too). Will they result in people being made happier, in people having
better lives? Or will they result in people being made more miserable?
According to Bentham, our decisions should be made on that basis and
*only* on that basis.

But Bentham did not stop when he had articulated this as a theoretical idea. He was concerned with bringing about social change and
not merely with voicing a philosophy. Bentham became the leader of
a group of philosophers, economists, and politicians who sought to
reform the laws and institutions of England along utilitarian lines, and
the social and intellectual life of people in the English-speaking countries has not been the same since. Bentham argued, for example, that
in order to maximize happiness, the law should not seek to enforce
abstract moral rules or meddle in the private affairs of citizens. What
consenting adults do in private is strictly their own business, and the

law has no right to interfere. The law should concern itself with people's behavior only when they may do harm to others. This idea, now so familiar a part of liberal ideology, was radically new when the Benthamites first urged it on their fellow Englishmen.

The implications for euthanasia were obvious. For the utilitarians, the question was simply this: Does it increase or decrease human happiness to provide a quick, painless death for those who are dying in agony? Clearly, they reasoned, the only consequences of such actions will be to decrease the amount of misery in the world; therefore, euthanasia must be morally right. Moreover, as Bentham's famous follower John Stuart Mill (1806–1873) put it, the individual is sovereign over his own body and mind; where one's own interests are concerned, there is no other authority. Therefore, if one wants to die quickly rather than linger in pain, that is strictly a personal affair, and the government has no business intruding. Indeed, Bentham himself requested euthanasia in his last moments.

## §10 RECENT DEVELOPMENTS

The utilitarian movement changed the way people think. Today, the calculation of benefits and harms is routinely accepted as a primary way of determining what is right and what is wrong. (The fact that contemporary philosophers spend so much time criticizing and arguing about utilitarianism only attests to its tremendous influence.) As a result, more and more people have come to favor euthanasia. In 1936, there was organized in England the Voluntary Euthanasia Society, with an eminent surgeon as its first president and many physicians among its sponsors. This was followed in the United States by the organization of such groups as the Euthanasia Society of America, the Euthanasia Educational Council, and the Society for the Right to Die. Advocacy of active euthanasia is no longer confined to a few figures on the fringes of academic thought. It is publicly supported by thousands of doctors, lawyers, scientists, and members of the clergy (including many Catholics) as well as philosophers; and although active euthanasia is still illegal, bills are being introduced in various legislative bodies every year in an attempt to legalize it.

## §11 THE POSITION OF THE AMERICAN MEDICAL ASSOCIATION

The preceding historical sketch must be qualified in an important way. Throughout the history of our subject, most people have thought that the distinction between active euthanasia and passive euthanasia is morally important; many of those who condemned active euthanasia raised no objection against passive euthanasia. Even when killing was thought to be wrong, allowing people to die by not treating them was thought in some circumstances to be all right. Four centuries before

Christ, we find Socrates saying of a physician, with approval, "bodies which disease had penetrated through and through he would not have attempted to cure . . . he did not want to lengthen out good-for-nothing lives."[11] Neither the Christians nor the Jews, in the centuries following, significantly altered this basic idea; both viewed *allowing to die*, in circumstances of hopeless suffering, as morally permissible. It was killing that was zealously opposed.

The morality of allowing people to die by not treating them has become critically important in recent years because of advances in medical technology. By using such devices as respirators, heart-lung machines, and intravenous feeding, we can now keep almost anybody alive indefinitely, even after he or she has become nothing more than a "human vegetable," without thought or feeling or hope of recovery. The maintenance of life by such artificial means is, in these cases, sadly pointless. Virtually everyone who has thought seriously about the matter agrees that it is morally all right, at some point, to cease treatment and allow such people to die. No less a figure than the Pope has concurred: as recently as 1958, Pius XII reaffirmed that we may "allow the patient who is virtually already dead to pass away in peace."[12]

In 1982 the American Medical Association (AMA) approved a set of guidelines with the title "Principles of Medical Ethics." These guidelines commented on a variety of matters, with four paragraphs devoted to the treatment of hopeless or terminal conditions. The traditional ban on mercy killing is reaffirmed, but allowing patients to die (in some circumstances) is said to be all right. The "Principles" include these paragraphs:

> *Quality of Life.* In the making of decisions for the treatment of seriously deformed newborns or persons who are severely deteriorated victims of injury, illness or advanced age, the primary consideration should be what is best for the individual patient and not the avoidance of a burden to the family or to society. Quality of life is a factor to be considered in determining what is best for the individual. Life should be cherished despite disabilities and handicaps, except when prolongation would be inhumane and unconscionable. Under these circumstances, withholding or removing life supporting means is ethical provided that the normal care given an individual who is ill is not discontinued.

> *Terminal Illness.* The social commitment of the physician is to prolong life and relieve suffering. Where the observance of one conflicts with the other, the physician, patient, and/or family of the patient have discretion to resolve the conflict.
>
> For humane reasons, with informed consent a physician may do what is medically indicated to alleviate severe pain, or cease or omit treatment to let a terminally ill patient die, but he should not intentionally cause death. In determining whether the administration of potentially life-prolonging medical treatment is in the best interest of the patient, the physician should consider what the possibility is for

extending life under humane and comfortable conditions and what
are the wishes and attitudes of the family or those who have responsibility for the custody of the patient.

Where a terminally ill patient's coma is beyond doubt irreversible,
and there are adequate safeguards to confirm the accuracy of the
diagnosis, all means of life support may be discontinued. If death does
not occur when life support systems are discontinued, the comfort
and dignity of the patient should be maintained.

The substance of this statement has been reaffirmed by numerous
other groups. Most recently, a group of distinguished physicians published a statement entitled "The Physician's Responsibility Toward
Hopelessly Ill Patients" in *The New England Journal of Medicine* for
April 12, 1984. If anything, these doctors go even further than the
AMA policy. The AMA policy implies a distinction between providing
food and water and other kinds of life-sustaining treatment: it implies
that, while other kinds of treatment may be withheld, food and water
may not be withheld. (Consider the last sentence quoted above, which
envisions the possibility that a patient may not die even if treatment
is withheld; obviously, in this situation, nourishment is still being provided.)

The doctors' statement goes further in that it countenances the
omission of *all* treatments, including the provision of food and water.
Several categories of patients are considered: patients in a "persistent
vegetative state"; "severely and irreversibly demented patients" who
do not initiate purposeful activity but passively accept care; and "elderly patients with permanent mild impairment of competence," that
is, "pleasantly senile" persons with only limited ability to engage in
purposeful activity or communicate. The doctors emphasize the desirability of following the patient's wishes, even if expressed only through
a "living will" or a proxy; they also emphasize the importance of
keeping such patients comfortable. But, with these preliminaries duly
stressed, it is said that there is nothing wrong, medically or morally,
with withholding treatment and allowing the patients to pass away in
peace.

Compared with active euthanasia, then, passive euthanasia is relatively uncontroversial. Therefore, in what follows, most of our attention will be given to active euthanasia.

## III. ARGUMENTS SUPPORTING THE MORALITY OF ACTIVE EUTHANASIA

### §12 THE IMPORTANCE OF ARGUMENT

We come now to the most important part of our investigation. So far
we have seen that there is widespread agreement that passive euthanasia is morally all right in at least some cases but that active

euthanasia is much more controversial. We have seen that in the course of Western history, some thinkers have approved of active euthanasia, but most have condemned it. We have seen that in some other cultures, a more tolerant attitude is taken toward active euthanasia. And finally, we have examined the posititition of the medical establishment in our own country, according to which active euthanasia is always "contrary to that for which the medical profession stands," even though passive euthanasia is said to be in some circumstances all right. But, while all of this is valuable as background information, none of it directly touches the most important issue. We want to know, most of all, whether euthanasia—active or passive—*really is moral,* or whether in fact it is immoral.

How are we to go about answering this question? We cannot discover whether euthanasia is immoral simply by consulting our feelings. Our feelings may be nothing more than irrational prejudice; they may have nothing to do with the truth. At one time most people "felt" that people of other races were inferior and that slavery is God's own plan. Our feelings about euthanasia may also be mistaken, so we cannot rely on them.

If we want to discover the truth about euthanasia, there is only one way this can be done, namely, by examining and analyzing the *arguments,* or reasons, that can be given for and against it. If cogent, logical arguments can be given in favor of euthanasia and if at the same time the arguments against it can be refuted, then it is morally acceptable, no matter what emotions or preconceptions one might have. And likewise if, upon analyzing the arguments, we find that the strongest case is against euthanasia, we shall have to conclude that it is immoral, no matter what our feelings were previously.

This is true not only of euthanasia but of any moral matter whatever. A moral judgment—*any* moral judgment—is true only if there are good reasons in its support. If someone tells you that you ought to do something or that a certain action would be wrong, you may ask *why* you ought to do it or why that action would be wrong; if no answer can be given, you may reject that advice as arbitrary and unfounded. In this way moral judgments are very different from mere expressions of preference. If someone says "I like coffee," there does not have to be a *reason;* this is merely a statement about individual tastes. And if someone else says "I don't like coffee," this is merely a statement about *different* personal tastes. There is nothing for these two to argue about, and there is no question of who is right and who is wrong (they are both right). There is no such thing as "rationally supporting" one's like or dislike of coffee. However, when *moral* claims are being made, rational support is in order; and the truth is simply the position that has the best reasons on its side. The attempt to determine what is true in morals, then, is always a matter of analyzing and weighing up reasons. Otherwise, morality degenerates into nothing more than prejudice, propaganda, and crass self-interest, without claim on any rational person.

## §13 THE ARGUMENT FROM MERCY

*Preliminary Statement of the Argument* The single most powerful argument in support of euthanasia is the argument from mercy. It is also an exceptionally simple argument, at least in its main idea, which makes one uncomplicated point. Terminally ill patients sometimes suffer pain so horrible that it is beyond the comprehension of those who have not actually experienced it. Their suffering can be so terrible that we do not like even to read about it or think about it; we recoil even from the descriptions of such agony. The argument from mercy says euthanasia is justified because it provides an end to *that.*

The great Irish satirist Jonathan Swift took eight years to die, while, in the words of Joseph Fletcher, "His mind crumbled to pieces."[13] At times the pain in his blinded eyes was so intense he had to be restrained from tearing them out with his own hands. Knives and other potential instruments of suicide had to be kept from him. For the last three years of his life, he could do nothing but sit and drool; and when he finally died it was only after convulsions that lasted thirty-six hours.

Swift died in 1745. Since then, doctors have learned how to eliminate much of the pain that accompanies terminal illness, but the victory has been far from complete. So, here is a more modern example.

Stewart Alsop was a respected journalist who died in 1975 of a rare form of cancer. Before he died, he wrote movingly of his experiences as a terminal patient. Although he had not thought much about euthanasia before, he came to approve of it after rooming briefly with someone he called Jack:

> The third night that I roomed with Jack in our tiny double room in the solid-tumor ward of the cancer clinic of the National Institutes of Health in Bethesda, Md., a terrible thought occurred to me.
>
> Jack had a melanoma in his belly, a malignant solid tumor that the doctors guessed was about the size of a softball. The cancer had started a few months before with a small tumor in his left shoulder, and there had been several operations since. The doctors planned to remove the softball-sized tumor, but they knew Jack would soon die. The cancer had metastasized—it had spread beyond control.
>
> Jack was good-looking, about 28, and brave. He was in constant pain, and his doctor had prescribed an intravenous shot of a synthetic opiate—a pain-killer, or analgesic—every four hours. His wife spent many of the daylight hours with him, and she would sit or lie on his bed and pat him all over, as one pats a child, only more methodically, and this seemed to help control the pain. But at night, when his

pretty wife had left (wives cannot stay overnight at the NIH clinic) and darkness fell, the pain would attack without pity.

At the prescribed hour, a nurse would give Jack a shot of the synthetic analgesic, and this would control the pain for perhaps two hours or a bit more. Then he would begin to moan, or whimper, very low, as though he didn't want to wake me. Then he would begin to howl, like a dog.

When this happened, either he or I would ring for a nurse, and ask for a pain-killer. She would give him some codeine or the like by mouth, but it never did any real good—it affected him no more than half an aspirin might affect a man who had just broken his arm. Always the nurse would explain as encouragingly as she could that there was not long to go before the next intravenous shot—"Only about 50 minutes now." And always poor Jack's whimpers and howls would become more loud and frequent until at last the blessed relief came.

The third night of this routine, the terrible thought occurred to me. "If Jack were a dog," I thought, "what would be done with him?" The answer was obvious: the pound, and chloroform. No human being with a spark of pity could let a living thing suffer so, to no good end.[14]

The NIH clinic is, of course, one of the most modern and best-equipped hospitals we have. Jack's suffering was not the result of poor treatment in some backward rural facility; it was the inevitable product of his disease, which medical science was powerless to prevent.

I have quoted Alsop at length not for the sake of indulging in gory details but to give a clear idea of the kind of suffering we are talking about. We should not gloss over these facts with euphemistic language or squeamishly avert our eyes from them. For only by keeping them firmly and vividly in mind can we appreciate the full force of the argument from mercy: If a person prefers—and even begs for—death as the only alternative to lingering on *in this kind of torment,* only to die anyway after a while, then surely it is not immoral to help this person die sooner. As Alsop put it, "No human being with a spark of pity could let a living thing suffer so, to no good end."

*The Utilitarian Version of the Argument*   In connection with this argument, the utilitarians should be mentioned again. They argued that actions and social policies should be judged right or wrong *exclusively* according to whether they cause happiness or misery; and they argued that when judged by this standard, euthanasia turns out to be morally acceptable. The utilitarian argument may be elaborated as follows:

1.  Any action or social policy is morally right if it serves to increase the amount of happiness in the world or to decrease the amount of misery. Conversely, an action or social policy is morally wrong if it serves to decrease happiness or to increase misery.
2.  The policy of killing, at their own request, hopelessly ill pa-

tients who are suffering great pain would decrease the amount of misery in the world. (An example could be Alsop's friend Jack.)

3. Therefore, such a policy would be morally right.

The first premise of this argument, (1), states the Principle of Utility, which is the basic utilitarian assumption. Today most philosophers think that this principle is wrong, because they think that the promotion of happiness and the avoidance of misery are not the *only* morally important things. Happiness, they say, is only one among many values that should be promoted: freedom, justice, and a respect for people's rights are also important. To take one example; people *might* be happier if there were no freedom of religion, for if everyone adhered to the same religious beliefs, there would be greater harmony among people. There would be no unhappiness caused within families by Jewish girls marrying Catholic boys, and so forth. Moreover, if people were brainwashed well enough, no one would mind not having freedom of choice. Thus happiness would be increased. But, the argument continues, even if happiness *could* be increased this way, it would not be right to deny people freedom of religion, because people have a right to make their own choices. Therefore, the first premise of the utilitarian argument is unacceptable.

There is a related difficulty for utilitarianism, which connects more directly with the topic of euthanasia. Suppose a person is leading a miserable life—full of more unhappiness than happiness—but does *not* want to die. This person thinks that a miserable life is better than none at all. Now I assume that we would all agree that the person should not be killed; that would be plain, unjustifiable murder. Yet it *would* decrease the amount of misery in the world if we killed this person—it would lead to an increase in the balance of happiness over unhappiness—and so it is hard to see how, on strictly utilitarian grounds, it could be wrong. Again, the Principle of Utility seems to be an inadequate guide for determining right and wrong. So we are on shaky ground if we rely on *this* version of the argument from mercy for a defense of euthanasia.

*Doing What Is in Everyone's Best Interests*   Although the foregoing utilitarian argument is faulty, it is nevertheless based on a sound idea. For even if the promotion of happiness and avoidance of misery are not the *only* morally important things, they are still very important. So, when an action or a social policy would decrease misery, that is *a* very strong reason in its favor. In the cases of voluntary euthanasia we are now considering, great suffering is eliminated, and since the patient requests it, there is no question of violating individual rights. That is why, regardless of the difficulties of the Principle of Utility, the utilitarian version of the argument still retains considerable force.

I want now to present a somewhat different version of the argument from mercy, which is inspired by utilitarianism but which avoids the difficulties of the foregoing version by not making the Principle of Utility a premise of the argument. I believe that the following argument is sound and proves that active euthanasia *can* be justified:

1. If an action promotes the best interests of *everyone* concerned and violates *no one's* rights, then that action is morally acceptable.
2. In at least some cases, active euthanasia promotes the best interests of everyone concerned and violates no one's rights.
3. Therefore, in at least some cases, active euthanasia is morally acceptable.

It would have been in everyone's best interests if active euthanasia had been employed in the case of Stewart Alsop's friend Jack. First, and most important, it would have been in Jack's own interests, since it would have provided him with an easier, better death, without pain. (Who among us would choose Jack's death, if we had a choice, rather than a quick painless death?) Second, it would have been in the best interests of Jack's wife. Her misery, helplessly watching him suffer, must have been almost equal to his. Third, the hospital staff's best interests would have been served, since if Jack's dying had not been prolonged, they could have turned their attention to other patients whom they could have helped. Fourth, other patients would have benefited, since medical resources would no longer have been used in the sad, pointless maintenance of Jack's physical existence. Finally, if Jack himself requested to be killed, the act would not have violated his rights. Considering all this, how can active euthanasia in this case be wrong? How can it be wrong to do an action that is merciful, that benefits everyone concerned, and that violates no one's rights?

## §14 THE ARGUMENT FROM THE GOLDEN RULE

"Do unto others as you would have them do unto you" is one of the oldest and most familiar moral maxims. Stated in just that way, it is not a very good maxim: Suppose a sexual pervert started treating others as he would like to be treated himself; we might not be happy with the results. Nevertheless, the basic idea behind the Golden Rule is a good one. The basic idea is that moral rules apply impartially to everyone alike; therefore, you cannot say that you are justified in treating someone else in a certain way unless you are willing to admit that that person would also be justified in treating *you* in that way if your positions were reversed.

*Kant and the Golden Rule* The great German philosopher Immanuel Kant (1724–1804) incorporated the basic idea of the Golden Rule into his system of ethics. Kant argued that we should act only on rules that we are willing to have applied universally; that is, we should behave as we would be willing to have *everyone* behave. He held that there is one supreme principle of morality, which he called "the Categorical Imperative." The Categorical Imperative says:

> Act only according to that maxim by which you can at the same time will that it should become a universal law.[15]

Let us discuss what this means. When we are trying to decide whether we ought to do a certain action, we must first ask what general rule or principle we would be following if we did it. Then, we ask whether we would be willing for everyone to follow that rule in similar circumstances. (This determines whether "the maxim of the act"—the rule we would be following—can be "willed" to be "a universal law.") If we would not be willing for the rule to be followed universally, then we should not follow it ourselves. Thus, if we are not willing for others to apply the rule to *us,* we ought not apply it to *them.*

In the eighteenth chapter of St. Matthew's gospel there is a story that perfectly illustrates this point. A man is owed money by another, who cannot pay, so he has the debtor thrown into prison. But he himself owes money to the king and begs that *his* debt be forgiven. At first the king forgives the debt. However, when the king hears how this man has treated the one who owed him, he changes his mind and "delivers him unto the tormentors" until he can pay. The moral is clear: If you do not think that others should apply the rule "Don't forgive debts!" to *you,* then you should not apply it to others.

The application of all this to the question of euthanasia is fairly obvious. Each of us is going to die someday, although most of us do not know when or how. But suppose you were told that you would die in one of two ways, and you were asked to choose between them. First, you could die quietly, and without pain, from a fatal injection. Or second, you could choose to die of an affliction so painful that for several days before death you would be reduced to howling like a dog, with your family standing by helplessly, trying to comfort you, but going through their own psychological hell. It is hard to believe that any sane person, when confronted by these possibilities, would choose to have a rule applied that would force upon him or her the second option. And if we would not want such a rule, which excludes euthanasia, applied to us, then we should not apply such a rule to others.

*Implications for Christians*   There is a considerable irony here. Kant, as we have already noted, was personally opposed to active euthanasia, yet his own Categorical Imperative seems to sanction it. The larger irony, however, is for those Christians who have for centuries opposed active euthanasia. According to the New Testament accounts, Jesus himself promulgated the Golden Rule as the supreme moral principle —"This is the Law and the Prophets," he said. But if this is the supreme principle of morality, then how can active euthanasia be always wrong? If I would have it done to me, how can it be wrong for me to do likewise to others?

R. M. Hare has made this point with great force. A Christian as well as a leading contemporary moral philosopher, Hare has long argued that "universalizability" is one of the central characteristics of moral judgment. ('Universalizability' is the name he gives to the basic idea embodied in both the Golden Rule and the Categorical Imperative. It means that a moral judgment must conform to universal principles, which apply to everyone alike, if it is to be acceptable.) In an article called "Euthanasia: A Christian View," Hare argues that Christians, if they took Christ's teachings about the Golden Rule seriously, would not think that euthanasia is always wrong. He gives this (true) example:

> The driver of a petrol lorry [i.e., a gas truck] was in an accident in which his tanker overturned and immediately caught fire. He himself was trapped in the cab and could not be freed. He therefore besought the bystanders to kill him by hitting him on the head, so that he would not roast to death. I think that somebody did this, but I do not know what happened in court afterwards.
>
> Now will you please all ask yourselves, as I have many times asked myself, what you wish that men should do to you if you were in the situation of that driver. I cannot believe that anybody who considered the matter seriously, as if he himself were going to be in that situation and had now to give instructions as to what rule the bystanders should follow, would say that the rule should be one ruling out euthanasia absolutely.[16]

We might note that *active* euthanasia is the only option here; the concept of passive euthanasia, in these circumstances, has no application.

We have looked at two arguments supporting the morality of active euthanasia. Now let us turn to some arguments that support the opposite view, that active euthanasia is immoral.

## IV. ARGUMENTS OPPOSING THE MORALITY OF ACTIVE EUTHANASIA

### §15 THE ARGUMENT FROM THE WRONGNESS OF KILLING

Almost everyone accepts, in one form or another, the principle of the value of human life. Religious people speak of the "sanctity" of life, and although nonreligious people may not like the theological overtones of the word 'sanctity', they nevertheless agree that human life is precious and ought to be protected. They all agree that it is wrong to kill people. The simplest and most obvious objection to active euthanasia, then, is that it is a violation of the moral rule against killing.

But to this the advocate of euthanasia has an easy answer. The rule against killing is not absolute; it has exceptions. People may disagree about exactly which exceptions should be allowed, but there is general agreement that there *are* exceptions. Most people would agree that it is permissible to kill in self-defense if that is the only way to prevent someone from murdering you. Others would add that it is permissible to kill in time of war provided that the war is just and you are observing the rules of war. Some think that capital punishment is morally permissible, as a way of dealing with vicious murderers. Others believe that abortion is a justified exception to the rule. Thus, even though killing people is *usually* wrong, it is not *always* wrong. And once this much is admitted, defenders of euthanasia can simply claim that euthanasia is one of the justified exceptions to the rule.

There are two arguments that might be given to show that euthanasia is a justified exception to the rule. First, killing is objectionable only because, in normal cases, the person who is killed loses something of great value—life itself. In being deprived of life, a person is *harmed*. In euthanasia, however, this is not true. If a dying person whose life holds nothing but torment says that such a life no longer has value, that surely can be a reasonable judgment. We are not doing harm by putting an end to the person's misery. So, in the special case of euthanasia, we do not have the same reasons for objecting to killing that we have in the normal cases. Second, killing a person is, usually, a violation of the individual's right to life. But if a person *asks* to be killed, the killing is not a violation of individual rights. (This is a general point that applies to other rights as well. If, for example, you steal something that belongs to me, you violate my property rights; but if I ask you to take it, and you do, then you do not violate my rights.) For these reasons, saying that euthanasia is a violation of the rule against killing is not enough to prove that it is wrong.

## §16 RELIGIOUS ARGUMENTS

Religious people often oppose euthanasia and claim that it is immoral, but there is often nothing particularly religious about the *arguments* they use. The argument from the wrongness of killing, for example, does not require any theological assumptions. Therefore, when assessing that argument, we did not need to get into any matters of religion at all.

There are some other arguments, however, that are distinctively religious. Since these arguments do require theological assumptions, they have little appeal to nonreligious people or to religious people whose presuppositions are different. Here are three of the most popular such arguments:

A. *What God Forbids*   It is sometimes said that active euthanasia is not permissible simply because God forbids it, and we know that God forbids it by the authority of either Scripture or church tradition. Thus, one eighteenth-century religionist wrote that, in the case of aged and infirm animals,

> God, the Father of Mercies, hath ordained Beasts and Birds of Prey
> to do that distressed creature the kindness to relieve him his misery,
> by putting him to death. A kindness which *We* dare not show to our
> own species. If thy father, thy brother, or thy child should suffer the
> utmost pains of a long and agonizing sickness, though his groans
> should pierce through thy heart, and with strong crying and tears he
> should beg thy relief, yet thou must be deaf unto him; he must wait
> his appointed time till his charge cometh, till he sinks and is crushed
> with the weight of his own misery.[17]

When this argument is advanced, it is usually advanced with great confidence, as though it were *obvious* what God requires. Yet we may well wonder whether such confidence is justified. The Sixth Commandment does not say, literally, "Thou shalt not *kill*"—that is a bad translation. A better translation is "Thou shalt not *murder*," which is different, and which does not obviously prohibit euthanasia. Murder is by definition *wrongful* killing; so if you do not think that a given kind of killing is wrong, you will not call it murder. That is why the Sixth Commandment is not normally taken to forbid killing in a just war; since such killing is (allegedly) justified, it is not called murder. Similarly, if euthanasia is justified, it is not murder, so it is not prohibited by the commandment. At any rate, it is clear that we cannot infer that euthanasia is wrong *because* it is prohibited by the commandment.

If we look elsewhere in the Christian Bible for a condemnation of euthanasia, we cannot find it. These scriptures are silent on the question. We do find numerous affirmations of the sanctity of human life and of the Fatherhood of God, and some theologians have tried to infer a prohibition of euthanasia from these general precepts. But we also find exhortations to kindness and mercy, and the Golden Rule proclaimed as the sum of all morality; and these principles, as we have seen, support euthanasia rather than condemn it.

We *do* find a clear condemnation of euthanasia in church traditions. Regardless of whether there is scriptural authority for it, the church has historically opposed mercy killing. It should be emphasized, however, that this is a matter of history. Today, many religious leaders favor active euthanasia and think that the historical position of the church has been mistaken. It was an Episcopal minister, Joseph Fletcher, who in his book *Morals and Medicine*[18] formulated the classic modern defense of euthanasia. Fletcher does not stand alone among his fellow churchmen. The Euthanasia Society of America, which he heads, includes many other religious leaders; and the recent "Plea for Beneficent Euthanasia," sponsored by the American Humanist Association, was signed by more religious leaders than persons in any other category.[19] So it certainly cannot be claimed that *contemporary* religious forces stand uniformly opposed to active euthanasia.

It is noteworthy that even Roman Catholic thinkers are today reassessing the church's traditional ban on mercy killing. The Catholic philosopher Daniel Maguire, of Marquette University, has written one of the best books on the subject, *Death by Choice.*[20] Maguire maintains that "it may be moral and should be legal to accelerate the death process by taking direct action, such as overdosing with morphine or injecting potassium"; moreover, he proposes to demonstrate that this view is *"compatible with historical Catholic ethical theory,"* contrary to what most opponents of mercy killing assume! Historical Catholic ethical theory, he says, grants individuals permission to act on views that are supported by "good and serious reasons" even when a different view is supported by a majority of authorities. Since the morality of active euthanasia *is* supported by "good and serious reasons," Maguire concludes that Catholics are permitted to accept that morality and act on it. At the very least, they do *not* have to assume that euthanasia is immoral because "God forbids it."

B. *The Idea of God's Dominion*   Our second theological argument starts from the principle that "The life of man is solely under the dominion of God." It is for God alone to decide when a person shall live and when he shall die; therefore, we have no right to "play God" and arrogate this decision unto ourselves. So euthanasia is forbidden.[21]

The most remarkable thing about this argument is that people still advance it today, even though it was decisively refuted over two hundred years ago by the great British philosopher David Hume. Hume made the simple but devastating point that *if it is for God alone to decide when we shall live and when we shall die, then we "play God" just as much when we cure people as when we kill them.* Suppose a person is sick and we have the medicine to cure her. If we do cure her, then we are interfering with God's right to decide whether she will live or die! Hume put the point this way:

> Were the disposal of human life so much reserved as the peculiar providence of the Almighty that it were an encroachment on his right, for men to dispose of their own lives; it would be equally criminal to act for the preservation of life as for its destruction. If I turn aside a stone which is falling upon my head, I disturb this course of nature, and I invade the peculiar providence of the Almighty by lengthening out my life beyond the period which by the general laws of matter and motion he had assigned it.[22]

We alter the length of a person's life when we save it just as much as when we take it. Therefore, if the taking of life is to be forbidden on the grounds that only God has the right to determine how long a person shall live, then the saving of life should be prohibited on the same grounds. We would then have to abolish the practice of medicine. But everyone concedes that this would be absurd. Therefore, we may *not* prohibit active euthanasia on the grounds that only God has the right to determine how long a life shall last. This seems to be a complete refutation of this argument.

*C. Suffering and God's Plan*   The last religious argument we shall consider is the following: Suffering is a part of life; God has ordained that we must suffer as part of his Divine plan. Therefore, if we were to kill people to "put them out of their misery," we would be interfering with God's plan. Bishop Joseph Sullivan, a prominent Catholic opponent of euthanasia, expresses the argument in this passage from his essay "The Immorality of Euthanasia":

> If the suffering patient is of sound mind and capable of making an act of divine resignation, then his sufferings become a great means of merit whereby he can gain reward for himself and also win great favors for the souls in Purgatory, perhaps even release them from their suffering. Likewise the sufferer may give good example to his family and friends and teach them how to bear a heavy cross in a Christlike manner.
>
> As regard those that must live in the same house with the incurable sufferer, they have a great opportunity to practice Christian charity. They can learn to see Christ in the sufferer and win the reward promised in the Beatitudes. This opportunity for charity would hold true even when the incurable sufferer is deprived of the use of reason. It may well be that the incurable sufferer in a particular case may be of greater value to society than when he was of some material value to himself and his community.[23]

This argument may strike some people as simply grotesque. Can we imagine this being said, seriously, in the presence of suffering such as that experienced by Stewart Alsop's friend Jack? "We know it hurts, Jack, and that your wife is being torn apart just having to watch it, but think of what a good opportunity this is for you to set an example. You can give us a lesson in how to bear it." In addition, some might think that euthanasia is exactly what *is* required by the "charity" that bystanders have the opportunity to practice.

But, these reactions aside, there is a more fundamental difficulty with the argument. For if the argument were sound, it would lead not only to the condemnation of euthanasia but of *any* measures to reduce suffering. If God decrees that we suffer, why aren't we obstructing God's plan when we give drugs to relieve pain? A girl breaks her arm; if only God knows how much pain is right for her, who are we to mend it? The point is similar to Hume's refutation of the previous argument: This argument, like the previous one, cannot be right because it leads to consequences that no one, not even the most conservative religious thinker, is willing to accept.

*Conclusion*   Each of these three arguments depends on religious assumptions. I have tried to show that they are all bad arguments, but I have *not* criticized them simply by rejecting their religious presuppositions. Instead, I have criticized them on their own terms, showing that these arguments should not be accepted even by religious people. As Daniel Maguire emphasizes, the ethics of theists, like the ethics of all responsible people, should be determined by "good and serious reasons," and these arguments are not good no matter what world view one has.

## §17 THE POSSIBILITY OF UNEXPECTED CURES

We have seen that euthanasia cannot be proved immoral by the argument that killing is always wrong, and that the most popular religious arguments against it are unsound. There is one additional argument we must now consider. Euthanasia may be opposed on the grounds that we cannot really tell when a patient's condition is hopeless. There are cases in which patients have recovered even after doctors had given up hope; if those patients had been killed, it would have been tragic, for they would have been deprived of many additional years of life. According to this argument, euthanasia is immoral because we never know for certain that the patient's situation is hopeless. *Any* so-called hopeless case might defy the odds and recover.

Those who advance this argument usually intend it as an argument against active euthanasia but not passive euthanasia. Nevertheless, we should notice that if this argument were sound it would rule out passive euthanasia as well. Suppose we allow someone to die by ceasing treatment; for example, we disconnect the artificial life-support systems that are necessary to maintain life. It *may* be that, if we had continued the treatment, the patient would eventually have recovered. Therefore, we cannot appeal to the possibility of unexpected recovery as an objection to active euthanasia without also objecting to passive euthanasia on the same grounds.

It must be admitted that doctors have sometimes made mistakes in labeling patients as "hopeless," and so we should be *very* cautious in any given case before saying that there is no chance of recovery. But it does *not* follow from the fact that doctors have *sometimes* been mistaken that they can *never* know for sure that any patient is hopeless. That would be like saying that since some people have sometimes confused a Rolls Royce with a Mercedes, no one can ever be certain which is which. In fact, doctors do sometimes know for sure that a patient cannot recover. There may be spontaneous remissions of cancer, for example, at a relatively early stage of the disease. But after the cancer has spread throughout the body and reached an advanced stage of development, there will be no hope whatever. Although there may be some doubt about some cases—and when there is doubt, perhaps euthanasia should not be considered—no one with the slightest medical knowledge could have had any doubt about Alsop's friend Jack. He was going to die of that cancer, and that is all there was to it. No one has *ever* recovered from such a dreadful condition, and doctors can explain exactly why this is so.

The same goes for patients in irreversible coma. Sometimes there is doubt about whether the patient can ever wake up. But in other cases there is no doubt, because of extensive brain damage that makes waking impossible. This is not merely a layman's judgment. Some of the best minds in the medical profession have argued that, in carefully defined cases, persons in irreversible coma should be regarded as *already dead!* In 1968, the *Journal of the American Medical Association* published the report of a committee of the Harvard Medical School, under the chairmanship of Dr. Henry K. Beecher, containing such a recommendation.[24] This report spells out, in precise terms, "the characteristics of a *permanently* nonfunctioning brain." There are four clinical signs of brain death. First, there is no response to stimuli that would be quite painful if felt; second, there is no movement or spontaneous breathing; third, there are no reflexes, such as swallowing or contraction of the pupils in response to bright light; and finally, there is an isoelectric (sometimes mistakenly called a "flat") electroencephalogram. It is noteworthy that all these signs may be present even while the heart still beats spontaneously, without the aid of machines. Yet the Harvard committee assures us that when these signs are present for a twenty-four-hour period, we may as well declare the patient dead.

What, then, are we to conclude from the fact that doctors have sometimes been mistaken in declaring patients hopeless? We may surely conclude that extreme care should be taken so as to avoid other such mistakes, and we may perhaps conclude that in any case where there is the slightest doubt, euthanasia should not be considered. However, we may *not* conclude that doctors *never* know when a case is hopeless. Sadly, we know that in some cases there simply is no hope, and so in those cases the possibility of an unexpected cure cannot be held out as an objection to euthanasia.

## V. THE QUESTION OF LEGALIZATION

We turn now to the question of whether euthanasia ought to be illegal, which is different from the question of whether it is immoral. Some people believe that, even if euthanasia is immoral, it still should not be prohibited by law, since if a patient *wants* to die, that is strictly a personal affair, regardless of how foolish or immoral the desire might be. On this view, euthanasia is comparable to sexual promiscuity; both are matters for private, individual decision and not government coercion, regardless of what moral judgment one might make. Others take a very different view and argue that active euthanasia *must* remain illegal, even if some individual acts of euthanasia are morally good, because the *consequences* of legalizing active euthanasia would be so terrible. They argue that legalized euthanasia would lead to a breakdown in respect for life that would eventually make all of our lives less secure. We shall consider the merits of these two arguments in §§ 20 and 21 below. But first, let us study something of the present legal situation respecting euthanasia.

## §18 HOW MERCY KILLERS ARE TREATED IN COURT

In 1939, a poor immigrant named Repouille, living in California, killed his thirteen-year-old son with chloroform. The boy, one of five children in the family, had suffered a brain injury at birth that left him virtually mindless, blind, mute, deformed in all four limbs, and with no control over his bladder or bowels. His whole life was spent in a small crib.

Repouille was tried for manslaughter in the first degree—apparently the prosecutor was unwilling to try him for first-degree murder, even though technically that charge could have been brought—but the jury, obviously sympathetic with him, brought in a verdict of *second*-degree manslaughter. From a legal point of view their verdict made no sense, since second-degree manslaughter presupposes that the killing was not intentional. Obviously the jury was intent on convicting him on only the mildest possible offense, so they ignored this legal nicety. They further indicated their desire to forgive the defendant by accompanying the verdict with a recommendation for "utmost clemency." The judge agreed with them and complied by staying execution of the five- to ten-year sentence and placing Repouille on probation.[25]

What Repouille did was clearly illegal, but the lenient treatment he received is typical of those tried for "mercy killing" in American courts. (The court regarded this as a case of euthanasia, even though it does not fit our strict definition.) Sometimes, as in the case of Robert Weskin, the jury will simply find the defendant not guilty. Weskin's mother was dying of leukemia in a Chicago hospital, in terrible pain, and Weskin took a gun into the hospital and shot her three times. He made no attempt to hide what he had done, saying, "She's out of her misery now. I shot her." He was indicted for murder, and legally it was an open-and-shut case. But the jury refused to convict him.[26]

From a strictly legal point of view, the juries' actions in both the Repouille case and the Weskin case were incorrect. In practice, however, juries have great discretion and can do practically anything they choose. (About the only thing they can't do is convict a defendant of a *more* serious charge than is made in the indictment.) What juries choose to do depends very much on the details of the particular case. For example, if the *manner* of the killing is especially gruesome, or if the killer tries to lie his way out, a jury might not be so sympathetic:

> In one case a lawyer killed his six-month-old mongoloid son by wrapping an uninsulated electrical cord around his wet diaper and putting the baby on a silver platter to insure good contact before plugging the cord into the wall. At the trial he claimed that the child's death was an accident, and he was convicted of first-degree murder and sentenced to electrocution himself, although the sentence was later commuted to life.[27]

There have been only two occasions on which *doctors* have been tried for mercy killing in this country. In New Hampshire in 1950, Dr. Herman Sander gave a patient four intravenous injections of air and then noted on the patient's chart that he had done so. The patient, who had terminal cancer, had asked to be put out of her misery. At the trial, the defense claimed that the patient was already dead at the time of the injections—which was a bit strange, since if the woman was already dead why were the injections given? Anyway, the jury acquitted Dr. Sander. The next such trial of a physician, and the only other one in the United States to date, occurred twenty-four years later in New York. Dr. Vincent Montemareno was charged with giving a lethal injection of potassium chloride to a patient with terminal cancer. At first the prosecutor announced that the case would be tried as a case of mercy killing; Dr. Montemareno, he said, had killed the patient to put her out of misery. But by the time the trial opened, the prosecutor had changed his mind and claimed that the doctor had murdered the patient for his own convenience, so that he would not have to return to the hospital later in the evening. At the conclusion of the trial the jury promptly voted to acquit.

But whatever juries may or may not do, active euthanasia is clearly against the law. The legal status of passive euthanasia is more uncertain. In practice, doctors do allow hopelessly ill patients to die, and as we have seen, the American Medical Association officially endorses this policy when the patient or his family requests it and when "extraordinary" means would be required to keep the patient alive. The legal status of such actions (or nonactions) is uncertain because, although there are laws against "negligent homicide" under which criminal charges could be brought, no such charges have been brought so far. Here district attorneys, and not juries, have exercised their discretion and have not pressed the issue.

It makes an important difference from a legal point of view whether a case of passive euthanasia is voluntary or nonvoluntary. Any patient—except one who has been declared legally "incompetent" to withhold consent—always has the right to refuse medical treatment. By refusing treatment, a patient can bring about his own death and the doctor cannot be convicted for "letting the person die." It is *nonvoluntary* passive euthanasia, in which the patient does not request to be allowed to die, that is legally uncertain.

## §19 THE CASE OF KAREN ANN QUINLAN AND OTHER RELATED CASES

There has been one famous case in which the question of nonvoluntary passive euthanasia was put before the courts. In April 1975, a twenty-one-year-old woman named Karen Ann Quinlan, for reasons that were never made clear, ceased breathing for at least two fifteen-minute periods. As a result, she suffered severe brain damage, and, in the words of the attending physicians, was reduced to "a chronic persistent vegetative state" in which she "no longer had any cognitive function." Accepting the doctors' judgment that there was no hope of recovery, her parents sought permission from the courts to disconnect the respirator that was keeping her alive in the intensive-care unit of a New Jersey hospital. The Quinlans are Roman Catholics, and they made this request only after consulting with their priest, who assured them that there would be no moral or religious objection if Karen were allowed to die.

Various medical experts testified in support of the Quinlans' request. One doctor described what he called the concept of "judicious neglect," under which a physician will say: "Don't treat this patient anymore. . . . It does not serve either the patient, the family, or society in any meaningful way to continue treatment with this patient." This witness also explained the use of the initials 'DNR'—"Do Not Resuscitate"—by which doctors instruct hospital staff to permit death. He said:

> No physician that I know personally is going to try and resuscitate a man riddled with cancer and in agony and he stops breathing. They are not going to put him on a respirator. . . . I think that would be the height of misuse of technology.[28]

The trial court, and then the Supreme Court of New Jersey, agreed that the respirator could be removed and Karen Quinlan allowed to die in peace. The respirator was disconnected. However, the nuns in charge of her care in the Catholic hospital opposed this decision, and anticipating it, had begun to wean Karen from the respirator so that by the time it was disconnected she could remain alive without it. (Reviewing these events, one prominent Catholic scholar commented angrily, "Some nuns always were holier than the church."[29]) So Karen lingered on in her "persistent vegetative state," emaciated and with deformed limbs and with no hope of ever awakening, but still alive in the biological sense. Finally, she died in June 1985.

Karen remained alive because, even though the respirator was disconnected, the intravenous tube supplying nutrition was *not* disconnected. Traditionally, a distinction has been made between (1) supplying food and water and (2) supplying other kinds of life-sustaining treatment. Even when it has been thought permissible to cut off other kinds of treatment, it has not been thought permissible to cut off food and water. However, this distinction has been brought into question in two more recent cases.

*The Case of Clarence Herbert.* In August 1981, two California physicians, Robert Nejdl and Neil Barber, were charged with murder when they terminated intravenous feeding for a fifty-five-year-old patient named Clarence Herbert. Herbert had suffered a heart attack while in the recovery room following an operation. He went into a coma and was placed on a ventilator and an intravenous (I.V.) feeding setup. After the judgment was made that he was unlikely to recover, his family requested that the life-sustaining equipment be removed. The ventilator was removed, and two days later the I.V. was taken away. Then Herbert died.

A nurse, who did not approve of all this, copied the patient's charts and took them to the authorities, who filed charges against the doctors. The magistrate hearing the case dismissed the charges, and when the state took the case to the appeals court, the appeals court affirmed the magistrate's decision.

The prosecutors objected to the removal of all the life-sustaining equipment, but the argument in court focused especially on the cessation of the I.V. feeding. The appeals court seemed to take it for granted that it was permissible to discontinue the respirator. The question that occupied attention was whether there is an important difference between the respirator and the I.V. The judge said that there was not:

> Medical procedures to provide nutrition and hydration are more similar to other medical procedures than to typical human ways of providing nutrition and hydration. Their benefits and burdens ought to be evaluated in the same manner as any other medical procedure.[30]

Thus, if it is permissible to allow a patient to die by unplugging a respirator, this judge said that it is equally permissible to disconnect an I.V. tube.

*The Case of Claire Conroy.*   However, a New Jersey judge reached a very different sort of conclusion. Claire Conroy was an eighty-three-year-old woman suffering from "organic brain syndrome." During the legal controversy that came to surround the case, a judge visited her and said "She does not speak. She lies in bed in a fetal position. She sometimes follows people with her eyes, but often stares blankly ahead. . . . she has no cognitive or volitional functioning."[31]

The controversy began in July 1982 when Mrs. Conroy developed necrotic ulcers on her foot as a result of diabetes. She had been in a nursing home for three years, and now she was moved to a hospital where doctors recommended that her leg be amputated. Mrs. Conroy's guardian would not permit the amputation and also demanded that the nasogastric tube supplying nutrition be removed. The doctor would not remove the tube, and so the guardian obtained a court order to force its removal. But before it could be removed, the patient died.

Because of the general interest and importance of the case, the New Jersey appeals courts continued to deliberate the legal issues involved, even though Mrs. Conroy's death had rendered the practical point moot. In mid-1983 an appeals court reversed the lower court's order that the tube be removed. The appeals court held that, in removing the nasogastric tube, the doctors would be purposefully killing the patient and so would be committing murder. The judge declared:

> If the trial judge's order had been enforced, Conroy would not have died as the result of an existing medical condition, but rather she would have died, and painfully so, as the result of a new and independent condition: dehydration and starvation. Thus she would have been actively killed by independent means.[32]

When the courts decided that it was all right to disconnect Karen Quinlan's respirator, it was widely assumed that now passive euthanasia was legally acceptable. However, these more recent cases show that the legal situation is much more complex than that. In the United States, at least, whether it is legally acceptable to allow a patient to die depends very much on the details of the case: on the patient's condition, on the kind of treatment that is withheld, and, moreover, on which judge hears the case.

Nevertheless, passive euthanasia is much less controversial than active euthanasia. Passive euthanasia has been accepted in at least *some* circumstances, while active euthanasia is altogether illegal. So, we will have little more to say about passive euthanasia. Instead we will focus attention on the question of active euthanasia: should *it* be legally accepted?

## §20 AN ARGUMENT FOR LEGALIZING ACTIVE EUTHANASIA: THE RIGHT TO LIBERTY

Should active euthanasia be legalized? We have already reached a number of conclusions that bear on this issue. We have seen that there are powerful arguments supporting the view that active euthanasia is morally permissible and that the arguments opposing it are weak. If active euthanasia is moral, as these arguments suggest, why should it not be made legal? We have noted that whenever charges have been brought against "mercy killers," prosecutors have had great difficulty securing convictions. Juries have not wanted to punish genuine mercy killers, and judges have not been willing to impose heavy sentences. So if active euthanasia were legalized, it would seem little more than an official acknowledgment of attitudes that already exist in the courtroom.

However, none of this really proves that active euthanasia ought to be legalized. We need to turn now to arguments that are addressed more directly to the issue of legalization. One such argument is the "argument from the right to liberty." According to this argument, each dying patient should be free to choose euthanasia or to reject it simply as a matter of personal liberty. No one, including the government, has the right to tell another what choice to make. If a dying patient wants euthanasia, that is a private affair; after all, the life belongs to the individual, so that individual should be the one to decide.

*Mill's Principle*   This argument starts from the principle that people should be free to live their own lives as they themselves think best. But of course the right to liberty is not completely unrestricted. We should not be free to murder or rape or steal. It is an interesting theoretical problem to explain why *those* restrictions should be placed on our freedom while many other restrictions are unacceptable. The classical solution to this problem was provided by Bentham, who observed that in murder, rape, and theft, *we are doing harm to other people.* That, he reasoned, is what makes the difference. So he suggested this principle: people's freedom may be restricted only to prevent them from doing harm to others. Bentham's famous disciple John Stuart Mill gave this principle its most elegant expression when he wrote:

> . . . the sole end for which mankind are warranted, individually or collectively, in interfering with the liberty of action of any of their number, is self-protection. The only purpose for which power can be rightfully exercised over any member of a civilized community, against his will, is to prevent harm to others. His own good, either physical or moral, is not a sufficient warrant . . . Over himself, over his own body and mind, the individual is sovereign.[33]

With apologies to Bentham, I will call this "Mill's Principle." There are two general classes of interferences that Mill's Principle would prohibit. First, we cannot force a person to conform to our ideas of right and wrong so long as the person is not harming others. Take homosexuality, for example. Many people think that homosexual behavior is immoral. The implication of Mill's Principle is that, even if it were immoral, we have no business trying to force people to stop being homosexuals; so long as they harm no one else, it is no one else's business what they do in private. It is important to notice that this argument does *not* depend on the assumption that homosexuality is morally all right (although, indeed, it well might be). It simply does not matter, so far as this argument is concerned, whether it is moral or immoral. All that matters is whether homosexuals, as a result of their homosexuality, do any harm to other people. If they do not, then others have no right to force their moral views on them.

Second, if Mill's Principle is correct, then we may not interfere with a person's actions "for his own good." We may think people are behaving foolishly, for example, if they invest their money in a highly speculative stock. And suppose they are. The point is that, if it is *their* money and only they will be hurt by it, then it is their business and we have no right to interfere. Now we might have the right to *advise* them against the investment and urge them not to make it, but in the end it is their decision and not ours. The same goes for other, similar cases. If someone is feeling poorly, we may advise or urge a visit to a doctor, but we have no right to force this on a person, even "for his own good." It is one's own health, and, as Mill put it, "Over himself, over his own mind and body, the individual is sovereign." (Mill excluded children and mental incompetents from the scope of this rule on the grounds that they are incapable of making rational choices concerning their own interests.)

*Implications for Euthanasia*   If Bentham and Mill are correct, a terminally ill patient who wishes to end his or her life rather than continue suffering certainly has the right to do so. The life belongs to the individual; no one else has the right to interfere; and that's that. But this only establishes a right to *suicide* in such cases. A further, additional step is required to reach the conclusion that we may kill the person. It is, however, easy to see how to provide the extra step in the argument. Mill's Principle covers not only the actions of individuals acting alone but of groups of individuals who voluntarily agree to act together. Homosexual alliances, for example, do not involve individuals acting alone but groups of two or more. The relevant question is: Does their conduct affect anyone other than themselves, the "consenting adults" who are involved in the affair? If not, then others have no right to interfere. An act of euthanasia, in which the patient requests a lethal drug and the doctor provides it, is a "private affair" in this sense; those participating are "consenting adults," and no one else's interests need be involved. Therefore, if we are to respect the right to liberty of dying patients, we must respect their right to enter into euthanasia agreements with their doctors, or with any other competent adults willing to help them.

This argument can also be made to apply to patients in irreversible coma, in the following way. Of course patients in irreversible coma are not able to request that they be killed or allowed to die. Nevertheless, they may leave instructions beforehand that if their condition becomes hopeless, they are to be killed or allowed to die. Some state medical societies have actually encouraged patients to leave such instructions and have designed forms for this purpose. Like the American Medical Association, these societies do not condone killing, but they do approve allowing patients to die by ceasing treatment. So in 1973, the Connecticut State Medical Society endorsed a "background statement" to be signed by patients, which includes this sentence: "I value life and the dignity of life, so that I am not asking that my life be directly taken, but that my life not be unreasonably prolonged or the dignity of life destroyed." Other state medical groups followed suit, and in 1976 the state of California enacted legislation that recognized the legal right of doctors to allow the deaths of patients who sign such statements. Following Mill's Principle, we could say that the right of patients to leave such instructions and to have them carried out is just one implication of their right to control their own affairs, regardless of whether other people think their decisions are right or wrong or wise or foolish.

## §21 AN ARGUMENT AGAINST LEGALIZING ACTIVE EUTHANASIA: THE SLIPPERY SLOPE

Now we shall examine the most widely used argument *against* legalizing active euthanasia, the slippery-slope argument.

*Statement of the Argument*    The basic idea of the argument is that if euthanasia were legally permitted, it would lead to a general decline in respect for human life. In the beginning, we might kill people only to put them out of extreme agony. Our motives would be honorable, and the results might be good. However, once we had started cold-bloodedly killing people, where would it stop? Where would we draw the line? The point is that once we accept killing in some cases, we have stepped onto a "slippery slope," which we will inevitably slide down, and in the end life will be held cheap. Sometimes a different analogy—called the "wedge" argument—is used; then it is said that once we admit the thin edge of the wedge, we are on the way to abandoning our traditional view of the importance of human life.

Bishop Sullivan puts the argument this way:

> . . . to permit in a single instance the direct killing of an innocent person would be to admit a most dangerous wedge that might eventually put all life in a precarious condition. Once a man is permitted on his own authority to kill an innocent person directly, there is no way of stopping the advancement of that wedge. There exists no longer any rational grounds for saying that the wedge can advance so far and no further. Once the exception has been made it is too late; hence the grave reason why no exception may be allowed. That is why euthanasia under any circumstances must be condemned.

More specifically, Sullivan says:

> If voluntary euthanasia were legalized, there is good reason to believe that at a later date another bill for compulsory euthanasia would be legalized. Once the respect for human life is so low that an innocent person may be killed directly even at his own request, compulsory euthanasia will necessarily be very near. This could lead easily to killing all incurable charity patients, the aged who are a public care, wounded soldiers, all deformed children, the mentally afflicted, and so on. Before long the danger would be at the door of every citizen.[34]

Although Sullivan writes from a Catholic point of view, it is clear that this argument is not a religious one. It requires no religious assumptions of any kind. And, in fact, non-Catholics have used this argument, too. Philippa Foot is a leading British moral philosopher. Unlike Sullivan, she thinks that in some individual cases, active euthanasia is *morally* all right. However, she thinks it should not be legalized, because of "the really serious problem of abuse":

> Many people want, and want very badly, to be rid of their elderly relatives and even of their ailing husbands or wives. Would any safe-guards ever be able to stop them describing as euthanasia what was really for their own benefit? And would it be possible to prevent the occurrence of acts which were genuinely acts of euthanasia but mor-ally impermissible because infringing the rights of a patient who wished to live? . . . the possibility of active voluntary euthanasia might change the social scene in ways that would be very bad. As things are, people do, by and large, expect to be looked after if they are old or ill. This is one of the good things that we have, but we might lose it, and be much worse off without it. It might come to be expected that someone likely to need a lot of looking after should call for the doctor and demand his own death. Something comparable could be good in an extremely poverty-stricken community where the children genu-inely suffered from lack of food; but in rich societies such as ours it would surely be a spiritual disaster.[35]

The conclusion of the argument is that no matter what view you take of individual instances of mercy killing, as a matter of social policy we ought to enforce a rigorous rule against it. Otherwise, we are courting disaster.

To assess this argument, we need to distinguish between two very different forms it might take. We may call these the *logical* version of the argument and the *psychological* version.

*The Logical Interpretation of the Slippery Slope*   The logical form of the argument goes like this. Once a certain practice is accepted, from a logical point of view we are committed to accepting certain other practices as well, since there are no good reasons for not going on to accept the additional practices once we have taken the all-important first step. But, the argument continues, the additional practices are plainly unacceptable; therefore, the first step had better not be taken.

Interpreted in this way, the slippery-slope argument makes a point about *what you are logically committed to* once certain practices are accepted. It says that once you allow euthanasia for the patient in terrible agony, *you are logically committed* to approving of eu-thanasia in other cases as well. Bishop Sullivan, in the passage previ-ously quoted, apparently intends this, for he says that "Once a man is permitted on his own authority to kill an innocent person directly . . . *there exists no longer any rational grounds* for saying that the wedge can advance so far and no further." But this is clearly false. There *are* rational grounds for distinguishing between the man in agony who wants to die and other cases, such as that of an old infirm person who does not want to die. It is easy to say what the rational ground is. It is simply that in the first case the person requests death, whereas in the second case the person does not request it. Moreover, in the first case, the person is suffering terribly, and in the second case the person is not. These are morally relevant differences to which we can appeal in order to distinguish the cases; therefore, we are *not* logically committed to accepting "euthanasia" in the second case merely because we approve it in the first. Thus, the logical form of the slippery-slope argument does not work in the case of euthanasia. It does not prove that active euthanasia ought to be legally prohibited in every case.

*The Psychological Interpretation of the Slippery Slope* This form of the argument is very different. It claims that once certain practices are accepted, *people shall in fact* go on to accept other, more questionable practices. This is simply a claim about what people will do and not a claim about what they are logically committed to. Thus, this form of the argument says that if we start off by killing people to put them out of extreme agony, we shall *in fact* end up killing them for other reasons, regardless of logic and nice distinctions. Therefore, if we want to avoid the latter, we had better avoid the former. This is the point that Mrs. Foot is making, and it is a much stronger argument than what I have called the "logical" version of the slippery slope.

How strong is the psychological version of the argument? Does it show that active euthanasia ought to be illegal? The crucial question is whether legalizing active euthanasia would in fact lead to terrible consequences. This is an empirical question—a question of fact—about which philosophers have no special inside information. But then, neither does anyone else; there is no definitive "scientific" answer to this question. Each of us is left to form his or her own best estimate concerning what would happen in our society if active euthanasia came to be accepted. For myself, I do *not* believe that it would lead to any sort of general breakdown in respect for life, for several reasons.

First, we have a good bit of historical and anthropological evidence that approval of killing in one context does not necessarily lead to killing in different circumstances. As has been previously mentioned, in ancient Greece, people killed defective infants without any feeling of shame or guilt—but this did *not* lead to the easy approval of other types of killing. Many instances of this kind could be cited. In Eskimo societies, the killing of infants and feeble old people was widely accepted as a measure to avoid starvation; but in at least some Eskimo communities, murder was virtually unheard of. Such evidence suggests that people are able to distinguish between various types of cases, and keep them separated fairly well.

Second, in our own society killing has been, and still is, accepted in many circumstances. For example, we allow killing in self-defense. But what if it were argued that we should not allow this, on the grounds that acceptance of killing in self-defense would inevitably lead to a breakdown in respect for life? Of course, we know that this is not true, because we know that acceptance of killing in self-defense *has not* led to any such consequences. But why hasn't it? Because, first, it is rather unusual for anyone to have to kill in self-defense—most of us never face such a situation—and second, we are not so stupid that we are unable to distinguish this case, in which killing is justified, from other cases in which it is not justified. Exactly the same seems to be true of killing people who ask to be killed to put them out of misery. Such cases would be fairly rare—most of us know of such cases only by reading of them—and we can distinguish them from other, very different cases fairly easily.

Third, Mrs. Foot fears that "It might come to be expected that someone likely to need a lot of looking after should call for the doctor and demand his own death." But this situation would become possible *only if* it were legal for doctors to kill *anyone* who requests it. It would not be possible under a legal arrangement that authorized doctors to administer euthanasia only to terminal patients of special kinds.

Finally, it must be admitted that if active euthanasia were legalized, there would inevitably be *some* abuses, just as there are abuses of virtually every social practice. No one can deny that. The crucial issue is whether the abuses, or the bad consequences generally, would be *so* numerous as to outweigh the advantages of legalized euthanasia. We must remember that the choice is not between a present policy that is benign and an alternative that is potentially dangerous. The present policy has its evils too, and for patients like Stewart Alsop's friend Jack those evils are all too real. We must not forget that these evils have to be weighed against any feared disadvantages of the alternative. For these reasons, my own conclusion is that the psychological version of the slippery-slope argument does *not* provide a decisive reason why active euthanasia should be kept illegal. The possibility of bad consequences should perhaps make us proceed cautiously in this area; but it should not stop us from proceeding at all.

## §22 HOW TO LEGALIZE ACTIVE EUTHANASIA

Opposition to the legalization of active euthanasia comes from those who believe it is immoral, from those who fear the consequences of legalization, and from those who believe that, although it may be a fine idea in theory, in practice it is impossible to devise any workable laws to accommodate active euthanasia. This last point is important. If we wanted to legalize active euthanasia, exactly how could we go about doing it? Who should be granted the awesome power to decide when a person may be put to death? Should patients or doctors or the patient's family be allowed to decide on their own? Or should some sort of hospital committee be authorized to make the decision? And if so, exactly who should sit on such a committee? What if those who are given the power abuse it? Shall they then be liable to charges of murder? If so, then it would seem that they do not really have the power to decide; but if not, their power is unchecked and they have a license to do as they please. It is easy to think of objections to almost any proposed scheme, so it is no wonder that even those who approve active euthanasia in theory are often wary of actually legalizing it.

I want to make a modest proposal concerning how active euthanasia might be legalized so as to avoid all these problems. Before outlining this proposal, I need to make some elementary points about American law.

Individuals charged with a crime have no obligation to prove their innocence. The burden of proof is on the prosecution, and the defense may consist entirely in pointing out that the prosecution has not decisively proven guilt. If the prosecution has not discharged its obligation to prove guilt, the jury's duty is to acquit the defendant.

However, if the prosecution does establish a strong case against the defendant, a more active defense is required. Then there are two options available. The defendant may deny having done the criminal act in question. Or, while admitting to the act, the defendant may nevertheless argue that he or she should not be punished for it.

There are two legally accepted ways of arguing that a person should not be punished for an act even while admitting that the act is prohibited by law and that the person did it. First, an *excuse* may be offered, such as insanity, coercion, ignorance of fact, unavoidable accident, and so on. If it can be shown that the defendant was insane when the crime was committed or that he was coerced into doing it or that it was an unavoidable accident, then the defendant may be acquitted. Second, a *justification* may be offered. A plea of self-defense against a charge of murder is an example of a justification. The technical difference between excuses and justifications need not concern us here.

Here is an example to illustrate these points. Suppose you are charged with murdering a man, and the prosecution can make a strong case that you did in fact kill the victim. You might respond by trying to show that you did *not* kill him. Or you might admit that you killed him, and then have your lawyers argue that you were insane or that the killing was a tragic accident for which you are blameless or that you had to kill him in self-defense. If any of these defenses can be made out, then you will be acquitted of the crime even though you admittedly did kill the victim.

When such a defense is offered, the burden of proof is on the defense, and not the prosecution, to show that the facts alleged are true. The prosecution does not have to show that the defendant was sane; rather, the defendant (or the defendant's lawyers) must prove that he or she was insane. The prosecution does not have to prove that the killing was not done in self-defense; instead the defense must prove that it was. Thus it is not quite accurate to say that under American law the burden of proof is always on the prosecution. If the defendant concedes to having performed the act in question but claims an excuse or justification for the act, the burden of proof may shift so that the defense is required to show that the excuse or justification should be accepted.

Now, my proposal for legalizing active euthanasia is that a plea of mercy killing be acceptable as a defense against a charge of murder in much the same way that a plea of self-defense is acceptable as a defense. When people plead self-defense, it is up to them to show that their own lives were threatened and that the only way of fending off the threat was by killing the attacker first. Under my proposal, someone charged with murder could also plead mercy killing; and then, if it could be proven that the victim while competent requested death and that the victim was suffering from a painful terminal illness, the person pleading mercy killing would also be acquitted.

Under this proposal no one would be "authorized" to decide when a patient should be killed any more than people are "authorized" to decide when someone may be killed in self-defense. There are no committees to be established within which people may cast private votes for which they are not really accountable; people who choose to kill from the motive of mercy bear full legal responsibility, as individuals, for their actions. In practice, this would mean that anyone contemplating mercy killing would have to be very sure that there are independent witnesses to testify concerning the patient's condition and desire to die; for otherwise, one might not be able to make out a defense in a court of law—if it should come to that—and would be legally liable for murder. However, if this proposal were adopted, it would *not* mean that every time active euthanasia was performed a court trial would follow. In clear cases of self-defense, prosecutors simply do not bring charges, since it would be a pointless waste of time. Similarly, in clear cases of mercy killing, where there is no doubt about the patient's hopeless condition or desire to die, charges would not be brought for the same reason.

Thus, under this proposal, the need to write difficult legislation permitting euthanasia is bypassed. The problems of formulating a statute, which were mentioned at the beginning of this section, do not arise. We would rely on the good sense of judges and juries to separate the cases of justifiable euthanasia from the cases of unjustifiable murder, just as we already rely on them to separate the cases of self-defense and insanity and coercion. Some juries are already functioning in this way but without legal sanction: when faced with genuine mercy killers, they refuse to convict. The main consequence of my proposal would be to sanction officially what these juries already do.

## VI. CONCLUSION

We have now examined the most important arguments for and against the morality of euthanasia, and we have considered arguments for and against legalizing it. It is time to summarize our conclusions. What do the arguments show?

First, in the central case of the terminal patient who wants to be killed rather than die slowly in agony, we are led inescapably to the conclusion that active euthanasia is morally acceptable and that it ought to be made legal. The morality of euthanasia in this case is supported by such diverse ethical precepts as the Principle of Utility, Kant's Categorical Imperative, and the Golden Rule. Euthanasia here serves the interests of everyone concerned: it is a mercy to the patient, it reduces the emotional strain of death on the patient's family and friends, and it conserves medical resources. Moreover, if doctors are legally forbidden to provide a painless death to such patients at their request, it is an unwarranted restriction on the freedom of the patients, for it is *their* life and so their right to decide. The arguments opposing euthanasia, both morally and legally, are not nearly so strong.

Second, in the case of the patient in an irreversible coma, we are struck by the fact that as far as *the patient's own* interests are concerned, it does not really matter whether he or she lives or dies. Although this unfortunate patient is still alive in the biological sense, life was over when consciousness was lost for the final time. That is why it seems so pointless to continue maintaining life by artificial means, especially when doing so is emotionally destructive to those who love the patient, and when medical resources could be used better to help those who still can be helped. In this type of case, then, our conclusion must also be that euthanasia is justified. The only qualification, suggested by the argument from the possibility of unexpected cures, is that we must be certain that the coma really *is* irreversible.

These are our main conclusions. Some readers may find them hard to accept. This is understandable, for the idea of deliberately killing someone goes against very deep moral feelings. The principle of the value of life is an especially fundamental one, not to be taken lightly. Nonetheless, I believe that the arguments we have considered show that in these tragic cases, killing may be not only permissible but mandatory.

## NOTES

1. *De. Ira.* i, 15.
2. *Dissertations,* I, IX, 16.
3. *De. Ira.* i, 15.
4. *De Corona,* 11.
5. E. Westermarck, *Christianity and Morals* (1939), p. 239.
6. *Mishneh Torah, Book of Judges,* "Laws of Mourning," 4:5.
7. Raanan Gillon, "Suicide and Voluntary Euthanasia: Historical Perspec-

tive," in A. B. Downing, ed., *Euthanasia and the Right to Die* (Los Angeles: Nash, 1969), p. 181.

8. Gillon, pp. 182–183.
9. From Book II of More's *Utopia*.
10. *New Atlantis* (1626).
11. Plato, *Republic*, III, 407-e.
12. *The Pope Speaks*, IV, 4: "Address to the International Congress of Anesthesiologists."
13. *Morals and Medicine* (Boston: Beacon, 1960), p. 174.
14. "The Right to Die with Dignity," *Good Housekeeping* (August 1974), pp. 69, 130.
15. *Foundations of the Metaphysics of Morals*, 422.
16. *Philosophic Exchange*, II:1 (Summer 1975), p. 45.
17. Humphrey Primatt, *A Dissertation on the Duty of Mercy and the Sin of Cruelty to Brute Animals* (London, 1776), p. 65.
18. See footnote 13 above.
19. *The Humanist* (July–August 1974), p. 5.
20. Garden City, New York: Doubleday, 1973. Also see Maguire's article "A Catholic View of Mercy Killing," in Marvin Kohl, ed., *Beneficent Euthanasia* (Buffalo, New York: Prometheus, 1975), pp. 34–43, from which the following quotations are taken.
21. See Joseph V. Sullivan, "The Immorality of Euthanasia," in Kohl, ed., *Beneficent Euthanasia*, p. 14.
22. "Of Suicide" (1784).
23. Kohl, ed., *Beneficent Euthanasia*, p. 19.
24. "A Definition of Irreversible Coma," *Journal of the American Medical Association*, 205 (1968), pp. 85–88.
25. *Repouille* v. *United States*, 165 F.2d 152 (1947).
26. *Miami News*, July 3, 1973, p. 3-A.
27. Yale Kamisar, "Some Non-Religious Views Against Proposed Mercy-Killing Legislation," *Minnesota Law Review*, 6, May 1958, p. 1022.
28. Supreme Court of New Jersey, 70 N.J. 10, 355 A.2d 647 (1976).
29. Andrew M. Greely, review of *Karen Ann: The Quinlans Tell Their Story* by Joseph and Julia Quinlan, in *The New York Times Book Review*, 9 October 1977, pp. 10–11.
30. Cf. *Barber and Nejdl* v. *Sup. Ct.*, 2 Civil No. 69350, 69351, Ct. of App. 2d Dist., Div.2 Oct. 12, 1983.
31. *In the Matter of Conroy*, Sup. Ct. N. J. App. Div., A-2483-82, July 8, 1983.
32. Ibid.
33. J. S. Mill, *On Liberty*, chap. 1.
34. Kohl, ed., *Beneficent Euthanasia*, p. 24.
35. "Euthanasia," *Philosophy and Public Affairs*, 6:2 (Winter 1977), pp. 111–112.

## SUGGESTIONS FOR FURTHER READING

Further readings are mentioned below in connection with the sections of the essay to which they are most pertinent.

§2 On the case of Elizabeth Bouvia, see George J. Annas, "When Suicide Prevention Becomes Brutality," *The Hastings Center Report*, 14 (April 1984), pp. 20ff.

§§5–9 For information on the history of attitudes toward euthanasia, see Edward Westermarck, *The Origin and Development of the Moral Ideas*, 2 vols. (London: 1906–1908), and W. E. H. Lecky, *History of European Morals,* 2 vols. (New York: 1919).

§11 In James Rachels, "Active and Passive Euthanasia," *New England Journal of Medicine,* vol. 292 (1975), pp. 78–80, it is argued that the distinction between killing and letting die has no moral importance; therefore, contrary to the traditional doctrine, active and passive euthanasia are morally equivalent. This article is reprinted in *Social Ethics,* edited by Thomas Mappes and Jane Zembaty (New York: McGraw-Hill, 1977). This anthology also contains a defense of the distinction by Tom L. Beauchamp, "A Reply to Rachels on Active and Passive Euthanasia."

On allowing patients to die, see Sidney H. Wanzer et al., "The Physician's Responsibility Toward Hopelessly Ill Patients," *The New England Journal of Medicine* 310 (April 12, 1984), pp. 955–959.

§§13–14 For additional arguments in favor of euthanasia, see Joseph Fletcher, *Morals and Medicine* (Boston: Beacon Press, 1960); Daniel Maguire, *Death by Choice* (Garden City, N.Y.: Doubleday, 1973); and various essays in *Beneficent Euthanasia,* edited by Marvin Kohl (Buffalo, N.Y.: Prometheus, 1975), and in *Euthanasia and the Right to Die,* edited by A. B. Downing (Los Angeles: Nash, 1969).

On the argument from the Golden Rule, see especially R. M. Hare, "Euthanasia: A Christian View," *Philosophic Exchange* II:1 (Summer 1975).

§§15–17 For additional arguments opposing euthanasia, see various articles in the anthologies edited by Kohl and Downing. "The Immorality of Euthanasia," by Joseph V. Sullivan (in the Kohl volume) is especially interesting; Sullivan advances almost all the antieuthanasia arguments considered in this essay. Another article in the Kohl volume, "Jewish Views of Euthanasia," by Byron L. Sherwin, is a good source of information about Jewish attitudes, which are generally antieuthanasia.

§18 Daniel Maguire provides a good, readable account of the present state of the law, together with arguments for changing it, in *Death by Choice.*

§19 The parents of Karen Ann Quinlan have written their own account of the events leading up to the court's decision to allow disconnection of the life-support systems: *Karen Ann: The Quinlans Tell Their Story,* by Joseph and Julia Quinlan (New York: Doubleday, 1977). For negative reactions to the court's decision, see a special issue of *Christianity and Crisis,* January 19, 1976. The February 1976 issue of *Hastings Center Report* contains a number of articles on the case reacting more favorably to the decision.

The Herbert case and the Conroy case are discussed in a number of articles in *The Hastings Center Report.* "Nonfeeding: Lawful Killing in CA, Homicide in NJ," by George J. Annas (vol. 13, no. 6, December 1983) is especially helpful in understanding these types of cases.

§§20–22 In *The Sanctity of Life and the Criminal Law* (New York: Knopf, 1957), the British jurist Glanville Williams argues that euthanasia ought to be legalized. Yale Kamisar, a professor of law at the University of Michigan, criticizes Williams's proposals in an article, "Euthanasia Legislation: Some Non-Religious Objections," which is included in *Euthanasia and the Right to Die,* edited by Downing. Downing's book also contains a rejoinder by Williams.

R. M. Hare, in the article previously mentioned, takes the view that although active euthanasia may be justified in some individual cases, still it probably should not be legalized because of possible abuses (the slippery-slope argument). On this point, also see Hare's article "Medical Ethics: Can the Moral Philosopher Help?" in *Philosophical Medical Ethics,* edited by Spicker and Engelhardt (Dordrecht: Reidel, 1977).

# 3

# Suicide

## TOM L. BEAUCHAMP

Families often conceal the fact that a death in the family was a suicide, and, generally speaking, we all tend to be puzzled and stunned when our friends take their lives. Many react to suicide with an instinctive revulsion. Such attitudes reflect a social situation in which motivations toward suicide are not well understood and the serious dimensions of the social problem are seldom confronted or discussed.

Yet suicide is a fact of everyday life. It is the second-ranking cause of death among college students (behind accidents), and approximately 25,000 people kill themselves every year in the United States. According to the World Health Organization, it can be reasonably estimated that (in reporting nations) about 1,000 people commit suicide every day. Moreover, the persons most knowledgeable about problems of suicidal patients commit suicide more often than any other segment of the population: the physician suicide rate is variously estimated at two to three times the rate of the general population, and the rate for psychiatrists increases to two to three times that of the physicians. These are only a few of the staggering statistics about suicide gathered in recent years.

Suicides present unresolved moral problems about the value of life. Philosophers have talked about the moral permissibility or impermissibility of suicide at least since Plato (430–350 B.C.) and Aristotle (384–322 B.C.), and several major writings on suicide have been bequeathed to us from major figures in the history of philosophy. There are at least two reasons why interest in the morality of suicide has increased in recent years. First, biomedical technology has made it possible for ill and seriously injured persons to prolong their lives beyond the point at which, in former times, they would have died. Many of these patients are seriously ill and in agony. Numerous people have come to think that suicide is justified in such cases, even that those who are incapacitated should be assisted in their acts of suicide. Slogans such as "the right to die" and "death with dignity" have grown up around such cases. Second, although suicide laws have been repealed recently in many jurisdictions in the United States, repeal is a matter of present debate in others. Whether "assisted suicide" should be decriminalized is also under active discussion. These debates turn more on moral than legal considerations.

The major objective of this essay is to evaluate various views—classical and contemporary—about the morality of suicide. In §1 through §6, I shall characterize and assess proposed analyses of the concept of suicide. After arguing for one particular analysis, I shall identify four moral principles relevant to the morality of suicide (§7 through §10). These principles will then be applied to the thought of two of the most influential writers on suicide: In §11, the position of the philosophical theologian St. Thomas Aquinas (1224–1274) is discussed, while in §12, the position of the eighteenth-century Scottish philosopher David Hume (1711–1776) is explored. In the concluding section (§13) to this part of the essay, Hume's position is defended. Only when we reach §14 do I raise the question of the morality of trying to prevent someone from committing suicide. The morality of suicide intervention is under discussion there and in the remainder of the essay.

## I. THE DEFINITION OF SUICIDE

### §1 SOME CONCEPTUAL DIFFICULTIES

Although debate about the legality, rationality, and morality of suicide has increased in recent years, minimal attention has been devoted to the development of an adequate definition of suicide. Yet definitions have important practical consequences. The way we classify actions is indicative of the way we think about them, and in the present case such classifications have immediate relevance for medicine, ethics, and law.

The following 1968 case illustrates some of the conceptual difficulties involved in correctly classifying a case as a suicide or as a nonsuicide:

*N.Y. Times,* February 7, 1968: Phoenix, Ariz., Feb. 6 (AP)—
Linda Marie Ault killed herself, policemen said today, rather than make her dog Beauty pay for her night with a married man.
" 'I killed her. I killed her. It's just like I killed her myself,' " a detective quoted her grief-stricken father as saying.
" 'I handed her the gun. I didn't think she would do anything like that.' "

The 21-year-old Arizona State University coed died in a hospital yesterday of a gunshot wound in the head.

The police quoted her parents, Mr. and Mrs. Joseph Ault, as giving this account:

" 'Linda failed to return home from a dance in Tempe Friday night. On Saturday she admitted she had spent the night with an Air Force lieutenant.' "

The Aults decided on a punishment that would "wake Linda up." They ordered her to shoot the dog she had owned about two years.

On Sunday, the Aults and Linda took the dog into the desert near their home. They had the girl dig a shallow grave. Then Mrs. Ault grasped the dog between her hands, and Mr. Ault gave his daughter a .22-caliber pistol and told her to shoot the dog.

Instead, the girl put the pistol to her right temple and shot herself.

The police said there were no charges that could be filed against the parents except possibly cruelty to animals.

Linda Marie Ault killed herself, as this story recounts, but is she a suicide? Does the coercive intervention of her parents render her intentional act of self-destruction *not* an act of suicide? Why?

Such questions surround a great many "suicides," and they are by no means idle questions or of interest only to those who compile dictionaries. For example, the accuracy of statistics about suicide depends on knowledge that reported suicides are really *suicides.* Credible statistics, then, depend not only on careful reporting but on our concept of suicide. This problem plagues those who plan programs for the prevention of suicide, insurance agents who assess the legitimacy of claims, and lawyers and judges who ascertain the extent of protections afforded by the law. Social scientists have registered similar difficulties:

> The following questions remain: how does the researcher identify his subjects (i.e. suicides) for study, if he does not know what 'suicide' means; how does one locate 'suicidal statements' or a 'suicidal action'? There seems to be the assumption that the individual understands himself better than any observer. This is not necessarily true. In defining the situation wholly in terms of the definitions offered by the patient, error can occur by accepting that definition as the *only* one. In doing so, the researcher may have become so personally involved in the relationship that he could no longer stand outside it. . . .[1]

One important reason for confusion over the precise nature of suicide is that social attitudes and customs are commonly reflected in the definitions accepted in a culture. If suicide is socially disapproved, then the definition may reflect this disapproval by excluding all praiseworthy actions from the category of "suicides." That is, an act will not be *called* suicide unless it incurs disapproval. Thus, if self-killing is generally disapproved in a society—while great value is placed on being buried with one's spouse—the act of ending one's life in order to be buried with one's spouse may be called "sacrificial," not suicidal.

A second and related reason for definitional confusion about suicide has to do with different assessments of the suicide's exact intentions. Sacrificial actions are especially troublesome: an act of self-killing is generally called "suicide" if performed for one's own sake or personal relief; it is generally called "sacrifice" if performed for others' sake or benefit. For example, when a spy takes a lethal poison in order to avoid revealing secrets, or when the driver of a runaway car rams into a hill in order to avoid killing others (knowing that he or she will die), or when a person stops using life-support equipment in order to relieve the family's anguish, we may be perplexed as to whether the action is a suicide even if it is in a reasonable sense an *intentional* self-caused death.

These are some of the issues we must now face. But before turning to them, brief mention should be made of the method I shall employ in attempting a conceptual analysis of "suicide." Various human actions are *easily* and *correctly* classified as acts of suicide; others are less clearly instances of suicide; and still others are borderline cases between suicide and, for example, accidental death or heroic sacrifice. Any satisfactory definition of suicide must be able to account for the clear cases and to pinpoint why borderline cases are troublesome. I shall attempt to provide a definition of this order that captures the ordinary English meaning of the term 'suicide'. On the other hand, there can be valid reasons for resisting the use of ordinary meanings if they are misleading or reflect morally prejudicial conclusions. I believe that 'suicide' presents problems of this sort, and I shall return to this issue after a discussion of the ordinary English meaning.

## §2 STANDARD DEFINITIONS

In recent years, three definitions have been widely accepted as ways of understanding suicide. The first is simple and might be called the prevailing definition: suicide occurs if and only if there is an intentional termination of one's own life. Contemporary moral philosophers such as R. B. Brandt and Eike-Henner Kluge have employed similar definitions, and this definition also is found in *Gould's Medical Dictionary* and *The Encyclopedia of Bioethics*.[2] The second definition, by contrast, supposedly does not rely on the intent to terminate life and derives from the sociologist Émile Durkheim:

> The term suicide is applied to all cases of death resulting directly or indirectly from a positive or negative act of the victim himself, which he knows will produce this result.[3]

This second definition broadens the scope of 'suicide', but the third definition is still broader than the other two and has fittingly been called the "omnibus definition." As contemporary sociologist Ronald Maris has stated it:

Suicide occurs when an individual engages in a life-style that he knows might kill him (other than living another day)—and it does [kill him]. This is an omnibus definition of suicide, which includes various forms of self-destruction, such as risk-taking and many so-called "accidents."[4]

It is easy both to see why these three definitions have been popular and to grasp the connection between them. The first seems consistent with ordinary linguistic usage, as most dictionaries define 'suicide'. Durkheim accepted the second and rejected the first because the first appeals to the presence of an intention *to die*—something not easily verifiable. Whether or not Durkheim's substitution of knowledge for a specific motivation or intention is any improvement is surely debatable, but at least we can understand his reasons for seeking a modification of definitions based on an unverifiable, specific intention if knowledge alone will suffice.

The word 'know' in Durkheim's definition seems objectionable to those who support the third definition, because the suicidal person may not *know* that a given act or life-style will produce death. If the words "he *knows* will produce" in Durkheim's definition are replaced by some weaker expression, such as "might produce," then the second definition has in effect been transformed into the third. Because a great many risk-taking behaviors such as heavy smoking may produce death (though this will not be *known* in advance), the number of suicides will be greatly expanded by this third definition and will far exceed the figure quoted earlier of a thousand per day (worldwide).

Erwin Stengel, a contemporary psychiatrist, supports this third definition. He contends that the majority of "suicides" have ambivalent intentions about whether to take their lives and cannot correctly be said either to want to live or to want to die.[5] Yet their tendencies toward self-destruction lead them to take extreme risks and to inflict various types of severe damage on their bodies. Among fifteen- to twenty-four-year-olds, suicides are the second leading killer, behind traffic accidents. Yet many suicidologists and police authorities believe that these traffic "accidents" are often the result of suicidal gambles or are disguised suicides. Because such persons are not clearly suicides according to either the first or the second definition, some writers maintain that neither of the first two definitions should be accepted; thus we get another reason for the third or omnibus definition.

## §3 THE INADEQUACIES OF STANDARD DEFINITIONS

What, if anything, is wrong with these standard definitions? Despite expressions such as "he drank himself to death," the third definition seems unacceptable. It would significantly and unduly warp the concept of suicide as we know it: those who engage in waterfall rafting, hang gliding, police bomb-squad work, mountain diving (into oceans), and space explorations of an adventuresome sort—and who die as a result of these activities—would be suicides if this definition were accepted. Smokers, excessively fast drivers, and those who serve in a dangerous division of the armed services would similarly have to be declared suicidal. Moreover, the definition fails to preserve the distinction between accidental death and suicide in all cases where high risks are systematically taken—as, for example, by terrorists. This result seems to require too much of a sacrifice of our ordinary notion of suicide, and for insufficiently powerful reasons. True, we do in a loose sense speak of drunks and heavy smokers as killing themselves; but this is comparable to speaking of television comics as "geniuses," even though they exhibit no real capacities of genius. As this usage is too loose, I reject this third definition and will concentrate exclusively on the first two.

The first problem to notice about each of these two definitions is that they omit all mention of *the precise nature of the intention or knowledge* involved in a suicide. Durkheim, of course, eliminated all mention of intentions because of the difficulty of ascertaining what someone's intentions are. Those who accept the first definition apparently accept it rather than Durkheim's because, to their way of thinking, an act of self-induced death cannot be *unintentional* and remain a suicide, and it also cannot be a suicide if there is some other primarily intended consequence besides self-caused death. (These writers do not, however, insist that suicide is the exclusively intended consequence.) But is the matter this simple? While I am willing to concede to supporters of the first definition (for present purposes) that suicide must be an *intentional* self-killing (a matter that is far from obvious),[6] more needs to be said about precisely *what* may or must be intended.

Consider, as an example of these problems, a captured soldier who, given the "choice" of being executed or of executing himself, chooses self-execution. Because coercion is instrumental in this self-killing, we do not classify it as a suicide, just as we do not think that Socrates committed suicide by intentionally drinking the hemlock, thereby causing his death.[7] Now change the case slightly: suppose that our imagined soldier intentionally terminates his life solely in order to avoid divulging critical information that an enemy would otherwise surely extract. He chooses to terminate his life by making a feigned escape attempt, since he is certain that he will be shot as a result. It seems inappropriate to say without further explanation that because he *intentionally* terminated his life he therefore committed suicide. Surely, some will say, the nature of the intention—the agent's precise and primary reasons for acting—as well as the circumstances under which the intention was formed, make a difference, although neither definition takes account of such considerations.

Some initial problems with cases like these two cases of suicide, and consequent attempts to define suicide, have been noticed by the American philosopher Joseph Margolis:

A man may knowingly, and willingly, go to his death, be rationally
capable of avoiding death, deliberately not act to save his life, and yet
not count as a suicide. In this sense, we usually exclude the man who
sacrifices his life to save another's, the religious martyr who will not
violate his faith, the patriot who intentionally lays down his life for
a cause. Not that men in such circumstances may not be suiciding;
only that they *cannot be said to be suiciding solely for those reasons.*
Some seem to have thought otherwise [such as] Durkheim. . . .[8]

Although I shall later reject part of Margolis's reasoning, we can safely
assume, for the moment, the correctness of his views about the relevant intentions in order to construct a more satisfactory definition of
suicide than those found in the above three definitions.

Here is a start—but merely a start—in the direction of a more
adequate definition: The death of person A is a suicide only if (1) A's
death is intentionally self-caused[9] by A and (2) A's self-caused death is
noncoerced. Although these two conditions conform to our intuitions
and judgments about common suicides—as where notes confessing
depression are left, nonaccidental drug overdoses are taken, and re-
volvers are employed—the matter cannot be as simply resolved as this
start suggests. We shall now see that matters are considerably more
complicated.

## §4 THE PROBLEM OF TREATMENT REFUSAL

Some difficult cases for such a definition involve persons who suffer
from a terminal illness or mortal injury and who refuse some medical
therapy without which they will die but with which they could live
(longer anyway). Refusal to allow a blood transfusion or an amputation
and refusal of further kidney dialysis are now familiar facts of hospital
life. But when death occurs, are these acts suicides?

Obviously, these acts *can* be suicides, because *any* means productive of death can be used to the end of suicide. Pulling the plug on
one's respirator is not relevantly different from plunging a knife into
one's heart if the reason for putting an end to life is identical in the
two cases.

The widely discussed case of Elizabeth Bouvia illustrates this point.
Ms. Bouvia since birth suffered from cerebral palsy that left her with
virtually no motor function in her limbs or skeletal muscles, although
she maintained enough control in her right hand to operate the controls of an electric wheelchair and could move her mouth enough to
eat if fed by someone else. She was in constant, uncontrollable pain
from muscle contractions, increased spasticity, and arthritis. Her mind
was totally unaffected, and she had obtained a quality education, including a college degree in social work. She found her pain difficult to
endure, and she found her dependence on others "humiliating" and
"disgusting." On September 3, 1983, she directed her father to take
her to Riverside General Hospital in Riverside, California, where she

sought admission. *After* admission, she disclosed her intention to starve herself by gradually discontinuing caloric intake. She said "I am choosing this course of action due to my physical limitation and disability."[10]

Whatever we may think of the *justifiability* of Ms. Bouvia's actions —a topic we shall later discuss—it seems incontestable that her action, if carried out, would have constituted a *suicide* attempt. She was not terminally ill, intended her death, took active steps to bring about her death, and ultimately was judged by a court to have made a free, "rational decision" and to be a "mentally competent adult." Still, the seriously suffering person with end-stage renal disease who refuses to continue dialysis and dies a "natural" death does *not* seem to be a suicide. Why?

Three features of such situations need to be distinguished in order to answer this question:

1.  Whether the death is *intended* by the agent
2.  Whether an *active* means to death is selected
3.  Whether a *nonfatal condition* is present (there is no terminal disease or mortal injury)

The closer we are to having unmistakable cases of actions by an agent that involve an *intentionally caused death* using an *active* means where there is a *nonfatal* condition, the more inclined we will be to classify such acts as suicides; whereas the more such conditions are absent, the less inclined we are to call the acts suicides. For example, if a seriously but not mortally wounded soldier turns his rifle on himself and intentionally brings about his death, the act is a suicide. But what about the seriously ill patient of ambiguous intentions who is suffering from a terminal illness and refuses yet another blood transfusion?

Although considerations of terminal illness and of intention are important, the main source of our present definitional problem is the active/passive distinction. A passively allowed, "natural" death seems foreign to the notion of suicide, both because the death is at least in part not caused by the agent and because the 'cide' part of 'suicide' entails "killing," which is commonly contrasted with "allowing to die." Here our concept of suicide begins to make contact with that to which suicide specifically stands in contrast, namely, a naturally caused death. Yet, because of the relevance of the agent's intention, not all naturally caused deaths can be eliminated from consideration as suicides. The person might be using such a "passive" means (for instance, failing to take requisite drugs) as a socially acceptable and convenient way of ending it all. People who so intend to end their lives cannot be excluded from suicides merely because they select a passive means to this end.

In the face of this complex mixture of elements, the following generalizations may be formulated as an hypothesis: An act is *not* a suicide if the person who dies suffers from a terminal disease or from a mortal injury which, by refusal of treatment, he or she passively allows to cause death—even if the person intends to die.[11] However, this analysis does not seem adequate for all cases. For example, think of a patient with a terminal condition who could easily avoid dying for a long time but who chooses to end his or her life immediately by not taking cheap and painless medication. This counterexample might incline us toward the view that a time restriction is also needed. But this restriction probably could not be reasonably formulated, and I am inclined to think that we have come as close to a tight definition of suicide as the concept permits in ordinary English.

I conclude that the notion of suicide seems to require the two conditions earlier mentioned (intended death and noncoercion) plus the qualification required by refusal-of-treatment cases. This conclusion will be more readily understandable after we examine a final set of difficult cases.

## §5 THE PROBLEM OF SACRIFICIAL DEATHS

There remains the problem, mentioned by Margolis, of altruistically motivated suicide. Lifeboat situations have provided some famous examples. Suppose a lifeboat will not sustain the number of people who scramble aboard, and some must die in order that others live. A person of advanced years and questionable health, without the ability to swim, voluntarily jumps overboard, drowning immediately. A life has been sacrificed for the welfare of others. Is this act a suicide? Many believe it is not. They draw a distinction between suicidal self-killing and merely self-caused death (where both involve intentional acts). Such a distinction is clearly at work in the coerced, self-inflicted, but nonsuicidal death of the soldier, for example.

The key notion responsible for our not classifying some intentional self-killings as suicides may be *sacrifice*. Perhaps those who sacrifice their lives are not conceived as "suicides" for an interesting reason: Because such actions have, from the suicide's point of view, plausible claim to justification for *other-regarding*—not *self-regarding*—reasons, we exclude these self-sacrificial acts from the realm of the suicidal. We may not regard them as *actually* justified, but rather as justified from the point of view of the agent who causes or perhaps fails to prevent his or her own death.[12]

Joel Feinberg writes about our intuitions about suicide and sacrifice as follows (though Feinberg does not endorse a particular definition of suicide based on this approach):

> We tend to exclude self-sacrificial acts of heroism such as diving in front of a speeding truck to push a small child out of danger, or falling on a live hand grenade to save one's buddies. Traditionally such forms of self-destruction have not been considered suicide at all. Yet most traditional moralists would deny the right of a terminal patient to volunteer to be killed on the operating table so that his organs might

be used to save the lives of injured children. That would not be called "suicide" only because a doctor would be the instrument of the patient's will, but if the patient himself injected the fatal fluid into his own arm it would probably be called "suicide" despite his altruistic motives. By and large, however, the term "suicide" has been reserved for self-killings done from self-serving motives, particularly from the desire to avoid suffering or humiliation for oneself. But usage has been inconsistent in respect to this requirement, generating considerable puzzlement.[13]

Sadly, exclusions based on self-sacrificial acts will not help much in structuring a definition of suicide unless further qualifications are introduced. The monk in Vietnam who pours gasoline over his body and burns himself to death as a protest against his government does not do so for his own sake but for the sake of his beloved countrymen, just as the father who kills himself in the midst of a famine so that his wife and children have enough to eat acts from self-sacrificial motives. Many cases of this general description would have to be declared nonsuicides if the approach were taken that other-regarding, sacrificial acts are excluded as suicides.

In the face of this new complexity, a course paralleling the one for refusal-of-treatment cases may be taken: An act is *not* a suicide if one is caused to die by a life-threatening condition that is not intentionally brought about through one's own actions. In exploring the parallels between this kind of case and the refusal-of-treatment cases previously discussed, three ingredients again need to be distinguished:

1. Whether the death is *intended* by the agent (rather than not intended)
2. Whether the death is *caused by* the agent (rather than caused to the agent)
3. Whether the action is *self-regarding* (rather than other-regarding)

Here the main source of confusion is not the "active/passive" distinction but the similar "caused by/caused to" distinction. To cause one's own death in order to die is to kill oneself, but to have death caused by some alien condition in the course of an action with multiple objectives may not be. Here the killing/being killed distinction is involved, and it functions rather like the killing/letting die distinction previously discussed.

A good test case for the above analysis is the classic case of Captain Oates, who walked into the Antarctic snow to die because he was suffering from an illness that hindered the progress of a party attempting to make its way out of a severe blizzard.[14] According to the contemporary English philosopher R. F. Holland, Oates was not a suicide because: "in Oates's case I can say, 'No [he didn't kill himself]; the blizzard killed him.' Had Oates taken out a revolver and shot himself I should have agreed he was a suicide."[15]

I cannot agree with Holland's estimate. On the above analysis, Oates's heroic sacrifice is plausibly a suicide because of the active steps that he took to bring about his death. Although the fierce climatic conditions proximately caused his death, he *brought about* the relevant life-threatening condition causing his death *with the intention* that he die. To me, Oates is *not* like the soldier who, in falling on a grenade, brings about a fatal exposure to the grenade. An exploding grenade is *in itself* no more threatening than a blizzard, but the soldier does not intend to end it all by causing his own death. Oates does.

True, in Oates's case "the blizzard killed him" and he intended to free his buddies of a burden, but he also intended to kill himself by his action. In the case of the soldier with the grenade, the soldier acts not with any intent to kill himself but only with the intent to save his buddies. But I admit that this distinction is difficult to formulate precisely and that the case of the soldier turns on the ambiguities of the actual intentions and actions involved. "The grenade killed him" is far from a fully adequate explanation of what occurs. This does not mean, of course, that the two acts are not equally heroic and praiseworthy. R. C. K. Ensor has a valuable historical outlook on the Oates case: "The death of Captain Oates illustrates the shifting moral emphasis at this time. Oates committed suicide. But because he did it in hope to save his fellows, his action was universally approved. Clergymen preached sermons in praise of it."[16]

Still, the Oates case is not *easily* classified as a suicide, and I admit it. It is a borderline case, precisely because there is both multiple causation and multiple intent: The action is an heroic way of being *causally responsible* for placing oneself in *conditions that cause* death, and death was intended as a merciful release from an intolerable burden, not only because of Oates's suffering but also because of his knowledge that he was imperiling the lives of his colleagues. No wonder the Oates case has become a classic in literature on the definition of suicide.[17]

Although the analysis I have now proposed shares parts of Margolis's perspective, the point at which we part company is now evident. Margolis argues as follows:

> The Buddhist monk who sets fire to himself in order to protest the war that he might have resisted in another way will not be said to have committed suicide if the *overriding* characterization of what he did fixes on the ulterior objective of influencing his countrymen. . . . [If there is] some further purpose that he serves instrumentally, then we normally refuse to say he has suicided. . . .[18]

In my view the matter is more complicated than this "overriding reason" analysis suggests and has little to do directly with notions of sacrifice, martyrdom, and patriotism. In the end, the *sacrificial* nature of an action is not a legitimate reason for excluding it from the suicidal.

It has rather to do with whether death is caused by a person's own intentional arrangement[19] of the life-threatening conditions causing death *for the purpose of bringing about death* (whether this purpose be the primary reason or not). Because the monk arranges the conditions precisely for this purpose (although for other primary reasons as well) he is a suicide, as is Captain Oates. Because the soldier falling on the grenade does not hurl his body over the grenade for this purpose (of ending it all), he is *not* a suicide.

## §6 CONCLUSION

We have arrived, then, at a fairly simple understanding of suicide, although it is more complicated than the definitions with which we began: An act is a suicide if a person intentionally brings about his or her death in circumstances where others do not coerce him or her to the action except in those cases where death is caused by conditions not specifically arranged by the agent for the purpose of bringing about the agent's death. I admit that there may be (minor) counterexamples to this analysis that show, for example, that precisely this form of intention may not be required.[20] Suicide is an ill-ordered concept not easily captured in a one-sentence definition that states brief exceptive conditions, and I claim only to have set out the main lines of an adequate definition.

In fact, there is more that we should like to know about this definition than can be pursued here. In particular, four features of the definition deserve further analysis:

1. What counts as *coercive?*
2. What counts as *intending one's own death?*
3. What counts as a *condition specifically arranged by an agent?*
4. What counts as a *relevant cause of death?*

Until these matters are further clarified, the kind of precision in a conceptual analysis that we would like to see will be missing. For example, what are we to say of people who intentionally starve themselves in order that ill members of their families may have an increased food supply? Are such people coerced? What is the causally relevant factor in their deaths? Is the condition that ultimately kills them not a condition specifically arranged by an agent? Do these people intend their own deaths?

While I would agree that my analysis does not have the rigor we would like to see in a fully sharpened conceptual analysis, the essential lines of an adequate analysis of the ordinary-language concept of suicide have now been set out with sufficient precision that we can move on to a discussion of the morality of suicide. In broaching the moral problems, we shall not entirely leave behind the definitional confusions discussed above. Many of our *moral* views turn in significant respects on our conceptual (or definitional) views. For example, many physicians and theologians believe that suicide and assisting a suicide fall wholly outside the boundaries of permissible practice in medicine, and yet these physicians and theologians are quick to add that health professionals often morally should permit terminally ill patients to refuse medical treatment if its continuation is burdensome, painful, risky, or costly, even though the refusal will bring death more quickly. One's ability to implement this moral perspective will turn in important ways on how one defines the boundary (if it can be defined) between suicide and refusal of treatment.

## II. PRINCIPLES RELEVANT TO DISCUSSING THE MORALITY OF SUICIDE

How are we to determine whether a particular act of suicide is or is not immoral? Understandably, this question is complex, and we shall not be able to answer it with confident finality. But this much, at least, seems reasonable to assume: If a particular act of suicide is wrong, then it will have certain similarities, certain shared features, with other wrong actions; conversely, if a particular act of suicide is not morally wrong, then it will share similar features with other actions that are not morally wrong. Those philosophers who have tried to develop a *general normative theory of right and wrong* have tried to discover what these shared features are, both in the case of all those actions that are morally right and in the case of all those actions that are morally wrong.

Some moral philosophers have argued that the fundamental theory determining right action rests on the following claim:

> An action is morally right if and only if it produces at least as great a balance of value over disvalue as any available alternative action.

This principle is known as the *Principle of Utility,* and philosophers who subscribe to the view that this alone is the basic principle of morality are referred to as *utilitarians.* Though they frequently disagree concerning exactly what things are valuable and how value is to be determined, utilitarians are united by their belief that the Principle of Utility determines the rightness and wrongness of all moral actions.

Other moral philosophers have argued that one or more fundamental principles of ethics differ from the Principle of Utility. For example, the following is offered as a nonutilitarian principle determining right action:

> An action is morally right if and only if it is the action required by a duty that is at least as strong as any other duty in the circumstances.

Philosophers who accept this nonutilitarian account of the principles of moral duty are referred to as *deontologists*. They are united by their conviction that the rightness of actions may be determined by features of the action other than the balance of value over disvalue produced by the action.

Theories of these two general sorts are used by moral philosophers to support a great many other derivative moral principles (and rules, such as that it is right to keep our promises and wrong to break them). Not all of these principles are needed for or even applicable to a discussion of the morality of suicide. But in order to take a reasoned approach to this otherwise emotionally charged subject, we need to have on hand those principles that permit us to take a consistent position on the issues. I shall propose, without further argument, that four moral principles are directly relevant to discussions of suicide. Most types of ethical theory recognize two or more of these principles as valid, although theories differ over their relative significance and rank them in different orders of priority. But let us examine these principles before discussing the question of priority.

## §7 THE PRINCIPLE OF UTILITY AS A BENEFICENCE PRINCIPLE

The first of these principles is the Principle of Utility itself, here understood as a general moral principle of beneficence. This principle should not be construed as the sole ethical principle but rather as one moral consideration among others. As we have seen, utilitarians look to the consequences of actions, to the value and the disvalue produced, to see what the impact on the interest and welfare of all concerned will be if a particular action is performed. The interests of the person contemplating suicide, the interests of dependents, the interests of relatives, and the like must all be considered in the calculation of positive values and disvalues that would result from the action. The fact that people love the person contemplating suicide and that they value the person's contribution to the community are both to be considered in moral evaluations of the acceptability of the contemplated action. So are the interests of those to whom the person owes financial debts, obligations of gratitude, and so on.

In the majority of possible cases of suicide, a calculation would show that *more disvalue* in the form of grief, guilt, and deprivation would be produced than value gained were someone to commit suicide. If so, the Principle of Utility would dictate that an act of suicide is not justified. However, there are cases where value might *outweigh* disvalue. For example, imagine someone who has neither dependents nor debts and is suffering from massive pain. Suppose further that this person's family has suffered greatly and that everyone in the family believes death would be a merciful release. An intentional overdose taken by the person could satisfy the utilitarian injunction that the greatest possible amount of value, or at least the smallest possible amount of disvalue, should be brought about by one's action.

## §8 THE PRINCIPLE OF AUTONOMY AS A PRINCIPLE OF RESPECT

The second principle deserving mention is sometimes referred to as the Principle of Respect for Persons, by which is usually meant that individuals should be allowed to be self-determining agents making their own evaluations and choices when their own interests are at stake. In order to be specific, I shall refer to this principle as the Principle of Autonomy. This principle is rooted in the liberal Western tradition of the importance of individual freedom and choice both for political life and for personal development. (The importance of the individual has been defended on both utilitarian and nonutilitarian grounds.)

The autonomous individual is conceived in this tradition as one who is capable of deliberation and of actions based on such deliberations. The decisions made by a truly autonomous individual are intentional, based on adequate knowledge, internally nonconstrained, and externally nonconstrained. This means that the autonomous person must be able to grasp and appreciate the significance of pertinent information, form relevant intentions, and not be controlled either by internal forces that the person is not capable of resisting or by external forces or influences that the person cannot resist—such as the coercive or exploitative interventions of others. These are the broad outlines of the autonomous person, or at least of the conditions of autonomous choice.

To respect such self-determining agents is to recognize them as having a right to determine their own destiny. Such respect entails a due regard for their considered evaluations, choices, and view of the world even if it is strongly believed that their evaluation, choice, or outlook is wrong and even potentially harmful to them. To "respect their autonomy" it is not necessary to respect their actual *views* but only to accord to them the *right* to have their opinions and to act upon them. Rules of respect in society are not rules that we respect the person's autonomy in all respects but more narrowly only that we respect a person's right to make autonomous choices. To grant persons such a right is to say that they are entitled to autonomous expression without external restraint. It follows that to show a lack of respect for an autonomous agent is either to show disrespect for that person's right to make deliberate choices or to deny the individual the freedom to act on those choices when such interference would affect in important ways that person's present and future interests. It would, therefore, be a showing of disrespect to deny such persons the right to commit suicide when, in their considered judgment, they ought to do so.

Respect for autonomy thus suggests a morally appropriate attitude, sometimes described as "respectfulness." Usually, however, the *right* to be respected rather than the *attitude* is appealed to in discussions of suicide. A main point of the appeal to the principle of respect for autonomy is to indicate that the burden of proof rests on one who would intervene by restricting or preventing a person's exercise of an autonomy right. Autonomy rights protect us against intervention without our consent. This is not to imply that autonomy rights always have *overriding* authority. If there are serious adverse consequences for other persons, then the principle of utility (or other principles) may override the principle of respect for autonomy—as we shall later see when we come to the subject of suicide intervention.

While some philosophers have believed that respect for autonomy takes precedence over *all other* moral considerations, this principle, like that of utility, will here be recognized as only *one* important moral principle governing the morality of suicide and not as the sole or overriding consideration on all occasions.

## §9 THE PRINCIPLE OF RESPECT FOR LIFE

A third principle often appealed to in discussions of suicide may be called the Principle of Respect for Life. According to this principle, human life has value in itself that deserves respect. Suicide is wrong because it destroys something of inherent value[21]—that is, a life that is valuable not for any other value it brings into existence but simply because of its own inherent value. This principle is variously expressed through concepts such as "the value of life" and "the sanctity of life."

As this principle is commonly construed, it is sometimes permissible to *allow someone to die* instead of attempting heroic efforts to save the person. For example, if someone is terminally ill and destined to die imminently, it is believed acceptable for such a person or the person's family to decide to allow a natural death. But it is not acceptable to *kill*, because one then becomes causally and morally responsible for an active destruction of life. This act of killing is not wrong *because* it produces social disutility or *because* it violates autonomy. Rather, it is wrong simply because it is an intentional, active termination of human life. The Principle of Respect for Life is thus entirely independent of the two principles previously discussed.

One could have a number of different reasons for holding this principle. It might be believed that life is a gift from God and therefore is only to be terminated at God's own appointed moment. Or one might think that human life, unlike life in the rest of the animal kingdom, is characterized by a dignity that sets it apart from the life of all other creatures. These and related issues are explored in several essays in this anthology. It is not important for our purposes, however, to canvass all the possible reasons for holding this view. All such views coalesce into a single, perhaps fundamental belief: Human life is valuable in itself, and it is always a wrong-making characteristic of any action that it is an intentional termination of human life.

Despite this coalescence into a single central belief, there are stronger and weaker ways of interpreting this principle. The strongest possible view is complete pacifism: It is always wrong intentionally to terminate any human life, whatever the circumstances—whether in capital punishment cases or as an act of self-defense, or by abortion, suicide, or any means whatever. A noticeably weak version of the principle is that the inherent value of life itself is always a relevant consideration when one is contemplating the intentional termination of a life—but is *only a consideration* and not necessarily the most important one.

Few would now defend either the strongest or the weakest version of this principle. A middle position—the interpretation that perhaps most defenders of this principle would support—is that killing is permissible only if another *moral principle* of equal or greater weight in the circumstances *justifies* the killing—for instance, if it is necessary to save the life of at least one other innocent person or if it is necessary to preserve the very existence of a (morally worthy) society. Henceforth, when I speak of the Principle of Respect for Life, I shall be referring to versions of the principle construed in this way as a prima facie principle. Thus, this principle, like utility and respect for autonomy, is not to be understood as an absolute moral principle.

## §10 THE THEOLOGICAL PRINCIPLE

A fourth principle, often appealed to in discussions of suicide, will here be termed the Theological Principle. According to this principle, suicide and other acts are morally wrong because they violate a direct command of God against the taking of human life.

Those who support this principle commonly attempt to ground morality in theology rather than in philosophy, culture, tradition, or whatever. Several quite specific appeals are found in literature opposed to suicide. It has been argued, for example, that human persons (or perhaps their souls) receive the gift of life from God; therefore suicides sin against their Creator by the act of destroying their lives. It has also been contended that because murder is specifically prohibited by God's direct command and because suicide is self-murder, suicide is therefore morally wrong—unless directly commanded by God. Many theologically based arguments against suicide turn on an account of some special design of providence, e.g., suicide violates an obligation to God by interfering with the divinely ordained order of the universe. It is not always clear what God's "order" is, but the notion of God's appointing a special purpose for each human life is especially prominent in these arguments.

Some philosophers and theologians have believed that the Theological Principle is so fundamental to morality that theological considerations alone determine the morality of an act of suicide. One who espouses this view argues that suicide is always morally wrong unless there exists a theological reason, probably based on a direct command of God, that excuses the act of suicide. Philosophers opposed to the Theological Principle have pointed out that there are grave difficulties in determining what God's purposes and commands are, and that whether God's commands are morally right is something that must be proved, not merely assumed.

However, it deserves repeating that the Theological Principle rests squarely on *theological* grounds rather than philosophical ones. If theology provides reasons that are valid independently of philosophy, then philosophical objections will not refute these reasons. Thus, the Theological Principle is also independent of the other three principles.

We have now completed our survey of the four basic principles that play a major role in ethical thinking about suicide. Few philosophers would today accept any one of them as an *absolute* principle that can never be overridden. One could hold to some version of two or more of the principles, thereby giving moral force to a plurality of principles that must be weighed and balanced in different circumstances. However, as we shall now see, major philosophers in the history of Western thought have tended to promote one or two of these principles as having *some* form of priority over the others.

## III. TWO OPPOSED PHILOSOPHIES OF SUICIDE

In this section two starkly different and historically prominent philosophies of suicide will be considered: the philosophies of St. Thomas Aquinas and David Hume. These philosophers illustrate the application of the ethical principles mentioned in the previous section to moral problems of suicide. For both philosophers, arguments about the permissibility and impermissibility of suicide have typically centered on questions of whether suicide violates one or more of three obligations: to oneself, to others, and to God. Their essays on suicide are both structured specifically to answer these questions.

Aquinas's answers rely almost exclusively on the use of the Principle of Respect for Life and the Theological Principle, while Hume's answers rely almost exclusively on the other two principles, the Principles of Utility and of Respect for Autonomy. Virtually everything asserted by Aquinas is disputed by Hume, because each relies heavily on different and conflicting principles.

### §11 THE POSITION OF ST. THOMAS AQUINAS

During the medieval period, many arguments using a theological basis were developed to demonstrate the immorality of suicide. These arguments became the dominant view of the most influential theologians of the Catholic church and of Orthodox Judaism, and they continue today to exert powerful influence on the views of many religious persons. Their arguments range from straight biblical injunctions against killing, as in the Sixth Commandment ("Thou shalt not kill") to the rather more reasoned philosophical arguments on which we shall concentrate. St. Augustine (A.D. 354–430) was an early and influential Christian writer against suicide, but St. Thomas's views were ultimately more influential.

Aquinas advances three primary moral arguments against suicide —or, as he says (*Summa Theologica*, II–II, Q. 64, Art. 5), three "reasons" that show that it is "altogether unlawful to kill oneself." Here are slightly abbreviated versions of his arguments, as found in the *Summa Theologica*:

> It is altogether unlawful to kill oneself, for three reasons:
> [1] because everything naturally loves itself, the result being that everything naturally keeps itself in being. . . . Wherefore suicide is contrary to the inclination of nature, and to charity whereby every man should love himself. Hence, suicide is . . . contrary to the natural law and to charity.
> [2] because . . . every man is part of the community, and so, as such, he belongs to the community. Hence by killing himself he injures the community. . . .
> [3] because life is God's gift to man, and is subject to His power. . . . Hence whoever takes his own life, sins against God. . . . For it belongs to God alone to pronounce sentence of death and life. . . .

How are we to understand these cryptic arguments? The first Thomistic argument [1] may be reconstructed in the following form.

1. It is a natural law that everything loves and seeks to perpetuate itself.
2. Suicide is an act contrary to self-love and self-perpetuation.
3. (Therefore) suicide is contrary to natural law.
4. Anything contrary to natural law is morally wrong.
5. (Therefore) suicide is morally wrong.[22]

It is easy to misapprehend this argument. Here is one common misunderstanding by a careful writer on suicide, the English legal thinker Glanville Williams:

> The first argument . . . is, in fact, an application of the usual Catholic method of arguing from an assumed "nature" to morals. Actually, the assumption here is wrong; if suicide were always contrary to man's inclinations, it would not occur. The moral question arises because the individual is, in some circumstances, tempted to suicide. . . . Not every disregard of a fundamental instinct is wrong. . . .[23]

This interpretation overlooks the fact that Thomistic philosophers draw an important distinction between laws of nature and natural laws. Presumably the former are descriptive statements derived from scientific knowledge of regularities in nature (for example, the law of gravity or Charles's law), while the latter are prescriptive statements derived from philosophical knowledge of the essential properties of human nature (for example, the law "Thou shalt not kill"). In this theory, natural laws do not empirically *describe* behavior, and they do not tell us how we *do* behave; rather, they delimit the behavior that is morally appropriate for a human being; they tell us how we *ought* to behave because of our very nature as humans. What is proper for a human differs from what is to be expected from other creatures insofar as their "natures" differ; and their natures differ because they possess different essences with different potentialities. In particular, while humans share with animals a natural tendency toward sexual reproduction, only through human reason can there be a tendency toward universal goods, such as concern to promote the interests of others.

St. Thomas is here building a distinctive natural law theory on the foundations of Aristotle's theory that the good of any creature in nature consists in the actualization of its distinctive natural potentialities. The good of a snail consists in the actualization of its distinctive natural potentialities, and the good of a human person consists in the fulfillment of its (quite different) complement of natural potentialities— namely, those properties distinctive of human persons. All living organisms flourish if and only if their parts function harmoniously as they should—where "should" is understood in terms of the way nature dictates or "legislates." A person's body, mind, and emotions must be coordinated and in accordance with natural functions in order to be healthy: one is mentally and physically healthy only if the mind and body function as nature has legislated, and one is morally healthy only if one attempts to fulfill one's own potentialities as well as the potentialities of others. Thus, those human inclinations related to the actualization of basic potentialities are elevated in the Thomistic theory to the status of natural laws, while others that destroy the possibility for the actualization of these potentialities are labeled unnatural deprivations.

Suicide is regarded in this theory as wrong precisely because it violates a natural inclination to the conservation of one's own existence and well-being (and, as we shall see, because the suicide does not exclusively intend a truly good outcome). This theory also permits the Thomist to admit that it is an empirical psychological fact that powerful inclinations to suicide do occur, and in this respect are "natural," while denouncing them as in a different respect *unnatural* deprivations.[24]

Aquinas's second argument [2] is quite simple by comparison to the first. It is an argument from social obligations and asserts that every individual belongs to family and neighbors and thus has obligations that are violated by an act of suicide. While Aquinas does not believe that society is sovereign over the individual, he does believe that individual decisions cannot be properly made in even so personal a matter as suicide without reference to the interests of other persons in the state. He regards an act of suicide as undermining social authority and human relations and therefore as harming all those affected by the action. This particular argument has close affinities to utilitarian thinking about suicide.

Aquinas's third argument has exerted massive influence among Christian believers, perhaps because it is squarely rooted in the Theological Principle. According to this argument, each human life is a gift from God and all individuals therefore belong to their Creator, much as a piece of property belongs to its owner. To commit suicide is tantamount to the sin of theft, for it deprives God of that which He created and is rightfully His. This argument presupposes that it is in general the will of God that we remain alive; for, if not, then suicide may be an act of obedience to His will.

Throughout St. Thomas's arguments, attention to right motives is essential. He excuses suicide if (and perhaps only if) one takes one's life *because* divinely commanded to do so. The so-called Principle of Double Effect allows him this conclusion.[25] This principle may be formulated as follows: Whenever from an action there occur two effects, one good and the other evil, it is morally permissible to perform the action and to permit the evil only if:[26]

1. The intention is to bring about the good effect and not to bring about the evil effect (which is merely foreseen).
2. The action intended must be truly good or at least not evil.
3. The good effect must bring at least as much good into the world as the evil effect brings evil into the world.

Aquinas apparently thinks that the suicide necessarily intends evil effects except when specifically commanded by God to perform the act.[27]

## §12 THE POSITION OF DAVID HUME

In his essay "On Suicide,"[28] David Hume presented the strongest set of arguments for the moral permissibility of suicide in the classical history of the subject. He offered arguments against the Thomistic contention that suicide is morally condemnable and was especially critical of theological views such as St. Thomas's.

Hume identified with pre-Christian, classical writings, especially those of Greek antiquity, where suicide had been considered an honorable and praiseworthy act in the instance of persons facing painful and chronic diseases. Christian beliefs such as Aquinas's were largely unknown in classical Greek culture, as was the Christian belief that pain and suffering serve a redemptive purpose. Hume also identifies with the Greek view that life is not worth living if ill health seriously undermines one's potential for enjoyment.

*Hume's Negative Arguments.* Hume's strategy in opposing St. Thomas's theological arguments is not that of challenging belief in the existence of God. Rather, he critically analyzes the following general theological proposition: The act of suicide violates an obligation to God and provokes divine indignation *because it encroaches on God's established order for the universe.*[29] This proposition is a general paraphrase of Aquinas's third argument and is of course closely related to what we have called the Theological Principle. Hume serially rejects several possible theological meanings of the italicized phrase—a sensible approach, since it is not clear in Aquinas's philosophy precisely what this phrase might mean. Hume's arguments focus on the meaning of "God's established order," and he tries to show that on any meaningful interpretation, the theology underlying it is either deficient or is compatible with the moral acceptance of suicide.

Among the possible meanings of "encroaching on God's established order"—and of the wrongfulness of encroachment—Hume focuses on the claim that it is wrong to disturb the operation of any general causal law, because all causal laws taken together constitute the divine order. Hume construes this "natural-law" thesis to mean that human beings must be absolutely passive in the face of natural occurrences, for otherwise they would disturb the operations of nature by their actions. Hume ridicules this theology as absurd: unless we resisted *some* natural events by counteractions, he reasons, we "could not subsist for a moment," because exposure to the weather or some other "natural" event would destroy us. But if it is morally permissible to disturb *some* operations of nature, Hume reasons, then would it not also be morally permissible to avert life itself by diverting blood from its natural course in human vessels? Does not this action relevantly resemble turning one's head aside to avoid a falling stone, since both alike simply divert the course of nature? "It would be no crime in me to divert the Nile or Danube from its course, were I able to effect such purposes. Where then is the crime of turning a few ounces of blood from their natural channel?" (155)

Hume's argument seems to me to fail as an argument against Thomists (as do R. B. Brandt's and Sidney Hook's similar arguments[30]), because the Thomistic contention that laws of nature and natural laws are distinct is not confronted. As we previously noted, Thomists hold that natural laws do not describe behavior but rather delimit the natural behavior that is morally appropriate for a human being; suicide is wrong precisely because it violates a natural inclination to live and flourish, in this special sense of 'natural'. While it is true that the Thomistic distinction between laws of nature and natural laws is obscure—far too obscure to be convincing—it is an essential feature of natural-law ethics. If the distinction is allowed, then there arguably is a morally relevant difference between diverting the Nile from its normal course and taking one's life by diverting blood from its normal channel, for human nature is different from river nature.

Hume's central contention—that it is *arbitrary* to permit resistance to the effects of some laws while prohibiting intervention against the effects of others—would be acceptable *if the accusation of arbitrariness were demonstrated.* That is, his argument would be conclusive if he successfully showed the arbitrariness of accepting some law-governed natural processes as authoritative while excluding others. In the end, the Thomistic argument may in fact be arbitrary because such a distinction cannot be upheld, but Hume's conviction to this effect is only asserted, not argued, and hence fails to refute the Thomist.

This criticism of Hume does not suffice, however, to disqualify his entire array of arguments. He offers—almost offhand—an interesting antitheological argument based on the importance of motives. Quoting Seneca, he observes that it is consistent that a man should take his life in virtue of his misery, while at the same time expressing sincere gratitude to God "both for the good which I have already enjoyed, and for the power which I am endowed of escaping the ills that threaten me." (156) This one-sentence suggestion constitutes an important objection to Aquinas's theological arguments, because it challenges the moral and theological roots of the Thomistic position. It does so by calling into question the unproven supposition that God has *willed* that we should never take our lives in virtue of our misery. The following is a reconstruction of Hume's argument: The removal of misery is a truly good effect and the intention to produce it cannot by itself be a condemnable motive, even if suicide is the unfortunate means to the end of removing the misery; additionally, it cannot be regarded as evil or sinful in intent if accompanied by a sincere expression of gratitude to God.

Under my previous interpretation of Aquinas's views, this argument has moral force, but the exact force depends on further specification of Aquinas's account. If one construes his position narrowly, so as to allow only a severely restricted set of motives to excuse suicide (such as fulfillment of a divine command as the sole allowed motive), then the Humean objection seems powerful. But the more broadly one construes Aquinas's position as allowing a range of excusing intentions, the more one blunts the force of Hume's counterargument. On an extreme liberal interpretation of acceptable Thomistic intentions and effects, it would no longer be possible to say that Hume and Aquinas have a principled disagreement at all because Hume's motive would be *allowed as a valid excusing condition.*

*Hume's Positive Arguments.* In addition to the criticisms he offers of St. Thomas's position, Hume provides some constructive arguments in support of the moral permissibility of suicide. His major argument is based almost exclusively on the Principles of Utility and Autonomy. Hume first tries to show that in some cases resignation of one's life from the community "must not only be innocent, but laudable." The strategy of the argument is that of analyzing hypothetical cases[31] that stand as counterexamples to St. Thomas's claim (in his second argument) that "by killing himself [a person] injures the community."

Hume begins with an analogy: Suppose a man retires from his work and from all social intercourse. He does not thereby harm society; he merely ceases to do the good he formerly did by his productivity and amiability. Hume advances a general claim about the reciprocity of obligations that launches his argument:

> All our obligations to do good to society seem to imply something reciprocal. I receive the benefits of society, and therefore ought to promote its interests; but when I withdraw myself altogether from society, can I be bound any longer? But [even] allowing that our obligations to do good were perpetual, they have certainly some bounds; I am not obliged to do a small good to society at the expense of a great harm to myself: when then should I prolong a miserable existence, because of some frivolous advantage which the public may perhaps receive from me? (158)

Hume then considers a series of both hypothetical and actual cases of suicide. Each case contains some new element not contained in previous cases that increases the personal or social value of death for the suicide. In his first hypothetical case, Hume envisages a sick person who is still marginally productive in society. If his social contribution is small in proportion to the largeness of his misery, then Hume thinks there is no social obligation to continue in existence. The claim is utilitarian: If the value of removing misery by taking one's own life is greater than the value to the community of one's continued existence, then suicide is justified.

Hume then moves to his second and third hypothetical cases.[32] In the second, the potential suicide's existence is so bleak that he is not only miserable and relatively unproductive but a complete burden to society. In the third, a political patriot spying in the public interest is seized by enemies and threatened with the rack, and is aware that he is too weak to avoid divulging all he knows. In both cases, Hume stipulates that these unfortunates shall remain miserable for the remainder of their days. He then proclaims suicide under such conditions praiseworthy because it both satisfies the individual's primary needs in the circumstances and is in the larger public interest. He even maintains, dubiously, that "most people who live under any temptation to abandon existence" act from such utilitarian motives. (159)

These case examples of suicide point to the possibility that a person might be so situated that everyone in society actually benefits from the suicide. Whether the state is advantaged or disadvantaged by citizen involvement is relative to the citizen's situation, and Hume thinks that there are cases where suicide not only promotes the interest of the individual but in fact honors and shows respect for the person's family.

*Can St. Thomas Refute Hume?* Hume's positive arguments in defense of suicide can be read as a critique of St. Thomas's second (nontheological) argument against suicide. We can now ask whether Hume's general claims about the reciprocity of obligations, his hypothetical cases, and his utility and autonomy-based arguments succeed in refuting Aquinas.

Aquinas's views depend on the thesis that the state actually is *injured* by removal of the part from the whole. Hume's carefully contrived examples point to the possibility that a person might be so situated that everyone actually benefits from the suicide. Should this result occur, then the Thomist would seem compelled in principle to *require* suicide in order to avoid injury to the state, or at the very least to *permit* suicide. More specifically, Hume's counterexamples show the Thomistic premises to be too feeble to support the desired conclusion in prohibition of suicide. Whether the state is advantaged or disadvantaged by citizen involvement is relative to the citizen's situation, and it is implausible to insist that the state is always advantaged by the "participation" of all its members under all circumstances.

Aquinas's real grounding principle, it seems, is the absolutistic one that it is *always* illegitimate to take one's own life when the motive is either utility-based or an autonomous, self-regarding action. Aquinas's grounding principle thus seems a rather strong variant of what we earlier called the Principle of Respect for Life. He gives this principle far greater weight than he gives to either of the principles employed by Hume. But if the Thomist presupposes this principle—or even the Theological Principle—as a basis for his second argument, then the argument has in effect abandoned the point presumably at issue about whether the state is advantaged or disadvantaged. Obviously, Hume's argument does not deviate from this point, and to this extent seems more satisfactory than Aquinas's, even if in the end one believes Aquinas's two moral *principles* more pertinent and defensible than Hume's two principles.

## §13 A DEFENSE OF THE UTILITARIAN AND AUTONOMY POSITIONS

Anyone who inferred from the previous section that my own sympathies in matters of the morality of suicide lie with Hume would have made a correct inference. In general, the position defended by Hume, and the one that I defend as well, gives predominant weight in matters of the morality of suicide to the Principles of Utility and Autonomy. An autonomous suicide is then judged permissible (and even on occasion laudable) if, on balance, more value is produced for the individual (using the Principle of Respect for Autonomy as the overriding principle) or more value is produced for society (using the Principle of Utility as the overriding principle) by the action than would be produced by not performing the act of taking one's own life.[33]

But at this point a certain problem arises. Hume is not only a utilitarian but a particular *type* of utilitarian, namely, a rule-utilitarian: He believes that the Principle of Utility justifies the moral rules that should be operative in society, and that particular acts are right if and only if they conform to these rules. The question arises whether there are substantial objections to rule-utilitarianism that have direct implications for suicide.

*Donagan's Objections.*   One such objection has been advanced by the American philosopher Alan Donagan.[34] Donagan constructs a general theoretical objection to rule-utilitarianism by appealing to the distinction between (1) *morally obligatory actions* (those required by a moral duty) and (2) *supererogatory actions* (those over and above the demands of moral duty and done from one's personal ideals). His strategy is that of imagining situations where an action is *supererogatory* rather than obligatory and yet where utilitarians must (mistakenly) regard the action as *obligatory* because "there would be more good and less evil in society as a whole if the rule were adopted."[35] Donagan would regard an act of suicide performed solely for the sake of other persons as a near perfect illustration of a supererogatory act and yet in some cases he thinks utilitarians are required by their principle to construe the supererogatory as obligatory and die for the people by committing a suicide. That is, utilitarians necessarily present a confused and unacceptable picture of the moral life because they demand that the supererogatory—including sacrificial suicide— be made obligatory, as a moral rule.

Donagan's criticism of rule-utilitarianism can be explicated as a *direct* reply to Hume's essay on suicide as follows: According to Hume, there are occasions when human existence has become personally and socially burdensome and has ceased to benefit both that person and other persons. Here, he says, suicide sets "an example, which, if imitated, would preserve to everyone his chance for happiness in life." Even more strongly, Hume argues that "both prudence and courage *should* engage us to rid ourselves at once of existence when it becomes a burden." (160, italics added) It seems to follow that for reasons of utility we should adopt a moral rule that obliges every person so situated to commit suicide[36]—for instance, utilitarianism seems to support the rule that "Suicide ought to be performed whenever it is the case both that one has become more of a burden than a benefit to society and that there is more intrinsic disvalue than value in one's personal life."[37]

Not only is this alleged Humean requirement counterintuitive, it is blatantly violative of our deepest moral convictions about autonomy and "the right to life," for one might *want* to live even if, by living, personal disvalue outweighs personal and even social value. This outcome seems a perfect instance of Donagan's claim that utilitarians cannot account for the distinction between morally obligatory acts and supererogatory acts. That is, that utilitarians necessarily construe some supererogatory acts as obligatory.

If this criticism is sound, it shows that Hume's prosuicide argument is too broad, for it justifies too much: it dictates a moral rule *requiring* suicide, not a moral rule that merely grants a *right* to commit suicide. (Hume's argument, on Donagan's construal, would presumably also dictate rules requiring various forms of euthanasia, abortion, cessation of lifesaving therapy, murder, and so on.)

*A Reply to Donagan's Objection*   Though there may be other ways to defend utilitarianism against Donagan's criticism, I shall dispute his criticism in the following way only: Against Donagan, I shall argue that it is a mistake both to suppose that utilitarian thinking dictates that a *rule* requiring suicide ought to be made current in our moral code and to suppose that Hume's essay justifies too much by requiring such a rule. My argument will take this guarded route to the defense of a utilitarian and autonomy-based position on suicide, as well as a defense of Hume.[38]

Donagan's argument assumes that a rule-utilitarian position requires the acceptance of moral rules formulated so that they *directly require* such bizarre obligations as suicide and judicial murder. There is no reason, however, that a rule-utilitarian must accept this characterization of the position. Here a distinction must be introduced between actions that fulfill what may be called *direct* obligations and those that fulfill what may be called *indirect* obligations—where the obligations in both cases are rule-governed. An action of the sort that fulfills a direct obligation is itself specifically described in and required by a valid rule in the moral code. The rule is universalizable for actions of that type. Truth-telling rules, for example, require that we tell the truth when faced with the temptation of lying, and they specifically govern truth-telling contexts. An action that fulfills an indirect obligation, by contrast, is not itself specifically described in and required by a valid rule referring to actions of that type; yet the action is required by some valid rule.

For example we presumably do not have a direct obligation to be sterilized, for there is not and ought not to be a moral rule in our code specifically requiring actions of that type. Still, circumstances can arise where an indirect obligation to be sterilized is acquired in order to fulfill the requirements of *some* valid moral rule—for example, a promise to one's spouse to be sterilized requires being sterilized because of the moral rule that one must keep one's promises. This raises the question whether (1) there *ought to be* a rule that itself refers to and requires suicide *or* (2) there *ought not to be* such a rule, even though suicide *might* be required as a means to the fulfillment of moral obligations generated by other moral rules. A rule-utilitarian like Hume must allow for the *possibility* of both 1 and 2—as Hume and Donagan both recognize[39]—since the acceptance or rejection of any rule in such theories depends upon actual social conditions. Because 2 is intuitively more acceptable than 1, I shall begin with 2 and return later to a consideration of 1.

INDIRECT OBLIGATIONS TO SUICIDE    Consider Hume's case of the pliable spy, a case Hume believes historically genuine, in the figure of Strozi of Florence. The spy possesses secrets "in the public interest" that could be extorted because of his own weakness. He knows this, and so commits suicide. This case is similar to Kant's fascinating case of Frederick the Great, who carried a quick-acting poison into battle. He intended to use the poison if captured, in order to protect the nation from having to pay an intolerably burdensome ransom for his release.[40] In these two striking cases, is it plausible to invoke the Donagan thesis that these actions are both supererogatory, but utilitarians must make them matters of moral duty?

Before capitulating to Donagan, we ought to build on these cases in order to see if his thesis can withstand an even tougher trial. Suppose that the first two men on the moon had returned to earth with an incurable, deadly, and perilously contagious microorganismic disease with a forty-eight-hour incubation period. If the two do not die within forty-eight hours of their return (or are not sent into space exile), the disease will be incubated and the human species will be annihilated. But if the two do die, then so will the microorganisms of disease. I would say that, under these unprecedented circumstances, these two astronauts, who are themselves doomed to certain death, have a moral *obligation* to commit suicide.

A less fanciful, and indeed nonhypothetical, case supports the same conclusion. At the Treblinka concentration camp, some of those incarcerated were ordered to exterminate their fellow prisoners by opening the gas valves. Many committed suicide rather than carry out the order. Their reasons for suicide were that they had an obligation not to kill innocent persons and that suicide at their own hands was a better, or at least less cruel, fate than death by Nazi extermination. One might say that they committed suicide for the instrumental purpose of preserving their own moral integrity, which could be maintained only by fulfilling their moral obligations. However, the principled or rule-governed reason for the obligation to suicide (let us suppose suicide is here the only morally satisfactory alternative) is the requirement *to protect* (themselves and others) *from harm* and *not* a rule that itself requires suicide.

DIRECT OBLIGATIONS TO SUICIDE    It has now been shown that from a Humean rule-utilitarian perspective, an *indirect* obligation to commit suicide is sometimes generated by some valid moral rules. But should there also be a rule that specifically governs suicide and that requires it under certain circumstances? That is, should the moral code be such that there are rules like truth telling and promise keeping specifically to commit suicide?

To this question, I think the answer is almost certainly no, at least under social circumstances as we conventionally know them. Such rules would serve a disutilitarian rather than utilitarian result. There is a point of diminishing returns in any moral code concerning how many rules can be or ought to be publicly promulgated and how many circumstances such rules can anticipate and govern. There ought not to be so many rules that people cannot acquaint themselves with all the rules; neither should there be rules that apply only infrequently or rules so heavily qualified that their interpretation is difficult. Because moral rules restrict human freedom, the social value derived from the having of a rule must be greater than the value of the freedom that would be gained by not having the rule. A rule requiring suicide would obviously limit one's autonomous choice as to whether one wished to commit suicide. Indeed, such a rule would be in direct conflict with the Principle of Autonomy on many occasions. Most importantly, it is doubtful that any rule directly requiring suicide could achieve any positive end that indirect-obliging rules could not. In short, it is doubtful that the public utility gained by having direct-obliging rules about suicide would exceed the disutility produced by disrespect for autonomy, confusion, insecurity, and misunderstanding.[41]

These reasons make it possible to see the germ of truth in the antiutilitarian argument offered by Donagan as well as its deficiencies. Generally, other-regarding or altruistic suicides *are* supererogatory, not morally obligatory. They are supererogatory because they confer a benefit on others, but not the sort of benefit that it would seem in general either significant enough or valuable enough to require. Thus such suicides are beyond the call of *duty*.[42] It is most doubtful that having a direct-obliging rule in our code that required suicide as a service to others would produce actions with better consequences than would be produced by leaving the choice of suicide up to the individual's personal *ideals* (the instruments of supererogatory actions) and to rules that indirectly require it in such highly dilemmatic situations as those previously mentioned.

On the other hand, any rule-utilitarian following Hume's lead must leave it an open question whether *under some social conditions* a rule requiring suicide *might validly be made current*. A rule-utilitarian must, for example, applaud the Eskimo rule that required suicide by the elderly. Survival at a decent level of human existence depended upon the institutionalization of the rule in their moral code, and it was fairly applied.[43] One can also imagine dire social circumstances into which any of us might fall that would similarly demand such a rule.[44]

Consider, for example, those recent cases where a large plane has been forced down in a remote snowy region that is invisible from the air, and outsiders do not know where the plane has crashed, thus precluding rescue efforts. (Hume himself considers similar cases of shipwreck.) Imagine a moral code being devised in such a minisociety, where it was freely decided by all (as a form of social contract) that in order for some to attempt escape after the spring thaw, cannibalism was necessary, that those who would die and be devoured would be chosen by a random method, that one so selected is obligated to commit suicide (so that none could later be judged "guilty" and prosecuted), and that normal rules against murder would prevail.

Rule-utilitarians must hold that under these and other unaccustomed circumstances, *a rule requiring suicide validly controls everyone's conduct and deserves its prominent place in the moral code.* Under these exotic circumstances, not committing suicide would encourage and perhaps even produce a general breakdown in the orderly system such that none could live—clearly the greatest disutility. It seems to me that any utilitarian who took this line—Hume included —would not in the least be subject to Donagan's censure, for what in other cases is either supererogatory or excusably wrong (because beyond a *normal* obligation) is here *obligatory, even if desperate.*

A general point of theoretical interest follows from this discussion. Those who attack utilitarianism often do so by adducing Donagan-type counterexamples. Cases of broken promises made in secret and cases of killing the innocent are legion in the antiutilitarian literature. But once the distinction between direct obligations and indirect obligations is recognized, it becomes obvious that counterintuitive *rules* about what one *should* do are not dictated except in highly unusual circumstances, such as the cannibalism case just mentioned. Thus, a Donagan-type objection fails to make any advance against either Hume's rule-utilitarianism or his position on suicide, based as it is in the Principles of Autonomy and Utility.

## IV. PROBLEMS OF SUICIDE INTERVENTION

If the Principle of Autonomy is heavily weighted in the justification of suicide, as it has been thus far, then it would seem that there is a *right* to commit suicide so long as a person acts autonomously and without so seriously affecting the interests of others that one's right is overridden by the weight of one's obligations to others. Yet we certainly do not always act as if the suicide has such a right, for we often intervene to prevent a person from committing suicide. In days past, for example, it was not uncommon for rescuers to place themselves at risk of death in order to prevent a person from jumping on subway tracks in the path of an oncoming train.

The Principle of Respect for Life may incline one to believe that we are justified in intervening in the lives of such individuals. But if they have a *right* to commit suicide, are we *really* justified? In the case of almost any similarly intrusive action, the person interfered with could sue those who intervene. A physician, for example, might be sued for malpractice by a similarly coercive treatment of patients. Yet in the case of suicide, some feel strongly inclined to say that we have obligations to suicidal human persons even when they are acting autonomously. These are obligations both to prevent suicide and to intervene to stop it. Can we morally justify this conviction that intervention in the name of respect for life and beneficence is better than nonintervention in the name of autonomy?

In a widely discussed case of a burn patient—Mr. Donald Cowart —this problem arose because Mr. Cowart had instructed his physician that he intended to commit suicide after being released from the hospital—a familiar reaction and ambition in the dire circumstances faced by burn patients.[45] A psychiatrist had judged Mr. Cowart competent to decide about such matters as hospital release despite second- and third-degree burns over 68 percent of his body. His physicians felt strongly that it was not in his best interest to be released. They cited factors that might influence or fail to influence Mr. Cowart's judgment, such as stress, inexperience, medical ignorance, severe pain, and lack of appreciation of the future. They forcibly prevented him from jumping six stories out of a hospital window and prevented his release from the hospital when he insisted on being released. They also gave him painful daily treatments against his will. Despite the judgment of a hospital psychiatrist that he was competent, the case has subtle problems of interpretation: Did the circumstances of his injury and the therapeutic maneuvers that were undertaken cause Mr. Cowart's reaction? Or had he made an autonomous choice? How are we to assess the reasons for and causes of his convictions?

One account of our obligations to such persons, by a strong advocate of the principle of autonomy, is the following by Glanville Williams:

> If one suddenly comes upon another person attempting suicide, the natural and humane thing to do is to try to stop him, for the purpose of ascertaining the cause of his distress and attempting to remedy it, or else of attempting moral dissuasion if it seems that the act of suicide shows lack of consideration for others, or else again from the purpose of trying to persuade him to accept psychiatric help if this seems to be called for. Whatever the strict law may be (and authority is totally lacking), no one who intervened for such reasons would thereby be in danger of suffering a punitive judgment. But nothing longer than a temporary restraint could be defended. I would gravely doubt whether a suicide attempt should be a factor leading to a diagnosis of psychosis or to compulsory admission to a hospital. Psychiatrists are too ready to assume that an attempt to commit suicide is the act of a mentally sick person.[46]

Many do not agree with Williams's estimate, primarily for two reasons. First, failure to intervene may indicate both a lack of concern about others and a diminished sense of respect for life and moral responsibility in a community. Attempts to save persons from suicide in subways are now comparatively rare; this seems to indicate how times have changed in large cities—and how disastrous the change has been. Second, many believe that most suicides are mentally ill or at least seriously disturbed and therefore are not capable of autonomous action. Notoriously, suicidal persons are often under the strain of temporary crises (as in Cowart's case), under the influence of drugs or alcohol, or beset with considerable ambivalence. Let us next consider these motives for suicide.

## §14 NONAUTONOMOUS SUICIDES

Many psychiatric and legal authorities can be cited in support of the belief that suicides often result from maladaptive attitudes needing therapeutic attention. The underlying conviction held by these authorities—especially orthodox psychoanalysts—is that many suicidal persons suffer from some form of disease or irrational drive toward self-destruction and that it is the business of medicine or behavioral therapy to cure the illness and prevent the patient from taking this action. While no single theory presently suffices for understanding the motivation to suicide, numerous accounts characterize the performance of suicides as substantially nonvoluntary and therefore as nonautonomous. Other suicidal persons are not depicted as ill but rather as not in a position to act autonomously, because they are immature, ignorant, coerced, or in a vulnerable position in which they might be manipulated by others.

How large one thinks the class of nonautonomous suicides is will have a major impact on how one responds in practice to particular persons. As we shall see, in discussing paternalism (§15), the larger one envisions the class of nonautonomous persons, the easier it is to set aside a suicidal person's preferences and choices and to intervene to treat them in terms of the Principle of Respect for Life, setting aside the Principle of Autonomy. Deep theoretical differences are often at work in using labels such as 'nonautonomous.' In his book *The Killing of Bonnie Garland,* psychiatrist Willard Gaylin reflects on how different theories of human motivation function in law and psychiatry. He argues, correctly I believe, that the premise of law is generally the autonomy of the person, while the premise of psychiatry is that the self is a geyser of impulses erupting in various irrational behaviors. The law assesses responsibility and fault; psychiatry seeks to cleanse our vocabulary of such terms.[47] Moral problems about nonautonomous suicides are both logically and historically tied to these theoretical and disciplinary differences.

Nonautonomous persons are of course due all the same protections of moral rules afforded to autonomous persons. One way of respecting them as persons is by direct intervention in their lives, which is intended to protect them against harms resulting from their illness, immaturity, psychological incapacitation, ignorance, coercion, or possible exploitation. We might directly intervene, for example, by coercively preventing their suicides. Those who are defenders of the Principle of Autonomy have never denied that this interference is valid, and this is because they regard such suicidal actions as *non-autonomous*. They regard the Principle of Autonomy and the derivative right to commit suicide as extending only to persons capable of autonomous choice. As Williams hints, suicide prevention and intervention are justified in many instances in order to determine if a serious defect, encumbrance, misunderstanding, or mental constraint is affecting the causal agent. Indeed, virtually everyone is agreed that nonautonomous suicidal actions should be prevented by intervention. The controversial questions concern how large the class of *nonautonomous* suicides is (which no one knows) and whether *autonomous* suicides can justifiably be prevented, a topic to which we now turn.

## §15 PATERNALISM AND AUTONOMOUS SUICIDES

Issues of intervention with autonomous action properly fall under the problem of paternalism. Some defenders of the view that autonomous suicides may be justifiably prevented take this position because they believe the Principle of Respect for Life creates a duty to prevent suicide that overrides all duties based in the Principle of Autonomy. This is a patently paternalistic viewpoint, and we must begin with an understanding of this problem and of the options available in suicide intervention.

'Paternalism' is used in current moral philosophy to refer to practices that restrict the autonomy of individuals without their consent, where the justification for such actions is either the prevention of some harm they will do to themselves or the production of some benefit for them that they would not otherwise secure. The following, then, may serve as our definition of 'paternalism': Paternalism is the intentional limitation of the autonomy of one person by another, where the person who limits autonomy exclusively invokes grounds of beneficence for the person whose autonomy is limited. The essence of paternalism is an overriding of the Principle of Autonomy on grounds of a principle of beneficence. The *Paternalistic Principle,* then, asserts that limiting people's autonomy is justified if through their own actions they would produce serious harm to themselves or would fail to secure important benefits.

It is vital to appreciate that the person's *autonomy* must be limited. It is not paternalistic, for example, to put an unconscious injured person in an ambulance and send him or her to the emergency room. In the case of suicide intervention, a refusal to release a person from the hospital or an intervention to force-feed the person is paternalistic if it intentionally restricts autonomy and is performed for the person's own good rather than for the good of others. If the person is not autonomous, then no intervention is paternalistic under the above definition.

Many kinds of actions, rules, and laws are commonly justified by appeal to the Paternalistic Principle. Examples include laws that protect drivers by requiring seat belts, court orders for blood transfusions when it is known that patients do not wish them, and various forms of involuntary commitment to mental hospitals. Laws both allowing intervention to stop or prevent autonomous suicides and permitting the resuscitation of patients who have asked not to be resuscitated have been claimed to be justified on similar and even identical grounds.

The Bouvia case treated earlier has been widely discussed because of the paternalism-autonomy issues it presents. When Ms. Bouvia asked a court to be allowed to starve herself in a hospital because of her physical limitations and disability, the chief of psychiatry at the hospital, Dr. Donald E. Fisher, testified that he would force-feed her using a nasogastric tube even if ordered by the court not to do so. Such paternalism is often found in modern medicine, although generally with patients whose illness or disability seriously affects their judgment. The striking thing about Ms. Bouvia is that she is a well-informed person judged competent by the court, and whose decision the court has found to be "rational" and "sincere."

However, the court ultimately found that "The established ethics of the medical profession clearly outweigh and overcome her own rights of self-determination." Therefore, "forced feeding, however invasive, would be administered for the purpose of saving the life of an otherwise non-terminal patient and should be permitted. There is no other reasonable option."[48] But is this conclusion based on the Principle of Respect for Life as clear as the judge supposes? Does a person have a *right* rooted in the Principle of Autonomy to commit suicide under such circumstances? Is it a moral requirement that such a person be force-fed? The court also uses the Principle of Utility to weigh the "profound effect" Ms. Bouvia's action would have on the hospital staff and on other patients if her intention were allowed to be carried out. This illustrates how complicated such cases of paternalism often become, especially when interests other than those of the patient are at stake.

The physicians and the court are obviously distressed in the Bouvia case not only about her suicide but about her desire that the medical facility *help* her in performing her action. Assisted suicide has been denounced throughout the history of medical ethics. The Hippocratic Oath specifically says, "I will neither give a deadly drug to anybody if asked for it, nor will I make a suggestion to this effect."[49] Physicians have often argued the consequentialist thesis that their dedication would be undermined by assisting suicides, as would the trust of patients in their doctors. These particular reasons are not paternalistic, but the main lines of the traditional denunciation of assisted suicide in both medicine and law have been paternalistic.

This is not surprising in a profession with the special objectives found in medicine. Since the Greeks, the role of the physician has been expressed as the cure of disease and injury whenever there is a reasonable cure. This includes the avoidance, removal, and prevention of harm—and in general a balancing of *medical* goods over harms for the patient. Throughout the history of medicine, the physician has primarily functioned in care-giving and comforting roles, with *beneficence* serving as the moral foundation of these roles, not respect for autonomy. This model of the physician's responsibility is not inherently paternalistic in that it does not entail that the physician's medical judgment and professional commitment must always override the patient's judgment. Nonetheless, the model does frame the physician's obligations in terms of medically specific ways of providing benefits and avoiding harms; the model itself promotes beneficence rather than respect for autonomy as the overriding principle for medical practice. Defenders of autonomous suicide need not criticize this *model* as a general standard of conduct, but they will still demand that a justification be forthcoming for *particular* interventions into the lives of autonomous suicides.

Any supporter of a general paternalistic principle that would justify suicide intervention thus should specify with care precisely which goods, needs, and interests warrant paternalistic protection. In most recent formulations, it has been said that the state is justified in interfering with a person's liberty if by its interference the person is protected against either (1) his or her own extremely and unreasonably risky actions, or (2) those actions not in the person's own best interest when such a person's best interest is knowable by the state, or (3) those actions that are potentially dangerous and irreversible in effect. Some believe that acts of suicide fit all of these categories, and therefore that intervention is justified. A general justification of this view has been offered by the British legal philosopher H. L. A. Hart:

> Paternalism—the protection of people against themselves—is a perfectly coherent policy. . . . No doubt if we no longer sympathise with [John Stuart Mill's] criticism this is due, in part, to a general decline in the belief that individuals know their own interest best, and to an increased awareness of a great range of factors which diminish the significance to be attached to an apparently free choice or to consent. . . . Harming others is something we may still seek to prevent by use of the criminal law, even when the victims consent to or assist in the acts which are harmful to them.[50]

In a much discussed defense of paternalism, Gerald Dworkin has argued that a limited paternalism should be regarded as a form of "social insurance policy" that fully rational persons would take out for their own protection.[51] That is, the paternalistic principle is justified under conditions that would be unanimously consented to by an impartial rational agent, who would appreciate that he or she might be tempted at times to make decisions to commit acts like suicide that are potentially dangerous and irreversible. The agent might at other times be driven to do something that would be considered too risky if the person could objectively assess the situation—such as smoking or drinking heavily enough to endanger life. In still other cases, even autonomous persons might not sufficiently understand or appreciate the dangers of their conduct or might distort information about their circumstances.

In these different situations in life, the paternalist is convinced that a reasonable and justified perspective can be legitimately substituted for that of the person whose judgment is faulty. Dworkin even argues that a paternalistic act that denies a person an immediate liberty may nonetheless protect his or her deeper autonomy—that is, the person's deeper preferences about the preferences on which he or she ought to act. A doctor might lie to a patient, for example, in order to prevent a suicide, where the doctor knows that the patient will later calm down and not act to cause his or her own death, although the patient is presently in no position to appreciate this fact.[52]

By contrast, some moral philosophers believe that paternalism to prevent suicide is never justified after an initial temporary intervention to ascertain the cause (as mentioned by Williams). This position is the one classically supported by the nineteenth-century English philosopher John Stuart Mill (1806–1873) in *On Liberty*, though it can be supported on grounds other than the utilitarian ones offered by Mill. The following passage is Mill's own summary of his central theses:

> The only purpose for which power can be rightfully exercised over any member of a civilized community, against his will, is to prevent harm to others. His own good, either physical or moral, is not a sufficient warrant. He cannot rightfully be compelled to do or forebear because it will be better for him to do so, because it will make him happier, because in the opinion of others, to do so would be wise, or even right. These are good reasons for remonstrating with him, or reasoning with him or persuading him, or entreating him, but not for compelling him, or visiting him with any evil in case he does otherwise. . . . His independence is, of right, absolute.[53]

Mill supposed he had articulated a general ethical principle that properly restricted social control over individual liberty, regardless whether such control is legal, religious, economic, or of some other type. Autonomous suicide would certainly seem to be included, much in the way Hume defended it.

Those who support this *antipaternalist* case, which is rooted in the Principle of Autonomy, would argue that it is legitimate to remonstrate with, to counsel, and to use other noncoercive measures to attempt to persuade the suicide not to perform the contemplated action—especially when the suicidal person appears voluntarily at a physician's office seeking help. But they would also maintain that in some cases it might be wise to counsel and assist persons in favor of suicide. This is, roughly speaking, the view that Ms. Bouvia and her attorney took of her desperate situation.

An analogy is often made by defenders of this antipaternalist view between committing an autonomous but "mentally disturbed" person against his or her will and preventing an autonomous suicide. It is illegal and immoral to cause the involuntary commitment of someone capable of autonomous actions merely on grounds that he or she is suicidal. By parallel reasoning, it is argued, it is immoral and should be illegal to coercively prevent someone from carrying out an intention to commit suicide. If people are autonomous, then they have the right to be left alone and to do with their lives as they wish so long as they are sufficiently free of responsibilities to others. From this Humean perspective, the intervention in the life of a suicide is simply an unjust deprivation of autonomy rights.[54]

## §16 MORAL ISSUES IN SUICIDE INTERVENTION

What now should be concluded about the justifiability of paternalistic intervention to prevent suicide? Here we confront a dispute that again centers on conflict between the four principles earlier adduced. Autonomy and Utility generally support nonintervention, while Respect for Life and the Theological Principle suggest intervention.

Consistent with the positions previously maintained, the sympathies of this author are for the noninterventionist position, once it has been *established* on sound evidence that the suicide's act is autonomous. At the same time, I do not deny that it is proper to praise those who intervene to prevent suicides by persons perched on ledges, frightened in psychiatric hospitals, or lying on train tracks. It is reasonable to presume until it can be ascertained otherwise that such individuals are not autonomous and so not competent. However, ascertaining level of competence will be most difficult when a train is moving down the tracks or a person's stomach must be pumped. Patients in psychiatric units present no less troublesome cases, and health professionals can scarcely be denounced for intervening to prevent suicides in these units. Interventions in these circumstances are patently reasonable and acceptable.

But when it has been ascertained that a person is acting autonomously, the burden of proof in defending an intervention shifts dramatically. This is the whole point of individual rights erected on the basis of the Principle of Autonomy. Ms. Bouvia's physician—Dr. Fisher—proclaimed that he would intervene until she had established a six-month history of competence.[55] This requirement is oppressive, a form of medical despotism that sets impossible conditions. As Mill argued, it is one thing to intervene forcibly for a short while and to continue to attempt to persuade such a person, but it is quite another to continue for months to intervene by force-feeding. Courts and physicians need to be sensitive to the limits of permissible interventions where the will of the person is subjected to the will of another. None of us should be eager to draw the line of intervention so that those who, deep down, want to live wind up dead; and this is the well-intentioned thought underlying Dr. Fisher's rule. But we should be no less eager to strip a demonstrably autonomous person of the only decisions of real importance in his or her life. As Ms. Bouvia's attorney eloquently argued, we need a flawless justification in order to require her to endure what *to her* is unendurable.

Moreover, there may be another level of unfairness at work if a patient is subjected to moral judgments—made by physicians and courts—that are by no means widely shared in the culture or fixed in law and medicine. During the same period in which Ms. Bouvia's case was decided in the courts, a judge in upstate New York ruled that an eighty-five-year-old (unnamed) man in a Syracuse nursing home who wished to starve himself to death could do so, without intervention from the operators of the home who had sought to force-feed him.

Courts have often defended the autonomy of patients in relevantly similar cases, and rightly so, in my view. Consider, for example, the case of *Satz* v. *Perlmutter*.[56] Seventy-three-year-old Abe Perlmutter was mortally ill in a hospital in Florida, suffering from advanced stages of Lou Gehrig's disease (amyotrophic lateral sclerosis). There is no cure for this disease, and normal life expectancy from the point of diagnosis is two years. Mr. Perlmutter could breathe only with a respirator and was desperately miserable; the prognosis was death in a short period of time. He was capable of making autonomous decisions and was fully aware of his perilous circumstances. He requested, with the concurrence of every family member, that the respirator be removed from his trachea, but his physicians refused to comply because he would die as the direct result. Mr. Perlmutter then managed to remove the respirator himself. An alarm sounded and hospital personnel reconnected the respirator, contending that they had an overriding duty to preserve life. The matter wound up in court. The patient contended that, in the face of his misery, his physicians had an obligation to allow him to make his own choices, even though his choice would cause his death. His physicians, and legal representatives of the state of Florida, argued that they had a duty to preserve life and to prevent suicide. Here the duty to preserve and protect life—as derived, roughly, from the Principle of Respect for Life—is in direct conflict with the Principle of Autonomy. A Florida court then had to fix the *actual* or *overriding* duty of the hospital and physicians. In a complicated balancing act, the court argued that the patient's choice should be overriding in this case because considerations of autonomy were *here* (although not *everywhere*) weightier than considerations of respect for life. The court reasoned that "the cost to the individual" in this case of refusing to recognize his choice in a circumstance of terminal illness could not be overridden by the duty to preserve life.

The commitments of medicine are such that physicians often over-interpret their paternalistic privileges in circumstances where their patients desire more information or disagree with an intervention. As a consequence, insufficient weight is given to the patient's view of what is in his or her interest. Certainly we ought to be skeptical that physicians and other authorities have the ability in many cases to know our interests better than we do. As physicians Paul Appelbaum and Loren Roth observe, "Teaching and writing about [paternalism and] death with dignity has clearly made an impact on the medical profession, but not enough of an impact to overcome in all cases the natural tendency of physicians to treat what can be treated."[57]

Nonetheless, two qualifications are in order. First, others do sometimes know our best interests with more insight and foresight than we; and, second, it is often difficult to know how much ability a person has to act autonomously or how much insight he or she has into his or her best interests. These two cautions lend an air of credibility to paternalism; occasionally we will find a case where it is another who has the greater wisdom, and in such cases it is difficult to say flatly that a paternalistic intervention is unjustified. I do not, then, conclude that a paternalistic intervention is always unjustified, for this thesis is indefensible. Its indefensibility follows from the earlier claim that the Principle of Autonomy *can* be overridden by other moral principles such as Utility, and so on, if the stakes are high enough. This can occur if the patient is at significant risk of illness or injury, the risk of intervention is relatively low, the risk to the patient's future health and well-being from nonintervention or noncompliance is significant, and the claims of autonomy are minimal. I do think, however, that these conditions are *never* satisfied if a *suicide* is genuinely autonomous.

At the same time, it is also important not to let the Principle of Autonomy overshadow the Principle of Utility in discussions of the morality of suicide. Here is a case in point. On May 30, 1984 Leanita McClain committed suicide in Chicago. Having been named by *Glamour* magazine one of the ten most outstanding young working women in the United States and being the first black member of the *Chicago Tribune's* editorial board, McClain suffered from depression about her romantic life and over the state of race relations in her "beloved city" of Chicago. There can be little doubt that Leanita McClain had an autonomy right to commit suicide and that it would have been unjustifiably paternalistic of her psychiatrist to intervene to prevent her suicide. But such appeals to autonomy miss the moral essence of her case. A few environmental changes, and perhaps more concentrated psychiatric efforts, would have made life bearable and perhaps even highly enjoyable for this enormously talented young journalist.

Through her own journalistic writings, Leanita McClain was searching both for people to trust and for a release from hate. She could not find them, and so wound up dead from her own sleeping pills.

The major moral problem in this case is not autonomy but unfulfilled human need and a felt lack of human decency in her culture, a generalization that fits thousands of suicides every year. In his classic study of suicide, Durkheim argued that community support—not "moral prohibition"—is the most important factor in the prevention of suicide. In this vein, Alfred Alvarez has recently offered the following insightful observation:

> The Church's condemnation of self-murder, however brutal, was based at least on a concern for the suicide's soul. In contrast, a great deal of modern scientific tolerance appears to be founded on human indifference. The act is removed from the realm of damnation only at the price of being transformed into an interesting but purely intellectual problem, beyond obloquy but also beyond tragedy and morality.[58]

## V. CONCLUSION

Although Hume's convictions about the permissibility of suicide have been supported in this paper, we should note in conclusion that a suicidal action may be cowardly and even morally wrong. We have seen that there are occasions on which one has moral obligations not to commit suicide, just as there could be extremely rare occasions on which one has moral obligations to commit suicide.

When all interests are taken into account, the overriding obligation may—or may not—be to abstain from suicide. Moreover, weak duties are sometimes overridden not only by stronger duties but also by strong prudential interests. Even though a dependent daughter might beg her terminally ill father to stay alive for his last remaining month, his agony may be sufficiently great to override the daughter's interest in his remaining alive. As Hume said: I am not obliged to do great harm to myself in order to procure a small benefit for another.

It is of course true that in calculating whether or not to commit suicide, it is easy to be mistaken in one's assessment by taking an unconsidered view. One's desires, sufferings, and hopes in the present moment generally tend to overwhelm consideration of what one's desires, sufferings, and joys may be at future times. In the case of known terminal illness, which provides one of the strongest justifications of suicide, one is not likely to change to a more optimistic frame of mind. Indeed, the matter is likely to become worse daily. But in the event of depression (where there is not a terminal physiological illness), during which the majority of suicides are committed, it is easy to miscalculate by substituting present feelings for rational calculations of future possibilities. This, of course, is the perspective taken by Ms. Bouvia's physician on her state of mind.

Depression not only tends to foreclose consideration of the future but even to render it impossible to project an adequate picture of future possibilities and probabilities. Without depression, persons might make quite different calculations, even when their situation is dire. Often patients are absolutely convinced by their depression that their circumstances are intolerable, and they may even be successful in convincing their psychiatrists that the situation is every bit as bad as they feel it to be. But psychiatrists are trained to look out for a "false empathy" with depressed patients, because it so often happens that when the patient's depression improves, so do their feelings about the direness of their situations. Their refusals of treatment or expressions of suicidal desires may subsequently vanish.[59]

The reason for this concluding speculation about depression is the following: It is one thing to judge, as I have, that autonomous suicide sometimes is justified. It is another to frame a realistic appraisal of the circumstances and of the actual state of mind of persons who perform allegedly autonomous suicides. It would be hoped that a suicide might take account of a great many relevant variables and future possibilities; such is often not the case. This is especially true of adolescent suicide. Depressed adolescents have a tendency to think both that deep hurts and suffering will not go away and that they will never again experience satisfactory human relationships. They have not yet developed a well-formed picture of how troubles come and go in life. Thus, questions about our obligations to prevent suicide will always be difficult because of our uncertainty as to whether the suicides are or are not truly informed, autonomous, mature, responsible, and the like.

In any final assessment of the misguided nature of some acts of suicide, it is important to consider different judgments that might be reached about *excusability*. We can surely excuse some suicides if they act on false information, if they are of temporarily unsound mind, or when depression or some other psychological state overwhelms someone of an ordinarily even disposition.[60] A suicide might be seriously misguided but not blameworthy; alternatively, a suicide might be both blameworthy and misguided. The case of false information is generally the most compelling kind of excuse, as the latter two are somewhat obvious. Suicides often do act on information that is false or radically incomplete. This can occur if a physician conceals information, if the patient has a false belief about a medical condition, if a person mistakenly felt spurned by a lover, and so on. The tragically fascinating cases —and among the most easily excused—are those where a person acts altruistically in committing suicide but with false information. For example, one might falsely believe that one is ill with a dreadful disease that will produce prolonged agony and leave one's family in financial ruin. Here it is reasonable to say that such a person not only acted wrongly though excusably but even that he or she acted commendably though wrongly.

One problem with the discussion of suicide found in St. Thomas and similar thinkers is that they do not distinguish the wrongness of an action from the moral excusability and even praiseworthiness of the intention that underlies that same action. One advantage of the analysis of suicide offered throughout this paper is that it permits us to make these important distinctions and to adjust our moral judgments about suicide accordingly. As emphasized earlier, a suicide is not necessarily a person who denies the value or meaning of life, even of his or her own life. *Some* suicides view life as not worth living, and some even have irrational reasons for taking this viewpoint. But others sacrifice their lives for some greater purpose, thus making the value of their lives subordinate to the value of some other cause. This complexity is another reason for caution in the moral assessment of a suicide's intention and action.

## NOTES

1. Ronald Maris, "Sociology," in S. Perlin, ed., *A Handbook for the Study of Suicide.* New York: Oxford University Press, 1975, p. 101.
2. Cf. R. B. Brandt, "On the Morality and Rationality of Suicide," in S. Perlin, ed., *A Handbook for the Study of Suicide,* op. cit., p. 61. Eike-Henner W. Kluge, *The Practice of Death.* New Haven, Conn.: Yale University Press, 1975, p. 101. The article on suicide in *The Encyclopedia of Bioethics* is jointly authored by David Smith and Seymour Perlin. In fairness to Brandt, he does preface his definition with the word 'assuming.' Effectively he *assumes* this definition in order to discuss the morality and rationality of suicide. So I shall not be criticizing Brandt per se, but rather the definition that he assumes.
3. Emile Durkheim, *Suicide: A Study in Sociology,* trans. John A. Spaulding and George Simpson. New York: Free Press, 1966, p. 44.
4. Maris, op. cit., p. 100.
5. E. Stengel, in *Proceedings of the VI International Congress for Suicide Prevention.* Ann Arbor, Mich.: Edwards Publishing, 1972.
6. It seems to me that some active but involuntary killings of the self can plausibly be described as suicide—as when a frustrated lover heavily under the influence of LSD plunges through a sixteenth-floor window. Perhaps, then, we should speak here only about rational suicides.
7. Some believe that Socrates did commit suicide. See R. G. Frey, "Did Socrates Commit Suicide?" *Philosophy* 53 (January 1978), pp. 106–108, and reprinted in M. Pabst Battin and David J. K. Mayo, *Suicide: The Philosophical Issues.* New York: St. Martin's, 1980, pp. 35–38. A main source of disagreement between my analysis and Frey's is that he does not take Socrates to have been *coerced:* "Socrates had a choice between drinking the hemlock willingly and having it, so to speak, force-fed; and only by choosing to be force-fed would Socrates have been forced to drink the hemlock, that is, compelled to die against his will" (p. 37). For reasons expressed elsewhere, I believe Socrates was coerced and so was not a suicide.

8. Joseph Margolis, "Suicide," in chapter 2 of *Negativities: The Limits of Life*. Columbus, Ohio: Merrill, 1975, pp. 23f.

9. Important problems for the definition of suicide are presented by the indefinite meaning of the term 'cause'. Unfortunately, this difficult concept cannot be analyzed here and must be left as an undefined term.

10. *Elizabeth Bouvia* v. *County of Riverside* (Superior Court, Riverside County, California, December 16, 1983), no. 159780, tr. 1238–1250, opinion by Judge John H. Hews. See also George J. Annas, "When Suicide Prevention Becomes Brutality: The Case of Elizabeth Bouvia," *The Hastings Center Report* 14 (April 1984), pp. 20–21, 46.

11. Henderson Smith and Glanville Williams have coined the term 'voluntary death' as a surrogate. Cf. Williams's essay, "Euthanasia," *Medico-Legal Journal*, 41 (1973, Part 1), p. 30.

12. I do not think it would be correct, however, to hold that such justifying reasons *must be moral ones* or even must be thought to be moral ones, though they can be moral ones. Religious martyrs may act from the reason that an action being demanded of them is a violation of their religious convictions, and they may be willing to die for them, because they regard them, or at least their nonviolation of them, as more important than life. The political patriot is in a similar situation.

13. Joel Feinberg, "Introduction" to "The Sanctity of Life," in Tom L. Beauchamp, William T. Blackstone, and Joel Feinberg, eds., *Philosophy and the Human Condition*. Englewood Cliffs, N.J.: Prentice-Hall, 1980.

14. See Robert S. Scott, *Scott's Last Expedition*. London: 1935, Vol. I, p. 462.

15. R. F. Holland, "Suicide," in J. Rachels, ed., *Moral Problems*. New York: Harper & Row, 1971, pp. 352–353.

16. R. C. K. Ensor, *England: 1870–1914*. Oxford, England: Clarendon, 1949, p. 553.

17. Perhaps a harder case is found in Eskimo societies, where the elderly take a small amount of food and leave the village expecting death in a short period of time but do not directly force death upon themselves as did Oates.

18. Margolis, op. cit., pp. 27–28. Cf. his final definition on p. 33.

19. 'Arrangement' here *excludes* refusals of treatment in the cases discussed previously.

20. For some possible counterexamples and a definition based on the conviction that suicide is an open-textured concept, see Peter Y. Windt, "The Concept of Suicide," in Battin and Mayo, op. cit., pp. 39–47. See also the essay by Robert Martin, "Suicide and Self-Sacrifice," in the same volume, esp. p. 50.

21. For an exposition of this point of view and a use of this principle, see Eike-Henner W. Kluge, *The Practice of Death*. New Haven, Conn.: Yale University Press, 1975, chap. 2.

22. Premise 2 commits the Thomist to agreement with Hume that some suicides are rational and avoidable. Many philosophers and psychiatrists would deny this, of course, yet would use an argument similar to premises 1, 2, and 3. Premises 1 and 2 would be acceptable to them if and only if 1 is construed as a law of human nature that denies that there can exist a natural internal impulse to self-destruction, while it is admitted that "external" forces such as physical causes or psychological compulsion can cause suicide.

23. Glanville Williams, *The Sanctity of Life and the Criminal Law*. New York: Knopf, 1957, p. 264.

24. This reading of Aquinas is based primarily on selected passages in the *Summa Theologica* other than the suicide passages. Cf., e.g., I–II. 90–97 and II–II. 94. Some Thomists place more emphasis on the importance of

essential properties and/or rational intuition, but it makes little difference for our purposes.

25.  Cf. Aquinas, Reply to Objection 4 in Article 5 and Reply to Objection 1 in Article 6 for his excusing condition. Article 7 in Question 64 contains a rough formulation of the Principle of Double Effect. Below I consider the possibility that a Thomist would regard killing oneself for the sake of others as morally justified, while maintaining that it is not a case of suicide.

26.  It is generally held that a fourth condition must also obtain: the evil result must not be the cause of or means to the good effect. Whether this condition is a necessary condition of the principle is a substantive moral controversy into which we cannot here delve. Fortunately, it is irrelevant to any controversy pertaining to Hume's criticisms and, in any event, the condition seems not to be found in Aquinas's text.

27.  Aquinas discusses the case of Samson as follows: ". . . not even Samson is to be excused . . . except the Holy Ghost . . . had secretly commanded him to do this." Reply Obj. 4. Cf. Reply Obj. 1 in Art. 6. Before Aquinas wrote, St. Augustine had applied the excuse to Samson and also to martyred women who cast themselves into rivers in order to avoid being raped by ("menaced with outrage") pagans. Augustine had maintained that God instructed them to so act, but with the caution: "Only let him be very sure that the divine command has been signified." See *The City of God,* trans. Marcus Dods. New York: Modern Library, 1950, Book I, Art. 26, p. 31.

28.  Throughout I shall use page references to the reprinting of Hume's essay in *Of the Standard of Taste and Other Essays,* ed. John Lenz (Indianapolis, Ind.: Bobbs-Merrill, 1965). Hume's essay has been widely reprinted in textbooks of philosophical ethics (as a classic deserving equal consideration with writings on suicide by Seneca, Aquinas, Kant, Schopenhauer, and others), though its main influence may have come as a contribution to both late eighteenth-, nineteenth-, and twentieth-century English discussions of the morality of suicide and the acceptability of its legalization. The history of the English debate on suicide through Hume's early critics is discussed in S. E. Sprott, *The English Debate on Suicide from Donne to Hume* (LaSalle, Ill.: Open Court, 1961).

29.  Hume's exact words are: "What is the meaning of that principle, that a [suicide] . . . has incurred the indignation of his Creator by encroaching on the office of divine providence, and disturbing the order of the universe?" (154)

30.  Brandt, op. cit., p. 66. Cf. Sidney Hook's distinctly Humean approach in "The Ethics of Suicide," *Ethics,* 37 (1927), and reprinted in Marvin Kohl, ed., *Beneficent Euthanasia.* Buffalo, N.Y.: Prometheus, 1975, p. 62.

31.  His hypothetical cases have actual analogues. Many suicide notes reflect a belief that the suicide has become an unavoidable social burden.

32.  Hume imagines still other cases, such as that of a prisoner condemned to die and the presumably historical case of Strozi of Florence. But these cases do not constitute types of cases relevantly different from the third case.

33.  The reverse, however, does not follow from any argument thus far presented. That is, it does not follow that suicide *should* or *must be* performed if the utilitarian calculus indicates that it would maximize value in the circumstances. Autonomy should not be overridden by utility—at least no argument thus far addressed commits either me or Hume to this claim.

34.  Donagan's objection is pressed in particular against R. B. Brandt's rule-utilitarianism, but that fact is of little concern for our purposes. Cf. Rich-

ard B. Brandt, "Toward a Credible Form of Utilitarianism," and Alan Donagan, "Is There a Credible Form of Utilitarianism?" both in *Contemporary Utilitarianism*, ed., Michael D. Bayles. Garden City, N.Y.: Doubleday, 1968.

35. Donagan, op. cit., p. 196.
36. In the context of Hume's essay it is left unclear whether the "should" in the previous sentence is merely a matter of what he calls a "duty to ourselves" or is a moral matter and hence a matter of a "duty to our neighbors." By reference to the constraints of his rule-utilitarianism, it can plausibly be argued that Hume cannot consistently believe that it is merely a matter of self-duty. Following this interpretation, which is favorable to Donagan, Hume is committed to saying the following: Whenever a person regards his life as "not worth keeping" and is a social burden, utility would be maximized in this single circumstance by committing suicide. An act-utilitarian might stop here, but a rule-utilitarian would go on to say that if adoption of a general rule to this effect would maximize utility, then a society ought to make such a rule current.
37. That is, if social utility would be maximized by having such a rule, as it often would be, then the rule ought to be adopted. Donagan actually formulates a similar rule intended to govern judicial murder (p. 196) and one that governs unusual welfare payments (p. 194).
38. My defense is not a full defense of rule-utilitarianism, of course, since the perplexing problem of distributive justice is not considered.
39. Hume, *Second Enquiry*, pars. 147, 149. Donagan, op. cit., p. 195f.
40. Kant, *The Metaphysics of Morals*, Part II, published as *The Metaphysical Principles of Virtue*, trans. J. Ellington. Indianapolis, Ind.: Bobbs-Merrill, 1964, pp. 84f.
41. The above analysis is indebted to both Brandt, "Toward a Credible Form of Utilitarianism," op. cit., p. 158, and to Hume.
42. Drawn from Joel Feinberg, "Supererogation and Rules," *Ethics*, vol. 71 (1961), pp. 276–288, esp. 280.
43. For an interesting presentation of the Eskimo rule, cf. Margolis, op. cit.
44. Hume specifically considers such cases, using the example of a shipwreck. However, his case is the more radical one, where social order breaks down completely and "the strict laws of justice are suspended." He also considers famines, but his comments are not insightful (*Enquiries*, pars. 147 and 165).
45. This case is developed from the following sources: Robert B. White and H. Tristram Engelhart, Jr., "A Demand to Die," *Hastings Center Report* 5 (June 1975), pp. 9–10; and a videotape of Donald Cowart's case entitled "Please Let Me Die," University of Texas Medical Branch, Galveston, Department of Psychiatry.
46. Williams, "Euthanasia," op. cit., p. 27.
47. Willard Gaylin, *The Killing of Bonnie Garland: A Question of Justice*. New York: Simon & Schuster, 1982.
48. *Elizabeth Bouvia* v. *County of Riverside*.
49. "The Hippocratic Oath," in Ludwig Edelsetin, *Ancient Medicine*, ed. Owsei Temkin and C. Lilliam Temkin. Baltimore: Johns Hopkins University Press, 1967.
50. H. L. A. Hart, *Law, Liberty, and Morality*. Stanford, Calif.: Stanford University Press, 1963, pp. 31–33.
51. Gerald Dworkin, "Paternalism," *Monist* 56 (1972), p. 65. His view on this point is indebted to Rawls. Many writers have subsequently expressed similar views, usually based on the view that rational consent justifies paternalism. These writers include Jeffrie G. Murphy, "Incompetence and Paternalism," *Archives for Philosophy of Law and Social Philosophy*

60 (1974), pp. 481–482; Rosemary Carter, "Justifying Paternalism," *Canadian Journal of Philosophy* 7 (1977), pp. 133–145; and John D. Hodson, "The Principle of Paternalism," *American Philosophical Quarterly* 14 (1977), pp. 65ff.

52.  See Dworkin's essay, "Autonomy and Informed Consent," in President's Commission for the Study of Ethical Problems in Medicine and Biomedical and Behavioral Research, *Making Health Care Decisions.* Washington, D.C.: U.S. Government Printing Office, 1982, vol. III, p. 69.

53.  *On Liberty,* as reprinted in *Essential Works of John Stuart Mill.* New York: Bantam, 1961, p. 263.

54.  For one influential statement of this view, cf. Thomas Szasz, "The Ethics of Suicide," *Antioch Review* 31:1 (Spring 1971), pp. 7–17.

55.  See Annas, op. cit., pp. 21, 46.

56.  *Satz* v. *Perlmutter,* 362 So.2d 160 (Florida District Court of Appeals, 1978).

57.  Paul S. Appelbaum and Loren H. Roth, "Treatment Refusal in Medical Hospitals," in President's Commission, op. cit., vol. II, p. 475.

58.  Alfred Alvarez, "The Background," from *The Savage God,* as reprinted in Battin and Mayo, op. cit., p. 30.

59.  Appelbaum and Roth, op. cit., p. 433.

60.  This analysis draws heavily on Brandt's useful discussion of the subject in "The Morality and Rationality of Suicide," op. cit., p. 124.

## SUGGESTIONS FOR FURTHER READING

On the question of how suicide is to be defined (§§1–6), the following readings are especially noteworthy:

Douglas, Jack D., *Social Meanings of Suicide.* Princeton, N.J.: Princeton University Press, 1967.

Durkheim, Emile, *Suicide: A Study in Sociology,* trans. John A. Spaulding and George Simpson. New York: Free Press, 1966.

Holland, R. F., "Suicide," as reprinted in James Rachels, ed., *Moral Problems,* 2nd ed. New York: Harper & Row, 1975.

Margolis, Joseph, *Negativities: The Limits of Life.* Columbus, Ohio: Merrill, 1975, chap. 2.

Martin, Robert M., "Suicide and Self-Sacrifice," in *Suicide: The Philosophical Issues,* ed. M. Pabst Battin and David J. Mayo. New York: St. Martin's Press, 1980. (Hereafter: Battin and Mayo.)

Rachels, James, "Barney Clark's Key," *Hastings Center Report* (April 1983), pp. 17–19.

Windt, Peter Y., "The Concept of Suicide." In Battin and Mayo, *Suicide: The Philosophical Issues.*

St. Thomas's position (§11) and related positions are set forth in representative primary and secondary works, including the following:

Augustine, *The City of God,* trans. Marcus Dods. New York: Modern Library, Random House, 1950. Bk. I, sections 17–27, esp. sections 21–22, 26.

Novak, David, *Suicide and Morality: The Theories of Plato, Aquinas, and Kant and Their Relevance for Suicidology.* New York: Scholars Studies, 1975.

St. John-Stevas, Norman, *Life, Death and the Law: Law and Christian Morals in England and the United States.* Bloomington, Ind.: Indiana University Press, 1961.

Thomas Aquinas, *Summa Theologica*, trans. English Dominican Fathers. New York: Benziger, 1947. Q. 64, A. 5 and Q. 76, A. 4.

David Hume's position (§12) and related positions are found in commentaries or other sources where Hume's position plays a central role. These sources include:

Beauchamp, Tom L., "An Analysis of Hume's Essay 'On Suicide'," *Review of Metaphysics,* 30 (September 1976), pp. 73–95.
Hume, David, "On Suicide." Reprinted widely.
Mossner, Ernest Campbell, "Hume's *Four Dissertations:* An Essay in Biography and Bibliography," *Modern Philology,* 48 (1950), pp. 37–57.
Sprott, S. E., *The English Debate on Suicide.* LaSalle, Ill.: Open Court, 1961.

Important readings relevant to the problem of suicide intervention (§§14–16) include:

Battin, M. Pabst, *Ethical Issues in Suicide.* Englewood Cliffs, N.J.: Prentice-Hall, 1982, chaps. 5–6.
Brandt, Richard B., et al., "A Suicide Attempt and Emergency Room Ethics," *Hastings Center Report* 9 (August 1979), pp. 12–13.
Chodoff, Paul, "The Case for Involuntary Hospitalization of the Mentally Ill," *American Journal of Psychiatry,* 133 (1976), pp. 496–501.
Greenberg, David F., "Involuntary Psychiatric Commitments to Prevent Suicide," *New York University Law Review,* 49 (1974), pp. 227–269.
Ringel, Erwin, "Suicide Prevention and the Value of Human Life," in Battin and Mayo, op cit., pp. 205–211.
Slater, Eliot, "Choosing the Time to Die," in Battin and Mayo, op cit., pp. 199–204.
Szasz, Thomas, "The Ethics of Suicide," *The Antioch Review,* 31 (Spring 1971), pp. 7–17. Reprinted in Battin and Mayo, op cit.
Williams, Glanville, *The Sanctity of Life and the Criminal Law.* New York: Knopf, 1957.

The following are important classical writings on problems of suicide:

Kant, Immanuel, *Lectures on Ethics,* trans. Louis Infield. New York: Harper & Row, 1963, pp. 148–154.
————, *The Metaphysics of Morals,* Part II, published as *The Metaphysical Principles of Virtue,* trans. James Ellington. Indianapolis, Ind.: Bobbs-Merrill, 1964.
Montaigne, Michel de, "A Custom of the Isle of Cea," *Essays,* trans. John F. Florio. 3 vols. London: Dent, 1928, Bk. 2, chap. 3.
Schopenhauer, Arthur, "On Suicide," *Studies in Pessimism,* trans. T. B. Saunders. London: G. Allen, 1890, 1962.
Seneca, "On Suicide," *Epistles,* trans. E. Barker. Oxford, England: Clarendon, 1932.

The following are important books and anthologies on suicide:

Battin, M. Pabst, *Ethical Issues in Suicide.* Englewood Cliffs, N.J.: Prentice-Hall, 1982.
Battin and Mayo, op. cit.
Beauchamp, Tom L., and Seymour Perlin, eds., *Ethical Issues in Death and Dying.* Englewood Cliffs, N.J.: Prentice-Hall, chap. 2.
Perlin, Seymour, ed., *A Handbook for the Study of Suicide.* New York: Oxford University Press, 1975.

Robins, Eli, *The Final Months—A Study of the Lives of 134 Persons Who Committed Suicide.* New York: Oxford University Press, 1981.

Shneidman, Edwin S., ed., *Suicidology: Contemporary Developments.* Seminars in Psychiatry, ed. Milton Greenblatt. New York: Grune & Stratton, 1976.

Stengel, Erwin, *Suicide and Attempted Suicide.* Studies in Social Pathology. Harmondsworth, England: Penguin Books, 1973. Reprint, New York: J. Aronson, 1974.

The following are noteworthy articles on moral problems of suicide:

Barrington, Mary Rose, "Apologia for Suicide," in *Euthanasia and the Right to Death,* ed. A. B. Downing. London: Peter Owen, 1969; abridged in Battin and Mayo, op. cit., pp. 90–103.

Brandt, R. B., "The Morality and Rationality of Suicide," as reprinted in James Rachels, ed., *Moral Problems,* ed. 2. New York: Harper & Row, 1975.

Hook, Sidney, "Ethics of Suicide," *International Journal of Ethics,* 37 (1927), pp. 173–189.

Kluge, Eike-Henner W., *The Practice of Death.* New Haven, Conn.: Yale University Press, 1975, chap. 2.

Lebacqz, Karen, and H. Tristram Engelhardt, Jr., "Suicide," in *Death, Dying, and Euthanasia,* ed. D. J. Horan and D. Mall. Washington, D.C.: University Publications of America, 1977, pp. 669–705.

Important reference works include the following:

*Bibliographies and Information Sources*

Farberow, Norman L., *Bibliography on Suicide and Suicide Prevention, 1897–1957, 1958–1970.* DHEW Publication No. (HSM) 72–9080. Rockville, Md.: National Institute of Mental Health. Washington: U.S. Government Printing Office, 1972.

Lester, David, et al., *Suicide: A Guide to Information Sources.* Detroit: Gale Research, 1980.

Sollitto, Sharmon, and Veatch, Robert M., comps., *Bibliography of Society, Ethics, and the Life Sciences.* Hastings-on-Hudson, N.Y.: Institute of Society, Ethics, and the Life Sciences, 1973—Issued annually. See "Death and Dying: Suicide."

Walters, LeRoy, ed., *Bibliography of Bioethics.* Vols. 1—. Detroit: Gale Research Co., 1975—. Issued annually. See "Suicide."

Encyclopedia of Bioethics *Articles*

AGING AND THE AGED: *Health Care and Research in the Aged*—Ernlé Young

LIFE: *Value of Life*—Peter Singer

LIFE: *Quality of Life*—Warren T. Reich

PAIN AND SUFFERING: *Philosophical Perspective*—Jerome Shaffer

PAIN AND SUFFERING: *Religious Perspective*—John Bowker

PATERNALISM—Tom L. Beauchamp

SUICIDE—David H. Smith and Seymour Perlin

# 4

# At Arms' Length: Violence and War

## JAN NARVESON

▬▬▬▬▬▬▬▬▬▬▬▬▬▬▬▬▬▬▬▬▬▬▬▬▬▬▬▬▬▬▬▬▬

## I. INTRODUCTION

### §1 THE WAY THINGS ARE

In this essay we are concerned with two topics that are literally deadly serious: violence and war, especially nuclear war. Violence occurs at least occasionally in all societies and war in nearly all, though wars have been especially frequent and enormous in scale in this century. As this is written, for instance, about forty conflicts qualifying as "wars" are taking place in various parts of the world, and in one of them casualties are mounting into the hundreds of thousands. This is hardly comforting to most of us. But still, most people would probably agree that the number-one worry for humankind today is the possibility of full-scale nuclear war.

Nuclear war deserves our most sober attention. At this very moment, missiles in the thousands are poised in a state of readiness that, at the mere command of a very few people, could plunge the entire world into the most devastating inferno of human-made violence it has ever seen. If that were to happen, the result would dwarf history's total of violence in a matter of hours, possibly even resulting in the total extinction of human life on earth. No human-made phenomenon has equaled nuclear war in its potential for violence, and even the awesome powers of volcanos and earthquakes do not equal nuclear weapons in their potential for destruction of people and what people hold dear.

Nuclear war occupies a position at the uppermost end of the spectrum of what we may call "political" violence. The victims of nuclear war, were one to occur, would be extremely numerous (to put it mildly), although thus far, of course, the actual number of victims of nuclear weapons runs only to an estimated two hundred thousand or so, a number dwarfed by the 2 million or more killed in automobile accidents in North America alone since the end of World War II. Even the number of civilian murders in those years is appreciably greater (about twice as many, so far). Still, there are two important differences. For one thing, while it is logically possible that we shall all be murdered by someone or other within the forseeable future, it is too unlikely to be worth considering, whereas nuclear war, unfortunately, seems a very real possibility indeed. More interestingly for our purposes is that war is a *political* act, and that means that it is capable of being controlled in a way that private, random acts of violence are not. For war involves the intentional acts of people who think that what they are doing is justified. This is why it is an appropriate subject for us to reflect on in a philosophical way. Nobody thinks that private murders are morally justified; there is scarcely room for real discussion on the subject of whether one morally ought to murder someone. Not so with war which, depressing though this may be, is at least thought to be right by many of those who engage in it.

In order to reflect on these matters philosophically, we must define some terms. We have talked of 'war', 'violence', and 'political', and even the idea of 'morality' needs some attention. Just the effort to specify the meanings of these important terms with reasonable clarity quickly leads us into many thorny issues, as we will see. We proceed to that task next.

## §2 DEFINITIONS

*'Violence'*   The term 'violence' is used in at least three importantly differing ways—so different that it is hopeless to try to proceed with a conglomerate, single meaning. We shall have to pick and choose. The three are as follows:

1. Consider "Mt. St. Helens exploded violently this morning," or "The train went off the rails and crashed violently into the mountainside." Here the idea is that a great deal of physical force was suddenly released. A related use of the word: "Morgan objected violently to Jenkins' assertion."

2. When applied to the acts of responsible agents, 'violence' refers to the intentional infliction of damage, pain, injury, or death on other persons or their property, contrary to the consent of the persons on whom it is inflicted.

3. Finally, the term is sometimes used in a "moral" sense, as we may call it. In such cases, it is essentially the noun form of the verb 'to violate', as in "that would violate the rights of the natives." Thus we can in this sense "do violence" to principles, to the English language, to people's rights, and the like.

We will not be employing the term in either sense 1 or 3 here, generally speaking. Violence in the first sense may not be an act of a person at all, in which case it cannot be moral or immoral. In sense 3, on the other hand, to call an act violent is already to condemn it morally (at any rate, when the "violence" in question is done to someone's rights, say). But in that case, there could not be a sensible inquiry into why violence is wrong, for it would be true by definition that it was. We would be begging the question of wrongness rather than answering it. Since we want to know whether it is ever right to use violence (and in fact will be arguing that it sometimes is), we cannot profitably use the term in this loaded way.

Even sense 2 is not entirely satisfactory, for some weapons of war need not be forcible in the usual sense of the term. Poison gas or lethal radiation do not involve hitting, stabbing, breaking bones or skin, etc. Yet we think it is as wrong to injure people by those means as by blowing them to bits. In fact, we are inclined to condemn the use of radiation, say, even more than such more ordinarily "violent" ways of doing violence to people. We certainly want to include such things in the subject of this essay, so we must broaden the term to include these ways of inflicting pain, death, harm, and other injuries.

*'War'*  Although we occasionally speak of conflicts between individuals as 'war' ("Lydia, this means war!"), the primary sense, and the one we are employing here, refers to the coercive use of violence between organized groups or their agents. Not just any old organized groups will do, for that matter. We do speak of "gang wars" and the like, to be sure; but this is understood to be a secondary use of the term. In wars most literally so called, the groups in combat are either the agents of actual governments, or people intending or hoping to form a government, of a certain state or states. At least one of these groups is attempting to impose its *political* will on the other or to defend itself or its state from having the will of the other imposed on it. Political power is what they strive for.

*'Political'*  This refers to matters subject to the governing power of the community, state, or other formally identified social unit in question. Precisely what this "power" consists in is not easy to say, but what matters is that there be a known, established group of people in the community—the agents of government—who have the recognized authority and power to make and enforce rules (laws) in that community. They may have been elected or not. Their power may or may not be checked by a constitution, with an independent judiciary to keep them within prescribed limits; but what they say goes, in the sense that they can force us—anyone in their jurisdiction—to do their bidding. To say that a matter is "political" is to say that it concerns what governments do or ought to do, or what you or I or others should try to get them to do. The nub of it is the actual or possible exertion of authorized force over the members of the community in question.

*'Moral'*  With morality things are rather different. Morality has to do
with what we should or should not do, to be sure. But not just any old
matter is thereby moral. Morality is a set of general rules applying to
everyone—everyone in the community if it is the community's morality that is in question, or everyone in general. But these are rules that
no legislature can enact or revoke. Moreover, different people, even
in the same society, will often differ considerably about the content of
these rules. If there is a general consensus, then we may to that extent
speak of "the morality of" that group; if there is worldwide consensus,
then we may speak simply of "morality" without qualification. These
would be moralities in what we may call the "de facto" sense of the
term. But of at least equal importance (and much more important to
philosophers) is what we may call the "ideal" sense of the term, in
which it refers to that set of rules that people *ought* to observe,
whether they in fact do or not. Philosophers have long been concerned with *rational* morality, morality as it would be if it were determined by reason—that is, by the best reasons. In their view, what I
have called ideal morality would be rational in that sense. That is the
sense of concern to the present essay.

What about the relation between politics and morality—between
the political and the moral? Someone might believe that whatever the
government says to do is *ipso facto* right, as if governments were
"moral authorities." But whether or not one thinks that whatever the
government says is right *is* right, it cannot be for that reason, at any
rate. For there is no such thing as a moral authority—no such thing
as a committee or individual with the power to declare something
right or wrong in such a way that the declaration automatically *makes*
that thing right or wrong. Morality is not that kind of thing. Government, on the other hand, is: if the legislature, in the appropriate
manner, declares such-and-such to be illegal, then it *is* illegal. Thus
anyone can make moral judgments about the acts of legislatures,
kings, judges, dictators, mayors, and so forth; that is, anyone may
claim, meaningfully, that a certain law or other government action,
large or small, is morally right or morally wrong, just or unjust, a
flagrant abuse of people's rights or a noble upholding of them, and so
on. Which of these claims, if any, is correct is an open question, not
logically closed off by the sheer fact that the government did something. Governments may or may not pay attention to what is morally
right. But they *ought* to; indeed, that they ought to is part of the very
idea of morality.

With these preliminary definitions in mind, we proceed to the
issues before us. Our eventual aim is to consider the most important
kind of political violence: nuclear war. But the concept of violence is
most directly appreciated in the individual case. Violence, so to say,
begins at home. So let us start by asking what the moral status of
violence is (Part II); and since it will surprise no one to hear that
violence is at least normally wrong, we do well to proceed next to the

question whether it is ever right, and if so why (Parts III and IV). Then we will consider the bearing of politics on the matter: does it reverse any of the judgments arrived at before, and if so, why? Might violence of a kind wrongful for individuals be all right for governments? This brings us to our main subject, war (Part V), concluding with nuclear war (Part VI), whose distinctive features raise the question whether nuclear weapons could ever be justified.

## II. MORALITY AND VIOLENCE

### §3 THE "STATE OF NATURE"

Violence, we have said, is the intentional infliction of pain, damage, or death on persons or their property, contrary to their consent. These conditions—pain, death, damage, etc.—are evils. We need not dwell long on the notion of 'evil'. It is enough that evils are conditions we want, on reflection, to avoid. Do we want to avoid them, as some would have it, because they are evil? Or is it that we call them evil because we want to avoid them? Those are the questions we shall have to avoid; their proper answers will not, I think, affect the present inquiry. In the case of the listed items, scarcely anyone would deny that they are evils. But they are not the only things that have been so regarded: some would point to various spiritual conditions as not only important additions, but even as much more important ones than any of them. If A insults B's religion, B may take that as worse than bodily injury or damage to property. Perhaps we should extend the notion of violence to cover such cases, saying, for instance, that to do violence to others is to do something to them that they value negatively or that is contrary to their positive values. Putting it that way would remove the concept of violence yet farther from its ordinary use, but it has the advantage of bringing it into connection with the widest context of relevant considerations here. For if A does something to B to which B is utterly indifferent, then that could hardly qualify as a case of "violence"—or, at least, it would not raise issues we are concerned with here: if B doesn't care a stick what A does, there will certainly be no wars between them!

The evils inflicted by violence are evils *from the point of view of the victim*. Are they also evils from the point of view of the assailant? Here we come upon one of the standing questions of moral philosophy in this century: what commitments to actions and attitudes are conveyed by moral expressions such as 'evil' and 'wrong'? When A calls X "evil," does A imply that X is something that A is concerned to avoid or minimize? Or might A only mean that X is something the *other* person, A's victim for example, would want to avoid? What, in short, is the connection between moral beliefs and motivation?

At the semantic level, anyway, I doubt that this is decidable. We can always be explicit and say, "Too bad for him! Heh, heh!"—using the purely relative sense of such terms as 'bad', in which they imply no particular motivation for the person doing the assessing. Alternatively, though, we can say of the sadist and the aggressor that they don't really believe that harm, pain, and the rest *are* evils when they happen to others: they may be thoroughgoing ethical egoists, believing that the only considerations that matter are, ultimately, considerations pertaining to one's own states of well or ill being. We understand this language used in either of these ways.

What matters is not semantics but the psychological fact that it is possible for people to be indifferent to the sufferings of others, or at least, so it seems. And even if they are neither indifferent nor downright sadistic, they not only may but commonly do attach much less weight to the sufferings of strangers, at least, than to the sufferings of some relatively few persons whom they love and care for. Thus in wars, for instance, they are likely to be concerned only about the casualties on their own side; enemy deaths are either ignored or accounted as positively desirable.

Some people have hearts of stone, and even normal people like you and me are not likely to account the ills of others exactly on a par with our own. This creates problems that lead directly to the great issues of moral philosophy. One way to get into them is to ask how we might go about persuading not only people like ourselves but also the stone-hearted to take a less selfish view of the social situation. The key that unlocks the most important possibilities in this area is, I believe, provided by the English philosopher Thomas Hobbes (1588–1676). Hobbes asks us to consider a hypothetical situation in which there is no government, which he calls the "state of nature." There, he argues, the following conditions hold:

1.  People are equally vulnerable, at least to the extent that anyone can kill anyone else ("the weakest can kill the strongest," as Hobbes puts it).
2.  Nature is not very generous: it will not supply us, without effort on our parts, with what we need, let alone with luxuries, at least unless we enlist much help and cooperation from others.
3.  People have limited sympathies: they highly value their own lives and those of a few friends and loved ones, but value less or not at all those of strangers or casually known persons.
4.  People are rational, in the sense that they can calculate the best means to their ends; but as to those ends themselves, they can vary greatly.
5.  People have no *natural* consciences that would inhibit them from doing violence to each other.

It is evident that these conditions do not characterize some mythical or far-off state of affairs, for the most part. It seems to me that they come pretty close to describing the way things normally are. Then if we add the defining condition of the state of nature, namely the absence of any government, the result, Hobbes argues, would be a truly terrible condition, which he describes as a state of war, and "such a warre, as is of every man against every man." By 'war' Hobbes did not mean a state of continual actual battle, but rather of "the known disposition thereto, during all the time there is no assurance to the contrary." It would be a state of continual fear and uncertainty, in which you could never rely on others to refrain from killing you just as it suited them, and destroying or carrying off your property whenever they thought they could get away with it—which, since there would be no army or police to protect you, they almost always could. The result of such a state of affairs, Hobbes goes on to say (in an immortal bit of English prose) is that

> There is no place for Industry; because the fruit thereof is uncertain; and consequently no Culture of the earth, no Navigation . . . no commodious Building . . . no knowledge of the face of the Earth; no account of Time; no Arts; no Letters; no Society; and which is worst of all, continuall feare, and danger of violent death; and the life of man, solitary, poore, nasty, brutish, and short. (*Leviathan,* chap. XIII)

It is important to see that Hobbes's result depends on all of these conditions: change any one of them and things might be very different. If people naturally loved each other, they would not be disposed to "invade for gain" and might share even their very last apple with a fellow human. If they had strong natural consciences ordering them not to injure people, they would not harm their fellows, however much they might like to. If they were irrational, it might never occur to them that they could gain advantage by violence. If nature were extremely generous, they would never need to seize the goods of others by violence, being able, as the philosopher David Hume (1711–1776) pointed out, simply to stretch out their hands and get what they wanted. Or if one of us were naturally a Superman, invulnerable to the worst others could do and able to wreak any havoc on them at will, then he might keep us in line by force. Finally—Hobbes's solution—if we had a strong government, then it could keep law and order by credibly threatening with punishment all those who attempted to gain their ends by private violence.

But there is a snag with Hobbes's solution. How could a group of totally lawless, unruly people set up a government in the first place? They would have to trust each other enough to get it going; but this seems to be ruled out by the other conditions. And which of the other conditions could we change? Clearly we can't change the fact that people are physically able to inflict damage on each other. And we can't change the fact that they are rational even if we wanted to, since rationality is an inherent part of human nature. There is admittedly the occasional case in which someone succumbs to the incantations of a mystical leader who turns the subject into a virtual zombie, and sometimes considerable nations seem to succumb in that way. But this is hardly a desirable solution, and in any case it is not, in the long run, a possible one at all. Can we, perhaps, change the emotional condition specified in point 3? This is a little more promising, since some people in history do seem to have attained a state of universal and impartial love of humankind. But it isn't much more promising, as evidenced not only by the fact that it is considered truly remarkable to achieve such a condition but also, more powerfully, by the fact that the different religions of mankind, which are the only widespread efforts devoted in substantial degree to inducing some such states in those who practice them, have—far from being outstandingly successful in getting almost all people to love each other in impartial fashion—themselves fomented as many wars against rival sects, infidels, and the like as any other cause of dissension, if not more. Think of the Crusades, the Thirty Years' War, and the war between Iran and Iraq which is going into its fifth tragic year even as this is being written.

## §4 THE "SOCIAL CONTRACT"

But two factors on the list are alterable to greater or lesser extent: the second, scarcity, and the fifth, conscience. We can improve our situation indefinitely with the aid of technology; and if conscience is not, as Hobbes insisted, a *natural* faculty, there is nevertheless a capacity for developing it by familiar psychological and sociological methods. We spend much time and effort training our children to respect the rights of others, and we are usually quite successful in those endeavors.

Might we be able to avoid the Hobbesian result with technology alone? Indeed not! Not only can we cynically observe that by now, technology is itself what makes the Hobbesian condition potentially worse than ever, but we must realize that technology, taken by itself, is not an available option here. For technology *presupposes* morality, just as does the emergence of government. To see why, consider that the fund of technical knowledge on which all material progress depends grows by constant intercommunication among hundreds and thousands of researchers: by the availability of books, journals, and now computers, and by myriad means of communication. Yet all communication, all social use of language, is cooperative. Similarly, cooperation at the most extensive level is required in the production and distribution of the goods that technology makes possible. From the people down on the assembly line to the board rooms of corporation magnates, all depend on each other in that vast, complex social activity by which we overcome scarcity. Now think of the degree to which all these interdependent activities are triggered just by say-so: "I'll do this while you do that"; "We'll meet at 2:30 in room 447"; and so on. Without further ado, without the signing of any contracts or appointing of any policemen, even perfect strangers accomplish useful cooperative tasks by these simple devices. Put all such little arrangements together and we have a store of human riches whose contribution to our lives is virtually inconceivable. And it all rests absolutely on our ability to depend on each other to refrain from violence. When that seriously breaks down, civilized life rapidly goes down the drain, in the manner Hobbes so eloquently depicted. But a necessary condition for these blessings is an understanding, an *agreement*—though not a signed one, of course—that we will do our respective turns in all the little arrangements we make, without the other parties having to fear for their lives in the meantime.

To see what is involved here, let us imagine our way back to the Hobbesian state of nature and consider the situation of the typical rational animal therein. Suppose that the individuals in that condition have all read their Hobbes and appreciate that all the conditions are fully met: people are thoroughly selfish, have no love at all for their fellows, have no consciences at all, and live in conditions where there simply won't be enough to keep bodies and souls together without cooperation. Suppose that a few people have accumulated modest stores of food and a bit of shelter against the elements. What will others who know this do? They can choose between attempting to grow or build something themselves, or they can devote energy to robbing the lucky ones. Which to do? If they try to satisfy their needs by honest toil, still others will descend on the products of their labors: kill a deer, and before they've skinned it their neighbors will have skinned *them!* And the lucky ones who do have something aren't saints either: they'd take the goods of others if they wanted them and thought that they had a decent chance to do so. For remember, by hypothesis no one has a conscience at all.

The continual likelihood of violence is clearly the major culprit in this miserable condition. Suppose that you, seeing this, would like to improve the situation. What can you do? There is but one way, in fact. We are all rational, freely acting beings with minds of our own. If we are to desist from violence, we must do so voluntarily. We must *decide* to do so. You, let us imagine, are prepared to. But clearly, there is no use in this if others will not do likewise. If you proclaim your own nonviolence, you will be a sitting duck for the others—a chump. And on the other hand, if you have no conscience and you find the others interested in your idea of nonviolence, another thought might occur to you: as soon as they all commit themselves to nonviolence, you hit them while their backs are turned and make off with their goods. Now *they're* the chumps!

If this sounds underhanded, devious, evil, and positively slimy, it should, for that's what it is. However, if we are to describe it thus, we must be invoking *rules* forbidding such behavior. But the state of nature has no rules! It looks as though our rational animal in the state of nature, despite the extreme immorality of its actions in our eyes, is merely doing its best under the circumstances. What is wrong?

What's wrong, as Hobbes and some modern thinkers have seen, is that each of the individuals in that condition is adjusting his or her actions in the light of the actor's own values, in complete independence of others. That is what it is to be in the uncooperative condition. In the absence of even the smallest shred of trust, what we know as morality is impossible. But in the absence of morality, everyone will be utterly miserable throughout a short life. Yet the cause of this misery seems to be a myopic concern for our own good. An exclusive seeking of our own good, regardless of others, turns out to be self-defeating.

There is truly a profound paradox here. As rational beings, we do seek our own good, whatever else we may seek. But in order to have any reasonable chance of achieving it, we must live with others, as members of a society; and in order to do that, we must forswear the principle of exclusive self-interest. It is in our interest to abandon an all-absorbing self-interest as a principle of conduct. Modern thinkers have given a name to the problem: the prisoner's dilemma. The name comes from the original version of the problem, in which two apprehended criminals are each given their choice between confessing to a major crime, thus implicating the other one, or remaining silent. If both remain silent, the prosecutor won't be able to convict either of them, and they'll get off with a small sentence for a minor crime of which he can convict them. If one confesses, however, he gets off scot free, while the other gets a major sentence. Finally, if both confess, they both get a medium sentence, heavier than if both had remained silent but lighter than that of the one who remains silent when the other confesses. In this situation, interestingly, it seems to be in the interest of either one to confess, no matter what the other does. For if the other confesses, and you don't, then you'll be worse off; if the other doesn't confess and you don't, then you get a light sentence; whereas if you had confessed instead, you'd get off scot free. Being rational, you confess. Being rational, so does the other one. But then you both end up with heavier sentences than you'd have received if you'd both kept quiet!

How is humankind in general in a similar situation? The answer is that if everyone else refrains from violence in the pursuit of self-interest, then you would do still better if you did not; for you would have not only the benefit of security from their aggression but also the benefit of successful aggression. Of course, you might not see this as a benefit, and some very great philosophers such as Plato would insist that you are right, that it *isn't* a benefit. But we have to worry about the next person, who would be delighted to make his way to a mansion in the Bahamas with your fortune, leaving your dead body behind.

Yet even that knave would be better off making an honest living than in a state-of-nature situation where he could depend on no one. Even he, if given the choice between *universal* acceptance of rules that forbade ready resort to violence and *universal* readiness to resort to it, would choose the former if he was choosing rationally. His preference for using violent methods himself is conditional upon others not generally using them. Otherwise, he'd have nothing to steal, for there would be no property; and anyway, he'd most likely be dead. It is difficult to believe that anyone at all would choose the Hobbesian state of nature rather than almost any ordered, civilized society one can think of, let alone ones we could imagine. And if anyone did, then consider the situation such persons would be in. Most importantly, they would not be in a position to complain about anyone else's treatment of them. Accepting no principles, they cannot appeal to any; and so if others do their worst, there is nothing for them to do but defend themselves as best they can without any attempt to appeal to the reason of their tormentors. We tend not to do this, in fact. Even hardened criminals and psychopaths get relatively benign treatment from most modern societies. But this, we should understand, is a generous concession on our part, not something we are required in justice to do. Such is the logic of the social contract.

To sum up so far: We have agreed with Hobbes that conscience is not natural, not a part of our basic constitution. But the argument is that, nevertheless, basic moral behavior is so essential to any society worth living in that, if we had such a choice, virtually any of us would choose to live in a moral society rather than an immoral one. Do we, then, have that choice in any sense? I think we do.

If we talk of "choosing morality," we can think of several different things that might be so called. One, of course, is choosing to *do* the right thing in a situation where we have the choice between doing that and doing what is wrong. Let us put that kind of choice aside for a moment, to return to it below, for it is obviously very important and, from the point of view I am developing, very difficult. But is there anything else? A second idea to consider is that of a "primordial choice," a sort of inner ceremony where we face up to our fundamental options and elect, as it were, to "marry" morality, for better or worse, for good and all. Some have indeed talked as though the social-contract view of morality required that there be such an act. Now, we need not deny that people could go through such an inner ceremony, nor indeed that they could be put through a formal ceremony to that purpose, by their society or groups therein—initiating young people into the responsibilities of civilized life, for instance. But it would be chancy, indeed silly, to rely on this as the standard activity of soul that all must be assumed to engage in if the idea of the social contract is to be realized.

But there is a third sort of thing, far more substantial, open to view, and universally available. There are, namely, the activities of *reinforcing* morality in others (as well as oneself): of praising and blaming, of sometimes intervening physically to prevent or to punish, and more generally of engaging in interpersonally witnessable acts of kinds relevant to supporting the institution, as we may call it, of morality. There is no question that people exert a good deal of influence on each other by these means, and in the case of the treatment of children by their parents, the influence is profound and extensive.

Armed with this three-way distinction, we can now turn to the question of whether someone who met the Hobbesian description as I have expounded it would rationally "adopt" morality. Now I suggest that we can see that such a person would indeed do so in the sense of engaging in the third type of activity. The agent would attempt to exert such influence as she or he could manage in the effort to get others to adopt the restrictions of morality in their behavior. Not to do even this would invite mistrust from others and, indeed, remonstrances and other uncomfortable reinforcements that we all know from social experience. Since it is greatly to our advantage to have others becoming moral in their actions and costs us little to attempt to get them to do so in these ways, the case for adopting morality in this sense is extremely strong. The case for going through an inner ceremony in the second sense is another matter, and need not concern us here. Perhaps in order to become moral in the first sense—that is at the level of action, of actually living up to one's commitments, doing the right thing—we need some such encounter deep within our souls. But we needn't assume this. Instead, we must ask whether there is any direct inducement to be moral in this first and most important sense. Here you are at the supermarket counter, the clerk is elsewhere or her back is turned, and you could easily walk off with a bit of free merchandise that you could really use but can't afford to buy. Why not do it?

Of course, if one's conscience has been developed in the way that one's parents and fellow members of society have been concerned to have it develop, then you will refrain because an internal monitor tells you that what you are contemplating is wrong. Or you might find it hard to believe that you really can get away with it; and in any case, it isn't worth the discomfort of making the calculation. And so on. But most fundamentally, I think, one will just reason that one knows full well that it is in the interests of everyone that everyone else not do things like this, and this reflection will cause sufficient discomfort to bring about the desired behavior in most of us. Not all, to be sure; but most. Rational people will see the wisdom of having people become the sort of individuals who won't do things like this and will themselves become comfortable with the image of themselves as that sort of person. This, I think, is a reasonable description of the mechanisms of morality in society, and it is such mechanisms, much more fundamentally than the police, on the one hand, or any "deeper" spiritual resources, on the other, that constitute the fundamental fabric of civilized society and make it possible. To advocate behavior substantially contrary to what is in this way in everyone's interest is irrational.

Many theorists and moralists are inclined to posit "higher" sources of morality or to insist that there is some deeper, "transcendent truth" about it that we have overlooked in the above account. The difficulty with such claims, however, is that it is hard to see what force they can have with people who don't find any such things in themselves. What do we do next, in such cases? The Hobbesian argument establishes, I think, a basis for morality that makes sense to everyone, and in so doing offers the only hope of truly universal principles. On this view, *morality is a sort of general agreement, a general setting of oneself to restrict one's pursuit of one's various ends provided that others do likewise, and to engage in behavior designed to secure recognition of and compliance with the principles justified by such considerations.*

Prominent among such principles, I have suggested, are those condemning violence. We are to refrain from pursuing our various ends by inflicting pain, harm, disability, and so forth, or of pursuing them in ways that run a serious risk of such effects on others. And we are to respect the property rights on their part, and not simply take things that are in their sphere of activity and over which they appear to enjoy nonviolently obtained control unless there is a reasonable basis of principle for such appropriations. But what are the limits on this kind of restriction? We turn to that interesting question next.

## III. PACIFISM

### §5 HOW WRONG IS VIOLENCE?

We must now ask what the proscription on violence is going to look like. Shall we say that all violence, for whatever reason and of whatever kind, is wrong? Or are we to say that on some occasions its use is legitimate and other times not? If so, how will we account for the exceptions in a principled way?

One view on this matter that has had many adherents down through the centuries has it that all violence, without exception and regardless of the reasons or circumstances, is forbidden. This is the view known as "pacifism"—though we should immediately note that the term is also used in other senses, most of them considerably looser and more general. The looser uses referred to hold not that violence is never allowed in any circumstances but only that (1) one must first be very sure to explore all the peaceful alternatives or (2) that only *military* violence, rather than absolutely all violence, is forbidden. On this latter view, war would always be wrong, but civil police use of firearms where necessary, for example, might not. These special views can be interesting, but I suggest that they are put in perspective by first examining the "extreme," more rigorous doctrine that is defined above. There are two reasons for such apparent myopia. First, the less restrictive views have serious problems of definition and specification. For example, in the case of view 1 above, how could we ever know that we had explored "all" peaceful alternatives? And what counts as an alternative? What about simply giving in, for instance—welcoming the enemy with open arms, inviting him to take over your government, kill whomever he pleases, and so on? If that is one of the alternatives envisaged, then the "looser" doctrine becomes identical with the strict one in practice. As for 2, there would be the question what constitutes an army? If people resist an enemy by taking up arms on their own, without organizing into an army, is that O.K. when organizing would not be? Why? The "pure" doctrine, on the other hand, seems (at least at first sight) much less susceptible to either sort of problem. Since it forbids *all* use of violence, we don't have to worry about whether a given case is over the line between the permitted and the forbidden. And we don't have to worry about justifying exceptions and thus appearing arbitrary, since there are no exceptions to justify.

Nevertheless, the pure view soon runs into horrendous problems unless we defend it on grounds, such as religious ones, that are generally judged unacceptable by moral philosophers. It is no use arguing that we must avoid all violence because God forbids it, since many people do not believe in God and many who do believe that God positively requires violence in some cases and permits it in many others. There would be no way of resolving such disputes, and in any case we cannot proceed by cramming controversial doctrines down the throats of those who don't accept them.

On what possible grounds, then, might pacifism be maintained as a doctrine for the regulation of everyone's conduct? Here we must immediately make a distinction between two basically differing ways of defending pacifism, which we will mark by the terms 'tactical' and 'ideal'. *Tactical* pacifism is the view that violence does not work, that other ways of dealing with a problem are always certain to be better. Tactical pacifism, in other words, specifies some goal or end other than pacifism itself and argues that pacifism is a good or the best or only means to that end. *Ideal* pacifism, on the other hand, holds that nonviolence is a supreme end in itself, or that it is a duty that transcends any consideration of other ends; considerations about whether it "works" or not are, therefore, out of place on that view. Let us consider each of these very different defenses in turn.

## §6 TACTICAL PACIFISM

The tactical pacifist concedes that we might be justified in using violence if it were ever really necessary for the defense of some legitimate right—the right to life, for instance. But this theorist maintains that it never *is* necessary. There is always some other way to deal with the threat. And any such way would necessarily be morally preferable. Therefore, violence is always wrong. We are obligated to avoid it if we can, and we always can.

But how does this type of pacifist know that violence is never necessary? What would he accept as establishing necessity? We can hardly deny that in any given situation in which most of us would resort to violent methods, some other way of doing it (defending ourselves, say) might conceivably be effective, especially if the right people tried to use those other methods. Some persons of incredible moral powers might be able to stare down the attacker. Some incredibly eloquent ones might be able, somehow, to talk him out of it. Miracles do happen, and miracle workers would be able to avoid the resort to violence. Yes—but how about the *rest* of us? Which is to say, how about practically everybody? We do not have miraculous or even terrific or extraordinary powers of will or persuasion, or superhuman courage. All we see is someone rushing at us with a deadly weapon or pointing a loaded gun at us. We don't have time to think up all the nifty spiritual strategies that people like Buddha or Christ might have been able to trot out at the flick of an eyelash. So far as we can see, it's either him or us. And the pacifist seems to be insisting that it always ought to be *us*. But why? The *other* guy is the guilty party, for heaven's sake! *He's* the one with the rifle. We were just going about our ordinary business, and this other person suddenly descends on us, bent on violence as we queue up to order our hamburgers. Isn't it outrageous for the pacifist to chastise us for doing what, in the circumstances, we had every reason to think was the only means likely to be effective in warding off the attack? In short, this type of pacifism seems to fail on the score of irrelevance, irrelevance to real life. The fact that a nonviolent defense could conceivably have been effective if used by someone else, someone with fabulous powers, has no tendency to show that you and I, ordinary people, were not justified in using violence at the time. Even if we could acquire such powers with a mere twenty years' intensive study at the right monastery in Nepal, why should we have to do that? They can just send the assailant to a monastery if they like —but why bother *us*? In short, what we think is that we have the right to go about our ordinary business—selling used cars, playing the oboe, milking the cows—without making fundamental changes to our entire way of life merely in order that some would-be murderer won't get clobbered.

I conclude that tactical pacifism fails because the pacifist's claim that violence is never necessary for any legitimate purpose is false, on any reasonable construal of it, or else irrelevant because it doesn't apply to *us*. Violence, alas, is sometimes necessary.

## §7 IDEAL PACIFISM

The most extreme view is that violence is wrong even if it is necessary, no matter what is to be gained (or lost) by using it. This is an intriguing position, certainly, even if it is unlikely to appeal to very many of us. Part of its interest stems from its apparent "purity," both in the sense that it seems theoretically simple and uncompromising, an assertion of a moral "absolute," and in the sense that people who practice it might strike us as exceptionally moral people. So it may seem. But I will argue that the first sort of "purity" is not necessarily a virtue, and that the claim to purity of the second kind is importantly dubious.

What makes us think the position is so theoretically simple and pure? Surely this: We all agree that violence is wrong, I take it. But if it is, then it's always wrong, whether done by aggressors or anyone else, since, after all, it is still violence. And violence is violence. Right?

Well, no, actually. It will be recalled that the definition we have provisionally adopted states that violence is the "intentional" infliction of damage, pain, injury, or death by forcible means. So far as simply describing an act as violent is concerned, our definition doesn't distinguish between one intention and another. But when it comes to evaluating violent acts as right or wrong, it makes all the difference. We do want to distinguish, for example, between the sadist and the dentist, even though both inflict pain. But the one does it for its own sake, just because he likes to see people suffer, whereas the other does it in order to fix your teeth. We are interested in the ends for which such things are done: Is it merely for personal gain? Or is there some more important end involved, such as the defense of someone's rights? And what about the special case in which the violence in question is a punishment for some heinous crime? Or will it be claimed that when violent criminals are forcibly subdued and imprisoned or even executed, the agents of the law are acting just as wrongfully as were the criminals themselves in murdering, raping, or whatever? Most of us will not, and should not, be tempted to answer in the affirmative.

Our consensus on this matter is strongly supported by the "contractarian" approach to ethics briefly set out above. In a condition of total amorality, anything goes, including the use of every kind of force and violence. It is reasonable to commit oneself to refraining from this unrestrained use of force only if others will also do so, for if they do not, then the point of the commitment is lost: namely, to enable one to live a good life. One cannot do that if others feel free to bash one's head in whenever it happens to serve their purposes to do so; and with such people, if nothing but counterbashing will be effective, then if one is to have any chance of securing that good life one must reserve the right to use force if it is necessary to prevent such depredations. A unilateral surrender of one's powers in those circumstances would be folly. The contractarian view clearly supports the right to use violence in such cases.

There is another quite influential argument to consider. It may be urged that readiness to use force is the cause of the problem in the first place, and that the only way to a good and peaceful life for all is universal abandonment of that readiness. If everyone were pacifist, the argument continues, then there would be no more wars, no assault, no violence. Therefore, the pacifist concludes, we ought to be pacifists. What about this?

But the argument is invalid. From the premise that the world would be a much better place if we were all to embrace code X, it does not follow that you or I or anyone ought to embrace X. For there may be other codes, Y or Z say, quite different from X, that would have the same effect. And in the present case, there are indeed other codes. Some of these may be mentioned simply in order to illustrate the logical point. For example, if we all embraced the doctrine that one should devote all of one's time to playing the oboe, the world would also be a perfectly nonviolent (if somewhat cacaphonous) place. It hardly follows that we should do so, though. But more importantly, there is the doctrine that one ought to refrain from violence *except when it is necessary to defend someone against violence.* For if everyone adhered to this view, then again we would have a completely peaceful world. If there are no aggressors, then there can be no defensive use of violence either. Thus the pacifist's premise does not support his conclusion.

But that's not all. For suppose that only some people embrace pacifism while others remain in the amoral condition, feeling free to use violence when it serves their ends. There would then be room to question whether embracing pacifism might not actually make things worse instead of better. For perhaps the aggressors, who would be deterred by the threat of counterforce, would not be deterred by the moral will and "purity" of the pacifists. What if some violent persons are egged on to even greater depths of violence by the sight of pacifistic people who won't fight back? If that was so, then the world might well have less violence in it if nobody at all were a pacifist than if some were and some were not. If all the nonaggressive people were prepared to use force in defense of their rights, then less aggression might be employed by people inclined to be aggressive.

Of course, it is difficult to know whether this is so or not. History seems to suggest that some aggressors, such as the Nazis, were not deterred by the prospect of nonresistance or of only nonviolent resistance, though they certainly would have been deterred by a really adequate counterthreat. These things are hard to prove, as I say. But unless the tactical pacifist, as discussed above, can prove his case, surely the argument remains with those who insist on a right of forcible defense. They should not have to allow themselves to be raped, murdered, enslaved, or pillaged on the ground that it *might* not have been necessary to defend themselves against such activities by means of the sword or the gun.

Those who refuse, on these ideological grounds, to defend themselves are also unlikely to defend others in need—why should the case of others be any different from one's own, after all? And this has made the pacifist, historically speaking, someone who is feared, distrusted, or even hated by his neighbors. It is one thing, however, to doubt that people can have good grounds for refusing to defend themselves, and another to insist that they have a duty to defend their neighbors. Whether we have in general such a duty can, I think, be rationally questioned. But it may also be agreed that if we think we have the right to defend ourselves and others, then we are quite likely to be willing to do so. Though it is wrong to mistreat people because they are pacifists, one can hardly much blame people for being unhappy with neighbors who would not, on principle, help them in what would very likely, if it happens at all, be the most crucial need of their lives —namely, the defense of those lives. It is on this ground that the moral stance of the pacifist is questionable. Courage and discipline are no doubt admirable qualities which the true pacifist displays in remarkable degree, but those qualities were, after all, displayed by Nazis as well. The question is whether the pacifist displays them on behalf of the right principles. Our reflections suggest that the answer is in the negative.

## IV. THE SCOPE OF DEFENSE

In the preceding discussions, I argued that the contractarian approach would establish the individual's right to use violence defensively, for example, in the defense of his or her own life. What remains to be asked is *how much* we are entitled to defend by force. Suppose a putative "aggressor," A, is concerned to acquire certain areas of land or certain natural resources that you claim to own. And suppose that A says, "Look here, I mean no injury at all to your person—nary a scratch, let alone death—so long as you let me use this land for my crops and animals, or this oil for my heat and energy needs. Nothing more than that!" And A moves in and starts milking what you claimed to be your cows, sleeping in what you claimed to be your bed, and so on. Now suppose that having told him in no uncertain terms to desist, and A having not taken the advice, you then point a gun at him, giving him his choice between going back where he came from or being killed. A then accuses *you* of being the aggressor: after all, you threatened to use force first!

The plot thickens, perhaps, when we consider that A might have needed your land or resources. A might be anxious to have only a smallish portion of your large holdings and points out that you could do very well with the remainder whereas he, A, faces a very bleak future, perhaps even starvation, if he doesn't have some of what you claim to be "your" resources. If all these things are true, then what? Must you back down?

It is hardly possible to turn this essay into a full-fledged treatment of private property, but just suppose that A, in the above case, is not an isolated individual or family but instead a state, and that you are a neighboring state. Then the extreme importance of the institution of private property for our concerns becomes obvious. It is not too much to say that almost all of the wars in history have been fought over property—over who is to control which pieces of real estate and/or natural resources. On the one hand, battles are fought on, and in order to gain, territory, and the winners (generally) have been those who gained the territory in question (or successfully prevented others from gaining control over it). And on the other hand, the major issues that started the war in the first place often consisted in claims and counter-claims to territory. Enthusiasts for socialism should note that states claiming to be socialist have been no more ready to cede pieces of territory to needy neighbors than have the capitalists, nor has their record been spotless on the matter of refraining from helping themselves to their neighbors' territory by armed force when the occasion offered. Of course they will make the new property "public" property —but it will be the public property of *that* particular state; let others beware!

Clearly, we need some grip on the question of which claims to territory and resources are legitimate and which are not, for otherwise we will be unable, in almost all cases, to identify the "aggressor" in a given conflict. If area X *belongs* to person B, we can then say that if A marches across the boundary of X with his army, then A is the aggressor. And if A marches in without his army but only his group of unarmed would-be farmers and oil explorers, then B will be in the right in refusing A admission and forcing him to stay out. But if there is no such thing as legitimate ownership, we won't be able to say any such things. Note that we will not be able to say them about *either* party: we won't be able to say that A is in the right any more than B. And so our general principle—to the effect that aggressive violence is prohibited while defensive violence is allowable when necessary to defend one's rights—would be useless.

## §8 NEGATIVE AND POSITIVE RIGHTS

But the situation is not hopeless. Let us first make a distinction, one that reaches very far in these matters. This is the distinction between "negative" and "positive" rights:

> *Negative:* This is the right of *noninterference.* To say that A has a negative right to do X is to say that others may not prevent A from doing X or interfere with A's doing it. To say that A has a negative right to a given thing, Y, is to say that others may not take Y, or use Y without A's permission. If, of course, A doesn't have Y or cannot do X, then there is nothing to be said about A's rights except in the cases where A had previous possession of which he has been wrongfully deprived. That would create grounds for a positive right to have Y returned to A.

> *Positive:* Positive rights are rights to be helped, as opposed to rights merely not to be hindered. To say that A has a positive right to do X or to have Y is to say that under certain circumstances (e.g., that A lacks a Y or lacks the ability to do X), others would have a duty to help (by supplying Y or the means to do X, for instance).

Most rights could be either negative or positive. The right to life, for example, is the right not to be killed (negative) or the right to be saved (positive), as by a lifeguard's assistance or a medical operation. Thus someone who argues on the basis of the right to life that we ought to give starving people food, or poor people with ailing kidneys the use of a kidney dialysis machine, evidently believes that the right to life is positive. But a purely negative right to life can always be sufficiently respected by doing nothing at all.

It seems clear that when people talk of "property rights" or "the rights of property," they usually have negative rights in mind. These are the rights of the "haves" rather than the "have-nots." However, along with such rights goes the right to exchange or give away one's property: a property right is basically the right to do as you please with the thing in question so long as your use doesn't interfere with the rights of others. If you own X and B owns Y and both you and B would prefer to have the other person's item, then your property right includes the right to make an exchange. And if we count among a person's resources (though it isn't ordinarily called "property") the capacity to do things, to work, then the have-nots can soon become haves, with a bit of luck, by virtue of exchanges of services for goods. A moral principle that forbade the transferring of property among voluntary agents, apart from things whose transfer could be dangerous to others (such as weapons), would be generally unacceptable from the contractarian point of view.

Theorists of property have also taken it that we have the right to acquire property by virtue of certain activities other than voluntary exchanges with people who already have it. One such way is by finding it before anybody else does, in a condition where no one else has any prior claims: "finders, keepers," as we used to say in my childhood. Another is by making it, where the materials employed have been satisfactorily acquired in some other way. This right to whatever one has made follows from one's right to use one's bodily and mental resources as one likes; and the right to use them thus is another that contractarians will be loathe to part with. In general, the contract idea gives substantial pride of place to liberty, the right to act as one thinks best; and this applies in the economic sphere as well, on their view.

But what about a rule requiring people to transfer property from the rich to the poor, or even simply from the better off to the worse off, in the interests of equality, say? Such principles are very popular in many quarters nowadays, as among socialists, though by no means only among them. But again, if you substitute nations for individuals, they are not widely respected in practice. The state of Libya, which claims to be socialist, would not look kindly on a proposal to force it to share its substantial oil wealth with its poverty-stricken neighbor Chad (unless it began by conquering the latter, perhaps), and the Soviet Union feels no compulsion to transfer a large part of its gross national product to neighboring China, despite the greatly inferior wealth of the latter. Curious, perhaps; but instructive: for these facts suggest that when it comes to action in the real world, such factors as need or equality, often identified with "justice" (as lip service, anyway), take a distinctly back seat to claims based on sheer "I was here first" historical occupancy. The situation is analogous to that of individuals and their bodies. As the well-known Harvard philosopher Robert Nozick has pointed out, we do not think that, in the interests of fairness, we have a duty to give up one of our good eyes to a blind person, despite the fact that he or she needs one good eye a lot more than we need our second good one. We certainly do not think that the blind person has a *right* to one of our eyes on such grounds. What we think, in fact, is that we have the right to our eyes, our limbs, the use of our minds, and so on simply because they are naturally part of ourselves. We take this to be a sufficient reason for asserting a right to them—no further argument is necessary. And neither do we think that poor nations have literally a right to the natural resources of rich ones (or to any of their resources, for that matter, except in the special case where it can be plausibly maintained that the rich ones stole it from the poor ones, which is not often true, rhetoric aside). States do not defend their territorial rights on the ground that it is somehow better in the universal scheme of things for them to have these rather than some other state; instead, they simply insist on the right to what they find themselves with. They were there first, and that's all that's required. Where they were not "there first," having conquered it some time in the past, their claim is shakier. "First conquest" is a clearly less respectable basis for title than first occupancy by peaceful means. Yet if the conquest took place centuries ago, the present claims of those allegedly displaced become correspondingly weaker as well.

## V. NATIONALISM AND THE RIGHTS OF STATES

### §9 HOW STATES ARE DIFFERENT

"First conquest," we have said, would not in general be an acceptable basis for moral relations among individuals. If twenty years ago I forced you off your land at gunpoint and now some new claimant comes along, my own claim is hardly going to carry much moral weight. Why should the situation of states be any different?

There *are* some reasons, though—for states, though home to individuals, are not themselves individuals, and that makes a difference. Consider the intermediate case where not I but my remote ancestors forced the then-occupant of what I claim to be "my" land off of it; since then it has been handed down from parents to children—in itself a perfectly peaceable and legitimate method of property acquisition. Now suppose that you make a claim against my land on the ground that it is stolen property, which indeed it was, these two hundred years ago. What now? If you are a direct descendant of the persons my remote ancestors extracted it from, it is hard to deny that you have something of a case—though even here it is by no means certain that it is quite good enough. What about all the improvements that my intermediate ancestors and I have meanwhile made? You can scarcely claim to be entitled to those as well, can you? And if you are a third party with no connection to that original owner who was unjustly used, it is hard to see that you have a claim at all—not to mention the far more normal case in which not *my* remote ancestors but only *someone or other's* were the culprits, since which event it has been bought and sold many a time. Now turn to the case in which an army conquered the region, centuries back. Individual soldiers did not occupy individual pieces of land, for the most part. And enough water has flowed under enough bridges so that now no individual could identify what he or she was supposedly deprived of, as an individual, by that conquest. To be sure, states can sometimes argue that their *people* have been deprived, collectively, of some sizable piece of territory—though even if they have, it might well be that they are no worse off than they would have been if their remote ancestors had not been forcibly expelled at all. It is hardly surprising that such disputes are often intractable, and they are very typical of the issues at stake in wars.

But one thing is clear: parties to disputes of this kind are certainly not going to "settle" the issues by going to war over them. Not, at any rate, insofar as they are moral or legal issues. If you kill half of my family and hold a gun to my head, giving me my choice between remaining (dead) or leaving (alive), that is not going to tell us whose claim to property, mine or yours, has the greater weight. And the same is true of war. It doesn't settle issues, or at any rate, not those. It determines who will in fact be in possession, who will in fact be left living and who dead—but that is all, and isn't quite what we wanted to know if what we wanted to know was: Who is right?

It may reasonably be asked why we should bother with the question of who is right. For once a state has in fact won its battles and acquired whatever it intended to acquire thereby, it may be said that it has what it wants and can leave abstract questions of right and wrong to philosophers. And this may once have been so—but not now. What if the state subjugated by our hypothetical winner asks some further, perhaps more powerful state for help? Or several other ones? What does the "winner" do now? Gird up to fight the lot of them? Or does it, perhaps, now decide to take its case to court or to the negotiating table? If the latter, however, we are back to questions of right and wrong, for those are precisely the terms in which these questions are negotiated. And in the modern world, resort to arms is increasingly hazardous; in the extreme case of the superpowerful nations, armed with atomic weapons, the hazards are positively apocalyptic. The negotiating table, the World Court, the United Nations Assembly, are far better arenas for resolving disputes than the battlefield. Why so? For two main reasons: no one gets killed and the enormous costs of arms are saved so that they may be put to better use.

Or at least they *may* be put to better use unless the state in question (or perhaps its citizens) become so enthusiastic about war—or about national power and image or some kind of ideology their state's power might serve—that they prefer the military life and its risks to those of peaceful life. Glory might be preferred to the comforts and pleasures of peaceful civilization. For centuries men have fought for their countries—their countries, right or wrong, as some are inclined to put it.

## §10 AND HOW THEY ARE NOT

Is this the right way to put it, though? Or do states really have the kind of status that justifies all this bloodshed? Is the state above morality? Is it, perhaps, the creator and arbiter of morality, so that what it says on such matters goes? If so, then men have not fought for their countries "right *or wrong*," for on this view their countries *cannot* be wrong. And it must be admitted that people have often talked as if that were so. When their country gets itself into a war, for instance, they have supported it with their lives—and have questioned their country's wisdom only when it appeared that it might lose the war in question—rather than asking whether its cause was just to begin with.

Is anything to be said for the view that the state is superior to individuals, and superior in such a way as to give it authority over their very lives? It might be said that the state is "prior" to the individual, that it is like your parents, only even more so, since it was the state that enabled even your parents to come together and bring you up, and so forth. [Thus argued the great Greek philosopher Socrates (ca. 480–399 B.C.), as reported by Plato in the dialogue "Crito."] And certainly it is usually true that the state got here first, as it were; and certainly true that it is a lot bigger than any one of us, or any association to which we might belong. But none of this takes the case very far when one thinks about it. The state may not have been prior to you: it may have come into existence two years ago. And did it enable your parents to marry? More likely, your parents managed to marry because the state did not use its enormous powers to hinder them in their case—as it did until recently in South Africa, for instance, should the couple happen to have been of mixed race. And bigger does *not* mean (morally) better. Nothing but force of habit and brainwashing by the state could make any sensible person think very highly of the moral character of typical states, even very good ones (comparatively speaking) such as our own. But the ultimate consideration here is simply that the state can be *remade*. It is not a natural entity, like a mountain range, but more like a corporation, which comes into existence by agreement; and if enough people do the right kind of things, it can be disassembled or destroyed and put back together again or conceivably even dispensed with. Its power is due to the will, or at least the permissiveness, of the many individuals it governs. This being so, those people are obviously in a position to make up their own minds about its merits. The basis of their appraisal of those merits need *not* be provided by the state itself.

It is nevertheless true that states are not individuals and that the actions of states are not (simply) the acts of individuals. States are collectivities or the representatives of them. So we must ask whether *that* makes any difference. Do large groups of people have rights that individuals do not? States can do things that individuals can't—declare war, for example, and pass laws. But it doesn't follow that there are no restrictions on their doing of those things. Quite the contrary: all of these actions of states are, in the opinion of people like ourselves, to be done for the benefit of their citizens. We don't exist for the sake of the state: it's the other way around! And just as we may not pursue our interests against other people in just any way we like, without regard for their rights, so too the state may not pursue its interests— which, in a properly run state, are our interests—just any way it wants. States that throw their own citizens into jail or torture them because they are inclined to criticize the government are wronging those citizens; similarly, states that murder the citizens of other countries simply because they want to rule over them or because they want their resources are wronging *those* people. Big people are not excused by their size when they kill little people, and big states should not be excused by their size when they kill the citizens of little states.

## §11 POWER AND POLITICS

Big states do differ in a crucial way from big individuals. In the case of individuals, as Hobbes observed, "the weakest have strength enough to kill the strongest"; but in the case of states, that is not (yet) so—though when every state, large and small, has nuclear weapons, it might become so! Meanwhile, however, we must ask whether this makes a difference. If, as my oft-expressed contractarian theory has it, morality is a sort of contract among basically equal individuals, then we might wonder whether there can be morality among states, which are not basically equal. And this is not an easy question to answer.

One important possibility is that it might not be necessary to an-swer it. For states are not superindividuals but artificial "corporate" beings. Real morality holds among all individuals, of whatever states they may be citizens, and if we can see that rules against killing and other forms of depredation done out of mere self-interest are valid because they are to everyone's good, why should we make exceptions when groups of individuals join together in those large associations we call states? States are *not,* I hasten to add, just "large associations"— for one thing, membership in them is typically involuntary. But this makes matters worse, not better. The acts of states, we might insist, ought to be measured against the standard of voluntary associations. If no voluntary association ought to be permitted to do X, then certainly no *in*voluntary one, such as the state, ought to be permitted to do it either. Anything else is just knuckling under to naked power. And thus we could simply insist that states be held to the standards of individuals because *we* come first.

Another and perhaps still more powerful argument is simply that the rules to be applied to states are the rules which every state would find it in its interests to support for the general governance of states' behavior, just as the rules for individuals (so the contractarian will hold) are the ones that every individual would find it in his or her interest to support for the general governance of individuals' behavior. If states insist on resorting to violence to pursue their ends, then other states will have to do so too, and the condition of international affairs will be one of desperate chaos. And every state that violates such canons of decent behavior is also unjust, for it has taken advantage of the forbearance of its neighbors who have refrained from attacking it long enough to enable it to acquire its newly found military power (for instance).

No doubt we may "have to" resort to the language and tactics of power politics in dealing with other states. But this is not because power politics is superior to morality. It is, instead, because of the nature of power: once force is resorted to by A, B may simply have no choice but to play the same game. It may, however, be a losing game for everyone, and the fact that it is so is one of the major things we may have against those powers who insist on resorting to war. War, we may say, is a sort of affront to decency, an outrage against those canons of conduct that make civilization possible and life worth living. Let's not let the superior power of states brainwash us into thinking otherwise!

Individuals are not to pursue their ends by violence, even if those ends be the promotion of what they think is the good of the people to whom they do violence. I cannot convert you to my superior religion at gunpoint, even if it *is* superior. The restrictions on conduct of states would, if the analogy is proper, be similar. State A would not be allowed to convert state B to A's favored political philosophy at gunpoint even if A's philosophy *is* superior. Thus America, a superpowerful state, may not invade some small state even if its intention is to convert that state to democratic government and even though democratic government *is* the superior kind of government. It will have to restrict itself to peaceful means of promoting that end.

That this is the form the restriction would surely have to take—if we think of the moral laws that are to govern the behavior of states on close analogy with those governing the behavior of individuals— is, of course, food for thought. What if A could get away with its forcible intervention in state B's affairs *and* the resulting government would really be a great improvement for B? What if B's citizens over-whelmingly approve of the intervention and its results? If the ultimate laws of morality stem from the interests of all individuals, then it is difficult to see why we should insist on *condemning* A's behavior in this case. Difficult, that is, until we have to react to the contrary case where state C forces *its* system of government on some small state, D. Then, suddenly, the fairness of this clause will strike us as self-evident!

Such reflections, perhaps, force us to a compromise. We shall in general condemn interventions by states into the internal affairs of other states except in those special cases where the other state clearly has an extremely unpopular government and the intervention in question would *both* (1) help to unseat the government in power, *and* (2) make it highly probable that it will be replaced with a very much more popular one at extremely little loss of life. This would be comparable, actually, to what we think about individual cases: If B is about to do something very rash, A might forcibly prevent B from doing this if what B does instead is very much better and B agrees that it is. This is a rare exception, and it would be rash to think that typical interventions in the past have met this standard, though not rash to think that perhaps some few of them have. And in any case, note that our principle is a very far cry from the idea that states may do whatever they please!

On the other hand, the right of self-defense, or in general of the defense of innocent persons under attack who agree to be defended by the agent in question, remains. But how far does it extend in the age of nuclear weapons? That is a dauntingly difficult question, to which we turn in the final section of this essay.

## VI. NUCLEAR WAR

### §12 A NEW ERA

When the first atomic bomb fell on the Japanese city of Hiroshima some forty years ago, it was appreciated by many that a new era in history had arrived. Why so? The Hiroshima bomb killed about a hundred thousand people outright, in a matter of a few seconds; about an equal number died lingering deaths from cancer, genetic diseases, and the like in the weeks and years following. Yet the "conventional" strategic bombing of Hamburg and of Tokyo killed even more. The difference is that whereas it took hundreds of airplanes dropping thousands of bombs to destroy those cities, the Hiroshima catastrophe was due to a single bomb dropped from a single airplane. Not long after, the thermonuclear bomb was developed, followed by high-accuracy long-range ballistic missiles. There were not enough explosives manufactured during the entire Second World War to equal the destructive power of a single larger thermonuclear warhead, and delivering all of those explosives to a single area would have taken a concentration and organization of planes and supply vehicles that could not have been accomplished at all.

It is often said that there are currently enough nuclear weapons to kill everyone on earth ten times over. And that is true; but there are probably enough bullets and guns to kill them twenty times. Even in ancient times, such large-scale killing could likely have been done with swords, arrows, and slings. Mankind has had the capacity to destroy itself for ages. The difference made by thermonuclear weapons and missiles is that in former times, a stupendous feat of organization would have been called for, and a very large number of highly motivated people; whereas now it would be comparatively easy to organize a similar slaughter with nuclear weapons. A very small number of people sitting in control rooms really *could* kill a very large portion of all the people on earth. And if recent scientific research is right, the aftereffects of the holocaust would include environmental changes that would, before long, bring death to the few survivors as well. Never before has it been technically possible to put so much destructive power in the hands of so few people.

Those people, in turn, are at the behest of governments, among which is ours. But we have some control over our governments. And so there is a moral issue, requiring us to address ourselves to the question of nuclear war and to take a stand. More than one question is raised, certainly. There are, I think, three major questions:

1. Under what circumstances, if any, would it be morally right to use such weapons?
2. Under what circumstances would it be right to *threaten* to use them?
3. How does one decide whether one is in either of those sets of circumstances? And, of course, what can or should we do to get out of them if we are in them?

Further questions are raised by certain answers to these. Would a morally responsible state disarm itself if it already had nuclear weapons? Or should it try to negotiate a mutual disarmament pact? Or should it try to match or even exceed the enemy's capability? Underlying all these questions will be fundamental issues about values. What sort of values would sanction the use of nuclear weapons? Is self-defense sufficient justification for employing such terrible weapons?

A major problem for our thought about these matters is that the technical situation is changing even as we think about it. On few current issues is the technical aspect so prominent. Thus we who lack expertise in these respects must tread carefully. But the stakes are so great that it would be outrageous to suggest that all of the issues must be left in the hands of "experts." We shall therefore simply have to be careful to identify our technical assumptions and consider how the issues might change if they should be upset by technical developments.

## §13 THE STAKES

Meanwhile, we should perhaps begin by considering what is at stake. Primarily, of course, there is the destruction of lives—our own, other people's, and possibly the human race itself. For present purposes, we can usefully divide the destructive effects into three different levels:

1.  *Restricted.* For want of a better one, I use this term to refer to levels of destruction comparable to those of past wars. Since the Second World War involved the deaths of nearly 50 million people all together, this category is not meant to be one we can slough off. But it perhaps means that we might be prepared to contemplate such a war without radically new reasons from those that obtained in the past.
2.  *Very Large Scale.* By this I mean destruction of an unprecedented scale—lives in the hundreds of millions and the virtual extinction of whole nations.
3.  *Universal.* By this I mean the eventuality that the human race as a whole would be wiped out—meaning, then, not only that everyone now living would be killed but also that no further humans would exist on earth until, perhaps, it reevolved after many millions of years. This level of destruction would not be due to outright blast or even radiation effect but (so we are told by scientists) to the alteration of the earth's atmosphere in such a way as to make the growing of crops impossible. Morally, of course, the mechanism doesn't much matter. The results are what concern us.

We will leave the first alternative to one side for present purposes —not because it is unimportant, needless to say, but for lack of space. Plainly it is an important question whether it would be possible to confine the use of nuclear weapons in such a way as to keep us at level 1. Most writers on these matters doubt it; but some think so, and we are hardly in a position to take sides on the matter here.

What all of these levels, but especially the second and third, have in common is that by any reckoning, nearly all of the casualties of a nuclear "war" would be *noncombatants.* One reason this is so is that there would be so very few combatants in a strategic nuclear exchange. A comparative handful of people on each side are the only ones who would be actuating the weapons. But the destructiveness of those weapons is of such magnitude that it would be impossible to confine it to those whose fingers were on the buttons. Moreover, the strategy that has been mainly in the public mind is one in which the missiles would actually be targeted at cities. Whether they were or not, horrendous casualties are to be expected; but this raises the interesting question whether there is a morally relevant difference between the case where we aim at cities and the one where we don't aim at them but nevertheless do as much—or even more—damage as if we had.

The third level involves the destruction of humankind as a whole. The question about this uniquely catastrophic possibility is whether it should be classed as *infinitely* evil—one, in short, that changes the moral picture entirely.

These, then, are the two primary questions that concern us. Could we ever be justified in taking actions that might result in the deaths of hundreds of millions of innocent persons? And could we *ever* be justified in taking actions that might result in the extinction of the human race itself?

The arguments in the preceding parts of this essay have supported the conclusion that a state is justified in going to war—*any* war—only for reasons of defense. Only defense, then, could possibly justify going to a nuclear war. Let us, then, begin by considering the facts about "defense" when nuclear weapons are in question.

## §14 "DEFENSE" IN THE NUCLEAR ERA

When we think philosophically about practical applications, we are in a mixed area involving both fact and theory. Sometimes, the facts are reasonably well known and it is unlikely that the central issues will change radically as the result of new technical developments. But with modern technological warfare, the facts are crucial and new developments likely, indeed normal. It is essential that we get a fair idea of where things stand now and how changes might alter the issues.

The most significant factor in the present situation concerns the way in which nuclear bombs would be "delivered" to their targets: namely, by means of guided missiles operating over comparatively great distances—from hundreds to thousands of miles. So important was the development of rockets and guidance systems that we might with justice have referred not just to the "nuclear era" but to the "nuclear missile era." The difference made by rockets is this: So long as bombs are delivered by comparatively slow-moving airplanes, it is at least technically possible to shoot them down and for those who sent them to recall them before they reach their targets. But with the main type of missiles, namely ballistic missiles, the situation alters radically. Ballistic missiles, such as the ICBM (inter-continental ballistic missile) and the IRBM (intermediate-range ballistic missile), are shot into the air by rocket motors. All of the aiming or guiding is done very soon after the missile is launched, and after this, it moves solely by inertial and gravitational force. It is simply thrown at its distant target, but thrown with amazing precision. Once on its way, it also moves very fast—something like 10,000 miles per hour in the case of an ICBM. Thus it has been assumed that it is impossible to do anything to defend oneself from an attack by such missiles: they cannot be shot down, and when they explode at their targets, nothing can withstand their awesome blast. Much of what follows will be based on this assumption.

But the assumption is now technically shaky. For one thing, among the weapons figuring in current nuclear debates is the "cruise" missile, which, unlike the ballistic missile, is a slow weapon (a few hundred miles per hour rather than a few thousand) guided throughout its entire course by on-board navigation devices. It's small and hard to detect by radar but nevertheless in principle reversible right up to the final few seconds before impact; if it is detected, it can (in principle) be destroyed by enemy fighters or antiaircraft missiles. In any case, it would afford hours of warning to the victims living in the target area. A more fundamental factor is the development of the ABM (anti-ballistic missile). Even as this was first being written, Americans successfully test-fired one of these devices. Tracking the incoming missile over its 4,000 mile course, they succeeded in literally shooting it down, using a countermissile aimed with truly incredible precision. To appreciate the problem, consider hitting an object with a frontal area of perhaps 3 square feet, moving at 10,000 miles per hour, launched without warning only 20 minutes earlier, and coming from almost any direction. That is what would have to be accomplished in a real war. In the test case, the problem was made easier by the fact that the testers knew precisely where the missile would be launched from and when. Whether a reliable ABM system that would be highly effective in a real war situation is in the offing can't be said with certainty, but if it is, clearly the effect on our problem would be profound. ABMs launched from hovering satellites—being worked on now, the so-called "Star Wars" weapons—would likewise change the picture. For the next several years, however, the situation remains that if a state equipped with nuclear missiles should want to destroy a city or other target with them, there is no way to literally prevent it from doing so. How does one deal with such an unprecedented threat? There are only two answers at present: civil defense and deterrence.

*A. Civil Defense.*   No one directly at the center of a nuclear explosion can survive it, nor can anyone within a certain radius from that center (depending on the size of the weapon). However, people occupying suitably designed and equipped shelters would certainly be able to survive if they were more than the critical distance from that center —a couple of hundred yards in the case of the Hiroshima bomb, a couple of miles in the case of even the largest thermonuclear bombs. A satisfactory shelter would have to have a few feet of earth on its roof, supplies of food and water to last the inhabitants two to three weeks (after which the initial radiation would have dissipated to a survivable level), and equipment to provide fresh air uncontaminated by radiation. There would also have to be an effective warning system, giving everyone (or most people) in the area enough warning of an incoming missile to enable them to get to their shelters. Doing that in the case of an IRBM or a missile launched from a submarine operating within a few hundred miles of the city in question, however, would be impossible, since the travel time of such a missile is on the order of 5 minutes

—scarcely time to discover that the missile is on its way, let alone warn everyone in time to descend to their shelters. But in the case of an ICBM attack, all of these are possible, and while the investment per person would be high, it would be within the means of a wealthy nation like the United States.

Civil Defense clearly could not save everyone in the event of nuclear attack. While it probably could save the great majority, at least under favorable circumstances, there is the question of what the survivors would do when they emerged from their shelters. Everything that made life worth living would be gone, and since that includes essential normal services, it is not clear how long they could survive anyway. These facts make it questionable whether Civil Defense is worth devoting much effort to; in fact, it has not been taken seriously by either of the superpowers or by most other nations, among which only the Swiss have undertaken extensive programs. (The Swiss are probably the last Europeans who would be objects of intentional attack in a nuclear war, by the way.) But it is an option nonetheless.

Interestingly enough, many liberals in the West have been opposed to civil defense programs on the ground that they make it look to the enemy as though one is preparing for war. Many have opposed the ABM for a similar reason. These remarkable reactions are further indication of the strangeness of the nuclear era.

*B. Deterrence.* Shields, castles, earthworks, fighter planes or antiaircraft batteries to shoot down incoming bomber planes—these are standard defensive tactics. The idea of defense is to prevent the attack *by force,* that is, by rendering the will of the opponent *ineffective,* making his attack unsuccessful for reasons beyond his powers of decision. Deterrence is different. Here the idea is to threaten the opponent with a response to his attack which is so unwelcome to him as to make it *unreasonable* for him to launch the attack. Deterrence and defense are different but not incompatible. At any time in history, a threatened group would be able to make a counterthreat, including the threat to beat off the attack so efficiently as to make it pointless to launch it. But at the present time, as we noted above, the situation is that no defense other than deterrence is possible. Threatened *nuclear* retaliation is not the only form deterrence may take. In principle, one could threaten something else: all that matters for purposes of deterrence is that the threat will "hit home" to the prospective opponent. In domestic cases, a threat of reduced affection, for example, can be quite effective! And in international cases, it might be possible, sometimes, to threaten massive *nonnuclear* retaliation. But since the effects of a large-scale nuclear threat are so enormous, including often the effective elimination of the victim's conventional retaliatory forces, it is generally taken for granted that nuclear retaliation is the form that an effective deterrent would have to take against a major nuclear power.

Massive nuclear strikes kill enormous numbers of people, almost all of whom, as we noted, would be noncombatants. Almost none of those victims would have been involved in defense industries, let alone in the planning or execution of any nuclear attack. Again, the advance of technology must be borne in mind. The latest missiles, we are told, can achieve target accuracy on the order of 50 yards instead of several miles, and the smallest nuclear bombs would have radii of destruction of similar size. So it may again become possible to target nuclear bombs on military targets with reasonable expectations of not hitting much else. That will change (and complicate) the situation considerably, especially since the old option of indiscriminate destruction will always be with us. Still, it remains the main case at present that full-scale atomic warfare would consist in exchanges of incredibly destructive bombs that would kill enormous numbers of noncombatants, and that is what presents the most pressing of the moral questions we must ask. We turn to them next.

## §15 EVALUATING DETERRENCE

Deterrence is the policy of maintaining enough of a military establishment to be able to credibly threaten the enemy with enough destruction to make it a bad deal from his point of view to mount an attack. If deterrence is successful, there will be *no* war. That is important, for if there is no war, there will be no casualties, whereas if there is "only" a conventional war, there will be plenty. In the Second World War, the toll mounted into the tens of millions—close to fifty, as we have noted. That is not so very much less than the lowest estimate of probable casualties in a major nuclear exchange between the US and the USSR—though it is a lot less than the highest such estimate, not to mention the numbers involved in the complete extermination of mankind.

This raises a most interesting and difficult question: How are we to reason regarding the value of deterrence? Let us contrast two approaches. On one approach, our planning should be based on the idea of minimizing the overall *expected cost* of war in human terms. This means that we are to minimize the likelihood of death (etc.) for all concerned. If war A would kill many less people but be much more likely to happen than war B, we have to take both these factors into account. The obvious (and standard) procedure is to multiply the likelihood of the war times the number of people likely to be killed and then act so as to minimize the resulting figure, which is the "expected cost" in deaths in the war in question. (One of the interesting subquestions here is how one weights deaths in the enemy country against deaths in one's own. A classic view holds that we should count them equally. But not our contractarian view. I leave the reader to think about this one!) Of course there would be other important costs besides deaths. We ignore these other costs only for brevity and not because they are unimportant.

A very different view, however, says that we should avoid the worse war regardless of its probability. This is a species of what theorists have called the "maximin" strategy: to maximize the minimum gain or, in this case, to minimize the maximum loss. So in our envisaged case, we should avoid war B by all means, even if it means a great likelihood of numerous deaths. I find the second view unattractive. And so, surely, will the contractarian moralist. If a given person wants to maximize his chances of a good life (and, other things equal, a long life), then if one policy gives him a 10 percent chance of being in a situation (a war, in this case) where he has a 1 percent chance of being killed while another gives him a 0.01 percent chance of being in a situation with a 75 percent chance of being killed, he will prefer the latter, which gives him an overall probability of death of 0.000075 as against 0.001 for the first policy—about thirteen times safer overall. How one applies probabilities to cases such as deterrence, where we are calculating the likelihood of human beings acting in certain ways rather than certain things happening to inanimate objects, is, of course, difficult to say; but it would be rash to suppose that we have absolutely no ideas about these things. The probability of war between, say, the United States and Canada next year is too small to calculate; the probability that there would be war between Germany and England in 1938, on the other hand, was surely substantial. 'Probability' sounds artificially precise, but some such notion is certainly needed and available.

There is a further point. The logic of deterrence is such that the enemy will not strike if he is rational. If he does his homework properly (and we've done ours properly too), then the "probability" that he will start a war is zero. What we are really estimating when we attach probabilities to enemy actions in a deterrence context is the probability that he will not act rationally. Still a serious problem, to be sure. Yet we should not be too hasty in assuming that our opponents are insane—a point we will revert to at the end. Meanwhile, however, let us look at another view, a very influential one, according to which these calculations may be dismissed on the ground that the very idea of killing the innocent is impermissible from the start.

## §16 DETERRENCE AND THREATENING THE INNOCENT: THE RELEVANCE OF INTENTIONS

Why is nuclear deterrence so controversial? The main reason is that when we threaten to drop nuclear bombs on those who threaten to drop them on us, we know that what we are threatening to do is something that will kill enormous numbers of innocent people. Since we know that would happen (so long as current technological assumptions are applicable), we can hardly shrug these deaths off as "acciden-tal." To be sure, it wouldn't exactly be *intentional* either: it isn't as though we were *trying* to kill all those people. On one strategy, how-ever, we would be doing just that, for on one view of deterrence, the idea is to threaten to kill enough of the enemy's population to make it unwise for him to attack. But even if we were just trying to destroy the enemy's war-fighting capability, the fact that we would also kill 50 million or so of his innocent citizens, and that we know we would do so, makes that fact seem a bit lame.

On some influential views, however, this question of intentionality is crucial. There is a principle, prominent in Roman Catholic circles but widely respected elsewhere as well, according to which the inten-tional killing of an innocent person is "absolutely" wrong—meaning that one is morally forbidden to do it no matter how much good might come of it. To kill intentionally is to kill either as an "end" or as a "means." Killing as an end is killing for its own sake—doing some act *in order* to kill. Sheer hatred of the victim or sadism would presumably be examples. To kill as a means is to bring about some other end by killing, as when someone kills a relative in order to get money left in a will or kills a politician to eliminate a rival for a desired office. Of course, the ends in these examples are bad or at least petty. But suppose that the end is the saving of many innocent lives or the forwarding of some project immensely useful to society? And what if, as may well be the case in a nuclear war situation, the object is to save the lives or freedoms of millions?

However, the doctrine we are considering makes an interesting further distinction. Some killings are neither means nor ends but "side effects" of otherwise legitimate acts done for otherwise good ends. These deaths are not intended by the agent but are nevertheless foreseeably the result of the proposed actions. The doctrine says that these are O.K. in some cases—namely, where the end is good enough and no alternative means to the same end are available. Because of this distinction, the doctrine goes under the name of the Principle of Double Effect. It raises two questions: Is intentionality that important? And does it help us out in the nuclear situation?

One problem that troubles this writer is that the intended distinc-tion seems obscure or even untenable. During an uprising, some inno-cent person ducks into a side street. You know that she will trip a wire by doing so, which will ring an alarm that will cause the wrong people to be warned; they kill many people and even secure the government in evil hands. Warning isn't possible, the issue is urgent and of utmost importance. You shoot her just in time. Means or side effect? You shoot her in order to prevent great evil, which suggests that it is a means and thus prohibited by the principle; yet her death is a side effect relative to the act of preventing the wire from being tripped. If redescriptions of our acts in this manner so greatly affect things, the principle seems suspicious. Few people really intend that the means to their ends should be killings—they'd rather that some other causal process were involved and would gladly use it if available. Means, that is, are generally unintended to be means. Why should supposed nonmeans (which are nevertheless foreseeable and where your action is clearly responsible for them) make so much difference?

It is worth noting that the Principle of Double Effect will get little support from our contractarian point of view. Would people consent to be used as means in some circumstances? The innocent woman in our example would, let us suppose, suffer from the regime that will get into power if the wire is tripped. She would not consent, just like that, to sacrifice her life to the cause of keeping it from power; but she might consent to be put at a certain risk of being so sacrificed if she happens to be in the wrong place at the wrong time. A large number of people addressing themselves to such an issue might well agree that the importance of this issue is enough to justify becoming a member of a sort of "insurance pool," where one accepts the risk of possibly being killed in unhappy cases like that in return for the greater likelihood of good government. The risk is especially acceptable if the result of the bad government's being in power is that many people will be tortured or executed unjustly and (1) she is one of the people who might be one of those victims while also (2) the chance of her being killed in the preceding turmoil is less than the chance that she will be one of the victims. This seems to me a compelling argument for many cases, and perhaps the nuclear war cases will be among them. Certainly the argument makes the means/side-effect distinction relatively unimportant. What matters is whether the risks work out to a good "buy" from the point of view of the affected parties. In order to extend a principle allowing such an action as the shooting of our innocent to all cases (what if she were an unwitting foreigner, for instance?), we would have to argue that all persons everywhere are to some minimal extent "in this thing together," so that the presumption might be made in the case of just anyone that the risks of being caught out in unhappy situations such as these are worth taking in exchange for the benefits likely to come to that person in the long run from the activities that entail such risk. Not easy, especially if one is out to attach precise numbers to the various risks involved, but not, I think, beyond the bounds of plausibility. On the whole, therefore, I am inclined to reject arguments asserting an "absolute" duty to avoid killing of the innocent. We may reserve the category of "absolute" prohibitions for killings (and many other harmings) that are done simply for the pleasure of the agent and involve no reasonable consent at any level by the victim.

## §17 A SPECIAL CASE: THE END OF HUMANKIND

Here is where the end-of-the-world problem looms large. If a war would exterminate everyone, then obviously it would have more casualties than any war that didn't do that; but that's not all. For it would not only kill more of the people who existed at the time (namely, all of them) but would also prevent the existence of indefinitely many more. Not, notice, *infinitely* many, for the world will certainly come to an end by some other means eventually anyway, when a stray comet crashes into it or the sun goes out or whatever. (If it literally were infinitely many, then the two ways of thinking would coincide, for infinity times anything except zero is still infinity; so the expected cost of a war which killed everyone would, on this reasoning, be infinite so long as there was any chance at all, however small, of its coming about.) So it is a very important question whether we should count all those "people."

Why the quotation marks, you may ask? Well, the thing is, you would not be literally killing any of those "people," for they haven't even been born yet. They do not, as we would normally say, exist, and you can't kill, or indeed do anything at all, to what doesn't exist. The most you can do is prevent its being the case that there ever is a person of the kind in question: there never will exist any of those people if we are all exterminated in the near future, hence no one whose life is snuffed out by any war, this or any other. *All* that will happen is that no such people will ever exist. The question is whether that matters. It is worth noting that it evidently won't matter to a contractarian theorist, for nonexistent people cannot be parties to any agreement. It is not as if we were negotiating with future generations to see whether we should give them the right to exist! On the contrary: *we* are negotiating with each other *right now,* to decide whether we should restrict each other to activities that would not run a risk of exterminating mankind. And this we will decide on the basis of how much value each of *us* happens to attach to the continued existence of humans. If we don't care much about that, then the possibility of universal death won't faze us that much; if we do, then it will. But of course we need a unanimous decision, and since presumably a fair number of people will not be much concerned about this possibility, it is hard to see how we could get much of a moral case for requiring *everyone* to have high concern about it.

On some other moral theories, things would be different. Certain kinds of utilitarians, for instance, would want to count everyone equally, including, in a sense, people who don't presently exist. For them, if a given policy would bring it about that there is a happy person in the remote future, then that would add just as much value to the world as would be subtracted if we were to kill one happy person now (rather more, actually, since the happy person who exists now has already lived a good deal of his life and so would lose less than the future person who hasn't even begun). This is not, unfortunately, the place to discuss these problems at length. Suffice it to say that they make a lot of difference to the present subject.

## §18 SELF-DEFENSE AND DETERRENCE

Having looked at and rejected certain important arguments against the legitimacy of nuclear deterrence, let us now return to the central issue. Our question is when it is reasonable to build up a military establishment that includes nuclear weapons. This is a special case of the more general question of when it is reasonable to take up arms of any kind. Given the strong right of self-defense argued for earlier in this essay, the answer would seem to be that it is reasonable for a given person or state, A, to do this whenever the actions of some other party, B, are such as to make it reasonable to believe that B would attack A but for A's ability to defend itself. In that case, our principle would normally say that A may assemble a military force of sufficient strength to defeat such an attack. But a massive attack by nuclear missiles cannot, we are assuming, be "defeated," and thus the question is more complicated in this case. We shall have to extend the principle to say that A may assemble a military force of a magnitude sufficient to *deter* a rational opponent from launching the feared attack. (We consider the special case of a supposedly irrational opponent in the next section.) Whatever that magnitude is, if A's force becomes appreciably greater than that, then A gives B reason to fear that A may become the attacker rather than merely the defender, and thus gives B reason to engage in an "arms race." But arms are both expensive and dangerous, and it is not in the interest of any party to waste money or incur unnecessary risks. Thus we must say that A may assemble a military force of a magnitude *just* sufficient (that is, sufficient and no more than sufficient) to deter B's attack. We may also note that if state B is rational and knows that state A can defend itself successfully against B's proposed attack, then it will not attack, which means that it will have been deterred. Thus our principle of deterrence will cover our principle of defense, and we needn't say that A may assemble enough force either to defend *or*, if that is impossible, then at least to deter, the attack in question. This, then, is the complete statement of our Principle of Self-Defense (as addressed to states):

> *Whenever a state reasonably believes that another state intends, and has the capacity, to attack it, that state may assemble and maintain a military force just sufficient to deter the other state from rationally attacking.*

Two points need to be noted about this principle. First, it is only a principle of *self*-defense as it stands. We should need to think further about a principle allowing state A to defend not only itself but also its friends. Second, and for the same reason, it does not address itself to the possibility that B might deserve some kind of punishment for its aggression if attempted. It is an important question whether such a function as punishment is ever legitimate as a war aim, but if it is, it goes beyond the immediate purview of defense. We cannot become involved deeply in these matters, but my inclination would be to argue that the defense of friends is straightforwardly legitimate provided they really want the defense in question, and that the punishment function is at least prima facie unacceptable. (If a nation goes to war knowing that the other side is bent on punishing it as well as defeating it, it has an incentive to fight to the bitter end instead of settling on a less bloody outcome—as illustrated by Japan in World War II and by the Iran–Iraq war, which is in its fifth year as this is written.)

Applying this principle to the special case of nuclear arms, then, we would first have to ask the factual question whether an adequate deterrent or other disincentive to the use of atomic weapons can be provided by any other means than assembling a nuclear armament oneself. It should not be assumed without further investigation that this is never possible. If we suppose some small and weak state—Pakistan, for example—equipped with but a modest number of smallish nuclear bombs and no missiles to deliver them, attempting a nuclear threat against some major power such as the USSR, we can well imagine that it would not get very far even if the USSR had no atomic weapons at all. On the other hand, given a USSR armed with a truly formidable array of modern nuclear warheads and missiles, it is certainly within reason to argue that only a comparable array of the same weapons could provide a sufficient deterrent—*if* that is, we have good reasons for believing it to be bent on aggression. In principle, therefore, I do not see how we can reject deterrence. Where it is necessary, it is morally justifiable.

## §19 THREATENING AND DOING: THE PARADOX OF DETERRENCE

At the outset, we distinguished two issues: (1) When are we justified in using nuclear weapons? (2) When are we justified in threatening to use nuclear weapons? In the Principle of Self-Defense formulated above, it would seem that we have answered only the second of these two. The difficulty, in brief, is this. Suppose that an enemy has fired off a salvo of nuclear missiles. When they arrive, a few minutes from now, your country will be destroyed pretty completely. You have attempted to induce him not to do what he has just done by threatening to reply in kind. But you have failed in this attempt—the missiles are on their way. Do you now carry out your threat? If you do, the world will contain two ruined countries instead of one, but that would seem to be all. True, the other country will have "won" the "war" if you don't retaliate, although it isn't going to do him much good, since anything of value your country might have to offer is now destroyed and the countryside uninhabitable for a long time to come. This will doubtless be a very depressing prospect, but it is not clear that sour grapes is a sufficient justification for killing a hundred million innocent people, even if you get a few guilty ones along with them.

In some cases, there might actually be some use in replying. If the first round of missiles is not enough to destroy your country completely, you might be able to destroy his second round by firing yours off before his have arrived. In that case, it might be worth doing, though the costs are very high relative to the benefits, since your country will be in very bad shape after this first round and you almost certainly won't succeed in preventing him completely from firing a second one. Moreover, your replying round will very likely cause him to fire what he has left of that second round, which he might not have done if you hadn't replied. In either case, you will face the same paradox at some point—a point likely to be in the very near future!

What are the other alternatives?

1. You might be punishing the enemy for his crimes.
2. You can claim, simply, that you are carrying out a threat which you were justified in making. Rather like keeping a promise.

How much difference there is between 1 and 2 is questionable, but there would seem to be at least a conceptual distinction. So let's consider them separately. The trouble with 1, as the preceding discussion suggests, is that virtually all the people you will kill if you reply in kind are *innocent* people. What business do we have punishing them? The USSR has been notorious for punishing ten innocent people to get at one guilty one, but the present occasion doesn't seem much of a time to be emulating them in this particular injustice. We could try to modify the claim of innocence, perhaps. We could perhaps suggest that every citizen of the USSR is guilty of complicity, complicity in a government that could commit such a monstrous crime as it will undoubtedly have committed in our imagined case. (It is, I hasten to repeat, purely imaginary, but the image seems to have a lot of appeal in the contemporary Western mind.) But are they guilty enough to judge it a capital crime? Hard to believe—especially since the typical citizen of the USSR has even less control over his country's policies than the typical citizen of the United States, Canada, France, or any other large modern country. All in all, it's going to be very difficult to square the claim to be "punishing" all these people with the demands of justice.

There remains the second alternative. We have argued above that we must be justified in making nuclear threats in some circumstances, namely those in which an enemy is really ready to engage in nuclear aggression. The justification consists in the fact that you have no other alternatives: the prospect of nuclear aggression, given that the enemy has gotten so far as to set up a formidable nuclear establishment, is one that leaves us helpless except in this one way—namely, deterrence by threatening a reply in kind. If the enemy is rational, he will not commit his aggression if he believes that we will destroy his country if he should attack first. Why, then, did he do it in the present case? The main likely reason will be discussed further below—namely, that he fears that *we* are about to do it to *him*, so that he doesn't really view it as "aggression." Apart from that, he may have had a temporary lapse of rationality—always a possibility to worry about. That's one of the principal problems about sophisticated weaponry: it's so interesting that there is a temptation to use the things just to watch the show— fascinating! And then there's the very real possibility that he doesn't actually believe you will carry out your threat. For he may have read this very essay and realized that his enemy will be faced with a grim moral dilemma, the very one we are now discussing. He may conclude that any rational person, especially any *nice* rational person such as ourselves, would refuse to push the buttons at the crucial moment, since we will perceive that it can do no good.

This last point, however, may contain the seeds of our reply. We may say that *if* we are correct in deducing from the right of self-defense that we have the right to use deterrence as a strategy in situations of nuclear threat, *then*, and just for that reason alone, we also have the right to carry out the threat in the stipulated situation. A threat is, as noted above, rather like a promise. In fact, the present threat carries with it a promise, for we say, in effect: Look here, if you don't drop those things on us, then we won't drop them on you. But if you do, then we will too, and don't you forget it! Theoreticians who have addressed themselves to this awful problem over the past forty years have all stressed the need for a highly automatic reply to an enemy salvo. Ideally, they have suggested, we should have a "dooms-day machine," wired so that we *can't* undo things. Once the enemy missiles are on their way here, it will be impossible for us to change our minds or intervene. The outgoing missiles will simply be shot off, automatically, and we will be able to say truly that it was beyond our power to avoid responding in kind.

The doomsday machine is a chilling prospect. A major disadvantage of it to begin with is that it is difficult to see how one could wire such a machine to distinguish between an accidental enemy salvo and an intended one. (Wouldn't we want to make that distinction?) The United States does not have a doomsday machine, but it does have a cadre of people in charge of the buttons who would certainly push them if asked and a set of highest officials who would be hard put not to order them pressed in the appropriate circumstances. No one believes that the American deterrent is not credible; likewise with the Russian deterrent. The present point is not whether they are or not but whether we can properly criticize a nation for mounting such a threat if, as we have been assuming, it is literally the only thing it can do to defend itself. It is hard to see how we can.

Nuclear war is monstrous, and nothing brings out its monstrous nature more compellingly than reflection on this very question. Nothing makes it clearer, too, that we would be very well advised to find a solution that would involve disassembling all these frightful weapons rather than keeping them at arm's length.

## §20 HOW MUCH DETERRENCE?

The Principle of Self-Defense proposed above has it that one may assemble a nuclear capability that is "just sufficient" to deter a "rational" enemy. "How much is that?" we must now inquire. NATO countries, and most especially the United States, are currently spending an enormous amount of money on arms, both nuclear and conventional. From the point of view of the taxpayer, the question whether it is the right amount is obviously important. Americans, for example, are currently spending well over $1,000 per person per year on "defense." That's $4,000 per typical family—probably a good deal more per typical middle-class family and much more again for high-income families. If they could get by with a good deal less, it would make a major difference to everyone, so this issue is financially important to all. And if it turned out that their spending is counterproductive, that they are actually making themselves less secure rather than more so by all this expenditure, then that would be still more important. Naturally, questions about the security of other nations whose independence is important to us will also arise, among many others. Still, the immediate and major purpose of defense spending is security for the parties in question, and considerations immediately relevant to that will probably determine the issue for most of us. There will sometimes be a conflict of interest here. Defense industries get secure and lucrative contracts from government to build expensive arms, and the livelihoods of many, many workers, at least in the short run, will depend on them. Yet to vote in favor of a huge arms expenditure on the ground that it will promote employment in a certain area is to allow a much less important issue—just what one is going to do for a living—to determine a much more important one—whether you and everyone else are going to get fried to a crisp, irradiated, vaporized, or otherwise disassembled by nuclear explosions. And since it is not just your money but everyone's, extracted from them involuntarily by taxation, the moral issue here is substantial. When one thinks about this issue, one must forget where one lives, how much one enjoys designing fancy and technologically challenging weapons, or how much money one could make by selling them to an eager military bureaucracy, and address oneself to the clearly essential.

We may note in passing a further morally interesting aspect of the nuclear problem: nuclear weapons are (comparatively) cheap. Killing people with conventional weapons, or defending yourself by means of them, is immensely more expensive than having a few nuclear warheads and missiles around. And notoriously, the NATO nations have opted for nuclear defense in considerable part because of the greater cost of conventional arms and armies. But it could be argued that we ought to be willing to spend more if doing so would secure us without resorting to nuclear arms. Others, of course, insist that there is no way we could secure ourselves adequately without such resort. And so it goes. Would it be possible to attach dollar amounts to these considerations? And if so, which way would they go? It is not easy to say. For present purposes, we are assuming that nuclear deterrence is literally indispensable, but the assumption should be recognized to be a debatable one.

Meanwhile, the question is: How much is "enough"? Clearly this is not an easy question, and clearly too it will depend much on the particular character of our presumed enemies. But let us at any rate consider the possibilities. To put it in somewhat oversimplified form, there are five:

1. Superiority: more than the enemy has
2. Equality: the same as he has
3. Inferiority: less than the enemy has, but still quite a lot
4. Minimum deterrence: just enough to make it unwise for the enemy to attack
5. Nuclear disarmament: none (but retaining conventional capability)

Let us consider each—reserving the third, which I propose to advocate, for last.

*Superiority.* Our preceding principle virtually rules out superiority, even if it were technically possible, which no one thinks it is, at least for long. The other fellow always catches up, owing to the rapid dissemination of technical ideas. But worse than that, superiority seems sure to be "destabilizing," as the current terminology has it. If you get way ahead, how is the other party to know that you aren't planning something quite a lot more than just defense? If nation A is building up its missiles to the point where it could contemplate a "first strike" —that is, an attack which would destroy all of B's missiles, with some of A's left over for further attacks—then nation B would have a motive to attack now before it's too late. And obviously superiority gets you into an arms race, for A and B cannot both be superior to each other. There is no end in sight along this route—except, eventually, all-out war.

*Equality.* This would seem to be the natural option, and certainly no country could plausibly deny its enemy the right to an equal nuclear establishment, given that the alternative would seem to be acquiescence in an inferior position. By and large, equality is the stance that the USSR has insisted on during the atomic era. It is the cornerstone of arms negotiations, and in view of the importance of negotiated peace, it is worth a special note. I shall then go on to explain why the correct alternative is, contrary to what almost everyone seems to think, the third one.

The international arms race represents the most outstanding case of a "prisoner's dilemma" situation, of which the Hobbesian state of nature was our theoretical starting point in this essay. In such a situation, each "player's" best alternative is the other player's worst. If A has nuclear bombs and B doesn't, then (or so A thinks, anyway) A can lord it over B if A wants to and B can't do anything to A; and vice versa. However, if both have atomic weapons, then both are worse off than if neither had them, for atomic weapons are frightening, dangerous, and expensive. At their best, they are useless, for each nation fervently hopes that neither side will ever employ them—but that's where they'd be if they didn't have them at all! If their purpose is defense, then if they are successful, the objective situation will be that they have wasted hundreds of billions of dollars over the period of their deployment; if they are unsuccessful, their countries will lie in ruins and all will have been lost. The alternative situation, where neither has them, is far, far better from each country's point of view. But how to achieve this happier state? The only possible way is by an agreement: each must agree to forgo nuclear arms provided the other does. It would be irrational to abandon yours if the other fellow doesn't, for then he has the drop on you. But if we could agree, that would seem to offer the best outcome. Of course, it is an agreement which we would have to be sure the other party was keeping, for otherwise we might as well not have bothered.

And it is precisely this consideration that has led to the demise of many of the attempts to negotiate an end to the nuclear weapons era. A decides that B's proposal is unacceptable because A could not be sure that B would live up to its provisions unless B allowed A to have extensive on-site inspections, and B refuses to allow this (or seems to!).

But this is not the only cause of breakdown in serious negotiations. Many Americans are probably unaware that the history of the nuclear arms race has, by and large, been one of American technological leads followed by (more or less successful) Russian efforts to catch up. American generals and candidates for president have represented those Russian efforts as being hugely successful, clearly enough to justify the expenditure of enormous amounts more of your money to enable America to do some "catching up" on its own—though a few years later it is admitted that what they really did was to get ahead, the original estimates of Russian strength having somehow been mistaken. Occasionally there has been a genuine Russian "first," but those have been the exception, not the rule. Meanwhile, a problem arises: how do you judge when the two superpowers are "equal"? Each claims, and must concede to the other, the right to be equal. So when the other side seems to have any advantage, negotiations incorporating the retention of that advantage are doomed from the other's point of view. And so it goes. The fact is that arms treaties have been seen by each side as an invitation to look for loopholes, and even when the treaty is signed, consequently, the arms race does not stop. Anything not covered in the agreement is treated as a happy hunting ground by the designers of war equipment.

It is evident that so long as both sides have this attitude, the arms race will not stop in the foreseeable future. It is likewise evident that a negotiated settlement is the only obvious possibility. Something must change!

*The "Minimum."*   Each side in the present conflict of superpowers is equipped with enough warheads to kill everyone in the other's country several times, it is often said. In fact, neither can do anything of the sort, for people will not obligingly sort themselves into convenient clusters so that there won't be any left over to occupy the stretches of territory that would be left even if 25,000 nuclear explosions were set off in the 8 million square miles of Soviet territory or the 3 million square miles of American (or 7 million of American plus Canadian!) territory. Nevertheless, each side could destroy pretty thoroughly all of the major and minor cities of the other, and that's plenty of damage by any conceivable standard. And that's the job that each side could do several times over. Under the circumstances, therefore, there is a question what constitutes a "credible deterrent."

If you are deterred by the prospect of having all of your major and minor cities destroyed once, will you be further deterred by the prospect of having them all destroyed six times in quick succession? Obviously not. For that matter, wouldn't all your major cities be enough? (Especially since all the leaders of each country occupy major cities!) Indeed, if you were a responsible leader, wouldn't you be very uncomfortable at the prospect of having even just all your minor cities destroyed? Obviously the question of how much is enough is impossible to answer precisely. Unless it was a pretty large amount, there would always be the worry that maybe it wasn't quite enough. And if it was, then where is the sense of "minimality"? Why would it then be an improvement?

Further, if you retain what you consider to be a minimum, and even if the other party considers it so too, then you would seem to be committed to aiming at the enemy's cities, which is sure to cause maximum civilian casualties, rather than at his military establishment, which presumably would cause less. And despite the difficulties noted with the idea of double effect, few of us would prefer knowingly to *aim at* the innocent, even if we know they will be hit.

*Unilateral Nuclear Disarmament.*   Many have advocated this seriously, but we should begin by dividing the advocates into two classes: those who base their case on out-and-out pacifism and those who do not. I shall take it that our preceding deliberations sufficiently answer the former. What about the latter? In believing that conventional defense is morally preferable, they may be relying on special arguments about the illegitimacy of nuclear arms which I hope also to have dispelled. If not, then there is the question whether conventional war is all that much preferable. First, it is not certain that the enemy would refrain from using nuclear weapons just because we do. And indeed, if he sees us engaging in an enormous arms buildup in, say, Central Europe, then what is he to think? Would that not make him as nervous as a nuclear buildup? And second, conventional war is quite capable of killing civilians as well as soldiers. In the Second World War, more than half of those 50 million lives taken were civilian. Maybe the next conventional war would be different, but how do we know? Finally, there is the very difficult question whether nuclear deterrence is necessary.

Of course we do not know for sure whether nuclear deterrence has worked. There has been not the slightest bit of actual fighting between the two superpowers since the end of the Second World War, now over forty years ago—the peace following the First World War, remember, lasted a mere twenty-one years—but this *may* be for other reasons than that each side dreaded the possibly nuclear consequences of battle. On the other hand, it is difficult to quarrel with the fact that there has been no war, nor does anyone who knows much about it really think one is likely any time soon *unless* someone does something really stupid . . . And then there is the question whether war would have been resorted to if there were only conventional arms to contend with. Although that is an imponderable, the logic of nuclear deterrence asserts itself rather strongly here. Would *you* start a war, no matter what you otherwise thought you might gain by it, against an opponent armed with an unstoppable array of nuclear-tipped missiles?

*Inferiority.*   Whatever the precise answer to the question of how much nuclear weaponry is necessary for deterrence, there is one thing we can be reasonably sure of: it'll be much less than what is presently within the capability of the *other* side. So far as deterrence is concerned, it seems, we would have literally nothing to lose by retaining an arsenal substantially smaller than that of the Soviet Union, for instance. Indeed, it seems hard to deny in general that for any possible nuclear superpowers, A would have nothing to lose by having less than B, down to the point where B has so little that A requires no atomic weapons at all, since a single nuclear bomb could not eliminate the conventional capability of any modern country and A, we are supposing, has retained such capability.

But retaining a lesser capability would have enormous political advantages. For the moral stance of a country following a policy of inferiority would be one that made it clearly impossible for the other side to justify its own policies by insisting that it is only trying to "catch up," only trying to achieve equality. So long as A makes a point of being clearly less than equal in all measurable respects, B would have no case at all in any negotiating context. If B persisted in an arms race, then everyone would know whom to blame. (And why would he persist? For it would only be an invitation for A to keep one step behind, and one step, as we know, simply isn't enough if a disabling surprise attack were contemplated.)

Bear in mind that the above argument is not an argument about rights. Obviously we cannot say that each side has a right to the other's being inferior! The argument, rather, is that superiority is clearly not permissible and that equality seems to lead only to an indefinitely continued arms race that must end either in disaster or at least in a stalemate at fabulous wastage of human effort. The argument is, in short, that inferiority is the right moral strategy in roughly current circumstances. Only it can combine real deterrence with any real prospect of eventual disarmament.

## §21 SIZING UP THE ENEMY'S INTENTIONS

This entire section on nuclear war has been predicated on the assumption that a country might be faced with identifiable "enemies" equipped with nuclear weapons that they would use, given opportunity, to conquer their opponents. But the practical question for the citizens of Western countries at present is whether we are now faced with such an enemy. The Western nuclear arsenal has roughly the following history. At the end of the Second World War, by which time substantial mistrust had arisen between the Soviet Union and its erstwhile allies, the Americans had developed the atomic bomb, primarily out of fear that the Nazis would develop one first. They then used the bomb in order, as they supposed, to hasten the defeat of the Japanese (whether this was effective or necessary is much debated by historians). Meanwhile, the Soviet Union did two things that made the West nervous: it retained a far greater conventional army than the Americans did (American fighting strength was rapidly and drastically reduced after 1945), and it set about securing its European frontiers by seeing to it that Communist regimes came to power in eastern Europe. It used its military presence, which it had by virtue of its role in the war against Germany, to assure this insofar as necessary. Americans concluded that the Russians were out to conquer the rest of Europe too, if opportunity presented itself, and they concluded that the only way to stop the Russian hordes was by opposing them with the threat of nuclear weapons. In fact, though, this became an economic argument, for the fact is that between western Europe and the United States there was no problem about the capability of matching Russian conventional strength except that it would be much more expensive than nuclear weapons. And then, of course, the Russians got the bomb too, and that led to the arms race, and so it has gone.

But the West's strategies obviously depend on mistrust. The leaders of the Soviet Union profess only peaceful intentions, but the West does not believe them. We insist that they are out to dominate the world and to force their political and social system on everyone else, contrary to all such professions. But why? Obviously this is a complex matter, which cannot be investigated in this theoretical essay. But there *is* a theoretical point of importance here. Grant that there are serious disagreements between the superpowers on ideological matters. Where, then, do we go from here? Neither approves of the other's political system, but our interest in continued existence is much greater on both sides than our interest in forcing the other one to come around. Accordingly, we estimate the other's aggressive intentions by looking at the size of their military establishment (roughly speaking: many logistical considerations come into it, of course). The maintenance of a mighty arms establishment, and in particular of one that is clearly more formidable than the other's, is prima facie evidence of aggressive intentions under the circumstances. The American army is not evidence of aggressive intentions against the French, because the Americans and the French are friends. But it is evidence of aggressive intentions against the Russians, because they are not, in the same sense, friends—that is, it will understandably be so taken by them.

In a situation of this kind, someone must take a step. Someone must show that his professions of nonaggressive intent are meaningful, and he can only do this by forgoing the temptation to try for superiority (unattainable in any case, as we know) in arms, especially in nuclear arms. We must put a more "charitable construction" on what our supposed enemies do than we have. For what we have so far is a situation in which we have provided them with good reason, under the circumstances, for doubting our peaceful professions. The error on the side of the West is serious, and it could prove fatal, as our preparations for war make people more and more nervous. And considering that those preparations continue to be pressed in the name of "defense," what reply do we have to charges of hypocrisy?

## VII. POSTSCRIPT

There are many dimensions to anything as complex, involving so many people, as the current situation between the superpowers. One prominent dimension that we have ignored above, because the interest here is primarily on fundamental theory, is what we might call the "human factor." Reflections of the kind made above seem, in retrospect, commonsensical enough to make one wonder how the situation has come to be as it is. Part of the explanation, certainly, lies in the personalities of the various leaders since the Second World War—Churchill, Stalin, Roosevelt, Truman, and others. A good part of it also lies in the conflicts of interest to which we adverted briefly above. It is impossible to doubt that bureaucracy plays a major role here. People are hired to pursue defense, and in the course of this, they not only develop a suspicious cast of mind, exaggerating every move or appar-

ent move of the presumed "opponent," but also see that the survival
and growth of their departments depend on a continued lively perception of the dangers from which they are "defending" their country. A new weapons program sponsored by our department or our
company (it's exactly the same in the Soviet Union—ideology makes
no difference here) means a secure and, in its way, interesting livelihood for colleagues, friends, and self, and of course prestige and the
rest of it. These can become formidable obstacles to peace, and if we
eventually have an atomic holocaust, this writer's personal estimate is
that it will have been due primarily to bureaucracy and very little to
any real dispute about anything that sensible people on either side
would think it worth fighting such a war over.

Beyond this, one must also admit that there is a darker and more
difficult "human factor" at work. It seems difficult to resist the conclusion that people are fascinated by military power, not only by the show
of technology—which *is* certainly impressive—but also by the feeling
of power, of being able to dominate others. This last might, in the end,
be the fundamental enemy. What sort of enemy is it? There are two
aspects to it; an internal, we might perhaps say "existential" aspect, in
which the question is what quality of soul is to be found in such
dispositions; and then a more commonsense, overt matter of sheer
survival, survival to pursue whatever sort of life one proposes to live.
In this essay, the latter has predominated. Like Hobbes, I have argued
that life matters because without it, there is no achievement of any
sort. But I would also want, on the more personal level, to side with
Plato and innumerable other philosophers and humanists in rejecting
the urge to dominate by force as an unworthy one. Do all the Napo-
leans, Caesars, and other conquerers of history equal one Beethoven
or one Aristotle in the final reckoning of the humanly valuable? I think
not. But on this matter of ultimate opinion we need not, indeed must
not, rest our case. What matters is that all of us have an interest in life
that overwhelms any contrary consideration, *and* that we have a legitimate complaint against those who would use force. For they not only
want to use force, but they want to use it on *us*. Were they simply
gladiators, their way of life could be accommodated. We have, after
all, the Olympic games (and even they have been spoiled by politics
in the past decade): there is ample room for competition on many
levels by persons of similar mind. We can even imagine people playing
deadlier War Games in remote areas where the rest of us need not get
involved. But the weapons of war involve everyone, and nuclear
weapons even more than any of those that have gone before. There
is no hope of confinement with them. And those who brandish them,
consequently, intrude on the lives of people everywhere and make a
mockery of that freedom of each to pursue his own way that we in the
West rightly hold precious. Those who make war have the upper hand,
for there is no way to resist without going along. That is why it is

hateful to decent people and why we must ultimately extinguish this poison from the human soul. Let us hope that it can be done, sufficiently and in time; for the alternative is, humanly speaking, the end of time.

## SUGGESTIONS FOR FURTHER READING

### I. INTRODUCTION

*Defining Violence*
J. A. Shaffer, ed., *Violence* (New York: David McKay, 1971).

*Values*
E. J. Bond, *Reason and Value* (Cambridge, England: Cambridge University Press, 1983).
R. E. Ewin, *Co-operation and Human Values* (New York: St. Martin's, 1981).

### II. CONTRACTARIANISM

David Gauthier, "Reason and Maximization," *Canadian Journal of Philosophy* (March 1975).
*Thomas Hobbes, *Leviathan* (1651)—many modern editions, such as Everyman Library.
Jan Narveson, "Contractarian Justice," in Raymond Frey, ed., *Utility and Rights* (Minneapolis: University of Minnesota Press, 1985).

### III. PACIFISM

Peter Mayer, ed., *The Pacifist Conscience* (Chicago: Regnery, 1967).
Jan Narveson, "Pacifism: A Philosophical Analysis," *Ethics*, 1965 (vol. 75). Reprinted, with a reply by Tom Regan, in R. Wasserstrom, ed., *Today's Moral Problems* (New York: Macmillan, 1975), which also has an essay by Newton Garver, "What Violence Is"; see also the more substantial treatment of this topic by Narveson in the first edition of Tom Regan, ed., *Matters of Life and Death* (New York: Random House, 1980).

### V. WAR

*Count Carl von Clausewitz, *On War* (new edition by Howard and Paret, Princeton, N.J.: Princeton University Press, 1976).
William Earle, "In Defense of War" (originally in *The Monist*, 1973; reprinted in J. Narveson, ed., *Moral Issues* (Toronto & New York: Oxford University Press, 1983); see also the reply by Narveson in the same volume, "In Defense of Peace."
Ronald J. Glossop, *Confronting War* (Jefferson, N.C.: McFarland, 1983).
J. Glenn Gray, *The Warriors* (New York: Harcourt, Brace & World, 1959).
Michael Howard, *The Causes of Wars* (Cambridge, Mass.: Harvard University Press, 1984).
*Immanuel Kant, *Perpetual Peace* (Many editions; e.g., Bobbs-Merrill, Library of Liberal Arts).
Robert Phillips, *War and Justice* (Norman, Okla.: University of Oklahoma Press, 1984).

Michael Walzer, *Just and Unjust Wars* (New York: Basic Books, 1977).

R. Wasserstrom, ed., *War and Morality* (Belmont, Calif.: Wadsworth, 1970).

## VI. NUCLEAR WAR

Double-effect doctrine: for an approved exposition of the Roman Catholic view, see Austin J. Fagothey, *Right and Reason* (St. Louis: Mosby, 1963), pp. 107ff. Any general ethics text in the Roman Catholic tradition would have such an exposition. Although he is not expounding this particular viewpoint, an essay on the nuclear war issue along similar lines is Tom Donaldson's "Nuclear Deterrence and Self-Defense," in the *Ethics* issue cited next.

*Ethics*, April 1985: special double issue devoted to nuclear war. Many interesting papers in this; also a fuller exposition of the present author's point of view.

Lawrence Freedman, *The Evolution of Nuclear Strategy* (London: Macmillan, 1981).

Gregory Kavka, "Some Paradoxes of Deterrence," *The Journal of Philosophy*, LXXV.6, June 1978 (also reprinted in Narveson, *Moral Issues*).

Harvard Nuclear Study Group, *Living with Nuclear Weapons* (New York: Bantam, 1983).

Gwyn Prins, ed., *Defended to Death.* Cambridge University Disarmament Seminar's report (New York: Penguin, 1983).

*Denotes a classic on its subject.

# 5

# Capital Punishment

## HUGO ADAM BEDAU

━━━━━━━━━━━━━━━━━━━━━━━━━━━━━━━━━━━━━━━━━━━

## §1 INTRODUCTION

When we confront the task of evaluating punishments from the moral point of view, a host of questions immediately arises: Who should be punished? What offenses and harms should be made liable to punishment? What is involved in making the punishment fit the crime? Are some punishments too cruel or barbaric to be tolerated no matter how effective they may be in preventing crime? Are some criminals so depraved or dangerous that no punishment is too severe for them? What moral principles should govern our thinking about crime and punishment?

In order to give reasonable answers to such questions, we need to appeal to a wide variety of empirical facts. We will want to know, for example, what would happen to the crime rate if no one were punished at all, or if all offenders were punished more leniently or more severely than is usual. We would want to know whether the system of criminal justice operates with adequate efficiency and fairness when it metes out punishment, or whether the severest punishments tend to fall mainly upon some social or racial classes. But we will want to settle other things besides these matters of fact. Social values, moral ideals, ethical principles are also involved, and we will want to know which values and which ideals they are and how to evaluate them as well. Central among these ethical considerations are the value, worth, and dignity of persons—the victims of crime, the offenders, and the rest of society. How, exactly, does our belief in the value of human life, the worth of each person, our common humanity and our common dignity, bear on the nature and methods of punishment as seen from the moral point of view?

There is no better setting in which to examine these questions than the one provided by the controversy over the morality of capital punishment (the death penalty). From an historical perspective, one of the most important relevant ethical values is the idea of *the sanctity of life*. The fundamental idea of the sanctity of human life derives from some of the earliest passages in the Old Testament. The central biblical text is Gen. 1:27, where we are told that "God created man in his own image." Other peoples of antiquity—the Homeric Greeks, the ancient Egyptians, Persians, and Babylonians—showed interest in and concern for the value of human life. But the idea that human life is of transcendent worth, independent of the value that can be placed on a person by virtue of efforts, accomplishments, talents, or any other measure, and that this worth is equal for all and owing to something divine in human beings—this is an inescapably religious notion and it is biblical in origin.

With the rise of rationalist thought in European culture during the Renaissance and the Enlightenment and the concurrent decline in an exclusively religious foundation for moral principles, philosophers increasingly lent their support to the doctrine of *the rights of man* as the basis for constitutional law and public morality. This doctrine took many forms, and it is a prominent part of the moral, political, and legal thinking of the most influential European, British, and American writers of that era. Although these thinkers differed in their views about the nature of rights, all agreed that first and foremost among them is "the right to life."

Distinct as the sanctity of human life and the right to life are, they are held together by a common bond. Each idea is an attempt to express the view that it is morally wrong to take a purely instrumental view of human life. By 'instrumental view of human life' I mean any view that makes it permissible to kill persons in order to protect some other value (e.g., property) or in order to advance some social or political goal (e.g., national liberation). If every human life is sacred or if every person has a right to life, then the murder of an insignificant peasant is just as heinous as the assassination of a king. Likewise, deliberately killing thousands in order to advance the welfare of millions is forbidden. On an instrumental view of human life, however, when other things are assumed to be more "valuable" or "worthy" than the lives of some people, the deaths of many persons often can be justified as necessary to the accomplishment of various social goals. For example, in the eyes of the Nazis, the triumph of the "master race" justified the murder of millions of Jews and other "inferior" peoples. But if everyone has a right to life, or if everyone's life is sacred, then genocidal murder cannot be justified and stands condemned as a grave crime against humanity.

So far as the death penalty is concerned, it might seem that once it is granted that human life is sacred or that everyone has an equal right to life, the death penalty is morally indefensible. Such a punishment seems obviously inconsistent with such ideals of human worth and value. The opposite, however, is true if we let history be our guide. Chief among the traditional defenders of capital punishment have been religious and secular thinkers who sincerely believed in these ideals. In fact, they usually invoked the sanctity of human life and the right to life as part of their defense and justification of death for murderers and other criminals. To see how such a seemingly paradoxical doctrine can be maintained, as well as to begin our examination of the major issues involved in the moral evaluation of the death penalty, we must scrutinize the traditional doctrine of the right to life.

## I. THE RIGHT TO LIFE AND CAPITAL PUNISHMENT

### §2 THE DOCTRINE OF NATURAL RIGHTS

The general idea shared by many philosophers, beginning in the seventeenth century, was that each person by nature—that is, apart from the laws of the state and simply by virtue of being born a human being—had the right to live. It followed from this that it was a violation of that right to be killed by another person, and that it was the responsibility of government to protect human rights, prohibit murder, and try to arrest, convict, and punish anyone guilty of this crime. Thus, the right to life can be thought of, first, as underlying the prohibition against murder common to the criminal law of all countries. On some versions of the theory, God was thought to be the source of this and other "natural rights." Still, few philosophers assumed a necessary connection between everyone's having the right to life and the existence of God as the creator. Hence, the right to life can be understood without significant distortion as a secular notion, free of any essential religious overtones, and thus available to the moral philosophy of theist, atheist, and agnostic alike.

In addition to being *natural,* the right to life was traditionally understood to be *universal* and *inalienable.* A universal right is a right that everyone has, regardless of where one is born or lives and regardless of sex or race. An inalienable right is a right that the possessor cannot transfer, sell, or give away to another person. Thus, killing one person is as much a violation of the right to life as killing any other person, and we cannot authorize others to kill us by giving up to them our right to life.

The right to life seems to pose a problem for a policy of capital punishment. Even if a person has committed murder (so the argument runs) and has therewith intentionally violated another's right to life, the criminal still has his or her own right to life. Would it not be a violation of that right for the murderer to be put to death as punishment? If so, must not capital punishment be morally wrong? A few philosophers, notably Thomas Hobbes (1588–1679), Jean-Jacques

Rousseau (1712–1778), and Cesare Beccaria (1738–1794), show signs of having been troubled by these questions, but they are the exceptions. Most philosophical proponents of the doctrine of a natural right to life were not troubled by them at all, because they adopted one or another variant of the position influentially expressed by John Locke (1632–1704). It will suffice for our purposes to examine his views.

## §3 FORFEITING THE RIGHT TO LIFE

Locke argued that although a person's right to life is natural and inalienable, it can be "forfeited" and *is* forfeited whenever one person violates that right in another. A recent philosopher has put the point clearly: "The offender, by violating the life, liberty, or property of another, has lost his own right to have his life, liberty, or property respected. . . ."[1] The idea is a familiar one, although there are troubling and unanswered questions, such as whether this right, once forfeited, can ever be restored, and if so, by whom and under what conditions. Thanks to the doctrine of forfeiture, it was possible for Locke to assert without apparent contradiction both that everyone has a natural right to life and that the death penalty for a murderer does not violate that right.

Locke's actual reasoning was somewhat more complex and less plausible but more revealing than the account of it so far given. According to Locke, a person forfeits the right to life whenever he or she commits a criminal act "that deserves death."[2] The obvious objection to this formulation is that it permits the use of capital punishment not only for murderers but for almost any crime whatever. Not only treason and the other traditional felonies (arson, rape, robbery, burglary) but relatively minor offenses against property and public order could be said to be properly punished by death. All that is required is some good argument to show that crime $x$ "deserves" such punishment. It will then follow that anyone guilty of $x$ has "forfeited" the natural right to life. What criterion does Locke propose to decide whether a crime "deserves" death or some lesser penalty? He seems not to have given any thought to the problem. He did say, however, that in a "state of nature" we may punish "each transgression . . . to the degree, and with as much severity, as will suffice to make it an ill bargain to the offender, give him cause to repent, and terrify others from doing the like."[3]

This very sweeping doctrine of forfeiture as Locke formulated it was carried over intact a century after Locke by the jurist Sir William Blackstone in his monumental *Commentary on the Laws of England* (1776). Thus, the seeming inconsistency of English legal philosophy being founded on a doctrine of natural rights, including the right to life, and English criminal law authorizing capital punishment for dozens of minor offenses against property—by 1800, there were some two hundred capital offenses, ranging from arson in the dockyards to theft of goods from a bleaching ground—disappears. Locke's doctrine of forfeiture shows why the idea of a natural, universal, and inalienable right to life was not, historically, a rigid moral barrier to capital punishment. It was never an *absolute* right.

## §4 DIFFICULTIES IN LOCKE'S THEORY

There are various objections to the classic theory of the right to life, two of which deserve to be mentioned here. First, underlying Locke's doctrine of natural rights and wholly independent of it are two important assumptions. One is that punishment under law is necessary for social defense.[4] The other is that justice requires retribution—criminals deserve to be punished, and the punishment must fit the crime. The result of these beliefs is that the punishment for murder and other crimes should be death, and they force Locke to make some accommodation in his theory of natural rights. The device he hit upon, and one that generations of later thinkers have also adopted, is to declare that the right to life could be forfeited under certain conditions.

Against Locke's doctrine several objections deserve to be considered. First of all, there are other alternatives. Suppose it is argued (as some of Locke's successors, notably Hegel, did) that one of the offender's natural rights is the right to be punished. If there is such a right, one that governs the appropriate responses of society to the offender, then it is an open question whether the offender's life is to be taken as his punishment. Alternatively, suppose it is argued that although punishments typically constitute harms or deprivations to the person who undergoes them, this is not necessary; what is necessary is that the punishment be imposed on the offender regardless of his preferences and choice. On this view, while it would be necessary for the offender to forfeit some rights in order to be punished, it would not be necessary to forfeit the right to life. Yet another possibility is to regard the right to life as an absolute right, one that it is always wrong to violate. Whether any of these alternatives can be better supported than the doctrine of forfeiture need not be resolved here. They do show that forfeiture of rights as Locke presents it is not the only way to permit punishment under a theory of natural rights.

Another difficulty with Locke's doctrine is that it seems to collapse two distinct issues into one. It is one thing to appeal to forfeiting rights in order to permit society to punish the guilty offender in the first place. It is quite another to appeal to forfeiture of rights in order to decide which among the available punishments is the appropriate one. Forfeiture is a plausible, even if (as we have seen above) not a necessary, solution to the first problem; but Locke uses it primarily in regard to the second. On his own assumptions, he is correct only if retributive justice and social defense in general require the death penalty for murderers. Otherwise, Locke's argument that a murderer (or any other criminal) forfeits the right to life collapses. It is extremely important to grasp this criticism. There is no intrinsic feature of any natural right, including the right to life, that makes it subject to loss through forfeiture. The only basis for supposing that any right is forfeited rather than grossly violated by society when it punishes an offender by death is that just retribution and social defense together require the death penalty for offenders guilty of a crime of this sort. If this requirement turns out to be false, unsubstantiated, or doubtful, then the claim that a criminal's right to life has been forfeited turns out to be equally false, unsubstantiated, or doubtful. As so much turns, therefore, on these questions of the necessity of the death penalty for just retribution and social defense, we shall return to examine them in more detail later (in §20 through §29).

Even if it is concluded that a murderer or other felon does forfeit the natural right to life, it does not follow that a murderer *must* be put to death. This is the second objection. The doctrine of forfeiture does not involve the idea that once a person forfeits a right to *x*, then those to whom it is forfeited have a *duty* to take *x* away from that person. This is often overlooked by those who insist that the death penalty is justified because murderers forfeit their lives. Forfeiting one's *right* to life is not identical with forfeiting one's life. Just as a person may in fact continue to possess something for which he or she has forfeited the right of possession (by, say, failing to renew the lease on a house he or she still occupies), so the government may decide to let a person live who under the doctrine of forfeiture "deserves" to die. Furthermore, it may be that nothing wrong is being done—to the criminal's victims, to the rest of society, or even to the criminal. Another way of putting it is this: Although a person may have forfeited the right to life, it is within *our* rights to let him or her live; in doing so we do not necessarily violate any duty, and it may be that there is nothing morally wrong in what we do. What is true is that if a person has forfeited the right to life but nevertheless continues to live, he or she cannot claim to do so on the ground of that right. Whether we do the right thing in not killing someone who has forfeited the right to life is, of course, a further question. But enough has been said to show that even if someone can forfeit the right to life, that does not morally require that he or she be put to death.

Finally, we should note that Locke's doctrine of forfeiture makes his theory of natural rights vulnerable to utilitarian reasoning, and with devastating effect. What is chiefly attractive about the idea of natural rights is that it purports to provide each of us with moral armor (our rights) that protects us against burdens and deprivations that might otherwise be imposed, on the ground that they are in the interests of the many or good for society in the long run. But Locke's theory requires any offender to forfeit the right to life whenever that is "deserved" by virtue of the nature of the offense. Surely, the harm done in a crime is part of its nature. Hence, it can be argued that crimes other than murder (such as treason, espionage, arson, rape) also "deserve" the death penalty because no other punishment can provide comparable protection for society. One may well doubt whether a theory of natural rights not impervious to reasoning of this sort is worth defending.

## §5 THE DIGNITY OF PERSONS

Although Kant by no means repudiated the doctrine of natural rights, he elevated to primary importance a different idea, the supreme worth or dignity of each person. The most famous single passage in which this doctrine and Kant's views on the punishment of murder are brought together is the following:

> If . . . he has committed a murder, he must die. In this case, there is no substitute that will satisfy the requirements of legal justice. There is no sameness of kind between death and remaining alive even under the most miserable conditions, and consequently there is no equality between the crime and the retribution unless the criminal is judicially condemned and put to death. But the death of the criminal must be kept entirely free of any maltreatment that would make an abomination of the humanity residing in the person suffering it. Even if a civil society were to dissolve itself by common agreement of all its members (for example, if the people inhabiting an island decided to separate and disperse themselves around the world), the last murderer remaining in prison must first be executed, so that everyone will duly receive what his actions are worth and so that the bloodguilt thereof will not be fixed on the people because they failed to insist on carrying out the punishment; for if they fail to do so, they may be regarded as accomplices in this public violation of legal justice.[5]

We may ignore Kant's appeal here to the idea of the "bloodguilt" incurred by murder. The notion that murder, unlike other crimes, is a pollution that deeply stains the social fabric has ancient origins; but it cannot be taken literally and made part of the theory of punishment appropriate for a secular society today. The idea of the dignity of man, however, is more promising. For Kant, that idea enters explicitly only to rule out any aggravations and brutality attended upon the sentence of death and its execution. For Kant, the dignity of man underlies the whole idea of a society of free and rational persons choosing to submit themselves to a common rule of law that includes the punishment of crimes. Accordingly, in punishment, "a human being can never be manipulated merely as a means to the purposes of someone else . . . His innate personality protects him against such treatment. . . ."[6] Kant must therefore also reject the idea that a murderer should be punished with death because by doing so we prevent him from killing again and also discourage others from murder. Kant's appeal to the dignity of man requires him to rule out any role for incapacitative or deterrent benefits in the justification of capital punishment.

As the above passage also shows, underlying Kant's belief in the appropriateness of punishing murder with death is a principle of just retribution. This is reminiscent of Locke's view (recall the weight he attached to the idea of crimes that "deserve" the punishment of death), and it is probably also an echo of the ancient law of retaliation, *lex talionis* ("a life for a life"). The chief difference between Kant and Locke is that Locke thinks it is proper to take into account not only just retribution but also social defense to determine proper punishments, whereas Kant unequivocally rules out the latter. What Kant has done is to present us with two moral ideas—the dignity or worth of each person as a rational creature, and the principle of just retribution —that he regards as inextricably tied together. The latter principle he explained in the following way:

> What kind and what degree of punishment does public legal justice adopt as its principle and standard? None other than the principle of equality . . . , that is, the principle of not treating one side more favorably than the other. Accordingly, any undeserved evil that you inflict on someone else among the people is one that you do to yourself. Only the Law of retribution . . . can determine exactly the kind and degree of punishment . . . All other standards fluctuate back and forth and, because extraneous considerations are mixed with them, they cannot be compatible with the principle of pure and strict legal justice.[7]

Kant, as is obvious from his remarks, thought that retribution *required* the death penalty for murder. He is not alone in holding this view; it has widespread appeal even today.

## §6 THE MIND OF THE MURDERER

Although Kant does not stress the point in the passages we have quoted, he must have realized that in actual practice, apportioning punishments to crimes is not so simple as his principle of retribution seems to imply. A person deserves to be punished, by Kant's reasoning, only when there is no excuse or justification for the criminal conduct; that is, whenever one acts by virtue of an "inner viciousness," as when one has "rationally willed" to kill another person who is entirely innocent and undeserving of any harm.

If modern criminologists and psychologists are correct, however, most murders are not committed by persons whose state of mind can be described as Kant implies. Empirical (clinical, experimental) criminology requires us to test and verify our assumptions regarding the psychology (motivation, intention, state of mind) of each person who kills, whereas Kant's theory is formulated from beginning to end without regard to any empirical considerations at all. His position is more abstract and theoretical. He argues, in effect, that *if* anyone rationally wills the death of an innocent party and acts on that decision, *then* such a person deserves to be put to death. Such an abstract doctrine is quite consistent with the reality described by social and clinical scientists that few who perpetrate violent crimes act in such a coolly deliberate and rational fashion. Consequently, it is theoretically possible to accept Kant's doctrine of just punishment and the death penalty for murder and at the same time to oppose the actual execution of most (perhaps even all) convicted murderers—a possibility that Kant seems to have entirely overlooked, owing perhaps to his unfamiliarity with criminal psychopathology and to the primitive state of the social, behavioral, and clinical sciences of his day. Whether we should accept a doctrine of just retribution even in the abstract remains to be seen. In later sections (§25 through §29), we shall examine some of the most important retributive principles that bear on the death penalty controversy.

## §7 DIFFICULTIES IN KANT'S THEORY

In the course of presenting Kant's views, we have already identified three respects in which his theory is vulnerable. One is that, like Locke's, it assumes that just retribution requires capital punishment for murder, an assumption that may be unnecessary and in any case is not proved. Another difficulty is that, unlike Locke's theory, Kant's seems to make no room whatever for the role of social defense in the justification of punishment. Because Kant's theory excludes this, one cannot argue (as utilitarians would) that if social defense does not require capital punishment for murderers or other criminals, then it is to that extent morally wrong to inflict this punishment on them. But one should be able to argue against a mode of punishment in this way, even if one concedes to Kant that social defense cannot be the only consideration in a system of just punishment.

Finally, a third objection follows from the fact that Kant's theory is so obviously abstract and unempirical from beginning to end. If we really take seriously the idea of the dignity of man, then it may be that we will be led in case after case of actual crime to reject Kant's reasoning on the ground that it is inapplicable in light of the actual facts of the case before us. It is an objection to Kant's theory that it tells us what to do only with ideally rational killers; what we need is a theory that tells us how to cope with the actual persons who kill, and how to do that in a way that acknowledges our common humanity with both the victim and the offender, as well as the injustices to which all social systems are prone and the wisdom of self-restraint in the exercise of violence, especially when undertaken deliberately and in the name of justice.

## §8 UTILITARIANISM AND THE DEATH PENALTY

In sharp contrast to Kant, for whom social benefits deriving from the death penalty played no role in its justification, utilitarian thinkers from his day to the present view the beneficial and harmful consequences of any law or policy as the only factors to be taken into account in trying to evaluate it from the moral point of view. (Locke's theory, as we can now see more clearly, uneasily straddles the middle ground between these two extremes.) Just as Kant disregarded considerations of consequences in evaluating the morality of capital punishment, so utilitarians disregard any appeals to natural rights or the dignity of man. For them, these ideas at best mask a reference to social benefits; more likely, they are moral standards independent of (and thus potentially in conflict with) the principle of utility. At worst, they are rhetorical phrases of dubious content. The utilitarian, therefore, regards the death penalty as justified by the degree to which it advances the general welfare. Accordingly, its justification proceeds in the following manner: (1) consider the practice of the death penalty and all its present and future consequences—for the executed offenders, for the victims of crime, their friends and families, and the rest of society; (2) consider each of the alternative modes of punishment that might be imposed and their consequences were they to be employed instead; (3) decide in favor of the death penalty rather than any alternative only if, in light of all the facts, its practice would have the greatest balance of benefit over harm for everyone affected by it.

Two things are noteworthy about such a pattern of reasoning. First, everything depends on the facts, and diverse and complex facts are always in question. Moreover, these facts are not certain to remain constant in a given society decade after decade, much less from one society to another. The result is that it may be very difficult to reach agreement on all of them, as the unending debate over the deterrent efficacy of executions attests (see §21). When that happens, reasonable utilitarians will have to agree to disagree with each other over whether the death penalty should be retained, modified, or abolished for this or that crime. We have, in fact, a perfect illustration of precisely such a disagreement between the two most influential classic utilitarian philosophers. Jeremy Bentham (1748–1832) strongly opposed the death penalty throughout his life and in one of his last essays argued forcefully for its complete abolition in England and France. His student, John Stuart Mill (1806–1873), however, when he was a member of Parliament in the 1860s, argued with comparable firmness against abolition of the death penalty for murder in the England of his day. Thus, within the space of half a century, Bentham and Mill, both professing utilitarians, disagreed over the desirability of abolishing the death penalty. What should we make of this spectacle? Principally, that complex facts are subject to uncertain estimate and calculation at best, so that a moral outlook founded on nothing but considerations that a consistent utilitarian can acknowledge may be insufficient for resolving the question.

A second point of interest is that the general welfare is an extremely abstract, remote, and elusive end state to serve as the good to be aimed at in choosing among alternative penal policies. Utilitarians have devoted much energy to trying to give shape and content to this idea, or to what they regard as better-defined alternative conceptions. Still, even the utilitarian may have to be content, as a practical compromise, to rely on some intermediate moral principles less comprehensive in their scope than the principle of utility and more directly applicable to the problem of punishment and the death penalty controversy. As Mill himself once urged, "Whatever we adopt as the fundamental principle of morality, we require subordinate principles to apply it by . . . ."[8] Below (in §13), I shall propose a small set of such principles in the hope that, among other things, they will serve this need; they are not, however, principles that only a utilitarian could endorse.

## §9 CONCLUSION

So far, our investigation has been largely historical—and largely inconclusive. We have seen how natural rights thinkers have *not* attacked the death penalty on the ground that it violates inviolable human rights. On the contrary, both Locke and Kant argue that the death penalty, whether on retributive or other grounds, is justified as a punishment for murder and perhaps for other crimes as well. Among utilitarians it is possible to find arguments against the death penalty (witness Bentham) but equally possible to find the principle of utility used in connection with a different assessment of the facts to yield a defense of the death penalty (as in Mill). Of course, it is always possible that a more exact and complete statement of one of these theories would give us a fixed and definitive judgment, once and for all, on the morality of the death penalty. We must leave that possibility to be explored by others. A better approach, more contemporary and more conclusive, requires us to strike out in a different direction and to approach the entire subject more systematically. It is time now to begin that task.

# II. THE MORALITY OF PUNISHMENT

As a first step toward providing a fresh setting for the rest of our discussion, it is useful to have a general sketch before us of why it is rational for society to have a system of punishment at all, quite apart from whether or not the death penalty is used as one of the modes of punishment. We are not likely to assess the morality of capital punishment correctly unless we understand the morality of punishment in general. Accordingly, we need to have a general conception of why society should have a system of punishment, a conception that takes into consideration the value of human life.

## §10 THE NATURE OF PUNISHMENT

We may start with the fact that a punishment, by its very nature, is unpleasant, distressing, often painful, and in any case either a deprivation of something deemed to be of value or the imposition of something deemed to be a hardship. Freedom of bodily movement and assembly with others, disposing of one's money and property as one pleases, having one's body (and one's life) intact—all these it is good to have and to have free of interference. Why, then, does society always insist on a system of punishment when this means inflicting so much suffering and deprivation upon persons? Punishment is in need of justification because it is always the deliberate infliction of deprivation or hardship on a person and is thus the sort of thing no one would freely consent to have imposed on oneself.

Its justification must begin with the fact that we cannot avoid regarding some kinds of human conduct as harmful to innocent persons. This leads any rational society to prohibit and condemn such conduct. Condemnation is achieved by the imposition of punishment. The next step is to establish degrees of severity in the punishments as a function of such factors as the community's judgment of the gravity of the offense, the difficulty and cost in detecting offenders, and so forth. In a society such as ours, where individual freedom is so highly prized, there is a tendency to make punishments rather more severe in order to compensate for restricting the police and the courts to a role that hampers them in bringing offenders to justice lest they invade what we regard as our justifiable privacy.

## §11 THE RIGHT TO PUNISH

Society is organized by reference to common rules that forbid anyone and everyone to engage in certain sorts of harmful conduct. When anyone does deliberately, willfully, and knowingly violate such rules, and therewith harms the innocent, the offender has violated the rights of others and therewith immediately becomes liable to a punitive response. Since the rules were originally designed to provide protection to every person, and since (so we also assume) the culprit knew in advance that his or her conduct was prohibited because it would be injurious to others, and since he or she freely and knowingly chose nevertheless to violate the prohibition, society cannot simply ignore the violation and continue to treat the offender as if no wrong had been done. It must attempt to bring the offender to judgment. But the reason is not mainly to give a lesson to the offender or to set an example for others who might be inclined to imitate such lawless conduct. The reason is twofold. First, it is simply inconsistent for society to establish a set of fair rules, with penalties for their violation, and then ignore them when actual violations occur. Second, it is simply unfair for the law-abiding to have to suffer the harms inflicted on them by lawbreakers, as well as the inconvenience of their own self-discipline in complying with laws that they, too, might like to violate, while the criminals indulge their lawless inclinations and suffer nothing in return.

Crime, on the model being developed here, is viewed as an attempt to take more than one's fair share of something. Theft of material goods is an obvious example. Murder and other crimes of violence against the person can be seen in the same way as conduct in which the offender takes more than a fair share of liberty with the bodies of others and disregards the lack of the victim's consent. Punishment, therefore, serves the complex function of reinforcing individual compliance with a set of social rules deemed necessary to protect the rights of all the members of society. Once it has been determined that society needs rules to guide the conduct of its members, when one of these rules has been deliberately violated, then there is no alternative but to set in motion the system of punishment.

That system is essentially retributive in at least two respects: Crime must be punished, and the punishment must fit the crime. On the theory being developed here, the first of these contentions is certainly acknowledged. Punishment by its nature pays back to an offender suffering and indignity akin to what the offender inflicted on the innocent victim. Justice, more than any other consideration (social defense, reform of the offender), dictates that in principle all crimes be liable to punishment, and that a reasonable portion of social resources (public expenditures) be allocated to the arrest and conviction of offenders. The retributive principle that punishments must fit crimes is more difficult to implement, and we shall discuss it in detail later (in §25 through §29).

## §12 MODES OF PUNISHMENT

What sorts of punishments are available to society to inflict on offenders? What are the sorts of things any person could be deprived of that would count as punishment? Obviously, one could lose one's money or property, or the right to future earnings or an inheritance. But because so much crime against property and against the person is committed by the poor and untalented, by persons with no property and no prospects of any, and because the stolen property is so often disposed of prior to the offender's arrest, it is often pointless to levy punishments in the form of fines or confiscations. Where the crime in question is not against property but against the person, a new difficulty arises. If society were to punish assault and battery by, say, a fine of $1,000, it would be impossible for the very poor to be punished for the crime, and it would be merely a modest tariff on the conduct of the very rich, like higher taxes on their yachts and private planes—an inconvenience, but not much more. In either case, the victim of the assault and battery would have suffered injury quite incommensurate with the punishment (especially if the $1,000 were to go to the state rather than to the victim).

It is for reasons such as these that society has long preferred to take other things of intrinsic value from persons in the name of punishment —notably, their freedom and their bodily integrity. Everybody, rich and poor, young and old, male and female, has life and some degree of liberty to lose. Historically, the objection to making punishments mainly a deprivation of liberty was that considerable tax revenues were needed to build and staff prisons. It was in part for such economic reasons that the earliest punishments were neither pecuniary nor incarcerative, but corporal: flogging, branding, maiming, and killing. Inexpensive and quick to administer, acutely painful for the offender —it is hardly any wonder that every society today is heir to punitive practices involving widespread and varied use of corporal punishments.

What our discussion shows is that there is an argument on grounds of fairness for a system of punishment in the first place (given the fact that not everyone will always abide by fair rules that prohibit injury to others, and that it is necessary to have such rules), and another argument on grounds of fairness for modes of punishment that all can pay and that impose similar deprivations on all concerned. It is also clear from this sketch that a system of punishment does not require capital punishment. Even if in the case of murder the punishment of death is the punishment most like the injury the victim has suffered, and even if it is the one punishment that guarantees the offender will never again commit another crime, there are other deprivations that are available to society and they may be preferable as punishment.

## §13 THE VALUE OF HUMAN LIFE AND MORAL PRINCIPLES

We have had occasion to notice earlier that there is an important tie between the religious idea of the sanctity of human life and secular ideas of the right to life and the dignity of man. Their common factor is the way each of these ideas rules out as immoral the taking of a person's life on grounds of social usefulness and nothing more. From the standpo᷂ ᴄ of moral theory, this amounts to the claim that when the moral principle of overall social welfare conflicts with the moral principle of the individual's right to life, the latter shall prevail. We have also seen how the right to life and the dignity of man generate the requirement that society must forbid and punish severely the crime of murder. From the standpoint of moral theory, this is an instance where a moral ideal is the source of a social or legal rule.

With a little reflection it is possible to connect several other moral principles with the idea of the worth of human life. We may regard these principles as corollaries or theorems of that ideal taken as an axiom or first principle of morality. Each of these principles bears on the moral desirability or permissibility of the death penalty. Some of these subsidiary principles we have already encountered; others will emerge in the discussions that follow. Here, for future reference, is the full set:

1. Deliberately taking the life of anyone is not justified unless it is necessary, i.e., as long as there is a feasible alternative.
2. Unless there is a good reason to punish a crime severely, a less severe penalty is to be preferred.
3. The more severe a penalty is, the more important it is to inflict it fairly and equally, i.e., on all and only those who deserve it.
4. If human lives are to be risked, risking the life of the guilty is morally preferable to risking the life of the innocent.

All of the above principles can be seen, in one way or another, as expressive of ideas that have their origin in the worth of human life. In addition to the above principles, two others have emerged that express aspects of the idea of retribution, or justice in punishment. These are:

5. Crimes should be punished.
6. Punishments should be graded in their severity according to the gravity of the crimes for which they are imposed.

Our task is to determine the scope and application of these several principles so that we may render a judgment on capital punishment from the moral point of view. These six principles are not, of course, of equal weight or scope; some are more important than others. (Whether utilitarianism or Kantianism, for example, would give the better defense of these principles is not immediately obvious.) Nothing short of a full-scale moral theory could incorporate each of these principles to the extent that is proper, and there is no opportunity here for the development of such a theory. Instead, we will attempt to show how each of these principles enters into a line of reasoning relevant to the morality of capital punishment and thus how each can be accorded something like its proper weight, so that by the time we are finished, we will have found a role for each principle that seems plausible. None of these principles has any specific reference to the morality of capital punishment. That should not be surprising, and it is certainly no defect. In general, one prefers a moral principle of broader rather than narrower application, one that covers many different kinds of cases and situations. If such broad generalizations can withstand criticism and counterexamples to test their plausibility, then they are likely to be sound principles.

## III. THE INDIGNITY AND SEVERITY OF THE DEATH PENALTY

### §14 IS CAPITAL PUNISHMENT AN UNTIMELY AND UNDIGNIFIED DEATH?

Some critics of the opposition to capital punishment have complained that such opposition involves an overestimation of the value of human life, for it tends to ignore the fact that we are all bound to die eventually. According to these critics, all that capital punishment does is to schedule a person's death at a definite time and place, by a definite mode and for a definite reason. This raises a new question for us, namely, whether the ideas of the value, worth, dignity, or sanctity of human life can be made consistent with the fact of human mortality.

Even though death is a fact of life, emphasizing the worth of human life is a way of giving sense to the familiar notions of an "untimely" death and of an "undignified" death. These terms are admittedly vague, and have application in a wide variety of settings, but they also have a place where crime and punishment are concerned. Other things being equal, if a death is brought about by one person killing another, as in murder, then it is an untimely death. If a death is brought about in a way that causes terror during the dying and disfigurement of the body, then it is an undignified death. This, of course, is exactly what murder and capital punishment both typically do. (The French film "We Are All Murderers" (1956) rendered this theme vividly.)

Historically, however, the most brutal methods of execution have been practiced in public, despite any objection that might be brought on these grounds. Such brutality was thought necessary to enhance the deterrent effect of the execution and to pay back the guilty offender, with interest, for the crime that had been committed. Stoning, crucifixion, impalement, beheading, even hanging and shooting, have often been hideously painful, terrifying to anticipate and experience, and they have left the executed person in various degrees of bodily disfigurement. In principle, of course, there is no medical or technical barrier to the development of modes of inflicting the death penalty that do not conspicuously affront human dignity. The gas chamber was introduced in this country in the 1920s as an improvement on the electric chair, much as the electric chair itself had been introduced in the 1890s in the belief that it was a humane improvement upon hangings. During the 1970s, several state legislatures enacted laws to impose the death penalty by painless lethal injection.

Confronted by these considerations, what should be the reply of the defender of the death penalty? There are several alternatives. One can argue that (1) neither retribution nor social defense, each of which does require brutal methods or administering the death penalty, is part of the purpose or justification of capital punishment; or one could argue that (2) neither retribution nor social defense really requires any of the brutalities still characteristic of capital punishment; or one could even argue that (3) the idea that death should be neither untimely nor undignified is a moral consideration of little weight, and other moral principles favoring the death penalty easily outweigh it. It is difficult to imagine any defender of the death penalty resting content with alternative (1). Alternative (2) is more promising, but for reasons suggested above and to be examined below (in §21 and §28), it really will not withstand close scrutiny. It is most likely that the defender of capital punishment would prefer to stand on alternative (3). If so, the dispute between defenders and critics of the morality of capital punishment will turn on how that punishment fares when measured by the requirements of just retribution and social defense. Accordingly, the bulk of our discussion will eventually need to be devoted to resolving this dispute (see parts IV and V).

## §15 GRADING THE SEVERITY OF PUNISHMENTS

Punishments can be plausibly graded into three categories of relative severity: Fines (loss of property) are the least severe, imprisonment (loss of liberty) is much more severe, and death (loss of life) is the most severe of all. Fines, as we noted earlier, are often like a tax on conduct, and relatively little social disgrace is attached to illegal conduct if the main consequence for the offender is to incur a fine. Loss of liberty, however, not only curtails freedom of association and movement; it is also a stigma, as well as a reminder hour by hour to the offender that he or she is undergoing punishment in a form that makes one (at least for the time being) literally a social outcast. As for the death penalty, most of those who oppose it as well as those who favor it believe it is far more severe than imprisonment. Why it is so severe, however, is often in dispute. Because opposition to the death penalty rests largely on the belief that this unusual severity is unnecessary and unjustified, it is important to examine this issue with some care.

Prolonged imprisonment without hope of release except by natural death has figured in dozens of novels and stories as the ultimate horror, and this is hardly surprising, especially if the incarceration is compounded by wretched living conditions and solitary confinement. Thus, life imprisonment without the possibility of parole can verge on the borderline that normally divides imprisonment from death as the less from the more severe punishment. Occasionally, prisoners under life sentence will commit suicide rather than face a bleak future any longer. "Lifers" also occasionally report that if they had known what it would be like to serve thirty or forty years in prison, they would have made no effort to avoid a death sentence at their trial. For those of us with just enough exposure to prison life to be appalled by the thought of undergoing it, and with imaginations vivid enough to know what we would be deprived of once we were imprisoned behind bars, it is understandable that we might reach the sober conclusion that we would rather die than be imprisoned for life.

But do these considerations really show that death is not a more severe punishment even than life imprisonment? Do they indicate that life imprisonment can be as great or even a greater affront to the dignity of a person than the death penalty? Mainly at issue is whether personal preference of one penalty over another shows that the latter is more severe than the former. It does not. First of all, it is not really possible to tell which of two penalties one prefers, where the one is death and the other life, the way it is possible to tell which of two vacations one prefers, a week at the seashore or a week in the mountains. One can try each of the vacations and then, on the basis of actual experience, decide which is the preferable. But where death and life imprisonment are concerned, at most one can hope to *imagine* which of the two one would like the least. Any comparative judgment, in the nature of the case, must be based on no experience of the one (death) and very incomplete experience of the other (life imprisonment). If the severity of these two alternative punishments must be judged in this way, we would never be able to tell which is the more severe. Or we would have to conclude that severity of punishments is not a matter for objective evaluation, but only of individual preference or arbitrary decision.

## §16 WHY DEATH IS MORE SEVERE THAN IMPRISONMENT

If we reflect further on the matter, we will see that the issue of the severity of a punishment is a complex idea in which there are identifiable factors that permit clear comparison between modes of punishment. Roughly, of two punishments, one is more severe than the other depending on its duration and on its interference with other things a person so punished might do. Death is interminable, whereas it is always possible to revoke or interrupt a life sentence. Death also makes compensation impossible, whereas it is possible to compensate a prisoner for wrongful confinement even if it is not possible to give back any of the liberty that was taken away. Of most importance, death permits of no concurrent experiences or activities, whereas even a life-term prisoner can read a book, watch television, perhaps even write a book or repair a television set, and experience social relations of some variety with other people. Death eliminates the presupposition of all experience and activity: life itself. For these reasons, the death penalty is unquestionably the more severe punishment, no matter what any despondent life-term prisoner or sentimental observer may prefer (or thinks he or she prefers), and no matter how painless and dignified the mode of execution may be.

It is of course true that it is possible to make even short-term imprisonment a living hell for the prisoner. No doubt, methods of imprisonment have been designed that would make death a blessed relief. Opponents of the death penalty, however, need favor no such brutal alternatives. It is true that Europe's first outspoken opponent of the death penalty, the young Italian nobleman Cesare Beccaria, recommended imprisonment over the death penalty because of "the perpetual example" that life-term prisoners afforded the public of what could happen if one committed a felony. Beccaria thought this would make long imprisonment a better deterrent than death because of the "much stronger impression" on the imagination of a whole life in prison as opposed to a few moments on the gallows.[9]

Today most opponents of the death penalty would favor as an alternative punishment a prison term of relatively brief duration (say, ten years) and then eligibility for parole release, with actual release depending upon the likelihood of further violent offenses and upon the public acceptability of the offender's release. Thus, a Charles Manson might never be released, whereas an armed robber who shot a gas station attendant during a holdup might be released in fifteen years (as, in fact, happens today in many such cases). The day-to-day prison regimen, while it need not approximate a country club—as it is cynically said to do by those who have never been there—also need not involve mistreatment, neglect, and brutality of a sort to delight the Spanish Inquisition, either.

We should also not forget that, as history shows, it is possible to aggravate the severity of the death penalty by any of several well-known techniques. Burning at the stake, for instance, would do very nicely as a more severe mode of execution than the electric chair. However, even if it could be established that such severe methods accomplished a marvelous improvement in the deterrent effect over less brutal methods, or that they were superbly fitted to repay the criminal for the kind of murder he committed, the indignity of such cruelties would prohibit their use. They would be widely if not universally seen as a dangerous throwback to more savage times, in which respect for our common humanity was less prominent and less widespread than it is today. Thus we see that even retribution and deterrence have their moral limits, limits imposed in the name of human dignity.

## §17 THE INDIGNITY OF CORPORAL PUNISHMENTS

In addition to the severity of the death penalty, killing persons as punishment shares certain important features with other modes of corporal punishment—maiming, flogging, branding—once widely practiced in our society but now abandoned. All these other methods of corporal punishment have been abandoned in part because they are now seen to violate the dignity of the person being punished. It is undignified to carry for the rest of one's life the visible stigma of having been convicted of a crime. But this is exactly what branding and maiming (such as cutting off the hand of a thief) did. Since the

Freudian revolution earlier in this century, informed and reflective persons have become uneasy whenever violent physical abuse is deliberately inflicted by one person upon another who is helpless to do anything about it. Yet this is exactly what flogging involves. (By 'flogging' I do not mean the paddling a mother might administer to the bottom of her wayward child. I mean tying a person to a post or a railing and then beating him raw on the naked back so that bloody welts are raised that leave scars for life, a standard form of punishment only a few decades ago and still used within prisons until fairly recently.) Any attempt by the authorities to revive such modes of punishment would be denounced as an unacceptable return to primitive techniques of punishment, and as needless physical violence that only hardens both those who undergo it and those who inflict it.

Why has death as a punishment escaped the nearly universal social and moral condemnation visited on all these other punishments with which it is historically and naturally associated? In part, it may be owing to a failure of imagination. Whereas we all know or can easily and vividly imagine the pain and humiliation involved in other corporal punishments, an execution is carried out away from public view, it is quickly over, and the person punished by death is no longer in our midst as a constant reminder. There are other factors, too. One is the belief that in some cases there is truly no alternative, because if the criminal were not killed there would be too much risk that he or she would repeat the crime. If so, then neither retribution nor deterrence, but rather prevention turns out to be the last line of defense. We shall examine this line of reasoning more closely below (§19 through §23).

## IV. CAPITAL PUNISHMENT AND SOCIAL DEFENSE

### §18 THE ANALOGY WITH SELF-DEFENSE

Capital punishment, it is sometimes said, is to the body politic what self-defense is to the individual. If the latter is not morally wrong, how can the former be morally wrong? In order to assess the strength of this analogy, we need first to inspect the morality of self-defense.

Except for absolute pacifists, who believe it is morally wrong to use violence even to defend themselves or others from unprovoked and undeserved aggression, most of us believe that it is not morally wrong and may even be our moral duty to use violence to prevent aggression directed either against ourselves or against innocent third parties. The law has long granted persons the right to defend themselves against the unjust aggressions of others, even to the extent of using lethal force to kill a would-be assailant. It is very difficult to think of any convincing argument that would show it is never rational to risk the death of another in order to prevent death or grave injury to oneself. Certainly self-interest dictates the legitimacy of self-defense. So does concern for the well-being of others. So also does justice. If it is unfair for one person to inflict violence on another, then it is hard to see how morality could require the victim to acquiesce in the attempt by another to hurt him or her, rather than to resist it, even if that resistance involves or risks injury to the assailant.

The foregoing account assumes that the person acting in self-defense is innocent of any provocation of the assailant. It also assumes that there is no alternative to victimization except resistance. In actual life, both assumptions—especially the second—are often false, because there may be a third alternative: escape, or removing oneself from the scene of danger and imminent aggression. Hence, the law imposes on us the "duty to retreat." Before we use violence to resist aggression, we must try to get out of the way, lest unnecessary violence be used to resist aggression. Now suppose that unjust aggression is imminent, and there is no path open for escape. How much violence may justifiably be used to ward off aggression? The answer is: No more violence than is necessary to prevent the aggressive assault. Violence beyond that is unnecessary and therefore unjustified. We may restate the principle governing the use of violence in self-defense in terms of the use of "deadly force" by the police in the discharge of their duties. The rule is this: Use of deadly force is justified only to prevent loss of life in immediate jeopardy where a lesser use of force cannot reasonably be expected to save the life that is threatened.

In real life, violence in self-defense in excess of the minimum necessary to prevent aggression, even though it is not justifiable, is often excusable. One cannot always tell what will suffice to deter or prevent becoming a victim, and so the law looks with a certain tolerance upon the frightened and innocent would-be victim who in self-protection turns upon a vicious assailant and inflicts a fatal injury even though a lesser injury would have been sufficient. What is not justified is deliberately using far more violence than is necessary to prevent becoming a victim. It is the deliberate, not the impulsive or the unintentional use of violence that is relevant to the death-penalty controversy, since the death penalty is enacted into law and carried out in each case only after ample time to weigh alternatives. Notice that we are assuming that the act of self-defense is to protect one's person or that of a third party. The reasoning outlined here does not extend to the defense of one's property. Shooting a thief to prevent one's automobile from being stolen cannot be excused or justified in the way that shooting an assailant charging with a knife pointed at one's face can be. In terms of the concept of "deadly force," our criterion is that deadly force is never justified to prevent crimes against property or other violent crimes not immediately threatening the life of an innocent person.

The rationale for self-defense as set out above illustrates two moral principles of great importance to our discussion (recall §13). One is that if a life is to be risked, then it is better that it be the life of someone who is guilty (in our context, the initial assailant) rather than the life of someone who is not (the innocent potential victim). It is not fair to expect the innocent prospective victim to run the added risk of severe injury or death in order to avoid using violence in self-defense to the extent of possibly killing his assailant. It is only fair that the guilty aggressor run the risk.

The other principle is that taking life deliberately is not justified so long as there is any feasible alternative. One does not expect miracles, of course, but in theory, if shooting a burglar through the foot will stop the burglary and enable one to call the police for help, then there is no reason to shoot to kill. Likewise, if the burglar is unarmed, there is no reason to shoot at all. In actual life, of course, burglars are likely to be shot at by aroused householders because one does not know whether they are armed, and prudence may dictate the assumption that they are. Even so, although the burglar has no right to commit a felony against a person or a person's property, the attempt to do so does not give the chosen victim the right to respond in whatever way one pleases, and then to excuse or justify such conduct on the ground that one was "only acting in self-defense." In these ways the law shows a tacit regard for the life of even a felon and discourages the use of unnecessary violence even by the innocent; morality can hardly do less.

## §19 PREVENTING VERSUS DETERRING CRIME

The analogy between capital punishment and self-defense requires us to face squarely the empirical questions surrounding the preventive and deterrent effects of the death penalty. Executing a murderer in the name of punishment can be seen as a crime-*preventive* measure just to the extent it is reasonable to believe that if the murderer had not been executed he or she would have committed other crimes (including, but not necessarily confined to, murder). Executing a murderer can be seen as a crime *deterrent* just to the extent it is reasonable to believe that by the example of the execution other persons would be frightened off from committing murder. Any punishment can be a crime preventive without being a crime deterrent, just as it can be a deterrent without being a preventive. It can also be both or neither. Prevention and deterrence are theoretically independent because they operate by different methods. Crimes can be prevented by taking guns out of the hands of criminals, by putting criminals behind bars, by alerting the public to be less careless and less prone to victimization, and so forth. Crimes can be deterred only by making would-be criminals frightened of being arrested, convicted, and punished for crimes—that is, making persons overcome their desire to commit crimes by a stronger desire to avoid the risk of being caught and punished.

## §20 THE DEATH PENALTY AS A CRIME PREVENTIVE

Capital punishment is unusual among penalties because its preventive effects limit its deterrent effects. The death penalty can never deter the executed person from further crimes. At most, it can prevent a person from committing them. Popular discussions of the death penalty are frequently confused because they so often assume that the death penalty is a perfect and infallible deterrent so far as the executed criminal is concerned, whereas nothing of the sort is true. What is even more important, it is also wrong to think that in every execution the death penalty has proved to be an infallible crime preventive. What is obviously true is that once an offender has been executed, it is physically impossible for that person to commit any further crimes, since the punishment is totally incapacitative. But incapacitation is not identical with prevention. Prevention by means of incapacitation occurs only if the executed criminal would have committed other crimes if he or she had not been executed and had been punished only in some less incapacitative way (e.g., by imprisonment).

What evidence is there that the incapacitative effects of the death penalty are an effective crime preventive? From the study of imprisonment, parole, release records, this much is clear: If the murderers and other criminals who have been executed are like the murderers who were convicted but not executed, then (1) executing all convicted murderers would have prevented many crimes, but not many murders (less than one convicted murderer in five hundred commits another murder); and (2) convicted murderers, whether inside prison or outside after release, have at least as good a record of no further criminal activity as any other class of convicted felon.

These facts show that the general public tends to overrate the danger and threat to public safety constituted by the failure to execute every murderer who is caught and convicted. While it would be quite wrong to say that there is no risk such criminals will repeat their crimes—or similar ones—if they are not executed, it would be equally erroneous to say that by executing every convicted murderer many horrible crimes will be prevented. All we know is that a few such crimes will never be committed; we do not know how many or by whom they would have been committed. (Obviously, if we did know we would have tried to prevent them!) This is the nub of the problem. There is no way to know in advance which if any of the incarcerated or released murderers will kill again. It is useful in this connection to remember that the only way to guarantee that no horrible crimes ever occur is to execute *everyone* who might conceivably commit such a crime. Similarly, the only way to guarantee that no convicted murderer ever commits another murder is to execute them all. No modern society has ever done this, and for two hundred years ours has been moving steadily in the opposite direction.

These considerations show that our society has implicitly adopted an attitude toward the risk of murder rather like the attitude it has adopted toward the risk of fatality from other sources, such as automobile accidents, lung cancer, or drowning. Since no one knows when or where or upon whom any of these lethal events will fall, it would be too great an invasion of freedom to undertake the severe restrictions that alone would suffice to prevent any such deaths from occurring. It is better to take the risks and keep our freedom than to try to eliminate the risks altogether and lose our freedom in the process. Hence, we have lifeguards at the beach, but swimming is not totally prohibited; smokers are warned, but cigarettes are still legally sold; pedestrians may be given the right of way in a crosswalk, but marginally competent drivers are still allowed to operate motor vehicles. Some risk is therefore imposed on the innocent; in the name of our right to freedom, our other rights are not protected by society at all costs.

## §21 THE DEATH PENALTY AS A CRIME DETERRENT

Determining whether the death penalty is an effective deterrent is even more difficult than determining its effectiveness as a crime preventive. In general, our knowledge about how penalties deter crimes and whether in fact they do—whom they deter, from which crimes, and under what conditions—is distressingly inexact. Most people nevertheless are convinced that punishments do deter, and that the more severe a punishment is the better it will deter. For half a century, social scientists have studied the questions whether the death penalty is a deterrent and whether it is a better deterrent than the alternative of imprisonment. Their verdict, while not unanimous, is nearly so. Whatever may be true about the deterrence of lesser crimes by other penalties, the deterrence achieved by the death penalty for murder is not measurably any greater than the deterrence achieved by long-term imprisonment. In the nature of the case, the evidence is quite indirect. No one can identify for certain any crimes that did not occur because the would-be offender was deterred by the threat of the death penalty and could not have been deterred by a less severe threat. Likewise, no one can identify any crimes that did occur because the offender was not deterred by the threat of prison even though he would have been deterred by the threat of death. Nevertheless, such evidence as we have fails to show that the more severe penalty (death) is really a better deterrent than the less severe penalty (imprisonment) for such crimes as murder.

If the conclusion stated above is correct, and the death penalty and long-term imprisonment are equally effective (or ineffective) as deterrents to murder, then the argument for the death penalty on grounds of deterrence is seriously weakened. One of the moral principles identified earlier now comes into play. It is the principle that unless there is a good reason for choosing a more rather than a less severe punishment for a crime, the less severe penalty is to be preferred. This principle obviously commends itself to anyone who values human life and who concedes that, all other things being equal, less pain and suffering is always better than more. Human life is valued in part to the degree that it is free of pain, suffering, misery, and frustration, and in particular to the extent that it is free of such experiences when they serve no purpose. If the death penalty is not a more effective deterrent than imprisonment, then its greater severity is gratuitous, purposeless suffering and deprivation. Accordingly, we must reject it in favor of some less severe alternative, unless we can identify some more weighty moral principle that the death penalty protects better than any less severe mode of punishment does. Whether there is any such principle is unclear.

## §22 A COST/BENEFIT ANALYSIS OF THE DEATH PENALTY

A full study of the costs and benefits involved in the practice of capital punishment would not be confined solely to the question of whether it is a better deterrent or preventive of murder than imprisonment. Any thoroughgoing utilitarian approach to the death-penalty controversy would need to examine carefully other costs and benefits as well, because maximizing the balance of all the social benefits over all the social costs is the sole criterion of right and wrong according to utilitarianism (recall §8). Let us consider, therefore, some of the other costs and benefits to be calculated. Clinical psychologists have presented evidence to suggest that the death penalty actually incites some persons of unstable mind to murder others, either because they are afraid to take their own lives and hope that society will punish them for murder by putting them to death, or because they fancy that they, too, are killing with justification analogously to the lawful and presumably justified killing involved in capital punishment. If such evidence is sound, capital punishment can serve as a counterpreventive or even an incitement to murder; such incited murders become part of its social cost. Imprisonment, however, has not been known to incite any murders or other crimes of violence in a comparable fashion. (A possible exception might be found in the imprisonment of terrorists, which has inspired other terrorists to take hostages as part of a scheme to force the authorities to release their imprisoned comrades.) The risks of executing the innocent are also part of the social cost. The historical record is replete with innocent persons arrested, indicted, convicted, sentenced, and occasionally legally executed for crimes they did not commit. This is quite apart from the guilty persons unfairly convicted, sentenced to death, and executed on the strength of perjured testimony, fraudulent evidence, subornation of jurors, and other violations of the civil rights and liberties of the accused. Nor is this all. The high costs of a capital trial and of the inevitable appeals, the costly methods of custody most prisons adopt for convicts on "death row," are among the straightforward economic costs that the death penalty incurs. Conducting a valid cost/benefit analysis of capital punishment is extremely difficult, and it is impossible to predict exactly what such a study would show. Nevertheless, based on such evidence as we do have, it is quite possible that a study of this sort would favor abolition of all death penalties rather than their retention.

## §23 WHAT IF EXECUTIONS DID DETER?

From the moral point of view, it is quite important to determine what one should think about capital punishment if the evidence were clearly to show that the death penalty is a distinctly superior method of social defense by comparison with less severe alternatives. Kantian moralists, as we have seen (in §5), would have no use for such knowledge, because their entire case for the morality of the death penalty rests on the way it is thought to provide just retribution, not on the way it is thought to provide social defense. For a utilitarian, however, such knowledge would be conclusive. Those who follow Locke's reasoning would also be gratified, because they defend the morality of the death penalty both on the ground that it is retributively just and on the ground that it provides needed social defense.

What about the opponents of the death penalty, however? To oppose the death penalty in the face of incontestable evidence that it is an effective method of social defense violates the moral principle that where grave risks are to be run, it is better that they be run by the guilty than by the innocent. Consider in this connection an imaginary world in which by executing the murderer his victim is invariably restored to life, whole and intact, as though the murder had never occurred. In such a miraculous world, it is hard to see how anyone could oppose the death penalty on moral grounds. Why shouldn't a murderer die if that will infallibly bring the victim back to life? What could possibly be morally wrong with taking the murderer's life under such conditions? The death penalty would now be an instrument of perfect restitution, and it would give a new and better meaning to *lex talionis*, "a life for a life." The whole idea is fanciful, of course, but it shows as nothing else can how opposition to the death penalty cannot be both moral and wholly unconditional. If opposition to the death penalty is to be morally responsible, then it must be conceded that there are conditions (however unlikely) under which that opposition should cease.

But even if the death penalty were known to be a uniquely effective social defense, we could still imagine conditions under which it would be reasonable to oppose it. Suppose that in addition to being a slightly better preventive and deterrent than imprisonment, executions also have a slight incitive effect (so that for every ten murders an execution prevents or deters, it also incites another murder). Suppose

also that the administration of criminal justice in capital cases is inefficient, unequal, and tends to secure convictions and death sentences
only for murderers who least "deserve" to be sentenced to death
(including some death sentences and a few executions of the innocent). Under such conditions, it would still be reasonable to oppose the
death penalty, because on the facts supposed more (or not fewer)
innocent lives are being threatened and lost by using the death penalty than would be risked by abolishing it. It is important to remember
throughout our evaluation of the deterrence controversy that we cannot ever apply the principle (recall §13) that advises us to risk the lives
of the guilty in order to save the lives of the innocent. Instead, the
most we can do is weigh the risk for the general public against the
execution of those who are *found* guilty by an imperfect system of
criminal justice. These hypothetical factual assumptions illustrate the
contingencies upon which the morality of opposition to the death
penalty rests. And not only the morality of opposition; the morality of
any defense of the death penalty rests on the same contingencies. This
should help us understand why, in resolving the morality of capital
punishment one way or the other, it is so important to know, as well
as we can, whether the death penalty really does deter, prevent, or
incite crime, whether the innocent really are ever executed, and how
likely is the occurrence of these things in the future.

## §24 HOW MANY GUILTY LIVES IS ONE INNOCENT LIFE WORTH?

The great unanswered question that utilitarians must face concerns
the level of social defense that executions should be expected to
achieve before it is justifiable to carry them out. Consider three possible situations: (1) At the level of a hundred executions per year, each
additional execution of a convicted murderer reduces the number of
murder victims by ten. (2) Executing every convicted murderer
reduces the number of murders to 5,000 victims annually, whereas
executing only one out of ten reduces the number to 5,001. (3) Executing every convicted murderer reduces the murder rate no more than
does executing one in a hundred and no more than does a random
pattern of executions.

Many people contemplating situation (1) would regard this as a
reasonable trade-off: The execution of each further guilty person saves
the lives of ten innocent ones. (In fact, situation (1) or something like
it may be taken as a description of what most of those who defend the
death penalty on grounds of social defense believe is true.) But suppose that, instead of saving 10 lives, the number dropped to 0.5, i.e.,
one victim avoided for each two additional executions. Would that be
a reasonable price to pay? We are on the road toward the situation
described in situation (2), where a drastic 90 percent reduction in the
number of persons executed causes the level of social defense to drop

202 Hugo Adam Bedau

by only 0.0002 percent. Would it be worth it to execute so many more murderers at the cost of such a slight decrease in social defense? How many guilty lives is one innocent life worth? (Only those who think that guilty lives are *worthless* can avoid facing this problem.) In situation (3), of course, there is no basis for executing all convicted murderers, since there is no gain in social defense to show for each additional execution after the first out of each hundred has been executed. How, then, should we determine which out of each hundred convicted murderers is the unlucky one to be put to death?

It may be possible, under a complete and thoroughgoing cost /benefit analysis of the death penalty, to answer such questions. But an appeal merely to the moral principle that if lives are to be risked then let it be the lives of the guilty rather than of the innocent will not suffice. (We have already noticed, in §23, that this abstract principle is of little use in the actual administration of criminal justice, because the police and the courts do not deal with the guilty as such but only with those *judged* guilty.) Nor will it suffice to agree that society deserves all the crime prevention and deterrence it can get as a result of inflicting severe punishments. These principles are consistent with too many different policies. They are too vague by themselves to resolve the choice on grounds of social defense when confronted with hypothetical situations like those proposed above.

Since no adequate cost/benefit analysis of the death penalty exists, there is no way to resolve these questions from that standpoint at this time. Moreover, it can be argued that we cannot have such an analysis without already establishing in some way or other the relative value of innocent lives versus guilty lives. Far from being a product of cost/benefit analysis, a comparative evaluation of lives would have to be available to us before we undertook any such analysis. Without it, no cost/benefit analysis can get off the ground. Finally, it must be noted that our knowledge at present does not approximate to anything like the situation described above in (1). On the contrary, from the evidence we do have it seems we achieve about the same deterrent and preventive effects whether we punish murder by death or by imprisonment (recall §21). Therefore, something like the situation in (2) or in (3) may be correct. If so, this shows that the choice between the two policies of capital punishment and life imprisonment for murder will probably have to be made on some basis other than social defense; on that basis alone, the two policies are equivalent and therefore equally acceptable.

## V. CAPITAL PUNISHMENT AND RETRIBUTIVE JUSTICE

As we have noticed earlier in several contexts, there are two leading principles of retributive justice relevant to the capital punishment controversy. One is the principle that crimes should be punished. The other is the principle that the severity of a punishment should be proportional to the gravity of the offense. They are moral principles of recognized weight. No discussion of the morality of punishment would be complete without taking them into account. Leaving aside all questions of social defense, how strong a case for capital punishment can be made on their basis? How reliable and persuasive are these principles themselves?

## §25 CRIME MUST BE PUNISHED

Given the general rationale for punishment sketched earlier (§10 and §11), there cannot be any dispute over this principle. In embracing it, of course, we are not automatically making a fetish of "law and order," in the sense that we would be if we thought that the most important single thing to do with social resources is to punish crimes. In addition, this principle need not be in dispute between proponents and opponents of the death penalty. Only those who completely oppose punishment for murder and other erstwhile capital crimes would appear to disregard this principle. Even defenders of the death penalty must admit that putting a convicted murderer in prison for years is a punishment of that criminal. The principle that crime must be punished is neutral to our controversy, because both sides acknowledge it.

It is the other principle of retributive justice that seems to be a decisive one. Under the principle of retaliation, *lex talionis,* it must always have seemed that murderers ought to be put to death. Proponents of the death penalty, with rare exceptions, have insisted on this point, and it seems that even opponents of the death penalty must give it grudging assent. The strategy for opponents of the death penalty is to argue either that (1) this principle is not really a principle of justice after all, or that (2) to the extent it is, it does not require death for murderers, or that (3) in any case it is not the only principle of punitive justice. As we shall see, all these objections have merit.

## §26 IS MURDER ALONE TO BE PUNISHED BY DEATH?

Let us recall, first, that not even the Biblical world limited the death penalty to the punishment of murder. Many other nonhomicidal crimes also carried this penalty (e.g., kidnapping, witchcraft, cursing one's parents). In our own nation's recent history, persons have been executed for aggravated assault, rape, kidnapping, armed robbery, sabotage, and espionage. It is not possible to defend *any* of these executions (not to mention some of the more bizarre capital statutes, like the one in Georgia that used to provide an optional death penalty for desecration of a grave) on grounds of just retribution. This entails that either such executions are not justified or that they are justified on some ground other than retribution. In actual practice, few if any defenders of the death penalty have ever been willing to rest their case entirely on the moral principle of just retribution as formulated in terms of "a life for a life." (Kant seems to have been a conspicuous exception.) Most defenders of the death penalty have implied by their willingness to use executions to defend not only life but limb and property as well, that they did not place much value on the lives of criminals when compared to the value of both lives and things belonging to innocent citizens.

## §27 ARE ALL MURDERS TO BE PUNISHED BY DEATH?

European civilization for several centuries has tended to limit the variety of criminal homicides punishable by death. Even Kant took a casual attitude toward a mother's killing of her illegitimate child. ("A child born into the world outside marriage is outside the law . . . , and consequently it is also outside the protection of the law.")[10] In our society, the development nearly two hundred years ago of the distinction between first- and second-degree murder was an attempt to narrow the class of criminal homicides deserving the death penalty. Yet those dead owing to manslaughter, or to any kind of unintentional, accidental, unpremeditated, unavoidable, unmalicious killing are just as dead as the victims of the most ghastly murder. Both the law in practice and moral reflection show how difficult it is to identify all and only the criminal homicides that are appropriately punished by death (assuming that any are). Individual judges and juries differ in the conclusions they reach. The history of capital punishment for homicides reveals continual efforts, uniformly unsuccessful, to identify before the fact those homicides for which the slayer should die. Sixty years ago, Benjamin Cardozo, then a justice of the United States Supreme Court, said of the distinction between degrees of murder that it was

> . . . so obscure that no jury hearing it for the first time can fairly be expected to assimilate and understand it. I am not at all sure that I understand it myself after trying to apply it for many years and after diligent study of what has been written in the books. Upon the basis of this fine distinction with its obscure and mystifying psychology, scores of men have gone to their death.[11]

Similar skepticism has been expressed on the reliability and rationality of death-penalty statutes that give the trial court the discretion to sentence to prison or to death. As Justice John Marshall Harlan of the Supreme Court observed more than a decade ago,

> Those who have come to grips with the hard task of actually attempting to draft means of channeling capital sentencing discretion have confirmed the lesson taught by history. . . . To identify before the fact those characteristics of criminal homicide and their perpetrators which call for the death penalty, and to express these characteristics

in language which can be fairly understood and applied by the sentencing authority, appear to be tasks which are beyond present human ability.[12]

The abstract principle that the punishment of death best fits the crime of murder turns out to be extremely difficult to interpret and apply.

If we look at the matter from the standpoint of the actual practice of criminal justice, we can only conclude that "a life for a life" plays little or no role whatever. Plea bargaining (in which a person charged with a crime pleads guilty in exchange for a less severe sentence than he might have received if his case went to trial and he was found guilty), even where murder is concerned, is widespread. Studies of criminal justice reveal that what the courts (trial or appellate) in a given jurisdiction decide on a given day is first-degree murder suitably punished by death could just as well be decided in a neighboring jurisdiction on another day either as second-degree murder or as first-degree murder but without the death penalty. The factors that influence prosecutors in determining the charge under which they will prosecute go far beyond the simple principle of "a life for a life." Cynics, of course, will say that these facts show that our society does not care about justice. To put it succinctly, either justice in punishment does not consist of retribution, because there are other principles of justice; or there are other moral considerations besides justice that must be honored; or retributive justice is not adequately expressed in the idea of "a life for a life"; or justice in the criminal justice system is beyond our reach.

## §28 IS DEATH SUFFICIENTLY RETRIBUTIVE?

Those who advocate capital punishment for murder on retributive grounds must face the objection that, on their own principles, the death penalty in some cases is morally inadequate. How could death in the electric chair or the gas chamber or before a firing squad or on a gallows suffice as just retribution, given the savage, brutal, wanton character of so many murders? How can retributive justice be served by anything less than equally savage methods of execution? From a retributive point of view, the oft-heard exclamation, "Death is too good for him!" has a certain truth. Are defenders of the death penalty willing to embrace this consequence of their own doctrine?

If they were, they would be stooping to the methods and thus to the squalor of the murderer. Where the quality of the crime sets the limits of just methods of punishment, as it will if we attempt to give exact and literal implementation to *lex talionis,* society will find itself descending to the cruelties and savagery that criminals employ. What is worse, society would be deliberately authorizing such acts, in the cool light of reason, and not (as is often true of vicious criminals) impulsively or in hatred and anger or with an insane or unbalanced mind. Moral restraints, in short, prohibit us from trying to make executions perfectly retributive. Once we grant that such restraints are proper, it is unreasonable to insist that the principle of "a life for a life" nevertheless by itself justifies the execution of murderers.

Other considerations take us in a different direction. Few murders, outside television and movie scripts, involve anything like an execution. An execution, after all, begins with a solemn pronouncement of the death sentence from a judge; this is followed by long detention in maximum security awaiting the date of execution, during which various complex and protracted appeals will be pursued; after this there is a clemency hearing before the governor, and then "the last mile" to the execution chamber itself. As the French writer Albert Camus once remarked,

> For there to be an equivalence, the death penalty would have to punish a criminal who had warned his victim of the date at which he would inflict a horrible death on him and who, from that moment onward, had confined him at his mercy for months. Such a monster is not encountered in private life.[13]

## §29 DIFFERENTIAL SEVERITY DOES NOT REQUIRE EXECUTIONS

What, then, emerges from our examination of retributive justice and the death penalty? If retributive justice is thought to consist in *lex talionis,* all one can say is that this principle has never exercised more than a crude and indirect effect on the actual punishments meted out by society. Other principles interfere with a literal and single-minded application of this one. Some homicides seem improperly punished by death at all; others would require methods of execution too horrible to inflict; in still other cases any possible execution is too deliberate and monstrous given the nature of the motivation culminating in the murder. In any case, proponents of the death penalty rarely confine themselves to reliance on nothing but this principle of just retribution, since they rarely confine themselves to supporting the death penalty only for all murders.

But retributive justice need not be thought of as consisting in *lex talionis.* One may reject that principle as too crude and still embrace the retributive principle that the severity of punishments should be graded according to the gravity of the offense. Even though one need not claim that life imprisonment (or any kind of punishment other than death) "fits" the crime of murder, one can claim that this punishment is the proper one for murder. To do this, the schedule of punishments accepted by society must be arranged so that this mode of imprisonment is the most severe penalty used. Opponents of the death penalty need not reject this principle of retributive justice, even though they must reject a literal *lex talionis.*

## §30 EQUAL JUSTICE AND CAPITAL PUNISHMENT

During the past generation, the strongest practical objection to the death penalty has been the inequities with which it has been applied. As the late Supreme Court Justice William O. Douglas once observed, "One searches our chronicles in vain for the execution of any member of the affluent strata of this society."[14] One does not search our chronicles in vain for the crime of murder committed by the affluent. All the sociological evidence points to the conclusion that the death penalty is the poor man's justice; hence the slogan, "Those without the capital get the punishment." The death penalty is also racially sensitive. Every study of the death penalty for rape (unconstitutional only since 1977) has confirmed that black male rapists (especially where the victim is a white female) are far more likely to be sentenced to death and executed than white male rapists. Convicted black murderers are more likely to end up on "death row" than are others, and the killers of whites (whether white or nonwhite) are more likely to be sentenced to death than are the killers of nonwhites.

Let us suppose that the factual basis for such a criticism is sound. What follows for the morality of capital punishment? Many defenders of the death penalty have been quick to point out that since there is nothing intrinsic about the crime of murder or rape dictating that only the poor or only racial-minority males will commit it, and since there is nothing overtly racist about the statutes that authorize the death penalty for murder or rape, capital punishment itself is hardly at fault if in practice it falls with unfair impact on the poor and the black. There is, in short, nothing in the death penalty that requires it to be applied unfairly and with arbitrary or discriminatory results. It is at worst a fault in the system of administering criminal justice. (Some, who dispute the facts cited above, would deny even this.) There is an adequate remedy—execute more whites, women, and affluent murderers.

Presumably, both proponents and opponents of capital punishment would concede that it is a fundamental dictate of justice that a punishment should not be unfairly—inequitably or unevenly—enforced and applied. They should also be able to agree that when the punishment in question is the extremely severe one of death, then the requirement to be fair in using such a punishment becomes even more stringent. There should be no dispute in the death penalty controversy over these principles of justice. The dispute begins as soon as one attempts to connect the principles with the actual use of this punishment.

In this country, many critics of the death penalty have argued, we would long ago have got rid of it entirely if it had been a condition of its use that it be applied equally and fairly. In the words of the attorneys who argued against the death penalty in the Supreme Court during 1972, "It is a freakish aberration, a random extreme act of violence, visibly arbitrary and discriminatory—a penalty reserved for unusual application because, if it were usually used, it would affront universally shared standards of public decency."[15] It is difficult to dispute this judgment, when one considers that there have been in the United States during the past fifty years about half a million criminal homicides but only about 3,900 executions (all but 33 of which were of men).

We can look at these statistics in another way to illustrate the same point. If we could be assured that the nearly 4,000 persons executed were the worst of the bad, repeated offenders incapable of safe incarceration, much less of rehabilitation, the most dangerous murderers in captivity—the ones who had killed more than once and were likely to kill again, and the least likely to be confined in prison without chronic danger to other inmates and the staff—then one might accept half a million murders and a few thousand executions with a sense that rough justice had been done. But the truth is otherwise. Persons are sentenced to death and executed not because they have been found to be uncontrollably violent or hopelessly poor confinement and release risks. Instead, they are executed because they have a poor defense (inexperienced or overworked counsel) at trial; they have no funds to bring sympathetic witnesses to court; they are transients or strangers in the community where they are tried; the prosecuting attorney wants the publicity that goes with "sending a killer to the chair"; there are no funds for an appeal or for a transcript of the trial record; they are members of a despised racial or political minority. In short, the actual study of why particular persons have been sentenced to death and executed does not show any careful winnowing of the worst from the bad. It shows that the executed were usually the unlucky victims of prejudice and discrimination, the losers in an arbitrary lottery that could just as well have spared them, the victims of the disadvantages that almost always go with poverty. A system like this does not enhance human life; it cheapens and degrades it. However heinous murder and other crimes are, the system of capital punishment does not compensate for or erase those crimes. It only tends to add new injuries of its own to the catalogue of human brutality.

## VI. CONCLUSION

Our discussion of the death penalty from the moral point of view shows that there is no one moral principle the validity of which is paramount and that decisively favors one side of the controversy. Rather, we have seen how it is possible to argue either for or against the death penalty, and in each case to be appealing to moral principles that derive from the worth, value, or dignity of human life. We have also seen how it is impossible to connect any of these abstract principles with the actual practice of capital punishment without a close study of sociological, psychological, and economic factors. By themselves, the moral principles that are relevant are too abstract and uncertain in application to be of much help. Without the guidance of such principles, of course, the facts (who gets executed, and why) are of little use, either.

My own view of the controversy is that, given the moral principles we have identified in the course of our discussion (including the overriding value of human life), and given all the facts about capital punishment, the balance of reasons favors abolition of the death penalty. The alternative to capital punishment that I favor, as things currently stand, is long-term imprisonment. Such a punishment is retributive and can be made appropriately severe to reflect the gravity of the crime. It gives adequate (though hardly perfect) protection to the public. It is free of the worst defect to which the death penalty is liable: execution of the innocent. It tacitly acknowledges that there is no way for a criminal, alive or dead, to make complete amends for murder or other grave crimes against the person. Last but not least, it has symbolic significance. The death penalty, more than any other kind of killing, is done by officials in the name of society and on its behalf. Yet each of us has a hand in such killings. Unless they are absolutely necessary they cannot be justified. Thus, abolishing the death penalty represents extending the hand of life even to those who by their crimes have "forfeited" any right to live. It is a tacit admission that we must abandon the folly and pretense of attempting to secure perfect justice in an imperfect world.

Searching for an epigram suitable for our times, in which governments have waged war and suppressed internal dissent by using methods that can only be described as savage and criminal, Camus was prompted to admonish: "Let us be neither victims nor executioners." Perhaps better than any other, this exhortation points the way between forbidden extremes if we are to respect the humanity in each of us.

# NOTES

1. W. D. Ross, *The Right and the Good* (1930), pp. 60–61.
2. John Locke, *Second Treatise of Government* (1690), §§23, 172.
3. Ibid., §12.
4. By 'social defense' is meant the prevention of crime, by means of deterrence and incapacitation, as well as by the avoidance of incentives and opportunities for the commission of crimes. Thus, prisons, police forces, controlling the sale of firearms, locks on doors, and threats of punishment can all be regarded as methods of social defense.
5. Immanuel Kant, *The Metaphysical Elements of Justice* (1797), tr. John Ladd, p. 102.
6. Ibid., p. 100.

7. Ibid., p. 101.
8. J. S. Mill, *Utilitarianism* (1863), chap. 2, penultimate paragraph.
9. Cesare Beccaria, *Of Crimes and Punishments* (1764), tr. Henry Paolucci, p. 50.
10. Immanuel Kant, op. cit., p. 106.
11. Benjamin Cardozo, "What Medicine Can Do for Law" (1928), reprinted in Margaret E. Hall, ed., *Selected Writings of Benjamin Nathan Cardozo* (1947), p. 204.
12. *McGautha* v. *California*, 402 U.S. 183 (1971), at p. 204.
13. Albert Camus, *Resistance, Rebellion, and Death* (1961), p. 199.
14. *Furman* v. *Georgia*, 408 U.S. 238 (1972), at pp. 251–252.
15. NAACP Legal Defense and Educational Fund, Brief for Petitioner in *Aikens* v. *California*, O.T. 1971, No. 68-5027, reprinted in Philip English Mackey, ed., *Voices Against Death: American Opposition to Capital Punishment, 1787–1975* (1975), p. 288.

# SUGGESTIONS FOR FURTHER READING

Further readings are mentioned below in connection with the section (§) of the essay to which they are most pertinent.

§§2–4 For general discussions of natural or human rights, see the essays collected in A. I. Melden, ed., *Human Rights,* Belmont, Calif., Wadsworth, 1970, or in David Lyons, ed., *Rights,* same publisher, 1979. The best recent discussions by philosophers—Ronald Dworkin, *Taking Rights Seriously,* Cambridge, Mass., Harvard University Press, 1977; J. Roland Pennock and John W. Chapman, eds., *Human Rights: Nomos XXIII,* New York, New York University Press, 1981; Theodore M. Benditt, *Rights,* Totowa, N.J., Rowman and Littlefield, 1982; Alan Gewirth, *Human Rights,* Chicago, Ill., University of Chicago Press, 1982—ignore the death penalty. An exception is A. I. Melden, *Rights and Persons,* Berkeley, Calif., University of California Press, 1977, see pp. 233–235. I have discussed some of the relevant issues in more detail in "The Right to Life," *The Monist,* 52 (1968), pp. 550–572, and in "Prisoners' Rights," *Criminal Justice Ethics,* 1 (1982), pp. 26–41.

§§5–7 On the moral and political philosophy of Kant, see H. B. Acton, *Kant's Moral Philosophy,* New York, St. Martin's Press, 1970, and Jeffrie G. Murphy, *Kant: The Philosophy of Right,* New York, St. Martin's, 1970. See also Don E. Scheid, "Kant's Retributivism," *Ethics,* 93 (1983), pp. 262–282.

§8 For a more extensive discussion of utilitarianism and the death penalty, see my essay, "Bentham's Utilitarian Critique of the Death Penalty," *The Journal of Criminal Law and Criminology,* 74 (1983), pp. 1033–1065.

§§10–12 See in general H. L. A. Hart, *Punishment and Responsibility,* Oxford University Press, 1968; Ted Honderich, *Punishment: The Supposed Justifications,* London, Hutchinson, 1969; H. B. Acton, ed., *The Philosophy of Punishment,* London, Macmillan, 1969; Gertrude Ezorsky, ed., *Philosophical Perspectives on Punishment,* Albany, N.Y., SUNY Press, 1972; Andrew von Hirsch, *Doing Justice: The Choice of Punishments,* New York, Hill and Wang, 1976; Nigel Walker, *Punishment, Danger and Stigma,* Totowa, N.J., Barnes and Noble Books, 1980; and Hyman Gross and Andrew von Hirsch, eds., *Sentencing,* New York, Oxford University Press, 1981.

§§15–16 For discussion of the relative severity of punishments, see Leslie Sebba, "Some Explorations in the Scaling of Penalties," *Journal of Research in Crime and Delinquency,* 15 (1978), pp. 247–265; and Maynard L. Erickson and Jack P. Gibbs, "On the Perceived Severity of Legal Penalties," *The Journal of Criminal Law and Criminology,* 70 (1979), pp. 102–116.

§17 A graphic account of the historic shift from corporal to incarcerative punishments can be found in Michel Foucault, *Discipline and Punish: The Birth of the Prison,* New York, Pantheon, 1977. A recent defense of physical pain as the best punishment for criminals may be found in Graeme Newman, *Just and Painful: A Case for the Corporal Punishment of Criminals,* New York, Macmillan, 1983.

§18 On the use of force in self-defense and in defense of property, see the cases and materials in John Kaplan, *Criminal Justice: Introductory Cases and Materials,* 2nd ed., New York, Foundation Press, 1978, pp. 43–45. Deeper issues have been explored by Judith Jarvis Thomson in *Self-Defense and Rights,* The Lindley Lecture, University of Kansas, 1976.

§19 The best general discussion of deterrence and related issues is in Jack Gibbs, *Crime, Punishment and Deterrence,* New York, Elsevier, 1975.

§§20–21 The factual issues surrounding the death penalty as a preventive and deterrent of crime are explored in H. A. Bedau, ed., *The Death Penalty in America,* 3rd ed., New York, Oxford University Press, 1982, chap. 4; Thorsten Sellin, *The Penalty of Death,* Beverly Hills, Calif., Sage Publications, 1980; and William J. Bowers, *Legal Homicide: Death as Punishment in America, 1864–1982,* Boston, Northeastern University Press, 1984, chaps. 8 and 9. The most recent review is by Richard Lempert, "The Effect of Executions on Homicides: A New Look in an Old Light," *Crime and Delinquency,* 29 (1983), pp. 88–115.

§22 For discussions of a cost/benefit analysis of the death penalty, see Barry Nakell, "The Cost of the Death Penalty," *Criminal Law Bulletin,* 14 (1978), pp. 68–80, reprinted in Bedau, *The Death Penalty in America,* cited above; and the report prepared by the New York State Defenders Association, *Capital Losses: The Price of the Death Penalty for New York State* (1982).

§§25–29 For the most influential recent retribution-based theory of punishment, see von Hirsch, *Doing Justice,* cited above; also Richard G. Singer, *Just Deserts: Sentencing Based on Equality and Desert,* Cambridge, Mass., Ballinger, 1979. I have criticized this theory in "Retribution and the Theory of Punishment," *The Journal of Philosophy,* 75 (1978), pp. 601–620.

§30 The best brief discussion of the inequities of the death penalty as currently provided in American law is in Charles L. Black, Jr., *Capital Punishment: The Inevitability of Caprice and Mistake,* 2nd ed., New York, Norton, 1981. See also Bowers, *Legal Homicide,* cited above, chaps. 7 and 10; and the death penalty symposium in *The Journal of Criminal Law and Criminology,* fall 1983.

§31 Discussions of the death penalty controversy by other philosophers may be found in various essays and chapters of books. See especially chap. 3 of Hart's *Punishment and Responsibility,* cited above, and Richard Wasserstrom, "Capital Punishment as Punishment: Some Theoretical Issues and Objections," *Midwest Studies in Philosophy,* 7 (1982), pp. 473–502; and the essays by Jeffrey H. Reiman and Stephen Nathanson in *Philosophy and Public Affairs,* Spring 1985. The death penalty is defended in chaps. 18 and 19 of Ernest van den Haag's *Punishing Criminals,* New York, Basic Books, 1974; in chap. 8 of Burton M. Leiser's *Liberty, Justice, and Morals,* 2nd ed., New York, Macmillan, 1979; and Walter Berns, *For Capital Punishment,* New York, Basic Books, 1979.

Omitted from the discussion in the foregoing essay but prominent in public debate during the past decade is the extent to which the death penalty violates the federal constitution because it is a "cruel and unusual punishment." The basic Supreme Court rulings on this issue during the 1970s, beginning with *Furman* v. *Georgia,* 408 U. S. 238 (1972), have been discussed and reprinted in Bedau, *The Death Penalty in America,* cited above, chap. 6. The most vigorous defense of the death penalty as not unconstitutional is in Raoul Berger, *Death Penalties,* Cambridge, Mass., Harvard University Press, 1982; his views have been equally vigorously criticized by David A. J. Richards in *California Law Review,* 71 (1983), pp. 1372–1398; Stephen Gillers in *The Yale Law Journal,* 92 (1983), pp. 731–748; and by me in *Michigan Law Review,* 81 (1983), pp. 1152–1165.

# 6

# Whither Baby Doe?

## DONALD VANDEVEER

To everything there is a season . . .
a time to plant, and a time
to pluck up that which is planted.

Eccles. 3:1, 2

## I. INTRODUCTION

### §1 THE QUESTIONS

In the spring of 1982, a six-day-old infant known as "Baby Doe" died in Bloomington, Indiana.[1] His parents, with the support of the courts, chose to deny him food, water, and surgery.[2] "Sure as shootin'," one might say, it was predictable—given such treatment—that Baby Doe would die. Was it infanticide? Was it wrong? As I write, in the fall of 1984, in Raleigh, North Carolina, a twenty-two-year-old mother is being prosecuted for periodically dosing her normal baby with warfarin (a substance that prevents blood coagulation) and thereby attempting to kill him. Are these two cases relevantly similar? Why or why not? More details, of course, would be needed to decide. Baby Doe apparently had a tracheoesophageal fistula—a condition in which the esophagus is not connected to the stomach—which is correctable by standard surgery. Baby Doe also had Down's syndrome, the victims of which have moderate to severe mental retardation (about 95 percent have an "IQ" below 50—if IQ tests are at all reliable), and one-third to one-half have other problems (such as congenital heart defects). Still, such children commonly are thought to have happy dispositions.

Ostensibly, the parents did not want to raise a retarded child. Did they have a right to so decide? Did they decide rightly? Is it permissible to let defective neonates die? If so, should they be allowed to starve—or be painlessly killed? If it is wrong to terminate such infants, should the government seek to intervene? Would complaints about "governmental meddling" carry much weight if we were discussing sexual child abuse? Questions assault us from all sides—hard questions about which considerable investigation is in order and about which reasonable, well-informed persons of good will often disagree. Still, as much was true about the controversy over whether the earth, as Ptolemy claimed, was the center of the universe, and there was a right answer in that case; eventually it won common acceptance.

We have certain deeply entrenched convictions (e.g., that we shouldn't kill everyone) which we do not surrender readily. Reflection and argumentation may move us to view some of our initial convictions as arbitrary, prejudicial, or unsustainable. One widely shared conviction is that if anything is wrong, then killing (human) babies is wrong. Such a matter initially does not seem a "borderline case"—one lending itself to sincere, reasoned disagreement. Many are tempted by the view that it is always wrong to kill (or, perhaps, let die as well) human newborns. A contrary suggestion may be viewed as the product of a corrupt mind. Such conviction often is shaken quickly, however. For example, consider a hypothetical case. Suppose that a couple in their thirties, with two children, are struggling financially but choose to go ahead with a planned third child. The husband loses his second job near the end of the pregnancy. To their surprise, their new baby suffers from trisomy 13 (or Patau's syndrome). Some key features of this syndrome are holoprosencephaly (incomplete development of the brain, with midline facial defects), cleft lip and palate, eye abnormalities (e.g., no eyes), severe mental deficiency, deafness, polydactyly (an extra digit) of the hands or feet, congenital heart disease, and apneic spells (trouble in breathing). Less than one in five such babies survives the first year; those who do have seizures and severe mental defects. Some will think that the case for letting the trisomy 13 infant die is stronger than in doing the same with Baby Doe. Even those most vehemently (morally) opposed to letting defective infants die tend to make an exception or two. For example, it is not unusual to encounter the concession that anencephalic (brainless or partly brainless) infants may be allowed to die. In considering the diverse range of defects, one also might compare the case of an infant born with a finger missing on each hand.

What may be done in such cases? What ought to be done? Why? Answering such questions requires, in turn, addressing some quite fundamental issues of moral philosophy. We cannot explore them fully here, but we can make a start. Those who prefer simple answers to apparently simple questions might be reminded that questions, though simple (such as "What causes cancer?"), often demand cau-

tious, thorough, complex investigation. Further, anyone initially inclined to adopt a certain form of moral subjectivism—that anyone's
answer to a moral question is as good (as reasonable?) as anyone else's
—might contemplate two points: (1) society "enforces morality" on
related matters (for instance, one may be treated as a murderer if one
kills a normal child even if one believes the act to be one's duty [as did
one mother in recent years who explained that she roasted her child
in the oven in order to drive out the demon who possessed him]) and
(2) the mentioned subjectivist view implies that a belief such as "Killing children for recreational purposes is all right" is as good as any
other belief—an implication few will accept (imagine organized "child
hunts" on the order of fox hunts). Fortunately, people enamored of the
slogan "morality is subjective" tend to ignore it—except when in philosophy classes (alas).

Our central moral questions—regarding (1) what treatment of defective neonates is permissible and (2) what treatment ought to be
extended to such neonates—have proved to be a source of deep and
continuing controversy. Partly, no doubt, this is due to strong emotional attachments people have to certain outlooks; it may also be
partly due to the absence of or disarray in pretheoretical moral beliefs
about such matters. For example, we are tempted to think that if
anything is wrong, surely killing innocent human babies is; on the
other hand, we may feel deep opposition to the suggestion that society
should criminally punish (for homicide) a health-care professional who
hastens the death of an anencephalic newborn. We need not dismiss
our initial prereflective convictions (or "moral intuitions") as of no
weight or relevance. Once we sort out cases and more fully articulate
and scrutinize our beliefs, perhaps we shall find firmer ground for this
or that conclusion about how we may treat newborns. We should also
resist the opposite (albeit inviting) inclination to rest uncritically content with what we already are inclined to think—since that is the path
taken by those distinguished for their prejudice, anti-intellectualism,
and dogmatism.

The primary moral question on which I shall focus is the question
of permissibility noted earlier: What treatment of defective neonates
is permissible? The question is highly general. In the end, what is
needed is a reasoned defense of an answer, an answer sufficiently
specific to provide guidance daily in neonatal intensive care units. The
needed answer and its defense would be sufficiently complex to deserve the label 'theory'. The identification of a fully adequate theory
is beyond my grasp, but in what follows we shall take steps in that
direction. Our general moral question requires answering a number
of other not-so-small questions. In each case I attempt to sketch and
assess the main arguments surrounding these questions.

However, we begin to examine the arguments directly only in §5.
In §4 a brief look at the diverse types of neonatal defects will provide
a useful background prior to getting down to the philosophical core

of things, namely, assessing the arguments for the competing views. And before that, some further stage setting is in order.

## §2 MATTERS OF LANGUAGE

We are reluctant to talk plainly about death and killing. Instead, we often use euphemisms and potentially misleading expressions (for example, children are sometimes surprised to learn that animals "put to sleep" or "put down" do not wake or get up). Consider also our diverse uses of the term 'euthanasia'. In a strict sense, to euthanize a being is to kill it (or, perhaps, let it die) *for its sake,* for example, to prevent or alleviate suffering. To kill a being or let it die because its continued existence promises a great burden to others or because fairness dictates no further expenditure of funds to keep it alive is *not* in the strict sense to euthanize the being.[3] For practical philosophical reasons, the ultimately important question is whether the killing (or letting die) is morally justifiable or not. Our classificatory labels ('euthanasia', 'suicide', 'active', 'passive', 'punishment', and so on) should facilitate, not impede, the task of determining what we must or may do.

To be clear about our focus we also should reflect on the terms 'infant', 'neonate', 'handicapped', and 'defective'. Unless otherwise indicated, the use here of such terms will refer only to members of *Homo sapiens.* In the law, 'infant' may refer to humans between birth and one year later—or, on occasion, to any human between birth and eighteen years later. Although it is somewhat arbitrary, I shall restrict my use of such terms to humans no more than one month beyond the time of birth. This restriction accords with a rather standard usage of 'neonate'. It is natural to speak of 'premature infants' and, thus, to use the term 'infant' even for a human only twenty-six weeks beyond conception. Should we call any viable fetus *ex utero* (outside the womb) an 'infant' or 'neonate'? What if, because it has been surgically removed (with or without the intent to abort it), it was not "born"— that is, not a byproduct of "giving birth"—is it then not to be called a "newborn"? We need not stipulate an answer to all these questions here. We should be alert to the possibility of conceptual confusion, however, which is why I call attention to such matters. In general I shall not hesitate to use 'newborn' or 'infant' to refer either to viable human fetuses *ex utero* (however they have gotten to be *ex utero*) under forty weeks since conception or to the stage between forty and forty-four weeks—those normally "newborn." Almost invariably, given current technology, our concern will be with *ex utero* humans between twenty and forty-four weeks after conception. Our typical focus, however, is on those "born" and between birth and "one month old."

Aside from reminding us of potential conceptual tangles, these reflections tend to emphasize the significance of a certain moral puzzle. Can we consistently believe both that abortion is morally permissible and that terminating defective neonates is impermissible (to set aside the killing/letting die distinction let us use 'terminate', or cognates, to mean deliberately kill or deliberately let die)? It is possible that in a late-stage abortion, say at twenty-four weeks, the fetus that is removed will prove to be viable. If we think abortion morally permissible, may the fetus be terminated? What if it is seriously defective? What if not?

I shall note here simply that some believe that the abortion of fetuses and termination of neonates are morally on a par—that is, that they are either both permissible (one position) or that they are both impermissible (a second position). Others take the view that the two practices can have divergent moral values—that is, one can be permissible and the other not (a third position). This third position seems to presuppose that there is a *morally relevant difference* between abortion and infanticide. What that difference might be is, on the face of things, not obvious when one recalls that the to-be-aborted fetus may be "older" and more developed than a "born" premature infant. Those who have never pondered this fact are often deeply impressed by it, but the nest of issues to be explored suggests the wisdom of not expecting any easy or obvious path to truth. After all, we have not yet examined a single explicit argument.

## §3 THE CONCEPT OF THE DEFECTIVE

Since our main concern is with defective neonates, we must consider what is meant by 'defective'. The drawback to not "paying attention to words" is failing to know, or obscuring, what is at issue. Those who breed collies as show dogs regard rigid pointed ears in collies (if not in Dr. Spock) as a fault—a defect of sorts. Yet there is, to my knowledge, no reason to believe that this trait, apart from human reactions to it, is likely to impair a canine possessor of it from leading a contented, successful, canine life. This point should call attention to two things that might be meant by 'defective', roughly: (1) possessing a trait likely to impair the possessor from achieving what is *in its own* interests or (2) possessing a trait likely to impair *another,* a nonpossessor, from achieving what is in *its* interests. It is worth observing that in discussions of the moral permissibility of terminating defective neonates, there is virtual unanimity that the only serious controversies concern those defective in sense (1) (which might be called the Possessor Regarding Conception, in contrast to (2), the Other Regarding Conception). Some people no doubt believe that aborting a male fetus is all right if one wants a female child, but no one, to my knowledge, conceptualizes "being a male" as a defect in sense (1).

The concept of a defect is more complicated than I have suggested, but I shall note only a few further features. Not all statistically abnormal traits are defects; for example, compare natural capacities to develop exceptional mathematical skills. The impairments associated with defects are evidently a matter of degree. Polydactyly (possession of an extra digit) is not as limiting as mental retardation. In a trivial sense, we are all "genetically defective" in that we are all said to possess a half-dozen or so genetic traits which, if expressed, result in impairments to the possessor; for example, I am genetically defective in that I am slightly myopic (without corrective lenses my vision is not 20-20). Some traits—such as severe scoliosis or severe retardation—impair under almost all prevailing conditions. Some traits are disadvantageous under some conditions but not others; for example, the sickle cell trait, which can result in anemia but also provides greater protection against malaria.

If we define, as I have, 'defect' in terms of what impairs the possessor's interest, what will count as a defect depends on how we identify what is in someone's interest and whether the latter is thought dependent on a person's desires. Subtleties arise which, however, it is better to avoid here. For most purposes, a useful if rough way to conceive of a defect is as any trait which in itself reasonable, well-informed persons would prefer not to have under most circumstances.

Given the above considerations, it is clear that it can be a grave mistake to generalize about "defective neonates," "handicapped newborns," or "the genetically defective." If there is a compelling case for terminating some defective neonates, it surely will not apply to all. Although "defective" is evaluative and presupposes certain standards of appraisal, there should be no suggestion that defective neonates are blameworthy or "deserving of death." Not all evaluations are moral evaluations.

Further, I have persisted usually in using "defective" rather than 'handicapped' since it seems misleading to speak of certain sorts of defective neonates as handicapped. For example, the anencephalic infant, perhaps the Tay-Sachs or Lesch-Nyhan infant as well, dubiously are said to be handicapped; it is not as if they have pursuits that are impaired. (The technical terms are explained in §4.) They arguably have *no* pursuits, *no lives to lead.* By way of further comparison, it would be odd to report "Oh, Max is all right except for one setback: he went into an irreversible coma." Conceptually, a handicap is a disadvantage under which the one handicapped nevertheless can get on living his life, pursuing some goals, and so on. Thus, lacking the capacity for consciousness or for reasoned formulation of goals dubiously are labeled "handicaps."

## §4 THE RELEVANCE OF DEFECTS

Infants may have various sorts of defects resulting from different causes: malformed genetic material, traumatic conditions during the gestational period (such as drug usage by the mother), or difficulties during birth (such as insufficient oxygen to the brain). Shortly we shall survey some of the important anomalies that may exist. With the possible exception of anencephaly, few are usually thought to provide reason to deny that the neonate is a "human being." In this respect, controversy over terminating neonatal life contrasts with the debate over abortion, especially early-stage abortion, concerning which some deny that the human zygote or human embryo should count as a human being. For those who find this latter view puzzling, it should be observed that being alive and being human are not sufficient for being a human being (otherwise, my thumb is a human being). Generally, with regard to the neonates in question, there is no dispute that they are human beings.

As we shall observe, some think that there is either no presumption against terminating the lives of any neonates or that there is only an overridable presumption (perhaps not a very strong one at that). The reasons for either view seem roughly the following ones, and I set them out here so that we can begin to think about the *relevance* of neonatal anomalies when we come to survey a sample of them. First, some philosophers defend the position that the right to life attaches only to *persons,* and the category of persons includes only some entities in the category of human beings. On this view, to be (to count as) a person one must exhibit certain psychological traits (such as self-awareness), ones not possessed by all humans—in particular not possessed, so it is claimed, by neonates. On this view *both* normal *and* defective neonates lack a right to life and, hence, that source of a moral presumption against termination simply does not exist. On this view, then, it is a mistake to assume, as many people do, that normal infants have a right to life not possessed by seriously defective infants; *neither* have such a right. Of some interest is the point that defenders of this rather "liberal" view may agree with some "conservatives" in denying that moral significance attaches to the presence of serious defects in deciding the permissibility of termination. The main argument surrounding the "personhood" approach will be set out in §9.

Some writers do not focus on the question of whether the defective neonate is a person and do not deny its status as a member of *Homo sapiens,* but they question whether the infant is capable of living a "truly human" life. If an infant, such as the Tay-Sachs child, is doomed to live only a few years and irremediably suffer on balance during that span, its prospective life seems so distant from a normal human life that one can see why some are tempted to say it is not a "truly human" existence. However, if it is granted that the infant is a human being (as a Tay-Sachs child surely is), its life is, quite literally, a human life —albeit an unusual and a tragic one. Perhaps what can be extracted from questions about whether the life is "truly human" is a judgment about the value or quality of the prospective life of the defective neonate. In short, sometimes the suggestion is that severe limitations make the life of little or no value.

When it is said that the life of a being (B) is of lesser or little value, it is important to determine whether the claim concerns (1) the value of B's life (or disvalue) to others or (2) the value of B's life (or disvalue) to B. Some deny the appropriateness of engaging in "quality of life" conjectures, but given the ambiguity of such an expression, we need to know whether what is being denied is the relevance of considerations associated with 1 or with 2 or both.

It may be held, then, that the presence of serious defects is relevant, since (to explore one view) their presence makes the newborn less valuable to others—or even a disvalue to others. Clearly, most parents would prefer a child without serious defects and, in that sense, abstractly value less a child with such defects. Further, it is clear that raising a seriously defective infant typically involves significant objective burdens (whatever offsetting rewards issue from the experience) —for example, fear, anxiety, surrender of certain hopes, expenditure of considerable time, energy, and money, and so on. In an abstract discussion such as this it is difficult but important to "emotionally appreciate" in a vivid, imaginative way both the enormous psychological burdens as well as the great satisfactions that parents *may* derive from caring for a seriously defective child. Clearly, one ought not generalize glibly here; experiences vary from case to case. Further, those who have rewarding experiences may be more likely to voice them publicly than those who do not; after all, it is not "becoming" or "gracious" to reveal one's regret, bitterness, or self-regarding complaints.

The question of moral interest here is not whether the presence of serious defects in an infant causes its parents to value it less but whether such defects and the prospective increased *burden* on the parents or other possible caretakers is morally relevant in making decisions about whether to prolong (or terminate) the neonate's life. That is, should such a prospective burden have any weight at all in deciding on life-sustaining treatment? If so, why—and how much? If not, why not? To these matters we shall return in §13.

We have identified two views about the relevance of neonatal defects. One is that they are not particularly relevant, since all neonates lack a right to life (on the "no right to infringe" view; see §9). A second view is that they are relevant since serious neonatal defects burden others, and this burden has weight in deciding whether to prolong life. A third view focuses on the prospective value of the life of the neonate to *it*. That is, given its defects and the probable limits to remedying them, can the infant have a decent life or one that is satisfying (to it) on balance? Alternatively, will its life be so limited or so filled with suffering—and the absence of offsetting satisfactions— that, as the point is sometimes put, it "would be better off dead"? In contrast to the second approach mentioned, this one cannot be accused of assuming that the value of a neonate's prospective life is solely a function of others' preferences and attitudes. On this third approach, those deciding whether to extend life-prolonging treatment— imaginatively and on the basis of the most expert medical diagnosis and prognosis—must judge whether such a life is worth living. To the tiresome cliché "who's to say" whether another's life is worth living, this approach says "we are" (or "others are") on the basis of the best empirical data available and with the greatest sensitivity and impartiality we can muster. If to do so is to assume that whether a life is worth (continued) living depends importantly on whether it will be a satisfying one (to the one living it) and on the quality of prospective life span remaining, so be it. This position seems incompatible with one asserting that "all human life is of unlimited, or infinite, value." That is one reason, among others, for the controversy that surrounds the position. Frequently, the Best Interest Principle is invoked, namely, that "we should do whatever is in the best interest of the child." On the third approach to the relevance of defects— the presence of *some* defects and the absence of effective remedies—there may be good reason to judge, in selected cases, that it is in an infant's best interest to live no longer. However, the Best Interest Principle may be associated with a different assumption about *what* is in an infant's best interest. For example, some maintain that it is best for anyone to *live as long as possible no matter what the quality of the living* (some call this view "vitalism") or that suffering is redemptive or will be rewarded in an afterlife. In any case, if a specific conclusion about treatment is to be derived, the Best Interest Principle must be supplemented by specific criteria for determining what is in a being's best interest.

We have surveyed briefly some different grounds for appraising the relevance of serious defects in newborns. In §6 we will join the issues more directly. The motivation for ethical inquiry has its roots in practical questions, and the goal of answering those questions rationally cannot be achieved in an empirical vacuum. Our space is limited, but to make matters less abstract it is useful to survey some types of defects found in newborns. To such matters I turn.

## §5 TYPES OF DEFECTS OR ANOMALOUS CONDITIONS

A fuller catalog of anomalous conditions in neonates would be out of place here. That which follows is a sketch of some of the more common and most discussed conditions.[4]

*A. Prematurity*  If not a defect in itself, prematurity of birth is often associated with, or likely to result in, defects. An infant is categorized as *premature* if born prior to thirty-seven weeks of gestation, *moderately premature* if born between thirty-one and thirty-six weeks, and *extremely premature* if born between twenty-four and thirty weeks. Half of the moderately premature have birth weights over 2500 grams (5 ½ pounds); those under are classified as "low-birthweight" infants. The extremely premature usually weigh between 500 and 1,500 grams. Although 90 percent of those born after twenty-nine weeks and treated in neonatal intensive care units (NICUs) survive, the premature often risk pneumonia, anemia, meningitis (inflammation of the sheath enveloping the spinal cord), heat loss, respiratory distress, and intraventricular hemorrhage.

*B. Hyaline Membrane Disease (HMD)*   Also called respiratory distress syndrome, HMD is a failure of the lungs to expand at birth or within six hours. About one-third of premature neonates have it; of those that do, 60 percent die from it. It is a disorder in which the lungs have trouble making the transition from an aquatic to a gaseous environment. Oxygen therapy is employed, but excess oxygen can be harmful; for example, it can result in retrolental fibroplasia (a disease of the retina in which an opaque membrane appears behind the lens of the eye).

*C. Congenital Heart Disease*   Congenital heart disease involves various sorts of heart lesions; it accounts for one-third of all neonatal deaths.

*D. Anencephaly*   This defect involves the absence of the cerebral hemispheres or the total absence of the brain (and brain stem). It occurs once in every thousand births. The infant dies before or within days after birth. An hydranencephalic infant (whose brain was destroyed during pregnancy) may live for a few years.

*E. Spina Bifida Cystica*   Some cases involve meningocele, a hernial protrusion of membrane tissue and fluid in the lumbosacral region of the spinal column. Some involve meningomyelocele, an opening in the lumbosacral region and a protrusion that leaks cerebrospinal fluid. It is caused by failure of the spinal tube to close during the first trimester of pregnancy. It may be associated with hydrocephalus (cerebrospinal fluid within the cranial cavity), neurological (nervous system) dysfunction, sensory loss below the lesion, paralysis, and bowel incontinence. Some untreated neonates may live for a year or more; some who are treated may have severe handicaps.

*F. Phenylketonuria (PKU)*   Those afflicted with PKU are usually severely retarded; they have a light complexion, jerky movements, and musty body odor. Only one in four lives beyond age thirty. Mainly northern Europeans are afflicted. Excessive levels of phenylalanine cause the damage. In 1961, a blood test was developed to detect abnormal levels of phenylalanine during the first neonatal days. Further, a special synthetic diet low in phenylalanine can be introduced, which radically improves the infant's prospects.

*G. Trisomy 21*   Also called Down's syndrome, this is the most common pattern of congenital malformation (1 per 660 births). For mothers under thirty, the chance of bearing a Down's syndrome child is 1 in 1,500; for those over forty, it is 1 in 130. Such infants usually have an extra chromosome 21, thus forty-seven chromosomes in all (instead of the normal forty-six). Aside from minor physical abnormalities, Down's syndrome adults typically have an IQ range from 25 to 60. A study in the 1950s supports the view that, on IQ testing, about 25 percent score below 25; 72 percent between 25 and 50; and 4 percent between 50 and 69; about 4 percent learn to read with comprehension. Also, one-third to one-half will have other problems such as higher susceptibility to infection, esophageal atresia, and congenital heart defects.

*H. Trisomy 18*   Also called Edwards' syndrome, it is the second most common malformation (1 in 3,500 births). Usually death occurs before birth. Those surviving have many physical abnormalities, such as congenital heart disease, and difficulty in breathing. Mental deficiency is common. About half die in the first two neonatal months and 90 percent by the end of the first year.

*I. Tay-Sachs Disease*   This condition is not evident until three or four months after birth (as is true of Lesch-Nyhan syndrome also; see J, below). Due to brain and spinal cord deterioration, the infant becomes retarded, progressively blind, and paralyzed; and dies by the age of three or four years. There is no known cure. Of those affected, 90 percent are of Jewish heritage.

*J. Lesch-Nyhan Syndrome*   Infants with Lesch-Nyhan syndrome usually appear normal for the first three to six months. After that, progressive cerebral deterioration develops and mental retardation results. Spasms and self-mutilating behavior occur. Currently there is no effective treatment for this syndrome. This genetic condition can be detected by amniocentesis; if detected, the fetus is usually aborted.

## §6 DIRECT AND INDIRECT DUTIES

In examining the arguments, our central question, as noted, will be whether it is *permissible* to let defective neonates die. Only if that is permissible could there be a duty to let them die. A persistent question in many cases concerns whether certain omissions are permissible—such as the deliberate omission of surgery or other therapeutic interventions—with the foreseen consequence of probable hastening of death.

It is useful to keep in mind a distinction commonly employed in moral philosophy, namely, that between *direct* and *indirect duties.* Suppose it were claimed that cars over fifteen years old are usually an eyesore, dangerous, and a source of pollution and that we ought therefore to eliminate them. It is doubtful that anyone would oppose this suggestion by maintaining that such cars have a right to continued existence, a sort of "right to life," as it were. Perhaps no one would maintain that we owe a duty of preservation *to* the cars or that we could *wrong* the cars (even though there is little doubt that we could *harm* them). Nevertheless, the mentioned proposal might be resisted on the ground that we have duties not to harm people wrongfully or that we have duties to respect their rights—including their property rights. Since these old cars are owned and connoisseurs may care about the cars' destiny even if such car buffs do not own them, it may be claimed that we have a *derivative* set of duties not to destroy such vehicles. That is, we owe no duties directly *to* the cars (they, for reasons not elaborated, are not the sorts of things that can be owed duties or properly be said to possess rights); but because of the direct duties we have *to* persons, we have indirect duties *regarding* the old cars (for example, not to harm or destroy them). Indeed, it seems that virtually anything might be something I have a duty not to destroy or harm. In the absence of other relevant considerations, if I promise to take care of your collection of movie-ticket stubs, I have a duty to do so and my destroying them would be impermissible.

The point of our little detour is that it might be argued, and has been, that we ought to care for and not terminate defective neonates *not* because they are directly owed duties or are bearers of a right to life but because adults care about what happens to them and/or because many people are shocked, disturbed, or horrified at practices that deliberately take innocent human life or deliberately fail to preserve it. Thus, it is claimed that we have an indirect duty to care for defective neonates even if they are not directly owed duties.

I shall not much explore this argument. It is doubtful, however, that it can provide a firm ground for concluding that it is in *all* cases wrong to terminate defective neonates. First, many people do not care whether the lives of certain seriously defective infants are preserved (indeed, some want them terminated and some believe it is wrong *not* to terminate them). Second, there is often a great burden (partly financial) in prolonging such lives and in rearing such children. It is not obvious that the public is willing to fund the care of *all* defective neonates. Similarly, many people care about the plight of historic buildings, works of art, wilderness areas, and wild animals—but not enough people are willing to fund the preservation of all of them. It is not obvious that those who are disturbed or saddened by the demise of some historic buildings (for example) have been wronged by those who are unwilling to contribute to preservation efforts.

The line of thought we are considering now will strike some as outrageous—somehow comparing defective babies to old cars or buildings! Indeed, we are considering an "extreme" view in one sense, and its place in the larger array of arguments will come into perspective only after we have surveyed further the intellectual landscape. The argument—that because of the mentioned indirect duties toward other adult persons we have a duty not to terminate defective infants —deserves consideration mainly because we *may* have no direct duties to such infants (a question to which we soon will turn). So it is sometimes claimed. However, if we have no direct or indirect duties to such neonates, then it is permissible to let them die (and perhaps actively to hasten death as well). In contrast, it looks as if those who think that it is always or generally impermissible to let such neonates die must rest their case *either* on an argument that we have direct duties to such neonates *or* on an argument that our indirect duties prohibit terminating them. I have suggested that the appeal to indirect duties seems less than compelling and that it is not well suited to ground a rigorous and uniform policy against terminating defective infants. If that is correct, *the crucial question concerns whether we have certain direct duties to such infants and, if so, just how stringent* they are. These are matters deserving careful exploration; the bulk of the rest of the essay focuses on various approaches to these matters.

## II. IS THERE A NEONATAL RIGHT TO LIFE?

### §7 NEONATAL RIGHT TO LIFE: FORFEIT AND WAIVER

Normally it is presumed that we have a rather stringent direct duty not to kill humans. This duty is often thought to be correlative to a right to life possessed by humans—a right often analyzed as a right not to be killed. But many of us believe, though I shall not much argue the point, that some killings of humans are, or would be, morally justifiable. For example, there are powerful arguments in favor of the view that some suicides are justifiable, that some instances of voluntary euthanasia are justifiable, that some killings in self-defense are justifiable, and that some killings to prevent large-scale catastrophe are permissible (for instance, suppose that by killing one innocent person we could prevent terrorists from killing a million people). Even many of those who wave the banner of "sanctity of life" or talk of being "pro-life" (typically *human* life, not all forms of life), often agree. Anyone who agrees cannot rationally accept also the extremist claim that it is always wrong deliberately to take human life. It is unfortunate that many who in fact think that there are justified exceptions to the prohibition against killing humans nevertheless rely on the principle, and pretend otherwise, in the arena of other debates (often in that of abortion).

A brief word about the concept of a right to life is in order here. Shortly, we shall question a widely held answer to the question: What sorts of things have this right? The widely held answer is all and only humans. Here we shall consider how a believer in the right to life and its normal possession by humans can attempt to reconcile such a belief with the view that some killings of humans are justified (although there is too little opportunity here to assess this position fully). In brief, the rights theorist may argue that a person (P) who had the right to life ceased to have it because (1) P forfeited it by a seriously wrongful deed such as homicide or (2) P waived it by voluntarily and knowingly consenting to being killed or being subject to the risk of such. The appeal to forfeit supposes that one can cease to have the right to life (hence, the right to life is "alienable" in the sense of "losable") and that one does lose it by virtue of committing certain serious wrongs. This reasoning is one possible way of *trying* to show why capital punishment is, in principle, justifiable and why some killings in self-defense (possibly in war) are justifiable. Such killings, it is said, infringe no right to life since the unjust aggressor has forfeited the right. How is this related to our question about neonates? A plausible answer is this: If the notion of forfeiting a right supposes justified blame (and thus the capacity for moral responsibility for one's acts), then it is doubtful that an infant, defective or not, can forfeit any rights it possesses. If so, forfeiture cannot be invoked to justify killing infants. If that is correct, a possibly successful type of justification for selected killings of adult persons is unavailable to justify terminating defective neonates. Another major type of justification for imposing burdens or the risk of such (for example, surgery on an adult patient) relies on the fact that a competent adult may give voluntary, informed consent to the procedure. For obvious reasons this plea is unavailable as a defense of terminating neonates. No neonate has waived its right to life by consenting.

## §8 NEONATAL RIGHT TO LIFE: JUSTIFIED INFRINGEMENT

Since a neonate cannot forfeit or waive any right to life it has, must we conclude that terminating a neonate violates its right to life and therefore must be morally wrong? Not necessarily. From the standpoint of a rights theorist, two possibilities remain. One concerns what might be called the *justified infringement argument*. Another concerns the *no right to infringe argument*. This latter argument will be examined in §9. Our present concern is limited to the former argument.

If one thinks that Jones is an innocent (adult) person but that it would be all right (albeit tragic) to kill him if that were the only way to prevent terrorists from killing a million people, how can such a view be reconciled with the belief that Jones has a right to life (a right not to be killed)—a right that he has neither waived nor forfeited? One might take the view that rights, or the right to life in particular, are not "absolute" (a weasel word unless clarified) in the sense of being *always* wrong to infringe. On this view, to say that P has a right to X is to say (in part) or imply that there is a very strong presumption against another's interfering with P's having, enjoying, or experiencing X but that there may be reasons that justify going ahead and infringing P's right. Anyone who accepts this seemingly reasonable view is committed to the possibility of giving (or there existing) a coherent and plausible account of what sorts of reasons justify infringements of rights. It seems, of course, that many of us do believe in "human rights" of various sorts, but we also hold that rights to property, privacy, and free speech are justifiably overridden under *certain* conditions. A fully adequate theory of rights would tell us just when this can be done.

The application of the justified infringement argument to our neonatal cases generally would maintain that infants have a right to life that, nevertheless, can be infringed under certain conditions. Presumably, plausible conditions would involve prevention (or amelioration) of significant harms. One sort of condition concerns the neonate's well being. Suppose the right to life is understood as a right not to be killed (or, perhaps, also a right not to be allowed to die). In some cases a neonate's prospects do not include consciousness or, alternatively, do include only a life of regular net pain and suffering. In such cases continued life is no benefit to the neonate. Hence it is not in the neonate's interest to continue to live. Indeed, it is *in its best interest* not to live. Thus, if we accept the Best Interest Principle, we must terminate the neonate's life. On such a principle then, we sometimes must infringe a right to life. This line of thought is a reasonable conjecture as to how right to life advocates *consistently* might concede that it is permissible to terminate some neonates. In this regard, compare the remark of C. Everett Koop, the extremely conservative current surgeon general of the United States, who said of the anencephalic and cephalodymus (one-headed twin) neonate that "neither medicine nor law should prolong these infants' process of dying."[5] I have suggested one principled ground for such "exceptions." There is a dilemma here, however, for many "right-to-lifers." If they accept or defend no principled ground for allowing such exceptions, their view seems arbitrary. If they accept a principled ground such as that noted, their more extreme claims seem unsupported, and such grounds may require accepting, as permissible, a greater range of terminations of defective neonates. For example, on what grounds is it permissible to terminate a one-headed twin? If the answer is categorizable as a "quality of life" consideration (presumably any evaluative consideration not focusing solely on life span), then why the often espoused (by right-to-life advocates) rejection of quality-of-life appeals? Why is this not just sheer inconsistency?

A second sort of circumstance under which it may be justifiable to infringe a neonatal right to life concerns not the interests of the neonate but the interests of others. It is a matter of some controversy as to whether it is all right to sacrifice innocents to prevent serious harm to others, and if so just when (under what conditions). This perplexity exists if the focus is on normal, innocent adults—prior to considering what to do about defective neonates. Although it is not difficult to elicit the rather useless (as a guide) response that "sometimes it's all right to infringe rights" by, for instance, reciting our prior terrorist example, what about other cases? For example,

1.  May we kill one nonconsenting innocent adult if that is the only way to prevent the deaths of a thousand innocent adult persons?
2.  May we kill one nonconsenting innocent adult if that is the only way to prevent the deaths of one hundred innocent adult persons?
3.  May we kill one nonconsenting innocent adult if that is the only way to prevent the deaths of ten adult persons?
4.  May we kill one nonconsenting innocent adult if that is the only way to prevent the deaths of two innocent adult persons?
5.  May we kill one nonconsenting innocent adult if that is the only way to prevent a broken leg for a hundred innocent adult persons?
6.  May we kill one nonconsenting innocent adult if that is the only way to prevent a broken leg for ten innocent adult persons?
7.  May we kill one nonconsenting innocent adult if that is the only way to prevent bankruptcy for a hundred innocent adult persons?
8.  May we kill one nonconsenting innocent adult if that is the only way to prevent bankruptcy for ten innocent adult persons?
9.  May we kill one nonconsenting innocent adult if that is the only way to prevent chronic depression for ten innocent adult persons?
10. May we kill one nonconsenting innocent adult if that is the only way to prevent chronic depression for two innocent adult persons?

Other imaginable cases can be sketched as one sees fit. Reflection tends to suggest that the justification of infringing a serious right (consider different rights here, the diverse effects of infringement, and so on) is less obvious as one goes through the list. That is, if we agree that it is permissible to infringe significant rights so as to promote or protect the interests of others, it seems that doing so is justifiable at best only to obtain important benefits for them or to protect them from very serious harms.

How do these reflections help us consider life-and-death decisions about defective neonates? The approach being considered, even if the neonate has a right to life, is that that right justifiably can be infringed if doing so is the only way to prevent serious harm. Aside from the rather obvious point that a great deal more needs to be said about what constitutes "serious harm," some degree of clarity may be achieved by distinguishing (1) the harm that may accrue to the infant if it continues to live and to be treated and (2) the harm that may accrue to other persons if the infant continues to live and to be treated.

In a given case, we may think that the "prospective harm" includes harms of types 1 and/or 2. As we have noted, on the Best Interest Principle the killing or letting die of a defective neonate is justified if and only if its prospective existence if treated is worse than no further life at all. Hence, out of concern for the infant, termination is appropriate.

One feature of this approach is its *exclusive* emphasis on the interests of the infant. If it is to be claimed, in contrast, that termination of the infant (thus infringing its right to life) is justified in order to prevent harms to *others* (or the infant and others), we get a broader focus. In cases involving defective infants, the prospective others who may suffer harm (understood broadly as burdens of time, effort, financial sacrifice, anxiety, peace of mind, and so on) primarily are the natural parents or those who will provide ongoing care for the infant if the parents refuse to do so. In spite of many acknowledged instances in which parents of defective neonates raise them and in which such parents are happy with that choice and even believe it to be a very (or the most) rewarding aspect of their lives (all things considered), it is clear that providing care for certain defective neonates objectively is extremely demanding and is not always offset by compensating benefits. Some parents regret the choice to continue to provide care. It is psychologically more likely, of course, that we encounter public expressions of satisfaction in a choice to provide care. *Reader's Digest* is not likely to please its readership with an article, entitled "Why Our Lives Are a Wreck," written by parents who regret a choice to continue to care. My question here, however, is whether realistically expectable, significant burdens on parents or other care providers should count *at all* or should count *much* in making a life-and-death decision regarding the care of a defective neonate. It seems unreasonable to claim that their interests have no weight in such decisions. Even in deciding to conceive (if there was a deliberate effort), parents do not thereby consent to making unlimited sacrifices for the benefit of their progeny (for example, on the order of a lung or heart transplant). Thus, they normally do not waive all rights that they have against others, including their own children. Further, when there is no adequate financial assistance from others, it seems callous and unjust to expect parents of normal means somehow to shoulder a $200,-000 debt to alleviate or remediate the burdens of a severely defective newborn. The parents as well as the infant are normally relevantly innocent in these cases. It is not clear why the normal prohibition on using people as a mere means—or elemental considerations of fairness —do not sometimes justifiably override the Best Interest Principle.

I have claimed that it is hard to defend the attribution of a right to life of the always-wrong-to-infringe sort to anyone. If so, no appeal to a neonatal right to life will support a total prohibition on terminations. Further, I have argued that it is dubiously fair to abide by a principle claiming that one always must do *whatever* is in the neonate's best interest (and thereby ignore the relevant interests of others). However, some claim that neonates have no right to life at all. If this view is accepted, discussion of grounds for justified infringement of their right to life is out of place. To a consideration of this matter we turn.

## §9 THE NO-RIGHT-TO-INFRINGE ARGUMENT

To avoid losing sight of the forest while examining a few trees, recall that we have noted in §7 that if neonatal humans have a right to life at any time, it cannot be lost by waiver or forfeit. Next we observed (in §8) that it seems reasonable to think that it *may* be justifiable to infringe even the right to life on occasion. Hence, even if the infant has such a right, that is not an insurmountable obstacle to the conclusion that it is sometimes permissible to terminate the infant's life. Much, at this point, would seem to depend on whether the interests of the infant, others, or both ever provide a justification for infringing its assumed right. We also noted but did not explore a no-right-to-infringe argument. We will approach it indirectly.

First, let us consider an important related concept: *moral standing.* As I shall use the term here (usage varies somewhat in moral philosophy) something has moral standing if and only if the well-being or continued existence of that thing is *in itself* important and rationally must be taken into account by moral agents when they make a decision significantly affecting the well-being or continued existence of that thing. The well-being and life of a thing with moral standing counts positively. Things thought to possess such standing often are said to be "members of the moral community." A very deep question that all ethical theories must address is: What things have moral standing? A rather common traditional assumption has been: All and only members of *Homo sapiens* have moral standing. Traditionally then (with notable exceptions), membership in a certain species (ours) has been regarded as both necessary and sufficient for possessing moral standing. On this *criterion of moral standing,* rocks, rivers, and rhinoceroses lack moral standing (recall, this claim means something with serious practical import: their well-being or lives in themselves do not count), but normal persons as well as both defective neonatal and normal neonatal humans have moral standing. The abortion debate has arisen *in part* over the dispute as to whether microscopic human zygotes, human embryos, and human fetuses count as "human beings" (not the misconceived question, mentioned ad nauseam, of "when human life begins").

An important question, which we examine shortly, asks: What is the most defensible criterion of moral standing? First, however, let us somewhat stipulatively suggest a relationship between the concepts of a right, a duty, and moral standing. To be a bearer of a right *or* an entity to whom a *direct* duty is owed is to have moral standing, and conversely. Employing these concepts in this manner, it is crucial whether normal or defective infants have moral standing. If they do not, then they lack rights and no duties are directly owed them (such as to provide for their care).

Now we are in a better position to state what I shall label the "no-right-to-infringe argument." There are numerous actual and possible close variants on this reasoning. I mention only one simplified version:

1. An entity, X, has a right to life only if X is capable of being aware of itself as an entity existing over time.
2. Human neonates lack this capacity.
3. Therefore human neonates lack a right to life.

If this argument is sound, then letting normal or defective infants die, or killing them, infringes no right to *life.* Thus, such acts cannot be deemed wrong, much less "murder," *for that reason.* The argument has certain attractions. As stated it is valid; we must accept the conclusion if we accept the premises. Further, its conclusion tends to support a view I believe to be widely shared, namely, that killing a newborn or letting it die is somehow less serious than so acting toward a fully developed person.

Several further points about the argument deserve comment. Implicit in it is the reasonable supposition that what rights an entity has depends in part on what empirical traits it has. For this sort of reason, it seems silly to attribute a right to life to a dead organism or a right to vote to a toddler. Michael Tooley, a contemporary philosopher, has defended in a series of essays and an important book a (far more sophisticated) variant of the argument we are considering.[6] Tooley believes that the appropriate neurological capacities sufficient to ground a right to life normally develop in infants only some months after birth. If one accepts the self-awareness condition as necessary for possessing a right to life, the *empirical* question of when such a condition comes to pass is absolutely crucial. Tooley is right to emphasize that philosophers, politicians, parents, students, or anyone else cannot just say whatever they want here. The best scientific evidence is needed. There is not room to recapitulate Tooley's serious survey of the scientific literature on this occasion; I suggest only that Tooley's data create a presumption in favor of premise 2.

In regard to premise 2, it is worth observing that some recent discussions, some understandably embedded in antiabortion arguments, speak of fetuses as being able to feel pain and of perceiving, responding to, and preferring this or that. There is a question here, partly analogous to questions about the "anthropomorphization" of animals, as to whether the evidence supports attributions of such psychological capacities to fetuses or neonates. In the absence of developed linguistic capacities (such as the ability to say "Help! I'm in pain"), we infer psychological states from knowledge of physiology, biochemistry, presence of a developed central nervous system, and other observations of the structure of an organism, or we rely on behavioral considerations, such as reactions to certain stimuli. The fact that a newborn will suck more during the playing of a tape of a story read to him before birth than he will during the playing of other tapes hardly seems sufficient to attribute a "preference" to the infant or sufficient to infer that it "remembers" or "recalls" the earlier events. What seems evident is that the trend of research on newborns in the past two decades is to discern various capacities heretofore denied infants. At the same time I am suggesting the need for a certain caution. The data collected, when neutrally described, frequently seem insufficient evidence to make certain psychological attributions. When a fetus absorbs more sweet than sour liquid or a newborn sucks more often on hearing one tape than another, we find differential reactions to different stimuli. The same phenomenon, generally put, is found in plants. Leaves droop in the absence of moisture and perk up when enough is present. It is only in an extended, loose sense that we say that plants prefer moisture, or that trees prefer sunshine, or that—since fall leaf colors are affected by it—trees remember the drought during the summer. It may be objected, reasonably, that in contrast to the case of plants we know that (most) infants have functioning brains as well. So the basis for psychological attributions is, in fact, more complex. The point is well taken. I shall leave open the question of just what follows. A further cautionary factor in interpreting newborn behavior is that to achieve a balanced perspective on the psychological capacities of newborn humans we would need a rather thorough comparison with the behavior of other neonatal primates. A consistent view may force us either to attribute self-consciousness to most neonatal humans and many nonhuman neonates or to deny self-consciousness to both groups. If we think self-consciousness (or the capacity for such) morally significant, the result, whatever it is, cannot be ignored.

It may be insisted that newborn humans normally are conscious, sentient, learning creatures who rapidly develop diverse psychological and intellectual capacities. As far as I can tell, nothing in Tooley's position denies this. Suppose, at least for the sake of discussion, that we agree that newborn humans normally possess the traits just noted. Several points deserve emphasis. First, such traits fall short of constituting self-consciousness, the claimed necessary condition of possessing a right to life. Tooley's guiding general assumption seems to be that for something to have a certain right it must possess the relevant corresponding capacity. Thus, for an entity to have a right to life (to continued existence as the sort of thing it is), it must be self-aware or must have the capacity for self-awareness (that is, to be aware of itself as a distinct entity over time). A distinction between being conscious (roughly, a scanner of the environment) and self-conscious (a self-scanning scanner) is presupposed here. There seems no reason to deny that newborn humans normally are conscious—or, for that matter, that newborn eagles, cats, or horses are conscious. Tooley's claim is that if an entity lacks the wherewithal for self-awareness, it psychologically cannot matter to it whether it continues to exist (how could it—in the absence of any concept of its own continued existence?). Perhaps the deeper assumption in Tooley's argument, put abstractly, is that it makes no sense, or is irrational, to attribute a right to X to anything not capable of caring about having X or not. Thus, if it is true that fetuses, neonates, or irreversibly comatose humans lack the relevant capacity to desire their own continued existence, then, on this view, they all lack a right to life. If this is correct, there is no problem of how to justify infringing a neonatal right to life; there simply is no right to life that could be infringed. This view cannot be dismissed by urging that, to the contrary, being-alive-and-being-human is sufficient to possess a right to life; to do that is merely to beg the question at issue.

## III. NEONATAL MORAL STANDING

### §10 THE RELEVANCE OF SENTIENCE

As I have characterized "moral standing," even if neonates lack a right to life, they still may be said to possess moral standing (to count positively and nonderivatively in the moral calculus) and thus be owed certain direct duties. Because of some unsettled substantive questions (about the relation of rights and duties) and a certain lack of standardized terminology, we can do a bit of slipping around between "duty talk" and "rights talk." However, the *moral bottom line* would seem to be *whether we have any sort of direct duties* (stringent, weak, or whatever) *to preserve the lives of defective neonates.* It may be claimed, then, that such neonates (or some of them) have moral standing even if they are rightless. Indeed several features (being sentient, being human, or being potentially rational and self-aware) that we have yet to discuss often are proposed as criteria for possessing moral standing (or certain rights as well). We consider these matters in this section as well as in §11 and §12. Whether an argument is formulated in terms of "rights" or "duties," it is well to remember the "bottom line" to avoid confusion.

As noted, a widely accepted criterion (logically necessary and sufficient condition) of moral standing is membership in *Homo sapiens*. To accept, instead, a psychological trait (such as capacity for certain desires) as the appropriate criterion is to reject membership in our or any particular species as a criterion. Recall that, as I have defined moral standing, what lacks moral standing does not in itself count. Does the view that newborns lack a right to life mean that it is permissible to do whatever we want to do to neonates, since they lack moral standing? It is important to see why the answer is negative even on a Tooley-like view. His argument, if sound, establishes only that newborns lack a right to life—not that they lack moral standing.

I shall not much develop the point here, but it is reasonable to think that one sufficient condition of possessing moral standing is *sentience*—the capacity to experience satisfaction or dissatisfaction. To so accept sentience is to reject the anthropocentric view—that membership in our species is the correct criterion. To paraphrase Jeremy Bentham, if it is true of a creature that it can suffer, then we ought to take its suffering into account. Thus, we ought to exhibit positive concern for its well-being. The point is a substantial and controversial one. But if sentience is a sufficient condition of moral standing and if most defective neonates are sentient, then most possess moral standing—even if they lack self-awareness. If so, what (direct) duties do we have to them? What rights do they have? I maintain that if they have a capacity to suffer, it is reasonable to think that they have a right against moral agents not to be deliberately and unfairly caused to suffer. That most neonates have this right is a point with implications for decisions about treatment, one to which we will return in §13.

At this juncture, it is important to recognize that it is logically *consistent* to claim:

1. That virtually all neonates have moral standing
2. In particular, that most neonates have a right not to be deliberately and unfairly caused to suffer
3. That all neonates lack a right to life

Such a position partly follows from the claims that sentience is sufficient for moral standing and that the capacity for self-awareness is necessary for possession of a right to life.

It is worth observing that the logically consistent position just characterized exhibits features central to the position *some* philosophers defend with regard to sentient animals—that they have moral standing and that the capacity for self-awareness is necessary for possession of a right to life. I note this parallelism in passing only to press a bit the point that there is a need for an overall, all things considered, view of how we may treat organisms that are not normal adult persons, and commitments on one matter (such as defective neonates) do not seem logically unrelated to commitments on other pressing issues (such as our dealings with sentient animals). Such a claim is likely to provoke, in some quarters, the response that the discussion here ignores the difference between human beings on the one hand and animals on the other. For this reason, we will consider the relevance of membership in *Homo sapiens* in the next section.

## §11 THE RELEVANCE OF BEING HUMAN

Traditional moral principles (such as the Golden Rule) commonly have been cast, implicitly or explicitly, as prohibitions on mistreating members of one biological species, *Homo sapiens.* A common implication has been that such prohibitions do not extend to organisms outside this species. What justifies this discrimination? Why is it thought all right to (kill to) eat chickens but not people? "They [the chickens] are only animals!" comes the reply. Of course, we know that. The challenge is to provide a rational justification for what Richard Ryder has called "speciesism," if by that label we mean the assumption that all and only humans have moral standing (thus, "anthropocentrism" may be more fitting).[7] Why think that species membership in itself is of moral significance any more than membership in itself in a certain race or a certain gender? Is there some feature or set of features about all and only humans in virtue of which they deserve a special concern, in contrast to other organisms? It may be said in reply that, unlike animals, humans are self-aware, can reason abstractly, or both. Two points are relevant here. First, such a claim is just false—as an assertion about *all* humans—for obvious reasons. Second, if it is such psychological traits that are sufficient for moral standing (or rights, or being owed direct duties), then it follows that it is not membership in *Homo sapiens as such* that is morally significant; rather it is possession of the relevant psychological trait or traits. Being a human is presumptive evidence that an entity possesses such traits, but the presumption is a defeatable one. It is reasonable to think, for example, that Karen Ann Quinlan (before her death in June 1985) was a human being but lacked all capacity to reason or be aware. It may be a useful fiction to state moral principles so as to imply that membership in *Homo sapiens* in itself is morally significant, but it is hard to see why anyone should believe this. If there were more space here, an objection—based on the claims that all and only humans have souls (of some sort) and that this is morally significant—should be considered. However, I here will note only that I think the objection fails and refer readers to the essay in this volume by Peter Singer.

The insignificance of species membership *as such* is strongly supported by thought experiments others have mentioned. If we were to encounter (or ever *do* encounter) members of other species, such as extraterrestrials, who were sentient, could reason, and act purposefully, should we regard them as possessing moral standing? I have never encountered anyone who answered negatively, even though the view that "all and only humans count" frequently seems presupposed, but perhaps uncritically. Strictly, what the thought experiment shows, at most, is that being a human is not *necessary* to possess moral standing; it does not show that it is not sufficient. However, to believe it sufficient is to be committed to the view that having genes of a certain type, a certain set of morphological traits, or certain breeding capacities, or particular habits (see the standard definition of 'species') is sufficient for moral standing. Put this way, it is again puzzling why rational beings would believe as much.

## §12 THE RELEVANCE OF POTENTIALITY

If it is agreed that membership in *Homo sapiens* as such is not sufficient (or necessary) for possessing moral standing but that being sentient is sufficient, then virtually all human neonates possess moral standing—but not because they are human. Further, their sentience provides good reason to believe that we owe them a direct duty not to cause them (on balance) pain deliberately and unfairly. This duty (and correlative right if one prefers) does not obviously morally prohibit the termination of life. At least in the case of sentient animals, it is held widely that it is wrong to inflict unnecessary suffering on the animals in circumstances in which termination of their lives is thought permissible. However, the suggestion that the duties directly owed certain neonatal humans may be similar to those owed sentient animals will shock many. That many react in this manner is not in itself a decisive consideration against the suggestion; at one time many found shocking the suggestion that slaves should be liberated or that women ought not be regarded as property of males.

Aside from the relevant similarity between most neonates and sentient animals (their sentience) and assuming, for the sake of inquiry at least, that species membership as such is not morally significant, cannot the opponents of terminating defective neonates rest their case on the fact that most such neonates have a potential for rationality and self-awareness—a possibly relevant difference between most neonates and all (or virtually all) animals?

There is a source of confusion in talk of "potentiality," "capacity," and similar terms. In one sense an apple seed has the "potential" to produce apples; in another sense it does not. To avoid a certain lengthy and tedious analysis and to stipulate a bit, let us call the relevant traits of the apple seed—the traits sufficient, under favorable conditions, for it to grow into a tree—its *potential.* If the seed develops naturally into a tree with the characteristics sufficient for apple production, let us say that the tree has the *capacity* to produce apples. From the fact, then, that an entity X at time T has the potential to do F (produce apples, reason, be self-aware, or whatever) it does not follow that X at T has the capacity to do F.

Given this terminology, it *may* be conceded that neonates lack the capacity to reason or be self-aware but insisted that they (or most) have the potential for such. An opponent of the permissibility of terminating neonates may reason in this way, then: Not only that which has the capacity to reason and be self-aware has a stringent right to life but also that which has the potential for such. Thus, it is wrong to terminate all neonates who have such a potential, and this includes virtually all defective newborns with the exception, perhaps, of anencephalic, trisomy 13, trisomy 18, Tay-Sachs, and Lesch-Nyhan infants (among others).

Alternatively, the appeal to potentiality *may* proceed in the following manner:

1. If an entity is rational and self-aware, it has a stringent right to life.
2. Baby X potentially is rational and self-aware.
3. Baby X has a stringent right to life.

As stated, proposition 3 does not logically follow. Analogously, although adults may have a right to vote and a given baby is a potential adult, it does not follow that the baby has a right to vote.

However, those who think that an entity's potential is morally significant need not rely on such fallacious reasoning. Consider this "Potentiality Principle," P:

Any entity, X, that is potentially both rational and self-aware has a stringent right to life (as does any being that is actually rational and self-aware).

Now, using P along with 2 and 3 from the prior argument, consider:

1. P (If an entity is potentially rational and self-aware, it has a stringent right to life.)
2. Baby X is potentially rational and self-aware.
3. Baby X has a stringent right to life.

This argument is valid. The crucial question concerns whether P should be accepted.

One way of trying to defend P is the following. It is tempting to think that a being's potential is, in fact, morally significant. Suppose a thirty-year-old male, Wyatt, has an accident and enters a coma. May custodians dispose of his library since Wyatt, being comatose, cannot read? It would seem relevant that (let us assume) Wyatt naturally will recover; thus, while comatose he has the potential (but not the capacity) to read. Thus, "potentiality" is clearly relevant and must not be ignored. If correct, this point may go some distance toward a defense of P (although not literally a defense of P as stated). What is shown by these reflections? It seems that what is presupposed is that Wyatt's potential to read (once again) *will* be realized, that he *will* have the capacity to read. This point suggests a question. Perhaps what these reflections show to have moral significance is potentials (to develop morally significant traits) which (to our knowledge, at least) *will be* realized. But, if we are deciding whether to prolong the life of a being with potential for rationality and self-awareness, it is an *open question* as to whether this potential *will be* realized.

So if the question of whether a neonate's potential will be realized depends in part on whether we shall preserve its life or not, we cannot decide the latter matter on the assumption that its potential will be realized. One upshot here is that even if potential-for-self-awareness-and-rationality-which-will-be-realized is morally weighty, the mere potentiality itself is not thereby shown to bestow moral standing or a right to life.

Even if the *absence* of all potential for relevant traits (sentience, self-awareness, and so on) is sufficient for *not* having moral standing (a reasonable view; compare the irreversibly comatose—or rocks), it does not follow that the *presence* of such potential is sufficient for possessing moral standing. That is the mistake made, I believe, by "conservatives." The contrary mistake that, I believe, may tempt "liberals" is to think that if the potential noted is not sufficient for moral standing, then it is altogether morally irrelevant.

Appeals to bare potentiality, then, fail to show that possessors have moral standing. Moreover, among defective neonates some lack a potential for rationality and self-awareness (detailed factual investigation is essential on this score, but one might conjecture here that anencephalic and many Tay-Sachs, trisomy 13, and trisomy 18 neonates are in this category). Thus, *even if* it were true (contrary to my claims) that potentiality for agreed-on right to life-bestowing traits were sufficient for moral standing, many defective neonates could not be viewed as possessing moral standing on that ground.

## §13 ELEMENTS OF A THEORY

It is time to try to draw together the strands of argument developed so far, and weave a few more, in an attempt to sketch a reasonable and coherent approach to the perplexities that we confront. Some defective newborns lack any potential for self-awareness and any prospect for such. Even if one accepted the appeals to potentiality, such newborns fail to have a right to life on this criterion. This seems to be a good reason for concluding that anencephalic infants lack a right to life; they are human forms of life but are owed no stronger direct duty of preservation than other forms of life lacking self-awareness, potential for such, or capacities for sentience. One might concede that such an infant (if it could live on) is characterizable as possessing an "interest in continued life" (as is a tree); but theories implying this interest to be a morally weighty one are, I believe, implausible.

In the absence of a more persuasive view, I believe we must conclude that (1) beings lacking a capacity for self-awareness lack a right to life and that (2) current evidence suggests that neonates lack the requisite neural capacities for such—even though normally coming to have them very soon, within a few months after completion of the normal period of gestation. If 2 is correct (admittedly the matter is important, and I have said rather little about it here), then all neonates, normal or not, lack a right to life. However, if they are sentient, they possess moral standing and are owed a duty not to be caused to suffer unfairly. Most defective neonates are sentient. Allowing that, abstractly, they all have an interest in continued life, it is a further question as to whether the continuation of the life of a particular neonate is in its interest *all things considered.* If one knew that one's being saved from drowning would eventuate only in another five years of life and protracted torture by terrorists (so that life would be miserable, on balance, until death), it would be irrational, ceteris paribus, to prefer its continuation. For some defective neonates, continued life promises to be intolerable even if they receive heroic treatment. It seems unjustifiably cruel to preserve the lives of such infants in the name of the "sacredness of all life," "do no harm," or "the infinite value of human life."

Extremely difficult empirical judgments and slippery evaluative assessments are involved in arriving at such determinations. What is often underplayed or ignored is that this is the stuff of life. As individuals and as governments or other institutions, we commonly have to make hard choices on the basis of limited information and imperfect rationality.

Of the defective neonates mentioned at the very outset of this essay—Baby Doe (with Down's syndrome), the trisomy 13 infant, the anencephalic baby, and the newborn missing a few fingers—the trisomy 13 infant is both sentient and has a very dim future. *If* its life prospects are intolerable on balance even with heroic treatment, it seems permissible, perhaps even obligatory, to terminate its life. Implicit in the above remarks are the assumptions that it is important whether "treatment is futile" and that we must make responsible, well-informed, quality-of-prospective-life judgments even though that is a path we rightly are reluctant to tread and one where each step deserves great scrutiny. I do not wish to make or imply any moral generalizations about all trisomy 13 infants. It is significant that the prospects of infants in certain categories change with technological advances, such as recent developments in genetic engineering that may change radically the prospects for Lesch-Nyhan infants.

There is a certain amount of agreement about the permissibility of letting the anencephalic infant die, or the quite gravely impaired, even though the grounds for such judgments are disputed (or left unstated). Morally, more disputatious cases remain. We are considering three broad classes of defective neonates: (1) those lacking sentience and with no prospect of self-awareness (such as many of the anencephalic); (2) those who are sentient and with the potential for self-awareness (such as our hypothetical trisomy 13 infant) but whose life prospect is one of misery on balance; (3) those who are sentient, with a potential for self-awareness, who probably can have a decent life if they receive good treatment. Somewhat stipulatively, let us call them, respectively, *morally* (1) hard, (2) harder, and (3) hardest cases. I use 'morally hard' here to focus on the degree to which proposed termination is controversial. Our last broad class encompasses a diverse group, such as the baby with missing fingers and Baby Doe. Hardly any parents would desire to terminate a baby (theirs) because of a few missing fingers. Hence, disputes about such a proposal are not likely to arise (although there are also parents who choose to abort on learning the woman is carrying a "wrong-gender" fetus). The view I am defending is *not* the view that "only perfect infants should be cared for." Those "pro-life" advocates who so caricature their opponents only throw darts at a "straw man" of their own construction.

The case of Baby Doe is a paradigm of the "hardest cases." Again, Baby Doe has the right not to be caused to suffer unfairly. Like other neonates Baby Doe lacks a right to life, although it is in her interest to continue to exist (even if lacking self-consciousness). On the supposition that a given Down's syndrome neonate has a life prospect that is beneficial on balance, it is in its interest to continue to live. In my view this is a morally relevant interest even if it is not a morally weighty interest.[8] Here I may diverge from Tooley's view. Among cases in our third category (of "hardest cases"), the raising of the child will constitute a grave burden for some parents but not for others. Once an infant comes to have a right to life (a few months after birth), its natural parents have, I believe, a strong obligation to care for it and preserve it. Prior to that they do not. The prospective burden on parents is not morally insignificant. Parents' interests count too, and to talk of their genuine emotional, financial, and other struggles as "mere inconveniences for them" is insensitive at best. The interest of an infant in continued life when it lacks a right to life creates, I believe, a presumption (though not necessarily a weighty one) in favor of its preservation—one which other considerations may outweigh. If the prospective parental burden is significant (and it tends to be even when parental "reasons" for not wanting to rear a certain child are irrational), such parents need not keep the infant or submit themselves to great financial burdens to pay for medical care. Even those who voluntarily have a baby are not thereby "mere things to be used" to benefit the infant. It does not follow, however, that they have a right to kill the infant or secure its death (whether natural parents should have any special say about the destiny of "their" infant *once* they abandon raising it is doubtful). What is permissible is for them to raise it *or* to abandon it (that is, surrender it to others for adoption).

As Mary Anne Warren has observed, commonly there are others who (1) are ready and willing to adopt or (2) care enough about neonates to pay for their care or institutionalization.[9] The interests of such persons are not insignificant. Some, indeed, will be "right to lifers" whose moral beliefs are at odds with the views I have defended here; still, their interests count as well. In some societies no one may care to adopt. In effect all potential caregivers choose abandonment. If so, it is permissible to let Baby Doe die. If this can only occur slowly, with intense, unalleviated suffering on balance, Baby Doe should be killed painlessly. We should not allow useless, intense suffering to occur in order to foster a self-righteous avoidance of "dirty hands" or a "guilty conscience," a stance that may comfort us or others but not "Baby Doe." Further, those who now vigorously try to save fetuses or neonates from premature death must work hard to see to it that the resulting lives are not miserable on balance; otherwise piously announced "body counts" of "lives saved" will just be the provision of opportunities for misery.

Even if all the preceding remarks are correct, they do not settle certain issues—for example, how to make quality-of-prospective-life judgments or how to weigh certain clinical signs and symptoms. A delicate mixture of moral or evaluative questions—and empirical questions—must be answered in deciding about specific defective neonates. The pediatrician may be expert in telling us how long Tay-Sachs infants live or the specific prospect of this particular one. That life is "worth preserving" or that an infant has a right to life are not empirical claims and *cannot be settled by purely scientific inquiry.* They are matters of moral or evaluative justification and must be settled by philosophical analysis and moral argument, whether carried out by parents, plumbers, pediatricians, philosophers, or politicians.

## IV. THE ARENA OF PUBLIC POLICY

### §14 PUBLIC STANDS, POLITICAL PROPOSALS, PRESUPPOSITIONS

On matters so difficult, it is not surprising that there is persistent disagreement. In this section two goals dominate: (1) to address a number of objections to the position I have defended and (2) to comment on the suppositions behind certain political proposals. In areas in which passionate convictions conflict, it is best to rise above name calling (such as "baby killer" or "worshiper of mere cell functioning") even though opponents tend to regard each other as morally myopic and/or jaded. Still, the issues must be joined, and I shall try to spell out unequivocally where I think contrary positions run amuck.

*On the Stance of the American Academy of Pediatrics* First, I will comment briefly on the stance of the Committee on Bioethics of the American Academy of Pediatrics (AAP). From 1982 to 1984 the Department of Health and Human Services (DHHS) in the United States opposed basing life-and-death decisions for seriously ill newborns on the existence of handicapping conditions. In October 1983 the AAP agreed with this stance but stated that they strongly opposed the remedy proposed by the DHHS—various governmental modes of intervention to prevent "discrimination on grounds of the handicap" (for example, no lifesaving surgery because of Down's syndrome).[10]

The moral core of the AAP position seems constituted by these assumptions (my reconstruction):

1. "Withholding or withdrawing life-sustaining treatment" is permissible if (a) "death is imminent regardless of treatment" or (b) "treatment will serve only to maintain biological function."
2. Among less extreme cases not all infants should be treated.
3. The range of complex conditions makes it impossible to define clinical criteria for withholding treatment.
4. "The pediatrician's primary obligation is to the child."
5. "Withholding or withdrawing treatment is justified only if such a course serves the interest of the patient."
6. "Treatment should not be withheld for the primary purpose of improving the psychological or social well-being of others. . . ."
7. An institutional ethics review committee is desirable to make it more probable that decisions are "informed and consistent with the broadest moral values of our society."

A sensitive and thoughtful position. There is too little space here for much comment. Claims 1 and 2 accord with the position defended here. For reasons discussed, 5 is too strong; to so view the neonate is tantamount to regarding it as an involuntary moral master to slave-others. The next item, 6, is too vague to be helpful; is *avoiding* a $200,000 medical bill a parental choice to "improve their social well-being"? With regard to 7 one must say that in the end, it is not necessary that a policy accord with the broadest (existing) moral values. That is a recipe for the status quo; reflection on two historically valued outlooks, racism and sexism, should suggest another view. As I read the AAP position, it would require the preservation of neonates whose lives would be marginally satisfactory (to them) even if the burden to the parents would be catastrophic. Here I think the AAP arrives at the wrong conclusion and gets there from inadequate premises. Indeed, their stated *position* is quite indeterminate, sidesteps certain key issues, is evasive, and possibly is inconsistent. How reconcile 1 with 3? *Why not* preserve mere biological function? The reasons for these and other claims remain obscure. Pediatricians, however, should be commended for still searching for an adequate moral stance here; that is a continuing and difficult task for all of us.

*On "Discriminating against the Handicapped"*   Waving the banner of "equality," some assert a full and equal right to life (or to routine medical care) for all infants, normal and handicapped. If there is such a right, then it would seem presumptively wrong to discriminate against handicapped infants by denying them routine medical care. As noted earlier, the child known as Baby Doe was born handicapped with Down's syndrome and the parents refused to permit surgery to correct esophageal atresia (blockage of the esophagus). Since surgery routinely would be performed on a normal infant to correct such atresia, it seems that the only (or primary) reason for refusing for Baby Doe was the presence of Down's syndrome. This refusal seems to be a paradigmatic case in the eyes of those who oppose discriminating against the handicapped because of the handicap. Although it is true that, as described, there is discriminatory treatment in the sense of *differential* treatment (surgery versus no surgery) as well as a difference in the subjects (Down's syndrome versus normal), these facts by themselves leave open entirely whether such treatment is justified, and if so, why.

Two further points about "equal treatment" deserve mention here. First, the strong thesis that *all* defective neonates "have the same rights" or "deserve equal treatment" (as is assumed for normal newborns) is one that hardly anyone defends, even though there is much flag waving on this score. Virtually all defenders of aggressive therapy for neonates allow exceptions, as for the anencephalic infant. In a thoughtful letter to *The New York Review of Books* (June 14, 1984), Paul Stone initially states that ". . . retarded children have the same right to life as normal children," but, in the face of objections to assuming equal rights for all, he quickly qualifies his position by stipulating that his claim is about children who *will be self-aware*, talk, and interact socially. This is an important qualification for one who denies that certain defects are relevant to treatment decisions and is a concession to those who insist, as do I, that some types of "quality-of-life" judgments are reasonable (in principle) and morally defensible. Stone goes on to make a point that deserves greater attention than "both sides" have given it. It is this: one basis for opposing certain sorts of differential treatment, or nontreatment, of handicapped newborns, aside from the strong claim that "all human life is of equal worth," is the assumption that ". . . *some* handicapped children's lives (e.g., those who will be self-aware) are of equal worth or at least of sufficient worth to deserve self-protection." As Stone notes, this claim is compatible with the assumption that "some human lives are more valuable than others."

To emphasize a point, defenders of aggressive therapy toward defective infants may appeal to an extreme egalitarian principle (that all human lives are of equal worth) and argue that certain differential treatment violates the noted principle. Such a principle, in fact, is hard to defend for reasons discussed, as in view of the anencephalic infant (counting it as one form of human life). Defenders of aggressive therapy, however, may argue that certain minimal forms of therapy are owed to certain defective infants even if not all human lives are of equal worth and even if the lives of the infants in question (quite retarded Down's syndrome infants?) are of lesser worth. This latter line of reasoning, then, is not vulnerable to arguments seeking to show that not all human lives are equally valuable. That is, a knock-down argument in favor of this last claim will not suffice to show that terminating certain defective neonates is justified. What would show that certain defective infants may be terminated, actively or passively, would be a demonstration that (1) they lack moral standing entirely, or (2) they lack a right of life and their interest in continued life is outweighed by the legitimate interests of others, or (3) in a given case an existing neonatal right to life may be infringed justifiably. If any of these claims can be established, then certain "discriminatory" (differential) treatment may be morally justified; indeed, failure to so discriminate, arguably may be unjust. Such substantive moral claims should be the focus then (as they have been here) and not merely the point, albeit a significant one, that certain defective infants are and have been treated differently, presumably because of their defects.

## §15 ON APPEALS TO THE SANCTITY OF LIFE, THE HUMAN LIFE BILL, THE CHILD-ABUSE AMENDMENTS

Much of the moral opposition to terminating the lives of defective newborns and to abortion derives from suppositions about the value of *all* human life and a battery of associated positive and negative arguments. We have touched on such matters already, but it is worth commenting on a residue of popular and/or politically influential lines of thought.

Consider first the related, recently proposed human life bill, S.158.[11] Its key proposal is that the United States Code be amended to read that "(a) The Congress finds that the life of each human being begins at conception," and "(b) The Congress further finds that the fourteenth amendment to the Constitution of the United States protects all human beings." Another purpose of the bill is said to be "to affirm that every human life has intrinsic worth and equal value regardless of its stage or condition." The latter claim is, then, a crucial moral presupposition of the bill's proponents—along with a (later explicit) commitment to the view that "the right to life is a self-evident, inalienable right of every human being." This stance has implications for both the question of abortion and the termination of the lives of defective newborns.

For the strong conclusion to follow that it is always wrong to terminate (and the government ought to prevent such an act) the life of a zygote, embryo, or fetus generated by recognized members of *Homo sapiens,* the *mentioned* approach needs to accept and defend a number of assumptions:

1. Any of the entities just noted is a human being.
2. Every human being has a right to life.
3. That right to life is "absolute" (in the sense that any act of deliberately infringing it is wrong).

4.  It is justifiable that the government use its coercive powers to prevent, and presumably punish, such wrongs as well.

What we find in the Senate subcommittee's defense, however, is mainly a concentration on points 1 and 2. Indeed, the subcommittee emphasizes the importance of distinguishing a "scientific question" and a "value question." Consider the former. At times the subcommittee suggests that the scientific question is "when a human life begins." It seems to assume that this question is the same as "whether unborn children are living human beings." It should be noted, however, that the latter formulation tends to beg the question. Those who doubt the correctness of describing a fertilized egg or fetus as a "living human being" will not concede that the entity should be labeled an "unborn child" either. Further, a third or more fertilized eggs spontaneously abort (die). Therefore if the competent speaker of English really thought "unborn children" an appropriate label for human zygotes, there would be nothing unnatural about describing most women as having numerous, perhaps dozens, of "dead children." Virtually *no one* talks or thinks this way. Maybe a human zygote is "a human being" or "a human organism." It is not a (human) child. Perhaps, however, the subcommittee can gain by honest intellectual toil what cannot be gained by attempted conceptual theft.

Elsewhere the subcommittee complains that although the Supreme Court in its major abortion decision, *Roe* v. *Wade* (1973), conceded that it could not decide when a human life begins, it went on to decide ("by fiat" according to the subcommittee) that the constitutional protection of *persons* did not extend to human fetuses ("unborn children" in the subcommittee's question-begging language). This complaint reflects a confusion. If a fetus must count as a person (in whatever sense the Constitution employs the term) to be constitutionally protected, it is unnecessary to decide whether the fetus is a living human being in order reasonably to decide that the fetus *is not* a person. For example, if a necessary condition of being a person in the constitutional sense is that an entity must have a functioning brain, then it follows (assuming that fetuses [embryos] prior to eight weeks lack such functioning) that fetuses prior to eight weeks are not persons—*even if* they count as "living human beings." Abstractly, there may be other logically necessary conditions for counting as a "person" *even if* being a "living human being" is one also (a point doubtful on other grounds).

Let us return to the claim that the scientific question is settled. The subcommittee maintains that there is an overwhelming scientific consensus that "The life of a human being begins at conception." In the final analysis I have no great quarrel with this claim since (1) this leaves the important questions unsettled and (2) it is one reasonable view. It is disturbing, however, that the subcommittee fails to recognize that the debate about whether a zygote or fetus is a "living human being" is almost invariably *conceptual* in nature—that is, a debate about how to *describe* or *classify* an entity which otherwise is readily identifiable and about whose other empirical properties there is general agreement. It is not as if (for example) some protagonists in the abortion discussion think that brain function occurs typically at eight weeks and others at twenty-eight weeks. Embryologists and others who trouble to acquaint themselves with the scientific data overwhelmingly agree about such matters. Rather, disagreement about whether there is a living human being reflects the lack of completely settled *criteria* for the correct application of the expression "living human being." Some think, so it appears, that to be a living human the entity must be viable, others that it simply possess a complete genetic program to develop into an adult human, and some that it must have a complete brain structure or be morphologically complete. Employing different criteria, people are led to different conclusions. The subcommittee seems oblivious to this conceptual source of the dispute over when a human life begins. Of the zygotes in question, no one, to my knowledge, denies that they are *living* or that they are *human somethings* (so, of course, is my heart and my thumb). Analogously, a sprouting acorn is an oak something and is living—and, no doubt, the life of any oak tree begins with an acorn; still it is not obvious that it follows that acorns *are* oak trees—or, hence, that if oak trees had a right to life acorns would too. The subcommittee, in believing that its hearing of "renowned scientists" settles the queston of whether the fetus is a "living human being," has asked empirical experts about the fetus (zygote, embryo, etc.) to settle a matter (a conceptual issue) partly outside their domain of expertise.

If it is granted that zygotes, embryos, and fetuses of *Homo sapiens* are living human beings, then, as the subcommittee concedes, there is a further question—of "value" if one prefers. The subcommittee insists that on this matter there are just two basic alternatives: (1) a sanctity-of-life ethic—which regards all human life as of intrinsic worth, and (2) a quality-of-life ethic—which denies (1) and proposes criteria other than simply "being human" as a basis for value.[12] The subcommittee asserts that the Declaration of Independence affirms (1) in its declaring that ". . . all men are created equal, that they are endowed by their creator with certain inalienable rights, that among these are life, liberty, and the pursuit of happiness." One question here, *if* it be granted that "the sanctity-of-life ethic" is one of the values embodied in our Constitution (or its history), is why we *ought* to subscribe to all the values in our Constitution. After all, *if* it is so embodied, that is only another empirical fact. More significantly, it is worth recalling that our Constitution has not exactly regarded all adult humans as deserving equal representation (and thus in one sense as having equal intrinsic worth just because human):

Article I section (3) counted persons not free (slaves) as three-fifths of a person for purposes of representation. Not to mention that half the population (women) had no recognized constitutional right to vote until 1920. Did "all men are created equal" mean all males? Further, the 14th Amendment's guarantee of equal protection explicitly counts as citizens only those "persons born or naturalized" in the United States. Thus, it is puzzling why the subcommittee insists that "the fourteenth amendment embodies the sanctity of human life. . . ." There is a great gap between *that* doctrine and an amendment concerning itself only with "American" (United States) citizens.

I would like to return to a slippery point related to the "scientific" question. As noted, my thumb is living and human but not a human being. In contrast, a fetus normally has a potential to grow into a mature human *being*. Thus, it is more tempting to classify it as a living human being. The subcommittee insists that the key scientific question is whether an entity is "a living member of the human species." There is a question here about *what counts as a member*. Thumbs do not. It is not clear that being alive, being human, and having a potential for growth and development are collectively sufficient either. Perhaps this is why (or partly why) the Christian theologian (thirteenth century) Thomas Aquinas believed that the female fetus did not receive a human soul ("animation") until eighty days after conception and the male fetus not until forty days after. The recent Christian thinker E. L. Mascall expresses doubt that the "rational soul is infused" at conception in the case of human "monsters" and also allows that the early-stage human embryo may lack a rational soul.[13] Similarly, the Roman Catholic theologian Joseph Donceel suggests that the church should return to the view it once accepted (the "delayed animation" theory)—one that supports the permissibility of early abortions.[14]

There is, in short, a history of philosophical and theological doubt about whether to conceptualize fetuses on the one hand and radically anomalous infants on the other as human beings even when it is not doubted that they are living human somethings with a potential for continued existence and development of some sort. Indeed, the seventeenth-century English physician-philosopher John Locke, whose *Second Treatise on Civil Government* espouses the rights theory which inspired the early quotation from the Declaration of Independence, puzzled at length (see his *Essay Concerning Human Understanding*, 4:4) over what to make of monstrous births (deformed human neonates), of "changelings" (sometimes defined as the offspring of fairies or elves substituted for a comely human child) "who lived forty years without any appearance of reason." Locke queried whether they were "something between man and beast." He also denied that "whatever is of human birth must be so" and denied that a human soul was always matched with a body of certain shape. Compare further his comment: "Shall the want of a nose or a neck, make a monster, and put such an issue out of the rank of men; the want of reason and understanding, not?"

I do not wish to side with Locke, Aquinas, Mascall, or Donceel, but these remarks serve to show why reasonable people of good will may find it *not obvious* that zygotes, fetuses, or radically anomalous neonates count as human beings in the sense of living *members of Homo Sapiens.* The issue is a conceptual one concerning the most defensible criteria for applying the expression 'human being.' In that sense it is not "factual" or "scientific"—the subcommittee's naiveté to the contrary.

I have been addressing the arguments explicitly found in the human life bill, S.158. There are other standard stratagems employed by defenders of the sanctity-of-life concept that deserve comment. I will note three quasi-popular arguments and a question about the idea that there is a clear thesis denoted by the "sanctity-of-life" view.

*Appeals to the Sanctity of Life*   Two persistent ploys used by some defenders of a sanctity-of-life view involve "associating" a form of killing believed wrongful with Nazi practices. One maneuver is to suggest or presuppose that the Nazi effort to kill off the old, the unproductive, or the handicapped was a form of euthanasia. As C. Everett Koop has put it, "The first direct order for euthanasia came from Hitler in 1939."[15] A grim tale then follows. What is misleading is that 'euthanasia' is standardly defined in terms of terminating life with the intent to aid the one who dies; hence it is, by definition, "mercy-killing." What is obvious is that the ghastly killings of the Nazi regime were carried out for quite other reasons (hatred of Jews or to eliminate the burden posed by the economically unproductive). That is *not* euthanasia.

I turn to a second ploy used by some defenders of the sanctity of life. Suppose it were true that Nazis, for whatever reason, favored what *really* does count as euthanasia (apparently they did introduce a policy of "voluntary euthanasia" for aged and infirm Aryans)—or, specifically, killing defective newborns. Nazism was indeed evil. Sanctity-of-life advocates imply that therefore the mentioned practices are evil. However, conceding that we should be wary of people like Nazis, the argument mentioned simply fails. Nazis also advocated regular exercise. It hardly follows that exercise *therefore* is evil. To recognize this point hardly is to recommend Nazism; rather, it is to urge dissecting ideas with a scalpel instead of a bludgeon.

Yet another stratagem employed by some "pro-life" advocates is to suggest that if decisions are made to abort, or not preserve all newborns (perhaps due to quality-of-life considerations), then possibly an important or highly talented person (such as Beethoven) who had some nontrivial defect (blindness, for example) would be lost to humanity. Given the view of the sanctity-of-(all human)-life defenders, it is odd, of course, to focus on a life that is very valuable to others.

Would not a blind vagrant (or a mass murderer) disliked by all serve as well? Nevertheless, the implicit reasoning seems to be something like this:

1. A policy involving abortion or infanticide might have prevented Beethoven from living a full life.
2. We ought not accept any policy that would prevent the life of a valuable person [or anyone as valuable as Beethoven (equals anyone on the view considered?)].
3. We ought not accept abortion or infanticide.

Clearly, however, premise 2 has intolerable implications. The zygote from which Beethoven developed could have been destroyed by preventing its implantation in the uterine wall. If so, no Beethoven. Yet various intrauterine devices prevent this sort of implantation. Thus, if we accept premise 2, we must judge the use of such "contraceptives" wrongful. Further, if we suppose that Beethoven would not have come to be unless a particular ovum and a particular sperm had not met, then a practice that could have prevented Beethoven would have been masturbation. This also seems to be condemned by 2. In short, the reasonable judgment would seem to be the rejection of 2. Then, however, the "pop argument" concerning Beethoven is seen to be impotent.

Too often, the concept of the sanctity of life (almost invariably only *human* life is meant) in "the sanctity-of-life approach" is assumed to be clear and unproblematic. However, the opposite is true. The *expression* 'sanctity of life' is not a claim or a principle. Sometimes it seems to stand in for a claim that all human life is valuable or that it is always wrong to take innocent life. But then *these claims* are at issue and should be addressed. Thomas Shannon and James Digiacomo, authors of *An Introduction to Bioethics,* claim that "sanctity of life includes" claims such as "Humans ought to work for the survival, not the destruction of the race," "Families should be free to determine their own size . . . and persons should be free to exercise personal choice and to make decisions about matters that affect their own welfare."[16] It is astonishing that these authors think such claims are "included" in the sanctity-of-life concept. It is also astonishing that they imply that the latter two claims should be accepted unqualifiedly. Elsewhere they candidly suggest that the Roman Catholic church itself frequently relies on quality-of-life judgments, as in finally accepting usury and in its recent defense of a right to a living wage.

Flag waving and sloganeering have their place, but they are no substitute for serious arguments in favor of an aggressive policy of life preservation. There *are* serious defenses of such a view, and much of our earlier inquiry was aimed at their assessment. Those who instead circumvent the serious philosophical task will be seduced by simplifications and led to a mindless marching in lockstep with other "true believers" who piously announce with cocksureness that God is on their side. It is evident by now that the issues are not simple, that those who imply as much perform a public disservice, and that, for the reasons set out, the usual appeals to the sanctity of life utterly fail to achieve their aim.

*On the Child Abuse Amendments of 1984*   In October 1984, federal legislation in the United States known as the Child Abuse Amendments of 1984 was signed into law. This legislation is the by-product of much controversy over the extent to which defective newborns ought to be treated, whether nontreatment at some point is permissible, and what policy on such matters should be required by law. The key question for our purposes concerns when this legislation allows nontreatment and when, in contrast, it views nontreatment as a form of wrongful neglect. The crucial passage indicates that "medically indicated treatment" must be provided for infants with life-threatening conditions unless

> (A) the infant is chronically and irreversibly comatose; (B) the provision of such treatment would (i) merely prolong dying, (ii) not be effective in ameliorating or correcting all the infant's life-threatening conditions, or (iii) otherwise be futile in terms of the survival of the infant; or (C) the provision of such treatment would be virtually futile in terms of the survival of the infant and the treatment itself under such circumstances would be inhumane.[17]

From the standpoint of the position defended here, part of this legislation is morally suspect. Part A, which allows nontreatment of the irreversibly comatose, is reasonable; such neonates have no potential for conscious life and no weighty interest in continued existence. The gist of parts B and C is that infants who are not comatose must be given medical treatment if the treatment would be effective in causing them to survive (presumably for a decent span of life; treatment cannot "merely prolong dying"). Although the language of the provisions is not crystal clear, the legislation requires extremely aggressive therapeutic intervention. Basically, if a noncomatose infant's life can be perpetuated long enough so that the treatment does not count as merely prolonging dying (a year? two years?), nonfutile treatment must be provided. Thus, even in some cases in which an infant is grossly malformed (for instance, with no arms or legs), in which extreme retardation is certain, where regular physical discomfort or suffering is likely, and in which the prospective burden on parents is great, treatment must be provided. In many cases the legislation can serve only to force parents against their will to support the judgment that a life must be perpetuated for a few years (compare the Tay-Sachs infant who nearly always dies by age four or five) a life that probably will be pain-ridden and for whose deprivations there probably will not be later compensation.

I have argued that such newborns lack a right to life even if possessing an interest in continued existence. Recognition of this interest, however, is compatible with the judgment that (1) it is only one morally relevant interest among others (compare parental interests here) and (2) it may not be in the *all-things-considered interest* of an infant to continue to live. In many cases the prospective burdens and prospective satisfactions make for a most bleak outlook, even with the best remedial care. In such cases the federal legislation requires acting in ways that, I believe, are morally indefensible—ways insufficiently sensitive to parents and myopically committed to the value of all (noncomatose) human life in the abstract. Aside from being living members of our species, some seriously defective neonates entirely or virtually lack those psychological capacities (or potential) necessary for what we often describe as a "uniquely human life" (in reality, any life with a certain intentionality, rationality, and emotional depth). To believe that all such lives must be perpetuated is to be committed to the view that a very special value attaches to any being that is (1) alive, (2) not irreversibly comatose, and (3) a member, in some sense, of *Homo sapiens*. Put this way (and following an examination of the arguments for this view), the eccentric nature of this stand and of drawing the moral boundaries in this manner is, I think, more obvious. The persistence of such a view seems explicable only as a by-product of the tendency to think of our species as so special, so exclusively valuable, that even the most misshapen and radically impaired human anomalies are to be viewed as "sacrosanct," of "infinite value" or "absolute worth."

Consider a further troublesome implication of this position. Suppose, as some believe, that the alleged moral prohibition on not treating noncomatose neonates also applied to human fetuses, embryos, and zygotes. Suppose further that a super scanner were available that could, prenatally, clearly diagnose any defects possessed by such entities. Prenatal surgery of certain kinds is now becoming a reality. Must such treatment (supposing that it is not futile) be employed on seriously defective fetuses, embryos, or blastocysts on pain of invidiously discriminating against the handicapped? If so, aborting a Tay-Sachs fetus would be wrong. So also for a one-headed twin or a cyclopean fetus. Consider a case of in vitro fertilization. Suppose a multicellular human blastocyst develops but has trisomy 13. Must it then (given earlier intentions) be implanted in the uterus, and (if feasible) prenatal surgery (if not *ex utero*) begun?[18] Is a decision not to implant a decision to *murder*? The mind boggles at the implications of the view that we morally fail if we do not go to extraordinary lengths to preserve *all* noncomatose human life forms.

The tendency to focus almost exclusively on persistent human cell functioning and to ignore quality-of-life considerations has one main advantage: in a complex, problem-laden world yearning for simplicity, it offers a brief, easy answer. And the truth, when complicated, does not always fare well in competition with the simple but false. Let mathematics, medicine, or technology be complex—we expect as much—but somewhere along the way we were encouraged to believe that morality posed a challenge only to our wills, not to our intellects. At least Socrates knew better.[19]

## NOTES

1.  The expression "Baby Doe cases" generally is coming to be used to refer to various cases involving defective neonates even though a specific baby in Indiana in 1982 was called Baby Doe. Another baby, "Baby Jane Doe," a spina bifida infant in Long Island (see §5) has been the subject of much dispute involving intervention by the Department of Health and Human Services in the United States in 1983 and 1984.

2.  I rely here on Norman Fost, "Putting Hospitals on Notice," *The Hastings Center Report* (August 1982), pp. 5–8.

3.  On this point see Margaret Pabst Battin's essay "Euthanasia" in *Border Crossings,* edited by Donald VanDeVeer and Tom Regan (New York: Random House, 1985).

4.  In part, I here rely on Robert Weir's very helpful *Selective Nontreatment of Handicapped Newborns* (New York: Oxford University Press, 1984), pp. 38–48. Also, see E. Peter Volpe, *Human Heredity and Birth Defects* (Indianapolis: Bobbs-Merrill, 1979).

5.  See *Deciding to Forego Life-Sustaining Treatment,* the March 1983 Report of the President's Commission for the Study of Ethical Problems in Medicine and Biomedical and Behavioral Research. Available from the U.S. Government Printing Office.

6.  See Michael Tooley, "Abortion and Infanticide," *Philosophy and Public Affairs,* Vol. 2, no. 1 (Fall 1972), pp. 37–65, and his book *Abortion and Infanticide* (Oxford, England: Clarendon, 1983).

7.  Richard Ryder, *Victims of Science* (London: Davis-Poynter, 1975).

8.  In my view an interest can be morally significant or relevant without being weighty. How to weigh interests is a problem. I develop this view a bit in "Interspecific Justice," *Inquiry,* vol. 22, nos. 1–2 (Summer 1979), pp. 55–79. The essay is reprinted in a volume coedited by myself and Christine Pierce entitled *People, Penguins, and Plastic Trees: Basic Issues in Environmental Ethics* (Belmont, Calif.: Wadsworth, 1986).

9.  See Mary Anne Warren, "On the Moral and Legal Status of Abortion" (especially the 1982 postscript), reprinted in Joel Feinberg, ed., *The Problem of Abortion,* ed. 2 (Belmont, Calif.: Wadsworth, 1984), pp. 102–119. Originally published in *The Monist,* vol. 57 (1973).

10.  See the statement "Treatment of Critically Ill Newborns" by the American Academy of Pediatrics in *Pediatrics,* vol. 72, no. 4 (October 1983), pp. 565–566.

11.  I have relied on the reprint of the human life bill, S. 158, in James P. Sterba, ed., *Morality in Practice* (Belmont, Calif.: Wadsworth, 1984) pp. 177–180.

12.  It is somewhat puzzling that many Christians invoke the "sanctity of human life" to defend extraordinary efforts to postpone death for all human life forms. For if one believes that death—understood as the permanent cessation of conscious experience—never occurs for human beings (rather what is called "death" is only some transition to an eternal continuation of life), it is not clear why one ought to view death as

tragic for the one who dies. If "eternal life" is thought good (the best life), then "dying" should be looked on, generally, as a great improvement. Billy Graham, in this vein, once stated "I look forward to dying." St. Augustine believed, as do many Christians, that all people—babies included—"inherit" original sin (of "Adam") and thus are doomed to eternal suffering—barring divine intervention. If this were true, then for some postearthly existence well might be a loss and dying a bad thing. Normally, if a person declared that he would slit your throat unless you obeyed him, we would think that a nasty bit of coercion. People, however, seem to be very forgiving of their gods. If it were important for defective newborns to be around on the earth for a good while—for purposes of divine intervention or baptism—then it would seem that a sporting god would see to it that such occurred. The picture of the divine that emerges from the Old Testament suggests, arguably, limited patience. When one of his prophets, Elisha (it is reported in II Kings 2:23–24), was insulted by some little children (who called him "bald head"), two "she bears" came out of the woods and mauled forty-two of the children. Literal-minded Christians, among others, might be hard put to reconcile their verbal opposition to taking human life and a "biblical ethic" (or, at least, an Old Testament one which is sometimes quite ready to terminate human life. See also Exod. 21:17, Deut. 20:10–14).

13. E. L. Mascall, *Christian Theology and Natural Science* (New York: Ronald, 1956), pp. 283, 285.

14. Joseph F. Donceel, "A Liberal Catholic's View," in Joel Feinberg, ed., *The Problem of Abortion* (Belmont, Calif.: Wadsworth, 1984), pp. 15–20.

15. C. Everett Koop, "The Slide to Auschwitz," in *Abortion and the Conscience of a Nation* (Nashville, Tenn.: Thomas Nelson, 1984), p. 63.

16. Thomas Shannon and James Digiacomo, *An Introduction to Bioethics* (New York: Paulist, 1979), pp. 39, 85.

17. See Public Law 98–457—October 9, 1984; 98th Congress. Also cited as the Child Abuse Amendments of 1984. See Sec. 121.

    Many who argue against the permissibility of abortion or infanticide invoke "slippery-slope arguments," e.g., if we take a step away from a strict prohibition on deliberately taking innocent human life, we will inevitably slide down the slope toward evidently wrongful killings (thus, we should not take the first step). It is worth observing that the often made concession that it is all right to let anencephalic or irreversibly comatose infants die is a step "down the slope." So also, in spite of his normal pro-life rhetoric, President Reagan in the first campaign debate in 1984 allowed that abortion might be permissible when the mother's life is threatened by the pregnancy. It is noteworthy that a *parental interest* is given weight here (a good deal of weight), but those who advocate "doing whatever is in the infant's best interest" in other contexts theoretically disavow such a move. When a deviation from "it's always wrong to kill innocent humans" is proposed, we should question whether this is a step *on a slope* and if so whether the slope is a *slippery* one.

18. This point is due to Peter Singer and Helga Kuhse in "The Moral Status of the Embryo" in *Test-Tube Babies*, edited by William A. Walters and Peter Singer (Melbourne, Austr.: Oxford University Press, 1982), pp. 57–62.

19. With regard to this essay, I wish to thank Richard Wyatt, Tom Regan, and Robert Hambourger for their suggestions, reservations, and provocations (not necessarily in that order).

## SUGGESTIONS FOR FURTHER READING

§1-2 On questions about the killing/letting die distinction, see the essay by James Rachels in this volume; Bonnie Steinbock, ed., *Killing and Letting Die* (Englewood Cliffs, N.J.: Prentice-Hall, 1980). For discussions of the Baby Doe case and related cases, see: Carol Levine, "The Case of Baby Jane Doe," *The Hastings Center Reports* (February 1984), p. 10; Anthony Gallo, "Spina Bifida . . . ," *The Hastings Center Reports* (February 1984), pp. 10–13; Bonnie Steinbock, "Baby Jane Doe in the Courts," *The Hastings Center Reports* (February 1984), pp. 13–19; Kathleen Kerr, "Reporting the Case of Baby Jane Doe," *The Hastings Center Reports* (August 1984), pp. 7–9; George Annas, "Disconnecting the Baby Doe Hotline," *The Hastings Center Reports* (June 1983), pp. 14–16; Carson Strong, "The Tiniest Newborns," *The Hastings Center Reports* (February 1984), pp. 14–19; R. Stinson, *The Long Dying of Baby Andrew* (Boston: Little, Brown, 1983).

§3-5 For empirical description of certain types of neonatal anomalies, see the already cited volumes by Robert Weir and Peter Volpe. Also, see the thorough and vivid graphic depictions in E. L. Potter, *Pathology of the Fetus and the Infant* (Chicago: Year Book, 1961).

§7-9 On theories of rights and related distinctions, a most useful volume is Joel Feinberg, *Social Philosophy* (Englewood Cliffs, N.J.: Prentice-Hall, 1973). For a non-rights approach to our topic, see chapter 7 of Peter Singer's *Practical Ethics* (Cambridge, England: Cambridge University Press, 1979). See also Michael Bayles, *Reproductive Ethics* (Englewood Cliffs, N.J.: Prentice-Hall, 1984), chapter 5.

§10-11 On sentience and the relevance of species, see Peter Singer, *Animal Liberation;* Tom Regan, *The Case for Animal Rights* (Berkeley, Calif.: University of California Press, 1983); Harlan Miller and William H. Williams, eds., *Ethics and Animals* (Clifton, N.J.: Humana Press, 1983); Mary Midgley, *Animals and Why They Matter* (Middlesex, England: Penguin, 1983). See also the already cited volume, Donald VanDeVeer and Christine Pierce, eds., *People, Penguins, and Plastic Trees.*

§12 For a thorough but skeptical discussion of potentiality (and much more) see the already cited volume by Michael Tooley, *Abortion and Infanticide.* Also useful is L.W. Sumner's lucid and rich *Abortion and Moral Theory* (Princeton, N.J.: Princeton University Press, 1981).

§13 Various theoretical moral positions are taken in the following materials: Albert Jonsen and Michael Garland, eds., *Ethics of Newborn Intensive Care* (Berkeley, Calif.: University of California Press, 1976); Kenneth Kipnis and Gailyn M. Williamson, "Nontreatment Decisions for Severely Compromised Newborns," *Ethics* 95 (October 1984), pp. 90–111; John Arras, "Toward an Ethic of Ambiguity," *The Hastings Center Reports* (April 1984), pp. 25–33; Robert C. Coburn, "Morality and the Defective Newborn," *Journal of Medicine and Philosophy,* vol. 5, no. 4, pp. 340–357; Marvin Kohl, "Moral Arguments For and Against Maximally Treating the Defective Newborn," a currently unpublished essay (Kohl is in the Philosophy Department of the State University of New York at Fredonia, New York); Phillip Devine, *The Ethics of Homicide* (Ithaca, N.Y.: Cornell University Press, 1979); Germain Grisez and Joseph M. Boyle, Jr., *Life and Death with Liberty and Justice* (Notre Dame, Ind.: University of Notre Dame Press, 1979). See also chap. 3 in *Moral Problems in Medicine,* edited by Samuel Gorovitz et al. (Englewood Cliffs, N.J.: Prentice-Hall, 1976); Paul Ramsey, *The Ethics of Fetal Research* (New Haven, Conn.: Yale University Press, 1975). Many fine essays more generally on killing or euthanasia can be found in John Ladd, ed., *Ethical Issues Relating to Life and Death* (New York: Oxford University Press, 1979).

§14-15 In addition to materials cited in the text, see Glanville Williams, *The Sanctity of Life and the Criminal Law* (New York: Knopf, 1970); and the undernoticed volume of Susan T. Nicholson, *Abortion and the Roman Catholic Church* (Knoxville, Tenn.: Religious Ethics, 1978). For an extremely conservative view, see I. Jakobovits, *Jewish Medical Ethics* (New York: Bloch, 1975).

Note: Robert Weir's *Selective Nontreatment of Handicapped Newborns* (already cited) contains further extensive bibliographical help. Students also could canvass issues of the *Journal of Medicine and Philosophy,* the *Journal of Medical Ethics, Theoretical Medicine, Pediatrics,* the *Journal of Law and Medicine, Ethics, Philosophy and Public Affairs, Social Theory and Practice,* and the *New England Journal of Medicine,* among others. Also relevant is the *Encyclopedia of Bioethics.*

# 7

# Abortion

## JOEL FEINBERG

Abortion can be defined as the deliberate causing of the death of a fetus, either by directly killing it or (more commonly) by causing its expulsion from the womb before it is "viable," that is before it is capable of surviving outside its mother's body. The word 'fetus' in this definition refers to a human offspring at any stage of its prenatal development, from conception to birth. There is a narrower medical sense of the word 'fetus' in which it refers to the unborn entity from roughly the eighth week of pregnancy (when brain waves can first be monitored) until birth, normally at nine months. In this technical sense the word 'fetus' is used to contrast the relatively mature unborn being with its earlier stages when it is called a "zygote" (from conception to implantation a week later in the uterine wall) or an "embryo" (from implantation until the eighth week). I shall use the word 'fetus' as a convenient general term for the unborn at all phases of its development except when the contrast between fetus and embryo or zygote becomes central in the argument.

A number of serious practical questions are raised by the practice of abortion. Two in particular stand out. The first is a question of personal conscience: Under what conditions, if any, is abortion morally justified? The second is a question of public policy: What, if anything, should be done to increase or decrease the opportunities for abortion? Despite its importance, we will be able to consider this second question only partially in the "Postscript" at the end of this chapter.

The question of the moral permissibility of abortion demands that we answer two very hard philosophical questions. The first requires us to consider which traits of the developing fetus are relevant to deciding what morally may and may not be done to it. The general problem discussed in this regard is often called "the problem of the status of the fetus." This question will be discussed in the first part of this essay. The second question that demands our attention can be classified under the general heading "the problem of the conflict of claims." The problem here is that, even granting that the fetus is a person, the fetus is not the only person involved; there are also the mother, the father, possibly other family members, etc. The needs and interests of all the affected parties, not just those of the fetus, seem to have a bearing on the question of the moral permissibility of abortion. Therefore, we must determine *whose* claims are the strongest, if they happen to clash. This problem is explored in the second part of this essay.

## I. THE STATUS OF THE FETUS

The problem of the status of the fetus can be formulated as follows: At what stage, if any, in the development between conception and birth, do fetuses acquire the characteristic (whatever it may be) that confers on them the appropriate status to be included in the scope of the moral rule against homicide—the rule "Thou shalt not kill"? Put more tersely: At what stage, if any, of their development do fetuses become people? A variety of familiar answers have been given—for example, that fetuses become persons "at the moment of conception," at "quickening" (that is, at the moment of their first self-initiated movement in the womb), at viability (that is, when the fetus is able to survive independently outside the mother's womb). Debates about *when* the fetus becomes a person, however, are premature unless we have first explored *what* a person is. Answers to the question "When does the fetus become a person?" attempt to draw a *boundary line* between prepersons and persons; however, even if correctly drawn, a boundary line is not the same thing as a *criterion* of personhood. Indeed, until we have a criterion, we cannot know for sure whether a given proposed boundary is correct. Let us mean by "a criterion of personhood" a specification of the characteristic (or set of characteristics) that is such that (1) no being can be a person unless he or she possesses that characteristic, (2) any being who possesses that characteristic is a person, and (3) it is precisely that characteristic that directly confers personhood on whoever possesses it. The person-making characteristic, in brief, is that characteristic (or set of characteristics) that is common and peculiar to all persons and in virtue of which they are persons. "A criterion of personhood," as we shall understand the phrase, is some statement (true or false) of what the person-making characteristic is.

The statement of a mere boundary line of personhood, in contrast, may be correct and useful even though it mentions no person-making characteristic at all. Such a statement may specify only some theoretically superficial characteristic that happens to be invariably (or perhaps only usually and roughly) correlated with a person-making characteristic. For example, even if it is true that all persons can survive outside the mother's womb, it does not follow that being able to survive outside the mother's womb is what makes someone a person or that this is even partially constitutive of what it is to be a person. The "superficial characteristic," then, can be used as a clue, a test, or an indication of the presence of the basic personhood-conferring characteristic and therefore of personhood itself, even though it is in no sense a *cause* or a *constituent* of personhood. An analogy might make the point clearer. What makes any chemical compound an acid is a feature of its molecular structure, namely that it contains hydrogen as a positive radical. But it also happens that acids "typically" are soluble in water, sour in taste, and turn blue litmus paper red. The latter three characteristics, then, while neither constitutive nor causative of acidity, can nevertheless be useful and reliable indexes to, or tests of, acidity. The litmus test in particular draws a "boundary" between acids and nonacids. The question now to be addressed is whether a reasonable criterion for personhood can be found, one that enables us to draw an accurate boundary line.

## §1 HUMAN BEINGS AND PERSONS

The first step in coming to terms with the concept of a person is to disentangle it from a concept with which it is thoroughly intertwined in most of our minds, that of a human being. In an influential article, the young American social philosopher Mary Anne Warren has pointed out that the term 'human' has two "distinct but not often distinguished senses."[1] In what she calls the "moral sense," a being is human provided that it is a "full-fledged member of the moral community," a being possessed (as Jefferson wrote of all "men"—did he mean men and women?) of inalienable rights to life, liberty, and the pursuit of happiness. For beings to be humans in this sense is precisely for them to be people, and the problem of the "humanity" of the fetus in this sense is that of determining whether the fetus is the sort of being —a person—who has such moral rights as the right to life. On the other hand, a being is human in what Warren calls the "genetic sense" provided he or she is a member of the species *Homo sapiens,* and *all* we mean in describing someone as a human in the genetic sense is that he or she belongs to that animal species. In this sense, when we say that Jones is a human being, we are making a statement of the same type as when we say that Fido is a dog (canine being). Any fetus conceived by human parents will of course be a human being in this sense, just as any fetus conceived by dogs will of course be canine in the analogous sense.

It is possible to hold, as no doubt many people do, that all human beings in the moral sense (persons) are human beings in the genetic sense (members of *Homo sapiens*) and vice versa, so that the two classes, while distinct in meaning, nevertheless coincide exactly in reality. In that case all genetically human beings, including fetuses from the moment of conception, have a right to life, the unjustified violation of which is homicide, and no beings who are genetically nonhuman are persons. But it is also possible to hold, as some philosophers do, that some genetically human beings (for example, zygotes and irreversibly comatose "human vegetables") are *not* human beings in the moral sense (persons), and/or that some persons (for example, God, angels, devils, higher animals, intelligent beings in outer space) are *not* members of *Homo sapiens*. Surely it is an open question to be settled, if at all, by argument or discovery, whether the two classes correspond exactly. It is not a question closed in advance by definition or appeals to word usage.

## §2 NORMATIVE VERSUS DESCRIPTIVE PERSONHOOD

Perhaps the best way to proceed from this point is to stick to the term 'person' and avoid the term 'human' except when we clearly intend the genetic sense, in that way avoiding the ever-present danger of being misunderstood. The term 'person', however, is not without its own ambiguities. The one central ambiguity we should note is that between purely *normative* (moral or legal) uses of 'person' and purely *descriptive* (conventional, commonsense) uses of the term.

When moralists or lawyers use the term 'person' in a purely normative way they use it simply to ascribe moral or legal properties—usually rights or duties or both—to the beings so denominated. To be a person in the normative sense is to have rights, or rights and duties, or at least to be the sort of being who could have rights and duties without conceptual absurdity. Most writers think that it would be sheer nonsense to speak of the rights or duties of rocks, or blades of grass, or sunbeams, or of historical events or abstract ideas. These objects are thought to be conceptually inappropriate subjects for the attribution of rights or duties. Hence we speak of them as "impersonal entities," the types of beings that are contrasted with objects that can stand in personal relationships to us or make moral claims on us. The higher animals—our fellow mammalian species in particular—are borderline cases whose classification as persons or nonpersons has been a matter of controversy. Many of them are fit subjects of right-ascriptions but cannot plausibly be assigned duties or moral responsibilities. These ideas are examined in considerable detail in Peter Singer's essay in the present volume. In any case, when we attribute personhood in a purely normative way to any kind of being, we are attributing such moral qualities as rights or duties but not (necessarily) any observable characteristics of any kind—for example, having flesh or blood or belonging to a particular species. Lawyers have attributed (legal) personhood even to states and corporations, and their purely normative judgments say nothing about the presence or absence of body, mind, consciousness, color, etc.

In contrast to the purely normative use of the word 'person' we can distinguish a purely empirical or descriptive use. There are certain characteristics that are fixed by a rather firm convention of our language such that the general term for any being who possesses them is 'person.' Thus, to say of some being that he is a person, in this sense, is to convey some information about what the being is like. Neither are attributions of personhood of this kind essentially controversial. If to be a person *means* to have characteristics *a*, *b*, and *c*, then to say of a being who is known to have *a*, *b*, and *c* that he or she is a person (in the descriptive sense) is no more controversial than to say of an animal known to be a young dog that it is a puppy, or of a person known to be an unmarried man that he is a bachelor. What makes these noncontroversial judgments true are conventions of language that determine what words mean. The conventions are often a bit vague around the edges but they apply clearly enough to central cases. It is in virtue of these reasonably precise linguistic conventions that the word 'person' normally conveys the idea of a definite set of descriptive characteristics. I shall call the idea defined by these characteristics "the commonsense concept of personhood." When we use the word 'person' in this wholly descriptive way we are not attributing rights, duties, eligibility for rights and duties, or any other normative characteristics to the being so described. At most we are attributing characteristics that may be a *ground* for ascribing rights and duties.

These *purely* normative and *purely* descriptive uses of the word 'person' are probably unusual. In most of its uses, the word both describes or classifies someone in a conventionally understood way *and* ascribes rights, etc., to him. But there is enough looseness or flexibility in usage to leave open the questions of whether the classes of moral and commonsense persons correspond in reality. Although some may think it obvious that all and only commonsense persons are moral persons, that identification of classes does not follow simply as a matter of word usage, and must, therefore, be supported independently by argument. Many learned writers, after all, have maintained that human zygotes and embryos are moral persons despite the fact that they are almost certainly not "commonsense persons." Others have spoken of wicked murderers as "monsters" or "fiends" that can rightly be destroyed like "wild beasts" or eliminated like "rotten apples." This seems to amount to holding that "moral monsters" are commonsense persons who are so wicked (only *persons* can be wicked) that they have lost their moral personhood, or membership in our moral community. The English jurist Sir William Blackstone (1723–1780) maintained that convicted murderers forfeit their rights to life. If one went further and maintained that moral monsters forfeit all their human rights, then one would be rejecting the view that the classes of moral and commonsense persons exactly coincide, for wicked persons who are answerable for their foul deeds must first of all be persons in the descriptive sense; but as beings without rights, they would not be moral persons.

## §3 THE CRITERION OF COMMONSENSE PERSONHOOD

A criterion of personhood in the descriptive sense would be a specification of those characteristics that are common and peculiar to commonsense persons and in virtue of which they are such persons. They are necessary conditions for commonsense personhood in the sense that no being who lacks any one of them can be a person. They are sufficient conditions in the sense that any being who possesses all of them is a person, whatever he or she may be like in other respects. How shall we formulate this criterion? If this question simply raises a matter of fixed linguistic convention, one might expect it to be easy enough to state the defining characteristics of personhood straight off. Surprisingly, the question is not quite that simple, and no mere dictionary is likely to give us a wholly satisfactory answer. What we must do is to think of the characteristics that come at least implicitly to mind when we hear or use such words as 'person', 'people', and the personal pronouns. We might best proceed by considering three different classes of cases: clear examples of beings whose personhood cannot be doubted, clear examples of beings whose nonpersonhood cannot be doubted, and actual or hypothetical examples of beings whose status is not initially clear. We probably will not be able to come up with a definitive list of characteristics if only because the word 'person' may be somewhat loose, but we should be able to achieve a criterion that is precise enough to permit a definite classification of fetuses.

*Undoubted Commonsense Persons* Who are undoubted persons? Consider first your parents, siblings, or friends. What is it about them that makes you so certain that they are persons? "Well, they look like persons," you might say; "They have human faces and bodies." But so do irreversibly comatose human vegetables, and we are, to put it mildly, not so certain that they are persons. "Well then, they are males and females and thus appropriately referred to by our personal pronouns, all of which have gender. We can't refer to any of them by use of the impersonal pronoun 'it', because they have sex; so perhaps being gendered is the test of personhood." Such a reply has superficial plausibility, but is the idea of a "sexless person" logically contradictory? Perhaps any genetically human person will be predominately one sex or the other, but must the same be true of "intelligent beings in outer space," or spirits, gods, and devils?

Let's start again. "What makes me certain that my parents, siblings, and friends are people is that they give evidence of being conscious of the world and of themselves; they have inner emotional lives, just like me; they can understand things and reason about them, make plans, and act; they can communicate with me, argue, negotiate, express themselves, make agreements, honor commitments, and stand in relationships of mutual trust; they have tastes and values of their own; they can be frustrated or fulfilled, pleased or hurt." Now we clearly have the beginnings, at least, of a definitive list of person-making characteristics. In the commonsense way of thinking, persons are those beings who, among other things, are conscious, have a concept and awareness of themselves, are capable of experiencing emotions, can reason and acquire understanding, can plan ahead, can act on their plans, and can feel pleasure and pain.

*Undoubted Nonpersons*  What of the objects that clearly are not persons? Rocks have none of the above characteristics; neither do flowers and trees; neither (presumably) do snails and earthworms. But perhaps we are wrong about that. Maybe rocks, plants, and lower animals are congeries of lower-level spirits with inner lives and experiences of their own, as primitive men and mystics have often maintained. Very well, that is possible. But if they do have these characteristics, contrary to all appearances, then it would seem natural to think of them as persons too, "contrary to all appearance." In raising the question of their possession of these characteristics at all, we seem to be raising by the same token the question of their commonsense personhood. Mere rocks are quite certainly not crowds of silent spirits, but if, contrary to fact, they are such spirits, then we must think of them as real people, quite peculiarly embodied.

*Hard Cases*  Now, what about the hard cases? Is God, as traditionally conceived, a kind of nonhuman—or better, superhuman—person? Theologians are divided about this, of course, but most ordinary believers think of Him (note the personal pronoun) as conscious of self and world, capable of love and anger, eminently rational, having plans for the world, acting (if only through His creation), capable of communicating with humans, of issuing commands and making covenants, and of being pleased or disappointed in the use to which humans put their free will. To the extent that one believes that God has these various attributes, to that extent does one believe in a *personal* God. If one believes only in a God who is an unknown and unknowable First Cause of the world, or an obscure but powerful force sustaining the world, or the ultimate energy in the cosmos, then, it seems fair to say, one believes in an *impersonal* deity.

Now we come to the ultimate thought experiment. Suppose that you are a space explorer whose rocket ship has landed on a planet in a distant galaxy. The planet is inhabited by some very strange objects, so unlike anything you have previously encountered that at first you don't even know whether to classify them as animal, vegetable, mineral, or "none of the above." They are composed of a gelatinous sort of substance much like mucus except that it is held together by no visible membranes or skin, and it continually changes its shape from one sort of amorphous glob to another, sometimes breaking into smaller globs and then coming together again. The objects have no appendages, no joints, no heads or faces. They float mysteriously above the surface of the planet and move about in complex patterns while emitting eerie sounds resembling nothing so much as electronic music. The first thing you will wish to know about these strange objects is whether they are extraterrestrial *people,* to be respected, greeted, and traded and negotiated with, or mere things or inferior animals to be chopped up, boiled, and used for food and clothing.

Almost certainly the first thing you would do is try to communicate with them by making approaches, gesturing by hand, voice, or radio signals. You might also study the patterns in their movements and sound emissions to see whether they have any of the characteristics of a language. If the beings respond even in a primitive way to early gestures, one might suspect at least that they are beings who are capable of perception and who can be *aware* of movements and sounds. If some sort of actual communication then follows, you can attribute to them at least the mentality of chimpanzees. If negotiations then follow and agreements are reached, then you can be sure that they are rational beings; and if you learn to interpret signs of worry, distress, anger, alarm, or friendliness, then you can be quite confident that they are indeed people, no matter how inhuman they are in biological respects.

*A Working Criterion of Commonsense Personhood* Suppose then that we agree that our rough list captures well the traits that are generally characteristic of commonsense persons. Suppose further (what is not quite as evident) that each trait on the list is necessary for commonsense personhood, that no one trait is by itself sufficient, but that the whole *collection* of traits is sufficient to confer commonsense personhood on any being that possesses it. Suppose, that is, that consciousness is necessary (no permanently unconscious being can be a person), but that it is not enough. The conscious being must also have a concept of a self and a certain amount of self-awareness. But although each of these last traits is necessary, they are still not enough even in conjunction, since a self-aware, conscious being who was totally incapable of learning or reasoning would not be a person. Hence minimal rationality is also necessary, though not by itself sufficient. And so on through our complete list of person-making characteristics, each one of which, let us suppose, is a necessary condition, and all of which are jointly a sufficient condition of being a person in the commonsense, descriptive sense of 'person'. Let us call our set of characteristics *C.* Now at last we can pose the most important and controversial question about the status of the fetus: What is the relation, if any, between having *C* and being a person in the normative (moral) sense, that is, a being who possesses, among other things, a right to life?

## §4 PROPOSED CRITERIA OF MORAL PERSONHOOD

It bears repeating at the outset of our discussion of this most important question that formulating criteria of personhood in the purely moral sense is not a scientific question to be settled by empirical evidence, not simply a question of word usage, not simply a matter to be settled by commonsense thought experiments. It is instead an essentially controversial question about the possession of moral rights that cannot be answered in these ways. That is not to say that rational methods of investigation and discussion are not available to us, but only that the methods of reasoning about morals do not often provide conclusive proofs and demonstrations. What rational methods can achieve for us, even if they fall short of producing universal agreement, is to list the various options open to us and the strong and weak points of each of them. Every position has its embarrassments, that is, places where it appears to conflict with moral and commonsense convictions that even its proponents can be presumed to share. To point out these embarrassments for a given position is not necessarily to refute it but rather to measure the costs of holding it to the coherence of one's larger set of beliefs generally. Similarly, each position has its own peculiar advantages, respects in which it coheres uniquely well with deeply entrenched convictions that even its opponents might be expected to share. I shall try in the ensuing discussion to state and illustrate as vividly as I can the advantages and difficulties in all the major positions. Then I shall weigh the cases for and against the various alternatives. For those who disagree with my conclusion, the discussion will serve at least to locate the crucial issues in the controversy over the status of the fetus.

A proposed criterion for moral personhood is a statement of a characteristic (or set of characteristics) that its advocate deems both necessary and (jointly) sufficient for being a person in the moral sense. Such characteristics are not thought of as mere indexes, signs, or "litmus tests" of moral personhood but as more basic traits that actually confer moral personhood on whoever possesses them. All and only those beings having these characteristics have basic moral rights, in particular the right to full and equal protection against homicide. Thus, fetuses must be thought of as having this right if they satisfy a proposed criterion of personhood. The main types of criteria of moral personhood proposed by philosophers can be grouped under one or another of five different headings, which we shall examine in turn. Four of the five proposed criteria refer to possession of *C* (the traits we have listed as conferring *commonsense* personhood). One of these four specifies actual possession of *C*; the other three refer to either actual or potential possession of *C*. The remaining criterion, which we shall consider briefly first, makes no mention of *C* at all.

A. *The Species Criterion* "All and only members of the biological species *Homo sapiens,* 'whoever is conceived by human beings,' are moral persons and thus are entitled to full and equal protection by the moral rule against homicide." The major advantage of this view (at least for some) is that it gives powerful support to those who would extend the protection of the rule against homicide to the fetus from the moment of conception. If this criterion is correct, it is not simply because of utilitarian reasons (such that it would usefully increase respect for life in the community) that we must not abort human zygotes and embryos, but rather because we owe it to these minute entities themselves not to kill them, for as members of the human species they are already possessed of a full right to life equal in strength to that of any adult person.

The species criterion soon encounters serious difficulties. Against the view that membership in the species *Homo sapiens* is a *necessary* condition of membership in the class of moral persons, we have the possibility of there being moral persons from other planets who belong to other biological species. Moreover, some human beings—in particular, those who are irreversibly comatose "vegetables"—*are* human beings but doubtfully qualify as moral persons, a fact that casts serious doubt on the view that membership in the species *Homo sapiens* is a *sufficient* condition of being a moral person.

The species criterion might be defended against these objections if some persuasive reason could be given why moral personhood is a unique feature of all and only human beings. Aside from an arbitrary claim that this is "just obvious," a position that Singer argues amounts to a pernicious prejudice against nonhuman animals comparable to racism and sexism, the only possible way to defend this claim to uniqueness is by means of some *theological* argument: for example, that *all* human beings (including human fetuses) and *only* human beings (thereby excluding all nonhuman animals and possible beings from other planets) are moral persons *because God has made this so.*[2] Now, if one already believes on faith that God had made it true that all and only humans are moral persons, then of course one has quite conclusive reason for believing that all and only humans are moral persons. But if we leave faith aside and confine our attention to reasons, then we shall have to ask what grounds there are for supposing that "God has made this so," and any reason we might have for doubting that it *is* so would count equally as a reason against supposing that God made it so. A good reason for doubting that $7 + 5 = 13$ is an equally good reason for doubting that God made it to be the case that $7 + 5 = 13$; a good reason for doubting that cruelty is morally right is, if anything, a better reason for denying that God made it to be the case that cruelty is right.

*B. The Modified Species Criterion* "All and only members of species generally characterized by *C*, whether the species is *Homo sapiens* or another and whether or not the particular individual in question happens to possess *C*, are moral persons entitled to full and equal protection by the moral rule against homicide." This modification is designed to take the sting out of the first objection (above) to the unmodified species criterion. If there are other species or categories of moral persons in the universe, it concedes, then they too have moral rights. Indeed, if there are such, then *all* of their members are moral persons possessed of such rights, even those individuals who happen themselves to lack *C,* because they are not yet fully developed or because they have been irreparably damaged.

The major difficulty for the modified species criterion is that it requires further explanation why *C* should determine moral person-hood when applied to *classes* of creatures rather than to individual cases. Why is a permanently unconscious but living body of a human or an extragalactic person (or for that matter, a chimpanzee, if we should decide that that species as a whole is characterized by *C*) a moral person when it lacks as an individual the characteristics that determine moral personhood? Just because opposable thumbs are a characteristic of *Homo sapiens,* it does not follow that this or that particular *Homo sapiens* has opposable thumbs. There appears to be no reason for regarding right-possession any differently, in this regard, from thumb-possession.

*C. The Strict Potentiality Criterion*   "All and only those creatures who either actually or potentially possess *C* (that is, who either have *C* now or)would come to have *C* in the natural course of events) are moral persons now, fully protected by the rule against homicide." This crite-rion also permits one to draw the line of moral personhood in the human species right at the moment of conception, which will be counted by some as an advantage. It also has the undeniable advan-tage of immunity from one charge of arbitrariness since it will extend moral personhood to all beings in *any* species or category who possess *C,* either actually or potentially. It may also cohere with our psycho-logical attitudes, since it can explain why it is that many people, at least, think of unformed or unpretty fetuses are precious. Zygotes and embryos in particular are treasured not for what they are but for what they are biologically "programmed" to become in the fullness of time: real people fully possessed of *C.*

The difficulties of this criterion are of two general kinds, those deriving from the obscurity of the concept of "potentiality," which perhaps can be overcome, and the more serious difficulties of answer-ing the charge that merely potential possession of any set of qualifica-tions for a moral status does not logically ensure actual possession of that status. Consider just one of the problems raised by the concept of potentiality itself.[3] How, it might be asked, can a mere zygote be a potential person, whereas a mere spermatozoon or a mere unfertil-ized ovum is not? If the spermatozoon and ovum we are talking about are precisely those that will combine in a few seconds to form a human zygote, why are they not potential zygotes, and thus potential people, *now?* The defender of the potentiality criterion will reply that it is only at the moment of conception that any being comes into existence with exactly the same chromosomal makeup as the human being that will later emerge from the womb, and it is *that* chromosomal combination that forms the potential person, not anything that exists before it comes together. The reply is probably a cogent one, but uncertainties about the concept of potentiality might make us hesitate, at first, to accept it, for we might be tempted to think of both the germ cell (spermatozoon or ovum) and the zygote as potentially a particular person, while holding that the differences between their potentials, though large and significant to be sure, are nevertheless differences in degree rather than kind. It would be well to resist that temptation, however, for it could lead us to the view that some of the entities and processes that combined still earlier to form a given spermatozoon were themselves potentially that spermatozoon and hence potentially the person that spermatozoon eventually became, and so on. At the end of that road is the proposition that everything is potentially everything else, and thus the destruction of all utility in the concept of potentiality. It is better to hold this particular line at the zygote.

The remaining difficulty for the strict potentiality criterion is much more serious. It is a logical error, some have charged, to deduce *actual* rights from merely *potential* (but not yet actual) qualification for those rights. What follows from potential qualification, it is said, is potential, not actual, rights; what entails actual rights is actual, not potential, qualification. As the Australian philosopher Stanley Benn puts it, "A potential president of the United States is not on that account Commander-in-Chief [of the U.S. Army and Navy]."[4] This simple point can be called "the logical point about potentiality." Taken on its own terms, I don't see how it can be answered as an objection to the strict potentiality criterion. It is still open to antiabortionists to argue that merely potential commonsense personhood is a ground for *duties* we may have toward the potential person. But they cannot argue that it is the ground for the potential person's *rights* without committing a logical error.

*D. The Modified or Gradualist Potentiality Criterion* "Potential possession of *C* confers not a right, but only a claim, to life, but that claim keeps growing stronger, requiring ever stronger reasons to override it, until the point when *C* is actually possessed, by which time it has become a full right to life." This modification of the potentiality criterion has one distinct and important advantage. It coheres with the widely shared feeling that the moral seriousness of abortion increases with the age of the fetus. It is extremely difficult to believe on other than very specific theological grounds that a zygote one day after conception is the sort of being that can have any rights at all, much less the whole armory of "human rights" including "the right to life." But it is equally difficult for a great many people to believe that a full-term fetus one day before birth does not have a right to life. Moreover, it is very difficult to find one point in the continuous development of the fetus before which it is utterly without rights and after which it has exactly the same rights as any adult human being. Some rights in postnatal human life can be acquired instantly or suddenly; the rights of citizenship, for example, come into existence at a precise moment in the naturalization proceedings after an oath has been administered and a judicial pronouncement formally produced and certified. Similarly, the rights of husbands and wives come into existence at just that moment when an authorized person utters the words "I hereby pronounce you husband and wife." But the rights of the fetus cannot possibly jump in this fashion from nonbeing to being at some precise moment in pregnancy. The alternative is to think of them as growing steadily and gradually throughout the entire nine-month period until they are virtually "mature" at parturition. There is, in short, a kind of growth in "moral weight" that proceeds in parallel fashion with the physical growth and development of the fetus.

An "immature right" on this view is not to be thought of simply as no right at all, as if in morals a miss were as good as a mile. A better characterization of the unfinished right would be a "weak right," a claim with some moral force proportional to its degree of development but not yet as much force as a fully matured right. The key word in this account is "claim." Elsewhere I have given an account of the difference between having a right (which I defined as a "valid claim") and having a claim that is not, or not quite, valid. What would the latter be like?

> One might accumulate just enough evidence to argue with relevance and cogency that one has a right . . . although one's case might not be overwhelmingly conclusive. The argument might be strong enough to entitle one to a hearing and fair consideration. When one is in this position, it might be said that one "has a claim" that deserves to be weighed carefully. Nevertheless the balance of reasons may turn out to militate against recognition of the claim, so that the claim is not a valid claim or right.[5]

Now there are various ways in which a claim can fail to be a right. There are many examples, particularly from the law, where *all* the claims to some property, including some that are relevantly made and worthy of respect, are rejected, simply because none of them is deemed strong enough to qualify as a right. In such cases, a miss truly is as good as a mile. But in other cases, an acknowledged claim of (say) medium strength will be strong enough to be a right *unless* a stronger claim appears on the scene to override it. For these conflict situations, card games provide a useful analogy. In poker, three of a kind is good enough to win the pot unless one of the other players "makes claim" to the pot with a higher hand, say a flush or a full house. The player who claims the pot with three of a kind "has a claim" to the pot that is overridden by the stronger claim of the player with the full house. The strongest claim presented will, by that fact, constitute a right to take the money. The player who withdrew with a four flush had "no claim at all," but even that person's hand might have established a right to the pot if no stronger claim were in conflict with it.

The analogy applies to the abortion situation in the following way. The game has at least two players, the mother and the fetus, though more can play, and sometimes the father and/or the doctor are involved too. For the first few weeks of its life, the fetus (zygote, embryo) has hardly any claim to life at all, and virtually any reason of the mother's for aborting it will be strong enough to override a claim made in the fetus's behalf. At any stage in the game, any reason the mother might have for aborting will constitute a claim, but as the fetus matures, its claims grow stronger, requiring ever-stronger claims to override them. After three months or so, the fact that an abortion would be "convenient" for the mother will not be a strong enough claim, and the fetus's claim to life will defeat it. In that case, the fetus can be said to have a valid claim or right to life in the same sense that the poker player's full house gives him a right to the pot: it is a right in the sense that it is the strongest of the conflicting claims, not in the sense that it is stronger than any conflicting claim that could conceivably come up. By the time the fetus has become a neonate (a newborn child), however, it has a "right to life" of the same kind all people have, and no mere conflicting claim can override it. (Perhaps more accurately, only claims that other human persons make in self-defense to their own lives can ever have an equal strength.)

The modified potentiality criterion has the attractiveness characteristic of compromise theories when fierce ideological quarrels rage between partisans of more extreme views. It shares one fatal flaw, however, with the strict potentiality criterion. Despite its greater flexibility, it cannot evade "the logical point about potentiality." A highly developed fetus is much closer to being a commonsense person with all the developed traits that qualify it for moral personhood than is the mere zygote. But being almost qualified for rights is not the same thing as being partially qualified for rights; nor is it the same thing as being qualified for partial rights, quasi-rights, or weak rights. The advanced fetus is closer to being a person than is the zygote, just as a dog is closer to personhood than a jellyfish, but that is not the same thing as being "more of a person." In 1930, when he was six years old, Jimmy Carter didn't know it, but he was a potential president of the United States. That gave him no claim *then*, not even a very weak claim, to give commands to the U.S. Army and Navy. Franklin D. Roosevelt in 1930 was only two years away from the presidency, so he was a potential president in a much stronger way (the potentiality was much less remote) than was young Jimmy. Nevertheless, he was not actually president, and he had no more of a claim to the prerogatives of the office than did Carter. The analogy to fetuses in different stages of development is of course imperfect. But in both cases it would seem to be invalid to infer the existence of a "weak version of a right" from an "almost qualification" for the full right. In summary, the modified potentiality criterion, insofar as it permits the potential possession of *C* to be a *sufficient condition* for the actual possession of claims, and in some cases of rights, is seriously flawed in the same manner as the strict potentiality criterion.

*E. The Actual-Possession Criterion*   "At any given time *(t)*, all and only those creatures who actually possess *C* are moral persons at *t*, whatever species or category they may happen to belong to." This simple and straightforward criterion has a number of conspicuous advantages. We should consider it with respect even before we examine its difficulties if only because the difficulties of its major rivals are so severe. Moreover, it has a certain tidy symmetry about it, since it makes the overlap between commonsense personhood and moral personhood complete—a total correspondence with no loose ends left over in either direction. There can be no actual commonsense persons who are not actual moral persons, nor can there be any actual moral persons who are not actual commonsense persons. Moral personhood is not established simply by species membership, associations, or potentialities. Instead, it is conferred by the same characteristics *(C)* that lead us to recognize personhood wherever we find it. It is no accident, no mere coincidence, that we use the moral term 'person' for those beings, and only those beings, who have *C*. The characteristics that confer commonsense personhood are not arbitrary bases for rights and duties, such as race, sex, or species membership; rather they are the traits that make sense out of rights and duties and without which those moral attributes would have no point or function. It is because people are conscious; have a sense of their personal identities; have plans, goals, and projects; experience emotions; are liable to pains, anxieties, and frustrations; can reason and bargain, and so on— it is because of these attributes that people have values and interests, desires and expectations of their own, including a stake in their own futures, and a personal well-being of a sort we cannot ascribe to unconscious or nonrational beings. Because of their developed capacities they can assume duties and responsibilities and can have and make claims on one another. Only because of their sense of self, their life plans, their value hierarchies, and their stakes in their own futures can they be ascribed fundamental rights. There is nothing arbitrary about these linkages. For these reasons I am inclined to believe that the actual-possession criterion is the correct one.

Despite these impressive advantages, however, the actual-possession criterion must face a serious difficulty, namely that it implies that small infants (neonates) are not moral persons. There is very little more reason, after all, to attribute *C* to neonates than to advanced fetuses still *in utero.* Perhaps during the first few days after birth the infant is conscious and able to feel pain, but it is unlikely that it has a concept of itself or of its future life, that it has plans and goals, that it can think consecutively, and the like. In fact, the whole complex of traits that make up *C* is not *obviously* present until the second year of childhood. And that would seem to imply, according to the criterion we are considering, that the deliberate destruction of babies in their first year is no violation of their rights. And *that* might seem to entail that there is nothing wrong with infanticide (the deliberate killing of infants). But infanticide *is* wrong. Therefore, critics of the actual-possession criterion have argued that we ought to reject this criterion.

*The Killing of Normal Infants*   Advocates of the actual-possession criterion have a reply to this objection. Even if infanticide is not the murder of a moral person, they believe, it may yet be wrong and properly forbidden on other grounds. To make this clearer, it is useful to distinguish between (1) the case of killing a normal healthy infant or an infant whose handicaps are not so serious as to make a worthwhile future life impossible and (2) the case of killing severely deformed or incurably diseased infants.

Most advocates of the actual-possession criterion take a strong stand against infanticide in the first (the normal) case. It would be seriously wrong for a mother to kill her physically normal infant, they contend, even though such a killing would not violate anyone's right to life. The same reasons that make infanticide in the normal case wrong also justify its prohibition by the criminal law. The moral rule that condemns these killings and the legal rule that renders them punishable are both supported by "utilitarian reasons," that is, considerations of what is called "social utility," "the common good," "the public interest," and the like. Nature has apparently implanted in us an instinctive tenderness toward infants that has proven extremely useful to the species, not only because it leads us to protect our young from death, and thus keep our population up, but also because infants usually grow into adults, and in Benn's words, "if as infants *they* are not treated with some minimal degree of tenderness and consideration, they will suffer for it later, as persons."[6] One might add that when they are adults, others will suffer for it too, at their hands. Spontaneous warmth and sympathy toward babies then clearly has a great deal of social utility, and insofar as infanticide would tend to weaken that socially valuable response, it is, on utilitarian grounds, morally wrong.

There are other examples of wrongful and properly prohibitable acts that violate no one's rights. It would be wrong, for example, to hack up Grandfather's body after he has died a natural death, and dispose of his remains in the trash can on a cold winter's morning. That would be wrong not because it violates *Grandfather's* rights; he is dead and no longer has the same sort of rights as the rest of us, and we can make it part of the example that he was not offended while alive at the thought of such posthumous treatment and indeed even consented to it in advance. Somehow acts of this kind if not forbidden would strike at our respect for living human persons (without which organized society would be impossible) in the most keenly threatening way. (It might also be unhygienic and shocking to trash collectors—less important but equally relevant utilitarian considerations.)

*The Killing of Radically Deformed Infants*  The general utilitarian reasons that support a rather rigid rule against infanticide in the case of the normal (and not too abnormal) infant might not be sufficiently strong to rule out infanticide (under very special and strict circumstances) when the infant is extremely deformed or diseased. Very likely, a purely utilitarian-based rule against homicide would have exceptive clauses for extremely abnormal neonates. In this respect such rules would differ sharply from rules against infanticide that derive from the ascription to the newborn infant of a full-fledged right to life. If the deformed neonate is a moral person, then he or she is as fully entitled to protection under the rule forbidding homicide as any reader of these words; if the neonate is not a moral person, then in extreme cases there may be a case on balance for killing him. The Partisan of the actual-possession criterion of moral personhood actually takes this consequence of nonpersonhood to be an advantage of his view rather than an embarrassment for it. If his view is correct, then we can destroy hopelessly malformed infants *before* they grow into moral persons, thus saving them from a longer life that would be so horrible as to be "not worth living," and this can be done without violating their rights.

Indeed, *failure* to kill such infants before they reach moral personhood may itself be a violation of their rights, according to this view. For if we permit such children to grow into moral personhood knowing full well that the conditions for the fulfillment of their most basic future interests have already been destroyed, then we have wronged these persons before they even exist (as persons), and when they become persons, they can claim (or it can be claimed in their behalf) that they have been wronged. I have argued elsewhere that an extension of the idea of a birthright is suggested by this point. If we know that it will never be possible for a fetus or neonate to have that to which he has a birthright and we allow him nevertheless to be born or to survive into personhood, then that fetus or neonate is wronged, and we become a party to the violation of his rights.[7]

Not just any physical or mental handicaps, of course, can render a life "not worth living." Indeed, as the testimony of some thalidomide babies[8] now growing into adulthood shows, it is possible (given exceptional care) to live a valuable life even without arms and legs and full vision. But there may be some extreme cases where deformities are not merely "handicaps" in the pursuit of happiness but guarantees that the pursuit must fail. A brain-damaged, retarded child born deaf, blind, partially paralyzed, and doomed to constant pain might be such a case. Given the powerful general utilitarian case against infanticide, however, the defender of the "right to die" position must admit that in cases of doubt, the burden of showing that a worthwhile life is impossible rests on the person who would elect a quick and painless death for the infant. And there is almost always some doubt.

*Implications for the Problem of Abortion* The implications of the actual-possession criterion for the question of the status of the fetus as a moral person are straightforward. Since the fetus does not actually possess those characteristics *(C)* that we earlier listed as necessary and sufficient for possessing the right to life, the fetus does not possess that right. Given this criterion, therefore, abortion never involves violating a fetus's right to life, and permitting a fetus to be born is never anything *we owe* it, is never something that is *its due*.

It does not follow, however, that abortion is never wrong. As we saw earlier, despite the fact that infants fail to meet the actual-possession criterion and thus are not moral persons, reasons can be given, of a utilitarian kind, why it is wrong to kill them, at least if they are not radically deformed. It is possible, therefore, that similar reasons can be given in opposition to aborting fetuses at later stages in their development if they are likely not to be radically deformed when born.

Utilitarian reasons of the sort we have considered are so very important that they might suffice to rule out harsh or destructive treatment of *any* nonperson whose resemblance or similarity to real persons is very close: not only deceased ex-persons and small babies, but even adult primates and human fetuses in the final trimester of pregnancy. Mr. Justice Blackmun may have had such considerations in mind when in his majority opinion in *Roe* v. *Wade* he declared that even though no fetuses are legal persons protected by the law of homicide, nevertheless during the final trimester, "The State in promoting its interest in the potentiality of human life, may if it chooses, regulate, and even proscribe, abortion. . . ."[9] Whatever interest the State has in "the *potentiality* of human life" must be derivative from the plain interest it has in preserving and promoting respect for *actual* human life. It is not only potential persons who merit our derivative respect but all *near-persons* including higher animals, dead people, infants, and well-developed fetuses, those beings whose similarity to real persons is close enough to render them sacred symbols of the real thing.

In the light of these considerations, it seems that a gradualist approach similar to that discussed earlier is a more plausible solution to the general problem of the moral justifiability of abortion than it is to the narrow problem of the criterion of moral personhood. Even if the fetus as a merely potential person lacks an actual right to life, and even if it would not be homicide therefore to kill it, its potential personhood may yet constitute a *reason* against killing it that requires an even stronger reason on the other side if abortion is to be justified. If that is so, it is not implausible to suppose that the more advanced the potential for personhood, the more stringent the case against killing. As we have seen, there are reasons relevant to our moral decisions other than considerations of rights, so that sometimes actions can be judged morally wrong even though they violate no one's rights. Killing a fetus, in that case, could be wrong in certain circumstances, even though it violated no rights of the fetus, even though the fetus was not a moral person, even though the act was in no sense a murder.

## §5 SUMMARY AND CONCLUSION

Killing human beings (homicide) is forbidden both by our criminal law and by the moral rules that are accepted in all civilized communities. If the fetus at any point in its development is a human being, then to kill it at that point is homicide, and if done without excuse or mitigation, murder. But the term 'human being' is subtly ambiguous. The fetus at all stages is obviously human in the genetic sense, but that is not the sense of the term intended in the moral rule against homicide. For a genetically human entity to have a right to life it must be a human being in the sense of a person. But the term 'person' is also ambiguous. In the commonsense descriptive meaning of the term, it refers to any being of any species or category who has certain familiar characteristics, of which consciousness of the world, self-concepts, and the capacity to plan ahead are prominent. In the purely normative (moral or legal) sense, a person is any being who has certain rights and/or duties, whatever his other characteristics. Whether or not abortion is homicide depends on what the correct criterion of moral personhood is.

We considered five leading formulations of the criterion of moral personhood and found that they are all subject to various embarrassments. One formulation in terms of species membership seemed both too broad and too narrow, and in the end dependent on an arbitrary preference for our own species. A more careful formulation escaped the charge of being too restrictive and the charge of arbitrariness but suffered from making the status of an individual derived from his membership in a group rather than from his own intrinsic characteristics. The two formulations in terms of potential possession of the characteristics definitive of commonsense personhood both stumbled on "the logical point about potentiality," that potential qualification for a right does not entail actual possession of that right. The modified or gradualist formulation of the potentiality criterion, however, does have some attractive features, and could be reformulated as a more plausible answer to another question, that about the moral permissibility of abortion. Even if the fetus is not a person and lacks a right to life, ever stronger reasons might be required to justify aborting it as it grows older and more similar to a person.

The weaknesses of the first four proposed criteria of moral person-hood create a strong presumption in favor of the remaining one, the "actual-possession" criterion. It is clear that fetuses are not "people" in the ordinary commonsense meaning of that term, hence, according to our final criterion, they are not moral persons either, since this criterion of moral personhood simply adopts the criteria of common-sense personhood. The very grave difficulty of this criterion is that it entails that infants are not people either, during the first few months or more of their lives. That is a genuine difficulty for the theory, but a far greater embarrassment can be avoided. Because there are pow-erful reasons against infanticide that apply even if the infant is not a moral person, the actual-possession criterion is not subject to the dev-astating objection that it would morally or legally justify infanticide on demand.

## II. THE PROBLEM OF THE CONFLICT OF CLAIMS

The problem of the status of the fetus is the first and perhaps the most difficult of the questions that must be settled before we can come to a considered view about the moral justifiability of abortion, but its solution does not necessarily resolve all moral perplexities about abor-tion. Even if we were to grant that the fetus is a moral person and thus has a valid claim to life, it would not follow that abortion is always wrong. For there are other moral persons, in addition to the fetus, whose interests are involved. The woman in whose uterus the fetus abides, in particular, has needs and interests that may well conflict with bringing the fetus to term. Do any of these needs and interests of the woman provide grounds for her having a genuine claim to an abortion and, if they do, which of the two conflicting claims—the woman's claim to an abortion or the fetus's claim to life—ought to be respected if they happen to conflict? This is the second major moral question that needs to be examined with all the care we can muster. To do this, one very important assumption must be made—namely, that the fetus is a moral person and so has a valid claim to life. As we have seen in the previous section, this assumption might very well be unfounded and is unfounded in fact if we accept what appears to be the most reasonable criterion for moral personhood—namely, the ac-tual-possession criterion. For purposes of the present section, how-ever, we shall assume that the fetus is a moral person; this will enable us to investigate whose claim, the fetus's or the woman's, ought to be honored if both have genuine but conflicting claims.

### §6 FORMULATION OF THE "RIGHT TO AN ABORTION"

The right to an abortion that is often claimed on behalf of all women is a *discretionary right* to be exercised or not, on a given occasion, as the woman sees fit. For that reason it is sometimes called a "right to choose." If a pregnant woman has such a right, then it is up to her, and her alone, whether to bear the child or to have it aborted. She is at liberty to bear it if she choses and at liberty to have it aborted if she chooses. She has no duty to bear it, but neither can she have a duty, imposed from without, to abort it. In respect to the fetus, her choice is sovereign. Correlated with this liberty is a duty of others not to interfere with its exercise and not to withhold the necessary means for its exercise. These duties are owed to her if she has a discretionary right to abortion, and she can claim their discharge as her due.

As a discretionary right, a right to an abortion would resemble the "right to liberty," or the right to move about or travel as one wishes. One is under no obligation to leave or stay home or to go to one destination rather than another, so that it is one's own choice that determines one's movements. But the right to move about at will, like other discretionary rights, is subject to limits. One person's liberty of movement, for example, comes to an end at the boundary of another person's property. The discretionary right to an abortion may be limited in similar ways, so that the statement of a specific right of a particular woman in a definite set of concrete circumstances may need to be qualified by various exceptive clauses—for example, ". . . may choose to have an abortion *except* when the fetus is viable." Which exceptive clauses, if any, must be appended to the formulation of the right to an abortion depends on what the basis of this discretionary right is thought to be. For example, if a woman is thought to have a right to an abortion because she has a right to property *and* because the fetus is said to be her property, then the only exceptions there could be to exercising the right to an abortion would be those that restrict the disposing of one's property. What we must realize, then, is that the alleged right to an abortion cannot be understood in a vacuum; it is a right that can only be understood by reference to the other, more fundamental rights from which it has often been claimed to be derived. Three of these rights and their possible association with the right to an abortion deserve our closest scrutiny. These are (1) the previously mentioned property rights, (2) the right to self-defense, and (3) the right to bodily autonomy. We shall consider each in its turn.

## §7 POSSIBLE GROUNDS FOR THE WOMAN'S RIGHT

*Property Rights over One's Body* Within very wide limits any person has a right to control the uses of his or her own body. With only rare exceptions, surgeons are required to secure the consent of the patient before operating because the body to be cut open, after all, is the patient's own, and he or she has the chief interest in it, and should therefore have the chief "say" over what is done to it. If we think of a fetus as literally a "part" of a woman's body in the same sense as, say, an organ, or as a mere growth attached to a part of the body on the model of a tumor or a wart, then it would seem to follow that the woman may choose to have it removed if she wishes just as she may refuse to have it removed if she prefers. It is highly implausible, however, to think of a human fetus, even if it does fall short of moral personhood, as no more than a temporary organ or a parasitic growth. A fetus is not a constituent organ of the mother, like her vermiform appendix, but rather an independent entity temporarily growing inside the mother.

It would be still less plausible to derive a maternal right to an abortion from a characterization of the fetus as the *property* of its mother and thus in the same category as the mother's wristwatch, clothing, or jewelry. One may abandon or destroy one's personal property if one wishes; one's entitlement to do those things is one of the "property rights" that define ownership. But one would think that the father would have equal or near-equal rights of disposal if the fetus were "property." It is not in his body, to be sure, but he contributed as much genetically to its existence as did the mother and might therefore make just as strong (or just as weak) a claim to ownership over it. But neither claim would make very good conceptual sense. If fetuses were property, we would find nothing odd in the notion that they can be bought and sold, rented out, leased, used as collateral on loans, and so on. But no one has ever seriously entertained such suggestions. Finally, we must remember the methodological assumption that we shall make throughout this section, at least for the sake of the argument, that the fetus is a full moral person, with a right to life like yours and mine. On this assumption it would probably be contradictory to think of the fetus as *anyone's* property, especially if property rights include what we might call "the right of disposal"— to abandon or destroy as one chooses.

It is more plausible at first sight to claim that the pregnant woman owns not the fetus but the body in which she shelters the fetus. On this analogy, she owns her body (and particularly her womb) in roughly the way an innkeeper owns a hotel or a homeowner her house and garden. These analogies, however, are also defective. To begin with, it is somewhat paradoxical to think of the relation between a person and her body as similar to that of ownership. Is it possible to sell or rent or lease one's body without selling, renting, or leasing oneself? If one's body were one's property the answer would be affirmative, but in fact one's relationship to one's own body is much more intimate than the ownership model suggests. More important for our present purposes, the legal analogies to the rights of innkeepers and householders will not bear scrutiny. One cannot conceive of what it would be like for a fetus to enter into a contract with a woman for the use of her womb for nine months or to fall in arrears in its payments and thus forfeit its right of occupancy. Surely that cannot be the most apt analogy on which to base the woman's abortion rights! Besides, whatever this, that, or the other legal statute may say about the matter, one is not *morally* entitled, in virtue of one's property rights, to expel a weak and helpless person from one's shelter when that is tantamount to consigning the person to a certain death, and surely one is not entitled to shoot and kill a trespasser who will not, or cannot, leave one's property. In no department of human life does the vindication of property rights justify homicide. The maternal right to an abortion, therefore, cannot be founded on the more basic right to property.

*Self-Defense and Proportionality*   Except for the most extreme pacifists, moralists agree that killing can be justified if done in self-defense. If, for example, one man (A) is attacked with a lethal weapon by another (B), we think that A has a right to defend himself against B's attack. Sometimes, in fact, we think that A would be justified in killing B if this were the only way for A to defend himself. Now, some of those who urge the maternal right to an abortion believe that this right is associated with the more basic right to self-defense. There are many difficulties standing in the way to rational acceptance of this view. In particular, the innocence and the nonaggressive nature of the fetus need our special attention. We shall turn to these matters shortly. First, though, it is important to realize what reasons would not count as morally good reasons for an abortion if the right to an abortion were supposed to be founded on the more basic right of self-defense.

All parties to the abortion dispute must agree that many women can be harmed if they are required to bring an unwanted fetus to term. Unwanted sexual intercourse imposed on a woman by a rapist can inflict on its victim severe psychological trauma of a sort deemed so serious by the law that a woman is entitled under some rules to use deadly force if necessary to prevent it. Similarly, an unwanted pregnancy in some circumstances can inflict equally severe psychological injury on a woman who is forced to carry her child to birth. There are various familiar examples of such harm. To borrow an example from Judith Thomson, a philosophy professor at the Massachusetts Institute of Technology: A terrified fourteen-year-old high schoolgirl whose pregnancy has been caused by rape has already suffered one severe trauma. If she is now required, over her protests, to carry the child to full term despite her fear, anguish, deep depression, and fancied public mortification, the harmful ramifications may be multiplied a hundredfold. The forty-year-old housewife who has exhausted herself raising a large family in unfavorable economic circumstances while dependent upon an unreliable and unsympathetic husband may find herself, to her horror, pregnant again and rightly feel that if she is forced to give birth to another child, she will forfeit her last opportunity to escape the intolerably squalid conditions of her life. A man must be morally blind not to acknowledge the severe harms that enforced continuance of unwanted pregnancies can inflict on women. An unwanted child need not literally cost the woman her life, but it can effectively ruin her life from her point of view, and it is a useful moral exercise for men to put themselves imaginatively in the woman's place to share that point of view.

At this stage in the argument the antiabortionist has a ready rejoinder. A woman need not keep her child, assume the responsibilities of raising it to adulthood, and forfeit her opportunities for self-fulfillment, he might reply, simply because she forgoes an abortion. She can always put the child up for adoption and be assured in the process that it will find loving foster parents who will give it a good upbringing. All she really has to suffer, the rejoinder concludes, is nine months of minor physical inconvenience. This is an argument that comes easily to the lips of men, but it betrays the grossest sort of masculine insensitivity. In the first place, it is not always true that a woman can have her baby adopted. If she is married, that transaction may require the consent of her husband, and the consent might not be forthcoming. But waiving that point, the possibility of adoption does not give much comfort to the unhappily pregnant woman, for it imposes on her a cruel dilemma and an anguish that far surpasses "minor inconvenience." In effect, she has two choices, both of which are intolerable to her. She can carry the child to term and keep it, thus incurring the very consequences that make her unwilling to remain pregnant, *or* she can nourish the fetus to full size, go into labor, give birth to her baby, and then have it rudely wrenched away, never to be seen by her again. Let moralistic males imagine what an emotional jolt that must be!

Still, on the scale of harms, mere traumas and frustrations are not exactly equal to death. Few women would choose their own deaths in preference to the harms that may come from producing children. According to a common interpretation of the self-defense rule, however, the harm to be averted by a violent act in self-defense need not be identical in severity to that which is inflicted upon one's assailant but only somehow "proportional" to it. Both our prevailing morality and our legal traditions permit the use of lethal force to prevent harms that are less serious than death, so it is plausible to assume that the rule of "proportionality" can be satisfied by something less than equality of harms. But how much less? The late Jane English, a philosopher from the University of North Carolina, offers an answer that, though vague, is in accordance with the moral sentiments of most people when they think of situations other than that involving abortion:

> How severe an injury may you inflict in self-defense? In part this depends upon the severity of the injury to be avoided: you may not shoot someone merely to avoid having your clothes torn. This might lead one to the mistaken conclusion that the defense may only equal the threatened injury in severity; that to avoid death you may kill, but to avoid a black eye you may only inflict a black eye or the equivalent. Rather our laws and customs seem to say that you may create an injury *somewhat but not enormously greater* than the injury to be avoided. To fend off an attack whose outcome would be as serious as

rape, a severe beating, or the loss of a finger, you may shoot; to avoid having your clothes torn, you may blacken an eye.[10] [Emphasis added.]

Applying English's answer to the abortion case, and assuming that both the fetus and the woman have legitimate claims, we derive the conclusion that killing the "fetal person" would not be justified when it is done merely to prevent relatively trivial harms to the mother's interests. Not *all* cases of abortion, therefore, can morally be justified, even if there is a maternal right to abortion derived from the more basic right to self-defense.

*Self-Defense: The Problem of the Innocent Aggressor*   Suppose, however, that the harms that will probably be caused to the mother if the fetus is brought to term are not trivial but serious. Here we have a case where the mother's right to have her important interests respected clashes with the assumed right to life of the fetus. In these circumstances, don't the mother's claims outweigh the fetus's? Doesn't self-defense in these circumstances justify abortion?

There is a serious, previously undiscussed difficulty that calls out for attention. Consider a case where someone aggressively attacks another. The reason we think that, to use English's expression, we may in self-defense create a "somewhat but not enormously greater injury" than would have been caused by the aggressor is because we think of the aggressor as the party who is morally at fault. If he had not launched the aggression in the first place, there should have been no occasion for the use of force. Since the whole episode was the aggressor's fault, his interests should not count for as much as those of the innocent victim. It is a shame that anybody has to be seriously hurt, but if it comes down to an inescapable choice between the innocent party suffering a serious harm or the culpable party suffering a still more serious harm, then the latter is the lesser of the two evils. Aggressors of course, for all their guilt, remain human beings, and consequently they do not forfeit all their human rights in launching an attack. We still may not kill them to prevent them from stealing $10. But their culpability does cost them their right to equal consideration; we may kill them to prevent them from causing serious harm.

But now suppose that the party who threatens us, even though he is the aggressor who initiates the whole episode, is not morally at fault. Suppose the person cannot act otherwise in the circumstances and thus cannot justly be held morally responsible. For example, he was temporarily (or permanently) insane, or it was a case of mistaken identity (he mistook you for a former Gestapo agent to whom you bear a striking resemblance), or someone had drugged the person's breakfast cereal and his behavior was influenced by the drug. George Fletcher, a Columbia law professor, provides a vivid illustration of the problem in what he calls "the case of the psychotic aggressor":

> Imagine that your companion in an elevator goes berserk and attacks you with a knife. There is no escape: the only way to avoid serious bodily harm or even death is to kill him. The assailant acts purposively in the sense that his means further his aggressive end . . . [but] he does act in a frenzy or a fit . . . [and] it is clear that his conduct is non-responsible. If he were brought to trial for his attack, he would have a valid defense of insanity.[11]

The general problem, as lawyers would put it, is "whether self-defense applies against an excused but unjustified aggression."[12] To *justify* an act is to show that it was the right thing to do in the circumstances; to *excuse* an act is to show that although it was unjustified, the actor didn't mean it or couldn't help it, that it was not, properly speaking, his doing at all. In the "excused but unjustified aggression" we have a more plausible model for the application of self-defense to the problem of abortion, for *the fetus is surely innocent* (not because of insanity but because of immaturity, and because *it* did not choose to threaten its mother—it did not "ask to be born").

Upon reflection, most of us would agree, I think, that one would be justified in killing even an innocent aggressor if that seemed necessary to save one's own life or to prevent one from suffering serious bodily injury. Surely we would not judge harshly the slightly built lady who shoots the armed stranger who goes berserk in the elevator. If we were in her shoes, we too would protect ourselves at all costs to the assailant, just as we would against wild animals, runaway trucks, or impersonal forces of nature. But while the berserk assailant, as well as those persons mentioned in the last paragraph, all are innocent—are not *morally* responsible for what they do—they all *are* assailants, and in this respect they differ in a quite fundamental respect from the fetus. For the fetus is not only innocent but also not an aggressor. *It* didn't start the trouble in any fashion. Thus, it would seem that while we are justified in killing an innocent assailant if this is the only way to prevent him from killing us, it does not follow that we are similarly justified in killing a fetal person, since, unlike the innocent aggressor, the fetus is not an aggressor at all.

Judith Thomson has challenged this argument. She presents the following farfetched but coherent hypothetical example:

> Aggressor is driving his tank at you. But he has taken care to arrange that a baby is strapped to the front of the tank so that if you use your anti-tank gun, you will not only kill Aggressor, you will kill the baby. Now Aggressor, admittedly, is in the process of trying to kill you; but that baby isn't. Yet you can presumably go ahead and use the gun, even though this involves killing the baby as well as Aggressor.[13]

The baby in this example is not only "innocent" but also the "innocent shield of a threat."[14] Still it is hard to quarrel with Thomson's judgment that you *may* (not that you *should*) take the baby's life if necessary to save your own, that it is morally permissible, even if it is not morally obligatory, to do so. After all, you are (by hypothesis) perfectly innocent too. This example makes a better analogy to the abortion situation than any we have considered thus far, but there are still significant dissimilarities. Unless the fetus is the product of rape, it cannot conceivably be the shield of some third-party aggressor. There is simply no interpersonal "aggression" involved at all in the normal pregnancy. There may nevertheless be a genuine *threat* to the well-being of the mother, and if that threat is to her very life, then perhaps she does have a right to kill it, if necessary, in self-defense. At any rate, if the threatened victim in Thomson's tank example is justified in killing the innocent shield, then the pregnant woman threatened with similar harm is similarly entitled. But all that this would establish is that abortion is justified only if it is probably required to save the mother's life. So not only could we not use the self-defense argument to justify abortion for trivial reasons, as was argued earlier; it appears that the only reason that authorizes its use is the one that cites the fact that the mother will probably die if the fetus is not aborted.

*Bodily Autonomy: The Example of the Plugged-in Violinist* The trouble with the use of self-defense as a model for abortion rights is that none of the examples of self-defense makes an *exact* analogy to the abortion situation. The examples that come closest to providing models for justified abortion are the "innocent aggressor cases" and these would apply, as we have seen, only to abortions that are necessary to prevent death to the mother. Even these examples do not fit the abortion case exactly, since the fetus is in no way itself an aggressor, culpable or innocent, but is at most a "nonaggressive, nonculpable threat," in some respects like an innocent shield.[15] And the more we change the examples to bring them closer to the situation of the fetus, the less clear is their resemblance to the central models of self-defense. Once we are allowed to protect ourselves (and especially to protect interests less weighty than self-preservation) at the expense of nonaggressive innocents, it becomes difficult to distinguish the latter from innocent bystanders whom we kill as means to our own good, and that, in turn, begins to look like unvarnished murder. The killing of an innocent person simply because his continued existence in the circumstances would make the killer's life miserable is a homicide that cannot be justified. It is not self-defense to kill your boss because he makes your work life intolerable and you are unable to find another job, or to kill your spouse because he or she nags you to the point of extreme misery and will not agree to a divorce,[16] or (closer to the point) to kill your shipwrecked fellow passenger in the lifeboat because there are provisions sufficient for only one to survive and he claims half of them, or to kill your innocent rival for a position or a prize because you can win only if he is out of the running. In all these cases the victim is either innocent or relatively innocent and in no way a direct aggressor.

Partly because of deficiencies in the hypothetical examples of self-defense, Thomson invented a different sort of example intended at once to be a much closer analogy to the abortion situation and also such that the killing can be seen to be morally justified for reasons less compelling than defense of the killer's very life:

> You wake up in the morning and find yourself back to back in bed with an unconscious violinist. A famous unconscious violinist. He has been found to have a fatal kidney ailment, and the Society of Music Lovers has canvassed all the available medical records and found that you alone have the right blood type to help. They have therefore kidnapped you, and last night the violinist's circulatory system was plugged into yours, so that your kidneys can be used to extract poisons from his blood as well as your own. The director of the hospital now tells you, "Look, we're sorry the Society of Music Lovers did this to you—we would never have permitted it if we had known. But still they did it, and the violinist now is plugged into you. To unplug you would be to kill him. But never mind, it's only for nine months. By then he will have recovered from his ailment, and can safely be unplugged from you." Is it morally incumbent on you to accede to this situation? No doubt it would be very nice of you if you did, a great kindness. But do you have to accede to it? . . . What if the director . . . says . . . "Granted you have a right to decide what happens in and to your body, but a person's right to life outweighs your right to decide what happens in and to your body. So you cannot . . . be unplugged from him." I imagine you would regard this as outrageous . . . .[17]

Suppose that you defy the director on your own, and exercise your control over your own body by unplugging the unconscious violinist, thereby causing his death. This would be to kill in defense of an interest far less important than self-preservation or the prevention of serious injury to oneself. And it would be to kill an innocent nonaggressor, indeed a victim who remains unconscious throughout the entire period during which he is a threat. We have, therefore, an example which—if it works—offers far more encouragement to the proabortion position than the model of self-defense does. We must now pose two questions: (1) Would you in fact be morally justified in unplugging the violinist? and (2) How close an analogy does this bizarre example make to the abortion situation?

There is no way to argue conclusively that unplugging the violinist would be morally justified. Thomson can only make the picture as vividly persuasive as possible and then appeal to her reader's intuitions. It is not an easy case, and neither an affirmative nor a negative judgment will seem self-evident to everyone. Still the verdict for justification seems as strong as in some of the other examples of killing innocent threats, and some additional considerations can be brought to bear in its support. There is, after all, a clear "intuition" in support of a basic right "to decide what happens in and to one's own body," even though the limits of that right are lost in a fog of controversy. So unless there is some stronger competing claim, anyone has a right to refuse to consent to surgery or to enforced attachment to a machine. Or indeed to an unconscious violinist. But what of the competing claim in this example, the violinist's right to life? That is another basic right that is vague around the edges.

In its noncontroversial core, the right to life is a right not to be killed directly (except under very special circumstances) and to be rescued from impending death whenever this can be done without unreasonable sacrifice. But as Warren has pointed out, one person's right to life does not impose a correlative duty on another person to do "whatever is necessary to keep him alive."[18] And though we all have general duties to come to the assistance of strangers in peril, we cannot be forced to make enormous sacrifices or to run unreasonably high risks to keep people alive when we stand in no special relationship to them, like "father" or "lifeguard." The wife of the violinist perhaps would have a duty to stay plugged to him (if that would help) for nine months; but the random stranger has no such duty at all. So there is good reason to grant Thomson her claim that a stranger would have a right to unplug the violinist from herself.

But how close an analogy after all is this to the normal case of pregnancy? Several differences come immediately to mind. In the normal case of pregnancy, the woman is not confined to her bed for nine months but can continue to work and function efficiently in the world until the final trimester at least. This difference, however, is of doubtful significance, since Thomson's argument is not based on a right to the protection of one's interest in efficient mobility but rather on a right to *decide* on the uses of one's own body, which is quite another thing. Another difference is that the mother and her fetus are not exactly "random strangers" in the same sense that the woman and the violinist are. Again the relationship between mother and fetus seems to be in a class by itself. If the person who needs to use the woman's body for nine months in order to survive is her mother, father, sister, brother, son, daughter, or close friend, then the relationship would seem close enough to establish a special obligation in the woman to permit that use. If the needy person is a total stranger, then that obligation is missing. The fetus no doubt stands somewhere between these two extremes, but it is at least as close to the "special relationship" end of the spectrum as to the "total stranger" end.

The most important difference, however, between the violinist case and the normal pregnancy is that in the former the woman had absolutely nothing to do with creating the situation from which she wishes to escape. She bears no responsibility whatever for being in a state of "plugged-in-ness" with the violinist. As many commentators have pointed out, this makes Thomson's analogy fit at most one very special class of pregnancies, namely those imposed upon a woman entirely against her will, as in rape. In the "normal case" of pregnancy, the voluntary action of the woman herself (knowingly consenting to sexual intercourse) has something to do with her becoming pregnant. So once again, we find that a proabortion argument fails to establish an *unrestricted* moral right to abortion. Just as self-defense justifies abortion at most in the case where it is necessary to save the mother's life, the Thomson defense justifies abortion only when the woman shares no responsibility for her pregnancy, as, for example, when it has been caused by rape (force or fraud).

*Voluntariness and Responsibility*   If we continue the line of reasoning suggested by our criticism of the violinist example, we will soon reach a general principle, namely, that whether or not a woman has a duty to continue her pregnancy depends, at least in part, on how responsible she is for being pregnant in the first place, that is, on the extent to which her pregnancy is the consequence of her own voluntary actions. This formula, in turn, seems to be an application of a still more general moral principle, one that imposes duties on one party to rescue or support another, even a stranger and even when that requires great personal sacrifice or risk, to the degree that the first party, through his own voluntary actions or omissions, was responsible for the second party's dependence on him. A late-arriving bystander at the seaside has no duty to risk life or limb to save a drowning swimmer. If, however, the swimmer is in danger only because the bystander erroneously informed him that there was no danger, then the bystander has a duty to make some effort at rescue (though not a suicidal one), dangerous as it may be. If the swimmer is in the water only because the "bystander" has pushed him out of a boat, however, then the bystander has a duty to attempt rescue at any cost to personal safety,[19] since the bystander's own voluntary action was the whole cause of the swimmer's plight.

Since the voluntariness of an action or omission is a matter of degree, so is the responsibility that stems from it, as is the stringency of the duty that derives from that responsibility. The duty to continue a pregnancy, then, will be stronger (other things being equal) in the case where the pregnancy was entered into in a fully voluntary way than it will be in the case that fits the violinist model, where the pregnancy is totally involuntary. But in between these two extremes is a whole range of cases where moral judgments are more difficult to make. We can sketch the whole spectrum as follows:

1. Pregnancy caused by rape (totally involuntary).
2. Pregnancy caused by contraceptive failure, where the fault is entirely that of the manufacturer or pharmaceutical company.
3. Pregnancy caused by contraceptive failure within the advertised 1 percent margin of error (no one's fault).
4. Pregnancy caused by the negligence of the woman (or the

man, or both). They are careless in the use of the contraceptive or else fail to use it at all, being unaware of a large risk that they *ought* to have been aware of.

5. Pregnancy caused by the recklessness of the woman (or the man, or both). They think of the risk but get swept along by passion and consciously disregard it.

6. Pregnancy caused by intercourse between partners who are genuinely indifferent at the time whether or not pregnancy results.

7. Pregnancy caused by the deliberate decision of the parties to produce it (completely voluntary).

There would be a somewhat hollow ring to the claim in case 7 that one has no obligation to continue one's bodily support for a moral person whose dependence on that support one has deliberately caused. That would be like denying that one has a duty to save the drowning swimmer that one has just pushed out of the boat. The case for cessation of bodily support is hardly any stronger in 6 and 5 than in 7. Perhaps it is misleading to say of the negligence case (4) that the pregnancy is only partially involuntary, or involuntary "to a degree," since the parents did not *intentionally* produce or run the risk of producing a fetus. But there is no need to haggle over that terminological question. Whether wholly or partially involuntary, the actions of the parents in the circumstances were faulty and the pregnancy resulted from the fault (negligence), so they are to a substantial degree responsible (to blame) for it. It was within their power to be more careful or knowledgeable, and yet they were careless or avoidably ignorant. So they cannot plead, in the manner of the lady plugged to the violinist, that they had no control over their condition whatever. In failing to exercise due care, they were doing something else and doing *it* "to a degree voluntarily." In these cases—4, 5, 6, and 7—the woman and her partner are therefore responsible for the pregnancy, and on the analogy with the case of the drowning swimmer who was pushed from the boat, they have a duty not to kill the fetus or permit it to die.

Cases 2 and 3 are more perplexing. In case 2, where the fault was entirely that of the manufacturer, the woman is no more responsible for being pregnant than in case 1 where she is the unwilling victim of a rape. In neither case did she choose to become pregnant. In neither case was she reckless or negligent in respect to the possibility of becoming pregnant. So if she has no duty to continue to provide bodily support for the dependent fetus in the rape case, then equally she has no duty in the other case. To be sure, there is always *some* risk of pregnancy whenever there is intercourse, no matter how careful the partners are. There may be only 1 chance in 10,000 that a contraceptive pill has an undetectable flaw, but there is no chance whatever of pregnancy without intercourse. The woman in case 2, then, would seem to have *some* responsibility, even if vanishingly small, for her pregnancy. She could have been even more careful by abstaining from sex altogether. But notice that much the same sort of thing could be said of the rape victim. By staying home in a locked building patrolled round the clock by armed guards, she could have reduced the chances of bodily assault from, say, 1 in 50,000 to effectively nil. By staying off the dangerous streets, she would have been much more careful than she was in respect to the risk of rape. But surely that does not entitle us to say that she was "partially responsible" for the rape that made her pregnant. When a person takes all the precautions that she can *reasonably* be expected to take against a certain outcome, then that outcome cannot fairly be described as her responsibility. So in case 2, where the negligence of the manufacturer of the contraceptive is the cause of the pregnancy, the woman cannot be held responsible for her condition, and that ground for ascribing to her a duty not to abort is not present.

Case 3 brings us very close to the borderline. The couple in this example do not choose to have a baby and, indeed, they take strong precautions against pregnancy. Still they know that there is a 1 percent danger and they deliberately chose to run that risk anyway. As a result, a woman becomes pregnant against her will. Does she then have a right to abandon to a certain death a newly formed moral person who is even less responsible for his dependence on her than she is? When one looks at the problem in this way from the perspective of the fetus to whom we have suppositively ascribed full moral rights, it becomes doubtful that the pregnant woman's very minimal responsibility for her plight can permit her to abandon a being who has no responsibility for it whatever. She ran a very small risk, but the fetus ran no risk at all. Nevertheless, this is a borderline case for the following reason. If we extend to this case the rule we applied to case 2, then we might be entitled to say that the woman is no more responsible than the fetus for the pregnancy. To reach that conclusion we have to judge the 1 percent chance of pregnancy to be a *reasonable* risk for a woman to run in the circumstances. That appraisal itself is a disguised moral judgment of pivotal importance, and yet it is very difficult to know how to go about establishing it. Nevertheless, *if* it is correct, then the woman is, for all practical purposes, relieved of her responsibility for the pregnancy just as she is in cases 1 and 2, and in that event the fetus's "right to life" does not entail a duty on her part to make extreme sacrifices.

## §8 SUMMARY AND CONCLUSION

Assuming that the fetus is a moral person, under what conditions, if any, is abortion justifiable homicide? If the woman's right to an abortion is derived from her right to own property in her body (which is not very plausible), then abortion is never justifiable homicide. Property rights simply can't support that much moral weight. If the right is derived from self-defense, then it justifies abortion at most when necessary to save the woman from death. That is because the fetus, while sometimes a threat to the interests of the woman, is an innocent and (in a sense) nonaggressive threat. The doctrine of proportionality, which permits a person to use a degree of force in self-defense that is likely to cause the assailant harm greater (within reasonable limits) than the harm the assailant would otherwise cause the victim, has application only to the case where the assailant is culpable. One can kill an "innocent threat" in order to save one's life but not to save one's pocketbook. The right of bodily autonomy (to decide what is to be done in and to one's own body) is a much solider base for the right to abortion than either the right to property or the right to self-defense, since it permits one to kill innocent persons by depriving them of one's "life-support system," even when they are threats to interests substantially less important than self-preservation. But this justification is probably available at most to victims of rape, or contraceptive failure caused by the negligence of other parties, to the risk of which the woman has not consented. That narrow restriction on the use of this defense stems from the requirement, internal to it, that the woman be in no way responsible for her pregnancy.

It does not follow automatically that because the victim of a homicide was "innocent," the killing cannot have been justified. But abortion can plausibly be construed as justifiable homicide only on the basis of inexact analogies, and then only (1) to save the mother from the most extreme harm or else (2) to save the mother from a lesser harm when the pregnancy was the result of the wrongful acts of others for which the woman had no responsibility. Another possibility that was only suggested here is (3) when it can be claimed for a defective or diseased fetus that it has a right *not* to be born. These narrow restrictions on the right of the woman to an abortion will not satisfy many people in the proabortion camp. But if the assumption of the moral personhood of the fetus is false, as was argued in the first part of this essay, then the woman's right to bodily autonomy will normally prevail, and abortions at all but the later stages, at least, and for the most common reasons, at least, are morally permissible.

## III. POSTSCRIPT

Since this article was written there have been numerous legislative attempts to undermine the constitutional right to an abortion declared by the United States Supreme Court in *Roe* v. *Wade* (1973). Perhaps the most prominent of these efforts was the bill, S. 158, introduced in the Senate in 1982 by Senator Jesse Helms, which resolves that "human life shall be deemed to exist from conception." The Congress, had it passed this bill, would have created a legal status for human fetuses and embryos that presumably would imply their possession of various constitutional rights, including "the right to life." Among the other intended legal consequences of this new status is that the killing of a fetus at any stage of its development would be a kind of criminal homicide.

Whatever difficulties might attend a legislative or constitutional rule endorsing some particular point in mid or late pregnancy as the starting point of moral personhood (and they, too, would be considerable), the consequences of the criterion endorsed by S. 158, or any other rule dating personhood from "the moment of conception," are intolerably paradoxical. Consider how this essay has treated the question: Is the single-cell zygote a moment after conception already a full-fledged human being? Depending on how we interpret the question, Senator Helms's affirmative answer is either self-evidently, but trivially and irrelevantly, true, or else absurd. The one-celled conceptus, the product of a human spermatozoan and a human ovum, is, of course, itself human. No scientist who counted its chromosomes could possibly classify it as feline, canine, or equine. The species to which it belongs is obviously the human species. Moreover, unless or until it aborts along the way, it is clearly a living thing as opposed to an inert piece of dead tissue. Therefore, the newly conceived "zygote" (the word for the fertilized egg before it becomes a hollow sphere of cells or "blastocyst" on the sixth day) is —in the most trivial and obvious sense—a form of "human life." There would appear to be nothing to quarrel about in this innocent claim—except, of course, whether the zygote is already "human life" in the sense that is morally significant, namely that of a person with rights, the legal status Senator Helms wishes to establish.

To show that living human zygotes have rights, it is not enough to point out that they are living things associated with the human species. One must also show that they are *people*, in all morally relevant respects like you and me. Fertilized human eggs, of course, are *potential* people. That is to say, that they will develop into actual people if all goes well in the normal course of pregnancy. But that obvious truth is not sufficient to establish their present rights. To be a potential human person, as we have seen, is to be only a potential bearer of human rights; actual rights must await actual personhood. To infer actual possession of rights from future qualification is a mistake that seems peculiar to the abortion controversy; we are rarely tempted to make it in other contexts. A twelve-year-old American child, for example, is a potential voter in American elections in the sense that he will have an actual right to vote six years from now if all goes well in the natural course of his adolescence. But we are not tempted to admit him to the voting booths now simply on the grounds that he is a "potential voter" who will be qualified later.

The relevant question, then, is whether human zygotes, a few minutes after conception, are already *actual* people. Senator Helms's affirmative answer to this question conflicts violently with common sense. The only people who are likely to agree with it are those who are prepared to abandon common sense or those who confuse this question with the obvious but irrelevant questions about life and species membership that we have already dismissed. The one-celled speck of protoplasm, or small cluster of cells, of which we speak has none of the characteristics we normally have in mind when we speak of persons. No one believes that this tiny entity is *already* conscious of itself and the world, capable of sensation and emotion, able to understand and reason, remember and anticipate, make plans and act, be pleased or frustrated or hurt. Nor do we take seriously the logical consequences of "deeming" human embryos in their earliest stages to be people. In particular our attitudes toward spontaneous miscarriage ("natural abortion") show that we do not regard embryos as full-fledged moral persons. We may be disappointed when a pregnancy miscarries because our desire to produce a child has been at least temporarily frustrated, but we do not grieve for the embryo's sake. Funeral rites are not performed for tiny clusters of cells; baptism and extreme unction are not given upon the arrival of a tardy menstrual period over menses that may have contained an embryo; names and "conception dates" are not recorded; death certificates are not required. Why would we be so casually negligent if we believed with Senator Helms that a real person has died?

More importantly, if zygotes and embryos are actual people, why do we not make a monumental effort to "rescue" the millions who are bound to perish each year from natural causes? If there are a dozen trapped coal miners in a caved-in mine or a million persons threatened by starvation in a foreign famine, we are prepared to spend millions of dollars to save them because they are, after all, undeniably fellow human beings. Why then do we not budget millions more for research toward the discovery of a drug that would prevent spontaneous abortions? Embryologists have estimated that only 58 percent of fertilized ova survive until implantation (seven days after conception) and that the spontaneous abortion rate after that stage is from 10 to 15 percent. If we left that many miners and farmers to die each year without rescue efforts, we would be very callous indeed. But if we did save all the fetuses with some wonder drug, then, according to one embryologist, instead of a population in which approximately 2 percent suffer from relatively minor congenital defects, we would have a population in which 10 to 20 percent would be abnormal "and most of the defects would be gross and incapacitating." (Malcolm Potts, *Biology and Ethics,* The Academic Press, 1969). Does Senator Helms intend to prepare us to face this consequence, or is he content to let millions of salvageable "human lives" perish?

Other absurd consequences of the redefinition in the "human life statute" have been more widely publicized. Women who use contraceptives that make the uterine wall unreceptive to implantation, for example, would themselves be murderers since they deliberately cause the death of fertilized human ova. Government could take vigilant steps to protect unborn persons, and many of these would involve intrusions into women's private affairs—requiring monthly pregnancy tests, for example, to determine whether any unborn persons exist in her womb, or requiring registration of all suspected pregnancies. If we really took seriously the view that fertilized eggs are people with the full panoply of human rights, these absurd practices would not seem implausible.

It seems to me that a case can be made for taking a human life statute that dates the origin of personhood at conception to be an "establishment" of religious doctrine. The argument runs as follows. For reasons given above, it is quite contrary to common sense to claim that a newly fertilized human ovum is already an actual person. Employing the term 'person' in the normal fashion, no one thinks of a fertilized egg in that way. The only arguments that have been advanced to the conclusion that fertilized eggs *are* people, common sense notwithstanding, are arguments with theological premises. These premises are part of large theological and philosophical systems that are very much worthy of respect indeed, but they can neither be established nor refuted without critical discussion of the whole systems of which they form a part. In fact, many conscientious persons reject them, often in favor of doctrines stemming from rival theological systems; so for the state to endorse the personhood of newly fertilized ova would be for the state to embrace one set of controversial theological tenets rather than others, in effect to enforce the teaching of some churches against those of other churches (and nonchurches), and to back up this enforcement with severe criminal penalties. The state plays this constitutionally prohibited role when it officially affirms a doctrine that is opposed to common sense and understanding and whose only proposed arguments proceed from theological premises. This case, it seems to me, is a good one even if there is reason, as there might be, for affirming the personhood of fetuses in the second or third trimester of pregnancy.

## NOTES

1. Mary Anne Warren, "On the Moral and Legal Status of Abortion," *The Monist* 57 (1973), pp. 43–61. Reprinted in J. Feinberg and H. Gross (eds.), *Liberty: Selected Readings*, pp. 133–143. The quotation is from the latter source, p. 138.
2. See Paul Ramsey, "The Morality of Abortion," in D. H. Labby (ed.), *Life or Death: Ethics and Options* (Seattle and London: University of Washington Press, 1968), pp. 60–93.
3. These problems are discussed in more detail in Joel Feinberg, "The Rights of Animals and Future Generations" (Appendix: The Paradoxes of

Potentiality), in W. T. Blackstone (ed.), *Philosophy and Environmental Crisis* (Athens, Ga.: University of Georgia Press, 1974), pp. 67–68.

4.  Stanley I. Benn, "Abortion, Infanticide, and Respect for Persons," in J. Feinberg (ed.), *The Problem of Abortion* (Belmont, Calif.: Wadsworth, 1973), p. 102.

5.  Joel Feinberg, *Social Philosophy* (Englewood Cliffs, N.J.: Prentice-Hall, 1973), p. 66.

6.  Benn, op. cit., p. 102.

7.  Joel Feinberg, "Is There a Right to Be Born?" in James Rachels (ed.), *Understanding Moral Philosophy* (Encino, Calif.: Dickenson, 1976), pp. 353–354.

8.  Thalidomide is the trade name of a potent tranquilizer once manufactured in Europe but never permitted in the United States. In the late 1950s, thousands of deformed babies were born to European women who had taken thalidomide during pregnancy.

9.  From Mr. Justice Blackmun's opinion in *Roe* v. *Wade* 410 U.S. 113 (1973).

10. Jane English, "Abortion and the Concept of a Person," *Canadian Journal of Philosophy* 5 (1975), p. 242.

11. George Fletcher, "Proportionality and the Psychotic Aggressor: A Vignette in the Comparative Criminal Law Theory," *Israel Law Review* 8 (1973), p. 376.

12. Fletcher, loc. cit.

13. Judith Jarvis Thomson, "Self-Defense and Rights," The Lindley Lecture, 1976 (Lawrence, Kans.: University of Kansas Philosophy Department, 1977).

14. The term comes from Robert Nozick, *Anarchy, State, and Utopia* (New York: Basic Books, 1974), p. 35.

15. Even when self-defense is acceptable as a defense to homicide in the case of forced killings of nonaggressive innocents, that may be because it is understood in those cases to be an excuse or a mitigation rather than a justification. If a criminal terrorist from a fortified position throws a bomb at my feet and I can escape its explosion only by quickly throwing it in the direction of a baby buggy whose infant occupant is enjoying a nap, perhaps I can be *excused* for saving my life by taking the baby's, perhaps the duress under which I acted mitigates my guilt, perhaps the law ought not to be too severe with me. But it is not convincing to argue that I was entirely justified in what I did because I was acting in self-defense. But the problem is a difficult one, and the case may be borderline.

16. See Ludwig Lewisohn's remarkable novel, *The Case of Mr. Crump* (New York: Farrar, Straus, 1947).

17. Judith Jarvis Thomson, "A Defense of Abortion," *Philosophy and Public Affairs* 1 (1971), pp. 48–49.

18. Warren, op. cit., p. 135.

19. The examples are Sissela Bok's. See her article "Ethical Problems of Abortion," *Hastings Center Studies* 2 (1974), p. 35.

## SUGGESTIONS FOR FURTHER READING

Further readings are mentioned below in connection with the section (§) of the essay to which they are most pertinent.

§3. A very helpful collection of articles on the concept of a person is *The Identity of Persons,* edited by Amélie O. Rorty (Berkeley, Los Angeles, London: University of California Press, 1976). In particular, the editor's introduction and postscript and Daniel Dennett's "Conditions of Personhood" are especially useful. A very penetrating and original analysis of commonsense personhood (not in the Rorty collection) is Harry Frankfurt's "Freedom of the Will and the Concept of a Person," *Journal of Philosophy* 68 (1971), reprinted in J. Feinberg (ed.), *Reason and Responsibility*, 4th ed. (Belmont, Calif.: Wadsworth, 1978). For articles that defend particular accounts of personhood in the context of the abortion problem, see especially Mary Anne Warren, "The Moral and Legal Status of Abortion," *The Monist* 57 (1973), and Joseph Fletcher, "Indicators of Humanhood: A Tentative Profile of Man," *The Hastings Center Report* 2 (1972). See also Lawrence C. Becker's "Human Being: The Boundaries of the Concept," *Philosophy and Public Affairs* 4 (1975).

§4. The most influential recent defenses of a species criterion are probably those of the Catholic legal scholar John T. Noonan, Jr., and the Protestant theologian Paul Ramsey. See Noonan's "Abortion and the Catholic Church: A Summary History," *Natural Law Forum* 12 (1967), and his rejoinder to critics, "How to Argue About Abortion" (New York: Ad Hoc Committee in Defense of Life, Inc., 1974). Ramsey's views are well stated in "The Morality of Abortion," in *Life or Death: Ethics and Options*, edited by D. H. Labby (Seattle: University of Washington Press, 1968).

A nicely nuanced defense of a kind of synthesis of the strict potentiality and species principles can be found in Philip E. Devine's book, *The Ethics of Homicide* (Ithaca, N.Y.: Cornell University Press, 1978). Although Devine's conclusions differ from those of this essay, the methodology is very similar to that employed here.

A thorough presentation of a modified potentiality criterion can be found in Daniel Callahan's learned and thoroughly moderate book, *Abortion: Law, Choice, and Morality* (London and New York: Macmillan, 1970). See especially chapters 10 and 11.

The most uncompromising defense of an actual-possession criterion is that of Michael Tooley, "Abortion and Infanticide," *Philosophy and Public Affairs* 2 (1972). Tooley defends not only abortion but, under certain circumstances, infanticide as well. His view on the latter question is criticized on utilitarian grounds by Stanley Benn and Jane English in the articles mentioned in the text of this essay.

§7. An eloquent account of the serious psychological harms that can be done to women by enforced pregnancies can be found in Lorenne M. G. Clark's "Reply to Professor Sumner," *Canadian Journal of Philosophy* 4 (1974). Baruch Brody argues forcefully that "self-defense" cannot justify abortion in his *Abortion and the Sanctity of Human Life: A Philosophical View* (Cambridge, Mass., and London: M.I.T. Press, 1975). An authoritative and very accessible discussion of the application of "self-defense" and other justifications to borderline cases of justifiable homicides of all kinds is Sanford Kadish's "Respect for Life and Regard for Rights in the Criminal Law," *California Law Review* 64 (1976), reprinted in S. F. Barker (ed.), *Respect for Life in Medicine, Philosophy, and the Law* (Baltimore and London: Johns Hopkins University Press, 1976).

Judith Thomson's use of the "plugged-in violinist" example is sharply criticized by John Finnis in his "The Rights and Wrongs of Abortion," in *Philosophy and Public Affairs* 2 (Winter 1973). Thomson's rejoinder to Finnis, "Rights and Deaths," is included in the same issue. Both articles can be found in *The Rights and Wrongs of Abortion*, edited by M. Cohen, T. Nagel, and T. Scanlon (Princeton, N.J.: Princeton University Press, 1973). Another useful anthology with more recent articles is *The Problem of Abortion*, 2nd ed., edited by Joel Feinberg (Belmont, Calif.: Wadsworth, 1983).

# 8

# The Moral Perplexities of Famine and World Hunger

## ONORA O'NEILL

### §1 ARE FAMINE AND WORLD HUNGER NEW MORAL PROBLEMS?

Moral problems aren't usually new. Most of the questions that give us pause or sleepless nights have been faced by others ever since (no doubt also before) the beginnings of systematic reflection about what to do. We know very well, for example, that we are not the first to be tempted to put career before everything else. If the temptation persists, we may want to consult our predecessors or other authorities. We may find ourselves thinking about Macbeth's vaulting ambition, perhaps comforted by the thought that, unlike him, we do not put career above everything—no murder for advancement, for example.

But when we wonder what we or others should do about global famine there are fewer familiar literary or religious traditions or philosophical discussions to which to turn. This is not because famine is new but because there is today far more that we (or others) can do—or refrain from doing—that will affect the risk and course of famine. Through history millions have died of sheer starvation and of malnutrition or from illnesses that they might have survived with better food. Whenever there were such deaths, nearby survivors may have realized that they could help prevent some deaths and may have done so, or wondered whether to do so. But nobody sought to prevent faraway deaths. Distance made an important difference; with few exceptions there was nothing to be done for the victims of faraway famines.

In a global economy things are different. Food from areas with agricultural surplus (nowadays mainly North America, Australia, and western Europe) can be distributed to the starving in Bangladesh or

Somalia. Longer-term policies that affect economic development, fertility levels, and agricultural productivity may hasten or postpone far-off famines or make them more or less severe. Consequently we can now ask whether we ought to do some of these newly possible actions. Ought we (or others) to try to distribute food or aid, to control fertility, or to further economic development? Who should foot the bills and suffer the other costs? To whom (if anyone) should aid be given and to whom should it be denied? How much hardship or sacrifice, if any, is demanded of those who have the means to help?

In answering these questions, traditional moral theories are often not very useful. Consider, for example, the Christian injunction to love your neighbor as yourself. Christ explained who your neighbor is in the parable of the good Samaritan.[1] The Samaritan, though an alien, helped the man who fell among thieves, so was neighbor to that man. Suppose the Samaritan had found on the road to Jericho someone who had not been mugged but who was starving. We have no doubt how to extend the Christian principle here: it is neighborly to feed the starving when we come upon them in distress. But what is neighborly when the starving are not lying on a lonely road where we are walking, but are numerous and scattered in distant parts of the world? What should a Christian do then? Should the Christian send money? If so, to whom? Or should Christians seek to influence the aid and trade policies of their own (or of other) countries to the advantage of starving persons or regions? If so, how is this to be done? How much aid should be sent and how much effort expended? May or ought Christians send so much that they or their families or community suffer hardship? Or are these approaches futile? If all the world's distressed people are neighbors, even the wealthiest and most dedicated Christian can help very few of them. And how are these few to be selected? Are some people nearer neighbors than others, contrary to the apparent message of the parable of the good Samaritan? If so, who are the nearer? If charity begins at home, should Christians perhaps devote their efforts to nearby, less acute distresses? And should Christians take into account the likelihood that fortunate others will (or won't) help the hungry?

The more we think about these questions, the more we see how important it is in the Christian parable that the good Samaritan encountered an isolated person in distress, for whose relief he had means. In saying this, we belittle neither the Samaritan's kindness nor his courage (he too might have been mugged). But we realize that famines in faraway places confront us with moral problems to which the Christian parable does not provide obvious answers. The parable leaves answers to the above questions *undetermined,* and if we are looking for a moral theory that will help us work out what we may or ought to do, we shall need one whose answers to these questions are more *determinate.* Indeterminate or abstract answers to problems rule out some solutions but don't offer enough to guide action.

It is not only Christian ethics that leaves many problems about distant famines unanswered. Other moral theories also fail to answer many questions sufficiently determinately. I will try in this essay to show how certain moral theories *can* help us think about some questions about famine (perhaps not others) and also to use considerations about famine to show some of the strengths and limitations of these theories.

# I SOME CRITERIA FOR MORAL ARGUMENT

## §2 MORAL THEORIES AND MORAL PROBLEMS

The project I've just described of simultaneously using and criticizing moral theories may strike you as about as likely to succeed as the proverbial task of pulling oneself up by one's own bootstraps. Once we've got a moral theory, we can use it to solve (some) moral problems. We use the theory plus an account of certain facts or examples and try to work out what we ought to do. But having done so, it seems we can't use those implications to criticize the theory from which they were (in part) derived. It may seem that if the criticism worked, it would undermine its own starting point. But this self-defeating circle can be avoided by using the criticism that we derive from a theory not so much to undermine as to revise and improve it. Just as scientists may use the inaccurate predictions their theories produce to work out better theories, so in moral thinking we can take hints from the implausible or inadequate results a theory may lead to in working out a better theory. To understand this process of building, checking, and improving moral theories, we need to know a bit about such theories and at least *some* of the things that would show them to be inadequate.

## §3 MORAL THEORIES AND MORALLY ACCEPTABLE THEORIES

Moral theories typically include a number of rather general principles that enjoin or forbid, commend or condemn some types of action. Examples of such general principles of action include the Good Samaritan principle and principles like "Injure nobody" or "Do whatever will produce the best results for everybody," or "Do as you would be done by." Many moral theories consist of more than one such principle, and when there is more than one, the theory usually explains their relationship. For example, a moral theory that includes the principle "Always do what produces the best results for everybody" will probably include a principle for settling what sorts of things count as good or bad results.

This minimal account of moral theories accepts that there can be many different moral theories. Some may be incompatible with others. For example, one moral theory might include the principle "Always do the act likely to have the best total results," and another the principle "Do what appeals to you most, even when it will produce less good total results than you could achieve by suiting yourself less well."

If we want moral theories to help us decide about difficult moral problems, then we need to choose one of these theories. If we do not, we would face various theories that enjoin or forbid, commend or condemn incompatible actions and so cannot give us guidance. In making this choice, we want to pick not just *any* moral theory, but one that is *morally acceptable.*

Moral theories enjoin or forbid, commend or condemn *types of acts* (or results or persons or lives—but all of these involve acts of certain sorts). Theories that are not moral theories do other things. They may be geological or ecological theories or sociological theories. These theories are all *nonmoral theories.* However, nonmoral theories are not generally morally unacceptable or immoral. (There may be some exceptions, where a nonmoral theory, or the holding of such a theory, would be judged immoral. An example might be certain Nazi theories about race.)

The theories we want to avoid in working out solutions to moral problems are not these nonmoral theories but inadequate moral theories that fail to pick out morally acceptable types of act. However, our moral perplexity over a matter like famine means that we are often unsure which results are morally acceptable. So we cannot simply discover the acceptable theories by seeing whether they give us the results we think acceptable. (If we were quite sure what was acceptable in all cases, we would probably not be looking at moral theories at all.) The best we can do is to examine the theories themselves and see how good they are *as theories.* In this way, although we may not discover a moral theory that is the only morally acceptable one, we may be able to show that some theories are inadequate in whole or in part or that they are adequate for some purposes and not for others.

In §4 and §5 I shall suggest two standards for assessing the adequacy of theories. These standards are of very general use and can be applied to nonmoral (for example, scientific) theories as well as to moral theories. Initially I shall use some scientific analogies to explain and show the appeal of these standards by which we can judge theories. In later sections I shall apply the standards to moral theories.

## §4 THE SCOPE OF MORAL THEORIES

One way of showing that a moral theory is not morally adequate is by finding out whether it can deal with a considerable range of problems. If a theory can deal with only a few problems, then its *scope* is small. It is, at best, a fragment of a morally acceptable theory. It is unacceptable as a complete theory because it doesn't resolve enough problems. Consider, for example, someone who claims to live by a moral theory consisting just of the principle "Never give or ask help." We may disagree whether this principle is strange or odious or admirable. But there is no doubt that it is not going to be much use in lots of circumstances. Where no question arises of help being given or received, this principle is silent. Someone who tries to get along with just this moral principle will often be at a loss. The principle has too narrow a scope.

Moral theories are in *some* ways like scientific theories. Both moral and scientific theories can have greater or lesser *scope*. One theory has greater scope than another if it can deal with more problems. A scientific theory is considered superior to a rival theory if it can account for more or more varied phenomena. For example, the seventeenth-century natural philosophers (physicists) who worked out a single science of motion created a theory whose scope included what had previously been handled in two separate theories, the theory of celestial dynamics and the theory of terrestrial dynamics.[2] Previously these two distinct theories had been used to explain respectively the movements of the heavenly bodies and those of "sublunar" (earthly) bodies. The heavenly bodies were thought to move in circles, while sublunar bodies fell down toward the solid earth. These earlier theories were ingenious in explaining deviations from apparent circular and downward motion. Ptolemaic astronomers used an elaborate theory of epicycles (orbits on orbits) to explain why some heavenly bodies appear to move on noncircular orbits. The theory of the elements explained why some sublunar bodies—like fire—move upward by attributing different weights to different sublunar bodies and theorizing that the heavier ones move down faster that the lighter ones. But the earlier theories never brought both sorts of motion under a single theory. Newton's theory did, and *one* of the reasons why it was a superior theory was that its scope was so much greater than the scope of either terrestrial or celestial dynamics. Similarly, we might expect any acceptable moral theory to have a relatively large scope—to give answers to a large range of important problems. Of course, we may find that we can't come up with any moral theory that will deal with *all* moral problems. If so, we'll have to accept that limitation, just as we accept the fact that no scientific theory covers all known natural phenomena.

## §5 ACCURACY AND PRECISION IN MORAL THEORIES

Not every theory of large scope is a good theory. There is little use for a moral (or scientific) theory that tells us very little about a great deal. A scientific theory that says merely that bodies move at varying speed would have large scope but be useless because so vague. We want scientific theories that not only have sufficient scope to cover an important range of cases but also give reasonably *accurate* predictions.

Scientific theories are also admired if they are not merely accurate but *precise*, that is if their predictions and implications are not only broadly correct but also expressed with mathematical precision.

In an acceptable moral theory, accuracy is also important but precision less so. A theory can help guide action even if it does not offer precise rules for every possible contingency (although we sometimes hanker for precision). Many writers on ethics doubt that much precision is possible (or necessary) in moral thinking. But we can't do without theories that, however lacking in precision, are generally accurate. A theory whose implications often point in what we think is the wrong direction, or that comes up with very unstable recommendations, or that offers recommendations which are constantly disputed, or reversed by trivial changes in circumstances, is not likely to be an acceptable moral theory. Accuracy is a matter of getting results that are broadly on target, and precision is a matter of getting results that are finely differentiated. Accuracy without precision is well worth having, but precision without accuracy is worthless in practical matters.

It follows that not every theory that has large scope and offers determinate answers to moral problems is acceptable. If the theory offers determinate answers because it has detailed, precise implications, but these are inaccurate, it will not be acceptable. In practical affairs it is more important to find a theory whose recommendations reliably point in the right direction than it is to find one that will provide a finely detailed code of conduct.

There is no reason to think that any moral theory with reasonably large scope and implications that do not seem inaccurate is acceptable. These are *necessary* but not *sufficient* conditions for an acceptable moral theory. They are, however, enough to provide us with a framework within which to begin looking at the merits and difficulties of the ways in which various moral theories can handle questions about famine.

## §6 LIMITING THE DISCUSSION

At this point I shall take *two* major shortcuts. The first is to concentrate on questions of scope and determinancy and say little about other requirements for an adequate moral theory, such as its justification or its compatibility with plausible accounts of human action and freedom. The second is to examine only two possible moral theories. One of these is utilitarianism; the other is a (simplified) version of Kantian ethics.

Many writers on ethics in the English-speaking world today think some version of one of these two theories is likely to be a morally acceptable theory (but others are more impressed by the promise of theories of human rights: I shall only indicate briefly why I do not think that approach promising).[3] I shall sketch both utilitarianism and Kantian ethics and then ask whether each has the scope and accuracy to help us deliberate about some of the moral problems that famines raise.

Before I start this investigation of the adequacy of utilitarian and Kantian ethics in dealing with famine dilemmas, I shall consider whether there really is any likelihood that famines will occur. If famines are *very* unlikely, we don't need a moral theory that can handle famine problems. There is little point in strenuous thought about unlikely problems when there are so many problems that we know will arise and require decisions, if not of us, then of many of our contemporaries. The other problems discussed in this book—problems raised by war and abortion and penal systems and terminal illness—are problems we *know* will arise. Famine is one that we might, after all, escape. So I shall now try to show why I think that even if we escape future famines, we cannot escape the moral problems raised by the risk of famine. Therefore it is worth our time and effort to think about those problems.

## II THE FACTS OF FAMINE

An enormous amount is known about the numbers of people now living and about the resources they have to live on. There are also many careful and scrupulous studies of the likely rate of growth of population and resources in various regions and countries. It may then seem easy to discover whether the world either is or will be over-populated, whether there will be famines, and when and where they are most likely to occur. But it turns out that this is not easy, indeed, that the experts disagree passionately. They don't, on the whole, disagree with passion about the particular figures (which all accept as being no more than careful estimates). They often do disagree about the import of these figures. But some matters are not controversial, and I shall sketch these briefly.[4]

### §7 THE LOOK OF FAMINE

Famine is a hidden killer, a dark horse. In the Book of Revelation, other killers are symbolized by highly visible horses and horsemen: the white horse of Conquest, the red horse of War, and the pale horse of Death itself.[5] But Famine is symbolized by a black horse and horseman. And so it is in human experience. When famine strikes, relatively few people die "of hunger." They die for the most part of illnesses they would easily have survived if hunger had not weakened them. They die of 'flu and of intestinal troubles, and disproportionately many of those who die are very young or old. When there is famine, the survivors too are affected in hidden ways. Children may suffer brain damage as a result of early malnutrition; whole populations may be listless and lethargic, unable to muster the energy needed for economic advance, still living but permanently weakened.

We have all seen pictures of starving, skeletal children in the appeals of famine-relief charities. But such emaciation is only the visible and publicizable fraction of the damage the black horse can do. When we wonder whether famine is likely, we must remember that most of the impact of hunger is less dramatic. Whenever death rates are higher than they would be with adequate nutrition, hunger is *already* taking its toll. Perhaps there will be future famines that are far more visible than today's hunger, large-scale versions of the disastrous famines that have recently occurred in the southern Sahara, in Bangladesh, and in Ethiopia. Perhaps there will be nothing so dramatic but rather many lives of unrelenting hunger and premature death, without mass migration in search of food or any of the other horrors of extreme famine. If we remember that most of the impact of hunger is of this sort, then we can see that famine is not some unknown evil that might strike human populations in the future, but a more virulent case of evil suffered by many now living. The question that divides the experts is less whether there will be future, dramatic episodes of famine than whether the endemic hunger and malnutrition that millions now live with can be ended or will become more intense and severe as time goes on.

Hunger does not have to produce dramatic and catastrophic episodes of famine to inflict acute suffering. Hunger destroys lives in two senses: it literally kills—destroys—the biological basis of life, and it also destroys the lives persons lead, their biographical lives, even when it leaves the biological organism functioning. The survivors of famines and near famine suffer the biological deaths of those they love, and their own biographical lives are often shattered by hunger and the destruction of ways of life.

## §8 THE EXTENT OF FAMINE

To get a feel for the extent of these miseries, it helps to have a few figures. The population of the world is around 4 ½ billion—and rising very fast. If we project present rates of growth, we can imagine a world whose human population doubles and redoubles every few decades. But a *projection* of existing trends is not *prediction*. There is no point in projecting this sort of figure and entertaining the fantasy of a world without resources but weighed down by or literally covered with living humans. Long before this point is reached, the availability of resources will limit the population that can remain alive.

The history of the last two centuries is one of rapid increases in available resources, which have permitted a corresponding growth in human population. Two centuries ago there were only 800 million human beings alive. We do not know how many there will be in another two centuries. But however few or many there are, there will not be more alive than there are resources to sustain them. (There may be fewer, since some or all persons may live at a higher-than-subsistence standard.) Sustained overpopulation is impossible: as soon as there are more people than there are resources, some people die. When populations expand beyond resources available to them, they are pruned by famine. But we do not have to be at the mercy of famines. Populations can control their own rates of growth and ensure that they don't grow faster than the resources available to them. A population that succeeds in this task (and some have) need not suffer or risk famine. It can be free not only of the spectacular miseries of catastrophic famines but also of the slower, hidden famine that shows itself in premature deaths, lack of resistance to illness, and lack of energy. On these matters the experts do not disagree.

## §9 CONTROVERSIES ABOUT AVOIDING FAMINES

When we ask *how* famine and hunger can best be ended and whether it is at all likely that they will be ended, there is great controversy. All agree that the task of ending famine is at best enormous and daunting. But even experts disagree about what is possible. Some awareness of these disagreements is helpful in considering moral problems raised by famine.

Some experts—often spoken of as neo-Malthusians[6]—think that the only secure way to end famine is by limiting population growth. In the long run no increase in available food could match population increase. Other experts—often called developmentalists—think that the first aim must be economic growth, which is a prerequisite of lowering population growth.

Developmentalists themselves disagree whether the most important changes are economic or political. They debate whether economic policies available within current political structures, such as foreign aid and international loans and investment by transnational corporations, provide an adequate framework to develop the now underdeveloped world. Are there—as some political economists believe—features of the present structure of aid and trade that prevent such policies from transforming the economic prospects of underdeveloped regions but which might be changed by political transformations? Is it even possible that the main obstacle to economic growth in the poorest regions lies in the present international economic order, despite its ostensible commitment to the goal of development?

These debates are ethically important because social inquiry itself is no matter of ethically neutral "facts." The debates between different experts often show that their disputes are *already* moral disagreements. There is no way in which those who want to do something about world hunger and poverty can hope that experts will present "the facts," and equally no way in which those who take action can shirk making informed judgments about what is possible.

## §10 MALTHUSIAN CONTROVERSIES

Neo-Malthusians take their name from Thomas Malthus (1766–1834), who noted in his *Summary View of the Principle of Population* (1830), "a tendency in mankind to increase, if unchecked, beyond the possibility of an adequate supply of food in a limited territory."[7]

Of course, Malthus knew well enough that such increase always was "checked." The check might be what he called "prudential restraint on marriage and population," or it might be high mortality. If there was much "imprudence," the ultimate check might even be the highly visible mortality of famine.

Recent neo-Malthusians hold that famine is not only the *ultimate* check on population growth but an imminent one. Some characterize population growth as a bomb that economic growth cannot defuse, whose explosion threatens all. Others compare the lives of those who appear well off to the plight of passengers on a lifeboat, who can rescue those who drown around them only at the risk of sinking and drowning everybody. Still others allege that the only responsible approach to the distribution of resources must follow the tough-minded principle of "triage," offering help neither to the better off nor to the destitute but only to the "best risks" for whom alone (they think) help can make a difference. These powerful images suggest that population growth cannot be sustained indefinitely and that, to avoid catastrophe, we must forthwith abandon rather than rescue the neediest.[8]

Various reasons are given for these views. Some neo-Malthusians claim that the rapid growth of population of recent centuries cannot be sustained because readily exploited natural resources have already been used and further exploitation will be harder because of pollution and low yields. The continued evasion of famine would require sustained technological advance, which we cannot guarantee. Other neo-Malthusians stress economic and political rather than natural barriers to sustained economic growth. It is apparent enough that there is nothing automatic about economic growth and that long periods of history have shown nothing more fundamental than succeeding lean and fat years. The risk of famine is greatest in just those places where economic growth will be hardest. Underdeveloped countries may lack investment capital and know-how; there may be resistance to the introduction of technology that will change existing and preferred ways of life, and an often accurate perception that not everybody will share the economic benefits which new technology is said to bring. Nor is it easy to transfer resources from areas of economic surplus to poorer regions. The richer nations are often reluctant to share their surplus, and the very process of transfer can harm the economic system of undeveloped regions.

In the eyes of neo-Malthusians, these obstacles to economic growth are matched by difficulty in controlling population growth. In spite of the "contraceptive revolution," it remains true that the only wholly safe and reliable modes of contraception are forms of sterilization that are not reliably reversible and are therefore unpopular. Reversible techniques (IUDs, rubber devices, chemical contraception) may be neither entirely reliable nor safe nor easy for those living in great poverty to use or to afford. They are also rejected by some on religious grounds. Abortion is even more widely rejected, and it is least available and safe where poverty is harshest.

Even if these difficulties were overcome, some neo-Malthusians argue,[9] the populations that most risk famine might not have the "prudence" to limit their increasing populations. Access to contraceptive technology does not guarantee smaller families; nor does lack of access always prevent reduction in family size. In the now developed countries of Europe and North America, a *demographic transition* has taken place, and these countries now have, despite long-lived populations and little emigration, either low or negative rates of population increase. By contrast, no such demographic transition has yet taken place in many now underdeveloped countries. Death rates have fallen, but fertility levels remain high and population increase is rapid. In other Third World countries (not generally in the poorest ones), fertility is now falling. This is particularly evident in some Southeast Asian countries.

An interesting and vitally important question to ask these neo-Malthusians is why they are so pessimistic about the longer-term prospects for economic development and fertility control in the Third World. Why, for example, do they not think the economic development and controlled population growth of the now developed world evidence that success is possible? After all, it is not so long since the whole world was underdeveloped. What is it that makes the development of the now underdeveloped world appear so hard that it demands abandoning those most at risk? Harsh measures may be necessary in certain emergencies, but we need to be sure that there is an emergency before we take or advocate emergency measures.

## §11 DEVELOPMENTALIST REJOINDERS

Developmentalist views of prospects for economic growth in the underdeveloped world and for ending the risk of famine are more optimistic. Like neo-Malthusians, these writers hold a great variety of views, and only a selection can be mentioned.[10] The optimism which developmentalist writers often show is only a *relative* optimism. Most of them do not think that economic development and ending the risk of famine can be either easy or rapid; many stress that huge political and social as well as economic changes may have to be made if the enterprise is to succeed.

The optimism is based on an awareness of the many ways in which economic advance takes place. Recent growth rates in the Third

World have often been high. However, the picture is one only of *qualified* optimism for several reasons. First, many of the poor do not benefit from growth; second, when population growth remains rapid, improvement in living standards must be slight even if the benefits of economic growth are evenly distributed. Few developmentalist writers today expect economic growth in poor countries to resolve all problems of dire poverty and hunger merely by some automatic "trickle down" of benefits toward the most vulnerable.

However, many of these more optimistic writers do not think that population growth is an insuperable barrier to economic growth. The most optimistic even argue that various countries are held back economically not by excess but by sparse population. More commonly, they think reduction in population growth rates is feasible. They point out that reduced fertility rates have generally succeeded rather than preceded economic growth. The demographic transition of the now developed world was not the prelude to but a result of increasing standards of living. They point out that, for the very poor, large families may appear an asset rather than a liability. Their children have a shorter period of economic dependence than children in more developed areas, and only children can provide for old age or illness or other contingencies which in richer countries may be handled by social or private insurance schemes. Developmentalists think that Third World populations will undergo a demographic transition *only when they begin to be less poor.* Trying to achieve economic growth by limiting population growth is going about the problem the wrong way round. "Prudence" in having children cannot be expected of those who can best secure their future by having many children.[11]

Developmentalists also view the present economic plight of poorer countries less as a natural inevitability, to which these countries must prudently adapt their expectations and their population growth, and more as the result of changeable economic and political structures. Many point out that the poverty of specific Third World countries is in part due to a history of colonialism, under which these economies stagnated because the imperial power either prevented or discouraged certain forms of trade or manufacture, or encouraged the production of goods that did not compete with the industries of the developed world (such as palm oil, coffee, rubber, and other tropical agricultural products that were often grown on the plantation system). While the *political* independence of former colonies is now virtually complete, the trade and economic policies of former imperial powers and other powerful developed nations often hinder development.

Developmentalist writers disagree not only about the detailed interpretation of the sources of economic vulnerability of Third World economies but also about the best strategy for economic progress and the part that redistribution has to play in it. Some stress the unnecessary consumption of developed countries and the grotesque size of their armaments expenditure, and the resulting possibilities for redistribution of resources. But many are unsure how these resources can be redistributed to the benefit of those whose poverty puts them at risk of famine.

One common view has been that policies stressing foreign aid, and in particular food aid, have a major part to play in overcoming the risk of famine. What could seem more sensible than the provision of food from the unsaleable agricultural surpluses of wealthier temperate-zone nations, particularly in North America and western Europe? But while such aid clearly benefits the farmers of the developed world, its impact on the Third World is often ambiguous. Food relieves hunger; in some emergencies, only the rapid delivery of food can prevent famine deaths. But when free or subsidized grain is standardly available, marginal farmers in poor regions may be unable to sell their crops; they may stop growing grain and even migrate to the shantytowns of Third World cities, where their chance of sharing in food aid is greater but their prospects of economic progress may be slight. Over the last twenty years, more and more countries have become dependent on food imports and food aid, especially in Africa.[12] The transfer of food can harm even when it is intended to benefit.

Many developmentalist writers have therefore focused less on the (far from simple) policy of transferring food to those who are hungry than on the (even more complex) requirements for achieving economic development within Third World countries. The underlying thought is the simple one expressed in the proverb often quoted by famine relief agencies: Give a man a fish and you feed him for a day; teach a man to fish and he will be fed for life. The proverb may have an obvious interpretation in a simple and traditional social world; but its interpretation in an interdependent world is no more obvious than the interpretation of the parable of the good Samaritan. Economic development needs capital investment, technological innovation, and trading opportunities. All three are scarce or difficult to acquire for most Third World countries. Poor countries cannot easily raise large capital sums for developmental projects: their problem is, after all, precisely that they still lack a developed economy in which there is accumulated capital. But they can attract international capital only if they offer comparatively favorable investment opportunities. Investment then has to reflect criteria other than those of need. For example, if irrigation or rural development projects would meet more needs but offer little return on investment, investment will not be in these areas; but if selling luxury goods to the small urban elite who already have more than subsistence incomes is profitable, then such less needed development will attract investment.

Technological innovation, even if successful, may not benefit most those who need most. For example, "miracle" strains of rice or wheat may need fertilizer and irrigation that only wealthier farmers can afford. Agricultural mechanization may reduce opportunities for work and earnings for the landless poor.

Trading opportunities nowadays are internationally regulated, and the developed world can often meet its own needs more cheaply without trading with Third World countries (except for a few tropical products). Even when Third World products are cheaper, developed countries may prevent their import, since competition from "cheap labor" is not acceptable to the high-earning workers of richer countries.

In spite of these difficulties, developmentalist writers argue that there is no more fundamental reason why the Third World should remain poverty-stricken forever than there was in the case of the developed world. Development is *always* difficult. It is true that Third World countries lack both colonies, whose imports they can keep cheap or whose markets they can preserve for their own industry, and a frontier or colonies for their own expanding population, and they do not control the international economic order. However, they have some advantages. Many forms of technology, including contraceptive technology, are already developed; there are interests and groups within the developed world that seek global development and are prepared to argue and agitate for aid, trade, and other policies that may help Third World countries develop. Above all, it is now well established that economic development and a better-than-subsistence standard of life can be reached by whole populations. We can no longer take it as given that "the poor are always with us."

## §12 SOCIAL AND MORAL INQUIRY

This brief account of issues that distinguish Malthusian and developmentalist perspectives on famine and world hunger may suggest that problems of famine aren't primarily *moral* problems at all. The controversies just mentioned arise within various lines of social inquiry; they are controversies between economists, demographers, political analysts and others. However, this does not show that we can do without moral inquiry into problems of famine. At most we might conclude that serious moral inquiry must take account of the divisions between different approaches to social and political inquiry and that it may not reach conclusions about some matters until these economic and social issues are better understood. We cannot, however, conclude that famine and world hunger are "purely" economic or demographic or social problems, to which moral inquiry is irrelevant. Even if we had complete social knowledge, for example, we would still need to work out what to do about famine and the risk of famine. We shall now consider whether either Kantian or utilitarian ethical reasoning can help us do so.

# III UTILITARIAN APPROACHES TO FAMINE QUESTIONS

## §13 SCIENTIFIC AND HUMANE UTILITARIANISM

The first person to call himself a utilitarian was an eighteenth-century polemicist and philosopher named Jeremy Bentham (1748–1832). Bentham is now best known for having written a work with the forbidding title *Introduction to the Principles of Morals and of Legislation*. But his aim was anything but forbidding. What he wanted was to increase human happiness, and he hoped that legal and moral reform undertaken in a systematic and organized way would do so. His object, he wrote, was "to rear the fabric of felicity by the hands of reason and law." The first principle of this task he called the Principle of Utility, and he meant by this

> . . . that principle which approves or disapproves of every action whatsoever, according to the tendency which it appears to have to augment or diminish the happiness of the party whose interest is in question.[13]

If faced with a decision, we should, according to Bentham's moral theory, ask ourselves which act will most increase the happiness of those affected. Legislators should ask which law would make the total happiness of those who have to live under it greatest. If we can discover the act or law that will do most for the happiness of the affected parties, then we have found the act that is right and required.

If we accept the Principle of Utility, we will solve all moral problems by working out which of the many courses of action we might take will produce the most happiness. This course of action is obligatory, and if more than one action is likely to yield maximal happiness, then it would be obligatory to do one or other of them, though perhaps not morally important which was picked.

Bentham realized that his theory required decision makers to go through long calculations in order to work out which available action (or legislation) would produce the greatest happiness. He was undaunted. He thought we could list all available courses of action, work out how much happiness each would produce, and then choose the happiness-maximizing action. He pointed out seven different aspects of happiness or pleasure that calculations should reckon with. If an act would affect only oneself, then one should consider the *intensity* of the pleasure or happiness; its *duration;* its *certainty* or *uncertainty* (counting unlikely pleasures like winning lotteries at a lower rate than sure things); its *propinquity* or *remoteness* (counting the pleasures we expect to enjoy soon at a higher rate); its *fecundity*, by which he meant its likelihood of being followed by more, similar pleasures; and its *purity*, which is the degree to which the pleasure is unmixed with pain. If an act would affect others as well as oneself, it becomes necessary to work out the pleasure's *extent* also, which is the number of persons who will be affected pleasurably or painfully by the proposed act. Bentham realized that using this "felicific calculus" would be strenuous: he even provided a mnemonic poem to help us to remember what we should take into account:

> *Intense, long, certain, speedy, fruitful, pure*—
> Such marks in *pleasures* and in *pains* endure.
> Such pleasures seek if *private* be thy end;
> If it be *public,* wide let them *extend.* [14]

But this is really not enough. Bentham's calculus requires us to make calculations for which we *nearly always* lack the necessary lists and information. We are standardly unsure which actions are available and can draw up only a short list of the more obvious candidates. We often don't know how much happiness an act or policy will produce, and how much unhappiness. In fact, we don't know who will be affected, to what extent, or for how long. Bentham apparently didn't find this sort of problem baffling. He was lifelong in the thick of political controversy, taking determined stands in favor of one or another proposal for reform on the basis of utility calculations he felt able to make. He agitated tirelessly for reform of harsh and pointless laws, for the extension of the franchise, and for the abolition of slavery. When he died in 1832, some of the reforms he had advocated had already been enacted by the British Parliament; others were fought for and achieved in the following decades.

If we assess Bentham's system soberly and discount some of his enthusiasm, we might conclude that its scope is large and that it aims at precision. But we may also think that some of this precision is spurious, for two reasons. First, it is unclear whether we can make the sort of quantifiable judgments about amounts of happiness and suffering and the probable outcomes of various lines of action that such calculations presuppose. Second, it is not clear whether such calculations, even if precise, are an accurate moral guide.

Bentham's successors, including some of his warmest admirers, have often been skeptical about the felicific calculus. Many have thought that his general picture was not inaccurate, but that he aimed for an unattainable and unneeded degree of precision. Sometimes they also worried that these precise calculations could lead to morally repugnant conclusions. Could utilitarianism, which makes beneficence basic, be acceptable if it implies that happiness for some can legitimately cost suffering for others (provided the suffering is outweighed)? Or are considerations of justice not equally fundamental? Might there not be an alternative form of utilitarianism that retains the wide scope and underlying commitment to human happiness of Bentham's approach but does not lead to repugnant conclusions or to spurious and unneeded precision?

A more humane conception of utilitarianism was first formulated by John Stuart Mill (1806–1873), Bentham's most famous successor, whose main work in ethics has as its very title the word 'utilitarianism'. Like Bentham, Mill took as his fundamental moral principle the Greatest Happiness Principle. He formulated it as follows: "Actions are right in proportion as they tend to promote happiness, wrong as they tend to produce the reverse of happiness."[15] Mill had grown up in Bentham's shadow as the heir to his reforming crusade, but he was not merely a disciple. He doubted that precise calculations about quantities of expected pleasure or happiness could be made. Pleasures, he thought, may vary in qualitative as well as in quantifiable respects. But if some pleasures are of higher quality than others, they can no more be added together than we can add Mill's height to Bentham's weight. We can add together only those quantities that are expressed in the same units, or in units that (like inches and centimeters) can be reduced to one another. But on Mill's view some pleasures are *irreducibly* superior to others. He wrote: "It is better to be a human being dissatisfied than a pig satisfied; better to be Socrates dissatisfied than a fool satisfied."[16] However intense, long, or fruitful the swinish or foolish pleasures are, they do not (on Mill's view) outweigh the pleasures of a nobler or more reflective life. This, he thinks, is shown by the fact that those who have tried both sorts of pleasures prefer the "higher" ones. This shift amounts to a rejection of "scientific" utilitarianism, with its striving for calculable precision; it also provides a way in which other and less explicitly formulated considerations can influence utilitarian reasoning.

The differences between Bentham and Mill did not end the influence of utilitarianism in moral and social thought but rather divided it into two streams. Some, including many economists and decision theorists, still hope for calculable precision in handling problems. These "scientific" utilitarians often find that their arguments lead to conclusions that appear morally repugnant. The staunchest of them are prepared to conclude that if *that* is where the theory leads, then hesitations and distaste must be set aside and the theory followed. But there are probably more utilitarians, especially among those who write on moral and political problems, who take their utilitarianism in a "humane" rather than a "scientific" way. They accept that precise calculations of expected happiness are impossible. They think it enough if utilitarianism achieves a tolerable accuracy in its implications. Their principal problem is that in throwing out methods of calculation, they have also thrown out the means for resolving disagreements between different utilitarians and so raise the question whether a humane form of utilitarianism can be accurate enough to be an acceptable moral theory. However, before discussing some general problems of "humane" forms of utilitarianism, it is useful to consider some of the ways in which it can be applied to famine problems.

## §14 SOME UTILITARIAN FAMINE CONTROVERSIES

No disagreement over famine and world hunger could be more fundamental than one between (1) those who think that either individual
citizens or social groups in the developed world are morally required
to take an active part in trying to reduce and end the poverty of the
Third World and (2) those who think that they are morally required
not to do so. Yet utilitarian arguments have been offered for both
conclusions. These arguments between utilitarians show how far all
utilitarian reasoning depends on comprehensive, yet often elusive,
calculations of consequences. In this section I shall describe some of
the disputes that have arisen between utilitarian writers on famine
questions. In the next section I shall consider some implications of
these disputes for the utilitarian enterprise.

One well-known utilitarian dispute about famine has been between the basically Malthusian perspective of Garrett Hardin and the
more optimistic, developmentalist perspectives of other utilitarian
writers. For the latter position I shall draw particularly on Peter
Singer's influential article, "Famine, Affluence and Morality".[17]

Hardin's argument may be summarized as follows: the citizens of
developed countries are like the passengers of a lifeboat around which
other, desperate people are swimming. Those in the lifeboats can
rescue some of the drowning. But if the affluent rescue some of the
starving, this will—unlike many lifeboat rescues—have bad consequences. It will mean that the affluent world will then have a smaller
safety margin. While this might in the short run be outweighed by the
added happiness and benefit of those who have been rescued, the
longer-run effects are grim. The rescued will assume that they are
secure; they will multiply, and next time that similar dangers arise
they will be more numerous and rescue will not be possible. It is
better, from a utilitarian point of view, to lose some lives now than to
lose more lives later. So it would be morally wrong to rescue those who
are desperate, and the starving must be left to starve.

Hardin's use of the lifeboat analogy has often been criticized.
Those in lifeboats risk a lot by attempting rescues: they may be
swamped. Anybody in a lifeboat faces genuine emergency. There are
also well-understood, if rough and ready, principles for allocating
spaces in lifeboats. Those in the boats may be entitled to their seats,
and they have no options except to stay put or to give up everything.
The affluent are in a different position. They may risk little in trying
to help the hungry, they may lack clear title to all that they have
(perhaps, for example, some of it has been acquired by unjust exploitation of parts of the Third World), and there are many ways in which
they can give up something without sacrificing everything. Hardin
does not take these points seriously because he thinks that the longer-
term balancing of beneficial and harmful results of attempting to help

the Third World point the other way. He holds that the rescued will increase their numbers imprudently, so that, on a finite globe, resources will ultimately be too scarce for everyone to survive (whatever assumptions we make about the rate of depletion). His crucial claim is that famine-relief efforts encourage population growth to a point that cannot be indefinitely sustained. If we pool resources, we shall all be in the same boat; the boat will not be stormworthy, but we will have sailed into stormy waters. He writes:

> If poor countries received no food aid from outside, the rate of their population growth would be periodically checked by crop failures and famines. But if they can always draw on a world food bank in time of need, their population can continue to grow unchecked, and so will their "need" for aid. In the short run a world food bank may diminish that need, but in the long run it actually increases the need without limit.[18]

From this perspective it follows that the prosperous ought, if they are utilitarians, to leave the starving to themselves to die or survive as best they may.

Singer's utilitarianism, by contrast, leads to interventionist conclusions. He starts from the standard utilitarian assumption that "if it is in our power to prevent something bad from happening, without thereby sacrificing anything of comparable moral importance, we ought, morally, to do it."[19] He then points out that contributions to famine relief, even if they amount to a large proportion of our income —say 50 percent—do not sacrifice anything of moral importance comparable to that of the famine they relieve. Hunger and starvation cause far greater suffering than the loss of minor luxuries: compare the results of doing without half your food with the results of doing without a car. So he concludes that the prosperous, even the modestly prosperous, ought to help feed the hungry and to give up their affluence until they have so reduced their own standard of living that any further giving would sacrifice "something of comparable moral importance."

Singer's position, like that of many other writers who bring a utilitarian moral perspective to famine issues, suggests that the most basic obligation of the prosperous is to provide food for the hungry. Our first task must be to give—individually or collectively—and to provide the food the starving need. More recently this claim has been challenged from within the famine-relief movement itself. Tony Jackson, an Oxfam food aid consultant, has argued in *Against the Grain* that giving food doesn't always benefit the starving.

Food aid commonly takes two forms. There is government-to-government food aid, which Third World governments obtain from food surplus countries and sell in their own countries. This food aid constitutes a form of budget and more general political support for Third World governments, and its harmful effects are often noted. It may do more to support a government that is failing to address needs than it does to meet those needs. The second form of food aid, so-called project food aid, is mostly channeled through the World Food Programme and various voluntary agencies. This food aid represents the very sort of action to relieve the greatest suffering that Peter Singer advocates on utilitarian grounds. To be sure, it is insufficient to meet all the food needs of the hungry and does not come near to costing the affluent anything of "comparable moral importance." But it is a considerable step toward the sort of transfer of needed resources that Singer advocates.

Jackson disagrees with Singer, not because he thinks the affluent should do nothing to meet the needs of the starving but because he thinks that providing food aid—even project food aid, which is intended to get the food where it is needed—has been shown to harm the needy. Project food aid competes with local food production, depriving vulnerable farmers of their living and driving them into the cities. Third World food production is then decreased rather than increased. Moreover, the food that is given often fails to reach those whose need is greatest and is diverted by others; where receipt of food aid is linked to some development project, the project is often distorted in order to spin out receipt of food aid. In some cases food-aid dependence is institutionalized and development hindered rather than helped. Apart from genuine short-term emergencies, such as the plight of refugees or results of sudden natural catastrophes, the provision of food aid often does more to benefit the prosperous farmers of the developed world, whose surplus is bought at subsidized prices, than it does to help the Third World. So the enormous international effort that goes into providing food aid preempts other and possibly more effective moves. In Jackson's view the final result is that "the food aid tail wags the development dog."[20] He comments that:

> On the surface project food aid seems to provide a morally and politically acceptable way of sharing the fruits of overproduction in the North with those in need in the South. Because of its appeal at this simple level . . . food aid's inherent weaknesses have been overlooked. But donors must recognise its ineffectiveness and the damage it can cause. . . .
>
> It has been assumed up to now that food aid is needed because there is a shortage of food in the Third World. The Third World is thus seen as a vast refugee camp with hungry people lining up for food from the global food aid soup kitchen. This view is false. Some disasters aside (and these are important areas for food aid), the basic problem is not one of food, but of poverty. Free handouts of food do not address this problem, they aggravate it.[21]

In Jackson's view the advocates of food aid have been mesmerized by their own publicity efforts. They have presented the Third World as a vast refugee camp—and have then pursued a remedy that would be appropriate in such a camp. Like Malthusian lifeboaters, the very differently motivated advocates of food aid have been blinded by their own lurid vision of global catastrophe.

## §15 RESOLVING UTILITARIAN DISPUTES ABOUT FAMINE

The radically different policy conclusions reached by different utilitarian arguments about famine policy raise sharp dilemmas. What implications do they have for the acts and policies that utilitarians should advocate or work for?

One view might be that these disputes can be settled once more social and economic information is available. Some writers think that the absent information can be acquired. For example, Hardin has been much criticized for treating projections of present rates of population growth as predictions. Projections provide predictions only if we know that all relevant factors are constant—which we don't in demographic or other social contexts. Since Hardin wrote, a number of more developed Third World countries have experienced reduced fertility. This suggests that reduced poverty is indeed a precondition of fertility control and not an incentive to "imprudent breeding," and that there are no sufficient reasons for doubting that a demographic transition will take place in the Third World *provided there is development.* Equally, we might think that new information provided by the problems of food-aid programs requires utilitarians now to advocate only development-oriented policies with Jackson rather than embracing Singer's more general advocacy of aid, including food aid.

Humane utilitarians would often back these specific claims with the more general point that it is unreasonable to look for total precision in moral reasoning.[22] However, precision is one thing and accuracy another. While we surely can and must do without complete precision in judgments about results, we can do nothing within a consequential pattern of thought when we cannot assess results either precisely or imprecisely. We have always to get along with what information we have, and we must accept that our conclusions will be subject to error and may need revision in the light of later and more precise information. However, the sort of disputes we have just considered reflect more than imprecision. Hardin, Singer, and Jackson point to *radically* different action and policies. If Hardin is right, Singer advocated not merely a suboptimal but a gravely wrong line of action, and conversely. Similarly if Jackson is right, both Hardin and Singer advocate action and policies that not merely could be improved but are actually wrong because likely to produce much more suffering and less benefit than alternative policies.

What, then, is a conscientious utilitarian to do? It is no answer to do nothing, since inaction itself might cause great harm. But if action is undertaken in the light of an inaccurate understanding of likely results, even with the best of motives, may we not cause more harm than by inaction? Is it enough to say that since matters are uncertain, we ought to do the best we can in the light of our understanding of the situation?

These thoughts may lead us back to an appreciation of the point of Bentham's advocacy of "scientific" utilitarianism. If we really could perform Benthamite calculations, then we could settle utilitarian disputes about famine and world hunger. But, as we have now seen, the Benthamite calculations would be available only if we had a full and accurate (even if not very precise) scientific understanding of the working of the global economy as well as complete demographic and political sciences. "Humane" utilitarians try to substitute approximate judgments for calculation. As a result, their reasoning may reach very varied conclusions. The action or policy that appears optimal in one line of utilitarian calculation may not even figure as available in another.

The long historical association between utilitarian moral thought and some social "sciences" (especially economics) runs very deep. Precisely because *results* are fundamental in utilitarian moral thinking, it is deeply dependent on accurate (even if imprecise) information about likely results. If we lack such information, we may do the utilitarian right thing by our lights yet fail to do what a utilitarian ought, given the actual situation, to do. The outcome may be not just a certain imprecision in utilitarian thinking but a radical diversity of conclusions, which could be overcome only by a genuinely scientific knowledge of society making it possible to predict the fundamental and long-term results of available action and policies.

It is not surprising that utilitarians disagree over famine and development policies. For utilitarians, it is *results* and not *principles* or *intentions* that count. The calculation of results must therefore be taken seriously and isn't adequate if it neglects remote and long-term consequences in global deliberations. Even if utilitarian thinking is accurate enough for settling personal dilemmas, where remote and long-term consequences aren't always so important, it is not accurate enough to guide either individual or institutional action on global problems.

If we are to work out the consequences of alternative available actions and policies, as utilitarianism demands, we shall repeatedly find ourselves confronted with impossible calculations. While accepting that precision is not generally possible or required in these matters, we cannot dispense with some accurate way of listing available options and the general character of the results of each. But our capacity to make accurate, if imprecise, judgments is on the whole restricted to matters that are relatively close at hand. We lack the sort of social science that provides an exhaustive list of available options or gives a generally accurate account of the long-term and overall likely results of each. Yet problems of world hunger, possible famine, and future population and resource growth cannot be considered without attending to the longer-term global results of available courses of action. If utilitarians lack a science of society and have only a limited ability to foresee results, they may have no general way to decide whether a proposed action or policy is morally required, forbidden, or neither.

## §16 UTILITARIANS ON JUSTICE AND BENEFICENCE

Some of the difficulty in utilitarian thinking which we have just considered may arise from the ambitious character of utilitarian thought. The very scope of utilitarian theory creates difficulties when predictions cannot be made with even approximate assurance. Might it not then be feasible to secure *parts* of utilitarian theory by giving up the claim that its scope is comprehensive? If we cannot generally deal with global and long-term problems because our knowledge of likely consequences is restricted to local and immediate results, which we can judge with reasonable accuracy, may we not reduce the scope of utilitarian reasoning so that it becomes unnecessary to make accurate assessments of the long-term and global results of all available lines of action?

Many moral theories draw some distinction between a limited core of action that is stringently required and a broader range of action that is not so strictly required. Action of the former sort is said to be a matter of *perfect duty;* action of the latter sort is seen as a matter of *imperfect duty.* Perfect duties to others are usually thought to be a matter of justice and respect, to whose performance others have a right. Imperfect duties are often thought to be a matter of beneficence, to whose performance nobody has a right. John Stuart Mill claims that utilitarians too can make this distinction. If he is right, utilitarian thinking may be able to make some claims about what is strictly due to others, even if there is no accurate social science, provided that we are able to foresee long-term and global results of a certain range of action.

If the duties of justice form a separate category for utilitarians, then a utilitarian approach can at least determine matters where others have a right to our performance. Duties of justice include both cases where all others have such a right (for example, a duty not to assault others) and cases where only specified others have such a right (for example, a duty to fulfill a promise or contract). Perfect duties of the first sort correspond to others' liberty rights: where A has a duty not to assault others, everyone has a right to be free of assault by A. Perfect duties of the second sort correspond to others' claim rights: where A has a duty to provide food for B, B (but not just anyone) has the right to be fed by A. By contrast, imperfect duties do not generate any rights in others; they are owed neither to all others nor to specifiable others. For example, if A has an imperfect duty to be kind or helpful to some (unspecified) others, nobody would be wronged by nonperformance, although A would do wrong in leading a life devoid of kind or helpful acts.

Mill was not the first to think justice more fundamental than beneficence. This is a much older claim that he fitted into utilitarian thought. The trouble is that borrowed clothes do not always fit well. Utilitarianism is, after all, a theory claiming that *all* right action is basically a matter of beneficence—that is, of producing happy results. From the start, skeptics have believed that utilitarian thinking cannot show what we ordinarily think matters of justice—where others have rights to our performance—to be either distinct from or of more moral significance than other sorts of duty. But if Mill is right and the distinction can be made within utilitarian thought, we may be able to isolate and make utilitarian calculations for the most important moral decisions.

## §17 GLOBAL JUSTICE IN A UTILITARIAN FRAMEWORK

The central problem in trying to find a determinate conception of justice within a humane utilitarian framework is that utilitarian thinking starts from a single foundation, namely, efficient contribution to human happiness. All duties are initially to be seen as duties of beneficence, but some of them are then said to be more stringently owed than others because they standardly affect human happiness more. Hence the claim to distinguish a core of justice within the class of beneficent acts requires us to pick out action that *standardly* produces more happiness or that *standardly* produces more misery. Acts of the first sort will be required as just; acts of the latter sort would be forbidden as unjust. Mill claimed in the final chapter of *Utilitarianism* that:

> Justice is a name for certain moral requirements, which, regarded collectively, stand higher in the scale of social utility, and are therefore of more paramount obligation, than any others.[23]

He is no doubt correct that some obligations are more important for utilitarians than are others. It is not so clear whether any of the traditional categories of obligation can be said to be *standardly* more productive of utility. In particular, it is unclear whether there can be any general arguments to show that what has traditionally been thought a matter of justice is more important than beneficence. Mill himself allowed that there were situations in which what is conventionally seen as just does not produce the greatest available happiness; and so on utilitarian grounds another act or policy is to be preferred. He wrote:

> Particular cases may occur in which some other social duty is so important as to overrule any one of the general maxims of justice.

> Thus, to save a life, it may not only be allowable, but a duty, to steal, or take by force, the necessary food or medicine, or to kidnap and compel to officiate the only medical practioner.[24]

Clearly Mill (and other utilitarians) don't think that what is conventionally thought just will *always* turn out to be most important on utilitarian grounds. We may not be able to pick out *any* central core of perfect duties to which utilitarians are stringently bound. When all duties are fundamentally a matter of beneficence, our only obligation is to do whatever is needed to maximize happiness. If the best way to reduce acute misery is to confiscate from the rich, or to enforce stringent rationing for everyone, or to institute benevolent dictatorships, or to reduce the numbers of the poor by draconian population planning measures, then these are the measures that a utilitarian must see as stringently required duties. Utilitarian reasons have been given for everything from "Robin Hood" strategies of redistribution to complete "hands off" attitudes to the poorest, who are not to be helped, lest the long-term result be more mouths and yet scarcer resources and so less happiness. Utilitarians can settle their debates over these varied actions and policies if, but only if, they know the appropriate laws of social science—not necessarily with complete precision but with sufficient accuracy to settle debates over which of various wholly incompatible policies is likely to maximize human happiness.

If utilitarians cannot draw a clear distinction between the requirements of beneficence and those of justice, we cannot hope for more accuracy in matters of justice than the theory as a whole offers us. Even over the most urgent and perplexing questions—for example the choice between centrally planned and market forms of economic organization, or the choice between alternative major development projects, or between providing food aid or refusing it in favor of development assistance—the theory may often be not merely imprecise but so inaccurate that it cannot guide our action.

Utilitarianism is an appealing theory for anyone who wants to deliberate morally about famine problems. Its scope is comprehensive and it offers a pattern of reasoning which, if we could get appropriate information, would give us accurate and precise resolution of moral problems. It appears to offer both institutions and individuals a method of discovering which available act or policy is best (hence morally obligatory), which next best, and so on. The difficulty is that the data utilitarians need are *usually* not available. Indeed, they could be available in the required form only if social scientists provided us with a comprehensive account of the available acts and their various results. While social science offers us only partial knowledge, utilitarian reasoning may go wildly astray. The range of options thought available may not even include the most important ones, and the calculations by which options are ranked may lead not merely to imprecise but to wholly inaccurate ranking of these options. At best, "humane" forms of utilitarian reasoning will be able to pick out certain types of action as likely to produce harmful or beneficial immediate results. This sort of conclusion can often be of great value, but it won't resolve all our perplexities about famine problems. The ambitious character of utilitarian thinking in the abstract is not sustained in determinate contexts. Where such reasoning is silent, we may have to look in other directions. For utilitarians cannot, without a science of society, establish more specific moral principles, such as conventional principles of justice.

## IV KANTIAN APPROACHES TO SOME FAMINE PROBLEMS

The second moral theory whose scope and determinacy in dealing with famine problems I shall consider was developed by the German philosopher Immanuel Kant (1724–1804). I shall offer a simplified version of Kantian ethics[25] in §18 through §22. In §23 through §25 I shall set out some of its implications for action toward those who are at risk of famine, and from §26 onward I shall summarize some differences between utilitarian and Kantian ethics.

### §18 A SIMPLIFIED ACCOUNT OF KANT'S ETHICS

Kant's theory is frequently and misleadingly assimilated to theories of human rights. It is, in fact, a theory of human obligations; therefore it is wider in scope than a theory of human rights. (Not all obligations generate corresponding rights.) Kant does not, however, try to generate a set of precise rules defining human obligations in all possible circumstances; instead, he attempts to provide a set of *principles of obligation* that can be used as the starting points for moral reasoning in actual contexts of action. The primary focus of Kantian ethics is, then, on *action* rather than either *results,* as in utilitarian thinking, or *entitlements,* as in theories that make human rights their fundamental category. Morality requires action of certain sorts. But to know *what* sort of action is required (or forbidden) in which circumstances, we should not look just at the expected results of action or at others' supposed entitlements but, in the first instance, at the nature of the proposed actions themselves.

When we engage in moral reasoning, we often need go no further than to refer to some quite specific principle or tradition. We may say to one another, or to ourselves, things like "It would be hypocritical to pretend that our good fortune is achieved without harm to the Third World" or "Redistributive taxation shouldn't cross national boundaries." But when these specific claims are challenged, we may find ourselves pushed to justify or reject or modify them. Such moral debate, on Kant's account, rests on appeals to what he calls the *Su-*

preme *Principle of Morality,* which can (he thinks) be used to work out more specific principles of obligation. This principle, the famous Categorical Imperative, plays the same role in Kantian thinking that the Greatest Happiness Principle plays in utilitarian thought.

A second reason why Kant's moral thought often appears difficult is that he offers a number of different versions of this principle, that he claims are equivalent, but which look very different. A straightforward way in which to simplify Kantian moral thought is to concentrate on just one of these formulations of the Categorical Imperative. For present purposes I shall choose the version to which he gives the sonorous name of *The Formula of the End in Itself.*

## §19 THE FORMULA OF THE END IN ITSELF

The "Formula of the End in Itself" runs as follows:

> Act in such a way that you always treat humanity, whether in your own person or in the person of any other, never simply as a means but always at the same time as an end.[26]

To understand this principle we need in the first place to understand what Kant means by the term *maxim.* The maxim of an act or policy or activity is the *underlying principle* of the act, policy or activity, by which other, more superficial aspects of action are guided. Very often interpretations of Kant have supposed that maxims can only be the (underlying) intentions of individual human agents. If that were the case it would limit the usefulness of Kantian modes of moral thought in dealing with world hunger and famine problems. For it is clear enough that individual action (while often important) cannot deal with all the problems of Third World poverty. A moral theory that addresses *only* individual actors does not have adequate scope for discussing famine problems. As we have seen, one of the main attractions of utilitarianism as an approach to Third World poverty was that its scope is so broad: it can be applied with equal appropriateness to the practical deliberations of individuals, of institutions and groups, and even of nation states and international agencies. Kantian ethical thinking can be interpreted (though it usually isn't) to have equally broad scope.

Since maxims are *underlying* principles of action, they may not always be obvious either to the individuals or institutions whose maxims they are, or to others. We can determine what the underlying principles of some activity or institution are only by seeing the patterns made by various more superficial aspects of acts, policies and activities. Only those principles that would generate that pattern of activity are maxims of action. Sometimes more than one principle might lie behind a given pattern of activity, and we may be unsure what the maxim of the act was. For example, we might wonder (as Kant does) how to tell whether somebody gives change accurately only out of concern to have an honest reputation or whether he or she would do so anyhow. In such cases we can sometimes set up an "isolation test"—for example, a situation in which it would be open to somebody to be dishonest without any chance of a damaged reputation. But quite often we can't set up any such situation and may be to some extent unsure which maxim lies behind a given act. Usually we have to rely on whatever individual actors tell us about their maxims of action and on what policymakers or social scientists may tell us about the underlying principles of institutional or group action. What they tell us may well be mistaken. While mistakes can be reduced by care and thoughtfulness, there is no guarantee that we can always work out which maxim of action should be scrutinized in the light of the Categorical Imperative.

It is helpful to think of some examples of maxims that might be used to guide action in contexts where poverty and the risk of famine are issues. Somebody who contributes to famine-relief work or advocates development might have an underlying principle such as, "Try to help reduce the risk or severity of world hunger." This commitment might be reflected in varied surface action in varied situations. In one context a gift of money might be relevant; in another some political activity such as lobbying for or against certain types of aid and trade might express the same underlying commitment. Sometimes superficial aspects of action may seem at variance with the underlying maxim they in fact express. For example, if there is reason to think that indiscriminate food aid damages the agricultural economy of the area to which food is given, then the maxim of seeking to relieve famine might be expressed in action aimed at limiting the extent of food aid. More lavish use of food aid might *seem* to treat the needy more generously, but if in fact it will damage their medium- or long-term economic prospects, then it is not (contrary to superficial appearances) aimed at improving and securing their access to subsistence. On a Kantian theory, the basis for judging action should be its *fundamental* principle or policy, and superficially similar acts may be judged morally very different. Regulating food aid in order to drive up prices and profit from them is one matter; regulating food aid in order to enable local farmers to sell their crops and to stay in the business of growing food quite another.

When we want to work out whether a proposed act or policy is morally required we should not, on Kant's view, try to find out whether it would produce more happiness than other available acts. Rather we should see whether the act or policy is required by, or ruled out by, or merely compatible with maxims that avoid using others as mere means and maxims that treat others as ends in themselves. These two aspects of Kantian duty can each be spelled out and shown to have determinate implications for acts and policies that may affect the risk and course of famines.

## §20 USING OTHERS AS MERE MEANS

We use others as *mere means* if what we do reflects some maxim *to which they could not in principle consent.* Kant does not suggest that there is anything wrong about using someone as a means. Evidently every cooperative scheme of action does this. A government that agrees to provide free or subsidized food to famine-relief agencies both uses and is used by the agencies; a peasant who sells food in a local market both uses and is used by those who buy it. In such examples each party to the transaction can and does consent to take part in that transaction. Kant would say that the parties to such transactions use one another but do not use one another as *mere* means. Each party assumes that the other has its own maxims of action and is not just a thing or prop to be used or manipulated.

But there are other cases where one party to an arrangement or transaction not only uses the other but does so in ways that could only be done on the basis of a fundamental principle or maxim to which the other could not in principle consent. If a false promise is given, the party that accepts the promise is not just used but used as a mere means, because it is *impossible* for consent to be given to the fundamental principle or project of deception that must guide every false promise, whatever its surface character. Those who accept false promises *must* be kept ignorant of the underlying principle or maxim on which the "undertaking" is based. If this isn't kept concealed, the attempted promise will either be rejected or will not be a *false* promise at all. In false promising the deceived party becomes, as it were, a prop or tool—a *mere* means—in the false promisor's scheme. Action based on any such maxim of deception would be wrong in Kantian terms, whether it is a matter of a breach of treaty obligations, of contractual undertakings, or of accepted and relied upon modes of interaction. Maxims of deception *standardly* use others as mere means, and acts that could only be based on such maxims are unjust.

Another standard way of using others as mere means is by coercing them. Coercers, like deceivers, standardly don't give others the possibility of dissenting from what they propose to do. In deception, "consent" is spurious because it is given to a principle that couldn't be the underlying principle of *that* act at all; but the principle governing coercion may be brutally plain. Here any "consent" given is spurious because there was no option *but* to consent. If a rich or powerful landowner or nation threatens a poorer or more vulnerable person, group, or nation with some intolerable difficulty unless a concession is made, the more vulnerable party is denied a genuine choice between consent and dissent. While the boundary that divides coercion from mere bargaining and negotiation varies and is therefore often hard to discern, we have no doubt about the clearer cases. Maxims of coercion may threaten physical force, seizure of possessions, destruction of opportunities, or any other harm that the coerced party is thought to be unable to absorb without grave injury or danger. A moneylender in a Third World village who threatens not to make or renew an indispensable loan, without which survival until the next harvest would be impossible, uses the peasant as mere means. The peasant does not have the possibility of genuinely consenting to the "offer he can't refuse." The outward form of some coercive transactions may *look* like ordinary commercial dealings: but we know very well that some action that is superficially of this sort is based on maxims of coercion. To avoid coercion, action must be governed by maxims that the other party can choose to refuse and is not bound to accept. The more vulnerable the other party in any transaction or negotiation, the less their scope for refusal, and the more demanding it is likely to be to ensure that action is noncoercive.

In Kant's view, acts done on maxims that coerce or deceive others, so therefore cannot in principle have the consent of those others, are wrong. When individuals or institutions, or nation states act in ways that can only be based on such maxims they fail in their duty. They treat the parties who are either deceived or coerced unjustly. To avoid unjust action it is not enough to observe the outward forms of free agreement and cooperation; it is also essential to see that the weaker party to any arrangement has a genuine option to refuse the fundamental character of the proposal.

## §21 TREATING OTHERS AS ENDS IN THEMSELVES

For Kant, as for utilitarians, justice is only one part of duty. We may fail in our duty, even when we don't use anyone as mere means (by deception or coercion), if we fail to treat others as "ends in themselves." To treat others as "Ends in Themselves" we must not only avoid using them as mere means but also treat them as rational and autonomous beings with their own maxims. If human beings were *wholly* rational and autonomous then, on a Kantian view, duty would require only that they not use one another as mere means. But, as Kant repeatedly stressed, but later Kantians have often forgotten, human beings are *finite* rational beings. They are finite in several ways.

First, human beings are not ideal rational calculators. We *standardly* have neither a complete list of the actions possible in a given situation nor more than a partial view of their likely consequences. In addition, abilities to assess and to use available information are usually quite limited.

Second, these cognitive limitations are *standardly* complemented by limited autonomy. Human action is limited not only by various sorts of physical barrier and inability but by further sorts of (mutual or asymmetrical) dependence. To treat one another as ends in themselves such beings have to base their action on principles that do not undermine but rather sustain and extend one another's capacities for autonomous action. A central requirement for doing so is to share and support one another's ends and activities at least to some extent. Since finite rational beings cannot generally achieve their aims without some help and support from others, a general refusal of help and support amounts to failure to treat others as rational and autonomous beings, that is as ends in themselves. Hence Kantian principles require us not only to act justly, that is in accordance with maxims that don't coerce or deceive others, but also to avoid manipulation and to lend some support to others' plans and activities. Since famine, great poverty and powerlessness all undercut the possibility of autonomous action, and the requirement of treating others as ends in themselves demands that Kantians standardly act to support the possibility of autonomous action where it is most vulnerable, Kantians are required to do what they can to avert, reduce, and remedy famine. On a Kantian view, beneficence is as indispensable as justice in human lives.

### §22 JUSTICE AND BENEFICENCE IN KANT'S THOUGHT

Kant is often thought to hold that justice is morally required, but beneficence is morally less important. He does indeed, like Mill, speak of justice as a *perfect duty* and of beneficence as an *imperfect duty*. But he does not mean by this that beneficence is any less a duty; rather, he holds that it has (unlike justice) to be selective. We cannot share or even support *all* others' maxims *all* of the time. Hence support for others' autonomy is always selective. By contrast we can make all action and institutions conform fundamentally to standards of nondeception and noncoercion. Kant's understanding of the distinction between perfect and imperfect duties differs from Mill's. In a Kantian perspective justice isn't a matter of the core requirements for beneficence, as in Mill's theory, and beneficence isn't just an attractive but optional moral embellishment of just arrangements (as tends to be assumed in most theories that take human rights as fundamental).

### §23 JUSTICE TO THE VULNERABLE IN KANTIAN THINKING

For Kantians, justice requires action that conforms (at least outwardly) to what could be done in a given situation while acting on maxims neither of deception nor of coercion. Since anyone hungry or destitute is more than usually vulnerable to deception and coercion, the possibilities and temptations to injustice are then especially strong.

Examples are easily suggested. I shall begin with some situations that might arise for somebody who happened to be part of a famine-stricken population. Where shortage of food is being dealt with by a reasonably fair rationing scheme, any mode of cheating to get more than one's allocated share involves using some others and is unjust. Equally, taking advantage of others' desperation to profiteer—for example, selling food at colossal prices or making loans on the security of others' future livelihood, when these are "offers they can't refuse" —constitutes coercion and so uses others as mere means and is unjust. Transactions that have the outward form of normal commercial dealing may be coercive when one party is desperate. Equally, forms of corruption that work by deception—such as bribing officials to gain special benefits from development schemes, or deceiving others about their entitlements—use others unjustly. Such requirements are far from trivial and frequently violated in hard times; acting justly in such conditions may involve risking one's own life and livelihood and require the greatest courage.

It is not so immediately obvious what justice, Kantianly conceived, requires of agents and agencies who are remote from destitution. Might it not be sufficient to argue that those of us fortunate enough to live in the developed world are far from famine and destitution, so if we do nothing but go about our usual business will successfully avoid injustice to the destitute? This conclusion has often been reached by those who take an abstract view of rationality and forget the limits of human rationality and autonomy. In such perspectives it can seem that there is nothing more to just action than meeting the formal requirements of nondeception and noncoercion in our dealings with one another. But once we remember the limitations of human rationality and autonomy, and the particular ways in which they are limited for those living close to the margins of subsistence, we can see that mere conformity to ordinary standards of commercial honesty and political bargaining is not enough for justice toward the destitute. If international agreements themselves can constitute "offers that cannot be refused" by the government of a poor country, or if the concessions required for investment by a transnational corporation or a development project reflect the desperation of recipients rather than an appropriate contribution to the project, then (however benevolent the motives of some parties) the weaker party to such agreements is used by the stronger.

In the earlier days of European colonial penetration of the now underdeveloped world it was evident enough that some of the ways in which "agreements" were made with native peoples were in fact deceptive or coercive or both. "Sales" of land by those who had no grasp of market practices and "cession of sovereignty" by those whose forms of life were prepolitical constitute only spurious consent to the agreements struck. But it is not only in these original forms of bargaining between powerful and powerless that injustice is frequent. There are many contemporary examples. For example, if capital investment (private or governmental) in a poorer country requires the receiving country to contribute disproportionately to the maintenance of a developed, urban "enclave" economy that offers little local employment but lavish standards of life for a small number of (possibly expatriate) "experts," while guaranteeing long-term exemption from local taxation for the investors, then we may doubt that the agreement could have been struck without the element of coercion provided by the desperation of the weaker party. Or if a trade agreement extracts political advantages (such as military bases) that are incompatible with the fundamental political interests of the country concerned, we may judge that at least some leaders of that country have been "bought" in a sense that is not consonant with ordinary commercial practice.

Even when the actions of those who are party to an agreement don't reflect a fundamental principle of coercion or deception, the agreement may alter the life circumstances and prospects of third parties in ways to which they patently could not have not consented. For example, a system of food aid and imports agreed upon by the government of a Third World country and certain developed countries or international agencies may give the elite of that Third World country access to subsidized grain. If that grain is then used to control the urban population and also produces destitution among peasants (who used to grow food for that urban population), then those who are newly destitute probably have not been offered any opening or possibility of refusing their new and worsened conditions of life. If a policy is imposed, those affected *cannot* have been given a chance to refuse it: had the chance been there, they would either have assented (and so the policy would not have been *imposed*) or refused (and so proceeding with the policy would have been evidently coercive).

## §24 BENEFICENCE TO THE VULNERABLE IN KANTIAN THINKING

In Kantian moral reasoning, the basis for beneficent action is that we cannot, without it, treat others of limited rationality and autonomy as ends in themselves. This is not to say that Kantian beneficence won't make others happier, for it will do so whenever they would be happier if (more) capable of autonomous action, but that happiness secured by purely paternalistic means, or at the cost (for example) of manipulating others' desires, will not count as beneficent in the Kantian picture. Clearly the vulnerable position of those who lack the very means of life, and their severely curtailed possibilities for autonomous action, offer many different ways in which it might be possible for others to act beneficently. Where the means of life are meager, almost any material or organizational advance may help extend possibilities for autonomy. Individual or institutional action that aims to advance economic or social development can proceed on many routes. The provision of clean water, of improved agricultural techniques, of better grain storage systems, or of adequate means of local transport may all help transform material prospects. Equally, help in the development of new forms of social organization—whether peasant self-help groups, urban cooperatives, medical and contraceptive services, or improvements in education or in the position of women—may help to extend possibilities for autonomous action. Kantian thinking does not provide a means by which all possible projects of this sort could be listed and ranked. But where some activity helps secure possibilities for autonomous action for more people, or is likely to achieve a permanent improvement in the position of the most vulnerable, or is one that can be done with more reliable success, this provides reason for furthering that project rather than alternatives.

Clearly the alleviation of need must rank far ahead of the furthering of happiness in the Kantian picture. I might make my friends very happy by throwing extravagant parties: but this would probably not increase anybody's possibility for autonomous action to any great extent. But the sorts of development-oriented changes that have just been mentioned may *transform* the possibilities for action of some. Since famine and the risk of famine are always and evidently highly damaging to human autonomy, any action that helps avoid or reduce famine must have a strong claim on any Kantian who is thinking through what beneficence requires. Depending on circumstances, such action may have to take the form of individual contribution to famine relief and development organizations, of individual or collective effort to influence the trade and aid policies of developed countries, or of attempts to influence the activities of those Third World elites for whom development does not seem to be an urgent priority. Some activities can best be undertaken by private citizens of developed countries; others are best approached by those who work for governments, international agencies, or transnational corporations. Perhaps the most dramatic possibilities to act for a just or an unjust, a beneficent or selfish future belongs to those who hold positions of influence within the Third World. But wherever we find ourselves, our duties are not, on the Kantian picture, limited to those close at hand. Duties of justice arise whenever there is some involvement between parties—and in the modern world this is never lacking. Duties of beneficence arise whenever destitution puts the possibility of autonomous action in question for the more vulnerable. When famines were not only far away, but nothing could be done to relieve them, beneficence or charity may well have begun—and stayed—at home. In a global village, the moral significance of distance has shrunk, and we may be able to affect the capacities for autonomous action of those who are far away.

## §25 THE SCOPE OF KANTIAN DELIBERATIONS ABOUT FAMINE AND HUNGER

In many ways Kantian moral reasoning is less ambitious than utilitarian moral reasoning. It does not propose a process of moral reasoning that can (in principle) rank *all* possible actions or all possible institutional arrangements from the happiness-maximizing "right" action or institution downward. It aims rather to offer a pattern of reasoning by which we can identify whether *proposed action or institutional ar-*

*rangements* would be just or unjust, beneficent or lacking in beneficence. While *some* knowledge of causal connections is needed for
Kantian reasoning, it is far less sensitive than is utilitarian reasoning
to gaps in our causal knowledge. The conclusions reached about particular proposals for action or about institutional arrangements will
not hold for all time, but be relevant for the contexts for which action
is proposed. For example, if it is judged that some institution—say the
World Bank—provides, under present circumstances, a just approach
to certain development problems, it will not follow that under all
other circumstances such an institution would be part of a just approach. There may be other institutional arrangements that are also
just; and there may be other circumstances under which the institutional structure of the World Bank would be shown to be in some ways
deceptive or coercive and so unjust.

These points show us that Kantian deliberations about famine and
hunger can lead only to conclusions that are useful in determinate
contexts. This, however, is standardly what we need to know for action, whether individual or institutional. We do not need to be able to
generate a complete list of available actions in order to determine
whether proposed lines of action are not unjust and whether any are
beneficent. Kantian patterns of moral reasoning cannot be guaranteed
to identify the optimal course of action in a situation. They provide
methods neither for listing nor for ranking all possible proposals for
action. But any line of action that is considered can be checked.

The reason this pattern of reasoning will not show any action or
arrangement the most beneficent one available is that the Kantian
picture of beneficence is less mathematically structured than the utilitarian one. It judges beneficence by its overall contribution to the
prospects for human autonomy and not by the quantity of happiness
expected to result. To the extent that the autonomous pursuit of goals
is what Mill called "one of the principal ingredients of human happiness" (but only to that extent),[27] the requirements of Kantian and of
utilitarian beneficence will coincide. But whenever expected happiness is not a function of the scope for autonomous action, the two
accounts of beneficent action diverge. For utilitarians, paternalistic
imposition of, for example, certain forms of aid and development
assistance need not be wrong and may even be required. But for
Kantians, whose beneficence should secure others' possibilities for
autonomous action, the case for paternalistic imposition of aid or development projects without the recipients' involvement must always
be questionable.

In terms of some categories in which development projects are
discussed, utilitarian reasoning may well endorse "top-down" aid
and development projects which override whatever capacities for
autonomous choice and action the poor of a certain area now have in
the hopes of securing a happier future. If the calculations work out
in a certain way, utilitarians may even think a "generation of sac-

rifice"—or of forced labor or of imposed population-control policies not only permissible but mandated. In their darkest Malthusian moments some utilitarians have thought that average happiness might best be maximized not by improving the lot of the poor but by minimizing their numbers, and so have advocated policies of "benign neglect" of the poorest and most desperate. Kantian patterns of reasoning are likely to endorse less global and less autonomy-overriding aid and development projects; they are not likely to endorse neglect or abandoning of those who are most vulnerable and lacking in autonomy. If the aim of beneficence is to keep or put others in a position to act for themselves, then emphasis must be placed on "bottom-up" projects, which from the start draw on, foster, and establish indigenous capacities and practices of self-help and local action.

# V. UTILITARIAN AND KANTIAN MORAL REASONING

## §26 RESPECT FOR LIFE IN UTILITARIAN REASONING

In the contrasting utilitarian and Kantian pictures of moral reasoning and of their implications in famine situations we can also discern two sharply contrasting pictures of the value of human life.

Utilitarians, since they value happiness above all, aim to achieve the happiest possible world. If their life plans remain unclear, this is because the means to this end are often unclear. But one implication of this position is entirely clear. It is that if happiness is the supreme value, then anything may and ought to be sacrificed for the sake of a greater happiness. Lesser possibilities of happiness and even life itself ought to be sacrificed to achieve maximal happiness. Such sacrifices may be required even when those whose happiness or lives are sacrificed are not willing. Rearing the fabric of felicity may be a bloody business. It all depends on the causal connections.

As our control over the means of ending and preserving lives has increased, utilitarians have confronted many uncomfortable questions. Should life be preserved at the cost of pain when modern medicine makes this possible? Or will happiness be greater if euthanasia is permitted under certain circumstances? Should the most afflicted be left to starve in famine situations if the happiness of all, and perhaps the average happiness, will be greater if those whose recovery is not likely to be complete are absent? Should population growth be fostered so long as total (or again perhaps average) happiness is increased, even if other sorts of difficulties arise? Should forced labor and enforced redistribution of income across national boundaries be imposed for the sake of a probably happier world? How far ought utilitarians to insist on the sacrifice of comforts, liberties, and even lives in order to "rear the fabric of felicity"?

Utilitarians do not deny that their moral reasoning raises many questions of these sorts. But the imprecision of our knowledge of consequences often blurs the answers to these questions. As we peer through the blur, we can see that on a utilitarian view lives must be sacrificed to build a happier world if this is the most efficient way to do so, whether or not those who lose their lives are willing. There is nothing wrong with using another as mere means, provided that the end in view is a happier result than could have been achieved any other way, taking account of the misery the means may have caused. In utilitarian thinking, persons are not ends in themselves. Their special moral status, such as it is, derives from their being means to the production of happiness. But they are not even necessary means for this end, since happiness can be located in nonhuman lives. It may even turn out that maximal happiness requires the sacrifice of human for the sake of animal lives.

In utilitarian thinking life has a high but derivative value, and some lives may have to be sacrificed for the sake of greater happiness or reduced misery in other lives. Nor is there a deep difference between ending others' lives by not helping (as some Malthusians suggest) and doing so as a matter of deliberate intervention or policy.

## §27 RESPECT FOR LIFE IN KANTIAN REASONING

Kantians reach different conclusions about human life. They see it as valuable because humans have considerable (but still quite incomplete) capacities for autonomous action. There may be other beings with more complete capacities, but we are not acquainted with them. Christian tradition speaks of angels; Kant referred to hypothetical beings he called Holy Wills; writers of science fiction have multiplied the varieties. There are certainly other beings with fewer capacities for autonomous action than humans standardly have. Whether we think that (some) animals should not be used as mere means, or should be treated as ends in themselves, is going to depend on the particular picture we have of partial autonomy and on the capacities we find that certain sorts of animals have or are capable of acquiring. This is a large question, around which I shall put some hasty brackets. It is quite an important issue in working out the famine and development implications of Kantian thinking, since development strategies have different implications for various animal species. For the moment, however, I shall consider only some implications of human capacities for (partially) autonomous action in Kantian thinking on respect for human life in contexts of acute vulnerability, such as destitution and (threatened) hunger.

The fundamental idea behind the Categorical Imperative is that the actions of a plurality of rational beings can be mutually consistent. A minimal condition for their mutual consistency is that each, in acting autonomously, not preclude others' autonomous action. This requirement can be spelled out, as in the formula of the end in itself, by insisting that each avoid action which the other could not freely join in (hence avoid deception and coercion) and that each seek to secure others' capacities for autonomous action. What this actually takes will, as we have seen, vary with circumstances. But it is clear enough that the partial autonomy of human beings is undermined by life-threatening and destroying circumstances, such as famine and destitution. Hence a fundamental Kantian commitment must be to preserve life in two senses. First, others must not be deprived of life. The dead (as well as the moribund, the gravely ill, and the famine-stricken) cannot act. Second, others' lives must be preserved in forms that offer them sufficient physical energy, psychological space, and social security for action. Partial autonomy is vulnerable autonomy, and in human life psychological and social as well as material needs must be met if any but the most meager possibility of autonomous action is to be preserved. Kantians are therefore committed to the preservation not only of biological but of biographical life. To act in the typical ways humans are capable of we must not only be alive, but have a life to lead.

On a Kantian view, we may justifiably—even nobly—risk or sacrifice our lives for others. When we do so, we act autonomously, and nobody uses us as a mere means. But we cannot justly use others (nor they us) as mere means in a scheme that could only be based on some deception or on coercion. Nor may we refuse others the help they need to sustain the very possibility of autonomous action. Of course, no amount of beneficence could put anyone in the position to do all possible actions: that is not what we need to be concerned about. What we do need to be concerned about is failure to secure for others a possibility of some range of autonomous action.

Where others' possibilities for autonomous action are eroded by poverty and malnutrition, the necessary action must clearly include moves to change the picture. But these moves will not meet Kantian requirements if they provide merely calories and basic medicine. The action must also seek to enable those who begin to be adequately fed to act autonomously. It must therefore aim at least at minimal security and subsistence. Hence the changes that Kantians argue or work for must always be oriented to development plans that create enough economic self-sufficiency and social security for independence in action to be feasible and sustainable. There is no royal road to this result and no set of actions that is likely to be either universally or totally effective. Too many changes are needed, and we have too little understanding of the precise causal connections that limit some possibilities and guarantee others. But some indication of ranges of required action, or ranges of action from which at least some are required, is possible.

# VI. PRACTICAL SUGGESTIONS

Moral inquiry is fundamentally a *practical* matter. One of its aims is to help us decide what action we might individually or collectively take or, if we can't get that far, to discover what we should perhaps avoid or what we should aim at. Yet moral discussions often leave us feeling that no practical issue has been resolved. That is probably true of many of the discussions in this book. When we are trying to get our minds around fundamental problems such as *how* we can best reason morally, we are apt not to reach conclusions about activity that should or should not be undertaken. Because famine and world hunger are urgent moral problems, it seems a good idea to finish with a short list of lines of action that may be morally important. Since all these issues are closely dependent on our knowledge of actual situations, I shall offer, in place of a set of recommendations, a list of pertinent questions from which to begin deliberation. The list isn't (and couldn't be) complete.

- A starting point is self-education. Many of us have heard the comment "If you aren't part of the solution, you're part of the problem." Until we know what particular situations arise and how we could affect them, we can't be sure that we aren't part of the problem. So information is a start. Various books are listed in the bibliography here; many more can be found in any library. It is worth considering whether the newspaper you regularly read has good coverage of Third World and development issues. Rather few newspapers in the English-speaking world are good on this. It may be useful to read a different or further magazine or newspaper.
- A second move might be to seek self-awareness of a more practical sort. What is it like to be hungry? How would it affect you? What degree of independence or autonomy would you expect of somebody who was eating only one meal a day? What aspects of your way of life seem wasteful? Which of them can be altered? Which alterations will seriously affect your happiness, and which your capacity for autonomous action? Which could release either funds or resources for others, and which would be only "exemplary" (that is, useful for altering your own awareness but not likely to have a wider impact)?
- A third move might be to help others to gain relevant information and awareness. Which others can you reach effectively? Which sorts of awareness is it most useful to encourage?

These three moves approach the question of action only by emphasizing the need to foster and secure further and effective possibilities for action for those in the developed world. Evidently it is more fundamental if we can foster and secure possibilities of action for those in the Third World. The next group of questions approaches these issues at various levels.

- Can you support the work of a voluntary organization? Is it one that stresses development aims? Or is it mainly involved in providing food aid? How efficient an organization is it? (How much of its funding goes into administration? How would you discover this?)
- Can you work for a voluntary organization? In what capacities? These might range from providing a skill that is needed in some Third World context to providing administrative and fund-raising help on a part-time basis.
- Can you work for another organization that affects the prospects of impoverished economies? For example, can you work for and through a business that has Third World involvements? Would the particular work you might take on be likely to harm or to help the development of the areas where the business is involved? How would you discover this? Where do the profits from this business get reinvested? Where is capital raised? Who can buy the products? What other uses might there be for the same investment capital and skills? How much employment does this business provide? Are its workers adequately paid? What standards of safety are observed? If you were to take such employment, would you have—or come to have—some scope for contributing to the happiness or autonomy of those in need?
- If you cannot join any organization, charitable or commercial, whose work impinges directly on the Third World, could you take part in setting up such an institution? (Some successful voluntary organizations have been set up relatively recently, and not all of them with massive institutional backing, such as that of a church.) Could you provide a market or a service for certain Third World organizations? Are there ways to affect the policies of institutions with which you *are* involved? Can institutions that haven't traditionally been much concerned with questions of world poverty change their interests and activities in that direction? What is it for a corporation or a university or a trades union to be "socially responsible" on a world scale?

No voluntary or commercial organization can affect the basic terms of relations between the developed and the underdeveloped world. But these terms of trade and of other relations aren't fixed by nature either —or even by "the market." Hence it is practical to ask what might be done to alter the international economic and political order in ways that are most conducive to the reduction of disabling poverty and endemic hunger. No individual can produce such changes alone. Political action and cooperation are indispensable if we are to affect basic matters.

- One focus of political involvement can be toward whichever government(s) we can most readily affect. We can examine and criticize our own government's record on foreign aid. How much is given in relation to the population and wealth? How does this compare with the record of the most generous developed nations (such as Norway)? How much of this aid is *really* development aid and how much is used to further the political and military objectives of the donor nation? Are the conditions and strings attached to foreign aid producing good results? Or does aid end up benefiting those in less need who are already able to act autonomously? How much of it goes into rural development? Is any of it earmarked to benefit the businesses of the donor nation, whose products must be purchased? What sorts of projects are being funded? Are they the sort that are most needed? How might effective lobbying for changes in priorities be undertaken?
- Should foreign aid be given only by *international* agencies, so that it is not distorted by the national interest of donor nations? What can be done to prevent Third World governments and officials from using aid arrangements to secure their own political base or personal fortunes, so diverting it from vital uses? What can be done to prevent corrupt misappropriation of aid?
- Are some international trade agreements damaging Third World countries? When can it be helpful to try to organize commodity agreements and cartels to secure the prices of Third World products and give producers some security? What moves can be made to secure better access to international markets for Third World products? What can be done to prevent the dumping of agricultural surpluses by Temperate Zone producers, while avoiding soaring food prices?
- Who can best institute which technical and medical changes? Which changes are really advances, and helpful to many people, and which are only helpful to the better-off classes in poorer countries? Which sorts of contraceptive services, agricultural innovations, and industrial development are actually needed in particular areas if more people are to have some control over their own lives?
- Which sorts of social changes are most vital if the benefits of development are to be shared? Is advance in a given area held back by a system of land tenure? Is it blocked by illiteracy? By the subservient and oppressed status of women or of certain ethnic and religious groups? By the oppressive activity of certain prominent families or religious or tribal leaders? Is the development of financial or legal structures a pressing need?

Practical questions of all these sorts demand answers that take account of detailed information about actual situations. This section has therefore not offered a list of *answers* or of required actions. Working out what to do and to avoid has to be done from the perspective of a particular agent or agency (whether a corporation, a charity, a government or an international agency) with determinate opportunities and abilities to act. Sometimes the information available in the actual context can lead us to some fairly detailed proposals. Sometimes we may find that the available information underdetermines what we might seek to do. Perhaps it will only rule out some possibilities as impermissible, without showing us just what (if anything) is required. But even this can be of practical importance. There is no reason to despair because nobody and no institution can do *everything* to resolve a global problem, particularly if nobody and no institution is prevented from doing *something* to help resolve it.*

## NOTES

1. Luke, 10:5.
2. For background to these comments on scientific theories, see Thomas Kuhn, *The Copernican Revolution: Planetary Astronomy in the Development of Western Thought,* Cambridge, Mass.: Harvard University Press, 1957.
3. Others are more impressed by the promise of a theory of human rights. See, for example, Henry Shue, *Basic Rights: Subsistence, Affluence and U.S. Foreign Policy,* Princeton, N.J., Princeton University Press, 1979. I shall not consider any such approaches as an *alternative* to theories discussed here because I suspect that human rights theories can be adequately defended only if they are embedded *within* a utilitarian or a Kantian approach. In the former framework the notions of good results and of right action are more fundamental than that of "a right," while in the latter the notions of moral worth and of obligatory action are more fundamental. Our understanding of what a right is will depend on the fundamental moral framework within which a theory of human rights is developed.
4. For the background to this summary of famine and hunger issues, see the works listed in the suggested reading for §7, below.
5. *Rev.* 6:5.
6. For a short list of "Malthusian" works and discussions of these views, see the suggested readings for § 9, below.
7. Thomas Malthus, *Summary View of the Principle of Population,* reprinted in *On Population: Three Essays,* ed. F. Notestein, New York: Mentor, 1960, p. 55.
8. Again, see the list under §9 below.
9. This line of argument has been pressed by Garrett Hardin; see references in 17 and in §9 below.
10. Again, see the list under § 7 below.

*I would like to acknowledge a variety of helpful comments on the first edition of this article, especially those made by Wendy Donner.

11.  See, for example, Ester Boserup, *Population and Technology*, Oxford, England: Blackwell, 1981, esp. chap. 14.
12.  See in particular Tony Jackson, *Against the Grain: the Dilemma of Project Food Aid*, Oxford, England: Oxfam, 1982.
13.  Jeremy Bentham, *Introduction to the Principles of Morals and of Legislation*, chap. I.; included in M. Warnock, ed., *Utilitarianism, On Liberty. . . . and Selected Writings of Jeremy Bentham and John Austin*, New York: World, 1971.
14.  Ibid., chap. IV.
15.  John Stuart Mill, *Utilitarianism*, in Warnock, op. cit., p. 257.
16.  Ibid., p. 260.
17.  Garrett Hardin, "Lifeboat Ethics: The Case Against Helping the Poor," *Psychology Today* September 1974; Peter Singer, "Famine, Affluence and Morality," *Philosophy and Public Affairs*, vol.7, no. 3, 1972. Both are reprinted in W. Aiken and H. La Follette, *World Hunger and Moral Obligation*, Englewood Cliffs, N.J.: Prentice-Hall, 1977.
18.  Garrett Hardin, in Aiken and La Follette, op. cit., p. 17.
19.  Singer, in ibid., p. 24.
20.  Jackson, op. cit., p. 92.
21.  Ibid., pp. 91–93.
22.  The point was first made by Aristotle. A recent utilitarian claim of this sort has been made by R. M. Hare in *Moral Thinking: Its Levels, Method and Point*, chap. 7. Professor Hare explains convincingly why we don't need (and can't get) precision (p. 121), but thinks that we can still get "tried and fairly general principles." Principles can, however, be "tried" and "fairly general" without being accurate; principles that are based on impression and judgment rather than scientific law are least likely to be accurate when dealing with global and long-term prospects. "Humane" utilitarians have to live with the implications of partial causal knowledge when reasoning practically as well as when criticizing Benthamite pretensions to precision. Their process of practical deliberation leans on overall causal claims, and not just on an ability to settle in context approximately what results are likely if one or another action is done.
23.  John Stuart Mill, *Utilitarianism*, in Warnock, op. cit., p. 320.
24.  Ibid., p. 321.
25.  The main Kantian text in which these points are articulated is the supposedly introductory, but actually rather difficult, *Groundwork of the Metaphysic of Morals*, tr. H. J. Paton as *The Moral Law*, London: Hutcheson, 1953. The interpretation I am offering is in some respects nonstandard; in particular I take it that the crucial Kantian notion of a maxim can be interpreted so that Kantian ethics is not committed either to individualism or to vacuous formalism or to a rigid ethic of rules of action. For textual and other arguments for this reading of Kant, see Onora O'Neill, "Kant After Virtue," *Inquiry*, 1984; "Paternalism and Partial Autonomy," *Journal of Medical Ethics*, 1984; "Between Consenting Adults," *Philosophy and Public Affairs*, 1985.
26.  Kant, op. cit., p. 430 (Prussian Academy pagination).
27.  John Stuart Mill, *On Liberty*, in Warnock, op. cit., p. 185

## SUGGESTIONS FOR FURTHER READING

The literature on world hunger, famine, and development problems is so large that any selection is in various ways arbitary. The books mentioned here are generally accessible and recent apart from some of the neo-Malthusian references. This is not to say that Malthusian perspectives have been wholly discredited or abandoned but only that current debates are less centered on them.

## FOR §7 AND LATER DISCUSSIONS OF DEVELOPMENT:

Frances Moore Lappé and Joseph Collins, *Food First: Beyond the Myth of Scarcity.* New York: Ballantine, 1979.

Tony Jackson, *Against the Grain.* Oxford, England: Oxfam, 1982.

Betsy Hartman and James Boyce, *A Quiet Violence: View from a Bangladesh Village.* San Francisco: Institute for Food and Development Policy, 1983.

Susan George, *How the Other Half Dies: The Real Reasons for World Hunger.* Montclair, N.J.: Allanheld, 1977.

Peter Brown and Henry Shue, eds., *Food Policy: The Responsibility of the United States in Life and Death Choices.* New York: Free Press, 1977.

Richard W. Franke and Barbara H. Chasin, *Seeds of Famine: Ecological Destruction and the Development Dilemma in the West African Sahel.* New York and Montclair, N.J.: Allanheld, 1980.

Amartya Sen, *Poverty and Famines: an Essay on Entitlement and Deprivation.* Oxford, England: Clarendon, 1981. (This is rather harder going, but well worth trying.)

Desmond McNeill, *The Contradictions of Foreign Aid.* London: Croom Helm, 1981.

Michael Perelman, *Farming for Profit in a Hungry World: Capital and Crisis in Agriculture.* Montclair, N.J.: Allanheld, 1977.

Colin Tudge, *The Famine Business.* London: Faber and Faber, 1977.

Keith Griffin, *The Political Economy of Agrarian Change: An Essay in the Green Revolution.* Cambridge, Mass.: Harvard University Press, 1974.

Onora O'Neill, *Faces of Hunger.* London: George Allen and Unwin, 1985.

## FOR §9 AND LATER DISCUSSIONS OF MALTHUSIAN POSITIONS

Thomas Malthus, *Essay on the Principle of Population as it Affects the Future Improvement of Society.* London: 1798, and see footnote 7, above.

George R. Lucas and Thomas W. Ogletree, eds., *Lifeboat Ethics: The Moral Dilemmas of World Hunger.* New York: Harper & Row, 1976. The bibliography in this book is a useful source of references.

Garrett Hardin, *Exploring the New Ethics for Survival.* New York: Viking, 1972; and see footnote 17, above, and the bibliography in Lucas and Ogletree, op. cit.

Paul Ehrlich, *The Population Bomb.* New York: Ballantine, 1971.

Paul and William Paddock, *Famine—1975.* Boston: Little, Brown, 1967.

# 9

# Animals and the Value of Life

## PETER SINGER

"Thou shalt not kill," says the Sixth Commandment, and we all nod our heads in solemn agreement. *Whom* should we not kill? Why, *people, human beings,* of course, we all answer. If pressed, we may narrow the scope of this answer still further, making exceptions for killing in self-defense and perhaps one or two other special cases; but we rarely think that our interpretation of the commandment could be too *narrow* and that it could apply to living things other than human beings.

The topic of this essay is the value of life and not the interpretation of the Sixth Commandment; but it is significant that we think it so obvious that the killing of nonhuman beings is not wrong that we do not even bother to spell out this qualification when we say "Thou shalt not kill"—or its equivalent—in more up-to-date language. That it is an immensely important qualification cannot be denied.

Take, for instance, chickens—just one of many species of nonhuman animals that humans kill for food. In the United States—just one of the countries where chickens are killed for human food—more than *3 billion* chickens are slaughtered every year. That is several times greater than the number of human beings killed in all the wars of the present century. In making this comparison, I am not saying that the death of a chicken is as bad as the death of a human being. That is something we shall consider later in this essay. At this stage, my aim is only to draw attention to the significance of the exception we make to the general principle that killing is wrong and thereby to indicate the importance of the question: Are we justified in making this exception? Is it morally all right to kill nonhuman animals? That, basically, is the question we shall be discussing.

# I. INTRODUCTION

Before we begin our discussion of the value of nonhuman life, there are two things that should be said by way of preliminaries.

## §1 FIRST PRELIMINARY: OTHER ISSUES IN THE TREATMENT OF ANIMALS

While any conclusion we may come to about the value of the lives of nonhuman beings will obviously be relevant to the issue of how we ought to treat nonhuman beings, it is not the only thing that is relevant to this issue. To see this, let us for the moment assume that the lives of the 3 billion chickens killed in the United States each year are of no value at all. Would this mean that there could be no moral objection to buying one of these chickens at your local supermarket, taking it home, and eating it? Not necessarily; for it is still the case that during their brief lives these chickens suffer from overcrowding, from having their beaks cut off with a hot knife, from rough handling during transportation, and finally from being hung upside down on a conveyor belt before they are killed. We might consider this a reason for holding that current methods of raising chickens for food are wrong and that we should therefore boycott chicken produced by these methods. We could think this even if we do not think that there is anything wrong with killing a chicken painlessly.

Similarly, one can quite consistently oppose hunting, the slaughter of seals for their fur, many of the 60 to 100 million experiments performed annually on animals in the United States, and a whole host of other practices involving animals without holding that killing an animal is in itself wrong. The suffering inflicted by these practices is grounds enough.

In my book *Animal Liberation* I argued at great length against unrestricted experimentation on animals, against the exploitation of animals in modern "factory farms," and for a vegetarian diet; yet I did not assert that killing an animal is wrong.[1] I based my arguments on the wrongness of making animals suffer, because this seemed to me the most straightforward argument against experimentation and factory farming. I used straightforward arguments that I hoped would have a wide appeal, because I wanted to increase public awareness of what is being done to animals. The argument about killing animals is a more difficult one, and I was (and remain) less certain about this issue than about the question of suffering. Despite my uncertainty about killing, I was not (and am not) at all uncertain about the wrongness of many of the things we do to animals.

Since we can make up our minds on many issues involving the treatment of animals without deciding whether it is wrong to kill animals, it might be thought that this latter issue becomes an idle one that can make no difference to what we ought to do and, hence, that it is not worth discussing. This suggestion—the exact opposite of the view that the wrongness of killing is the only thing relevant to our treatment of animals—is also mistaken. In some cases, we cannot decide what we ought to do without first making up our mind about the wrongness of killing. From my own experiences, three examples come to mind.

## §2 THREE QUESTIONS

*1.* A reader of *Animal Liberation* once said to me: "You don't eat meat because of the suffering the animals are forced to go through before they die, especially in modern intensive farms. I wouldn't eat an animal that had been made to live under these conditions either. But I live on a farm. Mainly we grow vegetables, but we do raise a few pigs. The pigs have a good life, with plenty of room to roam about. We do the slaughtering ourselves, so we know that it is quick and virtually painless. Do you think that's wrong? Would *you* eat our pork?"

*2.* A friend of mine who lives in New York City cannot pass a stray dog without trying to do something for it. Very often, when the dogs are especially thin, she will take them home to her apartment and feed them. Unfortunately there is a limit to the number of dogs one can keep in a small apartment. After a time my friend is forced to send the dogs back to the street, although she knows that they will soon be reduced to the miserable condition in which she found them. She does not take them to the dog pound, because she does not approve of the manner in which the animals are treated there. I once asked her whether it wouldn't be better to take her strays to a vet to have them killed painlessly by an intravenous injection. We were walking near the Bowery at the time, and by way of an answer she gestured toward a man slumped in a doorway, marked by his stubble and dirty overcoat as one of New York's derelicts. "He leads a miserable life," she said, "but we don't take him off for an intravenous injection. Why is a dog different?"

*3.* Working for a university as I do, I frequently meet researchers who perform experiments on animals. Some of these experiments involve suffering, but others do not. In physiology, for instance, many experiments are performed when the animal is under total anesthetic, and upon completion of the experiment the animal is killed before it recovers from the anesthetic. Provided it is properly looked after prior to the experiment, the animal suffers no more than if it had been taken to a vet to be killed painlessly. At the same time, many of these experiments are not really necessary. They are not urgent, lifesaving research. They may extend our knowledge of animal physiology in some small details, but this knowledge may not be applicable to human beings; or there may be alternative methods of finding these things out that do not use animals but are a little more laborious and expensive. What attitude should we take to such experiments? Are they wrong because they involve the needless death of an animal, or are they permissible because they do not cause suffering and because the life of a dog, cat, or mouse is of no value?

All these cases raise, in a practical form, the question we shall be discussing. Is it all right to raise animals for food if the animals lead a pleasant life and die painlessly? Should we "put to sleep" strays and other animals whose lives are likely to be miserable? Does the life of an animal count for more than the desire to further knowledge when we cannot foresee any benefits for humans from the knowledge gained? Does the life of an animal count for more than the convenience of the researcher? We will return to these questions at the conclusion of our investigation into the value of animal life (§19).

## §3 SECOND PRELIMINARY: THE VALUE OF HUMAN LIFE

If we could agree on exactly what value a human life has and why it has that value, the task of deciding on the value of nonhuman life would be greatly simplified. We could then consider to what extent members of the various species of animals possess the characteristics that give human life its value and evaluate their lives accordingly. For instance, if we were agreed that human life is valuable only because humans are self-conscious beings, aware of themselves and capable of evolving long-range purposes and plans of life, we could probably agree that the lives of animals like frogs, shrimps, fish, and lizards are of no value, since these animals appear not to be self-conscious or capable of making long-range plans. (There might be some valuable characteristic possessed by these animals and not possessed by humans, but it is not easy to see what it could be.) The lives of chimpanzees and whales, on the other hand, might well be regarded as worthy of protection, since there is now a good deal of evidence—details of which I shall give later—that these animals are self-conscious. In between these two groups of animals, some cases would be harder to decide, because it is difficult to be certain about what counts as evidence of self-consciousness and long-range planning; but at least we would know what we were looking for, because we had agreed that it is these characteristics that give value to life.

Similarly, if we were agreed that it is not self-consciousness but merely consciousness, or the capacity to experience pleasure or pain, that gives value to human life, we would know what to look for when trying to assess whether the lives of other animals have value. On this criterion we would have to proceed much further down the evolutionary scale before we came to beings whose lives have no value. Again, the exact cutoff point would not be easy to establish, but we would know that when we came to the boundary of consciousness, we had also reached the boundary of value.

Regrettably, as some of the other essays in this volume demonstrate, there are few ethical issues more hotly debated or more difficult to resolve than the question of why and when human life has value. Consider the differences of opinion that exist over the morality of abortion, euthanasia, and suicide. To a large extent, these differences of opinion can be traced to differing views about when human life is valuable or sacrosanct. Is the life of the human fetus worthy of protection simply because it is, biologically, a member of the species *Homo sapiens?* Or because of its potential for full rationality and self-consciousness? Or should we, instead, hold that if the fetus is not actually conscious, its life can be taken fairly lightly? Or take euthanasia: again we find deeply divergent views on the value of human life. If a dying person has nothing in store except six months of unbearable pain, is there any point in denying release from life if he or she should ask for death? What of the human being in an irreversible coma, or the defective infant who will never be able to walk, or talk, or recognize another human being?

The solution of these problems is beyond the scope of this essay; yet how can we proceed to discuss the value of animal life when we are so divided about the value of human life? We shall have to bear in mind the variety of opinion about the value of human life while we examine different proposals about the value of animal life, noting at the appropriate points the implications that adopting one particular view on the value of human life might have for one's position on the value of nonhuman life.

With these preliminaries out of the way, we can now make a start on our real task: the critical examination of the more important of the many possible views that have been held, or might be held, regarding the value of nonhuman life. I shall begin with the view that all human lives, and only human lives, possess some kind of special value or worth —sanctity, some have called it—that is not possessed by any other animals, and in comparison with which any value that animal lives might possess pales into insignificance.[2]

## II. IS HUMAN LIFE OF UNIQUE VALUE?

Most people think that the lives of human beings are of special value. They believe that any human life is so much more valuable than the life of any nonhuman animal that faced with a choice between saving the lowliest member of our own species or any member of any other species, they would always choose to save the human. So widespread is this belief in the supreme value of human life that the slightest hesitation over this choice is likely to be regarded as a sign of a warped moral sense. Even if the choice were between a thousand animals lives and one human life, most people would not doubt that it is right to save the human.

We can see the practical consequences of the attitude I have just described in our own daily lives. Our society takes great pains to save human life, spending millions of dollars on elaborate medical care for everyone from premature babies to geriatric patients. At the same time, we kill billions of animals and birds for the quite unnecessary purpose of providing ourselves with a diet containing large portions of animal flesh. If a dog is unwanted, it may be taken to a vet or the local pound to be destroyed; no one dreams of doing the same to unwanted humans. When a woman breaks her leg, the doctor will tell her not to worry because in a few weeks the leg will be as good as new again; when an animal fractures a bone, it is quite common to kill it in order to save the expense of medical treatment.

These dramatic contrasts in our attitudes to human and nonhuman animals do not show that our attitudes are wrong, but they do indicate a need for justification. I shall consider four distinct attempts to explain why all human life possesses unique value, incomparably greater than the value possessed by nonhuman life.

## §4 IS CONSCIOUSNESS UNIQUELY HUMAN?

Although most people in our society are prepared to take the lives of animals very lightly, we still think that there is more to killing a cow than there is to pulling up a plant or smashing a clock. The reason for this is not difficult to find: the clock, though it may move and emit noises, is neither alive nor capable of feeling; and the plant, while alive, is also, we presume, incapable of feeling.[3] The cow, on the other hand, is a living, feeling creature, a being with a mental life of its own, capable of experiences like pleasure and pain. To cut off the life of a being of this nature seems more serious than to destroy a plant, which lacks consciousness, or a machine, which lacks both consciousness and life.

More than three hundred years ago, the French philosopher, math-ematician, and scientist René Descartes startled his contemporaries by denying, in his celebrated *Discourse on Method*, that animals have minds. Animals, he said, are machines. Their movements and sounds are no more signs of consciousness than the movements and sounds of a clock; more complicated, to be sure, but this is to be expected, since clocks are machines made by humans, and animals are machines made by God. Descartes did not, of course, number humans among the animals. What distinguishes humans, he thought, is their possession of an immortal soul. It is this immortal soul, he said, that is responsible for our feelings and mental experiences.

Descartes was aware of the convenient implications of his theory about animals. It is, he wrote, "indulgent to men—at least to those who are not given to the superstitions of Pythagoras—since it absolves them from the suspicion of crime when they eat or kill animals."[4] By "the superstitions of Pythagoras" Descartes meant vegetarianism, for Pythagoras is said to have abstained from the eating of animals.

If the nonhuman animals truly are incapable of feeling anything, the gulf between humans and nonhumans is very great and the striking distinction commonly made between the value of a normal human life and an animal life can easily be defended. On the other hand, Descartes's view is so flagrantly contrary to common sense that it has never gained wide acceptance (except perhaps among those pioneer experimenters for whom, in view of their wish to cut open living animals—before the days of anesthetics—it was a most convenient doctrine).[5] Still, as philosophers we should not assume that common sense is always right. What grounds do we have for believing that animals are conscious?

We can start by asking how we know if any being, human or animal, is conscious. Take your own case. You know that you can feel because you are directly aware of your own feelings. When someone pricks you with a pin, you feel pain. Suppose, though, that you prick someone else with a pin. How do you know that he or she feels anything? You observe the person draw his or her arm away sharply, rub the spot where it has been pricked, and say "Ouch." None of these observations is a direct observation of pain, for it would be possible for a very complex doll to be wired up so that it reacted to a pinprick in precisely this manner. To that extent, Descartes was right. Indeed, his arguments go further than he thought and can be applied to humans too. A skeptical position about the consciousness of other beings is always possible. In practice, though, we do believe that other people are conscious, and we believe it on the basis of a perfectly reasonable inference from the similarity of their behavior to ours when we are in pain. The analogy is strengthened by our knowledge that other people are not robots but are similar to us in origin and in basic anatomical features, including those anatomical features that seem to be associated with pain, pleasure, and other mental states.

When we turn to nonhuman animals, we find that within those species most nearly related to our own, the situation is fundamentally the same as it is with humans. All the mammals and birds show by their behavior that they feel pain, as clearly as humans do. If you prick a dog with a pin it will jump away, yelp, and perhaps rub the spot where it was pricked. We know that all the mammals and birds have the same basic nervous system that we have, and scientists have observed that they respond physiologically to pain in much the same way that we do. We have a bigger brain than most other animals (although dolphins, whales, and elephants have larger brains than we do), but our large brain consists mainly of a more developed cerebral cortex. The cerebral cortex is the part of the brain that is associated with thinking functions and not with feelings and emotions. Feelings and emotions are associated with a part of the brain known as the diencephalon, which evolved long before the cerebral cortex and is well developed in many species of animals, particularly mammals and birds.

The common origin of our own and other species provides a further reason for believing that they are conscious as we are. The central features of our nervous systems were already in existence when the ancestors of our own species diverged from the ancestors of other modern species. The capacity to feel enhances an animal's prospects of survival, since it leads it to avoid contact with sources of danger. It is absurd to suppose that the nervous systems of animals function in a radically different way from our own, despite their common origin, evolutionary function, and anatomical structure and the similar forms of behavior to which they lead. Hence, if we accept that human beings are conscious, we should accept that mammals and birds, at least, are also conscious.

So far as other animals are concerned—reptiles, fish, crustaceans, molluscs, and so on—the analogy between them and us becomes weaker the further down the evolutionary scale we go. This is true of both the anatomical and the behavioral similarities. Nevertheless, in the case of vertebrate animals, at least, the analogies are sufficiently close to make it reasonable to suppose that they too possess consciousness. Even crustaceans (lobsters, crabs, prawns, and the like) have complex nervous systems, and their nerve cells are very much like our own.

Expert opinion on this matter is now virtually unanimous on the side of common sense against Descartes. The author of a scientific study of pain has written:

> Every particle of factual evidence supports the contention that the higher mammalian vertebrates experience pain sensations at least as acute as our own. To say that they feel less because they are lower animals is an absurdity; it can easily be shown that many of their senses are far more acute than ours—visual acuity in certain birds, hearing in most wild animals, and touch in others; these animals depend more than we do on the sharpest possible awareness of a hostile environment.[6]

Three separate expert committees appointed by the British government to look into different areas of cruelty to animals have agreed that animals are capable of suffering not only from physical pain but also from emotions like fear, anxiety, stress, and so on.[7]

Someone might object that all this talk of similarities between humans and other animals overlooks one vital difference: Humans can talk. Hence, humans can tell us what they feel and animals cannot. This alleged difference between humans and animals is too simply stated, for many species of animals do communicate in one way or another. There is evidence suggesting that whales and dolphins are able to communicate to each other precise descriptions of dangerous objects or of tasks to be performed.[8] Chimpanzees have now shown that they are capable of learning a form of sign language widely used by deaf and dumb people. Still, for present purposes, we may let that pass and agree that most nonhuman animals cannot tell us, in so many words, that they feel pain, or anything else.[9] But so what? What is the relevance of language to something as basic as feeling pain? We should not neglect nonverbal forms of communication. We ourselves are better at conveying our emotions—for instance love, joy, fear, anger, sexual desire—by a look or an action than by words. As Charles Darwin pointed out in *The Expression of the Emotions in Man and Animals*, many of the nonverbal means by which we convey our emotions are identical with or clearly related to those used by other species. Nonverbal communication crosses the species gap and provides as good a basis for belief in the existence of emotions in the nonhuman animals as it does in the human ones.

Descartes's attempt to show that animals are machines therefore fails; and with it fails the attempt to show that human life has unique value because human life is unique in possessing consciousness. Consciousness is something that we share with other animals, and if human lives possess unique value, it cannot be in virtue of our possession of consciousness alone.

## §5 MORTAL LIVES AND IMMORTAL SOULS

Descartes thought that human beings are not machines because they have immortal souls. We have seen that he was wrong to deny consciousness to nonhuman animals; but what of his assumption that the possession of an immortal soul is an attribute that marks out human beings from all the other species that inhabit our planet? In assuming this, Descartes was doing no more than expressing one of the cardinal tenets of orthodox Christianity.

According to orthodox Christian beliefs, humans alone among animals are made in the image of God and possess immortal souls. Hence, humans are not merely material beings, beings of this world, as the other animals are. Humans also have a spiritual side to their nature, a side that relates them to God and the angels. Christianity sees humans as the link between the material and the spiritual worlds.

When faced with the claim that human lives are infinitely more valuable than animal lives because only humans possess an immortal soul, there are two quite different questions we must ask. The first is: What is the basis for believing that humans, and only humans, have immortal souls? The second is: Why is the life of a being with an immortal soul so much more valuable than the life of a being without one?

To go into all the issues raised by the first of these questions would take us beyond the scope of the present essay (or the present book, for that matter). The first question can in turn be divided into two more questions: Does anyone have an immortal soul? and, If some beings do have immortal souls, and others don't, how do we know which ones do? Most atheists would deny that there is such a thing as an immortal soul at all. If there is no such thing, obviously we need not go on to consider which beings possess one. Orthodox Christians, on the other hand, would point to the Scriptures as the basis for their belief that humans have immortal souls. In my view, belief in the existence of immortal souls lacks rational justification, and we should not take things on faith when they cannot be defended on rational grounds. Since I cannot take the space to defend this view here, I shall simply refer the reader who disagrees to the works of those who have written specifically on this issue.[10]

Suppose, however, that we do believe that there is such a thing as an immortal soul. Which beings possess one? The orthodox Christian view is that of all material beings, only human beings are capable of immortality. This view is, again, one that is normally defended within the assumptions of Christianity. Even within those assumptions, there have been a few voices raised against it.[11] The Old Testament says very little about immortality at all, and although the New Testament, by contrast, says a great deal about the next world, it never says whether animals have any prospect of entering it. The doctrine that animals have no immortal souls seems to have become firmly entrenched in Christianity through the teachings of the great medieval theologian and philosopher Thomas Aquinas. Aquinas took over the views of the Greek philosopher Aristotle, who had held that only the rational part of the soul could be immortal, and only humans are capable of rationality. The argument by which Aristotle linked rationality and immortality has been regarded as fallacious by most philosophers, and his claim that only humans are capable of rationality is equally dubious. Thus, today's standard Christian position that only humans have immortal souls is, at least in part, based on the unsound arguments of a non-Christian philosopher.[12]

If, notwithstanding all the grounds for doubt, we persist in believing that there are immortal souls and that human beings are the exclusive possessors of them, we must still ask: Why is the life of a being with an immortal soul so much more valuable than the life of a being without one? To most theologians, the greater value of the life of the being with the immortal soul has seemed too obvious to require explanation; yet it can seem obvious only if we forget that it is the value of the *mortal* life that is at stake. If we believe that human beings really do survive the death of their bodies, then we cannot put an end to their lives, whatever we do; it is only their lives in this world, their lives as material beings, that we can end. Hence, the question at issue in any discussion of the wrongness of killing humans must be the wrongness of ending the life of a human being in this world. But why should the wrongness of killing a being in this world be increased by the fact that the being will live forever in another world? To put the matter another way: If we compare the value of the lives in this world

of two different beings, one human and the other nonhuman, is it not
a little odd to say that the life of the human being in this world is far
more valuable than the life of the nonhuman in this world because the
human's life in this world is only an infinitely small fraction of its entire
existence, whereas the nonhuman's life in this world is the entirety of
its existence? Might we not, with at least equal plausibility, draw
exactly the opposite conclusion?[13]

What probably did so impress the early Christians about killing a
being with an immortal soul was the idea that in so doing one con-
signed the person to his or her eternal fate. The early Christians had
a particularly vivid appreciation of what this meant. They believed
that to kill a person at a particular moment, when he or she might have
committed a sin and not yet repented, could mean roasting in hell
forever, instead of the eternity of heavenly bliss that might have been
in store had he or she lived a little longer and died in a state of grace.
Given these beliefs, it is understandable that the killing of a human
being should have been regarded with much greater abhorrence than
the killing of an animal. Nonetheless, this attitude is not entirely logical either, since for every murder that sends to hell an unrepentant
sinner who would otherwise have repented and gone to heaven, there
is presumably another murder that is responsible for adding one member to the heavenly choir who, while innocent at the time of death,
would have sinned mortally had he or she lived to have the chance.
So even this argument for respecting human life fails.

This last failure exhausts the line of argument that seeks to defend
the idea of the unique value of human life by reference to immortal
souls. We have not, however, exhausted Christian arguments for the
special sanctity of human life, for there is another, quite distinct, line
of argument that will be examined in the following section.

## §6 GOD'S RIGHTS AND HUMANITY'S DOMINION

More than 2,300 years ago, the great Greek philosopher Plato wrote
a work known as the *Phaedo.* Like Plato's other writings, the *Phaedo* is in dialogue form. Socrates is represented as one of the partici-
pants in the dialogue, and he is the one through whom Plato expresses
his own views. At one point in the dialogue Socrates is asked by Cebes,
another participant in the discussion, to explain his belief that suicide
is wrong. Socrates replies that he believes that human beings are
"chattels" of the gods, and then asks Cebes:

> If one of your own chattels, an ox or an ass, for example, took the
> liberty of putting itself out of the way when you had given no intima-
> tion of your wish that it should die, would you not be angry with it,
> and would you not punish it if you could?[14]

This argument against suicide is significant for our enquiry, because it implies that taking human life (whether one's own or that of

another) is quite different from taking the life of one's ox or ass. According to Socrates, to kill a human is to risk the wrath of the gods, but to kill an animal is merely to risk the wrath of the animal's owner. Consequently, if you own the animal yourself, you kill it or not as you please.

Plato was not, of course, a Christian, but a doctrine very similar to his has repeatedly been expressed by Christian writers. No Roman Catholic philosopher has had greater influence on the thinking of the Church than Thomas Aquinas, and Aquinas held that taking a human life is a sin against God, in the same way that killing a slave would be a sin against the master to whom the slave belonged.[15] On this view, God is the master of us all, and to kill a human being is to usurp His right to decide when we shall live and when we shall die. Many Protestant philosophers have taken a similar view, foremost among them Immanuel Kant. Kant uses a different metaphor but to the same end: "Human beings are sentinels on earth and may not leave their posts until relieved by another beneficent hand." The suicide, Kant says, "arrives in the other world as one who has deserted his post; he must be looked upon as a rebel against God."[16] This kind of position retains its influence to the present day. When we hear those who advocate the legalization of euthanasia being accused of seeking to "play God," we are hearing the echoes of Plato, Aquinas, and Kant.

What about nonhuman animals? Are not pigs and chickens God's creatures too? Certainly the Bible states that God created all of the animals, not just humans, and so one might think that to kill any animal is to destroy God's property, and thus to "play God." The catch, so far as animals are concerned, is to be found in the Biblical story of the Creation, where it is said that, after creating man and woman,

> God blessed them, and God said to them, "Be fruitful and multiply, and fill the earth and subdue it; and have dominion over the fish of the sea and over the birds of the air and over every living thing that moves upon the earth."

After the flood, God made the meaning of his gift of dominion more explicit still:

> And God blessed Noah and his sons, and said to them, "Be fruitful and multiply, and fill the earth. The fear of you and the dread of you shall be upon every beast of the earth and upon every bird of the air, upon everything that creeps on the ground and all the fish of the sea; into your hand are they delivered. Every moving thing that lives shall be food for you; and as I gave you the green plants, I give you everything."[17]

These verses have been understood by writers in the Judeo-Christian tradition to mean that God granted His rights over the nonhuman animals to humans. Humans are therefore in the same position vis-à-vis the "lower" animals as God is to humans. Augustine, for instance, refers to the "most just ordinance of the Creator" according to which "both their life and their death are subject to our use."[18] Aquinas quotes this opinion and concurs with it, adding that the very purpose for which animals exist is to serve human beings. He even goes beyond Augustine when he says: "It matters not how man behaves to animals, because God has subjected all things to man's power . . . and it is in this sense that the Apostle says that God has no care for oxen, because God does not ask of man what he does with oxen or other animals."[19]

We may call this view the *Dominion Theory*. It is not so much a view about the *value* of animal life as about the *right* of humans to take animal life when it suits them to do so. This distinction is important and will crop up again later in this essay. We can understand the difference between a view about the right to take life and a view about the value of life if we think for a moment about, for instance, the right that a soldier has—or is generally thought to have—to kill an enemy soldier in wartime. We may believe that soldiers have this right without believing that the value of the life taken will always be less than the value of the life of the soldier who takes it.

So we can distinguish between saying that human beings have a right to take the lives of animals and saying that the lives of human beings are more valuable than the lives of animals. Strictly speaking, the Dominion Theory is a theory about the right to kill and not a theory about the value of life. Nevertheless, we must remember that the Dominion Theory is a theory within the Judeo-Christian tradition, and it is a central tenet of that tradition that God is all knowing and all good. Hence, God would not have given humans the right to kill animals without good reason, and yet He must have known that humans do not need to kill animals for food to survive. It would therefore appear to be an implication of the Dominion Theory, in the Judeo-Christian context, that animal life is of little or no value—for why else would God have given humans dominion over the other animals and told us that we may kill them for food?

Some of the writers who espouse the Dominion Theory have realized that it does not provide a complete explanation of the differing status of humans and animals and have therefore offered reasons why God should be content to hand over the animals to human beings. Aquinas, for instance, adopts an argument from Aristotle to the effect that only reason or intellect is of intrinsic value, and God has made all those things whose nature is nonintellectual for the sake of those beings with intellectual natures. Animals, Aquinas holds, have no intellectual nature and therefore exist only for the sake of humans.[20] To prevent our discussion from becoming too complicated, however, we shall postpone discussion of this view, because it is logically distinct from the Dominion Theory. It is very close to the view of Immanuel Kant, and we shall discuss it when we come to consider his position.

Meanwhile, what can we say about the Dominion Theory itself? Obviously it rests on a number of questionable beliefs. To take the Dominion Theory seriously we must believe that God exists, that He has the right to decide which of His creatures shall live or die, that He has the right to delegate this right to others, and that He did delegate this right to human beings.

There are many who do take the Bible as authoritative, and within the limits of this assumption, the Dominion Theory is well founded. One can, of course, accept the biblical account without going to quite the lengths to which Aquinas goes when he claims that because God has granted us dominion over the animals, it doesn't matter how we behave to them. In opposition to this interpretation of the Dominion Theory, which makes humans despots over other animals, one could advance the interpretation that God's gift of dominion puts us in the position of stewards, that is, guardians of the property of another, who must take care to manage it well and keep it in good condition.[21] Adopting this "stewardship" interpretation of the Dominion Theory would make a significant difference to the way in which we are entitled to treat animals, particularly in respect of human activities that threaten to exterminate entire species of animals. It would not, however, make a fundamental difference to the principal implication of the theory, which is that we are entitled to kill individual animals if we wish to do so.

My own view is that belief in the existence of God cannot be justified. There is a dearth of convincing argument or evidence for the existence of a being who corresponds to the Judeo-Christian conception of God, and there are several reasons, of which the most important stems from the existence of so much unnecessary suffering and misery in the world, for believing that the universe is not under the control of an all-powerful and all-good God.[22] Whether I am right about this is, like the issue of immortality, a question for philosophy of religion rather than for ethics, and so I shall not elaborate here; but if I am right, the biblical account of the Creation must be rejected, and the Dominion Theory with it. We may then regard the Dominion Theory as an attempt to justify human attitudes and practices towards animals, including the killing of animals for food—a practice that was, no doubt, in existence long before *Genesis* was written.

## §7 HUMAN ENDS AND ANIMAL MEANS

If animals are capable of experiencing pleasure and pain as humans are, and if we reject the religious grounds for treating human life differently from animal life, what else can be said in favor of the sharp distinction we commonly make between ourselves and all other species? A lot of things have been said, although it is not clear that any of them helps very much.

Two hundred years ago the influential German philosopher Immanuel Kant lectured to his students as follows:

> Animals are not self-conscious and are there merely as a means to an end. That end is man. We can ask, "Why do animals exist?" But to ask, "Why does man exist?" is a meaningless question. Our duties towards animals are merely indirect duties towards humanity. . . . If a man shoots his dog because the animal is no longer capable of service, he does not fail in his duty to the dog, for the dog cannot judge, but his act is inhuman and damages in himself that humanity which it is his duty to show towards mankind.[23]

The most distinctively Kantian idea in this passage is the idea that human beings are "ends in themselves." As one contemporary philosopher has explained this, it amounts to saying, "Everything other than a person can only have value *for* a person. . . . Thus of everything without exception it will be true to say: if $x$ is valuable and not a person, then $x$ will have value for some individual other than itself."[24] Other philosophers have tried to make similar points in different words. They talk of "the intrinsic dignity of the human individual"[25] or the "intrinsic worth of all men."[26]

This kind of rhetoric is popular and meets with little opposition. After all, why should we not attribute "intrinsic dignity" or "intrinsic worth" to ourselves? Why should we not say that we are the only things in the universe that have intrinsic value? Our fellow human beings are unlikely to reject the accolades we so generously bestow upon them, and the other species to whom we deny the honor are unable to object. Indeed, if we think only of human beings it can be very liberal, very progressive, to talk of the dignity and worth of all humans. In so doing we implicitly condemn slavery, racism, and—if we eliminate the sexist references to the "intrinsic worth of all *men*" —the oppression of women. It is only when we recall that human beings are no more than one among the many species of animals living on this planet that we may realize that in elevating our own species we are at the same time degrading all other species.

Once we ask *why* it should be that all humans—including infants, mental defectives, criminal psychopaths, and tyrants like Adolf Hitler —have some kind of dignity or worth that no whale, gorilla, cow, or dog can ever achieve, we can see that the rhetoric of "human dignity" does not tell us much. More argument is needed to justify the claim that all and only humans have some special kind of dignity or worth or are ends in themselves. On the face of it, after all, shouldn't the mere fact that a being can experience pleasure or pain be sufficient to make it an "end in itself"? Isn't the experience of pleasure good in itself, and the experience of pain bad in itself? What this question really amounts to is: If, while everything else remained the same, we were able to increase the amount of pleasure experienced in the universe, or decrease the amount of pain experienced in the world, wouldn't both of these be improvements, things that make the world a better place? And isn't the answer to this question affirmative, irrespective of whether the beings whose pleasure is enhanced and whose pain is diminished are humans, gnus, or guinea pigs?

## §8 SPECIESISM

It is important to understand that the *mere* fact that all human beings are members of our species, while other animals are not does not provide a satisfactory justification for the view that all humans have greater moral worth than other animals. It is this view that I refer to as "speciesism" in my book *Animal Liberation,* and that is the main target of the philosophical arguments of that book. I use the term 'speciesism' to make the analogy between this attitude of preference for members of our own species, simply because they are members of our own species, and better-known attitudes like racism (preference for members of one's own race, simply because they are members of one's own race) and sexism (preference for members of one's own sex, simply because they are members of one's own sex).[27] Once the parallel between these attitudes has been recognized, it is easy to see why we cannot say that membership in our species alone is enough to give a being special worth. If we are prepared to say that a being has less worth because it is not a member of our own species, how can we object to the racist who says that a being has less worth if it is not a member of his race? If species is a morally significant criterion, why isn't race?

Someone might reply that the differences between species are more significant than the differences between races and sexes. After all, human beings can reason about abstract matters, use complex languages, plan for events in the distant future, make moral judgments, and so on. Perhaps this is what Kant had in mind when, in saying that animals are not ends, he asserted that they are not self-conscious, and when, in saying that a man does not fail in his duty to his dog if he shoots it when it can no longer serve him, he added that "the dog cannot judge." Nonhuman animals, it is commonly supposed, are not self-conscious and cannot judge, reason abstractly, use complex languages, plan for the future, etc. On the other hand, the differences that exist between humans and other animals in respect of these capacities do not exist between the different races and sexes of human beings.

The facts alleged by those who put forward this line of objection to the parallel between speciesism and racism may hold true when we compare normal adult humans with members of other species (though as we shall see, even this is not entirely true), but they clearly are not true of *all* human beings. Infants and mentally defective human beings are often not capable of abstract reasoning, using language, planning for the future, or judging morally. If, therefore, we think it is one of these capacities, or some combination of them, that gives human beings a worth or moral status that other animals do not have, we cannot hold that all human beings without restriction have this worth. Infants will have it only potentially, and some mental defectives whose brains have been irreparably damaged will not have it at all.

The view that beings with certain capacities—such as self-consciousness, the use of reason, or the capacity to make moral judgments —are of special worth is not a form of speciesism, for it is not the view that human beings have special worth *simply because* they are members of our species. It may be true that most human beings possess these capacities and most other animals do not, but the boundary of the class of specially worthy beings cannot be expected to run precisely along the boundary of our species. It is beyond dispute that there are nonhuman animals who are superior in terms of all mental capacities to some beings who are, in the biological sense, human. An adult chimpanzee, for instance, can solve problems that are beyond the reasoning capacity of most three-year-old children, and despite the special aptitude for language that humans are widely believed to have, chimpanzees have acquired language skills (using the sign language of the deaf and dumb) that are roughly equivalent to those of two-year-old human children. Many other species—baboons, dogs, dolphins, pigs, and others—are equally clearly superior in these respects to human infants under, say, one year old. Even if we decide that their potential for a higher level of rationality gives infants special value, we are still faced with the fact that some mental defectives are at the same mental level as human infants and have no potential to reach a higher level.

Thus, if we select any mental capacities as the basis of special worth, the class of special worthy beings will diverge considerably from the class of human beings. Those who attempt to eliminate this divergency by forging some logical link between these two classes will make themselves liable to the charge of speciesism. The alternative is to abandon belief that human life has unique value.

I think this widely accepted Western attitude does have to be abandoned. We have considered a number of attempts to defend it, and none of them has stood up to critical scrutiny. The accepted view must give ground. It is not yet clear, however, how much ground it has to give. The smallest possible modification would seem to be a shift from the idea that all *human* lives have unique value to the idea that it is the lives of *persons* that have unique value, where 'person' is defined in some manner not quite equivalent to 'human being'. It is this position that we shall examine next.

## III. THE VALUE OF A PERSON'S LIFE

### §9 WHAT IS A PERSON?

I have suggested that we may modify the idea that the lives of all humans have special value by substituting 'persons' for 'humans'. This may lead to some puzzlement, for 'person' and 'human being' are often used as if they meant the same thing. This usage masks a significant distinction. That the terms are not really equivalent can be seen from the fact that religious believers may describe God as a Divine Person without implying that He is a human being. According to the *Oxford English Dictionary*, one of the current meanings of the word 'person' is "a self-conscious or rational being." It is in something like this sense that the word is often used by philosophers, and it will be used in roughly this sense—the details will be discussed shortly—in the present essay.

Some writers have used the word 'human' to describe the kind of being I shall refer to as a person. For instance, Joseph Fletcher, an eminent Protestant theologian and ethicist, includes the following in a list of "Indicators of Humanhood": minimal intelligence, self-awareness, self-control, a sense of the future, a sense of the past, the capacity to relate to others, concern for others, communication, and curiosity.[28] There is no great harm in using the word 'human' in this way, as long as it is clearly understood that 'human' is then not equivalent to 'member of the species *Homo sapiens*'. They are obviously not equivalent because a newborn infant, an accident victim whose brain has been so damaged that he is in an irreversible coma, and an old man in a state of advanced senility are all members of the species *Homo sapiens*, though none of them possesses all of Fletcher's "indicators," and the road-accident victim, at least, possesses none of them.

So there are three terms that people are liable to confuse: 'person', 'human being', and 'member of the species *Homo sapiens*'. The important philosophical point is that the first and third of these be kept distinct. As for the middle term, 'human', it could be allowed to slop around between the other two, but it is more convenient to reject Fletcher's usage and treat 'human' as equivalent to 'member of the species *Homo sapiens*', since the former expression is so much briefer than the latter. We can then use the word 'person' to refer to the class of being for which Fletcher was suggesting indicators.

What, then, is it to be a person? What characteristics does a being have to possess to be a person? Let us start with the dictionary definition. What is it to be self-conscious? What is it to be rational? The concepts themselves need further analysis if they are to be made clear.

When philosophers refer to 'self-consciousness', they are not using the term in the popular sense in which I may say that I felt self-conscious when I realized that I was the only person at the state banquet not wearing a tie. 'Self-awareness' might be a better way of expressing what philosophers mean by 'self-consciousness'. A being is self-conscious if it is aware of itself as an entity, distinct from other entities in the world. We might add the requirement that the being be aware that it exists over a period of time, that it has a past and a future; for to be aware of oneself as an entity it may well be necessary to be aware of oneself as existing over some period of time, however brief. To be aware of oneself only in the instantaneous present is hardly to be aware of oneself as an entity at all, since an entity is something that exists over a period of time.[29]

Is the fact that a being is self-conscious in this sense enough to establish that the being is a person? Are there other characteristics one should add, like rationality or the ability to feel pleasure or pain? Rationality is probably already included in our conception of self-consciousness, since a being would not attain self-consciousness without possessing at least a minimally rational understanding of the world. The capacity to feel pleasure and pain is something that we might be able to separate from self-consciousness in theory, but in the world as we know it a self-conscious being will always be a being capable of feeling pleasure and pain—that is, if we interpret this capacity broadly enough so as to include any form of positive feeling, such as approval or satisfaction as a form of pleasure, and any negative feeling, such as disapproval or dissatisfaction, as a form of pain. Hence, our definition is roughly adequate as it stands.

## §10 UTILITARIANISM AND THE VALUE OF A PERSON'S LIFE

Let us, for simplicity's sake, define a "person" as a self-conscious being; and let us say that by 'self-conscious being' we mean a being aware of itself as a distinct entity, existing over time, with a past and a future. We can then ask: Is the life of a person especially valuable?

Let us put the question a little differently: Why might one think that taking the life of a person is more serious than taking the life of some other kind of being? One important line of argument runs as follows. If a being is aware of itself as a distinct entity, with a past and a future, it is capable of having desires about its own future. For example, a professor of philosophy may hope to write a book demonstrating the objective nature of ethics; a student may look forward to graduating; a child may want to go for a ride in an airplane. To take the life of any of these people, without their consent, is to thwart the victim's desires for the future, in a way that killing a snail or a day-old infant presumably does not.

This does not mean, of course, that when a person is killed, the dead person's desires are thwarted in the ordinary sense in which when I am hiking through dry country my desire for water is thwarted when I discover a hole in my water bottle. In this case, I have a desire that I cannot fullfill, and I feel frustration and discomfort because of the continuing and unsatisfied desire for water. When a person is killed, the desires he or she has for the future do not continue after death, and he or she does not suffer from their nonfulfillment. But does this mean that preventing the fulfillment of these desires does not matter?

Classical utilitarianism, as expounded by the founding father of utilitarianism, Jeremy Bentham, and refined by later philosophers like John Stuart Mill and Henry Sidgwick, judges actions by their tendency to maximize pleasure or happiness and minimize pain or unhappiness. Terms like 'pleasure' and 'happiness' are a little vague, but it is clear that they refer to something that is experienced, or felt—in other words, to states of consciousness. According to classical utilitarianism, therefore, there is no direct significance in the fact that a person's desires for the future go unfulfilled when he or she is killed. If death is instantaneous, whether he or she has any desires for the future makes no difference to the amount of pleasure or pain experienced. Thus for the classical utilitarian, the status of 'person' is not *directly* relevant to the wrongness of killing.

Indirectly, however, personhood may be important for the classical utilitarian. Its importance arises in the following manner. If I am a person, I have a conception of myself having a future. If I am also mortal, I am likely to realize that my future existence is liable to be cut short. If I think that this is likely to happen at any moment, my present existence will probably be less enjoyable than if I do not think it is likely to happen for some time. If I learn that people like myself are often the victims of unprovoked, murderous attacks, I will worry about the prospect of being killed; if I learn that people like myself are very rarely killed, I will worry less. Hence, the classical utilitarian can defend a prohibition on killing persons on the indirect ground that it will increase the happiness of people who would otherwise worry that they might be killed. I call this an *indirect* ground because it does not refer to any direct wrong done to the person killed but rather to a consequence of it for other people. There is, of course, something odd about objecting to murder not because of the wrong done to the victim but because of the effect on others. Only an exceptionally tough-minded classical utilitarian will be prepared to stomach this oddness. For our present purposes, however, the main point is that this indirect ground does provide a reason for taking the killing of a person, under certain conditions, more seriously than the killing of a being that is not a person. If a being is incapable of conceiving of itself as existing over time, we need not take into account the possibility of its worrying about the prospect of its future existence being cut short. It can't worry about this, for it lacks the necessary understanding of itself.

I said that the indirect classical utilitarian reason for taking the killing of a person more seriously than the killing of a nonperson holds "under certain conditions." These conditions are that the killing of the person may become known to other persons, who derive from this knowledge a more gloomy estimate of their own chances of living to a ripe old age. It is of course possible that a person could be killed under other conditions, in which case this classical utilitarian reason against killing would not apply.

That is, I think, the gist of what the classical utilitarians would say about the distinction between killing a person and killing some other type of being (although we shall return to classical utilitarianism in the next section). There is, however, another version of utilitarianism that may give more weight to the distinction. This other version of utilitarianism judges actions not by their tendency to maximize pleasure or minimize pain but by the extent to which they are in accord with the preferences of any beings who have preferences about the action or its consequences. This version of utilitarianism is known as "preference utilitarianism."

According to preference utilitarianism, an action contrary to the preference of any being is, unless this preference is outweighed by stronger contrary preferences, wrong. Killing a person who prefers to continue living is therefore wrong, other things being equal. Unlike classical utilitarianism, preference utilitarianism makes killing a direct wrong done to the person killed, because it is an act contrary to his or her preferences. That the victim is not around after the act to lament the fact that his or her preferences have been disregarded is irrelevant.

To the preference utilitarian, taking the life of a person will normally be worse than taking the life of some other being, since a being that cannot see itself as a distinct entity with a possible future existence cannot have a preference about its own future existence. This is not to deny that such a being might struggle against a situation in which its life is in danger, as a fish struggles to get free of the barbed hook in its mouth; but this indicates no more than a preference for the cessation of a state of affairs that is perceived as painful or threatening. Struggle against danger and pain does not suggest that the fish is capable of preferring its own future existence to nonexistence. The struggle of a fish on a hook suggests a reason for not killing fish by that method, but does not suggest a preference-utilitarian reason against killing fish by some other method that kills them instantly.

Although preference utilitarianism does provide a direct reason for not killing people, some may find the reason—even when coupled with the important indirect reasons that any form of utilitarianism will take into account—is not sufficiently stringent. Even for preference utilitarianism, the wrong done to the person killed is merely one factor to be taken into account, and the preference of the victim could sometimes be outweighed by the preferences of others. We commonly feel that the prohibition on killing people is more absolute than this kind of utilitarian calculation implies. A person's life, it is often said, is something to which he or she has a *right,* and rights are not to be traded off against the preferences or pleasures of others.

I am not myself convinced that the notion of a moral right is a helpful or meaningful one except when it is used as a shorthand way of referring to more fundamental moral considerations. Nevertheless, since the idea that we have a "right to life" is a popular one, it is worth asking whether there are grounds for attributing a right to life to persons as distinct from other living beings.

## §11 DO PERSONS HAVE A RIGHT TO LIFE?

Michael Tooley, a contemporary American philosopher now living in Australia, has argued that only 'continuing selves' have a right to life. To be a continuing self it is not enough to have merely momentary desires or interests. Instead, the being must possess some form of psychological continuity. This means that the being must, at some time, be able to see itself as existing over time. In other words, Tooley's notion of a 'continuing self' is closely akin to the notion of a person as we have used the term.

This argument, presented in Tooley's recent book *Abortion and Infanticide,* is a development from an earlier article that Tooley wrote as a contribution to the abortion debate. In this earlier article, Tooley claimed that there was a conceptual connection between the desires a being is capable of having and the rights that the being can be said to have. As Tooley put it:

> The basic intuition is that a right is something that can be violated and that, in general, to violate an individual's right to something is to frustrate the corresponding desire. Suppose, for example, that you own a car. Then I am under a *prima facie* obligation not to take it from you. However the obligation is not unconditional; it depends in part upon the existence of a corresponding desire in you. If you do not care whether I take your car, then I generally do not violate your right by doing so.[30]

If the matter really were as simple as this, one might argue that since the right to life is the right to continue existing as a distinct entity, the desire relevant to possessing a right to life is the desire to continue existing as a distinct entity. In that case, only a being capable of conceiving itself as a distinct entity existing over time—that is, only a person—could have this desire, and so only a person could have a right to life.

Tooley has since conceded that we cannot link rights and desires so tightly, because there are problem cases like people who are asleep or temporarily unconscious. We do not want to say that such people have no rights because they have, at that moment, no desires. So Tooley now acknowledges that rights can be based on *interests* rather than on *desires.*[31] But this change in Tooley's view makes little practical difference, because he then argues that to have an interest in one's continued existence one must desire, at that time, to continue to exist as a subject of consciousness, or one must have desires at other times. Moreover an individual does not, Tooley claims, have desires at other times unless there is at least one time at which the individual possesses the concept of a continuing self. While we can imagine an animal having desires at different times—the desire that pain stop, for instance—the desire will not be desires *of the same individual* if that animal has merely momentary desires without being able to link them under the concept of itself as a continuing self.

It therefore follows from Tooley's view that only beings that are or at some time have been capable of seeing themselves as existing over time will have a right to life. This is strikingly different from the conventional view that being a member of the species *homo sapiens* is what gives a being a right to life; and it seems that Tooley's view is an improvement over that view, because it is easy to see that the capacity to have an interest in continued existence is relevant to the possession of a right to life in a way that mere species membership cannot be relevant.

## §12 THE INHERENT VALUE OF A "SUBJECT OF A LIFE"

Tom Regan, in *The Case for Animal Rights,* has suggested a criterion which is in practice similar to that proposed by Michael Tooley, although Regan argues for his criterion in a different way. Regan asks what kind of beings have 'inherent value'—that is, which beings have value in themselves, not reducible to the intrinsic value of their pleasures or satisfactions. His answer is that a being has inherent value if it is a "subject of a life." To be a subject of a life, beings must, Regan says:

> have beliefs and desires; perception, memory and a sense of the future, including their own future; an emotional life together with feelings of pleasure and pain; preference and welfare interests; the ability to initiate action in pursuit of their desires and goals; a psychophysical identity over time; and an individual welfare in the sense that their experiential life fares well or ill for them. . . .[32]

Regan regards the claim that subjects of a life have equal inherent value as a postulate which we should accept because it avoids, on the one hand, arbitrary and inegalitarian distinctions and, on the other hand, the counterintuitive consequences of utilitarianism. Thus, like a rights-based view and unlike utilitarianism, Regan's view would not allow subjects of a life to be killed even if a greater good—perhaps the saving of a greater number of lives—could thereby be achieved. For those unhappy with both utilitarianism and Tooley's view of interests, Regan's position may therefore be an attractive third possibility.

## §13 WHICH ANIMALS ARE PEOPLE?

We have seen that if we accept either preference utilitarianism or Tooley's view of rights, it becomes important to know whether a being is a person—that is, whether it has the capacity to be aware of itself as a distinct entity existing over time. The same is true if we adopt Regan's view of inherent value, since memory and a sense of one's own future were among the elements of the subject-of-a-life criterion. To establish the relevance of these views to the treatment of animals we must therefore ask: Are any nonhuman animals persons?

This question is more difficult than it may appear at first glance. We do not normally think of animals as people, but this may be because of the confusion between the terms 'person' and 'human being', which I have already discussed. It does sound a little odd to refer to, say, a chimpanzee as a person. This oddness, however, may be no more than a linguistic echo of an unjustifiable prejudice. In any case, the real issue is whether any animals, other than human beings, are capable of conceiving themselves as distinct entities existing over time.

That some animals, at least, are self-conscious appears to have been shown by recent experiments in teaching American Sign Language to apes. The ancient dream of communicating with another species was realized when two American scientists, Allen and Beatrice Gardner, guessed that the failure of previous attempts to teach chimpanzees to talk was due not to the chimpanzees' lack of the intelligence required to use language but to their lack of the vocal equipment needed to reproduce the sounds of human language. The Gardners therefore decided to treat a young chimpanzee as if she were a human baby without vocal cords. They communicated with her, and with each other when in her presence, by using American Sign Language, a language widely used by deaf and dumb people.

The technique was a striking success. The chimpanzee, whom they called Washoe, could understand about 350 different signs and was able to use about 150 of them correctly. She also put signs together to form simple sentences. As for self-consciousness, Washoe did not hesitate, when shown her own image in a mirror and asked, "Who is that?" to reply, "Me, Washoe." She also used signs expressing future intentions.[33]

Suppose that on the basis of such evidence we accept that Washoe and the other apes who have now been taught to use sign language are self-conscious. Are they exceptional among all the nonhuman animals in this respect, precisely because they can use language? Or is it merely that language enables these animals to demonstrate to us a characteristic that they, and other animals, possessed all along?

Some philosophers have argued that for a being to think, it must be able to formulate its thoughts in words. The contemporary English philosopher Stuart Hampshire, for example, has written:

The difference here between a human being and an animal lies in the possibility of the human being expressing his intention and putting into words his intention to do so-and-so, for his own benefit or for the benefit of others. The difference is not merely that an animal in fact has no means of communicating, or of recording for itself, its intention, with the effect that no one can ever know what the intention was. It is a stronger difference, which is more correctly expressed as the senselessness of attributing intentions to an animal which has not the means to reflect upon, and to announce to itself or to others, its own future behavior. . . . It would be senseless to attribute to an animal a memory that distinguished the order of events in the past, and it would be senseless to attribute to it an expectation of an order of events in the future. It does not have the concepts of order, or any concepts at all.[34]

If Hampshire is right, no being without language can be a person. This applies, presumably, to young humans as well as to animals. Only those animals who can use a language could be persons. Apart from chimpanzees and gorillas who have been taught to use sign language, the other most likely group would be whales and dolphins, for there is some evidence that their buzzes and squeaks constitute a sophisticated form of communication that may one day be recognized as language.[35] With these few exceptions, however, the claim that language is necessary for reflective thought consigns the nonhuman animals to the level of conscious but not self-aware existence. But is this claim sound? I do not believe that it is. Hampshire's defense of it contains more assertion than argument, and in this respect he is representative of others who have advanced the same view. Attempts to decide a question of this nature by armchair philosophizing should be regarded with a certain degree of suspicion.

There is nothing altogether inconceivable about a being possessing the capacity for conceptual thought without having a language and there are instances of animal behavior that are difficult to explain except under the assumption that the animals are thinking conceptually. In one experiment, for instance, chimpanzees were taught to select the middle object from a row of objects. Even when the objects were not spaced regularly, the chimpanzees could pick out the middle object from a row of up to eleven objects. The most natural way to explain this is to say that the apes had grasped the concept of the "middle object." It is worth noting that many three- and four-year-old children, though accomplished language users, cannot perform this task.[36]

Nor is it only in laboratory experiments that the behavior of animals points to the conclusion that they possess both memory of the past and expectations about the future and that their behavior is intentional. Consider Jane Goodall's description of how a young wild chimpanzee she had named Figan secured for itself one of the bananas that

Goodall, to bring the animals closer to her observation post, had hidden in a tree:

> One day, sometime after the group had been fed, Figan spotted a banana that had been overlooked—but Goliath [an adult male ranking above Figan in the group's hierarchy] was resting directly underneath it. After no more than a quick glance from the fruit to Goliath, Figan moved away and sat on the other side of the tent so that he could no longer see the fruit. Fifteen minutes later, when Goliath got up and left, Figan without a moment's hesitation went over and collected the banana. Quite obviously he had sized up the whole situation: if he had climbed for the fruit earlier, Goliath would almost certainly have snatched it away. If he had remained close to the banana, he would probably have looked at it from time to time. Chimps are very quick to notice and interpret the eye movements of their fellows, and Goliath would possibly, therefore, have seen the fruit himself. And so Figan had not only refrained from instantly gratifying his desire but had also gone away so that he could not "give the game away" by looking at the banana.[37]

Goodall's description of this episode does, of course, attribute to Figan a complex set of intentions, including the intention to avoid "giving the game away" and the intention to obtain the banana after Goliath's departure. It also attributes to Figan an "expectation of an order of events in the future," namely the expectation that Goliath would move away, that the banana would still be there, and that he, Figan, would then go and get it. Yet there seems nothing at all "senseless" about these attributions, despite the fact that Figan cannot put his intentions or expectations into words.

There are other incidents, equally revealing of complex intentions, in Goodall's book, and many more in the scientific literature on animal behavior. The cumulative effect is to lead us to the conclusion that nonhuman animals do act intentionally and with expectations about the future. These observations are not limited to chimpanzees, nor are they all derived from efforts to obtain food.[38]

Finally, what of self-consciousness? I do not think that anything more is required as evidence for the existence of self-consciousness that the evidence already offered in support of the existence of intentional behavior. If an animal can devise a careful plan for obtaining a banana, not now but at some future time, and can take precautions against his own propensity to give away the object of the plan, that animal seems to be aware of himself as a distinct entity existing over time.

So some nonhuman animals are persons as we have defined the term. If Tooley's argument about the right to life is sound, these animals have a serious right to life, of the same kind as the right to life of an adult human. We cannot know which animals possess this right until many other species have been observed with the same kind of care and patience that Jane Goodall gave to her study of chimpanzees in the Gombe Stream area of Tanzania; but there is no reason to suppose that the chimpanzee is the only nonhuman animal with a right to life.

We can see, then, that if we accept the view that *persons* have a right to life that other beings do not have, we have come a long way from the position that all and only human beings have a right to life. In contrast to this latter view, we are now saying that many nonhuman animals have the same kind of right to life that normal humans have; and we are also saying that there are some human beings—newborn infants and gross mental defectives—who do not have this kind of right to life.

Some may regard the inclusion of infants in this category along with gross mental defectives as a mistake. Although newborn infants may not possess the actual capacity to conceive of themselves as entities existing over time, they do have the potential to conceive of themselves in this way, given normal development. In view of this potential, it may be suggested, infants should be regarded as having the same right to life as adult persons.

This issue is the same as that raised by the potential of the fetus in the debate about abortion; since it is more central to the issue of abortion than to the question of the treatment of animals and is discussed by Joel Feinberg in his essay on abortion in this volume, I shall not discuss it here. My own view is that the mere potential to possess a capacity does not necessarily carry with it the rights that arise from actual possession of the capacity. For our purposes, however, it does not matter too much whether the reader accepts this conclusion. Even readers who do not accept it have to recognize that there are still some humans—those with irreparable gross mental defects—who are not persons and who do not have the same right to life that persons, including nonhuman persons, have if it is true that all and only persons have this right.

If the evidence we have considered suggests that some nonhuman animals are persons, it also suggests that these nonhuman animals are subjects of a life, in Regan's sense. Thus both Tooley's and Regan's views have radical consequences for the way we may treat animals. We shall consider these consequences more fully below (§ 18).

## IV. ANIMAL LIFE

Although the arguments put forward in the preceding section would, if accepted, extend beyond our own species the respect for life that we now accord only to humans, it is doubtful that we have gone far enough. The sphere within which life is to be protected includes only the "higher" animals, possibly only mammals who, like ourselves, have the capacity to see themselves as distinct entities existing over time.

Perhaps a lizard or a fish is not capable of seeing itself in this way. Perhaps a chicken is not either. Some may think that the less intelligent mammals, like rabbits and mice, are not self-conscious. Yet as we saw earlier, birds and mammals are, almost certainly, capable of experiencing pleasure or pain, and the same is very likely true of reptiles and fish. All these animals possess a central nervous system, as we do, and the behavior of these animals, in situations in which we might expect them to be suffering pain, parallels our own pain behavior in many respects. There may therefore be animals who are *conscious* and capable of feeling but not *self-conscious* or capable of conceiving themselves as distinct entities existing over time. We must now consider what value the lives of these animals have and whether, even though they are not persons, they might not have some right to life.

## §14 CONSCIOUSNESS AS THE BASIS FOR EXTENDING THE RIGHT TO LIFE TO ANIMALS

One argument for attributing a right to life to all conscious living things can be derived from the implications that the arguments already discussed have for mentally defective human beings. We have seen that permanent mental defectives cannot be said to have a right to life merely because they are human beings. This would be speciesism. Nor can they be said to have a right to life because they are persons. Many of them are not persons. Therefore, if mental defectives are to have a right to life at all, it must be grounded on something else. What could this something else be? One possible candidate is the fact that all humans, even mental defectives—or at least those who are conscious—have positive interests in the shape of desires, goals, or preferences, the satisfaction of which provides them with intrinsically valuable experiences. Since one can seek to satisfy one's desires only if one is still alive, it is possible to draw from this argument the conclusion that there is value in the life of any being that has desires and that can derive some valuable experience from their satisfaction. One could also argue, on this basis, that any such being has a right to be left alive to seek to satisfy its desires and hence has a right to life. This argument for a right to life does succeed in encompassing all human beings; but it also encompasses all those nonhuman animals who are capable of having desires and seeking to satisfy them.[39]

One small qualification needs to be made to this argument. It does not quite cover all human beings. There are some human beings who are permanently unconscious and therefore have no desires. The argument from consciousness does not suggest that these humans have a right to life. Perhaps, though, this is an advantage rather than a drawback—for what point is there in keeping alive a human being who does not have, and never again will have, any conscious experiences? From the point of view of the permanently unconscious being, this state would appear to be indistinguishable from death.[40]

Similarly, the argument may not cover all animals. There is no reason to believe that the boundary between animals and plants (which is, in scientific terms, a very fine line) corresponds exactly to the boundary between conscious and nonconscious life. It is reasonable to believe that some relatively simple forms of animal life have no desires or conscious preferences. Perhaps animals like oysters and mussels fall into this category—or if they don't, there are still more simple animals, like the amoeba, that probably do. In any case, we can consider the argument without knowing precisely to which animals it applies. If the argument is sound, we can say this: Wherever the boundary of consciousness is to be found, there too is the boundary of the right to life.

But *is* the argument sound? It seems to me that its fundamental weakness is the extent to which the argument relies on the assumption that all human beings—including those with severe mental defects— have an equal right to life. If we come to consider a human who has such severe brain damage that he or she is not a person and can never become a person, it is plausible to hold that this human being does not have the same right to life as a normal adult human. If this seems shocking, recall the arguments we considered earlier in this chapter to the effect that merely being a member of the species *Homo sapiens* cannot carry with it any special moral status. Once this conclusion is accepted, it places humans who are not persons in the same category as nonhuman animals. It is this conclusion that is "shocking" to our conventional attitudes, for it forces us to alter our attitudes to one or the other of these groups, or to both. In other words, we must adopt one of the following positions:

1. While retaining our present attitudes to mentally defective humans, we change our attitudes to animals who are not persons, so as to bring them into line with our attitudes to mentally defective humans. This involves holding that animals have a right to life and therefore should not be killed for food or for the purposes of scientific experimentation.
2. While retaining our present attitudes to animals, we change our attitudes to mentally defective humans so as to bring them into line with our attitudes to animals. This involves holding that mental defectives do not have a right to life and therefore might be killed for food—if we should develop a taste for human flesh—or (and this really might appeal to some people) for the purpose of scientific experimentation.
3. We change our present attitudes to both mentally defective humans and nonhuman animals so as to bring them together somewhere in between our present attitudes. This involves holding that both mentally defective humans and nonhuman animals have some kind of serious claim to life—whether we call it a "right" does not matter much—in virtue of which,

while we ought not to take their lives except for very weighty
reasons, they do not have as strict a right to life as do persons.
In accordance with this view, we might hold, for instance, that
it is wrong to kill either mentally defective humans or animals
for food if an alternative diet is available but not wrong to do
so if the only alternative is starvation.

The argument for the first of these positions is inadequate, because
Tooley and Regan have provided plausible and nonarbitrary grounds
for distinguishing the value of the life of a person—or of a subject of
a life—from the value of the life of a being that is conscious but has
no sense of its own future. Preference utilitarianism also supports the
idea that there is a relevant distinction here.

## §15 CLASSICAL UTILITARIANISM AND THE VALUE OF
ANIMAL LIFE

The conclusion reached in the preceding section does not settle the
issue of the value of the life of an animal that is not a person. In that
section we distinguished three possible views, all consistent and none
of them speciesist, that one might take about both mentally defective
humans and nonhuman animals. We have now found that the first of
these positions is inadequate. There remain the other two positions,
one of which puts mentally defective humans in the same position as
animals now are, while the other brings our attitudes to mentally
defective humans and to animals together in some intermediate position between our present attitudes to the two. Assuming the foregoing
is sound, we must choose between these two positions.

The first of these two positions asks us to think about something
that is, for many people, utterly repulsive. The idea of killing mentally
defective human beings for food or to satisfy scientific curiosity involves a radical break with the widespread belief in the value of
human life. Yet if my arguments up to this point have been sound, we
must make a radical break with our current ethical beliefs at some
point: If we do not reject the belief that it is wrong to kill mentally
defective humans for food, then we must reject the belief that it is all
right to kill animals at the same level of mental development for the
same purpose.

If we remain strictly within the classical utilitarian position, we will
incline toward the former view and hold that killing is not in itself
wrong. The utilitarian view would, of course, take account of a wide
variety of external factors. It would note that many of the modes of
killing used on animals do not inflict an instantaneous death and involve considerable suffering. It would also take into account the effect
of the death of one animal on its mate or on other members of its social
group. There are many species of birds and animals in which the bond
between male and female lasts for a lifetime. Presumably in these

situations the death of one member of the pair causes something like sorrow for the survivor.[41] The mother-child relationship is also strong in most mammals and birds. In some species, too, the death of one animal may be felt by a larger group. This is the case when, for example, the leader of a wolf pack is killed.[42] All these factors would lead utilitarians to oppose much of the killing of animals that now goes on. They would not, however, lead them to oppose killing in itself. Killing can be instantaneous and painless, and it can be of an animal, or a mentally defective human being, who will not be missed by anyone else. In these special circumstances, killing will not increase the amount of pain or diminish the amount of pleasure in the universe, and hence it seems not, according to classical utilitarianism, to be wrong.

There is, however, a further question: Should utilitarianism take into account the pleasure that the human or animal would continue to experience if it were not killed? In the classical utilitarian view, if the chances are that the remainder of the life span of the being killed would contain more pleasure than pain, then, other things being equal, the killing diminishes the total surplus of pleasure over pain in the universe, and is for that reason wrong in the absence of counter-vailing considerations. Before classical utilitarians seize on this as a means of reconciling their theory with ordinary moral convictions, however, there is something else that needs to be noticed: the loss of pleasure associated with killing is, from a utilitarian point of view, of no greater moral significance than the loss of pleasure associated with failing to reproduce.

Let us look at this point more closely. Suppose that I am a utilitarian and I am considering killing a young boy, X. Let us say that there are no parents, friends, or relatives who will grieve over X's death, and the killing will be quite painless, so there are no relevant external factors; but I do, as a utilitarian, have to take into account the fact that X, living as he does in a pleasant community in which his basic needs can be satisfied, will probably experience a surplus of pleasure over pain in his lifetime. Therefore, I decide that it would be wrong to kill X.

Now suppose that I am a (female) utilitarian and I am considering whether to conceive and give birth to a child. We can call the possible child Y. It is, we shall suppose, reasonable to believe that if Y is born, he or she is likely to experience a surplus of pleasure over pain during life—in fact, let us say that Y's prospects of a happy life, once conceived, are exactly as favorable as the prospects of X's life continuing to be happy if he is not killed. Moreover, as in the case of X, there are, we shall say, no relevant external factors tipping the balance one way or the other. (The inconveniences of pregnancy are, for me, exactly balanced by the anticipated joys of becoming a parent.) Then, given all this, my reasons for not killing X are no more weighty than my reasons for conceiving Y, and my reason against killing X is, in utilitarian terms, equally a reason for conceiving Y. This means that the decision not to conceive Y is, other things being equal, as wrong as the decision to kill X.

All this is, again, very much at odds with our ordinary moral convictions. We do not ordinarily think that it is wrong to fail to conceive a child who would probably be happy. We certainly do not think that it is wrong in the way that killing a child is wrong. Someone might say that we do not think it wrong to fail to conceive a child because our world is already so overpopulated. This reply won't do; for why is killing a child a less acceptable way of reducing population than failing to conceive a child?

Essentially, the problem is that classical utilitarianism makes lives replaceable. Killing is wrong if it deprives the world of a happy life, but this wrong can be righted if another equally happy life can be created without any extra cost. Classical utilitarianism has this consequence because it regards sentient beings as valuable only insofar as they make possible the existence of intrinsically valuable experiences like pleasure. It is as if sentient beings were receptacles of something valuable and it did not matter if a receptacle got broken as long as another receptacle were available to which the contents could be transferred without any getting spilled in the process. The reasonableness of the classical utilitarian position turns on the reasonableness of this consequence. I shall have more to say on this matter shortly. First, though, it is worth noting that this argument has been used to justify meat eating. Leslie Stephen, for instance, once wrote:

> Of all the arguments for Vegetarianism none is so weak as the argument from humanity. The pig has a stronger interest than anyone in the demand for bacon. If all the world were Jewish, there would be no pigs at all.[43]

The thought here is that animals are replaceable, and that although meat eaters are responsible for the death of the animals they eat, they are also responsible for the creation of more animals of the same species. The benefit they thus confer on one animal cancels out the loss they inflict on the other. We shall call this the replaceability argument.

## §16 THE REPLACEABILITY ARGUMENT

The first point to note about the replaceability argument is that even if it is valid when the animals in question have a pleasant life, it would not justify eating the flesh of animals reared in modern "factory farms," where the animals are so crowded together and restricted in their movements that their lives seem to be more of a burden than a benefit to them.[44]

A second point is that if the replaceability argument applies to animals, it must apply to humans at a comparable mental level as well. Situations in which the argument would apply to humans might not be common, but they could occur. Some people carry genes that mean that any children they produce will be severely mentally retarded. As long as the lives of these children are pleasant, it would not, according to the replaceability argument, be wrong to perform a scientific experiment on a child that results in the death of the child provided another child could then be conceived to take its place. (Of course, one would need to consider the feelings of the parents—but then one should consider these feelings in the case of pigs too.)

A third point is that if it is good to create life, then presumably it is good for there to be as many people on our planet as it can possibly hold. With the possible exception of arid areas suitable only for pasture, the surface of our globe can support more people if we grow plant foods than if we raise animals.

These three points greatly weaken the replaceability argument as a defense of meat eating, but they do not go to the heart of the matter. Are sentient beings really replaceable? Henry S. Salt thought that the argument rested on a simple philosophical error:

> The fallacy lies in the confusion of thought which attempts to compare existence with non-existence. A person who is already in existence may feel that he would rather have lived than not, but he must first have the *terra firma* of existence to argue from: the moment he begins to argue as if from the abyss of the non-existent, he talks nonsense, by predicating good or evil, happiness or unhappiness, of that of which we can predicate nothing.[45]

When I wrote *Animal Liberation* I accepted Salt's view.[46] In a later attempt to defend Salt's position more systematically, I tried to formulate a plausible version of utilitarianism that accounts for the lack of symmetry in our attitudes to bringing a being into existence and putting a being out of existence. I ran into trouble as soon as I tried to apply this version of utilitarianism to situations in which the future population of the world is not fixed. In such a situation, a criterion for deciding upon the optimum population is required, and a plausible criterion is exceptionally difficult to find. An account of these difficulties would take us far beyond our present subject; it suffices to say that the adequacy of the reply that Salt and I have given to the replaceability argument must remain in doubt unless and until the difficulties are overcome.[47]

We must therefore conclude this section on a note of uncertainty. If the replaceability argument can be met, it would follow that from the classical utilitarian view the life of any being likely to experience more pleasure than pain is of value and not to be sacrificed without a very good reason. This would justify the third of the three possible positions outlined in §14 and would mean a radical change in our evaluation of the lives of animals. On the other hand, if the replaceability argument is sound, it would seem that in the absence of other considerations the second of the three positions is the one to take and it is our attitudes to mentally defective human beings that are in need of reconsideration.

# V. CONCLUSIONS

## §17 THEORETICAL ISSUES

It is now time to draw the discussion together and see what conclusions we have reached. In the first substantive section of this essay (§2) we scrutinized the position, so fundamental to Western attitudes to animals and nature, that human life has a unique value far beyond that of any animal. We considered four grounds for believing this:

1. That humans alone are conscious.
2. That humans alone have immortal souls.
3. That human lives are God's property, whereas God has given humans dominion over animals.
4. That human beings are "ends in themselves" and animals mere means.

None of these grounds stood up to critical examination, and so I maintained that—unless some better arguments appeared—the traditional Western attitude would have to be abandoned. It would seem impossible to hold, without arbitrary and unjustifiable discrimination, that the life of every member of our species is of higher value than the life of every nonhuman animal.

Next we distinguished between the terms 'human being' and 'person', using the latter term to refer to a self-conscious being, aware of itself as a distinct entity existing over time. In this sense it is possible for a human being—a member of the species *Homo sapiens*—not to be a person and also possible for a nonhuman animal to be a person.

We then asked if there were any reasons for holding that it was markedly more serious to take the life of a person than to take the life of a being that is not a person. We saw that this position can be defended on several grounds. The classical utilitarian can defend it only indirectly, in terms of the effects on others, but preference utilitarianism allows us to give direct weight to the desire for continued existence—a desire that only a self-conscious being can have. It is also possible to maintain, as Tooley does, that only a self-conscious being can have a *right* to life, in the fullest sense of the term; and we must also consider Regan's claim that "subjects of a life" have an inherent value.

If we accept that persons have a weightier claim to life than beings that are not persons, we still need to ask whether beings that are not persons have any kind of right to life at all or whether their lives are of any value. We examined an argument for an equal right to life for all sentient creatures but found it inadequate. We then considered the bearing of classical utilitarianism on this issue and found that a good deal depended on the very perplexing question of whether the loss of pleasure caused by the killing of one being can be made up for by the creation of another being. Only if a negative answer can be given to this question does classical utilitarianism allow the conclusion that killing is wrong in itself.

## §18 THREE QUESTIONS ANSWERED

What do our theoretical conclusions mean in practical terms? If they are correct, in what respects should our treatment of animals be modified? What should we think about the three cases of killing animals mentioned in the first section of this essay?

*A. Killing Animals for Food*  Let us consider, first, whether it would be right to kill and eat a pig if the pig lived happily under pleasant conditions and was killed painlessly. The first problem is to decide whether pigs are self-conscious. This is not an easy matter to settle. Pigs may not be as intelligent as chimpanzees, but it was not for nothing that George Orwell made them the elite of *Animal Farm*. Pigs are comparable in intelligence to dogs, and if we are prepared to allow that self-consciousness is possible without language, it is possible that pigs are self-conscious. If this is so, then preference utilitarianism, Tooley's view of rights, and Regan's view of inherent value all imply that we ought not to kill a pig, however painlessly it might be done, merely for the purpose of adding pork to our diet. Classical utilitarianism, on the other hand, would lead to this conclusion only if some justification exists for not setting against the loss of happiness occasioned by the death of the happy pig the happiness of future pigs that we will be able to raise only if we kill the one now alive.

My own position is that I am not certain that it would be wrong in itself to kill the pig; but nor am I certain that it would be right to do so. Since there is no pressing moral reason for the killing—the fact that one might prefer a dish containing pork to a vegetarian meal is hardly a matter of great moral significance—it would seem better to give the pig the benefit of the doubt.

There are also a number of other reasons why in most cases it is better not to raise and kill animals for food, even when they live happily and die painlessly. For a start, raising animals is an inefficient method of obtaining food for human consumption. Far more food— and more protein—can be produced by growing vegetables, grains, and soybeans than by raising animals—unless the land is not suitable for growing these crops. In a situation in which population growth is putting increasing pressure on all our resources, including food, it is important to encourage the most efficient possible use of the land we have available for agriculture.

Then there are some less tangible reasons against killing animals for food or for any other objective that is not a matter of life and death. For my own part, I cannot now, after being a vegetarian for many years, contemplate the killing and eating of an animal without a feeling of distaste amounting almost to revulsion. My meal would be tainted by the knowledge that I was dining on flesh from the corpse of an animal that was capable of relating to other animals, of caring for its young, and of having a pleasant or a miserable existence. This is an emotional attitude or perhaps an aesthetic judgment that would endure for some time even if I were to become convinced that on moral grounds the painless killing of a happy animal is not wrong. Moreover, there remains a doubt in my mind as to whether it is possible for those who kill animals for food to avoid slipping gradually into the attitude that animals are things for us to exploit for our convenience. If that attitude should take hold, the step to factory farming, with its ruthless sacrifice of the interests of animals to the dictates of commerce, is short indeed.

*B. Euthanasia for Strays*   The justifiability of euthanasia for stray dogs or cats, or for any animal whose future existence is likely to be wretched, is a very different matter. Here self-consciousness and the ability to understand and choose between alternatives is crucial. If an animal is not self-conscious and its future existence is likely to be wretched, utilitarian considerations and some views of rights agree that euthanasia is permissible. Instead of diminishing happiness, death then diminishes suffering. Even when self-consciousness is present, if the animal is not capable of understanding its future prospects and of choosing whether to live or die, it may be right for others to make this choice for the animal. Choosing on behalf of another can be defensible in situations in which one party understands the nature of a choice while the other party is totally incapable of appreciating what is at stake. Of course, such a choice is justifiable only if it is truly made in the interests of the being who is incapable of making the choice. But my New York friend with the small apartment would have been acting in the interests of the stray animals she could not look after if she had taken them to a vet to be killed by an intravenous injection; and while one can sympathize with her reluctance to take the animals to their death, it would not have been wrong to do so. We are responsible for the foreseeable consequences of our choices, whatever we choose, and we cannot escape responsibility for the fate of an animal by releasing it on the streets of New York and turning our back.

*C. Experimenting on Animals*   The third of the three cases with which this essay began is the case of animal experimentation. Again, it is not all animal experimentation with which we are here concerned but only experiments that raise the question of killing in isolation from other factors like the infliction of suffering; for example, an experiment in which the animal is made unconscious by an anesthetic prior to the experiment being performed and is then killed before it regains consciousness.

Animal experimentation does sometimes serve important and worthwhile purposes. Although many experiments are trivial and a waste of time and money (quite apart from being an abuse of animals), others do lead to significant gains in our knowledge of biological processes and the prevention and treatment of disease. It may in the long run be possible to obtain this knowledge by alternative techniques not involving animals, but the prospect of such alternatives in the future does not negate the benefits now being obtained by some experiments. This places animal experimentation in a different category from raising animals for food. Except in some simple subsistence economies, the use of animals for food does not contribute to vitally important human objectives. It does not save lives or reduce suffering. The knowledge gained from some experiments on animals does save lives and reduce suffering. Hence, the benefits of animal experimentation exceed the benefits of eating animals, and the former stands a better chance of being justifiable than the latter; but this applies only when an experiment on an animal fulfills strict conditions relating to the significance of the knowledge to be gained, the unavailability of alternative techniques not involving animals, and the care taken to avoid pain. Under these conditions the death of an animal in an experiment can be defended.

When the experimental animal may be self-conscious, the problem becomes more difficult. If either Tooley's argument about the right to life or Regan's view of inherent value is sound, it would appear that the lives of these animals should not be sacrificed in any experiments, no matter how important. Utilitarians, on the other hand, would be more flexible and would allow that some experimental goals are important enough to justify the death of even a self-conscious being. Preference utilitarians would require more in the way of likely benefits from the experiment than classical utilitarians, because they would take into account the animal's presumed desire to go on living. A utilitarian of either school would, in consistency, have to admit that an experiment important enough to justify the death of an animal would also justify the death of a mentally defective human at a similar mental level if for some reason the human were a more suitable subject for the experiment than the nonhuman animal. That fact may temper the readiness of experimenters to assume that their own experiments are important enough to justify killing animals.

## §19 CONCLUDING PRACTICAL POSTSCRIPT

Finally, it may be as well to remind the reader of the limitations on the scope of this essay and of the conclusions that, because of these limitations, do *not* follow from what I have said. We have been considering the issue of killing animals in isolation from other issues, like the infliction of suffering upon animals. This approach is necessary for a clear philosophical understanding of the separate issues involved, but it must not be taken as an indication of the way things are in the world. Killing animals for food normally means not only that the animals die but that they must be exploited throughout their lives in order to reduce the costs of production. Thus, the case for vegetarianism is strong whatever view we take of the value of animal life. Using animals in experiments, even when the experiments are painless, means housing animals for long periods before the experiment takes place, often in closely confined conditions. Moreover, many experiments are not at all painless, and many more are of no real importance. Thus the case for stricter control of animal experimentation is also independent of the issue of the value of animal life. To maintain that the lives of most animals are of less value than the lives of most humans is not to excuse what humans do to animals or to diminish the urgency of the struggle to end the callous exploitation of other species by our own.

## *NOTES*

1. *Animal Liberation* (New York, The New York Review, 1975), chap. 1.
2. The reader may note, in what follows, the absence of any discussion of the view, associated with Eastern religions and with Albert Schweitzer, that *all* life, whether animal or plant, conscious or not, has value. I do not believe that it has; but since this issue is discussed in William Blackstone's essay in the present volume, I have not argued for my belief here.
3. For a brief discussion of the contrary view about plants, see *Animal Liberation,* op. cit., pp. 261–263.
4. For Descartes's views, see the selections reprinted in *Animal Rights and Human Obligations,* ed. T. Regan and P. Singer (Englewood Cliffs, N.J., Prentice-Hall, 1976), pp. 60–66; for the passage quoted (from a letter to Henry More, February 5, 1649), see p. 66. Whether Descartes actually intended to deny that animals are *conscious* or merely that they can *think* is not altogether clear; but he has often been interpreted as making the stronger claim.
5. See L. Rosenfield, *From Beast-Machine to Man-Machine: The Theme of Animal Soul in French Letters from Descartes to La Mettrie* (New York, Oxford University Press, 1940).
6. Richard Sergeant, *The Spectrum of Pain* (London, Hart-Davis, 1969), p. 72.
7. See the reports of the Committee on Cruelty to Wild Animals (Command Paper 8266, 1951), paragraphs 36–42; the Departmental Committee on Experiments on Animals (Command Paper 2641, 1965), paragraphs 179–182; and the Technical Committee to Enquire into the Welfare of Animals Kept under Intensive Livestock Husbandry Systems (Command Paper 2836, 1965), paragraphs 26–28 (London, Her Majesty's Stationery Office).
8. John Lilly, *Man and Dolphin* (London, Gollancz, 1962), pp. 81–87. The authenticity of Lilly's evidence has been questioned.
9. See below, §8.
10. The classic argument against immortality is David Hume's essay "Of the

Immortality of the Soul," first published in 1777. A modern introduction to the topic can be found in T. Regan, *Understanding Philosophy* (Encino, Calif., Dickenson, 1974), chap. 6. See also B. Russell, *Why I Am Not a Christian* (New York, Simon & Schuster, 1957), and for a useful survey of the literature, Anthony Flew's article "Immortality" in *The Encyclopedia of Philosophy*, ed. Paul Edwards (New York, Macmillan, 1967).

11. See, for example, Joseph Butler, *The Analogy of Religion, Natural and Revealed* (Philadelphia, Lippincott, 1857), part I, chap. 1.

12. For Aristotle's position, see his *De Anima* II, 2, 3, 4; III, 12; for Aquinas, see *Summa Theologica* I, Q 76.3. See also C. W. Hume, *The Status of Animals in the Christian Religion* (London, Universities Federation for Animal Welfare, 1957), pp. 49–50.

13. At least one Christian *has* drawn the opposite conclusion. Cardinal Bellarmine is said to have allowed vermin to bite him, saying "We shall have heaven to reward us for our sufferings, but these poor creatures have nothing but the enjoyment of this present life." (Quoted from W. E. H. Lecky, *History of European Morals* [London, Longmans, 1892], vol. II, p. 172n.)

14. *Phaedo,* 62 6-c, in *The Dialogues of Plato,* 4th ed., tr. B. Jowett (Oxford, England, Clarendon Press, 1953), vol. 1, p. 412.

15. *Summa Theologica* II, ii. Q 64.5.

16. I. Kant, *Lectures on Ethics,* tr. L. Infield (New York, Harper & Row, 1963), pp. 153–154.

17. Genesis I, 29 and IX, 1–3.

18. *City of God* I, 20.

19. *Summa Theologica* II, ii Q64.1 and II, i Q102.6; the reference to "The Apostle" is to Paul, *Corinthians* IX, 9–10.

20. *Summa Contra Gentiles,* III, ii, ch. 112; reprinted in Regan and Singer, op. cit., pp. 56–59.

21. See John Passmore, *Man's Responsibility for Nature* (London, Duckworth, 1974), chap. 2.

22. For a careful presentation and discussion of this argument, see H. J. McCloskey, *God and Evil* (The Hague, Nijhoff, 1974).

23. Kant, op. cit., pp. 239–240.

24. Gregory Vlastos, "Justice and Equality," in *Social Justice,* ed. R. B. Brandt (Englewood Cliffs, N.J., Prentice-Hall, 1962), pp. 48–49.

25. William Frankena, "The Concept of Social Justice," in R. B. Brandt, op. cit., p. 23.

26. H. A. Bedau, "Egalitarianism and the Idea of Equality," in *Nomos IX: Equality,* ed. J. R. Pennock and J. W. Chapman (New York, Atherton, 1967).

27. The term is not of my own inventing; I first came across it in a pamphlet written by Richard Ryder, the author of *Victims of Science* (London, Davis-Poynter, 1975). Several reviewers of *Animal Liberation* objected to the term on stylistic grounds, but no one suggested anything equally concise and more euphonious. Species chauvinism or human chauvinism would also be possible.

28. *The Hastings Center Report,* vol. 2, no. 5 (1972).

29. This account has an impeccable philosophical ancestry. John Locke, for example, defined a person as "A thinking intelligent being that has reason and reflection and can consider itself as itself, the same thinking thing, in different times and places." (*An Essay Concerning Human Understanding,* bk. II, chap. 29, par. 9.) Locke distinguished 'person' and 'man', holding that an intelligent animal—he instances a parrot—might be a person, though it could not be a man. Immanuel Kant, too, referred

to the view that "that which is conscious of the numerical identity of itself at different times is in so far a *person.*" (*Critique of Pure Reason,* Paralogism 3.) For further references see "Persons," by Arthur Danto in *The Encyclopedia of Philosophy,* ed. Paul Edwards, vol. 6.

30. Michael Tooley, "A Defense of Abortion and Infanticide," in *The Problem of Abortion,* ed. Joel Feinberg (Belmont, Calif., Wadsworth, 1973), p. 60. An earlier version appeared in *Philosophy and Public Affairs,* vol. 2, no. 1 (1972).

31. Michael Tooley, *Abortion and Infanticide* (Oxford, England, Oxford University Press, 1984), chap. 5.

32. Tom Regan, *The Case For Animal Rights* (Berkeley, Calif., University of California Press, 1983), p. 243.

33. B. T. Gardner and R. A. Gardner, "Teaching Sign Language to a Chimpanzee," *Science,* vol. 165 (1969), pp. 664–672; see also W. H. Thorpe, *Animal Nature and Human Nature* (London, Methuen, 1974) pp. 283f.

34. Stuart Hampshire, *Thought and Action* (London, Chatto and Windus, 1960), pp. 98–99. Others who have espoused related views are Anthony Kenny, in A. J. P. Kenny, H. C. Longuet-Higgins, J. R. Lucas, and C. H. Waddington, *The Nature of Mind* (Edinburgh, Edinburgh University Press, 1972), p. 119, and in Anthony Kenny, *Will, Freedom and Power* (Oxford, England, Blackwell, 1925), pp. 18–21; Norman Malcolm, "Thoughtless Brutes," *Proceedings and Addresses of The American Philosophical Association* XLVI (1973), pp. 5–20 (but see the reply by Donald Weiss, "Professor Malcolm on Animal Intelligence," *Philosophical Review* LXXXIV [1975], pp. 88–95); and Donald Davidson, in "Thought and Talk," in *Mind and Language,* ed. S. Guttenplan (Oxford, England, Clarendon Press, 1975).

35. Lilly, op. cit.

36. F. H. Rohles and J. U. Devine, "Chimpanzee Performance in a Problem Involving the Concept of Middleness," *Animal Behavior* 14, pp. 159–162. (Cited in Donald Griffin, *The Question of Animal Awareness* [New York, Rockefeller University Press, 1976], p. 43.) See also Stephen Walker, *Animal Thought* (London, Routledge, 1983).

37. Jane van Lawick-Goodall, *In the Shadow of Man* (New York, Dell, 1971), p. 107.

38. For an example involving playful rather than food-gathering behavior, see Gary Eaton, "Snowball Construction by a Feral Troop of Japanese Macaques Living under Semi-Natural Conditions," *Primate* 13 (1972), pp. 411–414. It is also appropriate in this context to refer to the many well-authenticated reports of apparently intentional behavior by whales and dolphins.

39. This position was once defended by Tom Regan: see his "The Moral Basis of Vegetarianism," *Canadian Journal of Philosophy,* October 1975, and reprinted, in part, in T. Regan and P. Singer, op. cit., pp. 197–204. For Regan's present views, see the book referred to in note 32, above.

40. See the essay on euthanasia in this volume; and for a discussion of the value, if any, of life without consciousness, see the essay by William Blackstone.

41. For an example, see Farley Mowat, "The Trapped Whale," in Joan MacIntyre, *Mind in the Waters* (New York, Scribners, 1974).

42. Farley Mowat, *Never Cry Wolf* (Boston, Atlantic Monthly Press, 1963).

43. From *Social Rights and Duties,* quoted by Henry S. Salt, "The Logic of the Larder," in T. Regan and P. Singer, op. cit., p. 186n.

44. See *Animal Liberation,* chap. 3.

45. Salt, op. cit., p. 186.

46.   *Animal Liberation*, p. 254; for a similar view, see Mary Anne Warren, "Do Potential People Have Moral Rights?" *Canadian Journal of Philosophy*, vol. 7 (1977), pp. 275–289.
47.   For my attempt to formulate a criterion for deciding upon an optimum population, see "A Utilitarian Population Principle," in *Ethics and Population*, ed. Michael Bayles (Cambridge, Mass., Schenkman, 1976); and for damaging criticisms of this attempt, see Derek Parfit's "On Doing the Best for Our Children" in the same volume. For the best treatment to date of the problem, see Parfit's *Reasons and Persons* (Oxford, England, Oxford University Press, 1984), pt. IV.

# SUGGESTIONS FOR FURTHER READING

The following works are relevant to the general topic of the morality of our treatment of animals.

Clark, Stephen, *The Moral Status of Animals* (Oxford, England, Clarendon, 1977), pb. 1984.

Frey, R. G., *Interests and Rights: The Case against Animals* (Oxford, England, Clarendon, 1980).

Frey, R. G., *Rights, Killing and Suffering: Moral Vegetarianism and Applied Ethics* (Oxford, England, Blackwell, 1984).

Godlovitch, Stanley and Roslind, and Harris, John, *Animals, Men and Morals* (London, Gollancz, 1972).

Midgley, Mary, *Animals and Why They Matter* (Harmondsworth, England, Penguin, 1984).

Miller, Harlan, and Williams, William (eds.), *Ethics and Animals* (Clifton, N.J., Humana, 1983).

Paterson, David, and Ryder, Richard (eds.), *Animals' Rights: A Symposium* (Fontwell, Sussex, England, Centaur, 1979).

Regan, Tom, *All That Dwell Therein* (Berkeley, University of California Press, 1982).

Regan, Tom, *The Case For Animal Rights* (Berkeley, Calif., University of California Press, 1985).

Regan, Tom, and Singer, Peter (eds.), *Animal Rights and Human Obligations* (Englewood Cliffs, N.J., Prentice-Hall, 1976).

Rollin, Bernard, *Animal Rights and Human Morality* (Buffalo, N.Y., Prometheus, 1981).

Salt, Henry, *Animal Rights* (Fontwell, Sussex, England, Centaur, 1980; first published 1892).

Singer, Peter, *Animal Liberation* (New York, New York Review of Books, 1975; New York, Avon, 1977; Wellingborough, England, Thorsons, 1983).

The following works are specifically relevant to the use of animals for food:

Agriculture Committee, House of Commons, *Animal Welfare in Poultry, Pig and Veal Calf Production* (London, H.M.S.O., 1981). An authoritative government report which comes out firmly against many current practices.

Akers, Keith, *A Vegetarian Sourcebook* (New York, Putnam, 1983). The most comprehensive collection of up-to-date scientific information on the vegetarian diet.

Brambell, F. W. R. (Chairman), *Report of the Technical Committee to Enquire into the Welfare of Animals kept under Intensive Livestock Husbandry Systems* (London, H.M.S.O., 1965). The report of the first detailed government inquiry into factory farming.

Bryant, John, *Fettered Kingdoms* (Chard, Somerset, England, J.M. Bryant Ferne House, no date). A slim but powerful discussion of our abuse of animals.

Gold, Mark, *Assault and Battery* (London, Pluto, 1983). An examination of factory farming.

Harrison, Ruth, *Animal Machines* (London, Vincent Stuart, 1964). The book that started the campaign against factory farming.

Lappe, Francis Moore, *Diet for a Small Planet* (New York, Ballantine, 1971). This book argues on ecological grounds against meat production.

Mason, Jim, and Singer, Peter, *Animal Factories* (New York, Crown, 1980). The health, ecological, and animal welfare implications of factory farming, with an outstanding collection of photographs.

On the use of animals in research, see:

Rowan, Andrew, *Of Mice, Models and Men; A Critical Evaluation of Animal Research* (Albany, N.Y., State University of New York Press, 1984). An up-to-date examination by a scientist.

Ryder, Richard, *Victims of Science* (London, Davis-Poynter, 1975; London, National Anti-Vivisection Society, 1983). Still the best overall account of animal experimentation.

Sperlinger, David (ed.), *Animals in Research: New Perspectives in Animal Experimentation* (Chichester and New York, Wiley, 1981). A useful collection for those with a serious interest in the topic.

The following notes indicate further reading relating to specific sections of this essay:

§6. Two books on the place of animals within the Christian view of the world are Ambrose Aquis, *God's Animals* (Catholic Study for Animal Welfare, 1970), and C. W. Hume, *The Status of Animals in the Christian Religion* (Universities Federation for Animal Welfare, 1957). A strongly stated argument against vivisection by an influential twentieth-century Christian writer is C. S. Lewis's "Vivisection" (The National Anti-Vivisection Society Limited, 51 Harley Street, London, W1).

§7. A fuller account of Kant's position can be found in Alexander Broadie and Elizabeth Pybus, "Kant's Treatment of Animals," *Philosophy*, vol. 49 (1974). For a reply, see Tom Regan, "Broadie and Pybus on Kant," *Philosophy* (October 1976).

§8. The topic of speciesism is discussed in Bonnie Steinbock, "Speciesism and the Idea of Equality," *Philosophy* (July 1978). It is also touched upon by Michael Fox, "Animal Liberation: A Critique," *Ethics* (January 1978). For a reply, see Peter Singer, "The Parable of the Fox and the Unliberated Animals," *Ethics* (January 1978). See also Peter Singer, "All Animals Are Equal"; Kevin Donaghy, "Singer on Speciesism"; and Joseph Margolis, "Animals Have No Rights and Are Not the Equal of Humans," *Philosophical Exchange* (Summer 1974).

§§12–14. For the debate over the idea of animal rights, the following essays are relevant. Joel Feinberg, "What Sorts of Beings Can Have Rights?" in *Philosophy and Environmental Crisis*, ed. William T. Blackstone (Athens, Ga.: University of Georgia Press, 1974); R. G. Frey, "Animal Rights," *Analysis* (October 1977); and "Interests and Animal Rights," *Philosophical Quarterly* 27 (1977); Dale Jamieson and Tom Regan, "Animal Rights: A Reply to Frey," *Analysis* (January 1978); H. J. McCloskey, "Rights," *Philosophical Quarterly* vol. 15 (1965); Jan Narveson, "Animal Rights," *Canadian Journal of Philosophy* (March 1974); and Tom Regan, "Fox's Critique of Animal Liberation," *Ethics* (January 1978); "Frey on Interests and Animal Rights," *Philosophical Quarterly* (Winter 1977); "Narveson on Egoism and the Rights of

Animals," *Canadian Journal of Philosophy* (March 1977); "McCloskey on Why Animals Cannot Have Rights," *Philosophical Quarterly* (Fall 1976); and "Utilitarianism, Vegetarianism, and Animal Rights," *Philosophy and Public Affairs* (Fall 1979). The October 1978 issue of *Philosophy* and the Summer 1979 issue of *Inquiry* are devoted to essays relating to the nature and moral status of animals. A more complete bibliography is included in the *Inquiry* volume, and for the most complete bibliography of all, see Charles Magel, *A Bibliography on Animal Rights and Related Matters* (Washington, D.C., University of America Press, 1981).

# The Search for an
# Environmental Ethic

## J. BAIRD CALLICOTT

## I. INTRODUCTION

### §1 THE ENVIRONMENTAL CRISIS

During the mid-1960s an awakening occurred. People began to notice that many of the great rivers of the world had virtually become open sewers; that the atmosphere over many large cities was choked with noxious gases; that erstwhile open space and wildlife habitat had given way to highways, strip development, shopping malls, and suburbs; that soil was eroding faster than it could be rebuilt; and that industrial and agricultural toxins were showing up everywhere, including, of all places, in mothers' milk and raptors' eggs.

The scope and complexity of the dawning "environmental crisis" of the sixties defied standard methods of problem solving. Environmental problems could not be easily isolated, analyzed, and solved like some of the other challenges of that decade—putting a man on the moon, for example. Indeed, ecologists William Murdoch and Joseph Connell, in a celebrated discussion, argued that the application of the usual engineering methods of problem solving to environmental dislocations only made matters worse.[1]

Thus the environmental crisis soon came to be perceived as less a set of independent physical "problems" amenable to a coordinated program of engineering "solutions" than a massive ecological reaction that was and is symptomatic of modern technological civilization's maladaptation to the natural environment. And since modern technological civilization is rooted in and continuously inspired by deep-seated cultural attitudes, values, and beliefs, the first and most fundamental step toward amelioration of the environmental crisis, it then appeared, should be a program of *philosophical* criticism and invention. According to historian Roderick Nash, "Ideas are the keystone. . . . Machines, after all, are only the agents of a set of ethical precepts. . . . The most serious sort of pollution is *mind* pollution. Environmental reform ultimately depends on changing values."[2] It was recognized, in other words, that what was needed to "solve" environmental "problems" was not a new technology so much as a new "environmental ethic." Or, put more precisely, the invention and application of new technologies and the use of old technologies should be guided and restrained by an environmental ethic. As ecologist and amateur philosopher Aldo Leopold (1887–1948) had put it some two decades earlier, "We are remodeling the Alhambra with a steam shovel, and we are proud of our yardage. We shall hardly relinquish the shovel, which after all has many good points, but we are in need of gentler and more objective criteria for its successful use."[3]

Since its discovery a decade and a half ago, the environmental crisis has changed in complexion and, given that change, has grown more acute and critical. In the United States, surface waters and urban air are cleaner, highways are less littered, and more soil-saving methods of agriculture are at least recommended as a matter of policy. But the symptoms of our civilization's maladaptation to nature represented by resource depletion and pollution—in respect to which some progress has been made—pale in comparison with the alarming prospect of abrupt and massive species extinction, looming ominously on the horizon.

From the year 1600, when reliable records first began to be kept, to 1900, the average rate of species extinction has been roughly one every four years.[4] From 1900 to the mid-twentieth century, the rate of species extinction has been one per year and, according to conservationist Norman Myers, "if present patterns of exploitation persist," the rate of extinction during the last decade of the twentieth century may be something over a hundred species per day![5] By the end of the century, the total loss of species could exceed one million—one-tenth to one-twentieth of the earth's global complement of species! There is occurring today, particularly in the moist tropical regions of the world, a phenomenon we might call "biocide"; it is analogous to genocide except that its victims are not human "gens" or ethnic groups but nonhuman species. Harvard social entomologist Edward O. Wilson suggests that the biological impoverishment of the earth—the end result of massive species extinction—is the folly posterity is least likely to forgive us.[6] We are today, therefore, more certainly in need of an environmental ethic than ever.

## §2 "FACTS," VALUES, AND CRITERIA FOR THE EVALUATION OF ENVIRONMENTAL ETHICS

A living, practical morality, a real-world ethic—like the Homeric, Confucian, or Christian ethic—cannot be isolated from a larger conceptual matrix. A functional, practical ethic is woven into a larger tapestry of ideas. The world around is, for one thing, the theater of human action. How we picture the world, what we conceive it to be, will, at the very least, set limits on and suggest possibilities for action. What we imagine to be the rightful, natural, or intended "place" of people in the world, furthermore, serves as an ideal or model of human nature which most people, consciously or not, strive to realize or fulfill. As anthropologist Clifford Geertz has pointed out, "The powerfully coercive 'ought' is felt to grow out of a comprehensive, factual 'is' . . . . The tendency to synthesize world view and ethos at some level, if not logically necessary, is at least empirically coercive; if it is not philosophically justified, it is at least pragmatically universal."[7]

An ethic, like any other sort of rational pattern of ideas, must be self-consistent in order to be acceptable and persuasive. Nothing more effectively undermines an ethical system (or any other conceptual system) than to show that it is self-contradictory. A real-world ethic or "ethos," however, must also be consistent with the larger tapestry of ideas that Geertz calls "world view." To an orthodox Hindu, a logically impeccable *social* ethic, for example, that ignored the doctrines of reincarnation and karma would not be persuasive. A self-consistent *environmental* ethic, similarly, that is not also consistent with the whole fabric of scientific theory in which environmental destruction is perceived as a *moral* problem will be no more persuasive or acceptable than an internally incoherent one.

A second criterion for evaluating an ethic is adequacy. Does the ethic adequately address the moral problems with which it purports to help us cope? The Hippocratic code, for example, with its simple affirmation that a doctor's skills should be applied only to preserve and not to extinguish individual human life, is inadequate to deal with the newly emergent moral problems generated by modern medical technology, particularly artificial life-support systems. The reproductive ethic advocated by Pope John Paul II is an inadequate ethic to help us cope with the problem of human overpopulation, since it ignores and even implicitly denies that human *over*population exists or is a "problem" of distinctly *moral* concern. Similarly a putative *environmental* ethic would be inadequate and therefore unacceptable (or at least less acceptable than a more adequate candidate) if it cannot directly address or does not acknowledge as of moral concern those problems that together constitute the "environmental crisis" (as just characterized): biocide—massive *species* extinction, species extirpation (i.e., local extinction), biological impoverishment, and the simplification, degradation, and destabilization of local biotic communities— air and water pollution, soil erosion, and so on.

A third criterion for evaluating an ethic is practicability. Can one actually live in accordance with the precepts of the ethic? An ethic requiring equal consideration of the interests of other human beings may be difficult but not at all impossible to practice. An ethic, on the other hand, that would require the complete neglect of one's own interests would be literally unlivable and thus impracticable.

With the exception of self-consistency, these criteria admit of degrees. An environmental ethic may be more or less consistent with a larger conceptual framework, more or less adequate, and more or less practicable than another. The best environmental ethic would be self-consistent, of course, and *the most* consistent with the larger tapestry of ideas in which environmental problems are recognized as a moral crisis, *the most* adequate in relation to those problems, and *the most* practicable. Fortunately, one environmental ethic among the several that have been advanced by philosophers taking on the challenge of developing an environmental ethic *is* best in all three evaluative categories.

In the following discussion I shall review the several candidates for best environmental ethic, measure them against the criteria here set forth, and show how one approach excels above its competitors.

## II. HOW NOT TO DO ENVIRONMENTAL ETHICS

### §3 THE JUDEO-CHRISTIAN TRADITION: DESPOTISM

Under the leadership of church historian Lynn White, Jr., and landscape architect Ian McHarg, attention was directed to the so-called "Judeo-Christian tradition"—not, at first, as the ethical solution to environmental problems but as their cause.[8] Christianity has long been the established religion of the Western world and for centuries Western thought about everything was circumscribed by the Judeo-Christian world view. And, although presently all Western thought is not limited, as once it was, by the Judeo-Christian parameters of belief, the Judeo-Christian world view is still vigorously inculcated, at an early age, in virtually all members of Western civilization. Hence, White and McHarg claimed, the Judeo-Christian world view and its apparently human-centered ethical orientation must have permitted and even encouraged the abuse of the environment so typical of Western civilization.

The crucial scriptural passage which most invites such criticism is Gen. 1:26–28, in which people are declared to be created in the image of God, given "dominion" over the earth and over "every living thing that moveth upon the earth," and commanded to "be fruitful, and multiply, and replenish the earth and subdue it." At first glance, the implications of this passage seem quite clear: First, it segregates humanity from the rest of creation, then confers on people a special quasi-divine status. Finally, the rest of creation is delivered into human hands with the requirement that people crush other forms of life and fill the world from pole to pole and sea to sea with humankind. The contemporary mechanized, domesticated, biologically impoverished, overpopulated world seems to be nothing more nor less than the fulfillment of this biblical directive. We are in the environmental mess we're in, White and McHarg allege, because we have followed the biblical teachings, not because we have ignored them.

## §4 THE JUDEO-CHRISTIAN TRADITION: STEWARDSHIP

Apologists for the Judeo-Christian tradition countered the White-McHarg despotic interpretation with the stewardship interpretation. For example, biblical scholar James Barr insisted that "Man's dominion . . . contains no markedly exploitative aspect; it approximates to the well-known . . . idea of the Shepherd king."[9]

In the stewardship interpretation of Genesis, humanity's uniqueness among creatures—that is, to have been created in the image of God—confers upon people not only special rights and privileges but also special *duties* and *responsibilities*. Among these duties and responsibilities, it might well be supposed, is the duty to care for and the responsibility to pass on intact the earth and all its creatures, which God delivered into mankind's hands.

If we rest our decision as to which is the correct interpretation, despotism or stewardship, on the literal meaning of the Hebrew words translated as 'dominion' and 'subdue,' then the despotism interpretation would appear to have the most support. According to Barr, "the verb *rada* 'have dominion' is used physically of the treading or trampling down of the wine press; and the word *kabas* 'subdue' means 'stamp down.' "[10]

On the other hand, if we look beyond the passages upon which criticism has narrowly centered to the context in which they occur, the stewardship reading seems the most plausible. First, it might be mentioned that God seems to take a degree of delight and pride in his handiwork. After each day's creative efforts, God contemplated what he had created and found that "it was good." The other living creatures are also commanded to be fruitful and multiply and fill up the waters, the earth, and the sky. The text, in fact, seems to convey the impression that God desired a replete creation teeming with life of every possible variety. Any radical changes, especially destructive changes, people might impose upon the creation would seem to be contrary to God's creative designs.

The stewardship interpretation gains further support from chapter 2 of Genesis (which, however, was not originally narratively connected to the controversial passages in chapter 1). There humanity, represented by Adam, is not charged by God to have dominion over the earth and subdue it but is put into the garden of Eden by God expressly to dress and keep it. In light of the later statement in chapter 2 (later in the eventual arrangement of the texts, not in order of composition) of the role God intended for people in nature (if Eden may be understood to represent nature in general), the stewardship interpretation of the ambiguous notion of "dominion" is decisively confirmed.

## §5 THE ENVIRONMENTAL ETHIC OF THE JUDEO-CHRISTIAN TRADITION

From a philosophical point of view, the Judeo-Christian complex of ideas is an especially attractive intellectual resource for the construction of both an adequate and practicable environmental ethic. One of the most recalcitrant theoretical problems for formal environmental ethics has been the problem of establishing "intrinsic" (or as it is sometimes called, "inherent") value for nonhuman natural entities and/or for nature as a whole.[11] Everyone agrees that at least some nonhuman natural entities are *instrumentally* valuable—as means to human ends or as resources of one kind or another. But to be the direct subjects of *moral consideration* or, as this is sometimes expressed, to have independent *moral standing*, nonhuman natural entities and/or nature as a whole must have more than instrumental value; they must have *intrinsic* (or *inherent*) value.

The Judeo-Christian concept of God affords a possible ground for the intrinsic value of nonhuman natural entities and nature as a whole. On this view, God created the natural world, and by this creative act or by a subsequent fiat (declaring it to be "good"), invested his creation with intrinsic value.

Once intrinsic value and moral consideration has been established for nonhuman natural entities and nature as a whole, an apparently overwhelming practical problem for environmental ethics comes into view. To live at all in the world as it is so constituted, we must use— for food, shelter, clothing, fuel, medicines, and so on—nonhuman natural entities. This, in turn, affects nature as a whole, sometimes—as in the case of forestry, mining, damming, and agriculture—on a grand scale. How could such *exploitation* of *intrinsically* valuable entities ever be morally justifiable?

The Judeo-Christian environmental ethic of stewardship provides a ready solution to this difficulty. People *are* special, created in the image of God. The stewardship interpretation of this element of the Judeo-Christian complex of ideas focuses upon the moral *responsibility* that this divine hallmark imposes upon its bearer, because it is all too easy to suppose that it confers only *privilege*. But clearly it implies *both privilege and responsibility*. People thus have a right to use nature for their proper ends, although, to be sure, people also have the responsibility not to overuse, abuse, or destroy it.

Furthermore, in Genesis it is clear that when God is creating his creatures, he is creating or establishing *species*, not specimens: whales, not Moby Dick; trees, not the McArthur pine; and so on. Individuals come and go. It is natural forms or kinds—in a word, species—are understood to be the enduring elements of creation. Species and the creation as a whole, therefore, are intrinsically valuable (are declared "good"), not individual specimens. Hence, we human beings may in good conscience slaughter animals for food, cut trees for timber, plow the land for crops, etc. as long as these activities do not extirpate or endanger species or contribute to the overall degradation or biological impoverishment of the world. Nor is it necessary that they must. Careful cutting of forests enhances wildlife habitat and enriches biotic diversity; culling (for example, by hunting) specimens of some species can improve their populations and the populations of symbionts; the careful husbandry of land can build soil and benefit wildlife as well as feed people; and so on.

## §6 A CRITIQUE OF THE JUDEO-CHRISTIAN STEWARDSHIP ENVIRONMENTAL ETHIC

In view of the theoretical and practical advantages for an environmental ethic of the Judeo-Christian world view, it is surprising that it has not been more widely endorsed by environmentalists. There is one very basic reason why.

The stewardship environmental ethic of the Judeo-Christian tradition fails the test of consistency. While the classical Judeo-Christian world view may be self-consistent (and there is some question about even this), it is not consistent with a modern scientific concept of nature. What is now known about nature—from astronomy and astrophysics, geology, chemistry, and biochemistry—is not consistent with the hypothesis that the world as we find it was created out of nothing only a few thousand years ago. Indeed, what is now known about nature is not consistent with the idea that it was created or *made* at all. Instead, the evidence overwhelmingly supports the idea that the universe came gradually to be what we now find it to be—rather than coming into its present state all of a sudden—and that it is much larger, much older, and differently arranged than Genesis would lead one to suppose. Further, neither comparative anatomy and physiology nor the fossil evidence support the idea that human beings are a case apart from other creatures (which, of course, from a more informed point of view, are not "creatures" at all, in the literal sense of the term, but "evolvants"). This is not to deny that human beings possess some extraordinary capacities and exhibit some remarkable behaviors in comparison with other species; it is only to affirm that the same natural processes which account for the physical structures and behaviors of other species account equally well for the physical structures and behaviors of human beings.

Charles Darwin's (1809–1882) epic works, *The Origin of Species* and *The Descent of Man,* taken together are, as it were, a new, more naturalistic Genesis. They provide an account of the coming into being of the living world as we find it and a sense of the place or relationship of people in and to the organic world. As Australian philosopher Peter Singer puts it,

> Intellectually the Darwinian revolution was genuinely revolutionary. Human beings now knew that they were not the special creation of God, made in the divine image and set apart from the animals; on the contrary, human beings came to realize that they were animals themselves.[12]

Singer, who is primarily interested in "animal liberation," stops short of drawing a further implication: From the point of view of evolutionary theory as it has been extended in twentieth-century science, there is a historical continuity of human with animal life, *and* of animal with plant life, *and* of life in toto with nonliving chemical compounds, and so on right down to the most elementary physical constituents of nature.

## §7 THE EVOLUTIONARY CONNECTION: KINSHIP

From an evolutionary point of view, human beings are one with nature both physically and psychologically. The materials composing human beings were all forged probably some ten billion years ago in the nuclear cauldron of some giant star and made their way here after a stellar cataclysm, after a sojourn in interstellar space, and after participating in the process of the birth of our solar system. Later still, they jostled about in some caustic chemical soup on the surface of the primordial earth, combining and recombining in all sorts of protoorganic compounds—amino acids, proteinoids, and so on—until they finally formed primitive cells. They were in turn blue-green algae, zooplankton, amoebas, trilobites, arthropods, echinoderms, cephalopods, fishes, reptiles, fowl, insects, mammals, and now us.

Human beings are psychologically continuous with the rest of nature, because the psyche or consciousness is a natural "by-product" of organisms with backbones. The human brain is, to compare great things with trivial, something like a layer cake.[13] The richly laminated and fissured neocortex lies around and over the old brain that we human beings share with other vertebrates. The limbic and supralimbic lobes of the old brain are the locus of sensory, sensorimotor, and emotive experiences and responses. The cerebral cortex first appeared, although in a poorly developed form, at the phylogenetic level of reptiles. From there onward it evolved continuously until it reached its greatest size and complexity in primates, especially Homo sapiens, and cetaceans (whales and dolphins). Human beings, therefore, belong to a wide and varied *psychological community*. Our sensory and emotive capacities are our most widely shared psychological characteristics, but the regions of the cortex devoted to association and other "higher" mental capacities are present to one degree or another in many other species. Thus we are not, in this sense either, psychologically or mentally isolated from the rest of the natural world.

A vast array of other species share to one degree or another our conscious experiences. They experience sensations, pleasure and pain, fear and rage, love and affection. Some—by no means a small number —also "think" to one degree or another, judging by their thoughtful behavior and the presence in them of an organ of thought. This organ, though different in size and complexity, is not different in origin or general structure from our own. The pervasive presence of mind in nature (which is, in turn, the basis for a sense of community with nature), is one of the great moral legacies of the evolutionary epic.

Aldo Leopold summed up Darwin's contribution to a new world view with new moral implications in the following remark:

> It is a century now since Darwin gave us the first glimpse of the origin of species. We know now what was unknown to all the previous caravan of generations: that men are only fellow-voyagers with other creatures in the odyssey of evolution. This new knowledge should have given us, by this time, a sense of kinship with other creatures; a wish to live and let live; a sense of wonder over the magnitude and duration of the biotic enterprise.[14]

## §8 THE ECOLOGICAL CONNECTION: SYMBIOSIS

Evolution links human beings with the rest of nature diachronically (through time). It posits common origins, temporal continuity, and hence phylogenetic kinship and shared experience among species. Ecology unites human beings with the rest of nature synchronically (at one time). Prior to the emergence of ecology, the Western concept of living nature was characterized by a kind of conceptual fragmentation introduced by Plato (428–348 B.C.). According to Plato, each living thing derives its specific characteristics from a "form," an ideal model or pattern as Plato conceived it: elephants from the form of Elephant, crocodiles from the form of Crocodile, and so on. Each thing, thus, acquires an "essence." Logically speaking, species are therefore only *externally* related. Each is what it is by virtue of the impression upon it of its ideal model, a transcendent supranatural entity, not by virtue of its relations with other physical things.

The impression of the living natural world conveyed by Plato's theory of forms is that individual organisms, outfitted with their respective essences and understood as tokens of the ideal types, are just loosed into the physical arena to interact haphazardly, catch as catch can. Nature was thus perceived to be very much like a roomful of furniture—that is, a collection or mere aggregate of individuals of various kinds, relating to one another in an accidental and altogether external fashion. If one pictures the living natural world as an aggregate of physical representatives of ideal models, then "undesirable," "inconvenient," or just "useless" kinds of living things can simply be exterminated and replaced by exotic or domestic species—just as if one were remodeling one's home and rearranging the furniture to make things more comfortable and convenient—without fear of any systemic effects.

Aristotle (384–322 B.C.), whose magisterial work in biology virtually dominated all subsequent thought about living nature until the Darwinian revolution, staunchly and consistently opposed the independent existence of Plato's forms. However, Aristotle retained Plato's doctrine of essences. The forms or taxa (Elephant, Crocodile, etc.), according to Aristotle, do not "exist apart" from individual specimens; they exist, rather, "immanently" in individuals. But the effective picture of living nature remains the same on Aristotle's account as Plato's: it is still represented, in effect, as an aggregate of individuals of varying essential types *that have no functional connection with one another.* Upon Aristotle's taxonomic theory, organic beings remain only externally related.

From an ecological point of view, the living natural world is much more fully integrated and systemically unified than it had been represented to be in Platonic–Aristotelian classical taxonomy.[15] The biotic mantle of the earth, from an ecological point of view, is one because *its living components are reciprocally coevolved and mutually interdependent.* Each living thing is embedded in a matrix of vital relationships, a "web of life." A species' specific complex of characteristics, its *essence,* in classical terminology, is *inconceivable apart from such a matrix.* From the perspective of evolutionary–ecological biology, organisms acquire their specific characteristics through interactive adaptation to other organisms. Hence species, including *Homo sapiens,* are *internally* related to one another. That is, *each is what it is because of its relationships with other kinds.* Thus, we are the kind of beings that we are—psychologically and mentally as well as physically and physiologically—because of our relationships with other species. Human nature is inconceivable in isolation from the living matrix that has shaped it.

## §9 TWO ECOLOGICAL METAPHORS

Ecologists have attempted to express the peculiar integration and systemic unity of living nature disclosed by their science principally by means of two complementary metaphors. Early on, the ecosystem was compared to human socioeconomic organizations. Thus ecologists speak of the "economy of nature" and the "biotic community."[16] More recently, the ecosystem has been compared to a single organism, a planetary "whole earth organism."[17] Both comparisons are, I wish to stress, only metaphors (i.e., condensed similes). The systemic unity of the ecosystem is just what it is and not another thing. Perhaps it is, however, *like* a human economic community in some respects and *like* an organism in some other respects. If these metaphors are expanded into full-blown self-conscious analogies, the following relationships result.

1. The ecosystem and its various subsystems are analogous to human socioeconomic communities. Species are analogous to roles in the biotic community or professions in the economy of nature: butcher, baker, candlestick maker, doctor, lawyer, Indian chief. Specimens are analogous to persons who fill those roles: butchers, bakers, candlestick makers, doctors, lawyers, Indian chiefs. As in medieval society, one is born to one's trade in the economy of nature and there is little or no "social mobility."

2. The ecosystem and its various subsystems are analogous to an organism. Species are analogous to organs in the planetary organism: heart, liver, lungs, intestines, kidneys, and so on. Specimens are analogous to the several cells constituting those organs.

Both of these primary metaphors, similes, or analogies (depending on how they are expressed) characterizing the ecosystem have been very useful in the development of environmental ethics. The organic analogy is morally useful principally because the simultaneously descriptive and normative concepts of "health" and "disease" are conceptually bound up with it. Environmental degradation and destruction are thus represented as similar to disease or amputation in an organism. Pollution is like a sickening poison and species extinction is like random surgery. One may lose one's tonsils, appendix, or even a kidney and still continue to live a healthy, whole life. One may even lose an eye, a digit, or an appendage and still live well, though at some reduced level of function. Certain organs, however, are vital. Similarly, we may lose the Bengal tiger or blue whale and the whole-earth organism, though certainly esthetically impoverished, will continue to function. Which species are vital organs is hard to know. But certainly should an ecological class of organisms like the insect pollinators of plants or rhizobial nitrogen-fixing bacteria be exterminated, the chance of ecospasm—ecological death or life at a substantially reduced level of function—may be very real indeed.[18]

Environmental degradation and destruction, particularly in the form of biological impoverishment, is represented according to the community analogy as similar to a severely depressed human economy in which roles or professions begin to disappear. Ecologists identify three generic professions in the economy of nature: producer (green plants), consumer (animals), and decomposer (fungi and bacteria). Each of these categories is divisible into a myriad of specialities. Some specialized professions are more important than others in the economy of nature, as in human economies.

It will later be very important to remember that the currency, the coin of the realm, in the economy of nature is not a material—like minted gold or silver or paper money—but solar energy. In Aldo Leopold's characterization, the economy of nature, in the last analysis, consists of "a fountain of energy flowing through a circuit of soils,

plants, and animals. Food chains are the living channels which conduct energy upward, death and decay return it to the soil."[19]

We may think of present human activities as thus a bid for economic monopoly, diverting more and more of the river of energy, the
currency of the economy of nature, into fewer and fewer channels
that terminate in more and more fat-cat consumers, members of a
particularly inessential profession: namely human beings. Since the
solar energy budget is fixed, the diversion of energy into the human-
terminating channels reduces the energy flowing through the nonhu-
man-terminating channels, which then shrink or even dry up.
Environmental ethics may thus be conceived, from the point of view
of the socioeconomic model of the biosphere, as a theoretical foundation for a just distribution of the ultimate natural resource, solar energy, among all earth's working partners in the biotic community or
economy of nature.

## §10 THREE SECULAR APPROACHES TO ENVIRONMENTAL ETHICS

In the fifteen years or so since the emergence of a broad awareness
of the environmental crisis and an evolutionary–ecological world
view, professional philosophers have attempted to construct a logically coherent, adequate, and practicable *theory* of environmental
ethics without reference to God or to his "creation." Three main
secular theoretical approaches have, in this interval, clearly emerged.
They are as follows:

1. Traditional and Protracted Humanism—business-as-usual
   Western human-centered ethics, in which moral standing is
   sometimes accorded to human beings of future generations.
2. Extensionism—the extension of moral standing and/or moral
   rights from human beings inclusively to wider and wider
   classes of *individual* nonhuman natural entities.
3. Ecocentrism—moral consideration for the ecosystem *as a
   whole* and for its various subsystems as well as for human and
   nonhuman natural entities severally.

I shall argue that the third approach, ecocentrism, is the best approach to environmental ethics. It is, I think, by far the most coherent
in both senses, viz., that it is (1) self-consistent and, just as important,
(2) consistent with the larger pattern of ideas that gave rise to environmental awareness and concern in the first place. It is, I also think, the
most adequate: it *directly* and *effectively* addresses the moral problems that it is supposed to help us resolve. And finally, of the three
secular approaches to environmental ethics so far developed, I think
it is the most practicable—in the sense that the limitations it would
impose on human behavior vis-à-vis the environment are limitations

that will help the environment to prosper *and* human beings to live and live well.

## §11 TRADITIONAL AND PROTRACTED HUMANISM

The traditional humanistic approach to environmental ethics treats the environment merely as a "pool" of "resources" and as an "arena" of human interaction and potential conflict that the science of ecology has recently revealed to be much more complex than previously supposed. The adverse effects human beings may have upon other human beings *indirectly* through things they may do *directly* to the environment—like "developing" and consuming it and treating it as a sink for wastes—have recently become amplified, moreover, by ballooning human numbers and more powerful and/or more toxic technologies. According to philosopher Kristin Shrader-Frechette, a leading advocate of this approach,

> it is difficult to think of an action which would do irreparable damage to the environment or ecosystem, but which would not also threaten human well-being. . . . if a polluter dumps toxic wastes in a river, this action could be said to be wrong . . . because the "interests" of the river are violated, but also . . . because there are human interests in having clean water (e.g. for recreation and for drinking).[20]

Therefore, we don't need a *new* environmental ethic to set out what human beings may and may not do to nonhuman natural entities and nature as a whole. Our old ethics of equal moral consideration and/or justice for all human beings are quite adequate—especially if by "all" we intend future as well as presently existing human beings, as in protracted humanism.

## §12 A CRITIQUE OF THE TRADITIONAL AND PROTRACTED HUMANISM APPROACH

As philosopher Tom Regan has pointed out, the humanistic approaches to environmental ethics actually result not in an environmental ethic at all but in an ethic for the use of the environment, a "management" ethic.[21] That is, our duties to the environment would be only *indirect* duties; our only *direct* duties are to our "fellow man." "Well, so what?" an advocate of environmental humanism might reply. "If it gets the job done, if it prohibits overconsumption, pollution, and other human harms to the environment as strictly as an environmental ethic proper, why not go with it, rather than some controversial new alternative?"

Environmental philosophers Richard Sylvan and Val Plumwood have vigorously challenged the contention that the *practical* implications of an environmental ethic based upon humanism (which they unflatteringly call "human chauvinism") would be equivalent to the *practical* implications of an environmental ethic that accorded intrinsic value to nonhuman natural entities and to nature as a whole: "There is an enormous *felt* or *emotional* difference between feeling that a place should be valued or respected for itself . . .," they point out, "and feeling that it should not be defaced because it is valued by one's fellow humans. . . . These differences in emotional presentation are accompanied by or expressed by an enormous range of behavioral differences."[22]

I too doubt that a human-centered ethic for the use of the environment would in fact prohibit human harms to the environment as strictly as any other ethic. To take Shrader-Frechette's own example, a polluting industry might generously compensate the affected *people* for the loss of the recreational amenity afforded by a clean river and provide them an alternative source of drinking water. Upon this approach to environmental ethics, the industry could then ethically go on using the river as a dump for its toxic wastes. Although fish, birds, and the river itself would continue to suffer disease, death, and degradation, the "interests" of the affected human parties would be fairly balanced.

However, *even if Shrader-Frechette is right* that "existing utilitarian and egalitarian ethical theories [are adequate] to safeguard the environment," an inconsistency of the second sort (see §2) lies at the core of this approach to environmental ethics. Its advocates seem at once ecologically well informed and ecologically unenlightened. According to both the traditional and protracted humanistic approaches to environmental ethics, ecology only complicates human-to-human intercourse, both in the present and across generations; it does not transform our vision of what it means to be human.

Norwegian philosopher Arne Naess and his American exponents Bill Devall and George Sessions call these approaches to environmental ethics "shallow" as opposed to "deep" ecology.[23] Ecology is acknowledged or intellectually affirmed in one area or at one level of thought—relations of cause and effect in the nonhuman natural environment—but it is ignored or denied at another level or area of thought—the general structure of nature and the embeddedness of people within that structure. From an evolutionary–ecological point of view, we are "kin" to the fellow members of the biotic community. Our actions in respect to these fellow members should somehow be *directly* morally accountable, and the integrity of this community per se, the health of the planetary organism, should somehow be of *direct* moral concern.

Protracted humanism currently is the subject of intense controversy in a rapidly growing body of literature, since it involves moral consideration of, or duties to, nonexistent or at best only potentially existent people.[24] I am inclined to agree that we ought to bequeath a robustly healthy and copiously bountiful ecosystem to posterity. But that should be an ancillary or corollary duty, the fulfillment of which will follow naturally upon the implementation of a genuine *environmental* ethic, rather than vice versa.

## §13 EXTENSIONISM

A second approach to environmental ethics attempts conceptually to articulate and theoretically to ground moral concern *directly* for the environment by extending or stretching traditional Western humanistic moral theory so that it recognizes the moral standing of some nonhuman natural entities. It was first developed, most notably by Peter Singer, as a theory which would extend moral considerability to fellow *sentient* beings (beings capable of experiencing pleasure and pain) without reference to the environment at large or environmental problems per se.[25] As further developed and refined by Tom Regan, this first stage of extensionism—the extension of equal consideration and even (in Regan's formulation) basic rights to sentient animals[26]— was so compelling that a second, distinctly environmental stage was advanced.[27]

## §14 FIRST-PHASE EXTENSIONISM

If one demands a theoretical justification of traditional humanism (i.e., if one asks just why *all and only human* beings are morally considerable and/or possessed of rights), some characteristic of human nature is usually cited. *Secular* Western philosophical humanism has assiduously avoided citing some *nonempirical* characteristic, like the "image of God," as that which renders human beings exclusively morally considerable, since grounding human moral worth in the image of God or any other nonempirical characteristic would abrogate the commitment of moral philosophy to rational persuasion—it would rest ethics upon faith rather than reasoned belief. It might also open the way for similar nonempirical characteristics that could frustrate the goals of moral humanism: by parity of reasoning racists might speak of a "chosen people" or of races which bear "the mark of Cain." Or sexists might similarly argue that the subjugation of women is just since women are essentially only "Adam's rib." Any criterion for moral considerability must also be *relevant* to the benefit for which it selects. Just as traditional Western humanism rejects race and gender per se, albeit empirical characteristics, as irrelevant to moral standing, so traditional Western humanism must also reject an empirical characteristic like mere species membership as equally irrelevant.

*Secular* traditional Western humanism is thus exposed to a dilemma posed by recent advocates of animal liberation/rights: If the empirical characteristic upon which human moral worth allegedly rests is pitched high enough (e.g., rationality or the capacity for moral reciprocity) to exclude most animals, some "marginal" human beings (infants and abject morons are most frequently mentioned) will also be excluded from moral standing and thus may be treated as we please —experimented upon, hunted, and so on—contrary to the precepts of traditional Western humanism.[28] But if the empirical characteristic upon which human moral worth allegedly rests is pitched low enough to include the marginal cases, some nonhuman beings who also possess that characteristic will be included and thus they too will be (or, should be) extended equal moral standing—contrary to the precepts of traditional Western humanism.

The criterion of moral considerability advanced by Singer, following Jeremy Bentham (1748–1832), is sentience—the capacity to experience pleasure and pain. This is a capacity equally possessed by all human beings including marginal cases. It is, prima facie, a morally relevant criterion, since to be wronged often means to be caused to suffer. But many, many other nonhuman beings are also sentient subjects. Therefore, sentient nonhuman beings, Singer argues, should also be *extended* the same moral consideration that human beings accord themselves and one another.

Peter Singer's criterion of sentiency for equal consideration or equal moral standing is not an adequate basis for an ethical theory to address the major moral issues of animal welfare, let alone an adequate basis for a theory of environmental ethics. Singer himself considers meat eating immoral and, throughout his book *Animal Liberation*, insists that people ought, *morally* ought, to become vegetarians. Bentham, the original advocate of sentiency as a criterion for moral considerability, however, recognized that it is perfectly possible to raise animals in comfort and to slaughter them painlessly; thus he would support the view that human carnivorousness is perfectly consistent with a sentiency-based animal welfare ethic. If everyone were a vegetarian, many fewer cows, pigs, chickens, and other domestic livestock would be raised and thus many fewer animals would have the opportunity, for an alloted time, to pursue happiness. One might therefore argue, on Singer's own grounds, that people have a positive moral obligation to eat meat *provided that the animals raised for human consumption were raised in comfort and given the opportunity to live happily.* Even sport hunting—long regarded by some concerned about animal welfare to be the most odious because the most gratuitous abuse of animals—would be permissible on Singer's grounds *provided that hunters deliver a clean kill and by so doing preserve animals from greater suffering from the vicissitudes of life in the wild,* while as a bonus benefit also giving themselves pleasure.

Recognizing these (and other) inadequacies of Singer's moral theory in relation to the moral problems of the treatment of animals, Tom Regan has advocated a "rights" approach to address them.[29] Regan postulates that some individual animals have "inherent worth" because they are, like ourselves, not only sentient but *subjects of a life* that from their point of view can be better or worse. Inherent worth, in turn, may be the grounds of basic moral rights. I am persuaded that Regan's representation of animal rights in his book *The Case for Animal Rights* adequately supports the basic moral agenda of those concerned primarily for individual animal welfare: an end to (1) meat eating, (2) the use of animals in "scientific" experimentation, and (3) hunting and trapping.

## §15 A CRITIQUE OF FIRST-PHASE EXTENSIONISM IN RELATION TO ENVIRONMENTAL PROBLEMS.

Clearly, however, neither Singer's theory of animal liberation nor Regan's theory of animal rights will do double duty as an environmental ethic. For one thing, most obviously neither animal liberation nor animal rights provides for direct moral consideration of plants and all the many animals that may not be either sentient or, more restrictively still, "subjects of a life." But the brunt of environmental destruction is borne by plants helplessly in the path of chain saws and bulldozers, and the bulk of rare and endangered species are neither sentient nor subjects of a life as Regan defines this concept.

An apologist for the animal liberation and/or animal rights ethics might argue that they entail *indirect* duties to preserve plants and nonsentient/nonsubject animals for the sake of those sentient/subject animals whose welfare, like ours, depends upon plants and "lower" animals for food and shelter and more generally upon the integrity of the ecosystem. We could hardly expect Regan, however, to endorse such an argument since he has so eloquently and persuasively insisted (see §12) that a *human-centered* environmental ethic would not be a genuine ethic *of the environment* (but only, rather, a "management ethic") if it provided *direct* moral considerability exclusively for people but only *indirect* concern for nonhuman natural entities.

A *sentiency centered* and/or *subject-of-a-life centered* environmental ethic would result, no less than traditional and protracted humanism, in a mere management ethic, an ethic for using the environment by sentient or subject-of-a-life animals (including humans, of course) for their own sake. While not an anthropocentric ethic, it would nonetheless be a management ethic. Animal liberation/rights broaden the base class of morally considerable beings (the former more widely than the latter), but not by very much relative to the millions of plant and invertebrate forms of life making up earth's biotic community. So plants and invertebrate animals, the vast majority of earth's living denizens, remain mere means to be managed for the good of the morally privileged class of sentient or subject-of-a-life animals. (Tom Regan, it should be noted, argues only that the subject-of-a-life criterion is a sufficient, not necessary, condition of inherent value and thus rights. He leaves open the question of the inherent value of individuals who are not subjects of a life or even of groups or systems.)

Clearly, the ethics of animal welfare are inadequate precepts of human behavior in respect to environmental problems. Perhaps even more seriously problems of consistency of the second sort—analogous to those raised respecting traditional humanism (see §12)—have been raised respecting the animal liberation/animal rights ethics *if* they are offered as *environmental* as well as animal welfare ethics.[30]

Animal liberation/animal rights seems very well informed by one of modern biology's two great theoretical cornerstones, the theory of evolution, while not at all by the other, ecology. Animal liberation/ rights rests in part on the basic notion that there is no essential *morally relevant* difference between mankind and mankind's closest kin in the phylogenetic scale. But the *ecological* order of nature is premised on one fundamental principle—all life (even plant life, for plant nutrients must be recycled) depends upon death. Death and often pain are at the heart of nature's economy. To the extent that the animal liberation/animal rights ethics condemn the taking of life (as a violation of the rights of a subject of life) or the infliction of pain on a sentient being, they are irreconcilably at odds with the ecological "facts of life."

To develop this point more particularly, a ruthlessly consistent deduction of the consequences of both the Singerian and Reganic ethics *might* imply a program of humane predator extermination. For sound ecological reasons, the conservation and reintroduction of predators is among the highest priorities on the agenda of current environmental goals. Predatory fishes, reptiles, birds, and mammals, however, cause a great deal of suffering to other innocent animals. If carnivorous animals could be rounded up, housed comfortably in zoos, fed soyburgers, sterilized, and allowed to die natural deaths, then only herbivorous animals would remain in nature and the total amount of pain and suffering might be vastly reduced. Singer clearly recognizes this implication of his own ethical principles but, inconsistently, turns aside from it:

> It must be admitted that the existence of carnivorous animals does pose one problem for the ethics of Animal Liberation. . . . Assuming humans could eliminate carnivorous species from the earth and that the total amount of suffering among animals in the world were thereby reduced, should we do it? . . . We cannot and should not try to police all of nature. We do enough if we eliminate our own un-necessary killing and cruelty to other animals.[31]

We may not be able to police all of nature, but we should try—just as we should try though we may not succeed, in Singer's view, to police the factory farms and animal research laboratories for the same reason —our obligation to prevent needless suffering. Ongoing programs of "predator control" have already proven that removing what Aldo Leopold called the "apex of the food chain" will not destroy ecosystems, only impoverish and degrade them. And the pleasure that an environmentalist or nature aesthete takes in the soaring flight of a hawk or eagle must be judged as trivial and unnecessary, as the pleasure of wearing mink or dining on paté de foi gras, in comparison with the suffering of the thousands of mice, rabbits, and other mammals literally eaten alive by predators.

A consistent deduction of the implications for predator policy of Regan's "rights view" is not so clear cut. According to Regan, the goal of wildlife management should be to "defend wild animals in the possession of their rights, providing them with the opportunity to live their own life, by their own lights, as best they can, spared that *human predation* that goes by the name of 'sport.' "[32] Why should we not defend wild animals from *nonhuman predation* as well, no matter what name we give it? Regan's answer is that "animals are not moral agents and so can have none of the duties moral agents have, including the duty to respect the rights of other animals."[33]

It is at least arguable, however, that, on Regan's rights view, even so, innocent vegetarian animals should be protected from nonhuman predators as well as from human predators. We regard criminally insane human beings as "not moral agents" either. Hence, we do not try them in court and punish them as we do those who are sane. But neither do we permit them to remain free in society. We protect innocent *people* by incarcerating, in maximum-security psychiatric wards, destructive humans who are not moral agents. Likewise, it would seem that predators should be incarcerated in similar institutions (zoos or holding pens) to safeguard the rights of their would-be victims. Regan (inconsistently?) would protect human subjects of a life from "rabid foxes," who are not moral agents and have no duties. Why, then, would he not protect, say, rabbit subjects of a life from healthy foxes who are not moral agents and have no duties? Yet in both cases, indeed, more especially in the latter (since a healthy fox has a longer prospect of life), "their lives assure future attacks [upon people and rabbits respectively] if nothing is done."[34]

In his argument for the negative moral value of human predation and at the same time neutral moral value of animal predation, Regan says that "wildlife managers should be principally concerned with letting animals be, keeping human predators out of their affairs, allowing these 'other nations' to carve out their own destiny."[35] Regan here seems to want to have his cake and eat it too. If animals are *equally* subjects of a life with people and have the *same* basic moral rights as people, then they belong to the *same moral community* of inherently valuable, rights-holding beings. Our present publicly acknowledged and institutionalized human rights ethic does not acknowledge the moral relevance of national origin any more than it acknowledges the moral relevance of race or creed. Why then do not both rabbits and people deserve *equal* protection from foxes (regardless of the state of health of the foxes) and other predators? My question is not rhetorical; rather, I think the predator policy of Regan's "rights view" needs more detailed development and argument if it is persuasively to answer such criticisms as these.

If the animal welfare ethics of Singer and Regan require the (humane) phasing out of predators from nature, as possibly they may, then they would not only be inadequate but, from an ecological point of view, actually nightmarish. I wish to emphasize that the predator policy required by both the animal liberation and animal rights ethics is controversial, if for no other reason than that their principal advocates, Singer and Regan, respectively, do not themselves admit, what *seem* to me to be, the ecologically untoward implications of both theories.

Both Singer and Regan, however, quite openly admit that rare and endangered species are provided no special, preemptory status by their respective theories.[36] And yet species extirpation and extinction is today widely recognized as the single most pressing problem among the spectrum of problems collectively called the environmental crisis. The specimens of most endangered species, moreover, are neither sentient nor subjects of a life. They are, rather, plants and invertebrates. Hence, if there were a mortal conflict between, say, an endangered plant *species* and *individual* sentient or subject-of-a-life animals, there could be no *moral* reason to choose to save the plant species at the expense of the lives of plentiful individual animals, according to animal liberation/rights. Environmental philosopher Holmes Rolston III reports with approval an action of the National Park Service in which hundreds of rabbits on Santa Barbara Island were killed "to protect a few plants . . . once thought extinct and curiously called the Santa Barbara Live-Forever."[37] Since in this and similar cases, the animal liberation/rights ethics would give preference to the sentient/subject-of-a-life animals, the environmental problem of species extinction would be not merely ignored; it would be aggravated, at least for the vast majority of threatened species.

Animal liberation/rights, finally, does not discriminate between the value of domestic and wild animals, since both are equally sentient and/or subjects of a life. However, most environmentalists regard the intrusion of domestic animals into natural ecosystems as very destructive and therefore prima facie contrary to an environmental ethic. Naturalist John Muir (1838–1914), a prophet and pioneer of the modern environmental movement, referred to domestic sheep (benignly raised and tended not for meat but for wool) as "hooved locusts."[38] And Aldo Leopold, the first to suggest the need for an environmental ethic, remarked that "the farmer who clears the woods off a 75 percent slope, *turns his cows into the clearing,* and dumps its rainfall, rocks and soil into the community creek, is still (if otherwise decent) a respected member of society."[39] The farmer in Leopold's hypothetical example is almost certainly supposed to be a Wisconsin dairy farmer whose cows (benignly raised for milk, not meat) spend their days in comfort and contentment on a small family farm. Let us suppose that this farmer had become convinced by Singer and Regan that his action was intended to benefit directly his cows and only incidentally himself. Yet Leopold regards his creation of pasture for his cattle as a prime illustration of an *environmentally immoral* action. Had the same farmer fenced his cattle out of the woodlot and planted browse for deer, grouse, woodchucks, and other wild animals, Leopold would have regarded it as a prime illustration of an *environmentally moral* action. Since domestic livestock and wild animals are equally sentient and/or equally subjects of a life and a pasture can support more cows than deer in a woods of the same-size, the animal liberation/animal rights ethic cannot, as an environmentalist would prefer, condemn the former and commend the latter.

An ecologically well-informed environmental ethic would draw a moral distinction among animals along another axis than that drawn by animal liberation/rights. Rather than providing moral standing or rights to animals that are sentient or subjects of a life and withholding standing or rights from those that are not, an ecologically oriented environmental ethic would provide preferred moral consideration (and possibly rights) to wild animals, whether or not sentient or subjects of a life, and regard domestic animals as, for all practical purposes, a kind of human technology to be evaluated, like all other technologies, in terms of environmental impact. The environmental impact of domestic animals might be benign—as, for example, that of domestic bees—but from the ecological point of view, environmental impact should be the *primary* consideration governing the treatment of man-made animals originally designed for human utility.

## §16. SECOND-PHASE EXTENSIONISM

Philosopher Kenneth Goodpaster, recognizing the limitations of first-phase extensionism vis-à-vis environmental problems, proposed a "life-principle" ethic to address them. He turned Singer's critique of the humanists' criterion of moral considerability against Singer's own criterion of sentiency. Thus, if rationality (or any of the other criteria for moral considerability proposed by humanists) is arbitrary and irrelevant to the status that it would confer, how is sentiency (or being the subject of a life) any less arbitrary and irrelevant?[40] If humanists are, from the point of view of animal welfare ethics, "speciesists," advocates of animal liberation/rights are, from the point of view of a life-principle ethic, "vertebrate chauvinists"!

Goodpaster argues that sentience is not an end in itself but evolved as a means to further the goal of survival. Therefore, since sentience is ancillary to life, the capacity to live—rather than the capacity to experience pleasure and pain—should be the criterion of moral considerability. (A similar argument might be made respecting the set of capacities that together define the "subject of a life.") Further, though 'to harm' sometimes means to cause to suffer, it very often means something broader. One may *directly* harm a tree or any other plant, Goodpaster contends, in a straightforward, unproblematic sense. One may, therefore, quite intelligibly *morally consider* living but nonsentient (and non-subject-of-a-life) beings in deciding what to do. Goodpaster, following legal philosopher Joel Feinberg, suggests that a living being, as opposed to a "mere thing" (an inanimate object), may be defined, for the purposes of ethical analysis, in terms of *conations* (i.e., inherent tendencies, directions of growth, and natural fulfillments).[41] To harm a conative thing would be to interdict or to frustrate its growth and/or natural fulfillment.

## §17 A CRITIQUE OF SECOND-PHASE EXTENSIONISM AS AN ENVIRONMENTAL ETHIC

The second, more inclusive, phase of extensionism is designed to overcome the most obvious *environmental* inadequacy of the first, more restricted phase, since it includes plants as well as animals within the scope of morals. Even so extended, however, the life-principle ethic remains less than adequate as an environmental ethic because it does not directly address even the most important environmental problems which, according to its designer, Goodpaster, it is supposed to address.

First and foremost, according to Goodpaster, is the problem of species extinction. Conativism of the sort we find in Goodpaster cannot directly address species extinction for the simple reason that species per se are no more conative than they are either sentient or subjects of a life. Nor can his theory even theoretically provide *preferred* moral standing to a *specimen* of endangered species, since its conations can count for no more than the conations of a specimen of a plentiful species. For similar reasons, it cannot morally discriminate between domestic and wild animals and/or plants. A community of rare wildflowers, for example, would deserve no more consideration than a monoculture of corn plants or soybeans, since any plant is as conative as any other.

The life-principle ethic, as an environmental ethic, is less than adequate and, as even its advocates admit, hopelessly impracticable (as I shall more fully illustrate in a moment) for the same fundamental reason: The life-principle ethic—no less than animal liberation/rights and traditional Western humanism, which is the paradigm for both— is *individualistic* and reductive. An equitable system for resolving conflicts of interests among individuals is a reasonable, practicable goal if the individuals whose interests are to be equally considered are relatively few and far between. As more and more individuals are admitted into moral entitlement via a theoretical extension of moral considerability and/or moral rights, moral space becomes more crowded. More conflicts of interest inevitably arise, and their management becomes more hopeless. Finally, when *every living thing* is extended moral considerability, then moral standing becomes so diluted as to be practically meaningless. Either one must starve oneself to death, since even to eat vegetables is to violate the interests of some living things, or one must continually live in a condition of hypocrisy or bad faith. With conativism, the practicability quotient approaches zero; a point of moral overload is reached and the whole enterprise of ethics threatens to collapse into absurdity.

## III. AN ECOCENTRIC ENVIRONMENTAL ETHIC

### §18 A PLEA FOR A HOLISTIC APPROACH TO ENVIRONMENTAL ETHICS

Goodpaster, in a subsequent discussion, recognized the moral bankruptcy of extensionism for environmental ethics:

> What I want to suggest is that the *last* thing we need is simply another "liberation movement"—for animals, trees, flora, fauna, or rivers. More importantly, the last thing we need is to cling to a model of moral judgment and justification which makes such liberation movements (with their attendant concentric reasoning) the chief or only way to deal with moral growth and social change.
>
> What I am maintaining is *not* that the "individualistic" model cannot be pressed into service, epicycle after epicycle, to deal with our environmental obligations. Rather my point is that when this is the only model available, its implausibilities will keep us from dealing ethically with environmental obligations and ideals altogether. . . . [Extensionism] strains our moral sensitivities and intuitions to the breaking point. . . .[42]

Goodpaster then points the way to an alternative approach which, though not at all usual in *modern* Western philosophy, has precedents in *ancient* Western philosophy:

> The oft-repeated pleas by some ecologists and environmentalists that our thinking needs to be less atomistic and more "holistic" translates in the present context into a plea for a more embracing object of moral consideration. In a sense, it represents a plea to return to the richer Greek conception of man by nature social and not intelligibly removable from his social and political context—though it goes beyond the Greek conception in emphasizing that societies too need to be understood in a context, an ecological context, and that it is this larger whole which is the "bearer of value."[43]

A holistic or ecocentric environmental ethic was outlined in *A Sand County Almanac,* the widely read and admired "gospel" of environmental philosophy by Aldo Leopold. For the most part, contemporary moral philosophers searching for a coherent, adequate, and practicable environmental ethic have failed to explore and develop Leopold's "land ethic" to the extent that they have, for example, Bentham's even briefer remarks about the moral considerability of sentient animals. This is, in large measure, because a holistic approach to ethics is so unfamiliar and represents such a radical departure from long-established modern traditions of Western moral philosophy. One prominent moral philosopher has even called Aldo Leopold's land ethic "environmental fascism," because of its holistic characteristics.[44] This impression has unfortunately been invited and abetted by Leopold's few philosophical partisans who have imprudently emphasized the holistic aspects of the land ethic at the expense of its provisions for the moral consideration of individuals.[45] Nevertheless, Leopold's land ethic remains the only holistic or ecosystemic game in town. I shall accordingly first explore and develop its conceptual foundations and moral precepts, and then show how it does not, in fact, lead to the untoward moral consequences its critics have thought that it must.

## §19 ETHICS AS AN EVOLUTIONARY PARADOX

In sharp contrast to traditional Western humanism and its protracted and extended variations, the Leopold land ethic is firmly tied to evolutionary and ecological concepts, as the following remark indicates. "Ethics, so far studied only by philosophers, is actually a process in ecological evolution. Its sequences may be described in ecological as well as philosophical terms."[46] The conceptual foundations of the land ethic, at the outset, therefore, promise to be in harmony with the new organic outlook.

According to Leopold, "an ethic, ecologically, is a limitation on freedom of action in the struggle for existence."[47] This biological characterization of ethics suggests at once an evolutionary paradox: How could "a limitation on freedom of action" possibly have evolved—that is, have been first conserved and then spread through a population—given the unremitting "struggle for existence"? It would seem that an ethical organism, an organism that tended to *limit* its own *freedom* of action, would be severely disadvantaged in the struggle for existence and would, thus, fail to survive and reproduce. So how can evolutionary theory be squared with the manifest existence of moral behavior?

## §20 THE PARADOX RESOLVED

Darwin tackled this problem in *The Descent of Man* "exclusively from the side of natural history."[48] Darwin's explanation of how natural selection could produce "a moral sense or conscience" assumes that morality or ethical behavior is based less upon reason than upon *feelings* (love, affection, sympathy, and so on), as David Hume (1711–1776) had claimed. For an *evolutionary* account, to ground morality primarily in reason would be to put the cart before the horse. Reason appears to be a very *delicate* and *widely variable* human faculty and only *recently evolved*, dependent for its development upon a preexisting moral climate. Feeling, however, is a more primitive and far more general animal capacity.

Darwin begins with the observation that for many species, and especially mammals, prolonged parental care is necessary to ensure reproductive success. Such care, he argues, by extrapolation from our own animal experience, is *motivated* and facilitated by a certain strong *emotion* that adult mammals (in some species perhaps only the females) experience toward their offspring—parental *love* (or perhaps, motherly love). The capacity for such a feeling would thus be selected as part of a species' psychological profile, since such a capacity would strongly contribute to reproductive success.

Once established, Darwin argued, the "parental and filial affections" permitted, among the primate ancestors of *Homo sapiens,* the formation of small family or clan social groups, perhaps originally consisting only of parents and offspring. Now these and similar "social sentiments" or "social instincts," such as "the all-important emotion of sympathy," Darwin reasoned, "will have been increased through natural selection; for those communities which included the greatest number of the most sympathetic members would flourish best, and rear the greatest number of offspring."[49]

As family group competed with family group, ironically, the same principles that at first would seem to lead so directly and inevitably toward greater and greater mutual aggression and rapacity led instead toward increased affection, kindness, and sympathy, for now the struggle for limited resources is understood to have been pursued *collectively.* Those *groups* that included "the greatest number of the most sympathetic members" may be supposed to have outcompeted those whose members were quarrelsome and disagreeable. "No tribe," Darwin tells us, "could hold together if murder, robbery, treachery, etc., were common; consequently, such crimes within the limits of the same tribe 'are branded with everlasting infamy'; but excite no such sentiment beyond these limits."[50]

Not only did competition select for *more intense* sympathy and affection within group limits or boundaries, but for casting social sentiments even *wider,* since larger social groups make possible more division of labor and hence greater economic efficiency. Indeed, in competition among the most internally peaceable and cooperative groups, the *larger* will win out. Thus there arose a tendency for extended family groups to merge into larger social units.

## §21 THE DOUBLE CORRELATIVE RELATIONSHIP OF MORALITY AND SOCIETY

This evolutionary explanation of the origin of ethics, to which Leopold alludes near the beginning of "The Land Ethic," clearly issues in a fundamental principle, namely, that *ethical relations and social orga-*

*nization are correlative* in two ways: (1) the perceived boundaries of a society are also the perceived boundaries of its moral community and (2) a society's structure or organization is reflected in its ethical code of conduct.[51] Some comments on both points follow.

Original human societies consisted of extended families and clans. Subsistence hunting and gathering determined both their *size* and *organization* or structure. Correspondingly, original human ethics were narrowly circumscribed and xenophobic, stressing virtues that contributed to small-group survival—for example, the virtues of sharing, courage, loyalty, deference, obedience to elders, and so on. Ethical behavior toward out-group members was not enjoined. Indeed, such persons could be exploited, or even tortured and killed, without violation of the clan code of conduct.

When clans eventually merged into tribes, there occurred a corresponding growth in the *boundaries* of the moral community: one was required to behave morally toward members of one's tribe as well as members of one's family or clan. And as *tribal social structure* is more complex, involving specialized social roles as chieftain, warrior, priest, doctor, and so on, the corresponding ethical *code* became more elaborate and finely articulated.

As tribes eventually merged into larger social units—nations or countries—corresponding extensions of moral *boundaries* occurred along with corresponding modifications and amplifications of the older ethical *rules* and *precepts*. There also occurred radical changes in economic patterns of existence and in *social organization*. These changes in social organization were reflected in correlative changes in ethics. In large, heterogeneous societies, for example, there emerged the moral ideals of individual liberty, privacy, and equality. (Such modern moral principles are not only not recognized in familial and tribal ethics but are, in clan and tribal codes, regarded more as vices than virtues.)

Today we are witnessing the merger of nations into a global community. This "global village" has become an emergent reality because of multinational economic interdependence and because of transportation and communications technologies. Corresponding to this emergent global phase in human social evolution is the current humanitarian or "human rights" moral ideal.

## §22 TRANSITION FROM HUMANISTIC TO ENVIRONMENTAL ETHICS

According to Aldo Leopold, "All ethics so far evolved rest upon a single premise: that the individual is a member of a community of interdependent parts. . . . The land ethic simply enlarges the boundaries of the community to include soils, waters, plants, and animals, or collectively: the land."[52] Since ethics have evolved and changed correlatively to the growth and development of the putative social or communal organization, and since the natural environment is represented in ecology as a *community* or society, an ecocentric environmental ethic may be clearly envisioned.

Moral precepts—for example, against "murder, robbery, treachery, etc."—may be regarded as the cultural specification or articulation of the limitations on freedom of action to which our social sentiments predispose us. Moral behavior has a genetic basis, but it is not "hardwired." In the process of enculturation, we are taught both the appropriate forms of behavior and toward whom they should be directed. The people around us are socially classified. Some are mother, father, brothers and sisters; others uncles, aunts, or cousins; still others are friends and neighbors; and in former times, some were barbarians, aliens, or enemies. This *representation* plays upon and provides substance to our "open" or merely dispositional other-oriented feelings and produces subtly shaded moral responses. And should the cognitive representation of our relationships change, our moral responses would change accordingly. If one is told, for example, that a person previously thought to be a stranger is actually a long lost relative, then one's feelings toward him or her are likely to be altered whether it is true or not. Or when religious teachers tell us we are all "brothers" and "sisters" beneath the skin, our moral sentiments are stimulated accordingly. How the social environment is *cognitively represented*, therefore, is crucial to how it is valued and to our moral response to it.

Now, the general world view of the modern life sciences *represents* all forms of life on the planet Earth both as *kin* and as fellow members of a social unit—*the biotic community.* The Earth may now be *perceived* not, as once it was, the unique physical center of the universe but rather a mere planet orbiting around an ordinary star at the edge of a galaxy containing billions of similar stars in a universe containing billions of such galaxies. In the context of this universal spatial-temporal frame of reference, the planet Earth is very small and very local indeed, an island paradise in a vast desert of largely empty space containing physically hostile foreign bodies separated from Earth by immense distances. All the denizens of this cosmic island paradise evolved into their myriad contemporary forms from a simple, single-cell common ancestor. All contemporary forms of life thus are represented to be *kin, relatives, members of one extended family.* And all are equally members in good standing of one *society* or *community,* the biotic community or global ecosystem.

This cosmic/evolutionary/ecological picture of the Earth and its biota can actuate the moral sentiments of affection, respect, love, and sympathy with which we human mammals are genetically endowed. It also actuates the special sentiment or feeling (call it "patriotism"), noticed by both Hume and Darwin, that we have for the *group as a whole* to which we belong, the *family* per se, the *tribe,* and the *country* or *nation*. From the point of view of modern biology, the earth with its living mantle is our tribe and each of its myriad species is, as it were, a separate clan.

Thus the land ethic—in sharp contrast to traditional Western humanism and its protracted and extended variations—provides moral standing for both environmental *individuals* and for the environment *as a whole*. In Leopold's words, "a land ethic changes the role of *Homo sapiens* from conqueror of the land community to plain member and citizen of it. It implies respect for fellow-members *and also* respect for the community as such."[53]

## §23 HOLISM

Respect for wholes, for the community as such and its various subsystems, is a theoretical possibility for the land ethic because it is conceptually and historically related to the Humean–Darwinian theoretical complex. Both individual members of society and the community as such, the social whole (together with its component divisions), are the objects of certain special, naturally selected moral sentiments. Beauty may be in the eye of the beholder, but it does not follow from this that only the eye of the beholder is beautiful. Similarly, there may be no value without valuers, but it does not follow from this that only valuers are valuable. Both beauty and intrinsic value are bivalent concepts; that is, both involve subjective and objective factors. *Intrinsic value* is, as it were, "projected" onto appropriate objects by virtue of certain naturally selected and inherited *intentional* feelings, some of which (patriotism, or love of country, is perhaps the most familiar example) simply have social wholes as their natural objects. We may value our community per se, for the sake of itself, just as we may value our children for the sake of themselves. Wholes may thus have intrinsic value no less problematically than individuals.[54]

Leopold's interpreters have generally read his outline of the "ethical sequence"—the evolutionary development of ethics—in light of Darwin's more elaborate discussion in *The Descent of Man*. Leopold himself seems more concerned, however, with the interplay between the holistic and individualistic moral sentiments, and the potentially conflicting values to which they give rise, than to their expansion or extension.[55] For example, he makes the following cryptic remark:

> The first ethics dealt with the relation between individuals; the Mosaic Decalogue is an example. Later accretions dealt with the relation between the individual and society. The Golden Rule tries to integrate the individual to society; democracy to integrate social organization to the individual.
>
> There is as yet no ethic dealing with man's relation to land and to the animals and plants which grow upon it. . . .[56]

From an evolutionary perspective it is doubtful that the first ethics dealt with the relation between individuals and not at all with the relation between the individual and society. From what we know of the moral attitudes of tribal people, among them certainly the Hebrews, the social whole—the clan, tribe, or nation—is the object of intense sentiment for the sake of which individuals might willingly sacrifice themselves. The Golden Rule, on the other hand, does not mention society; rather, its primary orientation seems to be toward "others," that is, other human individuals. Democracy seems to further rather than to countervail the individualistic orientation of the Golden Rule.

In any case, as "The Land Ethic" proceeds, it becomes more and more holistic, that is, more and more concerned with the biotic community per se and its subsystems and less and less individualistic—less and less concerned with the individual animals and plants that it comprises. Finally, in the summary moral maxim of the land ethic, the individual drops out of the picture altogether, leaving only the biotic community as the object of respect and moral considerability: "A thing is right when it tends to preserve the integrity, stability, and beauty of the biotic community; it is wrong when it tends otherwise."[57]

The stress upon the value of the biotic community is the distinguishing characteristic of the land ethic and its cardinal strength as an *adequate* environmental ethic. The land ethic directs us to take the welfare of nature—the diversity, stability, and integrity of the biotic community or, to mix metaphors, the health of the land organism—to be the standard of the moral quality, the rightness or wrongness, of our actions. Practically, this means that we should assess the "environmental impact" of any proposed project, whether it be a personal, corporate, or public undertaking, and choose that course of action which will enhance the diversity, integrity, beauty, and stability of the biotic community, the health and well-being of the land organism. Quite obviously, then, environmental problems, from billboards and strip-development to radioactive-waste generation and species extirpation, are directly addressed by the land ethic. It is specifically tailored to be an *adequate* environmental ethic.

## §24 THE DANGERS OF AN UNTEMPERED HOLISTIC ENVIRONMENTAL ETHIC

But, as with so many things, the cardinal strength of the land ethic is also its cardinal weakness. What are the moral (to say nothing of the economic) costs of the land ethic? Most seriously, it would seem to imply a draconian policy toward the human population, since almost all ecologists and environmentalists agree that, from the perspective of the integrity, diversity, and stability of the biotic community, there are simply too many people and too few redwoods, white pines, wolves, bears, tigers, elephants, whales, and so on. Philosopher William Aiken has recoiled in horror from the land ethic, since in his view it would imply that "massive human diebacks would be good. It is our species' duty to eliminate 90 percent of our numbers."[58] It would also seem to imply a merciless attitude toward nonhuman individual members of the biotic community. Sentient members of overabundant species, like rabbits and deer, may be (as actually presently they are) routinely culled, for the sake of the ecosystems of which they are a part, by hunting or other methods of liquidation. Such considerations have led philosopher Edward Johnson to complain that "we should not let the land ethic distract us from the concrete problems about the treatment of animals which have been the constant motive behind the animal liberation movement."[59] From the perspective of both humanism and its humane extension, the land ethic appears nightmarish in its own peculiar way. It seems more properly the "ethic" of a termitarium or beehive than of anything analogous to a human community. It appears richly to deserve Tom Regan's epithet "environmental fascism."

## §25 THE RELATION OF THE LAND ETHIC TO PRIOR ACCRETIONS

Despite Leopold's narrative drift away from attention to *members* of the biotic community to the *community per se* and despite some of Leopold's more radical exponents who have confrontationally stressed the holistic dimension of the land ethic, its theoretical foundations yield a subtler, richer, far more complex system of morals than simple environmental holism. The land ethic is the latest step in an evolutionary sequence, according to its own theoretical foundations. Each succeeding step in social-moral evolution—from the savage clan to the family of man—does not cancel or invalidate the earlier stages. Rather, each succeeding stage is layered over the earlier ones, which remain operative.

A graphic image of the evolution of ethics has been suggested by extensionist Peter Singer. Singer suggests we imagine the evolutionary development of ethics to be an "expanding circle."[60] According to this image, as the charmed circle of moral considerability expands to take in more and more beings, its previous boundaries disappear. Singer thus feels compelled by the logic of his own theory to give as much weight to the interests of a person (or, for that matter, a sentient animal) halfway around the world as to the interests of his own children! "I ought to give as much weight to the interests of people in Chad or Cambodia as I do to the interests of my family or neighbors; and this means that if people in those countries are suffering from famine and my money can help, I ought to give and go on giving until the sacrifices that I and my family are making begin to match the benefits the recipients obtain from my gifts."[61] When he chooses to give preference to his own or his children's interests, he has, according to his own account, morally failed. This is because the basic moral logic of traditional Western humanism and its extensions rests moral considerability on a criterion that is supposed to be both morally relevant and *equally* present in the members of the class of morally considerable beings. Hence, all who equally qualify are *equally* considerable. The circle expands as the criterion for moral considerability is changed in accordance with critical discussion of it.

A similar but crucially different image of the evolution of ethics has been suggested by Richard Sylvan and Val Plumwood. According to them,

> What emerges is a picture of types of moral obligation as associated with a nest of rings or annular boundary classes. . . . In some cases there is no sharp division between the rings. But there is no single uniform privileged class of items [i.e., rational beings, sentient beings, living beings], no one base class, to which all and only moral principles directly apply.[62]

The evolutionary development of ethics is less well represented by means of Singer's image of an expanding circle, a single ballooning circumference, within which moral principles *apply equally to all* than by means of the image of annular tree rings in which social structures and their correlative ethics are nested in a graded, differential system. That I am now a member of the global human community, and hence have correlative moral obligations to all mankind does not mean that I am no longer a member of my own family and citizen of my local community and of my country or that I am relieved of the peculiar and special limitations on freedom of action attendant upon these relationships.

## §26 THE PLACE OF HUMAN BEINGS IN THE LAND ETHIC

Therefore, just as the existence of a global human community with its humanitarian ethic does not submerge and override smaller, more primitive human communities and their moral codes, neither does the newly discovered existence of a global biotic community and its land ethic submerge and override the global human community and its humanitarian ethic. To seriously propose, then, that to preserve the integrity, beauty, and stability of the biotic community we ought summarily to eliminate 90 percent of the current human population is as morally skewed as Singer's apparent belief that he ought to spend 90 percent of his income relieving the hunger of people in Chad and Cambodia and, in consequence, to reduce himself and his own family to a meager, ragged subsistence.

However, just as it is not unreasonable for one to suppose that he or she has *some* obligation and should make *some* sacrifice for the "wretched of the earth," so it is not unreasonable to suppose that the human community should assume *some* obligation and make *some* sacrifice for the beleaguered and abused biotic community. To agree that the human population should not, in gross and wanton violation of our humanitarian moral code, be immediately reduced by deliberate acts of war or by equally barbaric means does not imply that the human population should not be scaled down, as time goes on, by means and methods that are conscionable from a humanitarian point of view. How obligations across the outermost rings of our nested sociomoral matrix may be weighed and compared is admittedly uncertain—just as uncertain as how one should weigh and compare one's duty, say, to one's family against one's duty to one's country. In the remainder of this essay, I shall go on to discuss some general considerations applying to this problem.

## §27 INTRA- AND INTERSPECIES RELATIONSHIPS IN THE LAND ETHIC

Although I have, for purposes of illustration, stressed the differences between the evolved layers of *human* society and thus the differences in their correlative ethics, these differences pale in comparison with the difference between any and all *human communities,* on the one hand, and the *biotic community,* on the other. While an Ihalmiute village in the remote wilds of the arctic and the United States of America are both literally societies, the biotic community is a "society" only by analogy, as I earlier emphasized (§9). Its form or structure is, in some respects, *like* and, in other respects, *very unlike* that of a human community or society. And as I also earlier emphasized (§24), an ethic is, from an evolutionary point of view, *doubly* correlative to social organization. Hence, the *kind* of duties we have depend *both upon the size and structure* of the social organizations to which we simultaneously belong: our duties to our fellow citizens are not the same as our duties to family members. Similarly, an ecosystemic ethic, a land ethic, should not only embrace the entire biotic community but *its moral precepts should reflect and foster the peculiar structure or form of organization* of the biotic community as well.

Let us recall, once again, that energy is the "currency" of the "economy" of nature, the "coin" of the realm in the biotic community, and further, that energy is transferred by means of what ecologists euphemistically call phagic or trophic relations (more bluntly, by one thing *eating* another). The extensionist approach to an environmental ethic is utterly incapable of countenancing intrinsic value or moral considerability for wholes. Moreover, for the community per se and its various subsystems and populations, it cannot take into account the fundamental moral differences between intraspecies and interspecies "social" relationships. Extensionists contemplating the "expanding circle" thus think that since it is wrong to kill and eat a human being, a fellow member of the human community, it must also be wrong to kill and eat a fellow member of the expanded moral community. Hence, first-phase extensionists (animal liberationists/rightists) insist that human beings have a moral obligation to become vegetarians. Second-phase extensionists, life-principle extensionists (or plant liberationists), wonder if it is permissible for people to eat at all.

The land ethic requires neither vegetarianism, at least not for the same reasons, nor certainly self-starvation as moral imperatives (although a vegetarian diet might for other reasons, reasons I shall explain in §29, contribute to the integrity, stability, and beauty of the biotic community). To argue that since it is wrong to kill and eat a human being, it is wrong to kill and eat, say, a rabbit or deer, is, from the evolutionary ethical sequence here recommended, analogous to arguing that since it is wrong for one not to give one's personal attention and affection to one's own children, it is wrong not to give equal personal attention and affection to all children. In neither instance do the precepts of the ethic reflect or nurture the structure of the community that is correlative to it.

So, if the land ethic does not translate the precepts of the humanitarian or humanistic ethic, *simpliciter,* through the next step in the sequence, what provision does the land ethic make for non-human members of the biotic community *individually?* Leopold is quite clear about what the land ethic requires vis-à-vis the ecosystem or biotic community as a whole—the preservation of its diversity, integrity, and stability. But what about individual plants and animals?

## §28 THE PLACE OF INDIVIDUAL NONHUMANS IN THE LAND ETHIC

Richard Sylvan and Val Plumwood have developed the view that Leopold briefly suggests, namely, that an ecosystemic ethic primarily provides not rights but *respect* for individual nonhuman members of the biotic community. Although the concept of respect is singular and simple, its practical implications are varied and complex. These thinkers further suggest that American Indian environmental attitudes and values provide a well-developed, rich exemplar of *respectful* participation in the economy of nature, a participation that permits human beings morally to eat and otherwise consumptively to utilize their fellow citizens of the organic society:

> The view that the land, animals, and the natural world should be treated with *respect* was a common one in many hunting-gathering societies. . . . Respect adds a moral dimension to relations with the natural world. . . . The conventional wisdom of Western society tends to offer a false dichotomy of use versus respectful non-use . . . of using

animals, for example, in the ways characteristic of large-scale mass-production farming . . . *or* on the other hand of not making use of animals at all. . . . What is left out of this choice is the alternative the Indians . . . recognized . . . of limited and respectful use. . . .[63]

A great deal of controversy has surrounded the hypothesis of an American Indian land ethic. Recent studies, empirically based upon actual cultural materials, have shown beyond reasonable doubt that at least some American Indian cultures did in fact have an ecosystemic or environmental ethic *and* that such an ethic maps conceptually upon the Leopold land ethic.[64] In other words, some American Indian cultures—among them, for example, the Ojibwa of the western Great Lakes—represented the plants and animals of their environment as engaged in *social* and *economic* intercourse with one another and with human beings. And such a social picture of human–environment interaction gave rise to correlative moral attitudes and behavioral restraints. The Ojibwa cultural narratives (myths, stories, and tales), which served as the primary vehicles of enculturation or education, repeatedly stress that animals, plants, and even rocks and rivers (natural entities that Western culture regards as inanimate) are *persons* engaged in reciprocal, mutually beneficial exchange with human beings. A cardinal precept embellished again and again in these narratives is that nonhuman natural entities, both individually and as species, must be treated with respect and restraint. The Ojibwa were primarily a hunting-gathering people, which perforce involved them in killing animals as well as plants for food, clothing, and shelter. But they nevertheless represented the animals and plants of their biotic community as *voluntarily* participating in a mannerized economic exchange with people who, for their part, gave tokens of gratitude and reimbursement and offered guest friendship.

For example, in one such Ojibwa story called "The Woman Who Married a Beaver," we find a particularly succinct statement of this portrait of the human–animal relationship. Here is an excerpt from the story:

> Now and then by a person would they be visited; then they would go to where the person lived, whereupon the person would slay the beavers, yet they really did not kill them; back home would they come again. . . . in the same way as people are when visiting one another, so were the beavers in their mental attitude toward people. . . . They were very fond of the tobacco that was given them by the people; at times they were also given clothing by the people.
>
> When finally the woman returned to her own (human) kin, she was wont to say, "Never speak you ill of a beaver . . .! Just the same as the feelings of one who is disliked, so is the feeling of the beaver. And he who never speaks ill of a beaver is very much loved by it; in the same way as people often love one another, so is one held in the mind of the beaver; particularly lucky then is one at killing beavers."[65]

## §29 MODERN LIFE IN ACCORDANCE WITH AN ECOSYSTEMIC ENVIRONMENTAL ETHIC

Of course, most people today do not live by hunting and gathering. Nevertheless, the general ideal provided by American Indian cultures of respectful, restrained, mutually beneficial human use of the environment is certainly applicable in today's context. An ecosystemic environmental ethic does not prohibit human use of the environment; it requires, rather, that that use be subject to two ethical limitations. The first is holistic, the second individualistic.

The first requires that human use of the environment, as nearly as possible, should enhance the diversity, integrity, stability, and beauty of the biotic community. Biologist René Dubos has argued that Western Europe was, prior to the industrial revolution, biologically richer *as a result* of human settlement and cultivation.[66] The creation and cultivation of small fields, hedgerows, and forest edges measurably (objectively and quantitatively) enhanced the diversity and integrity and certainly the beauty of the preindustrial European landscape. Ethnobotanist Gary Nabhan has recently drawn a similar picture of the Papago inhabitation of the Sonoran desert.[67] Human occupation and use of the environment from the perspective of the quality of the environment as a whole does not *have* to be destructive. On the contrary, it can be, as both hunter-gatherers and yeoman farmers have proved, mutually beneficial.

The second, individualistic ethical limitation on human use of the environment requires that trees cut for shelter or to make fields, animals slain for food or for fur, and so on should be thoughtfully selected, skillfully and humanely dispatched, and carefully used so as to neither waste nor degrade them. The *individual* plant, animal, or even rock or river consumed or transformed by human use deserves to be used respectfully.

Surely we can envision an eminently livable, modern, systemic, *civilized* technological society well adapted to and at peace and in harmony with its organic environment. Human technological civilization can live not merely in peaceful coexistence but in benevolent symbiosis with nature. Is our current *mechanical* technological civilization the only one imaginable? Aren't there alternative technologies? Isn't it possible to envision, for example, a human civilization based upon nonpolluting solar energy for domestic use, manufacturing, and transportation and small-scale, soil-conserving organic agriculture? There would be fewer material *things* and more *services, information,* and opportunity for aesthetic and recreational *activities;* fewer people and more bears; fewer parking lots and more wilderness. I think it is possible. It is a vision shared with individual variations by designer Ian McHarg, biologist René Dubos, poets Wendell Berry and Gary Snyder, and philosophers Holmes Rolston and William Aiken, to mention only a few.

In the meantime, while such an adaptive organic civilization gradually evolves out of our present grotesque mechanical civilization, the most important injunction of ecosystemic ethics remains the one stressed by Leopold—subject, of course, to the humanitarian, humane, and life-respecting qualifications that, as I have just argued, are theoretically consistent with it. We should strive to preserve the diversity, stability, and integrity of the biotic community.

Before ending, it is appropriate to ask what the implications of an ecocentric ethic would be for our daily lives. After all, one value of this ethic, no less than any other, is that it gives meaning to choices that otherwise remain unconscious or arbitrary. If as I have claimed, an ecocentric ethic is the most practicable environmental ethic, how does it actually inform our real-life choices?

Integrating an ecocentric ethic into our lives would provide new criteria for choices we make everyday in virtually every arena of our lives. Some of these choices are obvious; others, less so.

Most obviously, because a vegetarian diet, more directly and efficiently than a meat-centered diet, conducts solar energy into human bodies, the practice of vegetarianism could not only help reduce human hunger and animal suffering, it would free more land and solar energy for the restoration of natural communities.[68] (Note that eating wild game, respectfully, lawfully, and humanely harvested, would be an exception to the vegetarian implications of ecocentric ethics. Only grain-fed, domestic livestock should in general be avoided.)

Above all, one should try to avoid fast-food beef (McDonald's, Hardee's, and the like) made mostly from the imported carcasses of cattle, not only because consuming such food contributes to the political and economic causes of hunger in the countries from which it is exported, but also because it is produced on lands once covered by rain-forests.[69] Hence, the consumption of such foods not only implicates one (in all probability) in the destructive politics of world hunger and the disrespectful use of animals, it implicates one (almost certainly) in the extinction of endemic species (those specifically adapted to particular rain-forest habitats).

But what we eat is only the most obvious link between our daily choices and the integrity of the biotic community of which we are part. In a multitude of other roles, our choices either contribute to its regeneration or its continued ruin. As *consumers,* do we weigh our purchases according to the environmental consequences of their production? As *students,* do we utilize our learning time to hone our knowledge and sensibilities so as to more effectively live an ecocentric ethic? As *citizens,* of both a nation and a community, do we elect leaders whose policies ignore the need for environmental protection and reparation? As *workers,* do we choose to be employed by corporations whose activities degrade the environment? As *parents and individuals whose opinions necessarily influence others,* do we work to impart to others an understanding of the importance of an ecocentric ethic? As *decisionmakers over resources*—from real estate to other large or small assets—do we assume responsibility for their use? Or do we simply turn a blind eye, allowing others to use them for environmentally destructive ends?

Asking ourselves such questions, we discover that the implications of an ecocentric ethic cannot be reduced to one or even several major life choices. Rather, the contribution of an ecocentric ethic is to be found in the myriad of mundane, even banal decisions we make everyday. A grounding in an ecocentric ethic would thus shape the entire unfolding of one's life.

The second most serious moral issue of our times—second only to our individual and collective responsibility to prevent thermonuclear holocaust—is our responsibility to preserve the biological diversity of the earth. Later, when an appropriately humble, sane, ecocentric civilization comes into being, as I believe it will, its government and citizens will set about rehabilitating this bruised and tattered planet. For their work, they must have as great a library of genetic material as it is possible for us to save. Hence, it must be our immediate goal to prevent further destruction of the biosphere, to save what species we can, and to preserve the biotic diversity and beauty that remains.

## IV. SUMMARY AND CONCLUSION

The "environmental crisis" of the mid-twentieth century is very real and very profound. It represents less a challenge to engineers than to philosophers, since in the final analysis technology only gives substance to our beliefs and serves our values. The eventual resolution of the environmental crisis and the ultimate viability of *Homo sapiens* will therefore turn upon the development of a world view and ethos more in harmony with the working principles and laws of earth's biotic mantle, mankind's nurturing natural home.

In our search for such an ethos, an "environmental ethic," I set out three general criteria against which we could test and measure candidates for *best* environmental ethic. They are (1) *consistency*—both self-consistency and, for a prospective environmental ethic, consistency with the larger tapestry of ideas which now represents nature and has revealed the environmental crisis; (2) *adequacy*—the capacity of a prospective environmental ethic both to recognize and directly to address as distinct *moral questions* those problems that, taken together, constitute the environmental crisis; and (3) *practicability*— the liberty, the elbow room, one is allowed to live within the constraints imposed by a prospective environmental ethic.

Since the advent of the environmental crisis, four basic approaches to environmental ethics have emerged: (A) the Judeo-Christian stewardship environmental ethic; (B) an environmental ethic based upon (i) traditional and (ii) protracted humanism; (C) extensionism in its (i) first, animal liberation/rights phase and (ii) second, life-principle (or conative) phase; and (D) ecocentrism, classically expressed by Aldo Leopold as the "land ethic."

These candidates for the best environmental ethic were taken up in order and measured against the three evaluative criteria. The Judeo-Christian stewardship environmental ethic admirably meets criteria 2 and 3 but fails to meet 1. The stewardship environmental ethic is both adequate and eminently practicable, but—though on the whole self-consistent (if generously interpreted)—the world view in which it is embedded and the premises upon which it is founded are not consistent with the representation of nature in contemporary science. And it is contemporary science, especially evolutionary and ecological biology, that has enabled us to better understand the structure and unity of nature and to appreciate that our civilization is not well adapted to its natural setting.

Traditional and protracted humanism more or less meet criterion 3, practicability, but fail, to one degree or another, to meet criteria 1 and 2, consistency and adequacy. While they may be adequate resource management ethics, they cannot be adequate *environmental* ethics because they do not regard human harms to the environment as of *direct* moral concern. The only thing wrong with, say, torturing an animal, hunting the great whales to extinction, setting fire to a forest just to see it burn, polluting a river, and so on are the untoward effects of such actions upon the sensibilities and/or material welfare of other people, those presently living or those yet to come.

Finally, traditional and protracted humanism as candidates for an *environmental* ethic fail to meet criterion 1, consistency, because the evolutionary–ecological world view, which has informed us of the environmental crisis and from which perspective environmental problems are perceived as *moral* problems, does not represent mankind as set apart from nature. But humanism, by definition, regards human beings as somehow a case apart and the environment as merely a shrinking "resource pool" and a maddeningly complex "[human] life support system."

Extensionism, speaking globally of its first- and second-phase forms, fails to meet all three criteria. Because it is primarily a formal philosophical approach to environmental ethics, extensionism—more deliberately than the previously mentioned, less well-defined candidates for an environmental ethic—strives to be self-consistent. With the exception, perhaps, of Singer's categorical vetetarianism and both Singer's and Regan's seemingly ad hoc insistence on morally condemning human but not nonhuman predation, first-phase extensionism—at least as represented by its ablest advocates—seems on the whole self-consistent. It is also consistent with the theory of evolution that binds mankind and other forms of life into a single community through ties of kinship. But it is patently inconsistent with ecology. Nature's economy is constituted by a system of trophic relationships.

Energy, the currency of nature's economy, flows through the ecosystem only when one thing eats another. Sudden, untimely death and often pain are fundamental and intractable ecological facts of life. An ecosystem purged of pain, which animal liberationist Peter Singer's theory *seems* to pose as a moral ideal, would be both vastly impoverished and critically destabilized. But setting aside this disputed issue, both first- and second-phase extensionism are more deeply inconsistent with ecology because ecology is, in its conceptual orientation, holistic and extensionism is, in its moral orientation, individualistic. Ecology is concerned with collective entities—species, populations, ecosystems, biomes—while extensionism is concerned exclusively with the moral considerability and/or rights of individual animal subjects of a life, sentient animals, or living beings. An ethic requiring equal consideration for and/or conferring rights upon "all" individual animals (i.e., all sentient and/or subject-of-a-life animals, as the theoretical case may be) would, if generally instituted and practiced, result in more harm than good for the environment as a whole.

Turning directly to criterion 2, adequacy, the individualistic orientation of extensionism makes both of its phases inadequate for environmental ethics. Neither can recognize nor address as moral questions the most important issues collectively called "the environmental crisis." Neither biological impoverishment per se nor species extinction can be of direct moral concern for extensionism, while environmentalists regard these as among the most pressing and profound moral issues of our time.

Regarding criterion 3, the practicability criterion, while first-phase extensionism may be demanding but livable, second-phase extensionism, the intended *environmental* version of extensionism, is utterly unlivable as even its own proponents confess.

Just as extensionism, judged by these criteria, is the worst approach to environmental ethics, ecocentrism is clearly the best. A historically expanded and conceptually developed version of Leopold's land ethic is as self-consistent as any other candidate *and* is deliberately built upon the conceptual foundations of evolutionary and ecological biology; hence it is consistent with the evolutionary–ecological world view in the context of which the environmental crisis is perceived as such.

The ecocentric environmental ethic is directly and straightforwardly adequate because it morally commends and condemns human actions in terms of their environmental impact: "a thing is right when it tends to preserve the integrity, beauty and stability of the biotic community; it is wrong when it tends otherwise." The welfare of the environment, in other words, is the benchmark against which the moral value of actions is measured.

Because of this very feature of ecocentrism, its practicability has been challenged. Wouldn't an ecocentric environmental ethic result in a kind of "environmental fascism" in which *individual* dignity and worth are ignored or, worse, actively suppressed? A reexamination and critical reappraisal of the conceptual foundations of the classic Leopold land ethic reveal that such concerns are baseless. The land ethic makes explicit provision for respect for individual members, both human and nonhuman, of the biotic community as well as for the community as a whole. The land ethic does not compete with familiar social ethics, nor does it swallow up earlier stages of moral natural history. Rather, the land ethic suggests an evolutionary interpretation of moral development in which it is the next step in a sequence of ethical accretions. All the previous accretions remain operative and in full force. Hence, instead of overriding familiar social ethics, the land ethic creates additional, less urgent obligations to additional, less closely related beings. Hence, our obligations to family and friends— and to human rights and human welfare generally—come first; they are not challenged or undermined by an ecocentric environmental ethic. The land ethic obliges us to look out for the health and integrity, the diversity and stability of nature in a way that is consonant with these prior duties to human beings and human aspirations. The land ethic envisions, as a moral ideal, a human civilization at peace and in harmony with nature. This ideal should not be construed as an unwelcome or onerous, barely practicable goal; it should be, rather, a desirable, eminently livable goal. An ecocentric ethic would imply significant changes in our values and our ways of living. But such changes would be a long overdue relief from the spiritual oppression of our overly mechanized environment and from the dissatisfied boredom of our consumptive, materialistic civilization.

## NOTES

1. William Murdoch and Joseph Connell, "All About Ecology," in Ian G. Barbour, ed., *Western Man and Environmental Ethics*. Reading, Mass.: Addison-Wesley, 1973, pp. 156–170.
2. Roderick Nash, *The Environmental Studies Program, 1983–84*. Santa Barbara, Calif.: University of California, 1983.
3. Aldo Leopold, *A Sand County Almanac with Essays on Conservation from Round River*. New York: Ballantine, 1966, pp. 263–264.
4. Cf. International Union for Conservation of Nature and Natural Resources (IUCN), *Red Data Book*. Morges, Switzerland, 1974.
5. Norman Myers, *The Sinking Ark: A New Look at the Problem of Disappearing Species*. New York: Pergamon, 1979, p. 4.
6. Edward O. Wilson, *Biophilia*. Cambridge, Mass.: Harvard University Press, 1984, p. 121.
7. Clifford Geertz, "Thick Description: Toward an Interpretive Theory of Culture," in Clifford Geertz, ed., *The Interpretation of Cultures*. New York: Basic Books, 1973, pp. 126–7. Cf. J. Baird Callicott, "Hume's Is/ Ought Dichotomy and the Relation of Ecology to Leopold's Land Ethic," *Environmental Ethics* 4 (1982): 163–174, for a discussion of the fact/ value dichotomy in the context of environmental ethics.
8. Cf. Lynn White, Jr., "The Historical Roots of Our Ecologic Crisis,"

*Science* 155 (1967): 1203–1207; and Ian McHarg, *Design With Nature.* Philadelphia: Falcon, 1969.

9. James Barr, "Man and Nature: The Ecological Controversy and the Old Testament," in D. and E. Spring, eds., *Ecology and Religion in History.* New York: Harper & Row/Torchbooks, 1974, p. 64. Cf. Francis Schaeffer, *Pollution and the Death of Man: The Christian View of Ecology.* New York: Hodder and Stoughton, 1970; and Albert J. Fritsch, *Environmental Ethics: Choices for Concerned Citizens.* Garden City, N.Y.: Doubleday/Anchor, 1980; for Protestant and Catholic discussions, respectively.

10. Ibid., p. 62.

11. Cf. J. Baird Callicott, "Non-anthropocentric Value Theory and Environmental Ethics," *American Philosophical Quarterly* 21 (1984): 299–309.

12. Peter Singer, *Animal Liberation: A New Ethics for Our Treatment of Animals.* New York: Avon, 1977.

13. Cf. Carl Sagan, *The Dragons of Eden: Speculations on the Evolution of Human Intelligence.* New York: Ballantine, 1977, for a readable discussion of the evolution of the human brain/psychology glossed in this paragraph.

14. Aldo Leopold, *A Sand County Almanac.* pp. 116–117.

15. Cf. Paul Shepard, "Ecology and Man: A Viewpoint," in P. Shepard and D. McKinley, eds., *The Subversive Science: Essays Toward an Ecology of Man.* New York: Houghton Mifflin, 1969, pp. 1–10.

16. Cf. Donald Worster, *Nature's Economy: The Roots of Ecology.* Garden City, N.Y.: Doubleday/Anchor, 1979, for a thorough history of this concept.

17. Cf. J. E. Lovelock, *Gaia: A New Look at Life on Earth.* Oxford, England: Oxford University Press, 1979, for a recent development of this idea.

18. For a development of the concept of "ecospasm," see Austin Meredith, "Devolution," *Journal of Theoretical Biology* 96 (1982): 49–65.

19. Aldo Leopold, *A Sand County Almanac,* p. 253.

20. K. S. Shrader-Frechette, *Environmental Ethics.* Pacific Grove, Calif.: Boxwood, 1981, p. 17.

21. Tom Regan, "The Nature and Possibility of an Environmental Ethic," *Environmental Ethics* 3 (1981): 19–34.

22. Richard Routley and Val Routley, "Human Chauvinism and Environmental Ethics," in D. Mannison, M. McRobbie, and R. Routley, eds., *Environmental Philosophy.* Canberra, Australia: Australian National University, 1980, p. 131.

23. Cf. Bill Devall, "The Deep Ecology Movement," *Natural Resources Journal* 20 (1980): 299–322, for a comprehensive discussion.

24. Cf. R. J. Sikora and B. Barry, eds., *Obligations to Future Generations.* Philadelphia: Temple University Press, 1978; and Ernest Partridge, ed., *Responsibilities to Future Generations: Environmental Ethics.* Buffalo, N.Y.: Prometheus, 1981, for representative literature.

25. Peter Singer, *Animal Liberation: A New Ethics for Our Treatment of Animals.* New York: Avon, 1975.

26. Tom Regan, "The Moral Basis of Vegetarianism," *The Canadian Journal of Philosophy* 5 (1975): 181–214.

27. Cf. Kenneth Goodpaster, "On Being Morally Considerable," *Journal of Philosophy* 75 (1978): 308–325.

28. Cf. Tom Regan, "An Examination and Defense of One Argument Concerning Animal Rights," *Inquiry* 22 (1975): 189–219, for a thorough discussion.

29. Tom Regan, *The Case for Animal Rights.* Berkeley, Calif.: The University of California Press, 1983.

30. Cf. John Rodman, "The Liberation of Nature," *Inquiry* 20 (1977): 83–131; and J. Baird Callicott, "Animal Liberation: A Triangular Affair," *Environmental Ethics* 2 (1980): 311–338, for examples.
31. Peter Singer, *Animal Liberation*, pp. 238–239.
32. Tom Regan, *The Case for Animal Rights*, p. 357.
33. Ibid.
34. Ibid., p. 353.
35. Ibid., p. 357.
36. Cf. Ibid., pp. 359–363; and Peter Singer, "Not for Humans Only: The Place of Non-humans in Environmental Issues," in K. E. Goodpaster and K. M. Sayre, eds., *Ethics and Problems of the 21st Century*. Notre Dame, Ind.: University of Notre Dame Press, 1979, pp. 191–205.
37. Holmes Rolston III, "Duties to Endangered Species," p. 8. Unpublished paper presented to the Environmental Ethics—New Directions Conference, Oct. 4–6, 1984, at the University of Georgia.
38. As quoted in Roderick Nash, *Wilderness and the American Mind*, rev. ed. New Haven, Conn.: Yale University Press, 1973, p. 130.
39. Aldo Leopold, *A Sand County Almanac*, p. 245.
40. Cf. Kenneth Goodpaster, "On Being Morally Considerable."
41. Cf. Joel Feinberg, "The Rights of Animals and Unborn Generations," in William Blackstone, ed., *Philosophy and Environmental Crisis*. Athens, Ga.: University of Georgia Press, 1974, pp. 43–68; and Tom Regan, "Feinberg on What Sorts of Beings Can Have Rights," *Southern Journal of Philosophy* 14 (1976): 485–498.
42. Kenneth Goodpaster, "From Egoism to Environmentalism," in *Ethics and Problems of the 21st Century*, p. 29.
43. Ibid., p. 30.
44. Tom Regan, *The Case for Animal Rights*, p. 362.
45. Cf. J. Baird Callicott, "Animal Liberation: A Triangular Affair."
46. Aldo Leopold, *A Sand County Almanac*, p. 238.
47. Ibid.
48. Charles Darwin, *The Descent of Man and Selection in Relation to Sex*, 2nd ed. New York: Hill, 1904, p. 97.
49. Ibid., p. 107.
50. Ibid., p. 118.
51. Cf. J. Baird Callicott, "Elements of an Environmental Ethic: Moral Considerability and the Biotic Community," *Environmental Ethics* 1 (1979): 71–81, for a more formal development of this double correlation.
52. Aldo Leopold, *A Sand County Almanac*, p. 239.
53. Ibid., p. 240.
54. Cf. J. Baird Callicott, "Non-anthropocentric Value Theory and Environmental Ethics," for a full discussion of intrinsic value for nature and nonhuman natural entities.
55. Cf. Roderick Nash, "Do Rocks Have Rights?" *The Center Magazine* 10/6 (November–December 1977): 2–12, for a representative interpretation.
56. Aldo Leopold, *A Sand County Almanac*, p. 238.
57. Ibid., p. 262.
58. William Aiken, "Ethical Issues in Agriculture," in Tom Regan, ed., *Earthbound: New Introductory Essays in Environmental Ethics*. New York: Random House, 1984, p. 269.
59. Edward Johnson, "Animal Liberation vs. the Land Ethic," *Environmental Ethics* 3 (1981): 271.
60. Peter Singer, *The Expanding Circle: Ethics and Sociobiology*. New York: Farrar, Straus & Giroux, 1982.
61. Ibid., p. 153.

62. Richard Routley and Val Routley, "Human Chauvinism and Environmental Ethics," p. 107.
63. Ibid., pp. 178–179.
64. Cf. Thomas W. Overholt and J. Baird Callicott, *Clothed-in-Fur and Other Tales: An Introduction to An Ojibwa World View.* Washington, D.C.: University Press of America, 1982; and J. Baird Callicott, "American Indian and Western European Attitudes Toward Nature: An Overview," *Environmental Ethics* 4 (1982): 293–318.
65. Ibid., pp. 74–75.
66. Cf. René Dubos, "Franciscan Conservation and Benedictine Stewardship," in *Ecology and Religion in History:* 114–136.
67. Gary Nabhan, *The Desert Smells Like Rain.* San Francisco: Northpoint, 1982.
68. Frances Moore Lappé, *Diet for a Small Planet* (New York: Ballantine Books, 1982).
69. Frances Moore Lappé and Joseph Collins, *Food First: Beyond the Myth of Scarcity* (New York: Ballantine Books, 1979).

## SUGGESTIONS FOR FURTHER READING

§§1–2 Among the earlier classics heralding the environmental crisis are Rachel Carson, *Silent Spring.* Boston: Houghton Mifflin, 1962; Stewart Udall, *The Quiet Crisis.* New York: Holt, 1963; P. Shepard and D. McKinley, eds., *The Subversive Science: Essays Toward an Ecology of Man.* Boston: Houghton Mifflin, 1969; and Barry Commoner, *The Closing Circle.* New York: Knopf, 1971.

§§3–6 Noteworthy discussions of the Judeo-Christian Tradition and the environmental crisis are Ian McHarg, *Design With Nature.* Philadelphia: Falcon, 1969; Francis Schaeffer, *Pollution and the Death of Man: The Christian View of Ecology.* New York: Hodder and Stoughton, 1970; D. and E. Spring, eds., *Ecology and Religion in History.* New York: Harper & Row, 1974; Elizabeth D. Gray, *Green Paradise Lost.* Wellesley, Mass.: Roundtable, 1979; Albert J. Fritsch, S.J., *Environmental Ethics: Choices for Concerned Citizens.* Garden City, N.Y.: Doubleday/Anchor, 1980; and Robin Attfield, *The Ethics of Environmental Concern.* New York: Columbia University Press, 1983.

§§7–9 Accessible discussions of evolutionary and ecological theory with an eye to environmental philosophy are Loren Eiseley, *The Immense Journey.* New York: Random House/Vintage, 1967; Edward J. Kormondy, ed., *Readings in Ecology.* Englewood Cliffs, N.J.: Prentice-Hall, 1965; Lewis Thomas, *The Lives of a Cell: Notes of a Biology Watcher.* New York: Viking, 1974; Michael Ruse, *The Darwinian Revolution: Science Red in Tooth and Claw.* Chicago: The University of Chicago Press, 1979; Donald Worster, *Nature's Economy.* Garden City, N.Y.: Doubleday/Anchor, 1979.

§§11–12 Noteworthy resources for the traditional and protracted humanistic approaches to environmental ethics are John Passmore, *Man's Responsibility for Nature: Ecological Problems and Western Traditions.* New York: Scribner's, 1974; William F. Baxter, *People or Penguins: The Case for Optimal Pollution.* New York: Columbia University Press, 1974; R. I. Sikora and B. Barry, eds., *Obligations to Future Generations.* Philadelphia: Temple University Press, 1978; K. S. Shrader-Frechette, *Environmental Ethics.* Pacific Grove, Calif.: Boxwood, 1981; Ernest Partridge, ed., *Responsibilities to Future Generations: Environmental Ethics.* Buffalo, N.Y.: Prometheus, 1981.

§§13–17 There is a large philosophical literature representing an extensionist approach. Only a few outstanding examples can be mentioned here. They are Albert Schweitzer, *Civilization and Ethics.* London: Black, 1946; Peter Singer, *Animal Liberation: A New Ethics for Our Treatment of Animals.* New York: The New York Review, 1975; Tom Regan and Peter Singer, eds., *Animal Rights and Human Obligations.* Englewood Cliffs, N.J.: Prentice-Hall, 1976; R. K. Morris and M. W. Fox, eds., *On the Fifth Day.* Washington, D.C.: Acropolis, 1978; Charles Birch and John B. Cobb, Jr., *The Liberation of Life: From the Cell to the Community.* Cambridge, England: Cambridge University Press, 1981; Tom Regan, *The Case for Animal Rights.* Berkeley, Calif.: The University of California Press, 1982.

§§18–26 By contrast there is a small body of philosophical literature representing an ecocentric approach. See Aldo Leopold, *A Sand County Almanac with Essays on Conservation from Round River.* New York: Ballantine, 1966; Christopher Stone, *Should Trees Have Standing?: Toward Legal Rights for Natural Objects.* Los Altos, Calif.: Kaufman, 1974; Daniel G. Koslovsky, *An Evolutionary and Ecological Ethic.* Englewood Cliffs, N.J.: Prentice-Hall, 1974; the essays of J. Baird Callicott and Holmes Rolston III in *Environmental Ethics* and other journals; the scattered essays of Richard Routley (now Sylvan), Val Routley (now Plumwood) and Richard and Val Routley; and the essays of John Rodman.

§§27–28 For sources of American Indian environmental attitudes and values see John G. Neihardt, *Black Elk Speaks.* Lincoln, Neb.: University of Nebraska Press, 1932; A. Irving Hallowell, *Culture and Experience.* Philadelphia: University of Pennsylvania Press, 1956; Calvin Martin, *Keepers of the Game: Indian–Animal Relationships and the Fur Trade.* Berkeley, Calif.: University of California Press, 1978; C. Vecsey and R. W. Venables, eds., *American Indian Environments.* Syracuse, N.Y.: Syracuse University Press, 1980; Thomas W. Overholt and J. Baird Callicott, *Clothed-in-Fur and Other Tales: An Introduction to an Ojibwa World View.* Washington, D.C.: University Press of America, 1982; J. Donald Hughes, *American Indian Ecology.* Lubbock, Texas: Texas Western Press, 1983.

Recent anthologies for general reading in environmental ethics are: K. E. Goodpaster and K. M. Sayers, eds., *Ethics and Problems of the 21st Century.* Notre Dame, Ind.: University of Notre Dame Press, 1979; D. Scherer and T. Attig, eds., *Ethics and the Environment.* Englewood Cliffs, N.J.: Prentice-Hall, 1983; R. Elliot and A. Gare, eds., *Environmental Philosophy.* University Park, Pa.: Pennsylvania University Press, 1983; and Tom Regan, ed., *Earthbound: New Introductory Essays in Environmental Ethics.* New York: Random House, 1984.

# INDEX

**425**

murder. *See* infanticide; killing
Murdoch, William, 281
Myers, Norman, 382

Nabhan, Gary, 415
Naess, Arne, 394
Nash, Roderick, 382
nationalism, 145–150. *See also* states
natural rights, 177–178
negative rights, 27–28, 143–145
Nejdl, Robert, 63
neo-Malthusian theory, 302–304
neonates
  defective. *See* defective neonates
  definition of, 216
  moral standing of, 233–241
    potentiality and, 236–238
    sentience and, 233–234, 236–239
  personhood of, 270–271
  public policy regarding, 241–252
    American Academy of
      Pediatricians and, 241–242
    Child Abuse Amendments of 1984,
      250–253
    human life bill, 244–248
    right to life and, 243, 250–251
    sanctity of life and, 248–250
  right to life of, 225–233, 238–241,
    269, 271–273, 364
    forfeiture of, 225–226
    infringement of, 226–233
    public policy and, 243, 250–251
  sentience of, 234, 236–239
nonconsequentialist theories, 23–25
normative ethics, 15–32
Nozick, Robert, 145
nuclear disarmament, 168–169
nuclear war, 125–126, 150–171
  defense against, 153–156
  deterrence of. *See* deterrence of
    nuclear war
  extermination of humankind and,
    159–165
  human factor and, 171–172
  recent history and, 170–171
  stakes of, 152–153

Oates, Captain, 86–88
opinions, moral judgments and, 9
Orwell, George, 372

pacifism, 137–142
  ideal, 139–142
  tactical, 138–139

paternalism
  definition of, 109
  suicide intervention and, 109–113
Perlmutter, Abe, 114–115
personal preferences, moral judgments
  and, 7–8
personhood. *See also* moral standing
  of animals, 361–364
  commonsense, 259–263, 270
  definition of, 257–258, 355–356
  of fetuses, 257–275, 288–292
    commonsense, 261–263
    moral, 264–274
    normative and descriptive,
      259–261
  of human beings, 258–259, 264–266,
    355
    moral, 259–261, 264–274
      actual-possession of, 270–271
      potentiality criterion of, 266–270
      species criterion of, 264–266
  of neonates, 270–271
  normative and descriptive, 259–261
  potentiality and, 266–270, 364
  right to life and, 359–360, 371–372
  self-consciousness and, 355–356
Plato, 147, 172
  on animals, 389–390
  on suicide, 348–349
Plumwood, Val, 393–394, 411, 413–414
politics. *See also* nationalism; states
  definition of, 127
  morality and, 128
  power and, 148–150
positive rights, 27–28, 143–145
potentiality
  of fetuses, 266–270, 274
  moral standing and, 236–238
  personhood and, 266–270, 364
Potts, Malcolm, 290
power, politics and, 148–150
principles. *See* moral principles; *and
  specific principles*
property rights over one's body,
  276–278
proportionality, 278–280
punishment, 175, 203
  capital. *See* capital punishment
  as crime deterrant, 196–201
  modes of, 187–188
  morality of, 185–189
  nature of, 186
  as right of society, 186–187
  severity of, 191–193
Pythagoras, 343–344

# ABOUT THE AUTHORS

TOM L. BEAUCHAMP was born in Austin, Texas, in 1939. He received an undergraduate degree from Southern Methodist University and graduate degrees from Yale University and The Johns Hopkins University. He is currently a member of the department of philosophy at Georgetown University. He is author of *Philosophical Ethics* and coauthor of *Hume and the Problems of Causation, Medical Ethics, A History and Theory of Informed Consent,* and *Principles of Biomedical Ethics.* He has edited or coedited seven other books, including *Ethical Issues in Death and Dying.* His main interests in philosophy are ethical theory, the philosophy of David Hume, and contemporary issues in causation. He has written extensively on each of these subjects in philosophical journals.

HUGO ADAM BEDAU was born in Portland, Oregon, in 1926. He entered the Navy Officer Procurement Program at the University of Southern California in 1944, served two years in the Naval Reserve, and graduated summa cum laude from the University of Redlands in 1949. He received his Ph.D. from Harvard University in 1961 and has taught at Dartmouth College, Princeton University, Reed College, and, since 1966, at Tufts University, where he is now Austin Fletcher Professor of Philosophy. He is the author of *The Courts, The Constitution, and Capital Punishment,* editor of *The Death Penalty in America, Justice and Equality,* and *Civil Disobedience,* and coauthor, with Edwin Schur, of *Victimless Crimes.* He has written widely on topics in political, legal, and social philosophy.

J. BAIRD CALLICOTT was born in Memphis, Tennessee, in 1941. He received his B.A. from Rhodes College (formerly Southwestern at Memphis). He was awarded a Woodrow Wilson Fellowship in 1963 and earned his M.A. and Ph.D. at Syracuse University. Currently he is Professor of Philosophy at the University of Wisconsin–Stevens Point. He is the author of *Plato's Aesthetics: An Introduction to the*

436 About the Authors

*Theory of Forms* and coauthor with Thomas W. Overholt of *Clothed-in-Fur: An Introduction to an Ojibwa World View,* and editor of *A Companion to a Sand County Almanac: Interpretative and Critical Essays.* He has published numerous essays in environmental philosophy and American Indian philosophy. He teaches courses in environmental ethics, environmental aesthetics, and American Indian environmental philosophies at UWSP as well as courses in more traditional fields of philosophy. He maintains an active interest in conservation issues, particularly the preservation of rare and endangered species.

JOEL FEINBERG was born in Detroit, Michigan, in 1926. He graduated from the University of Michigan, where he was awarded a Ph.D. in 1957. He has held regular teaching positions at Brown University, Princeton University, the University of California at Los Angeles, and Rockefeller University. At present, he is Professor of Philosophy at the University of Arizona, where he has taught since 1977. He is the author of *Doing and Deserving, Social Philosophy, Rights, Justice, and the Bounds of Liberty, Harm to Others, Offense to Others,* and numerous articles on moral, social, and legal philosophy.

JAN NARVESON is a native of Minnesota. He received his undergraduate degrees at the University of Chicago and Harvard University where he also received his Ph.D. in 1961. He has taught at the University of New Hampshire and, since 1963, at the University of Waterloo in Ontario, Canada, where he is now Professor of Philosophy. He has also served as Visiting Professor at The Johns Hopkins University, Stanford University, and the University of Calgary. His publications include *Morality and Utility* and numerous articles in professional journals and anthologies on ethics, political philosophy, and other subjects. His main nonprofessional interest is music, and he is founder and president of the Kitchener-Waterloo Chamber Music Society.

ONORA O'NEILL was born in Aughafatten, Northern Ireland, in 1941 and educated at Oxford and Harvard universities. She has taught at Barnard College (Columbia University) and is now at the University of Essex in Colchester, England. She is the author of *Acting on Principle,* and she has written on a variety of topics in ethics, social and political philosophy, and Kantian studies. Her most recent book is *Faces of Hunger.*

JAMES RACHELS was born in Columbus, Georgia, in 1941. He graduated in philosophy from Mercer University and received his Ph.D. from the University of North Carolina at Chapel Hill. He has held teaching positions at the University of Richmond, New York University, the University of Miami, and Duke University. At present he is Professor of Philosophy at the University of Alabama in Birmingham, where he has taught since 1977. His writings on moral philosophy have appeared in numerous books and journals.

TOM REGAN was born in Pittsburgh, Pennsylvania, in 1938. He received his undergraduate education at Thiel College and was awarded the M.A. and Ph.D. degrees by the University of Virginia. Since 1967 he has taught philosophy at North Carolina State University, where he has twice been elected Outstanding Teacher and, in 1977, was named Alumni Distinguished Professor. He has lectured throughout the world on a variety of moral topics, was Distinguished Visiting Scholar at the University of Calgary, and has served as Visiting Distinguished Professor of Philosophy at Brooklyn College. During the academic year 1984–85 he was a Fellow at the National Humanities Center, where he completed *Bloomsbury's Prophet: The Moral Philosophy of G. E. Moore*. The coeditor of three books, he is sole editor of *Earthbound: New Introductory Essays in Environmental Ethics* and *Just Business: New Introductory Essays in Business Ethics*. His other books include *Understanding Philosophy, All That Dwell Therein: Essays on Animal Rights and Environmental Ethics*, and *The Case for Animal Rights*. He is married to the former Nancy Tirk and has two children, Karen and Bryan.

PETER SINGER was born in Melbourne, Australia, in 1946 and educated at the University of Melbourne and Oxford University. He has taught at University College (Oxford), New York University, La Trobe University, and Monash University, where he is Professor of Philosophy and Director of the Centre for Human Bioethics. His books include *Animal Liberation, Practical Ethics, The Expanding Circle*, and (with Deane Wells) *The Reproductive Revolution*.

DONALD VANDEVEER is a native of Baltimore, Maryland. He received a Ph.D. in philosophy from the University of Chicago in 1968 and taught at the University of Illinois (Urbana) in 1969. Since then he has taught at North Carolina State University, where he is currently Professor of Philosophy. His published essays are in the fields of moral and political philosophy and biomedical ethics. He is coeditor (with Tom Regan) of both *And Justice for All* (1982) and *Border Crossings: New Introductory Essays in Health-Care Ethics* (1985) and coeditor (with Christine Pierce) of *People, Penguins, and Plastic Trees: Basic Issues in Environmental Ethics* (1985). He is the author of *Paternalistic Intervention* (1985).